In

New Americanists

A Series Edited by Donald E. Pease

Amy Kaplan and Donald E. Pease, Editors

Cultures of United States Imperialism

 Duke University Press   Durham and London   1993

© 1993 Duke University Press

All rights reserved

Printed in the United States of America on acid-free paper ∞

Designed by Cherie Holma Westmoreland

Typeset in Aster with Gill Sans display by Tseng Information Systems

Library of Congress Cataloging-in-Publication Data

Cultures of United States imperialism / Amy Kaplan and

Donald E. Pease, editors.

p.   cm.   —(New Americanists) Includes index.

ISBN 0-8223-1400-2 (cl).—ISBN 0-8223-1413-4 (pa)

1. United States—Territorial expansion. 2. Imperialism.

3. United States—Territories and possessions. 4. Racism—United

States. 5. United States—Race relations. 6. Political culture—

United States—History.   I. Kaplan, Amy.   II. Pease, Donald E.

III. Series.   E179.5.C96   1993   305.8'00973—dc20   93-19817   CIP

Contents

Contents

Introduction

Amy Kaplan

"Left Alone with America"

The Absence of Empire in the

Study of American Culture

One of the central themes of American historiography is that there is no American Empire. Most historians will admit, if pressed, that the United States once had an empire. They then promptly insist that it was given away. But they also speak persistently of America as a World Power.
—William Appleman Williams, 1955[1]

Through significant and underscored omissions, startling contradictions, heavily nuanced conflicts, through the way writers peopled their work with the signs and bodies of this presence—one can see that a real or fabricated Africanist presence was crucial to their sense of Americanness.
—Toni Morrison, 1992[2]

he field of American studies was conceived on the banks of the Congo. This genealogy appears in Perry Miller's well-known preface to *Errand into the Wilderness*, where Africa gives rise to the now legendary scene of intellectual awakening to the "meaning of America."[3] In the 1956 preface Miller recalls how as a college dropout in the 1920s he boarded an oil tanker for Africa in search of the "adventure" he had missed on the European battlefields of World War I. His perception of the "tawdry" reality of Africa, however, thwarted his romantic expectation of exotic exploits; yet it offered him, as though in compensation, an even more heroic "quest." With the force of an "epiphany," while he was unloading drums of oil, "the jungle of central Africa" vouchsafed to him "the pressing necessity for expounding my America to the twentieth century." The imagined blankness of Africa inexplicably crystallized in the fullness of America. His own journey into the fabled "Heart of Darkness" led Miller not to Marlow's "beginning of the world," but to the origins of American culture, not to Kurtz's breakdown of the European subject, but to the vocation of the American historian. Miller's expedition did for his intellectual development what he claims the Puritan errand did for American history; it founded the "beginning of a beginning" that gives coherence to all that follows. From the remote vantage of the Congo Miller discovered himself at home with a coherent national identity; there, like the Puritans in the wilderness, he found himself "left alone with America."

Miller's preface maps the boundaries of national identity by demarcating the narrative of American origins from the African setting of his epiphany. This distinction embraces other key oppositions that sever the European errand from the indigenous inhabitants of the wilderness; intellectual history from social history; domestic identity from foreign relations; and the Puritan migration from the middle passage of enslaved Africans. These conceptual borders, I will argue, delineate Miller's apprehension of the "uniqueness of the American experience" as antithetical to the historical experience of imperialism. The preface is remarkable, however, for the wealth of material it evokes and dismisses in order to forge the coherence of what Miller calls *the* fundamental theme." He turns Africa into the repository—and thus uneasy reminder—of those repressed alternatives, and it comes to embody an inventory of counter-evidence, from which one can plot shadow narratives of imperial histories underlying and contesting his story of Puritan origins. Miller's Africa thus both defines and threatens to destabilize his carefully negotiated boundaries of American identity.

Cultures of United States Imperialism takes for its subject what Miller relegated to the unnarrated background of Africa: the multiple histories of continental and overseas expansion, conquest, conflict, and resistance which have shaped the cultures of the United States and the cultures of those it has dominated within and beyond its geopolitical boundaries. The essays in this volume reconnect those realms severed by Miller's cartography of American uniqueness and attempt to reconstruct the competing cultural histories implicitly rejected and displaced onto the site of Africa. Miller's discovery of America in the Congo—his return of and return to the repressed—brings into conjunction key moments of the formation of U.S. cultures in the context of Western imperialism which this volume addresses: European colonization, slavery, westward expansion, overseas intervention, and cold war nuclear power.

Most histories of American studies single out Miller's preface as a "paradigm drama" in the foundation of the discipline. These readings, however, have ignored the centrality of the African context as the enabling condition that actively shapes that paradigm.[4] Instead they find that the incongruity of the exotic backdrop passively highlights the drama of intellectual self-discovery; Africa thus figures as distance itself, a foil or shadow for the Puritan "city on the hill." Toni Morrison, in contrast, has suggested that such distancing may conceal a more profound and unsettling intimacy, part of the process of constituting a dominant white national identity in relation to an Africanist presence: "through significant and underscored omissions, startling contradictions, heavily nuanced conflicts, through the way writers peopled their work with the signs and bodies of this presence—one can see that a real or fabricated Africanist presence was crucial to their sense of Americanness." My reading of the preface draws out the international and spatial dimensions of Morrison's argument by examining how Miller attributes the genesis of his "sense of Americanness" to his presence in Africa. What Morrison calls "the process of organizing American coherence through a distancing Africanism"[5] can be seen at work in the preface, where the apparently remote, exterior setting produces inner meaning and gives coherence to the central narratives: the origins of a life's work, of an academic discipline, and of America itself.

My introduction begins with Perry Miller in the Congo, even though his model for American studies has in many ways been superseded, to argue that the imperial dimensions of his founding paradigm have yet to be fully explored and still remain in place today. The first part of my introduction demonstrates how Miller represents a coherent America by constructing Africa as an imperial unconscious of national identity. From the decentering perspective of the African background, a close reading of Miller's preface foregrounds the ways in which imperialism has been simultaneously formative and disavowed in the foundational discourse of American studies. The second part of my introduction examines how this paradigm has persisted and shifted in the redefinition of empire and culture across different fields.

I

Miller's vision of America sharpens into focus against an African background that grows less and less distinct, metamorphosing from the named port of Matadi on the Congo, to "the edge of the jungle of Central Africa," to the "barbaric tropic," to the point where, finally, it is only evoked metonymically by Miller's own presence "among the fuel drums." As the colonial reality of Africa recedes from view, Miller charts his discovery of America's theological origins, while his language, with unintentional irony, rhetorically reenacts the material colonization of America that he rejects as the subject of his study. After his first reference to the "vacant wilderness" awaiting early settlement, America is next imaged at a further stage of colonization, as an "inexhaustible wilderness" mined for its natural resources, as Miller supervises the flow of oil to Africa. When Miller returns to graduate school, he employs an extended metaphor of agricultural development: "as for the interminable field which may be called the meaning of America, the acreage is immense and the threshers too few." Here he transforms "the meaning of America" into a field for study. From there he turns to the present of the United States as an industrial republic in the 1950s; the drums of oil no longer point back to the wilderness, but ahead to the "future of the world . . . tangible symbols of the republic's appalling power." Standing in counterpoint to Miller's insistence on theological origins, these images of American development uncannily mirror Miller's immediate setting—the unacknowledged colonial history of Africa.

The mirroring of "jungle" and "wilderness" effaces the inhabitants of both continents whose histories would undermine the coherence of both the Puritan errand and Miller's mission. In the opening of the preface, he describes the overall unity of his volume as "a rank of spotlights on the massive narrative of the movement of European culture into the wilderness of America." The acknowledgment that he has "silently expunged" what he calls his "more egregious lapses," suggests deeper silences and longer lapses that underwrite his massive narrative. In Miller's formulation, the origins of America stem from a dyadic relationship between Europe and an empty continent, while his presence in Africa introduces a triangular relationship that destabilizes this dyad. The presence of Africa—and the absence of its inhabitants—both reproduce the imaginary vacancy of the wilderness and threaten to disrupt this closed dyadic relationship by introducing a repressed third realm of the unnarrated stories of colonization, slavery, and resistance that link the histories of both continents.

Just as Miller implicitly distinguishes the narrative of American history from the unnarratable African setting, he more explicitly distinguishes his own historical method from prior alternatives. When he first describes his epiphany of *"the* fundamental theme," Miller differentiates his own intellectual "quest" from the material biases of "social history," which he ridicules as "the Wilmot Proviso and the chain store." Both examples to him of crude materialism are also telling instances of nineteenth-century expansion, one through territorial conquest in a war with Mexico (1846–48) and the other through later economic rationalization. Reference to the Wilmot Proviso also introduces the major theme Miller never touches in his work but silently evokes on the banks of the Congo: American slavery. Defeated in its effort to outlaw slavery in the newly conquered territories, the Wilmot Proviso brought into view the profound connection between westward expansion and slavery which would lead to the Civil War. This link was often denied by politicians, such as President Polk, who claimed that slavery "was purely a domestic question" and "not a foreign question."[6] A similar demarcation of the domestic from the foreign is central to Miller's conception of the meaning of America as well: that America—once cut off from Europe—can be understood as a domestic question, left alone, unique, divorced from the international conflicts—whether the slave trade or the Mexican War—in which that national identity takes shape. Miller's presence on the banks of the Congo evokes an earlier historical connection to Africa in the slave trade, with its later consequences in the Wilmot Proviso, which breaks down the absolute boundary between domestic and foreign at the same time that he insists upon them.

Slavery is thus invoked by the Wilmot Proviso only to be relegated to what Miller tellingly calls "the warp and woof" of American history, just as Africa is relegated to the backdrop of his own epiphany. Yet as the preface proceeds and America emerges as a field of study awaiting its earliest threshers, this silent backdrop gets more and more crowded and noisy. When the Puritan migration appears to Miller as the "beginning of a beginning," he feels compelled parenthetically to concede to and reject the priority of Virginia (which he does once home from Africa in the "security of graduate school"). His explanation is tautological: "what I wanted was a coherence with which I could coherently begin." Virginia, however, would obstruct coherence for reasons other than the insignificance of the white settlers and their lack of an articulate body of expression, as Miller claims. Beginning with Jamestown would evoke a counternarrative of migration to that of the Puritans: the forced migration of Africans on slave ships, and the unarticulated expression of another historical trajectory which Miller's student Edmund Morgan would describe twenty years later in *American Slavery, American Freedom.* Jamestown is incoherent as a beginning, because it would resonate with Miller's immediate setting in Africa to initiate an alternative narrative of beginnings in slavery, in the triangle of Europe, America, and Africa, not the neat dyad of the errand into the wilderness.

Indeed the locus of Miller's epiphany in Africa arises from the unacknowledged interdependence of the United States and European colonialism. To give coherence and clarity both to the "massive narrative" of American development and the consistency of his own career, Miller effaces the historical referents to his own position in what was then the Belgian Congo in the 1920s. He mentions neither Africans nor Europeans, nor the global conditions which would have brought Miller to Africa on an oil tanker, presumably delivering petroleum for cars and trucks that were crucial to the colonial apparatus at the time. Miller's account of raw material flowing out of the United States to Africa performs a curious reversal, since the primary economic circuit would have been the extraction and export of minerals *from* the Congo to Europe. By the 1920s, U.S. capital and individual engineers had major stakes in the largely Belgian mining industry of the Congo (where there was a settlement called "little America"). Miller's apparently random and quixotic arrival in Africa could only have been made possible by the longstanding economic, political, and cultural involvement of the United States in European colonialism, of which the Congo is a major case in point.[7] This triangulated relation of the United States, Europe, and the colonized world had added resonance in the 1950s when Miller wrote his preface on the eve of African independence, a process in which the United States was already playing a crucial neocolonial part in molding multiple struggles for decolonization to a dyadic script of cold war conflict. Thus the African setting of Miller's epiphany directly situates the United States in the broader history of Western imperialism, at the same time that his narrative of origins divorces him from it.

Miller more explicitly suggests and denies that he is writing imperial history in a tongue-in-cheek comparison of his epiphany to that of Edward Gibbon, who conceived of *The Decline and Fall of the Roman Empire* among Roman ruins, "while listening to barefooted friars chanting response in the former temple of Jupiter." Miller finds parallels to his own situation: "It was given to me equally disconsolate on the edge of a jungle of central Africa, to have thrust upon me the mission of expounding what I took to be the innermost propulsion of the United States, while supervising, in that barbaric tropic, the unloading of drums of case oil flowing out of the inexhaustible wilderness of America." Miller again draws startling parallels only to disclaim them. Gibbon saw in contemporary evidence of Christian spirituality a narrative of decline from the past glories of empire; Miller inversely looks at evidence of a contemporary empire, in the material forms of the oil drums, and transforms them into evidence of the spiritual origins of the past. In contrast to Gibbon, who started at "the beginning of a fall"—which made for aesthetic coherence—Miller starts at "the beginning of a beginning." He thereby transforms himself from a European historian into an American visionary as he evokes Walt Whitman (who, as Miller paraphrases him, never got beyond the beginning of his studies). Miller implicitly differentiates the American republic in its illimitable capacity for self-renewal and expansion—to always be at the beginning—from the inevitable decline of Old World empires. This differentiation from Rome Empire paradoxically allows the United States to assume the mantle of Old World empires, and safely inoculates it from their inevitable decline, while his playful tone undermines this distinction.

The racially inflected distinction between images of the "jungle" and "wilderness" underwrites the familiar opposition between Old and New Worlds in this passage. If America is not like the decaying empire of Rome, implies Miller, it is even less like the depleted undeveloped continent of Africa. In contrast to the enervated "barbaric tropic," marked by its unspoken connotations of blackness, the "inexhaustible wilderness" offers the challenging space of implicitly white achievement. In the reference to "barefoot friars," where we might expect to find barefoot Africans, Old World empire and African jungle come together as sites of decay and exhaustion, into which American vitality flows. Miller reverses the trajectory of the colonial "mission" from the backward barbarians to the "twentieth century," and thereby redeems Protestant doctrine from the decay of Gibbon's Catholic friars, just as he redeems the inexhaustible American wilderness from the already exhausted jungle. This implicit differentiation from black Africa is as crucial to the ascription of American uniqueness as is the more common opposition to Old World empires.

In the personal narrative of the preface, this reclamation of national vigor allows him to return home—rejuvenated as a "boy" in graduate school—where he would renew America's Puritan origins as a fertile field for study, against his teacher's warnings that the field was already "exhausted." While rejecting Turner's frontier thesis on intellectual grounds (in the preface to his titular essay), Miller's personal narrative reenacts a frontier tale: the rejuvenation of the lone white male in the wilderness, who submits to the power of a feminized and racialized landscape only to wrest control and separate himself from it, substituting in this case intellectual work for regeneration through violence.[8]

In the final oblique reference to his stay in Africa, Miller looks back typologically at the fuel drums to find not only the Puritan past, but also a portent of the future and his own present in the nuclear age. Miller, I believe, feared that nuclear destruction would become the tragically ironic fulfillment of the Puritan errand into the wilderness. He ends his first essay with the Puritan failure to "rivet the eyes of the world" on their "city on the hill" (15), and in the final essay, "The End of the World," nuclear power succeeds overwhelmingly in riveting the eyes of the world not on New England but on Hiroshima (238). In the preface, Miller refers to this "appalling power" as a problem, with which he can curiously see no way of "coping . . . except by going to the beginning of" Puritan theology. His mission to the twentieth century becomes more urgent at this point as part of a broader insistence that "the mind of man is the basic factor in human history." Thus the double meaning of the Puritan "errand" spawns two competing historical trajectories in the 1950s: one leading to the transcendent life of the mind, the other to nuclear destruction, "a point in time beyond which the very concept of the future becomes meaningless" (217). Miller's mission becomes an effort to recover the original meaning of the errand, as on some "incomprehensible behest" (217) to counter the threatened end of the world by writing intellectual history in protest against the nuclear flash.[9] In venturing out to Africa, where he receives his "mission," he completes the cycle from which the Puritans were severed, to return home as a light to the world. In his opening theatrical metaphor of writing history as "a rank of spotlights," Miller restores the international audience that the Puritans lost when they were left alone in the darkened theater called America.

At this point where nuclear power enters his narrative in the present, Africa disappears from the background of the preface. To elevate American history to the ongoing life of the mind, Miller rejects the frightening alternative view of American history culminating in nuclear power. To uphold this belief, he projects this possibility onto Africa, which then fades out as though it were weighted down with the material symbols of America's "appalling power." Yet in the 1950s of the preface, Africa lingers in the shadow of the "city on the hill" and threatens to disrupt its light with independent narratives of decolonization and resistance to the unilinear history of cold war nuclear policy.

Thus to maintain the consistency of his own intellectual quest and the coherence of American history in the origins of Puritan thought, Miller must reject alternative origins: "This was not a fact of my choosing: had the origin been purely economic or imperial I should have been no less committed to reporting." As his preface so painstakingly details, the "meaning of America" lay not in Virginia and the slave trade, not in the Wilmot Proviso and westward expansion, not in the chain store and economic development, not in the fuel drums Miller unloaded in Africa in the 1920s, not in the nuclear power which so appalls him in the 1950s; nor could the life of the mind in America be written as either social history or Gibbon's imperial history. Instead Miller's preface clears the ground for his "spacious theme" by forcing competing themes into the space called "Africa," the site which generates and challenges the coherence of the project that would become American studies.

II

The location of Miller in Africa reveals the discursive formation of what William Appleman Williams called "one of the central themes of American historiography": that "there is no American Empire." *Cultures of United States Imperialism* challenges this still resilient paradigm of American exceptionalism that links the political practice of empire with its academic study. The second part of my introduction discusses three salient absences which contribute to this ongoing pattern of denial across several disciplines: the absence of culture from the history of U.S. imperialism; the absence of empire from the study of American culture; and the absence of the United States from the postcolonial study of imperialism.

The study of American culture has traditionally been cut off from the study of foreign relations. From across this divide, however, the fields of American studies and of diplomatic history curiously mirror one another in their respective blind spots to the cultures of U.S. imperialism. In a classic work of American studies, for example (contemporaneous with Miller's *Errand*), Richard Chase defined the special features of the American romance by distinguishing it from the imperial tendencies of the English novel:

> The English novel, one might say, has been a kind of imperial enterprise, an appropriation of reality, with the high purpose of bringing order to disorder. By contrast . . . the American novel has usually seemed content to explore, rather than to appropriate and civilize, the remarkable and in some ways un-

exampled territories of life in the New World and to reflect its anomalies and dilemmas. It has not wanted to build an imperium but merely to discover a new place and a new state of mind.[10]

A "new place" devoid of inhabitants (like Miller's wilderness) is elided into a "new state of mind" (the secularized errand), subject to its own internal tensions, unshackled and unsullied by the imperial politics of appropriation and civilization. Furthermore, Chase draws on an enduring assumption that the American struggle for independence from British colonialism makes U.S. culture inherently anti-imperialist.

Whereas Chase, like Miller, would have considered an American Empire to be a contradiction in terms, historians of foreign policy often deny its existence even when addressing the subject, as a recent revaluation of "The Global Role of the United States and its Imperial Consequences" concludes:

> Empire has remained a mere episode in American foreign policy. The acquisition of colonies and permanent informal control were the goals of American foreign policy only from 1898 to 1912. . . . The United States rose to the level of a global power in the course of its two struggles with what it considered as German imperialism, and after 1945 in the wake of the "containment" of what was officially perceived as "Soviet imperialism."[11]

Distant from traditional concerns of American studies, this historian voices a theme held in common with literary critic Chase, in the ascription of American uniqueness: just as the presumed openness and exploratory nature of the American novel become essentially nonimperial in contrast to the British, the unique feature of American global power lies in its opposition to the imperialism of the Nazis and the Soviets. Furthermore, Miller's dyad reappears in the central opposition between American and English novels that makes Indians disappear from Chase's "unexampled territories," just as the colonized world disappears from the struggle between the United States and totalitarianism.

Both examples—one from American studies in the 1950s, the other from diplomatic history in the 1980s—speak from within a cold war discourse, which defines American exceptionalism as inherently anti-imperialist, in opposition to the empire-building of either the Old World or of communism and fascism, which collapse together into totalitarianism. Yet in the demise of the cold war, the disavowal of American imperialism persists in the opposition to new "evil empires." The following Op-Ed piece on the eve of the Gulf War, for example, by a professor of international affairs, defines United States global power as nonhegemonic because it is opposed to the imperial aggression of a postcolonial nation:

> It took the Iraqi invasion of Kuwait to reveal what should have been obvious all along to the foreign policy experts: the bipolar, cold war world has given way not to "multipolarity" but to "unipolarity," with the U.S. the only pole left. . . . But unipolarity is not the same as American hegemony. . . . A unipolar world is not the same as a hierarchical system dominated by a single power that creates the rules as well as enforces them. . . . America could have stood by while the world drifted into a dangerous multipolarity. But, provoked by Mr. Hussein, the Bush Administration stopped this drift in a flurry of military deployments and superlative diplomatic activity. . . . Unipolarity arrived in just one summer week.[12]

These passages bear out Williams's observation of a double dynamic whereby displacement accompanies denial: "World Power" not "American Empire"; "discovery" not "imperium"; "global power" not "imperialism"; "unipolarity" not "hegemony." Furthermore, to denial and displacement we can add projection; imperial politics denied at home are visibly projected onto demonic others abroad, as something only they do and we do not. If the vehemence and persistence with which something is denied mark its importance and even formative power, the characterization of a nation's ideological opponents reveals as much about that nation's self-conception as it does about its enemies. Whereas the anti-American imperialists of the cold war ranged from the Old World of Europe to the brave new world of totalitarianism, the nations of the former colonized world—embodied in the Satanic Hussein—have now emerged as the new imperialists threatening "multipolarity" against the New World Order.

A major challenge to what might be called the paradigm of denial was launched by William Appleman Williams in *The Tragedy of American Diplomacy* (1955, another book contemporaneous with *Errand*). By focusing primarily on the economic sources of imperial expansion, however, Williams and his school of "revisionists" tended to ignore the role of culture in the unfolding of imperial politics. They thereby inverted yet remained within Miller's paradigm, which divides the spiritual and intellectual origins of America from its imperial and economic roots. Within this broad division, Williams was reacting directly against George Kennan and his school of "realists." In *American Diplomacy* (1951), Kennan articulated a long historical tradition of explaining away U.S. imperialism as an aberration, or a fleeting episode in the brief period following the Spanish-American War. Historians of Kennan's school, who view imperialism as inconsequential to American history, tend to attribute its brief eruption to the motivations that we might now call cultural: whether the misguided "moral idealism" of foreign policy elites, "public opinion," or "mass hysteria" generated by the yellow press. This view of empire as a momentary psychological lapse was countered by Williams in his view of imperial expansion as the driving force in national history from the conquest of North America through the cold war. Williams attributed this imperial drive primarily to economic motivations in the ongoing search for foreign markets to alleviate economic crises and preempt domestic social upheaval.

Revisionist emphasis on economic causality may have stemmed in part from the effort to endow imperialism with reality and solidity against the subjective explanations given by those "realists" who relegated empire to a minor detour in the march of American history. The economic approach, however, embodied its own contradictions, which led to multiple debates among historians, for example, about whether the fabled markets of Asia—long the chief prize sought by advocates of expansion—were mere "illusions," as opposed to having "real" economic value. If economics is privileged as the site of the "real," then cultural phenomena such as the belief in markets, or racialist discourse, or the ideology of "benevolent assimilation" can only be viewed as "illusions" that have little impact on a separate and narrowly defined political sphere.

This volume aims to explore more fully Williams's later understanding, which goes beyond economics alone, of *Empire as a Way of Life*—not only for the "foreign" subjects of U.S. domination, but for the U.S. citizens who benefit from it, who are subjugated to it, and who resist it. To understand the multiple ways in which empire becomes a way of life means to focus on those areas of culture traditionally ignored as long as imperialism was treated as a matter of foreign policy conducted by diplomatic elites or as a matter of economic necessity driven by market forces. Not only about foreign diplomacy or international relations, imperialism is also about consolidating domestic cultures and negotiating intranational relations. To foreground cultures is not only to understand how they abet the subjugation of others or foster their resistance, but also to ask how international relations reciprocally shape a dominant imperial culture at home, and how imperial relations are enacted and contested within the nation.

If the importance of culture has gone unrecognized in historical studies of American imperialism, the role of empire has been equally ignored in the study of American culture.[3] The current paradigm of

American studies today, still under intense debate, emphasizes multicultural diversity and scholarly "dissensus" and analyzes American society and culture in terms of internal difference and conflicts, structured around the relations of race, gender, ethnicity, and class. This approach overturns the paradigm to which Miller contributed, of consensus and univocality, wherein the meaning of America could be distilled through the symbolic manifestations of its mind and its seamless historical narrative. Yet the new pluralistic model of diversity runs the risk of being bound by the old paradigm of unity if it concentrates its gaze only narrowly on the internal lineaments of American culture and leaves national borders intact instead of interrogating their formation. That is, American nationality can still be taken for granted as a monolithic and self-contained whole, no matter how diverse and conflicted, if it remains implicitly defined by its internal social relations, and not in political struggles for power with other cultures and nations, struggles which make America's conceptual and geographic borders fluid, contested, and historically changing.

By defining American culture as determined precisely by its diversity and multivocality, "America" as a discrete identity can cohere independently of international confrontations with other national, local, and global cultural identities within and outside its borders. The critical force of multiculturalism thus may lay itself open to recuperation by a renewed version of "consensus." In a recent introduction to "The New American Studies," for example, Philip Fisher reduces multiculturalism and the complex identities of gender, race, and ethnicity to what he calls a new "regionalism," set in dialectic tension with the unifying elements of American nationalism. He tellingly transcribes all conflicts as "civil wars" over representation, over boundaries internal to an isolated fixed nationhood, and these conflicts inevitably help to cement the center. Thus it is not surprising that such a formulation leads back to revoice the rhetoric of cold war exceptionalism:

> Analysis within American studies will always be characterized by the absence of a monopoly of power. Because America had no experience of monarchy, it has a permanent democratic core working not only against the centralization of power, but, more important, against its inheritance or preservation over time. In the absence of a state we find ourselves freed of the intellectual components of the systematic state: ideology.[14]

In this model, the lack of a state means that the borders of national identity appear infinitely porous, but in fact, remain inflexibly unchallenged by competing political claims, ideological conflicts, or historical change. To reconsider the meaning of imperialism in American studies is to make statehood unavoidable as precisely the site of the monopoly of power and the production of ideology which Fisher finds inherently un-American. Yet the power concentrated in an imperial state is not static as he implies but is amassed both as an ongoing political, social, and cultural process in struggle with oppositions it gives rise to and responds to at home and abroad, and as a monopoly whose contours change over time in relation to those struggles.

This volume contributes to the multicultural critique of American ethnocentrism, not by supplanting heterogeneity with a new synthesis of empire, but by relating those internal categories of gender, race, and ethnicity to the global dynamics of empire-building. *Cultures of United States Imperialism* explores how such diverse identities cohere, fragment, and change in relation to one another and to ideologies of nationhood through the crucible of international power relations, and how, conversely, imperialism as a political or economic process abroad is inseparable from the social relations and cultural discourses of race, gender, ethnicity, and class at home. The binary opposition of the foreign and the domestic is itself imbued with the rhetoric of gender hierarchies that implicitly elevate the international to a male, public realm, and relegate the national to a female, private sphere. Foregrounding imperialism in the study of American cultures shows how putatively domestic conflicts are not simply contained at home but how they both emerge in response to international struggles and spill over national boundaries to be reenacted, challenged, or transformed.

The domestic and the foreign have long met on "the Frontier," a major conceptual site in American studies, which has undergone revision from the vacant space of the wilderness to a bloody battlefield of conflict and conquest, and more recently to a site of contacts, encounters, and collisions that produce new hybrid cultures. Yet this most recent revision of the frontier risks downplaying the imperial dimensions of power and violence that structure, underwrite, and are informed by cultural "interpenetrations."[15] The field of Chicano studies has begun to redress the conceptual limits of the frontier, by displacing it with the site of "the borderlands."[16] Where the frontier implies a model of center and periphery, which confront one another most often in a one-way imposition of power, the borderlands are seen as multidimensional and transterritorial; they not only lie at the geographic and political margins of national identity but as often traverse the center of the metropolis. The borderlands link the study of ethnicity and immigration inextricably to the study of international relations and empire. At these borders, foreign relations do not take place outside the boundaries of America, but instead constitute American nationality. The borderlands thus transform the traditional notion of the frontier from the primitive margins of civilization to a decentered cosmopolitanism.

Chicano studies has brought an international perspective to American studies in part by reconceiving the concept of ethnicity (traditionally treated as a self-enclosed entity) through the theory and politics of postcoloniality. Most current studies of imperial and postcolonial culture, however, tend to omit discussions of the United States as an imperial power.[17] The history of American imperialism strains the definition of the postcolonial, which implies a temporal development (from "colonial" to "post") that relies heavily on the spatial coordinates of European empires, in their formal acquisition of territories and the subsequent history of decolonization and national independence. How would this Eurocentric notion of postcoloniality apply to the history of American imperialism, which often does not fit this model? What would postcolonial culture mean in relation to U.S. imperialism, both on its own territory and in parts of the world where the United States predominated more directly only after the formal independence of former European colonies, in a power relation often called neocolonial? Is it possible yet to speak of "postimperial" culture, and how might it differ from the postcolonial?

The absence of the United States in the postcolonial study of culture and imperialism curiously reproduces American exceptionalism from without. The United States either is absorbed into a general notion of "the West," represented by Europe, or it stands for a monolithic West. United States continental expansion is often treated as an entirely separate phenomenon from European colonialism of the nineteenth century, rather than as an interrelated form of imperial expansion. The divorce between these two histories mirrors the American historiographical tradition of viewing empire as a twentieth-century aberration, rather than as part of an expansionist continuum. By linking United States nation-building and empire-building as historically coterminous and mutually defining, the essays in this volume complicate the simple chronology that plots the U.S. empire emerging full blown at various stages of the twentieth century to step into the shoes of dying European empires; instead the essays explore in varied contexts how the United States, as Richard Drinnon has claimed, exports its past "metaphysics of Indian-hating" and Indian-fighting into new frontiers abroad and across new borders.[18]

The contrast we have seen in Miller between Old World and New World empires may still inform the current critical trajectories that separate British studies from American studies. While the former contests an ethnocentric national tradition by decentering it from the postcolonial vantage of commonwealth culture and imperial history, the deconstruction of a monolithic American tradition has revolved more around challenging the canon by competing domestic traditions. Two historically different yet interrelated definitions of empire—as external subjugation of colonies versus internal national consolidation—have been split between these two national cultures. Just as current studies of English nationalism are breaking down this split by examining the empire close to home, not only in Ireland but also in urban immigrant communities, this volume directs its focus on these interconnections between internal and external colonization in the imperial constitution of American national cultures. It links America as a colony and an empire to the imperial enterprises of other nations in a global system and insists on the historical specificity of the cultures of U.S. imperialism without either collapsing them into European models or propagating a new model of American exceptionalism.

The divergent yet intertwined histories of American and European imperialism might be found to cross paths where Perry Miller first conceived of the "meaning of America": the banks of the Congo. In a recent revision of Conrad's classic text of European imperialism, the documentary film *Hearts of Darkness*, by Eleanor Coppola, relocates the African site to Vietnam and the Philippines. Francis Ford Coppola would probably view *Apocalypse Now* (1979) as the reversal of Miller's paradigm of the denial of empire, as the antiwar film exposes the horrors of American imperialism in Vietnam. Furthermore, Coppola might be seen to counter American exceptionalism, by scripting the war through Conrad's text, and placing the Vietnam war in relation to the history of European imperialism. The documentary on the making of the film, however, which stands awkwardly between an exposé and a publicity reel, refuses recognition of the film's complicity with the imperial context that enables its production, at the same time that context is paraded dramatically on the screen.

Coppola located his "Congo" as the setting for his exploration of the meaning of America in the late 1970s, neither in Africa nor in Vietnam, but in the Philippines, a former United States colony with ongoing strong ties to the United States through the repressive regime of President Ferdinand Marcos. There for great sums Coppola bought the support of the regime, borrowed Marcos's bodyguards, and rented military equipment from the U.S. built army of the Philippines (since the U.S. military would not rent them equipment for an antiwar film). As the documentary covers the shooting of the famous scene of the helicopter attack on the beach, we watch the Filipino helicopters suddenly turn out of line as they are radioed by their commanders to fight a political insurrection in the immediate vicinity. The breakdown between fiction and history in these glaring parallels between the present in the Philippines and the past of Vietnam do not make Eleanor or Francis Coppola reflect on their participation as film makers in the dynamics of empire which the documentary explores as history. Instead, the blatant evidence of the surrounding reality of imperialism generates excitement in the voice-over about being in the "thick of the jungle," about being so close to a real battlefield. They find in the Philippines a way of retrieving nostalgically the intensity of the battlefield experience they may have rejected on political grounds. By turning the Philippines into a timeless "jungle" backdrop, outside of history, like the African "jungle" of Miller, the Coppolas deny the imperial history which brings them to the Philippines. Yet, like the setting of Africa, the backdrop of the Philippines speaks out of the cultures of U.S. imperialism which enable the production of this American epic film— as the helicopters break through the stage set to fight a real war. As we watch both the film and the documentary in the journey up the river, a river which conflates the Congo, Vietnam, and the Philippines and takes the viewer to "the beginning of time," indeed, as the productive political context of U.S. imperial culture fades from view, we are left alone with America.

Notes

I would like to thank Dick Burt, Leslie Moore, Michael Rogin, Priscilla Wald, and Don Weber for their helpful comments on earlier versions of this introduction.

1 William Appleman Williams, "The Frontier Thesis and American Foreign Policy," *Pacific Historical Review* 24 (November 1955): 379–95.

2 Toni Morrison, *Playing in the Dark: Whiteness and the Literary Imagination* (Cambridge: Harvard University Press, 1992), p. 6.

3 Perry Miller, "Preface," *Errand into the Wilderness* (Cambridge: Harvard University Press, 1956), pp. vii–x. Subsequent references to the preface are to this edition; quotations from the other essays in this volume will be cited parenthetically in the text.

4 Gene Wise, " 'Paradigm Dramas' in American Studies: A Cultural and Insti-

tutional History of the Movement," *American Quarterly* 31 (1979): 301–4; Myra Jehlen also views this scene as a typical American effort to locate national origins, in *American Incarnation: The Individual, the Nation, and the Continent* (Cambridge: Harvard University Press, 1986), pp. 28–29. Most studies of Miller's life and thought view this as a centrally defining scene; see, for example, Robert Middlekauff, "Perry Miller," in *Pastmasters*, ed. Marcus Cunliffe and Robin Winks (New York: Harper and Row, 1969), pp. 167–90. It is, after all, hard to imagine such a moment becoming as memorable in the lore of American historiography if it had taken place in, say, the mountains of Colorado or the streets of Greenwich Village (both places Miller visited as a college drop-out before he reached Africa).

5 Morrison, p. 8.

6 Quoted in Walter LaFeber, *The American Age: United States Foreign Policy at Home and Abroad Since 1750* (New York: Norton, 1989), p. 112.

7 In the late nineteenth century, for example, Henry Stanley's famous accounts of his travels both represented Africa to America and made him an active participant in the political and economic establishment of King Leopold's Free Congo. Stanley was a Welsh immigrant who, though he later resumed British citizenship, regarded himself as an American and was financed mostly by Americans at the time of his African explorations. He also advised the American delegates to the Berlin West Africa Conference (1884), the first major U.S. participation in the European colonial negotiations on the most effective principles for the occupation of Africa.

8 For Miller's rejection of Turner's thesis, see *Errand,* pp. 1–2.

9 For Miller's more direct statement of the need to turn to the intellect in the face of the nuclear threat of the machine age, see *Responsibility of Mind in a Civilization of Machines: Essays by Perry Miller,* ed. John Crowell and Stanford J. Searl, Jr. (Amherst: University of Massachusetts Press, 1979).

10 Richard Chase, *The American Novel and Its Tradition* (New York: Doubleday, 1957), p. 12.

11 Klaus Schwabe, "The Global Role of the United States and Its Imperial Consequences, 1898–1973," in *Imperialism and After: Continuities and Discontinuities,* ed. Wolfgang J. Mommsen and Jurgen Osterhammel (London: Allen and Unwin, 1986), pp. 13–33.

12 Richard Spielman, "The Emerging Unipolar World," *New York Times,* August 21, 1991, p. 27.

13 There are of course exceptions to this paradigm. See, for example, Robert Rydell, *All the World's a Fair: Visions of Empire at American International Expositions, 1876–1916* (Chicago: University of Chicago Press, 1984); and Drinnon, below.

14 Philip Fisher, *The New American Studies: Essays from Representations* (Berkeley: University of California Press, 1991), p. xxii.

15 This term is used by Annette Kolodny, who persuasively calls for redefining the literature of frontiers through "the evolving dialogue between different cultures and languages and their engagement with one another and with the physical terrain" (5) in "Letting Go Our Grand Obsessions: Notes Toward a New Literary History of the American Frontiers," *American Literature* 64, (March 1992): 1–18. Her analysis, however, risks reproducing the monolithic model of American identity now defined by this new frontier of cultural contact and negotiation.

16 See, for example, Gloria Anzaldúa, *Borderlands/La Frontera: The New Mestiza* (San Francisco: Spinsters/Aunt Lute, 1987); Renato Rosaldo, "Ideology, Place, and People Without Culture," *Cultural Anthropology* 3, (1988): 77–87; José David Saldívar, "The Limits of Cultural Studies," *American Literary History* 2, no. 2 (Summer 1990): 251–66.

17 A recent special issue of *Representations*, 37 (Winter 1992), for example, entitled *Imperial Fantasies and Postcolonial Histories*, includes no essays related to the United States. Lawrence Buell, in contrast, proposes that early American writers be understood as postcolonial; he thereby not only overlooks the history of American imperialism, but in a sense colonizes postcolonial theory by implicitly positing the United States as the original postcolonial nation; "American Literary Emergence as a Postcolonial Phenomenon," *American Literary History* 4.3 (Fall 1992): 411–42.

18 Richard Drinnon, *Facing West: The Metaphysics of Indian-Hating and Empire-Building* (New York: NAL, 1980).

Donald E. Pease

New Perspectives on U.S. Culture

and Imperialism

he idea for this volume germinated in the shadow of three macro-political events—the end of the cold war, the Persian Gulf War, and the Columbian quincentennial. While the breakdown of cold war ideology made formerly submerged heterogeneous cultural histories available to public and scholarly discourse, clashes over the celebration of the Discovery made visible an absent imperial history that the Gulf War, in its renewal of an imperial synthesis, threatened once again to eclipse.

Contested by alternative histories, the official celebration of the Discovery covered up what Richard Van Alstyne had demonstrated persuasively in *Rising American Empire;* namely, that U.S. culture was from its origins grounded on "an *imperium*—a dominion, state or sovereignty that would expand in population and territory, and increase in strength and power."[1] Although the United States' imperial nationalism was predicated on the superiority of military and political organization as well as economic wealth, it depended for its efficacy on a range of cultural technologies, among which colonialist policies (exercised both internally and abroad) of conquest and dominion figured prominently. The invasive settlement of the Americas provided a vast space wherein were linked as related claims on the "unmapped territories" the imperatives of reason and conquest. In shaping the "New World" according to the demands of the emergent sciences of geography, botany, and anthropology, imperialism understood itself primarily as a cultural project involved in naming, classifying, textualizing, appropriating, exterminating, demarcating, and governing a new regime.

The anthropological concept of culture depended upon the Americas as the theater for colonial encounters wherein it discovered its objects as well as its mode of knowledge. When resituated within the inexorable logics of imperialism, modernization, and world capitalism, these imperial encounters resulted in cultural technologies that in facilitating colonization and colonial rule had also spawned the utterly new sociopolitical categories of nationality, race, geography, history, ethnicity, and gender; prefigured political organizations that would later guarantee the authority of the modern U.S. security state (and legitimate resistance to its repressive apparatus) and later still would consolidate for the United States an international cultural hegemony. As an ongoing cultural project, U.S. imperialism is thus best understood as a complex and interdependent relationship with hegemonic as well as counterhegemonic modalities of coercion and resistance. When linked with the more inclusive project of global imperialism, U.S. cultural formations manifest themselves as heterogeneous and unevenly developed modes of internal colonization in complex relations with Second and Third World nations. Through an uncovering of reciprocal interanimations of U.S. cultures and U.S. imperialism, the contributors to this volume intend the restoration of heterogeneous cultural histories.

The Persian Gulf War threatened to eclipse such heterogeneous cultural histories with a monocultural image of the national identity predicated on the active suppression of the specificity of race, class, and gender relations as disruptive to this renewed synthesis of U.S. imperialism. Like other wars in U.S. history, the Gulf War derived its official self-representations from a symbolic economy already saturated with racial and gender hierarchies, and the discursive logic of the war also legitimated related forms of racism in the domestic sphere. The New World Order the Bush administration claimed to have achieved as an effect of the war was in fact a rebirth of a national mythology developed in the aftermath of the Second World War.

In "Left Alone With America" (this volume), Amy Kaplan uncovered as a cognitive gap in the inaugural moment of American studies the ideological disjuncture separating the diplomatic history of U.S. imperialism from academic study of the national culture and enabling imperialism to go unrecognized as an American way of life. In light of the linkages Kaplan has adduced between the founding mythology of American Studies and the official doctrine of American exceptionalism, the disciplinary map of the field of American studies over the last fifty years can be understood in relation to the geopolitical fortunes of that doctrine. For the purposes of this volume, the history of U.S. cultural studies can be divided into four periods: the "official nationalism" of the myth-symbol school, spanning 1945–68, the "critical nationalism" during the years of detente 1968–80, the neocolonialism of the Reagan-Bush era, and the more recent postnationalist initiatives of the so-called New Americanists.

In the relationship they have discerned between Americanist masterworks and their extrinsic historical environment, practitioners of the myth-symbol school proposed that the particulars of historical processes and the "concrete universals" of American literary history were involved in a homologous relationship. Previously the new critics had conceived the relationship between the part and whole of a literary artifact as a synchronic state and as such logically incompatible with extrinsic historical enactments. The myth-symbolists did not abandon the new critics' formalist criteria but misrecognized those criteria as motives for the historical actions which took place within the more inclusive Americanist metanarrative constructed out of their mythology.

While each of the masterworks of the myth-symbol school has provided slightly different accounts of the metanarrative that defined the practices of Americanists, all of them have presupposed a realm of pure possibility where a whole self internalized the norms of American history in a language and series of actions that corroborated American exceptionalism. When interpreted from within the ideal space of the myth-symbol school, Americanist masterworks legitimized hegemonic understanding of American history expressively totalized in the metanarrative that had been reconstructed out of (or more accurately read into) these masterworks. That metanarrative of American history, insofar as it involved a universal subject in a transhistorical action, should have been classified as political mythology rather than history. The complex mythological event informing this metanarrative cross-identified Columbus's discovery of the "New World" with the United States' successful War of Independence against the British Empire. As a consequence, referents embedded in this complex imaginary event came to name—that is to entitle—master texts within the scholarly field of American studies. In keeping with the myth-symbol school of interpretation, these referents engaged a prototypical American self (*American Adam*), in a quest romance (*Errand into the Wilderness*) to liberate "our" native land (*Virgin Land*) from "foreign" encroachment (*The Power of Blackness*).

In the place of accounts compatible with this metanarrative, Americanists writing between 1968 and 1980 criticized the political agenda at work within its ruling assumptions. Richard Slotkin's *Regeneration Through Violence* and Annette Kolodny's *The Lay of the Land*, to name two of the representative works of this period, redescribed "virgin land" and the metanarrative it supported to be, in both its conception and deployment, an ideological cover-up for Indian removal, frontier violence, government theft, land devastation, class cruelty, racial brutality, and misogyny. Slotkin and Kolodny and other critics of U.S. imperialism constructed out of the political unconscious of *Virgin Land* what might be called an alternative primal scene. Their books proposed this scene as the different context from within which Americanists could construct their critical personae, canonical objects, and disciplinary practices.[2]

After 1968, new historicism and multiculturalism emerged as more or less contemporary strategies in the field of American studies, but with two very different intentions. The new historicism declared the impossibility of subverting the national metanarrative that multiculturalists had found bankrupt. The contentious relations between these two strategies may well determine the future of the field. Because of its capacity to colonize resistance within already existing cultural spaces, the new historicism can be said to reenact as its methodology the imperializing power of U.S. nationalism. It imposes a binary framework that adapts the temporal logic of prior colonialism and subsequent postcolonialism to cultural forms and thereby proposes that such forms be understood as: (1) either already subsumed under the dominant social logic, or (2) that their "resistance" in miming the colonizing power reaffirms its hegemony.[3]

When practiced in the absence of the global social analytic Kaplan has invoked, multiculturalism can be understood as the new historicism pluralized. In associating the subjugated knowledges of race, class, gender, ethnicity, and nationality *solely* with the work of their emancipation, the new historicism evades the heterological sense in which cultural spaces are not answerable to binary social logic. While they do not refuse new historicism as a reading strategy, the contributors to *Cultures of U.S. Imperialism* have drawn insights from a broad range of interpretive practices: discourse analysis, post-Althusserian Marxism, Foucaultian genealogy, cultural materialism, critical legal studies, postcolonial and subaltern studies. Overall, they indicate how the introduction of a global analytic dimension to otherwise local struggle enables the subjects positioned there to understand the production of racial, gendered regional and class subjectivities as mutually implicated and to recognize, as a corollary, that a group who successfully overcame cultural oppression in the first world may have depended, for their surplus cultural resources, on class exploitation in the so-called Third World.

Partially as a result of the end of the cold war, the habit of binary thinking upon which the new historicism depended has been discarded and revisionist interpretations of the part imperialism has played in the history of U.S. culture have been taken up across the disciplines. *Cultures of U.S. Imperialism* addresses the relationships between recent changes in the understanding of U.S. diplomatic history and the emergent interest in the importance of imperialism to cultural constructions in general and for critical multiculturalism's understanding of race, class, and gender as culturally constructed categories specifically. Because the concept of U.S. imperialism has itself become the subject of political and scholarly debates, this volume, rather than foreclosing the contentions and contradictions at issue within any single understanding, intends their elaboration.

The emergent discourse of "global-localism" proposes the most challenging critique directed against the pre-constituted categories anchored in the discourse of anti-imperialism. It argues against the colonizer's power to construct the "other" out of figures within an ethnocentric unconscious. Because of its capacity to violate national boundaries, imperialism, according to this critique, should be understood instead as a phase in the process of globalization that, in disrupting the coherence of the geopolitical entities called nation-states, thereby enabled their openness to interconnection with all other nation-states.

Whereas critics of imperialism usually endorse a reading of the emergence of Third World colonies into nation-states as a more or less effective anti-imperialist project, global-localism construes Third World nationalism as itself a moment in colonial domination, and it understands social relations in the so-called Third World to be at once more complicated, unbounded, and interconnected than the anti-imperialist reading permits. This discourse thereafter insists that colonialism, nationalism, and imperialism be understood as interlinked phases in a decentered yet encompassing system.

In recasting imperialism and nationalism as more or less equivalent enframements of actual geopolitical conditions, however, globalist thought also would characteristically reconfigure such a conspicuous imbalance in the global system as the economic hierarchy (designed to support the globalist advantage of transnational corporations and multinational capital and foster other vertical rankings in matters of race, gender, and ethnicity) as if it were merely a temporary dysfunction rather than a component structural to the system.

The discourse of global localism should not be ignored, but neither should it displace the critique of imperialism. Taken together the two discourses configure an interpretative crossroads whereby each supplies key figures missing from the other. Whereas anti-imperialism loses track of the role imperialism played in a more inclusive process of global inter-

connection, global-localism loses sight of the economic and cultural exploitation at work in the process. To begin to keep track of the terms missing from each discourse, they should be taken together as equivalently
important modes of understanding cultures of U.S. imperialism.

To accommodate this more inclusive understanding, the concept of
culture has been treated with equal openness to conflicting interpretations, which include ways of life, symbolic actions and representations,
contradictory forms of common sense, social practices, and networks of
social institutions. The historical scope of the volume is not limited to one
period, but instead ranges across American history (without any pretense
of coverage) from early colonial culture as the outgrowth of European
colonialism, to continental expansion and conquest, to twentieth-century
international relations. Interdisciplinary in scope and historical and theoretical in approach, the volume strives to uncover these changing international relations and to examine how these dialectical relations contribute
to the formation of national and oppositional identities.

The volume is divided into four parts conceived to address and enable different questions. Under the rubric "Nation-Building as Empire-
Building" are gathered essays that investigate the cultural consolidation
of national identity through continental expansion in extricable relation
to various forms of imperial domination. Contributors to "Borderline
Negotiations of Race, Gender, and Nation" delineate the connections between representations of "foreign" cultures and peoples inside and outside U.S. national boundaries and investigate as well how the affiliations
and conflicts between the genders were shaped by imperialist and nationalist contexts. While the questions addressed by the several essays collected under "Colonizing Resistance or Resisting Colonization?" intersect
with those in "Borderline Negotiations," their focus is on the efficacy of
the national, mestizo, and diaspora identities constructed in opposition to
U.S. imperialism. With the exception of Brannen's, which scrutinizes the
similarities between Japan's cultural imperialism and the United States',
and the final essay on "Occidentalism," the essays in "Imperial Spectacles"
interpret the Gulf War as a representative instance of an emergent imperializing cultural formation.

The significance of Myra Jehlen's essay "Why Did the Europeans
Cross the Ocean? A Seventeenth-Century Riddle" to the volume's topic
and the heading ("Nation-Building as Empire-Building") under which it
appears derives from the unprecedented positionality Jehlen discerns at
the intersection between a discredited imperialist archive—represented
by Montaigne's essays—and an emergent postcolonialist problematic. In

pursuit of an answer to the riddle in the title, Jehlen traces the epistemo-logical fortunes of three key terms—"universal humanity," "other," and "difference"—which have a stake in both the imperialist archive and the anticolonialist problematic. Then she stages a purely fictive (and delayed) colonial encounter between a European, Montaigne, who was skeptical of imperialism's self-justification, and an Aztec, Motechuza, who shared Montaigne's skepticism. In "Of Cannibals," Montaigne refused the "other" as an adequate epistemological category, and preferred instead to de-scribe New World natives as only relatively different from Europeans. But without an alternative narrative in which to explain their efficacy, the differences Montaigne discerned in the natives' culture (their "wheel-lessness" in Jehlen's representative instance) rendered them susceptible to wholesale inclusion within the Enlightenment's imperial narrative of the Europeans' conquest. Jehlen proposes, as a supplement to Mon-taigne's essay, Motechuza's written account of his encounter with Cortes. In reading this text alongside Montaigne's essay, Jehlen constructs a here-tofore unrecognized "zone of contestation" *between* the Aztecs and the Europeans. In this space of mutual contestation, Jehlen argues, Cortes and Motechuza were neither reducible to the abstract negativity of "dif-ferences" nor able to recuperate the same identities; each was instead *potentially* able to define himself against but also in terms of the other.

Jehlen understands the boundary line separating colonizer from colo-nized as an occasion for mutuality but in "Terms of Assimilation: Legis-lating Subjectivity in the Emerging Nation," Priscilla Wald reinscribes this boundary within the "frontier" that the U.S. national narrative had sacralized. At this liminal site the line separating colonizer from colonized was recoded as the difference between insiders and outsiders. Thereafter the U.S. "frontier mentality" was associated with chronic anxieties over secure borders and stable cultural subjects with the right to expand the frontier if you were an insider and to be expropriated if not. The U.S. national narrative was itself to be understood as the product of ongoing border negotiations and comprised of a constellation of texts—political Supreme Court decisions ("Cherokee Nation," "Dred Scott"), legislative acts (Dawes Act), literary (*Hobomok*), and presidential (Lincoln's Second Inaugural)—all of which struggled to provide a stable referent for the "We the People" clause in the Declaration of Independence. Because that referent was vulnerable to internal decomposition—immigration, misce-genation, Native American mimicry—the boundary lines distinguishing a national people from others had to be continually reinstated (through the rhetorical and ideological strategies represented in the cited texts) whenever the "external" forces threatened to dissolve them.

Wald's historicist readings correlate the origins of the U.S. national narrative with territorial ancestry, but a rather different account of the origins of the national narrative informs Gauri Viswanathan's "The Naming of Yale College." In this essay, Viswanathan unearths from the imperialist archive abundant evidence of Yale University's embeddedness within Britain's imperialist enterprise. The party of Connecticut Dissenters who asked Elihu Yale to support the construction of Yale College were persuasive largely as a result of the homology they adduced between the college's purpose and Elihu Yale's prior service as a colonial agent in the East India Company. Because Elihu Yale believed England had to be the controlling center for both halves of the Empire (the American "West Indies" and the British East Indies), he found this rhetoric appealing. Their additional proposal that the college be named after Yale added symbolic patrimony to imperial urge as an equivalently persuasive motive for his philanthropy. Imperial wealth again supplied the precondition for this appeal. It inaugurated a complex system of circulating goods and capital that required the metaphorical translation of biological filiation into institutional affiliation as a more durable form of reproduction.

Viswanathan's association of a Yale education with its namesake's imperialism is startling partly because the imperial origins of his patrimony have been all but erased. In "Savage Law: The Plot Against American Indians in *Johnson and Graham's Lessee v. M'Intosh* and *The Pioneers*," Eric Cheyfitz proposes as a rationale for this erasure the following claim: Western imperialism founded its program on the disappearance of the other. As warrant for this claim Cheyfitz demonstrates the ways in which law and letters conspired to dispossess the Native American. Both Cooper's novel and the judicial decision it rationalized, Cheyfitz observes, were the result of a liberal ideology whose key terms—property, individual, and representation—were not applicable to Native American governance. Cases involving Native American societies could not be properly adjudicated within U.S. courts because they were grounded in incommensurate assumptions. They were constituted, that is, out of consensual rather than representative modes of governance. They occupied communal land rather than private property and were comprised of mutually acknowledged persons rather than private individuals.

Cheyfitz reads Cooper's *The Pioneers* as complicit with a dominant legal fiction whereby white settlers inherited legal title for their property as if from a vanished native American tribe. But, in "Science Fiction, the World's Fair, and the Prosthetics of Empire, 1910–1915," Bill Brown proposes that racism remained in the national psyche long after *The Pioneers* where it constituted the political unconscious of science fiction. The technological artifacts represented in turn-of-the-century U.S. science fiction produced a scenario akin to that of the universal subject in Enlightenment discourse. These figures enabled a complete separation of persons from bodies, placing what Brown calls a "prosthesis" (either as "universal subjects" or machine men) at the site of disembodiment and recycling antebellum race relations to rationalize the process. In *Engine Man*, to cite Brown's representative example, man and machine became white and black (and the "more and the less human"). Following an intricate reading of the posters featuring the body of Hercules as representative of international work on the Panama Canal, Brown concludes that Hercules's perfect body completes the separation of international labor from the bodies of individual laborers and that this international aspect of labor resulted as well in its denationalization.

The trajectory of Brown's argument tracked the erasure of the nation as well as the persons who embodied it from the scene of labor and culminated in a "body without a memory." In "Buffalo Bill's 'Wild West' and the Mythologization of the American Empire," Richard Slotkin argues that the mythology supplementing the national narrative was a defensive reaction against denationalization. Slotkin accounts for William Cody's Wild West Show as a representative instance of such a reaction. Organized at the turn of the century, this traveling show comprised at once an elegy for the death of the Western as a genre and the construction of a new role for the United States as a leader on the world stage. Concentrating on the symbolic exchange between such agents of real-world imperialism as Teddy Roosevelt's Rough Riders and William Cody the mythmaker, Slotkin concludes that the former put the latter to effective historical usage with the consequence that Cody's Wild West achieved something like diplomatic recognition in Teddy Roosevelt's Battle of San Juan Hill.

In concluding that the nation recycled its myth of the frontier as imperial policy, Slotkin implies that the national mythology was exportable. Vicente Rafael argues that Filipinos routinely demystified this mythology as a form of U.S. cultural imperialism. Throughout "White Love: Surveillance and Nationalist Resistance in the U.S. Colonization of the Philippines," Rafael painstakingly documents the natives' discrimination of the U.S. stipulated motive for intervention in the Philippines—altruistic regard for the natives—from its tragic and invariable consequence—brutal colonial relations. Upon distinguishing the U.S. administration's cover story from its actual consequences, Rafael underscores as well the fundamental contradiction between an imperial state able to acknowledge Filipinos' self-rule only as their internalization of U.S. ideology and a native people who understand this internalization as only another form of colonial surveillance. In its reduction of persons to statistics in the areas of health, education, and elections, the census became the primary instrument of U.S. domination. But the nationalist dramas which emerged coincidentally with the census, Rafael observed, supplied Filipinos with an alternative representational economy. These dramas contested the instrumentalities of American colonial rule and activated collective memories of the Filipino defeat of Imperial Spain as an oppositional resource.

Rafael's focus is on the effect of U.S. rule on native peoples and their nationalism as counterimperialist. In "Black and Blue on San Juan Hill," Amy Kaplan suggests a nationalist motive for a U.S. imperial adventure. As a "just war" directed against an external enemy, the Spanish-American War, according to Kaplan, reunified the nation. U.S. soldiers, in Kaplan's reading, did battle on two fronts: internationally against Spain in their colonies' struggle for national independence and nationally against Reconstruction and blacks' struggle for civil rights. In the complex interaction it thereby effects among race, nation, and empire, U.S. foreign policy becomes a medium as well for the policing of domestic racial tensions.

In "Teddy Bear Patriarchy: Taxidermy in the Garden of Eden, New York City, 1908–1936," Donna Haraway refigures Teddy Roosevelt from the context of U.S. imperial policies in Puerto Rico and New York City where Kaplan had him situated, relocating his cultural effects to the Roosevelt Memorial, where Roosevelt presided over African Hall, the central building of the American Museum of Natural History. In a complex tracking of the images, stuffed trophies, and photographs housed in the Roosevelt Memorial Archive, Haraway interassociates Roosevelt's cult of masculinity and the emergent science of eugenics with Carl Akeley's contributions to the science of taxidermy, exposing the three projects as functions of defensive reaction against decadence, "the dread disease of imperialist, capitalist, white culture."

Both Kaplan and Haraway demonstrated how U.S. imperial adventure renewed frontier mentality that was the topic of Wald's essay, and how this mentality then domesticated an official national history clearly reinscribed the terms of nationalist assimilation and exclusion in an imperialist adventure. But the borderland literature he analyzes in "Américo Paredes and Decolonization" enables José David Saldívar to propose empowering alternatives to this mentality. Drawing upon Raymond Williams's formulation of the notion in *The Country and The City*, Saldívar refines and extends Williams's understanding of border literature as counterhegemonic. The borderland conflicts represented in Paredes's novels, Saldívar claims, effectively counter Anglocentric hegemony and produce the culturally safe places needed for the construction of heterogeneous identities. The symbolic events represented in border literature supplant events in Anglo history and propose for readers an understanding of identity as processual rather than fixed and constructed within but also against official representation.

If Kaplan finds imperial adventure an American way of life, Rafael and Saldívar discern cultures constructed in opposition to U.S. imperialism. In "Pious Sites: Chamorro Culture Between Spanish Catholicism and American Liberal Individualism," however, Vicente Diaz further complicates the relationship between dominant and subversive. The Chamorro culture he describes is indebted to both of the dominant cultures represented in the title yet identifiable with neither. In his dramatic unfolding of the political vissitudes of two island issues—the suicide of the former governor of Guam and the controversy concerning an abortion decision—Diaz constructs a highly complex space; one that cannily solicits yet cunningly abrogates metanarratives (Spanish Catholicism, U.S. liberalism) that would otherwise definitively resolve them. As a consequence, Diaz accounts for Guam's hybridity as a multiform legacy comprised of colonial as well as countercolonial modes of expression and dizzingly asymmetrical narrative emplotments.

The dramatic tension in Diaz's essay originated in the ongoing cultural contestations to which he drew our attention—between representational economies capable of imposing order and Guam natives' ingenious capacity for evasion. In "Plotting the Border: John Reed, Pancho Villa, and *Insurgent Mexico*," Christopher Wilson discovers a related tension in representations of Pancho Villa by U.S. reporters. Because it conflated the Indian with the cowboy, the bandit with the border patrolmen, Pancho Villa's persona embodied the fluidity the press associated with the border. Focusing primarily on John Reed's correspondence and press reports, Wilson finds in their construction of Villa's Mexican campaign a comparable fluidity. According to Wilson, Reed's accounts of the Mexican insurgency seemed a version of what Saldívar had called border literature, rather than a journalist's representation of the phenomenon.

The essays included under the first two headings, "Nation-Building as Empire-Building" and "Borderline Negotiations of Race, Gender, and Nation," presupposed a political difference between imperialism and anti-colonialism, and they took the efficacy of resistance for granted. But the essays included under the heading "Colonizing Resistance or Resisting Colonization?" question these assumptions. In "Anti-Imperial American-ism," for example, Walter Benn Michaels explains that Thomas Nelson Page in *Red Rock* and Thomas Dixon in *The Clansman* and *The Leop-ard's Spots* correlated their Americanism with their opposition to U.S. imperialism. According to Michaels, these writers were representative of an Americanist reaction against the extension of U.S. rule to foreign protectorates. But unlike their precursors, isolationist "progressives" like Dixon understood national citizenship as a form of resistance to an *Afri-can* rather than British (or Soviet) Empire. And they thereby accepted *essentially* racial criteria for U.S. citizenship. Michaels largely contradicts the premises of the other contributors to the volume and finds that anti-imperialism *inevitably* promoted a cultural Americanism, and includes in this progeny present-day multiculturalists who espouse what Michaels provocatively labels racism without racists.

In "Appeals for (Mis)recognition: Theorizing the Diaspora," Kenneth Warren points up a difficulty in being properly recognized, with Langs-ton Hughes as the exemplar. Hughes's partial identifications—with Afri-cans, African Americans, intellectual elites, urban masses—resulted in a multiply interpellated identity and a more or less permanent crisis in self-legitimation. Hughes's plight was not singular, but representative of what Warren calls the "diaspora subject" who must always be aware of himself as from elsewhere even as "he" is in the process of making an appeal to be considered as if "he" belonged.

Warren's account of Hughes's experience solicits pathos, but in "Re-sisting the Heat: Menchú, Morrison, and Incompetent Readers," Doris Sommer argues for the virtues of such misrecognition as a productive re-fusal to become meaningful. Associating the will to interpretive mastery with other forms of imperial will, Sommer constructs, by way of read-ings of Toni Morrison's *Beloved* and Rigoberta Menchú's testimonial, a provisional vocabulary of the patterns and tropes of literary refusals of meaning.

In "Black Americans' Racial Uplift Ideology as 'Civilizing Mission'" Kevin Gaines examines the complex rhetorical strategy Pauline Hop-kins believed it necessary to adopt, one that was at once opposed to cruder forms of racism yet aligned with the civilizationist ideology that authorized what Gaines calls "metaracism." By identifying herself as an "agent" of progress for more disadvantaged blacks, Hopkins did not break down racial barriers and regain citizenship rights, as she had hoped. The "racial uplift" platform she espoused only legitimated the racist premises of Christian imperialism, which consigned black American and colonial subjects alike to a common category (of the politically unfit).

William Cain identifies W. E. B. Du Bois's identification with Stalinist Communism as responsible for a related cultural blind spot. In "From Liberalism to Communism: The Political Thought of W. E. B. Du Bois," Cain explains that Du Bois's life-long efforts to restore political agency to oppressed blacks resulted in his "entrapment," during the cold war era, within an unwavering Stalinist perspective. After pointing out such available options as C. L. R. James's anti-Stalinist cosmopolitanism, Cain characterizes Du Bois's identification with Stalinism as finally an abridgment of his freedom of speech.

Cain's explanations for Du Bois's abject refusal to find in Stalinism anything other than the Africanized America he desired are perforce speculative. Stalin may have been the interlocutor for the construction of his oppositional identity, Cain hypothesizes, because he enabled Du Bois to develop a reverse language for the personal betrayal he experienced in an America that would not keep its promises to African Americans. In "White Like Me," Eric Lott argues a correlative interlocutor for the construction of the white male identity. Through a subtle reading of John Howard Griffin's *Black Like Me*, the minstrel show tradition, and the U.S. white male's perennial attraction to racial impersonation, Lott argues that the white male's need to "go Negro" derived from his related need to transgress the color barrier even *after* it appeared intractable. Lott relates this drive to more pervasive strategies of global domination when he concludes that the mastery of the racial Other both at home and in oneself constituted the psychological precondition for global imperialism. That this internal colonization is never finally successful, that it is always exceeded or threatened by the same gender and racial arrangements upon which it depends reveals the most penetrating aspect of Lott's inquiry.

Lott's essay concludes the section entitled "Colonizing Resistance or Resisting Colonization?" with an account of race relations within U.S. borders that indicate their affinity with the U.S. foreign policy during the cold war era; that is, as a bipolar relationship between national identities whose oppositionality constituted the precondition for their self-identity. The essays in "Imperial Spectacles" investigate the appeal of that bipolar model to a society of spectacle. In his sequel to "'Make My Day!' Spectacle as Amnesia in Imperial Politics" Michael Rogin finds in the representations of the Gulf War a spectacular proof of the argument he advances in the first part of his essay: that "spectacle colonizes everyday life" and converts U.S. citizens into imperial spectators. Only the full-fledged absorption of U.S. foreign policy into nationalizing spectacles of successful U.S. intervention like the Gulf War could possibly mobilize, Rogin adds, a populace otherwise hopelessly diverted. By virtue of their power to reenact real events as national dramas, imperial spectacles, Rogin concludes, blur the difference between history and fantasy and thereby render amnesia the appropriate state of mind for their consumption.

But Susan Jeffords in "The Patriot System, or Managerial Heroism" finds a slightly different foreign policy assignment for the Gulf War. In rehabilitating the image of the managerial elite that had been thoroughly compromised during the Iran-Contra hearings, the Gulf War reaffirmed the importance of the CIA for the post-cold war epoch, Jeffords claims, and identified the U.S. "character" with the technocratic needs of the New World Order. Concentrating specifically on official representations of the Patriot Missile System, Jeffords argues that they rationalized the state control of the nation's information systems and legitimated the post-cold war agenda of the technocratic elite.

In "Hiroshima, the Vietnam Veterans' War Memorial, and the Gulf War: Post-National Spectacles," Donald Pease adds official national memory to Jeffords's and Rogin's explanation of the rehabilitative work of the Gulf War. In its efforts to forget the Vietnam syndrome, Pease argues, the Gulf War recalled World War II as the symbolic medium appropriate to postwar rememoration, but, according to the same symbolic logic, it also recalled Hiroshima as the agency for that war's end, along with the controversy attending the use of nuclear weapons. As a spectacular demonstration of U.S. power designed to promote a New World Order, Hiroshima predated the Gulf War as an imperial spectacle. But without the cold war to justify its usage, the collective memory of that nuclear spectacle proved threatening to the coherence of the U.S. national narrative.

Pease, Jeffords, and Rogin understand the Gulf War as a wish to remember a cultural mythology, but in "Techno-Muscularity and the 'Boy Eternal': From the Quagmire to the Gulf," Linda Boose proposes that it be understood contrarily as an effort to forget the Vietnam syndrome. Freed from prior checks on the overt display of U.S. military power as well as press and feminist censorship, the U.S. war machine reconstructed a militarist state in the Gulf War as a means of actively forgetting the lessons of Vietnam (which for Boose were instructions in how differently to construct gender identities) and remembering a national narrative within the image of the Eternal Boy.

Whereas the other accounts in this section presuppose an undeterred U.S. imperialism, Mary Yoko Brannen proposes an understanding of the cross-cultural relationship between the United States and Japan as a counterimperialism. In "'Bwana Mickey': Constructing Cultural Consumption at Tokyo Disneyland," Brannen persuasively argues against an explanation of Tokyo Disneyland as simply a one-way imposition of Western consumer culture on an "other," who is either passively receptive or absolutely rejecting of Western values. In their place, Brannen proposes that Tokyo's Disneyland be read as a zone of contestation setting Japan's cultural imperialism against that of the United States. In Tokyo the Japanese do not reconstruct their identities in the terms of the U.S. metanarrative Disneyland reproduces, but they reencode and thereby reincorporate Disneyland for their own purposes.

This volume began with Myra Jehlen's thoughtful analysis of an as yet unachieved effect, namely the colonial encounter's *potential* capacity to engender substantially different subject positions for *both* of the engaged parties. It concludes with an essay by two anthropologists, Frederick Errington and Deborah Gewertz, that would move beyond the concept of the "other." This final essay begins with a critique of Marianna Torgovnik's explanation in *Gone Primitive* of literary modernism's fascination with primitive culture. According to Torgovnik, that fascination masks a postmodern nostalgia for a clearly defined, largely patriarchal world, devoid of contingency and moral relativism. Gewertz and Errington find Torgovnik's reading to be primarily *textual*, resulting in an imaginative legitimation of a "generic primitive" rather than culturally embedded persons, and that this *textual* focus symptomatizes what they call "Occidentalism." In presuming to know the "other" but without being implicated in a shared world system, occidentalism always results in getting the other to some extent wrong. In place of the assumption that others are constructed largely out of Westerners' hopes and fears, in "We Think, Therefore, They Are? On Occidentalizing the World," these anthropologists correlate that assertion with the most insidious aspect of the imperial will and recommend contrarily that they be acknowledged nontextually as actual lives and in complex interaction "with our own." That recommendation constitutes a fitting last word for this volume on *Cultures of U.S. Imperialism.*

Notes

While it was conceptualized independently the volume takes its beginnings and owes its final shape to a conference made possible by the generosity of the Dickey Endowment and the Geisel Professorship, and held at Dartmouth College in November 1991. All but three of the essays grew from papers delivered there. Special gratitude is due to Sandy Gregg for her great organizational skills and attention to details, which made the conference possible.

1 Richard W. Van Alstyne, *The Rising American Empire* (New York: Norton, 1974), p. 1. See also Michael W. Doyle, *Empires* (Ithaca, N.Y.: Cornell University Press, 1986), and Walter La Feber, *The New Empire: An Interpretation of American Expansionism* (Ithaca, N.Y.: Cornell University Press, 1963).

2 For a further elaboration of this history, see Donald E. Pease, "New Americanists: Revisionist Interventions into the Canon," *boundary 2* 17, no. 1 (Spring 1990): 1–37.

3 Such a view enabled the editors of *The Empire Writes Back* to count the United States among the anticolonial nations.

> . . . the literatures of African countries, Australia, Bangladesh, Canada, Caribbean countries, India, Malaysia, Malta, New Zealand, Pakistan, Singapore, South Pacific Island countries, and Sri Lanka are all post-colonial literatures. The literature of the USA should also be placed in this category. Perhaps because of its current position of power, and the neo-colonizing role it has played, its postcolonial nature has not been generally recognized. But its relationship with the metropolitan centre as it evolved over the last two centuries has been paradigmatic for post-colonial literature everywhere. What each of these literatures has in common beyond their special and distinctive regional characteristics is that they emerged in their present form out of the experience of colonization and asserted themselves by foregrounding the tension with the imperial power, and by emphasizing their differences from the assumptions of the imperial centre. It is this which makes them distinctively post-colonial.

Bill Ashcroft, Gareth Griffiths, and Helen Tiffin, *The Empire Writes Back: Theory and Practice in Post-Colonial Literatures* (London and New York: Routledge, 1989), p. 2.

Nation-Building as
Empire-Building

Myra Jehlen

Why Did the Europeans Cross the Ocean?

A Seventeenth-Century

Riddle

laubert's *Dictionary of Received Ideas* offers, for the entry "Colonies (our)," a cautionary definition: "Register sadness in speaking of them." With this recommendation, the author, as is his wont, mocks his compatriots of good conscience, ridiculing hypocrisies that mask horrors. The empire here joins romance, bourgeois marriage, and the excellence of provincial virtue in Flaubert's catalog of foundational falsehoods of the nineteenth century. In his time, the creed of empire was as basic to French and European right-thinking as that of domesticity, was indeed the complement of domesticity since the common wisdom held until well into this century that an imperial impulse was the very pulse of Western man and colonies the natural fruit of his overflowing virility. Though the West's civilizing mission might occasionally lapse and was often disappointed (inducing sadness), colonizing lay in the order of things and those who questioned that order were alienated souls who probably also had doubts about conjugal love.

Now however, at the close of the millennium and concurrently nightfall in the empire whose day began five centuries ago, most Westerners living through the end of their era have taken skepticism for their familiar. If the empire seemed to rest on a natural foundation when it encircled the globe, for us who mainly fear having made the whole world unnatural, history is too clearly of human provenance. Even the annexation of the American continents, where Europeans made themselves so thoroughly at home they considered removing the former inhabitants just housekeeping, no longer seems so self-evident. It is not obvious any more that the Spanish, the French, and the English would naturally impose their civilizations upon two continents on the other side of the world. The conquest of America suddenly needs explaining.

At the same time, out of the empire's penumbra, the civilizations it long shadowed are emerging with renewed clarity. Indeed these formerly eclipsed civilizations themselves, particularly through the narrative of their colonization, seem to be coining the dominant idiom—as one would have said, the King's English—of the current international conversation. Postcolonial recuperations and reconstructions are providing the organizing terms of an increasingly influential revisionary history that attempts to turn the analytical tables on Europe itself (and as well on Europe-in-America). Such a refraction of Europe through the colonies is perfectly in line, of course, since European civilization is inconceivable without its empire. Equally, the experience of colonization fundamentally reshaped the colonized; so we ought not to be surprised if, even as it dissolves, the empire proves as adhesive as ever, conquest and colonization remaining central issues of national self-definition for former imperialists and imperialized alike. But though unsurprising, this adhesiveness needs noting, both in itself as a political and cultural phenomenon and because it glosses one of the key words of the current analytical discourse, the word "difference."

In turn, "difference" glosses another key word, "other," glosses it by attempting to replace it as oppressive to those so designated.[1] Naming them "other" seems to cast the speaker's cultural interlocutors in an inferior position by rendering them mere negative quantities defined by an opposition to which they do not contribute. The term "different" proposes to right this imbalance by granting others identities of their own. With the substitution of "difference" for "otherness," it is hoped that the imperial monologue becomes a two-sided exchange. Describing oneself or one's kind as "other," one would not only represent the very meaning of alienation but be incapable of further self-definition and even speech; while to declare oneself "different" leads logically to self-description, even to monologue. Let's just say "Rousseau" and move on.

Derridean deconstruction lends a certain formulaic rigor to the notion of difference as part of the neologism "différance." Différance, gerundial and antinomian, combines two verbs, to differ and to defer, to explain how (also why) no definition can ever attain a definitive authority. In time, difference is the stuff of Zeno's paradox, preventing any account from reaching a final truth. The race that never ends cannot go to the swift. In space, difference denies the centrality of any point of view and the all-encompassingness of any horizon. All this amounts to denying the ground for the transcending self-sufficiency that authorizes designating the Emersonian "Not-Me" as "the other." To return to our original vocabulary, difference is the anticolonial response to the imperial history of otherness.

Students of difference might be said to be the reluctant heirs of Europe's late empire, dismantling its house and marking for return piles of looted goods. Edward Said's analysis of "orientalism" suggests why the metaphysical goods have been especially difficult to catalog. In the American colonies, a mass of European presumption overwhelmed Amerindian cultures, perhaps beyond extricating. The arriving Europeans were so intent on taking over that few even registered the indigenous cultures. The discoverer himself began his first letter home not with what he found but what he did to it. "I reached the Indian sea," Columbus reported, "where I discovered many islands, thickly peopled, of which I took possession without resistance in the name of our most illustrious Monarch, by public proclamation and with unfurled banners."[2] (Proving, in this invocation of sonorous Spanish and snappy standards deployed on an innocent beach, that when you have the upper hand you can afford to look ridiculous.) Columbus's admirably succinct account of his landfall would do as the first example in a primer of imperial prose. "I reached . . . I discovered . . . I took," he writes; the objects of my actions were both abundant and anonymous, "many islands, thickly peopled," an indefinite, possibly infinite plenitude lacking only the agency to resist. Therefore imposing my will, which is the will of white civilization, was only natural and right. "I took possession" of this latent world and named it: in making it mine I made *it*, imparting to it political capability, bringing it into the Law. I baptized it in the name of "our most illustrious Monarch" with the ceremonies and symbols in which civilization inheres, with rhetoric and flags. I acted as a prime mover, creating order and meaning, making objects into subjects; or rather subjects into objects and thus subjects of the Spanish Crown.

An accounting follows: "The inhabitants of both sexes in this island," Columbus notes, ". . . go always naked as they were born, with the exception of some of the women. . . . None of them . . . are possessed of any iron, neither have they weapons, being unacquainted with, and indeed incompetent to use them, not from any deformity of body (for they are well-formed), but because they are timid and full of fear." The lineaments of the benign savage emerge, his simplicity, honesty, and rather foolish generosity. Withal he is not stupid "but of very clear understanding" demonstrated in one or two "admirable descriptions" local informants have contributed to Columbus's report. So far so good; the expropriation of the New World—which Columbus will never quite recognize as such— is progressing unproblematically through the arrogation not only of the Indians' land but of their intellectual resources which, in these first passages describing their cooperative quiescence, is simply another piece of the local treasure. Thus far too the difference between Indians and Spanish is both absolute and inert, that is, without implications beyond those that pertain to the New World generally as a place of yet untapped resources. At this point the relations between conqueror and conquered are still not political. One does not have political relations with a beach or a tree; in Columbus's first *Letter*, the inhabitants of San Salvador are not even properly other, do not yet comprise a negative term.

But when subsequent explorations discover a second and much different group of islanders, the bloodthirsty Caribs who will shortly lend their name to coin the appalling "cannibal," the process of mastering foreign peoples reveals itself more complicated than just taking over their land. The Arawaks are morally uninflected, benign like the local climate but not actually "good," until they come to contrast with the "bad" Caribs. This moral differentiation entails more than a refinement, a transformation of categories: the bad Caribs reveal the Indians as human beings not fruit trees. The rhetoric of oppression often characterizes victims as in- or subhuman but the meaning of that accusation is worth investigating further. "Inhuman" may not be meant literally but, like "unthinkable," as judgment rather than fact. Were inhumanity a fact it would preclude a self-justifying condemnation. The enemy on the battlefield arouses not only repugnance but anger, resentment, indignation, rage. These emotions directed at inanimate objects or animals involve an ancillary anthropomorphism. In the same way the Caribs/cannibals need to be granted a portion of humanity before they can be seen worthy of annihilation for their inhumanity.[3] Thus it is their categorical humanity that places them beyond the pale; savagery has its ethics just like civilization. Discovering the humanity of the New World savages when he finds that some are actively evil, Columbus tells a story ironically paralleling that of the Fall in which being bad similarly achieves a distinct human status defined basically as the capacity to choose between good and evil. The irony, of course, lies in acknowledging that the Indians are categorically people as a step toward enslaving them; down that road, the vision of the New World as potentially a second Eden will inspire the genocide of its first inhabitants whose difference from the Europeans is now qualified (limited), in that they *are* human, but insuperable and fraught with implications for their violent suppression. To kill Indians with conviction, Columbus had to attribute to them a mode of life whose very evil made it basically commensurate with his own.

That is a sword that cuts both ways. With the edge sharpened by a view of the savages as unworthy of humane treatment, it kills them with moral impunity. But Flaubert's ancestor, Montaigne, honed its other edge in an essay entitled "Of Cannibals" (1578–80) which argues that bad as New World anthropophagites may be, we (sixteenth-century Frenchmen) are worse, more deeply fallen and further alienated from our common human nature. Like us but unlike us, the cannibals deserve freedom for their—not otherness (since they are comparable) but difference. Human like us and therefore deserving humane treatment, they have an entirely different civilization which, to behave humanely, we ought to respect.

The concept of cultural difference as an autonomous, self-generated mode appears new to us, even post-new, but it dates back at least to Montaigne's response to what he too saw as a lethal notion of otherness. The response was not entirely successful, however, for a closer look will reveal that Montaigne's anticolonial notion of difference remains tied to an irresistibly emerging sense of European centrality; that indeed, for all he resists, "difference" tends perhaps irresistibly to slide toward "otherness."

Yet, in "Of Cannibals" Montaigne sets out precisely to separate difference and otherness, explicitly rejecting the attitude that makes one's kind the universal standard. A returning colonizer's tales of the wild men of Brazil have had a contrary effect on Montaigne. "I think," he muses, "there is nothing barbarous and savage in that nation, from what I have been told, except that each man calls barbarism whatever is not his own practice; for indeed it seems we have no other test of truth and reason than the example and pattern of the opinions and customs of the country we live in." Hopelessly provincial, we are convinced that where we are is the epitome of all good things. "*There* is always the perfect religion, the perfect government, the perfect and accomplished manners in all things."[4]

Recent discoveries of alien peoples leading vastly different lives ought to be teaching us that other ways can also make sense, even better sense. A Brazilian tribe of cannibals surely represents the epitome of difference,[5] yet these proverbial pariahs of civilized society nonetheless have their virtues. Montaigne finds much about them to admire, like their honesty and generosity, their innocence of any lust for riches. Comparison does not flatter Europe, for doing their worst, the cannibals still appear better people than the French. "I think there is more of barbarity," Montaigne observes referring to certain contemporary practices, "in eating a man alive than in eating him dead; and in tearing by tortures and the rack a body still full of feeling, in roasting a man bit by bit, in having him bitten and mangled by dogs and swine . . . than in roasting and eating him after he is dead" (155). "We surpass them in every kind of barbarity" (156). Instead of their masters, we ought to be the cannibals' pupils. But we are too parochial to learn from others; all that Montaigne's compatriots seem capable of recognizing in the cannibal culture is that "they don't wear breeches" (159).

Five years later, when Montaigne again took up the theme of cultural difference, it was not to mock but to mourn. "Of Coaches" (1585–88) denounces the Spanish slaughter of the Incas in terms at first familiar from the cannibals essay. Children in an infant world, the Incas differ from us by their proximity to nature. They are innocent of our civilized perversions, simple and direct where we lie and cheat, loyal and true where we will resort to any guile to satisfy our bloated greed. Beyond this precocious projection of the concept of the noble savage—it will be another century before Rousseau codifies him—Montaigne moves in this essay toward a still more precocious anticolonialism. True, he does not formulate this opposition to the conquest of America as an absolute principle, since he can imagine a worthy and even improving colonization by the ancient Greeks and Romans (694–95). But these benign tutors, far from scorning the Incas as other, would have actually helped difference unfold, "strengthened and fostered the good seeds that nature had produced in them" (694).

The Spanish, on the other hand, are nowhere more vile than in their insistence that the humiliated Incas abandon their gods along with their goods and lands. Having used every form of treachery to defeat the Peruvian king, his ignoble captors "permitted [him] to buy his way out of the torment of being burned alive by submitting to baptism at the moment of execution" (696). Montaigne opposed conversion at a time when it was the empire's major ethical justification. Even Bartolome de Las Casas did not abandon the missionary pursuit when he saw where it could lead; but Las Casas, for all his outrage at the brutality of Spanish exploitation, disputed the administration of the empire, not its existence. More radically, for Montaigne the Incas' "indomitable ardor" in "the defense of their gods" represents an equal capacity for autonomy.

In fact the Incas are generally not at all inferior to their invaders, even on the battlefield where, Montaigne speculates, "if anyone had attacked them on equal terms, with equal arms, experience and numbers, it would have been just as dangerous for him as in any other war we know of, and more so." Unequal odds decided the outcome of the battle not unequal opponents. "Eliminate [the] disparity, I say, and you take from the conquerors the whole basis of many victories" (694). Military disparity is not to be taken as a sign of the sort of cultural/racial inferiority that Europeans invoked to justify colonization; disparity does not imply a disparaging difference. The problem, however, lies in the converse, that difference does seem to engender a disparaging disparity. Over the course of the narrative of the Indian defeat, the notion of difference as the ground for arguing against colonization develops complications that were not evident in the mere statement of the principle. Never a justification for the subjection of the Incas, difference in "Of Coaches" does tend to become an *explanation*.

Montaigne essays are typically labyrinthine and "Of Coaches" especially so. Tracing the singular path of the idea of Indian difference requires a plan of the whole. The essay, then, starts with the observation that the classics are not always reliable; even Aristotle and Plutarch were capable of reporting legend as truth. This bringing to mind that not only the figurative but the actual ground under one's feet is not always entirely firm reminds Montaigne that he is phobically afraid of falling which can make his travels unpleasant, particularly in swaying vehicles like boats and coaches. We have arrived at our coaches. These come in many varieties including war coaches drawn in ancient times by all sorts of odd beasts—stags, dogs, naked women, ostriches. To be sure, it was the plebes who paid for such princely displays but still, they were magnificent in those days and Montaigne doubts we will see their like again.

On the other hand history can take unexpected turns. Here, for example, it has just revealed a whole new world. With this Montaigne enters on the account of the Incas as above and the essay ends with an anecdote proving the Incas' moral excellence in their devotion to their king. As Montaigne tells it, the Inca monarch rode to his last battle on a golden litter borne by trusted warriors. As fast as the Spaniards killed these bearers others took their places so that the king would never have fallen had not a Spanish soldier, raised astride his horse to the height of the litter, seized the king bodily and dashed him to the ground. Montaigne's fear of falling makes this episode especially dramatic and, recalling his earlier discussion of various means of conveyance, not an absolutely incoherent conclusion to an essay about coaches.

One may ask what coaches have to do with Peru in the first place? A Montaigne scholar, Marcel Gutwirth, has proposed a link whereby coaches represent a crucial difference between Spaniard and Inca: coaches, that is, wheels. The Spanish have wheels and the Incas don't.[6] To be sure, Montaigne hastens to acknowledge, the Incas have accomplished amazing things without the wheel, notably a magnificent road from Quito to Cuzco that is easily the match of any in Europe. Roads being the trademark of the Roman empire, this is a most telling example of Inca achievement. Wheel-less, therefore, the Incas are different but not lesser. Indeed in another sense, they are different and therefore greater, since it takes a greater effort to build roads without pulleys or carts.

Exactly here, however, even as Montaigne directly affirms the equal worth of Inca civilization, the ambiguity of that affirmation begins to emerge. This ambiguity lies in the blurred status of wheel-lessness—an *occasion* for Inca virtue that is sliding toward becoming its *condition*. Does the lack of wheels merely provide an occasion for demonstrating Inca virtue (which exists independently of such occasions)? or does the need to overcome their wheel-lessness generate a special virtue not extant among those possessed of wheels? The problem with that question, of course, lies in the very asking, for the Incas, lacking the concept of the wheel, cannot query that lack themselves. Only Montaigne can pose that question and, to make things worse, by posing it, he demonstrates not only the epistemological ascendancy of having wheels but the additional power that accrues to those who know that others don't.

In other words, while Montaigne insists on the fundamental equality of all human beings (and proves that conviction when he shudders in identification with the Inca king's fall), this equality turns out to be limited to the fundamentally human. The Incas are only *fundamentally* human: the technology of the litter only extends the body. But the Spanish control, in addition to their fundamental humanity, a technology that transforms their bodily energy into something of which bodies on their own are incapable. Montaigne may be terrified when he imagines himself falling from a litter but, thank Heaven, litters are not his problem which is, fearsome enough but not fatal, coaches: witness the title of his essay. The Indian litter-bearers are exceedingly brave as the workers who build the Mexican road are surpassingly skilled, but all in vain. From being the *occasion* for virtue, then its *condition*, lacking the wheel has become the sign of its *futility*. Tragically and to its shame, the modern world has rendered certain virtues futile. But inasmuch as these virtues are associated with the technology of litters, it is difficult to regret them in the sense of wanting them back for ourselves.

While coaches embody the corruption of Europe, they also carry the weight of a history that has traded innocence for knowledge. Cowering in his coach, Montaigne dreads the wheels that the Incas lack; dreads as well the technology that will destroy the Incas. But since fear is here the measure of knowledge, he can hardly wish himself ignorantly fearless, however brave. As "Of Coaches" develops the concept of difference beyond "Of Cannibals," it now figures as the remainder in a subtraction problem, so that the difference between the Spanish and the Incas equals the reason for the latters' defeat, a difference that, as the ground for anticolonialism, is as shaky as a coach.

In the twentieth century, Europe's former colonies being at least nominally independent, anticolonialism means cultural liberation. And since this new definition makes the recognition of difference central, what we might call the problem of the wheel becomes commensurately greater. Almost four hundred years after Montaigne, Tzvetan Todorov wrote his book *The Conquest of America: The Question of the Other* and defined its subject as "the discovery *self* makes of the *other*."[7] Todorov's purpose is the same as Montaigne's, to denounce the concept of the other as a chief weapon of colonial outrage, and, revisiting essentially the same site, he writes about the fall of the Aztec empire a decade before the Inca. But to explain the defeat of a civilization in many respects easily Europe's match, the late twentieth-century Todorov is unimpressed by technology and seeks the determining force of history rather in culture, specifically in a profound difference (as he sees it) in the Aztec and Spanish conceptions of language and communication.

In brief, his thesis is that the Aztecs could not counter the alien assault for lack of a concept of the other; while the Spanish in their encounter with the New World discovered otherness and how to manipulate it. Unlike the Spanish who, for all their religiosity, saw themselves first as men among men, the Aztecs located themselves first in relation to a sacred plan whose laws they were to implement. This precedence of universal over human order was expressed with special force in their conception of language as the articulation of a world order. For the Spanish, language functioned instead as an instrument of human relations and a means of reordering things to their liking. In a word, the Spanish knew how to lie. Lying is language taking power by overthrowing rightful meanings, and lying won the Spanish their empire. In control of communication, Cortes plunged his prey into fatal confusion. Control of communication, in Todorov's account, is a second Spanish wheel.

As appalled as Montaigne by the ravages of colonization and more knowing, Todorov regrets the epistemological imbalance that gave the conquistadors their bloody victory. But to understand this unhappy event, he has had himself to know something of which the vanquished were ignorant, and this imbalance he can hardly regret. For while knowing is associated with the guilt of the conquest, ignorance was and remains annihilative. Remains so because Todorov could not write his book nor we read it without knowing (indeed taking as fact) what the Spanish knew.

Is Todorov then doing what he denounces, rendering the Aztecs as Europe's negatives? This is certainly not what he intends. Indeed, some time after *The Conquest of America,* he took up the issue explicitly arguing in response to an essay by Abdul R. JanMohamed[8] that we should be careful not to exaggerate differences. Todorov finds JanMohamed's stipulation that understanding the other requires "'negating one's very being'" "excessively pessimistic." Even if "'one's culture is what formed that being,'... human beings are not trees, and they can be uprooted without provoking such dramatic consequences," he insists. For "We are not only separated by cultural differences; we are also united by a common human identity, and it is this which renders possible communication, dialogue, and, in the final analysis, the comprehension of Otherness—it is possible precisely because Otherness is never radical" (374).

In this concern that difference when it is cast as absolute precludes precisely the interactions it is intended to engender, Todorov joins a growing number of scholars, many themselves descended from or representing the peoples Europe designated "other," who are dissatisfied with studies that discover only divergence and distinctiveness.[9] Though these scholars are presumably the beneficiaries of a concept of difference that returns to them the agency of their own interpretation, they have been finding that what is represented as autonomy often turns out to be exclusion: that difference too easily reverses into otherness. The Native American writer Michael Dorris has complained that "the paradigm of European confusion"[10] which renders Indians "objects of mystery and speculation, not people" still organizes a current scholarship willy-nilly producing images that are the complementary opposites of the old myths. We need to "stipulate only a few givens," he writes with some impatience. "That human beings *qua* human beings, where and whenever they may live, share some traits; that Indians were and are human beings—then we have at least a start." And Dorris concludes his essay by urging that we "begin the hard, terribly difficult and unpredictable quest of regarding [Indians] as human beings" (104–5).

It is hard to disagree with such a program, but even harder to carry it out. The principle that one should explicate people's differences (in Dorris's words) "within the configurations of their own cultures," while at the same time "regarding [others] as human beings," seems clear enough stated abstractly, but its practice is another matter. Unfortunately, Todorov does not reflect upon his *Conquest of America* in relation to his later postulate that "Otherness is never radical." But the otherness of the Aztecs, defined as their inability to comprehend otherness, constitutes the very definition of "radical." At the same time, what content can one imagine imparting to the universal term "human being" that would render its universality genuinely multiform? If in the past the notion of the universal human being served the colonizing enterprise, as the anticolonial scholarship has been arguing for the last two decades, what is now going to make universality useful on the other side? What is a "human being" when he's at home? How do we keep him civil when he goes visiting?

In short, the universalities upon which Todorov falls back in order to temper radical otherness and transform it into relative difference are both vague with regard to future incarnations and discouraging in their past. Moreover, the logic that invokes universality as the counter to difference is the logic of otherness which reduces differences to an abstract negativity; and it is difficult to see how the same logic can organize an account of others that makes them *more* autonomously substantial. In that difference *is* substance or it collapses into otherness, resorting to universalities in order to correct extreme difference seems inauspicious, methodologically as well as politically. To qualify difference we need to know more about its content, not less. More content, in other words more history. Let's go back then and look more substantively at the history of the Aztecs.

As it happens, it is possible to reconstruct the Aztecs' own sense of their place in the history of American colonization with relative conviction in that, exceptionally among New World cultures at the time of the discovery, they had a written language in which they produced a conquest literature of their own.[11] The earliest of these Nahuatl writings by Aztec priests and wise men date from only seven years after the fall of Mexico. Their complicated account of the two-year war preceding the fall offers some unexpected perspectives.

For one thing, it comes as a surprise to find that, contrary to the European tradition of the first encounters, the Aztecs are not unambiguously impressed. Though amazed, as who would not have been, by their first sightings of the bedecked and bemetaled Spanish, they retain some critical distance from which they find the response to their welcoming gifts of gold and precious feathers less than inspiring. "They picked up the gold and fingered it like monkeys," recalls an Aztec observer. "Their bodies swelled with greed, and their hunger was ravenous; they hungered like pigs for that gold. They snatched at the golden ensigns, waved them from side to side and examined every inch of them." In this depiction the Spanish are flatly bestial, not super- but subhuman. Repugnantly different, others outside the pale: "They were like one who speaks a barbarous tongue," the writer continues: "everything they said was in a barbarous tongue" (51–52). In other words, they were of the category of person with whom by definition it is impossible to communicate. From the Aztec point of view, not surprisingly, it is the Spanish who cannot communicate.

At other times recounted in other passages, it seems true as tradition has it, that the Aztecs greeted the Spanish like gods, and overall the Mexicans perhaps understood their enemy less well than the reverse. But passages like the one just cited suggest that the Aztecs' perceptions were not entirely clouded, indicating that we might usefully look for other explanations besides cultural incapacity even for their misunderstandings. Explanations, for instance, like the fact that the invaders knew whence they came and to what end; while for the invaded the sudden irruption of strange peoples from unknown lands was an impenetrable mystery. The Aztecs' epistemological passivity seems a not unlikely response to impenetrable mysteries. Beyond this, granting that control of communication was a decisive factor in the Spanish victory, it seems well to note that Cortes controlled communication in large part through his control of a translator/interpreter, a slave woman whom he acquired upon landing on the Mexican coast and who then accompanied him on his progress to the capital city. Montezuma not only did not have a translator of his own, he depended on Cortes's: by this alone the Mexicans lost linguistic control to the point that they heard their own language speaking an enemy meaning. In the process of making available the world of the Mexicans along with their language, La Malinche, who is still referred to in Mexico as "the traitor" (and more ambiguously the "fucked one"), at several critical junctures in the campaign took the lead in manipulating the Indians, if not into submission, certainly into confusion. Alterity was not a mystery at least for her.[12]

Politics and biology can provide two other reasons for the Mexican defeat. The Aztecs were nomadic intruders who arrived in the region and established their city only around 1325. Thus the Aztec empire which at its height ruled several million people was rising, ironically, at the same time as the European. The opponents at the siege of Mexico City were politically more alike than either realized; and their resemblance may have worked as much as their difference to the advantage of the Spanish who were able to forge alliances with those the Aztecs had recently vanquished. By the end of the war the situation looked little like the puzzling story of a few hundred Spaniards in alien territory conquering hundreds of thousands of Indians on their home ground. The sides were probably roughly balanced, Cortes commanding, against no more than 300,000 Aztecs, at least 200,000 (some suggest 225,000) Indians in addition to his own men with their far more destructive arms.[13]

Finally, Alfred Crosby has argued that biology was the decisive factor, devastating the Mexican society so quickly that the role of technology and politics was essentially moot.[14] The Aztecs repelled the first Spanish assault on the city causing such losses among the attackers that their defeat became legend as "la triste noche." Upon his return, Cortes was reinforced not only by new Indian recruits but, within the walls, by the plague which, according to accounts on both sides, had heaped rotting corpses in all the streets of the city and left virtually none to defend it.

The factors suggested by Aztec documents as equally important in the conquest of Mexico as cultural difference are not inconsiderable: the possession of specific knowledge of the origins, the purposes, and the motives of the enemy; the balance of military force measured both in arms and men; the natural imbalance derived from the Aztecs' lack of biological immunity. Todorov stipulates all these, but seems not to consider them decisive in that they do not figure in his explanation of the final outcome. On the other hand, figuring them in profoundly changes the entire picture; though the Aztec defeat seems no less historically likely, it no longer appears inherently inevitable. Neither passive nor helpless, the Aztecs represent themselves in their own writings by acting, in relation to overwhelming odds, with reason (their own reasons) and will.

In traditional accounts of the Aztecs as helpless before the Spanish, one of the pieces of evidence is an account to be found in their conquest literature of omens said ten years before to have predicted the coming apocalypse. Of course the omens could be just that, in which case fate rules the world and there's nothing further to say about it. If however the omens are the creature of the conquest, there is another way to read them than as evidence of helplessness. For while they prophesy doom, they also hold out a certain hope. George Orwell wrote that who controls the past controls the future.[15] The catastrophic future predicted in the Aztec omens takes place, in relation to the invention of the omens themselves, in the present. The effect is to release the future—even if only for oppression—by restoring purposeful direction to a present that would otherwise appear to be the end of the world. If the present has grown out of the past, the future can be expected to grow out of the present, to *have* a future. In the omens, therefore, the Aztecs can be seen demonstrating instead of epistemological passivity, something like an opposite historical capability, one that is more congruent with the picture of interactions that emerges from their own accounts than with the view that they were culturally paralyzed.[16]

All these ways in which Aztecs and Spanish were not only unlike but also like (both relations, moreover, evolving over the course of their conflict)[17] seriously complicate notions of both difference and universality. Colonizer and colonized emerge as similar as they are different in that they profit and lose in the same ways from common situations: the imperialist Aztecs, for instance, lose out when their history in the region makes willing allies for Cortes who, when he wins, will kill and exploit like the Aztecs before him. On the other hand, it is difficult to talk of the Aztecs and the Spanish as simply universally "human" and let it go at that in the presence of their fundamentally different visions of the universe and of humanity's place in it. In that context, the term "universally human" just does not seem very useful.

This said, however, a solution or more modestly a strategy may be emerging out of these very difficulties. Dubbing them different, one reflects that they came together in related ways; dubbing them all human beings, one contrarily wants to point to the basic issues on which they oppose one another. In both cases, however, there is a common denominator which is precisely the commonality of their encounter, the common ground they construct, new to both, and on which they are neither the same nor different but only inextricably related; indeed neither the same nor different *through* their relation.

I would suggest that the encounter of Aztecs and Spanish offers the terms for avoiding, as the orientalist, exoticist tendencies of the concept of the other (the different) emerge, falling back into an equally worrisome universalism. From focusing on the history of the conquest—from locating oneself on the site of the encounter rather than attempting to project oneself simultaneously on both sides of it—a concept of commonality or common ground [18] emerges that is not a compromise between the universal and the different, but a distinct third term. This third term indeed stands opposed to both "human being" and "other/different." The shortcomings of "other" even when it is chastened into "different" we have already examined. As for "human being" shorn of its covert content—when it really means white man, prince of Denmark or president of the United States—one is hard put to say what it is. Besides mortality, the urge to satisfy three or four physical needs, a proneness to foregather, which human traits can be considered universal? On the contrary, commonalities abound being continuously generated by precisely the historical process that works to limit the realm of the universal.

One term that recurs in histories of difference is "contested zone," meaning cultural areas and social regions that different groups seek to define each its own way. The notion of "commonality" or common ground implies a reversal of that term, thus "zone of contest": a territory whose contours are sketched as overlappings rather than boundaries, a terrain of mediations and equally of confrontations. The history of the European empire seems exactly such a terrain upon which peoples define themselves as modalities of shared experience. The moment Columbus landed in San Salvador, as soon as the home of the Arawaks became San Salvador, the reason the European crossed the ocean became inextricable from what he found when he got to the other side. A passionate traveler, Montaigne sought, in difficult journeys he made more difficult by refusing an orderly itinerary, the same process of becoming he recorded in his essays. He understood that what he found upon his travels was inextricable from the finding, and that he himself would be transformed by both.

Put another way, all this has been to suggest that a difference so distinct as to constitute the opposite of universality cannot be. As vehicles of meaning, the ships that discovered America exploded on impact. After the landfall, all there was on the beach was a confusion of European timber and American sand. Difference being an analytical concept, its objective reality lies only in its construction of subjective realities. Thus while the Aztecs and the Spanish certainly existed before their encounter, the difference between them did not. *That* was the creature of the conquest. The children of difference as well as its students, we find ourselves, therefore, fulfilling the eighth and last Aztec omen, the appearance of "monstrous beings . . . : deformed men with two heads but only one body." Monstrous, deformed, two- and many-headed, "human beings" and "others" in postcolonial America have one body divisible only by its own parts.

Notes

A version of this chapter appears in *Discovering Difference: Contemporary Essays in American Culture,* ed. Christopher K. Lohman (Bloomington: Indiana University Press).

1 I am grateful to Rick Livingston for an illuminating discussion of the dynamic between the concepts of "difference" and of the "other."

2 Christopher Columbus, *Four Voyages to the New World,* trans. and ed. by R. H. Major (Gloucester, Mass.: Peter Smith, 1978), pp. 1–2.

3 Arkady Plotnitsky has brought to my attention in connection with this Marlow's account of the horrifying Africans in *Heart of Darkness.* The landscape, Marlow recalls shuddering, "was unearthly, and the men were—No, they were not inhuman. Well, you know, that was the worst of it—this suspicion of their not being inhuman," *Youth, Heart of Darkness, the End of the Tether* (New York: Oxford University Press, 1984), pp. 96–97.

4 Citations from both "Of Cannibals" and "Of Coaches" are from *The Complete Works of Montaigne: Essays, Travel Journal, Letters,* trans. Donald Frame (Stanford: Stanford University Press, 1957), pp. 150–59, 685–99, esp. p. 152. All subsequent page references in text.

5 It should be noted that there is no unimpeachable evidence for the existence of cannibals in the New World. For a particularly illuminating analysis of the evidence, see David Beers Quinn, "The New Geographical Literature," in *First Images of America: The Impact of the New World on the Old,* ed. Fredi Chiapelli (Berkeley: University of California Press, 1976), pp. 635–57. A more recent discussion of this ongoing controversy is in Peter Hulme, *Caribbean Encounters: Europe and the Native Caribbean, 1492–1797* (London: Methuen, 1986).

6 "Des coches, ou la structuration d'une absence," *L'Esprit Créateur* 15, nos. 1–2 (Spring–Summer 1975), pp. 8–20. Since Montaigne's time, anthropologists have determined that the Incas did make wheels but only on toys. Of course this only deepens the distinction between Europeans and Americans being projected here. I am indebted to Rolph Trouillot for this correction.

7 Translated by Richard Howard (Harper Torchbooks, New York 1987), p. 3. Originally published as *La conquête de l'Amérique* (Paris: Editions du Seuil, 1982).

8 "'Race,' Writing and Culture," ed. Henry Louis Gates, Jr., *"Race," Writing and Difference* (Chicago: University of Chicago Press, 1986), pp. 370–80. Todorov's essay responds to one published earlier in the Special Issue of *Critical Inquiry* which was the first version of this book: "The Economy of Manichean Allegory: The Function of Racial Difference in Colonialist Literature," *"Race," Writing and Difference,* Special Issue of *Critical Inquiry,* ed. Henry Louis Gates, Jr., vol. 12, no. 1 (Autumn 1985), pp. 59–87. The passage from which Todorov cites is on page 65. To clarify JanMohamed's part in this argument, I should say that Todorov seems to me to misrepresent it a little. JanMohamed also seeks a way out of the predicament of absolute alterity and, as I read him, only stresses the difficulties it entails on the way to proposing a way of overcoming them.

9 An interesting version of this argument is made in Rey Chow's " 'It's You, and not Me': Domination and 'Othering' in Theorizing the 'Third World,' " *Coming to Terms: Feminism, Theory, Politics*, ed. Elizabeth Weed (New York: Routledge, 1989), pp. 152–61. Rey Chow uses a short story by the twentieth-century Chinese writer Lu Xun to criticize current Western projections of an absolutely other Third World. Lu Xun's story, according to her, "foretells much that is happening in the contemporary 'Western' theoretical scene." This foretelling, of course, demonstrates a shared universe of concerns. An equally telling discussion occurs in V. Y. Mudimbe's *Invention of Africa: Gnosis, Philosophy, and the Order of Knowledge* (Bloomington: Indiana University Press, 1988) in a section of chapter 3, "The Power of Speech" entitled "The Panacea of Otherness: J. P. Sartre as an African Philosopher." Mudimbe here analyses the effect of the theory of "Negritude" set forth in Sartre's essay *Black Orpheus* which attempts precisely to identify a different culture without rendering it in any way inferior. On the contrary, Sartre is prepared to find in the values and energies of Negritude the next world-important culture to take over in the twilight of European culture. Without attempting to rehearse an exceptionally complex and dense argument, I want to invoke it here as a particularly penetrating treatment of the contradictions of the concept of difference and particularly of its fatal tendency to move toward an obliterating otherness.

10 "Indians on the Shelf," ed. Calvin Martin, *The American and the Problem of History*, (New York: Oxford, 1987), pp. 98–105. Interestingly, Calvin Martin himself argues the opposite in his introduction. Attempts to write Indian history in the conventional Western terms so distort its fundamental structures of meaning, Martin claims, as to render the results either meaningless or, worse, new instances of ethnic and racial suppression. A recent theoretical study of Indian literature urges on the contrary that the same models of interpretation be applied to it as to any literature and that not to do so is to continue excluding this literature from United States culture: Arnold Krupat, *The Voice in the Margin: Native American Literature and the Canon* (Berkeley: University of California Press, 1989).

11 A selection from these writings is available in a paperback collection, *The Broken Spears: The Aztec Account of the Conquest of Mexico*, ed. Miguel Leon-Portilla (Boston: Beacon Press, 1966).

12 La Malinche is a figure of enormous interest who would repay more attention from historians. A woman and a slave, Mexican and woman, she was at once helpless and decisively powerful, victim of an oppressive gender and class system, yet also a significant agent in the defeat of her people.

13 These are Indian figures (*The Broken Spears*, p. 124). They also estimate that of the 300,000 on the Aztec side, 240,000 were killed by the end of the final siege.

14 Alfred Crosby, *The Columbian Exchange: Biological and Cultural Consequences of 1492* (Westport, Conn.: Greenwood, 1972). Within five years of the arrival of Europeans, nine out of ten Americans were dead of diseases ranging from the common cold to smallpox. A contemporary account of the North American part of the holocaust, which puzzled the whites almost as much as it terrified the Indians, is in Thomas Harriot's 1588 *Briefe and True Report of the New Found Land of Virginia.*

15 The full citation, from *1984,* is "who controls the past controls the future; who controls the present controls the past." This is the Party's slogan.

16 Todorov interprets the same phenomenon differently, suggesting that what the Aztecs preserve through the invention of the omens is a meaningful past, demonstrating the orderliness of their universe by having it forecast its own end. I am suggesting on the contrary that what is safeguarded in the omens is the future, that is, after the end of their universe, the possibility of an ongoing orderliness however horrific the order.

17 One of the most problematical aspects of the Todorov account is its failure to incorporate any effects from the historical process itself of the conquest. The Spanish learn to see others as others, but this is already implicit or anyway potential in Spanish culture; the Aztecs do not learn about otherness and that is also implicit in their culture. The events and experiences of the conquest itself dramatize and illustrate, but they do not really inform, let alone form.

18 By "common ground" here I intend something quite different from "bridge." Bridging two cultures emphasizes their distinctness while on the contrary I want to sketch their interactions. I am once again grateful to Arkady Plotnitsky for suggesting this distinction.

Priscilla Wald

Terms of Assimilation

Legislating Subjectivity in

the Emerging Nation

In the nineteenth-century United States, debates concerning the status of indigenous tribespeople and slaves register unresolved legal conflicts that troubled claims of national unity. Two Supreme Court cases—*Cherokee Nation v. Georgia* (1831) and *Scott v. Sandford* (*Dred Scott*, 1857)—in particular demonstrate the genesis of these debates in the territorial expansion that similarly added urgency to the potent issue of states' rights. Both cases attempt to legislate the disappearance of the "Indians" and the "descendants of Africans," respectively, by judging them neither citizens nor aliens and therefore not legally representable. In so doing, however, these cases call attention to the symbolic processes through which the United States constitutes subjects: how Americans are made. The Courts' decisions turn the Cherokee and slaves into uncanny figures who mirror the legal contingency—and the potential fate—of all subjects in the Union, a fate made all the more plausible by the instability of the Union and the tenuousness of national unity.

Efforts to promote national unity did not originate in the nineteenth century. Nations typically derive their legitimacy from a unity that is presumed to give rise to an independent political entity; Thomas Jefferson's "one people," for example, declares the colonies' independence from England.[1] The Declaration of Independence must not only convert kinship ties into "political bands," a connection that can be "dissolved," but also political alliance into cultural identification, a more enduring connection. Rhetorical strategies designed to promote a collective identity emerge with particular clarity in Congress's emendations of Jefferson's draft. In the edited version, for example, the king incites the suggestively vague "domestic insurrections" rather than the more problematic "treasonable insurrections." "Treasonable" names a crime committed against an independent political entity, a charge that countermands the Declaration's claims to be calling forth such an entity. At the same time, "treasonable" too nearly calls attention to the colonists' own treasonous activities—and therefore to their political ties with England. "Domestic," on the other hand, lays claim only to a locale, although its resonance with "home" suggests a familial collectivity. By implication, the colonies form a homeland that predates and justifies the political entity. "Domestic insurrections" has the added advantage of referring at once to the uprisings of British Loyalists and of slaves. Thus Congress excises a lengthy passage in which Jefferson, assailing the king for inciting slave rebellions, raises the hotly contested issue of slavery.

The Declaration must point the way to an ongoing association among the "one people" who are renouncing the former ties. In the last paragraph, Jefferson's "good people of these states" becomes the Declaration's "good people of these colonies," and it is from these "good people" that the document derives its authority to turn those colonies into "free & independent states."[2] The Declaration defines the "one people" through contrasts—with the English, for example, or with Loyalists or with the "merciless Indian savages" whose hostility is allegedly encouraged by the king. But once the political bands are dissolved, what new ones will be put in their place? Who will comprise the "one people" of the emerging political entity? And how can it provide for an expansion—through territorial acquisition or through immigration—that will not challenge that unity?

At stake in both Supreme Court cases is, quite literally, the fate of the Union, the status of the political entity constituted in the name of "the people." Debates surrounding the extension of federal law into unincorporated territories generate both cases. *Cherokee Nation* concerns Georgia's right to violate federal treaties and extend its legislation into Cherokee territory contained within the state's borders but exempt from state law. *Dred Scott* considers the status of slaves taken to dwell for an extended period in free territory. Both cases, therefore, involve a conflict between state and federal law, and both immediately precede federal crises—the Nullification Crisis of 1832–33 entailing South Carolina's right to nullify the federal Tariff of 1832, and the sectional conflicts leading to the

Civil War. In the liminal spaces of territories neither foreign nor quite domestic, legal ambiguities resurface.

What begins as a question of territoriality ends in the Cherokee's and Dred Scott's exclusion from legal and social representation as the Courts strive to resolve or obscure those ambiguities. But the decisions in both cases disclose as much as they cover up when they make available the conventionality of the natural rights through which citizenship and, by implication, I will argue, cultural subjectivity is constructed. As G. Edward White also argues in his detailed analysis of *Cherokee Nation*, the legal treatment of both the indigenous tribes and the slaves profoundly troubled the concept of natural law—particularly the rights to own and inherit property, including property in the self.[3] The dispossessed subjects thus embody—or disembody—an important representational threat: human beings to whom *natural* property rights do not extend. The rhetoric of erasure evoked to justify this exclusion images the rhetorical process of the translation of a subject into a citizen (largely a rights discourse). Ironically, the legal unrepresentability designed to deflect the political issues itself ushers in the return of the cultural repressed, what is entailed in (and covered up by) the making of Americans. By positing human beings whom the law cannot represent, in other words, the Marshall and Taney courts actually return to the (repressed) legal ambiguities and, by extension, to the legal genesis of United States subjectivity. Positive law distinguishes among subjectivities, but *all* subjects depend on that law for their *natural* rights. I invoke the uncanny here because I want to stress that the threat that the indigenous tribespeople and descendants of Africans come to pose to the anxious confederation inheres at least as much in their resemblance to as in their differences from other cultural subjects.

Cherokee Nation demonstrates significant contradictions within both states' rights and nationalist arguments. Since the case turns on Georgia's violating federal treaties by legislating within Cherokee territory, which is itself circumscribed by the state of Georgia, the relative authority of state and federal legislation is in question. The interesting twist of the case is that an actual victory for Georgia entails the court's upholding the integrity of the state against the coexistence of sovereign governments within shared boundaries, which coexistence in effect echoes the states' rights argument. Conversely, a victory for the national government conceptually upholds that principle of coexistence. At deeper issue, then, is just what kind of entity the "Cherokee Nation" describes.

The decision of the Court, as explained by Chief Justice Marshall, turns on the unique "condition of the Indians in relation to the United States [which] is, perhaps, unlike that of any other two people in existence."[4] Marshall rejects the designation "foreign" that characterizes "nations not owing a common allegiance" when determining

> the relation of the Indians to the United States. . . . The Indian territory *is admitted* to compose a part of the United States. In all our maps, geographical treatises, histories and laws, it is so considered. In all our intercourse with foreign nations, in our commercial regulations, in any attempt at intercourse between Indians and foreign nations, they are considered as within the jurisdictional limits of the United States, subject to many of those restraints which are imposed upon our own citizens. . . . [I]t may well be doubted, whether those tribes which reside within the acknowledged boundaries of the United States can, with strict accuracy, be denominated foreign nations. (*CN*, 11–12, emphasis added)

The representational bind that Marshall expresses grows out of the expanding borders of the United States, an expansion that brings the Declaration's "merciless savages" on "our frontiers" within national boundaries. Once used to delineate geographical boundaries, these "savages" threaten to define the limits of a natural rights discourse. Marshall responds with an erasure marked by the (elided) subject of the passive construction in the phrase "is admitted." He assumes a consensus that has already refused the tribal nations representation: "In all *our* maps . . . it is so considered." The "Indians" are comprehended within an *American* discourse just as the Cherokee nation is circumscribed by Georgia's boundaries, a colonizing gesture that inscribes both collective identity and geographic totality. While national policy, articulated especially in treaties, had distinguished among the tribal nations, many legal cases had obscured such distinctions in the service of the cogently articulated national terms into which the growing number of immigrants and rapidly expanding national boundaries could be readily translated. By the 1830s, the terms are set for the simultaneous and often contradictory policies toward the indigenous tribespeople: assimilation (in the service of appropriations of both land and identity), or removal.[5] In both instances, the pretext of United States legislation of the indigenous tribespeople inheres in the struggle to construct a collective identity, "We the People," that sanctifies the independent political entity uttered into existence in the founding texts.

The expanding borders of the nation generate a great deal of legal activity, but *Cherokee Nation* and *Dred Scott* demonstrate the larger relevance of property disputes to the construction of subjectivity. In a government based on what C. B. Macpherson calls "possessive individualism," the natural right to own property is a critical component of the definition of personhood.[6] Both Supreme Court cases are troubled by competing claims to property that in turn manifest competing definitions of property and personhood in the emerging nation. The legal unrepresentability of nonwhite subjects upon which *Cherokee Nation* and *Dred Scott* resolve justifies the exclusion of these subjects from the right to own property and, by implication, from personhood.

At the end of one of the two dissenting opinions in *Dred Scott,* Justice Benjamin R. Curtis asserts the symbolic—and representational—function of the law through its creation of property: "Without government and social order there can be no property; for without law, its ownership, its use and the power of disposing of it, cease to exist, *in the sense in which those words are used and understood in all civilized States.*[7] Here the law names property into existence by standardizing linguistic structures if not language itself. The material fact of property is a function of owning and bequeathing, actions and relations that the law governs. The "law," in turn, expresses the terms that make experience comprehensible. By implication, the subject's desire to comprehend, to make experience meaningful, underwrites his/her obeying the law. Curtis depicts the law as a rhetorical-legal discourse that defends the subject against an implied anarchy that threatens both the physical body and meaningful experience, hence subjectivity itself.

Efforts to legislate kinship in the early Republic explain the more symbolic importance of inheritance to cultural identity. The Naturalization Act of 1790 explicitly adds citizenship to the terms of property and inheritance governed by the patronym. This act not only "naturalizes" the children ("under the age of twenty-one years") of naturalized parents and extends the (natural) boundaries of the nation to include children born of citizens abroad, but it also very specifically provides "[t]hat the right of citizenship shall not descend to persons whose *fathers* have never been resident in the United States" (my emphasis). By the 1830s, the trope of the family commonly represents the Union. Accordingly, from the ever more strict and complex Naturalization and Alien and Sedition Acts to the 1819 law requiring annual records of immigration; from the American Society for Colonizing the Free People of Color in the United States (founded in 1817) to the 1819 Indian Civilization Fund and the Indian Removal policy (formalized by James Madison in 1825 and made an act under Andrew Jackson in 1830), the logic of official legislation and de facto policies of this period protects personhood and property from threatened disruptions of both metaphysical and territorial inheritance. Miscegenation legislation during these years, as Eva Saks shows, simultaneously protects a social institution that governs "the transmission of property" and "formalizes the parties' social relation."[8]

Even in legislation not specifically prohibiting interracial marriage, kinship metaphors express the anxiety evoked by nonwhite subjects in the early Republic. Justice William Johnson, in a consenting opinion in *Cherokee Nation*, pointedly excludes the Indians from "the family of nations" (*CN*, 14, 17, 18) and, consequently, from representation within the United States legal system and even, by implication, from the human family. Johnson, in fact, deconstitutes "Indians" back into tribal affiliations to support his contention that "every petty kraal of Indians, designating themselves a tribe or nation, and having a few hundred acres of land to hunt on exclusively . . . should, indeed, force into the family of nations, a very numerous and very heterogeneous progeny" (*CN*, 17).

The catalog of anti-amalgamation laws (directed as much against "Indians" as "descendants of Africans") with which Chief Justice Roger Taney begins his opinion in *Dred Scott* similarly excludes descendants of Africans from "the whole human family, . . . civilized governments and the family of nations" (*DS*, 702–3). Taney pushes the nation's natural basis through the common currency of body and family tropes:

> citizens in the several States, became also citizens of *this new political body:* but none other; it was formed by them, and for them and their posterity, but for no one else. . . . It was the union of those who were at that time members of distinct and separate political communities into *one political family,* whose power . . . was to extend over the whole territory of the United States. (*DS*, 701, emphasis added)

Taney uses these metaphors to suggest the threats posed by nonwhites to the genealogy of a white "family of independent nations" (*DS*, 701). The anti-amalgamation laws "show that a perpetual and impassable barrier was intended to be erected between the white race and the one which they had reduced to slavery" (*DS*, 702); Taney's passive voice invokes what Robert Ferguson calls "the rhetoric of inevitability," establishing history itself paradoxically as a justification for and outgrowth of the laws of nature.[9] Marshall's consistent use of passive voice similarly constitutes a legal strategy in which subjectivity is rhetorically subordinated to a historical narrative that, circularly, (re)constructs it.

The family archetype evokes both the actual inheritance and the genealogical relations that legally govern it. *Cherokee Nation* enables at once the appropriation of land and the delineation of "the American people." The defense in an earlier case, *Johnson and Graham's Lessee v. William McIntosh* (1823), had appealed to the putative lack of a tribal concept of private ownership to obviate the validity of the plaintiffs' claim to contested land: "as grantees from the Indians, they must take according to their laws of property, and as Indians subjects [sic]. The law of every dominion affects all persons and property situate within it . . . ; and the Indians never had any idea of individual property." [10] The concentric circles of this argument geometrically articulate a need to circumscribe tribal property relations within an American discourse of property: the plaintiffs are within Indian dominion for the sake of their purchase, but the Indians are, in turn, contained within United States definitions of property. The United States government's explicit policy toward the Indians, from the aforementioned 1819 Indian Civilization Fund to its fullest articulation in the 1887 Dawes Act, had at its core the civilization (dissolution) of tribal societies through the institution of private property. [11]

Circumscribed within the Euro-American community, a situation that provokes both *Cherokee Nation* and the later *Worcester v. Georgia* (1832), tribal society presents an ongoing challenge to the physical and ideological representations of the Union and its subjects. The boundaries separating a "civilized," or (re)presentable, person from a "savage" are, therefore, directly at stake in these cases. Where citizenship is defined through the natural right to own property, and, following Locke, the most basic expression of this concept rests in the citizen's *self*-ownership, members of tribes and slaves (extending, at least in *Dred Scott,* to all "descendants of Africans") constitute two ways of not owning the self: the former in the tribal absence of an "American" concept of private property, and the latter in their being owned by someone else. [12]

Rhetorically, indigenous tribespeople and descendants of Africans are fashioned into monsters that fit Frantz Fanon's description of "the real Other" whom the "white man . . . perceive[s] on the level of the body image, absolutely as the non-self—that is, the unidentifiable, the unassimilable." But the exclusion intended to foster a sense of homogeneity among white Americans ironically raises the more dramatic specter of the status of any "American" self without the already tenuous cultural identity. White America could see its own alterity, or alienation, reflected in the fate, and often quite literally in the face, of the racialized other. [13]

The Marshall Court seeks resolution to this dilemma in erasure, as in Justice Henry Baldwin's declaration that "there is no plaintiff in [the *Cherokee Nation*] suit" (*CN*, 21). This ominous (and prophetic) elision rests in the Marshall Court's reading of

> the eighth section of the third article [of the United States Constitution] which empowers congress to 'regulate commerce with foreign nations, and among the several states, and with the Indian tribes.' In this clause, they are as clearly contradistinguished, by a name appropriate to themselves, from foreign nations, as from the several states composing the Union. They are designated by a distinct appellation; and as this appellation can be applied to neither of the others, neither can the application distinguishing either of the others be, in fair construction, applied to them. The objects to which the power of regulating commerce might be directed, are divided into three classes—foreign nations, the several states, and Indian tribes. (*CN*, 12)

The Court's reliance on the wording of the Constitution makes the Cherokee's legal representation contingent on their textual representation. When Justice Smith Thompson, in his dissenting opinion, labels the Court's reading "a mere verbal criticism," he unwittingly shakes the rhetorical foundation on which, as Justice Curtis will later suggest, society and subjectivity are constructed. Thompson returns to the original act of naming to counter the "argument . . . that if the Indian tribes are foreign nations, they would have been included, without being specially named, and being so named, imports something different from the previous term 'foreign nations'" (*CN*, 41). He offers two alternative readings of the Constitution's phraseology: stylistic, "avoid[ing] the repetition of the term nation"; and practical, allowing Congress to deal separately with each tribal nation. Again unwittingly, however, Thompson taps into precisely the anxiety over heterogeneity that Johnson has evoked in "every petty kraal of Indians." At stake is the colonizing gesture that naturalizes the land as it makes the many one.

Neither Curtis nor Thompson intends to deconstruct the law. On the contrary, they offer essentially nationalist arguments, using the logic of the Constitution's regulations of commerce, currency, and naturalization to bring the individual *states* of the Union within the terms of a common law. Curtis especially argues for a common vocabulary of private property that will Americanize all who accept its terms. This assimilation, however, means cultural erasure rather than integration, and it entails a proportionately greater sacrifice for non-European cultures. The dissenting arguments address whether or not, rather than how, non-Europeans can and ought to become "Americans." Curtis wants to apply, not reform, the law, and his opinion must be understood as a response to Taney's demonstration, through an appeal to the anti-amalgamation laws with which he opens his majority opinion, that the father is not willing to give his name to his darker-skinned (or, more consistently, -blooded) progeny.

Cherokee Nation is finally about the incomprehensible hole in the map within the perimeters of Georgia. It is in fact an increasing Cherokee nationalism, evidence of the Cherokee's plan to remain indefinitely in possession of the disputed territory, that precipitates Georgia's controversial legislation. Debates within the Cherokee community had entailed whether nationalism could best be expressed in traditional Cherokee or in United States terms, but it is the traditionalists' defeat, and the adoption of a Cherokee Constitution, to which Georgia would most blatantly respond. The 1827 *Constitution of the Cherokee Nation,* spearheaded by the mainly interracial (mixed Cherokee and white parentage) elite, signaled a victory for a Cherokee nationalism simultaneously modeled on and opposed to United States nationalism.[14] Andrew Jackson's political ascendancy in the 1820s encouraged, and was even largely predicated on, a federal policy that replaced the aforementioned ambivalence with a new and determined program of removal. The victorious Cherokee nationalists hoped that a demonstration of their "civilization," this parallel Constitution for example, would ensure their right to remain on their land. While United States policy changes guaranteed their ultimate removal, the trends signified by the Cherokee Constitution precipitated events that may actually have expedited it.

The putatively Americanized Cherokee, many of whom had become farmers and even slaveholders, evoked anxious responses in their neighbors, as typified by the director of the Office of Indian Affairs at this time, Thomas L. McKenney: "They seek to be a People. . . . It is much to be regretted that the idea of Sovereignty should have taken such a deep hold of these people."[15] His common nineteenth-century use of "a People" to express "a nation" suggestively articulates the rhetorical underpinnings of personhood's contingency upon national identity during this period. The public outrage, which McKenney echoes, stems from the anxieties exacerbated by the profound threat of Cherokee separatism to the collective identity. The Cherokee's becoming like but not of the United States political entity, mirroring without acceding to its claims, seems to threaten the terms of that identity. And the threat is literally embodied by the "mixed-bloods" who trouble both white exclusionists and integrationists in their *physical* as well as *legal* uncanniness.

The particular nature of the threat posed by the Cherokee Constitution is complicated in precisely those ways in which, as Homi Bhabha suggests, "mimicry is at once resemblance and menace."[16] As a colonial strategy, an imposed "mimicry" mandates "a reformed, recognizable Other, as a *subject of a difference that is almost the same, but not quite*" (MM, 126), which is also to say, "*almost the same, but not white*" (MM, 130). In response to an ideology that envisions Americans as cultivators, some Cherokee take up hoes and crosses, purchase slaves, and adopt a Constitution, hopefully preserving whatever indigenous culture can elude the disciplinary gaze. But the nationalist Cherokee, by imitating rather than by assimilating or by otherwise disappearing, recontextualize the logic of United States nationalism. A Cherokee nation would ironically recapitulate the relation of the pre-Revolutionary colonies to England: " *'imperium in imperio'* (a state within a state)," conceptually complicating ideas of American exceptionalism, absorptiveness, and republicanism.[17] It is also worth reiterating that *Cherokee Nation* introduced complications concerning the volatile federalist debates. Only blatant racism—specifically, the assertion that the white race alone could be capable of civilization— could resolve the contradictions, and the Cherokee's mimicry (civilization in United States terms) directly countermands those assertions.

Marshall's attempt to express the Cherokee's ambiguous relation to the United States depicts the untenability of this positioning; Marshall offers an apparent compromise that works hierarchically to erase any slippage in *Cherokee Nation:* "They may . . . be denominated domestic dependent nations. . . . [T]heir relation to the United States resembles that of a ward to his guardian. They look to our government for protection; rely upon its kindness and its power, appeal to it for relief to their wants; and address the president as their great father" (CN, 12). This rhetoric echoes the earlier colonial legislation of indigenous tribespeople that, as the defense argued in *Johnson v. McIntosh*, "treat[ed] them as an inferior race of people, without the privileges of citizens, and under the perpetual protection and pupilage of the government" (JGL, 251). Marshall responds to the aggressive removal policy of the Jackson government with a paternalism that paradoxically withholds the father's name from the adopted children.

Marshall's domestic fantasy had been effectively dramatized by the future abolitionist, Lydia Maria Child, in *Hobomok* (1824). In her literary work, Child can play out a scenario that Marshall can only imply in a legal decision. Yet their efforts to resolve an ideological predicament are strikingly similar. Set in colonial New England, the novel uses its white female protagonist's ill-advised marriage to Hobomok, chief of a neighboring tribe, to accomplish her Americanization. The fate of Charles Hobomok Conant, son of Hobomok and Mary Conant and adopted son of Charles Brown, accomplishes for a fictitious individual what Marshall rhetorically tries, unsuccessfully, to do for the tribal nations. The novel conscientiously depicts Mary's consent to marry Hobomok as the unfortunate outcome of her maddening grief at reports of the death of her Royalist fiancé, Charles Brown, and anger at her father's unrelenting fanaticism. When she awakens to the consequences of her impulsive behavior, Mary redeems herself for her early nineteenth-century audience by accepting her exile and renouncing her inheritance. Although her father "conjure[s] her not to consider a marriage lawful, which had been performed in a moment of derangement" and enjoins her to return both to him and to the inheritance bequeathed to her by a beloved paternal grandfather, Mary "urg[es] him to appropriate her property to his own comfort" since "her marriage vow to the Indian was [no] less sacred, than any other voluntary promise."[18] Mary must stay married to Hobomok because of a contract that cannot be declared illegal. Her inheritance, on the other hand, can be invalidated by her relinquishing a legal identity that is contingent upon her (consensual) membership in a community in which those laws apply. Those laws, in other words, hold between the tribespeople and the government but have no weight within tribal society (as within the Cherokee nation). Only Hobomok can release her from her contract.

Hobomok, however, turns out to be an appropriately cooperative noble savage. When Charles Brown appears, almost as though reborn, Hobomok concedes his entitlement to both Mary and the land and self-lessly agrees to "'go far off among some of the red men in the West. They will dig him a grave, and Mary may sing the marriage song in the wig-wam of the Englishman'" (*Hob*, 139). His emigration/death speaks more to the ambiguities of government policy than to any deep wish of mi-grating tribes, but, most importantly, his self-abnegation Americanizes those it leaves behind. Mary can no longer return to England as she had wished because, she explains, "'[m]y boy would disgrace me, and I never will leave him; for love to him is the only way that I can now repay my debt of gratitude'" (*Hob*, 148). Instead, she must remain in the New World to reconstruct the American family both by reconciling with her Puritan father and by reconstituting Charles Hobomok.

The significance of Hobomok and his son inheres in the reconstitution of the family according to the ideology of the early nineteenth century. Mary and Hobomok's amalgamation reconciles the austere Mr. Conant to Charles Brown, and her return re-forms her rigid father into an affectionate patriarch and, "[p]artly from consciousness of blame, and partly from a mixed feeling of compassion and affection" (*Hob*, 149), a doting grandparent. Hobomok's erasure is signaled rhetorically through Charles Hobomok's assimilation: "he departed to finish his studies in England. His father was seldom spoken of; and by degrees his Indian appellation was silently omitted" (*Hob*, 150). The tacit agreement, denoted by passive voice, that whitewashes Mary's son attests to a faith in consensus and in the ability of the community to absorb a dash of Indian blood. In fact, that blood seems to be just the seasoning necessary to de-anglicize, or nativize, the fledgling national culture. But Charles (Hobomok) Conant Brown's Indianness can metaphorically occasion his family's Americanization only if his father departs, a contingency that recalls the appropriating of tribal names, insignia, dress, customs, and even bastardized ceremonies as badges of Americanness. Hobomok occasions a transformation of the Conant family that symbolically links colonial and early nineteenth-century America as it distinguishes both from England. Hobomok's son can even be schooled in England precisely because he can never be anglicized, only further Americanized.

As an Indian, however, Charles Hobomok simply ceases to exist. And in the Supreme Court case of *Worcester v. Georgia* (1832), Justice John McLean similarly argues that their Americanization entitles the Cherokee to federal protection but, in turn, requires their complete acquiescence. "By entering into [these treaties]," asks McLean, "have we not admitted the power of this people to bind themselves, and to impose obligations on us?"[19] McLean recognizes that the United States assimilation policies, such as the Indian Civilization Fund ("the means adopted by the general government to reclaim the savage from his erratic life, and induce him to assume the forms of civilization"), have Americanized the tribal nations into certain entitlement; they have tended, for example, "to increase the attachment [and, by implication, the right] of the Cherokees to the country lands" (*WG*, 397). But it is precisely *as* Americans that the tribal nations must submit to the authority of the United States government to define rights:

> The exercise of the power of self-government by the Indians, within a state, is undoubtedly contemplated to be temporary. . . . [A] sound national policy does require, that the Indian tribes within our states should exchange their territories, upon equitable principles, or eventually consent to become amalgamated in our political communities. (*WG*, 400)

The use of "amalgamated," especially in light of the anti-amalgamation legislation, is startling here, although, like "domestic dependent nations," it subtly articulates the subtext of the legislation. Just as women were disenfranchised by marriage, so the "Indians'" amalgamation would necessarily entail a surrender of any property held in the name of a tribal affiliation. In light, moreover, of anti-amalgamation laws, even the most enlightened official policies did no more than advocate a national forgetting, such as the tacit agreement that allows Charles Hobomok to pass in the name of his adopted father. Of course, the exception of an individual whose features obscure his bloodline could certainly not hold true for an entire tribe. Hence, the national fairy tale of *Hobomok* and the failure of Marshall's efforts at peaceful resolution.

It is, then, as a *collective* entity that the tribe (and, by *extension*, each of its members) must cease to exist. And it is *Worcester v. Georgia* that, through the uncanny resemblance, most pointedly depicts the untold history of the fate of the racialized other within an American legal discourse as an extension of the fate of the American self within an American collective identity. Significantly, the federal intervention called for by the plaintiff in *Cherokee Nation* is conferred by the court in *Worcester*, where the case now involves "the personal liberty of a citizen" (*WG*, 364). The court's *apparent* reversal, which is actually not quite a reversal, of the *Cherokee Nation* decision attests to the national stake in maintaining the apparent priority of "the personal liberty of a citizen." The case rules on the claim of the plaintiff, Samuel A. Worcester, of rights violations—including wrongful detainment—on the part of the state of Georgia, and it revolves around the constitutionality of an act passed by the Georgia legislature on December 22, 1830, claiming state jurisdiction over tribal territory. Georgia charges Worcester and a small group of fellow missionaries with residing in Cherokee territory without a permit and without taking "an oath to support and defend the constitution and laws of the state of Georgia" (*WG*, 350). Worcester's defense calls forth the federal treaties that uphold Cherokee sovereignty within established boundaries. Not only is there now a "plaintiff in this suit," but the case, which links the American citizen's "personal liberty" to tribal land rights, comes dangerously close to demonstrating a correlation between the legal representational invisibility of the racialized other and the necessary self-abridgment of even the most apparently representative Christian white male within a collective identity. Hence the ruling *against* Georgia, although in favor of *Worcester* rather than the Cherokee.

The threat of the Cherokee's mimicry, which largely inheres in the conceptual resonance between an American citizen's "personal liberty" and Cherokee land rights, is fully enacted in the Cherokee Constitution. Land distinguishes the Cherokee *nation* from the original Cherokee. The first section of Article 1 spells out the "boundaries of this nation," which do not encompass the Cherokee who had migrated west in accordance with United States government colonization programs—who had, that is, allowed themselves to be translated out of Georgia's boundaries. The second section defines the land as the nation's exclusive property:

> The sovereignty and Jurisdiction of this Government shall extend over the country within the boundaries above described, and the lands therein are, and shall remain, the common property of the Nation; but the improvements made thereon, and in the possession of the citizens of the Nation, are the exclusive and indefeasible property of the citizens respectively who made; or may rightfully be in possession of them; Provided, that the citizens of the Nation, possessing exclusive and indefeasible right to their respective improvements, as expressed in this article, shall possess no right nor power to dispose of their improvements in any manner whatever to the United States, individual states, nor individual citizens thereof; and that whenever any such citizen or citizens shall remove with their effects out of the limits of this Nation, and become citizens of any other Government, all their rights and privileges as citizens of this Nation shall cease.[20]

The passage articulates the distinctly Lockean concept of entitlement ("ownership") based on work ("improvements"). But this proprietorship is contingent upon membership in the collective national identity.[21] Since this land is explicitly indefeasible, it cannot, strictly speaking, be said to *belong* to any single proprietor.

In mimicking the de facto United States policy of contingent entitlement, the Cherokee Constitution exposes the conventionality of inalienable rights. First, it rearticulates (with significant slippage) the decision in *Johnson v. McIntosh*, which involves the dispute over the title to land that the plaintiffs had purchased from the Piankeshaw Indians and that the United States had granted to the defendants. Marshall's uncontested opinion upholds the defense counsel's appeal to "the uniform understanding and practice of European nations, and the settled law, as laid down by the tribunals of civilized states, [that] denie[s] the right of the Indians to be considered as independent communities, having a permanent property in the soil, *capable of alienation* to private individuals" (*JGL*, 565, emphasis added). The brief report of the defense repeats "alienation" two more times: "the extent of their right of alienation must depend upon the laws of the dominion under which they live" and "the Indian title to lands [is] a mere right of usufruct and habitation, without power of alienation" (*JGL*, 567). The defense counsel invokes Locke, among other sources, to naturalize the inalienable rights of the indigenous tribespeople to their land: "By the law of nature, they had not acquired a fixed property, capable of being transferred" (*JGL*, 567).

The Cherokee Constitution signals the Cherokee's adoption of the concept of provisional land rights, but in the service of Cherokee rather than United States nationalism. That Constitution, however, makes apparent that these rights are the result of positive rather than natural law. A similar implication plays throughout Marshall's rhetoric:

> As the right of society to prescribe those rules by which property may be acquired and preserved is not, and *cannot, be drawn into question;* as the title to lands, especially, is, and must be, admitted, to depend entirely on the law of the nation in which they lie; it will be necessary, in pursuing this inquiry to examine, not simply those principles of abstract justice, which the Creator of all things has impressed on the mind of his creature man, and which are admitted to regulate, in a great degree, the rights of civilized nations, whose perfect independence is acknowledged, but those principles also which our own government has adopted in the particular case, and given us as the rule for our decision. . . . [I]f the principle has been asserted in the first instance, and afterwards sustained; if a country has been acquired and held under it; if the property of the great mass of the community originates in it, it becomes the law of the land, and *cannot be questioned.* (*JGL*, 572, 590, emphasis added)

Marshall insists on the irrefutability of established laws, especially governing property. In the interest of the "categorical authority" of the law, he blurs the distinction between the "principles of abstract justice" and "those . . . which our own government has adopted," a distinction upon which he ostensibly insists.[22] By accepting the concept of provisional land rights but implicitly rejecting its genesis in natural law, the Cherokee Constitution restores the questioning agent that Marshall's passive voice would erase.

The effect of the mimicry extends, more importantly, to the concept of inalienable rights. In its strictest sense, as the *Johnson* decision makes apparent, inalienability countermands the agency of the subject itself as well as of the larger community. The Indians cannot "alienate"— that is, sell—their land because they do not own it. This context adds a new and troubling perspective to the politically fundamental concept of inalienable rights. Jefferson intends a natural law argument when he asserts the inalienability of certain individual rights in the Declaration.

Nevertheless, rights that cannot be alienated are not, strictly speaking, *owned* by the individual. The rights protected by United States law are, technically, the *property* of American society conferred upon subjects recognized by United States law and who in turn (at least in theory) accept the terms of that law. Like the Indians' property, they are more accurately rights of proprietorship than (alienable) possessions. Hence Mary Conant's automatic forfeiture when she consents to join Hobomok's world. Natural rights are rights that inhere in a certain conception of personhood, but that conception—and those rights—extend only to certain persons. Personhood is itself conceptually constructed by convention. *Cherokee Nation* and *Dred Scott* demonstrate the contingency of inalienable rights upon a government that chooses to define and protect them as such; they also reveal persons within that government's borders to whom those rights do not extend.

The political complexity of these cases lies in the many ways in which they threaten to represent both the legal construction of identity in rights discourse and the shifting basis of the authority to confer and protect those rights. In his concurring opinion in *Worcester,* Justice McLean tries to cover up the justification for the claims, made by proponents of states' rights, "that the federal government is foreign to the state governments; and that it must, consequently, be hostile to them." McLean argues that "foreign" and "state governments . . . proceed[] from the same people," and that the people of the state are also "the people of the Union" (*WG,* 386). Yet no amount of insistence on national unity can obscure the fundamental question of the case that McLean himself must finally ask: "which shall stand, the laws of the United States, or the laws of Georgia?" (*WG,* 391). In the shifting field of inquiry, from the status of "the Cherokee Nation" (and hence, Cherokee's legal representability) to the "personal liberty" of white male United States citizens, the nature of citizenship—and, more fundamentally, personhood—in the Union emerges as the anxious inquiry of these cases. But the anxiety overtakes the inquiry, which is in turn displaced or suppressed. When, for example, the Nullification Crisis in South Carolina helps turn the *Worcester* decision into a threat to the Union, and to the authority of the Court, both the Court and the plaintiffs demonstrate a willingness to compromise.[23] Although the South balked at the economic nationalism signaled by the protective tariffs in the 1820s, and although John C. Calhoun emphasized an analogy between South Carolina's right to nullify federal tariff regulations and Georgia's right to supersede federal treaties with indigenous tribes, Indian legislation generally inspired more obvious divisions among partisan rather than sectional factions. What may at times have seemed to be an East/West division was complicated by an emerging nationalism. Between *Cherokee Nation* and *Dred Scott*, however, these debates would more clearly reinscribe "We the People" into two distinctly competing sectional narratives.

Divergent national narratives, in other words, coalesce into two dominant narratives, as the related issues of slavery and state sovereignty inescapably force constitutional ambiguities to the fore in the antebellum United States. The Taney Court must therefore resolve what the Marshall Court can still try to obscure. Taney's opinion, which becomes the Court's official opinion, returns to the language of eighteenth-century political discussions to maintain Dred Scott's legal unrepresentability.[24] Excluding descendants of Africans from "We the People," Taney insists that the Constitution prohibits their holding federal citizenship while any state precludes them from holding state citizenship. Nor, however, are they eligible for alien status. Dred Scott consequently cannot sue for his freedom because he is not and cannot be a citizen of the state of Missouri. Because of the centrality of the issues raised in *Dred Scott* to the mounting political crisis, however, Taney rules on other controversies touched on by *Dred Scott* as the case had made its way, in several incarnations, through other courts. Taney's majority opinion describes a Constitution that prevents the federal government from prohibiting slavery in a territory and that gives a state rather than the federal government jurisdiction over the regulation of domestic institutions, including slavery. Even if Dred Scott could sue in state or federal court, neither his master's sojourn in the free state of Illinois nor in the territory designated free under the Louisiana Purchase could legitimate his suit for freedom in Missouri. Thus the Taney Court upholds the "squatter sovereignty" of the 1854 Kansas-Nebraska Act and (necessarily) affirms the unconstitutionality of the 1820 Missouri Compromise.

Taney carefully distinguishes between Indians and descendants of Africans. By the late 1850s, the government's aggressive policy had substantially diminished any significant physical or representational challenge from the tribes. And by 1857, Taney could *contrast* the legal invisibility of "a negro, whose ancestors were imported into this country and sold as slaves" (*DS*, 700) with the status of "Indian governments [that] were regarded and treated as foreign governments, as much so as if an ocean had separated the red man from the white" (*DS*, 700). One must either question Taney's legal scholarship, or interrogate his willful mis-construal of *Cherokee Nation*. His decision reveals a deliberative shift of emphasis that elucidates an important difference between these groups:

> It is true that *the course of events* has brought the Indian tribes within the limits of the United States under subjection to the white race; and it *has been found necessary,* for their sake as well as our own, to regard them as in a state of pupilage, and to legislate to a certain extent over them and the territory they occupy. But they may, without doubt, *like the subjects of any other foreign government,* be naturalized by the authority of Congress, and become citizens of a State and of the United States; and if an individual should leave his *nation or tribe,* and take up his abode among the white population, he would be entitled to *all the rights and privileges which would belong to an emigrant from any other foreign people.* (*DS,* 700, emphasis added)

No longer a threat, the tribes could now comprise an alien nation, and their lack of proximity to the white family permits suggestions of their assimilability.[25] In contrast, each side of the slavery debate invokes the mulatto to depict the gruesome consequences of the other side's insti-tutions: the threat from within. Black subjectivity evidently presents the more serious danger in the antebellum United States. The descendant of Africans registers the uncanniness of the legally unrepresentable subject perhaps even more forcefully than the member of a tribal nation. "Indian governments" had represented the *collective* threat offered by the prox-imity of an alternative collectivity. A descendant of Africans, in Taney's narrative, embodies the *individual* threat of a human being deprived of choice and self-possession within (but not of) the Union.

Taney's reconstructed historical narrative seeks to legitimate—and moralize—slavery ("for their sake as well as our own"). At stake is the states' rights claim that the state rather than the federal government pro-tects the liberties of *all* citizens. The majority opinion in *Dred Scott* must establish the priority of both the master's property rights over the slave's right to self-possession and the state's right to regulate slavery over fed-eral legislation.

Taney's narrative must present a government dedicated to the preser-vation of individual liberty. Inconsistencies within that program must be rhetorically elided. Accordingly, Taney uses a rhetoric of inevitability to inscribe Indian removal within the progressive movement, the "manifest destiny," of the American people. His loose echo of the Declaration of In-dependence ("course of human events"; "found necessary") ensures that the subjection of tribes remains within the terms of the American Revolution, although emigration of these "nations or tribes" (the distinction is no longer so crucial) has removed the immediate risk of an imperial analogy between the United States and England that, for example, the Cherokee resemblance to the revolutionary colonies had promoted.[26] The prosperity of the Union inevitably results in the civilization or removal of the tribal nations (either way, the passing of tribal cultures). That same prosperity, on the other hand, extends to slavery, which is consequently as inevitable and beneficial to all concerned as Indian removal. Both are the outcome of civilization; hence, the familiar paternalistic rhetoric that enslaves Africans and their descendants, as it removes tribal cultures, "for their sake as well as our own."

Whereas Indian removal makes it possible to emblematize (and thus Americanize) tribal culture, however, the slave remains within United States culture as a visible symbol of nonpersonhood: neither *potential* citizen nor alien. The rhetoric of two southern Justices who concur with Taney's opinions evinces concern that *Dred Scott* somehow challenges the "*status* of [white] persons" in the United States. Justice John A. Campbell argues that the individual's inalienable rights curb Congress's power to "determine the condition and *status* of persons who inhabit the Territories" (*DS*, 744). Campbell imagines "an American patriot" who contrasts the European and American systems by affirming

> that European sovereigns give lands to their colonists, but reserve to themselves a power to control their property, liberty and privileges; but the American Government sells the lands belonging to the people of the several States (*i.e.*, United States) to their citizens, who are already in the possession of personal and political rights, which the government did not give, and cannot take away. (*DS*, 745)

Inalienable rights here restrict the United States *government's* rather than the individual's access, which was also Jefferson's intention. Largely on the basis of this distinction, the colonies declared their independence. Campbell, however, uses the "American Government" to conceptualize a transfer of rights that is regulated by a legal system. That system controls the distribution of those rights—not unlike the European sovereigns—by its power to decide exactly *who* is "already in the possession of personal and political rights, which the government did not give, and cannot take away." For Justice Peter V. Daniel, the slave's status as property makes citizenship unthinkable. Daniel insists that "the power of disposing of and regulating . . . vested in Congress . . . did not extend to the personal or political rights of citizens or settlers . . . inasmuch as citizens or persons could not be property, and especially were not property belonging to the United States" (*DS*, 735). Americans' self-ownership is evidently at issue in *Dred Scott*.

The counternarratives offered by the two dissenters, Justices McLean and Curtis, paradoxically maintain slavery's general legality and suggest the challenge that slavery poses to the law. Curtis's reluctance to contest the legality of slavery stems from the New Englander's conservatism. Justice John McLean, on the other hand, manifests a politician's fervency—and his own presidential ambitions. He summons the danger of the nation's dissolution, posed by slavery, in an effort to save the Union. McLean draws on precedent to "show that property in a human being does not arise from nature or from the common law, but, in the language of this court, it is a mere municipal regulation, founded upon and limited to the range of the territorial laws" (*DS*, 760). This precedent establishes Scott's right to freedom on the basis of his having lived in free territory. But he ambiguously (and ominously) evokes the crux of impending national crisis in labeling "[t]his decision . . . the end of the law" (*DS*, 760). To enslave a person is to push the law to its extreme: if a law that turns a human being into property "does not arise from nature," then what, he wonders, stops a government from making "white men slaves?" (*DS*, 757). Moreover, the law that creates slaves also, by extension, creates the natural rights that constitute personhood. This is to envision the *end*, in both senses of the word, of the law.

In the debate over the power of the federal government, each side had to establish itself as safeguarding "the people's" liberty (individual rights). But the focus on individual liberty was, as many argued, inconsistent with the slave's status as a potential citizen. Accordingly, the slave had to be either excluded from the possibility of citizenship or emancipated. *Dred Scott* manifests the social and legal consequences of the rhetorical elision of the black subject in the haunting possibility of a legally invisible subject.

Within a decade of the *Dred Scott* decision, Abraham Lincoln would connect the similar rhetorical disappearance of the white subject to the dissolution of the Union in his Second Inaugural Address. Lincoln ends the first paragraph of this brief speech, which looks ahead to the reconstruction of the Union, ambiguously: "With high hope for the future, no prediction in regard to it is ventured." Dangling modifier and passive voice defer a subjectivity apparently contingent upon the fate—the reconstitution—of the Union. Lincoln similarly constructs three of the four sentences that comprise this paragraph around the passive voice, and the first person—singular or plural—appears only embedded within a clause: "I trust." In the wake of a crisis concerning the collective identity, the subject, which certainly cannot act, can barely even exist—can only "trust." The deferred subject begs a central question of the conflict: whom does "We the People" include, and, more pointedly, who speaks in their (its?) name? Is the United States itself a plural or singular subject? Lincoln's rhetoric announces his stand; the American subject cannot exist without the Union, in the name of which it is held *in trust*. The contingency of the subject promotes a personal investment in the fate of the Union, now unobstructedly on the way to nationhood.

The questions raised in *Cherokee Nation* and *Dred Scott* motivate but are not finally resolved either by Lincoln's rhetoric or the reconstructive strategies it articulates. Instead, they resurface in the anxious efforts to legislate mimicry and difference out of official existence, efforts that emerge from, as they attest to, fundamental contradictions of United States subjectivity. These contradictions are not resolved in the Fourteenth Amendment, which establishes federal and state citizenship for all persons born in the United States, or in the postwar nation. Debates surrounding overseas expansion of the late-nineteenth and early-twentieth centuries evince renewed concerns for the stability of the nation and the fate of Americans as well as reinvigorated strategies of rhetorical erasure. In particular, the 1901 Supreme Court case of *Downes v. Bidwell* forcefully registers the return of the issues (and decisions) of *Cherokee Nation* and *Dred Scott*. The case, which explicitly sanctions the nation's right to own territory and legislate over subjects that it does not incorporate, declares inhabitants of United States overseas territories neither citizens nor aliens, hence, again, legally unrepresentable. Although *Downes v. Bidwell* divides the Court, both sides show marked concern for national stability. Those favoring the decision—and thus legislating imperialism—imagine a territory that is necessary to "the peaceful evolution of national life" but inhabited by a "people utterly unfit for American citizenship." Dissenting justices are equally troubled by the alleged power of Congress to turn such a territory into "a disembodied shade, in an intermediate state of ambiguous existence for an indefinite period."[27] In legislating the ambiguous status of (nonwhite) inhabitants of overseas territories, however, the Court creates disembodied subjects who bear witness to the fate most feared by both sides.

In *Downes v. Bidwell,* as in *Cherokee Nation* and *Dred Scott,* the perceived threat to national stability (actual or imagined) gives rise to an almost apocalyptic anxiety over the fate of American subjects. These cases do not interrogate the source of that concern, the rhetoric through which the nation constitutes its subjects, and that concern continues to motivate the creation of subjects who embody precisely that fate. From the judgments of *Cherokee Nation* and *Dred Scott* to Lincoln's Second Inaugural Address and into the twentieth century with *Downes v. Bidwell*, the disembodied subject continues to haunt the imperial nation. The history of these subjects is a "tale twice-told but seldom written": the story of subjectivity in the United States.[28]

Notes

I wish to thank Sacvan Bercovitch, Joseph Donahue, Robert Ferguson, Jay Fliegelman, Elaine Freedgood, Barbara Gelpi, Howard Horwitz, Amy Kaplan, Karl Kroeber, and Michael Tratner for extraordinarily helpful suggestions for revising this work. I am also grateful for a summer research grant from the Council for Research in the Humanities of Columbia University and a Mellon Fellowship from Stanford University, both of which afforded me the time to research, write, revise. This essay first appeared in *boundary 2* 19, no. 3 (Fall 1992): 77–104.

1 With E. J. Hobsbawm, I would maintain that "nationalism comes before nations." *Nations and Nationalism since 1780: Programme, Myth, Reality* (Cambridge: Cambridge University Press, 1990), p. 10. See also Benedict Anderson, *Imagined Communities: Reflections on the Origin and Spread of Nationalism* (London: Verso, 1983), and Ernest Gellner, *Nations and Nationalism* (Oxford: Oxford University Press, 1983).

2 Thomas Jefferson, *The Papers of Thomas Jefferson*, vol. 1: 1760–76, ed. Julian Boyd (Princeton, N.J.: Princeton University Press, 1950). Future references to the Declaration are from this work.

3 G. Edward White, *The Marshall Court and Cultural Change, 1815–35: The History of the Supreme Court of the United States*, vol. 3–4 (New York: Macmillan Publishing, 1988), esp. pp. 703–40.

I am also indebted, in this discussion, to James Kettner's theoretical formulations of United States citizenship in *The Development of American Citizenship, 1608–1870* (Chapel Hill: University of North Carolina Press, 1978).

My interest in the uncanniness of nonwhite subjects and in the anxieties concerning the conception of personhood in legal and political rhetoric has been inspired by Allen Grossman's "The Poetics of Union in Whitman and Lincoln: An Inquiry toward the Relationship of Art and Policy," *The American Renaissance Reconsidered: Selected Papers from the English Institute, 1982–83*, ed. Walter Benn

Michaels and Donald E. Pease (Baltimore: Johns Hopkins University Press, 1985), pp. 183–208.

4 *Cherokee Nation v. the State of Georgia, United States Reports,* vol. 30, pp. 1–53; p. 11. Future references are cited in the text as *CN.*

5 Lucy Maddox offers an especially rich analysis of Indian legislation in light of the "persistent otherness of the Indians" (8) who "continued to frustrate white America's efforts . . . to include them within the discourse of American nationalism and, concomitantly, within the structure of the country's laws and institutions" (7) and of how that dilemma shaped the culture of the early Republic. *Removals: Nineteenth-Century American Literature and the Politics of Indian Affairs* (New York: Oxford University Press, 1991).

Robert Berkhofer, Jr., contends that *Cherokee Nation* made the Cherokee the point of reference for this question as well as for removal. I have benefited greatly from Berkhofer's discussion of *Cherokee Nation* in *The White Man's Indian: Images of the American Indian from Columbus to the Present* (New York: Vintage Books, 1979), esp. "Democracy and Removal: Defining the Status of the Indian," pp. 157–66.

6 C. B. Macpherson, *The Political Theory of Possessive Individualism, Hobbes to Locke* (Oxford: Oxford University Press, 1962).

In *"Ronald Reagan," the Movie and Other Episodes in Political Demonology* (Berkeley: University of California Press, 1987), Michael Paul Rogin uses a similar phrase, "propertied individualism," to theorize a liberal American society. He offers a fascinating psychoanalytic reading of the threat that tribal communalism posed to "American" society that also considers the simultaneous threat and attraction emblematized by the "Indian savagery" onto which white aggression projected itself.

See also Eric Cheyfitz, *The Poetics of Imperialism: Translation and Colonization from The Tempest to Tarzan* (Oxford: Oxford University Press, 1991). Cheyfitz discusses the translation of "Native American land . . . into the European identity of *property*" (43). Whereas Cheyfitz demonstrates the translation of the other into alienating terms, I am more concerned with how that translation destabilizes the subjectivity of the dominant group as it exposes the already alienating terms on which that subjectivity is predicated.

7 *Scott v. Sandford, United States Reports,* vol. 60, pp. 691–795, esp. pp. 787–88. Future references are cited in text as *DS.*

8 Eva Saks, "Representing Miscegenation Law," *Raritan* 8, no. 2 (1988): 39–69.

9 Robert Ferguson, "The Judicial Opinion as Literary Genre," *Yale Journal of Law & the Humanities* 2, no. 1 (Winter 1990): 201–19.

10 *Johnson v. McIntosh, United States Reports,* vol. 21, pp. 240–67; p. 251. Future references are cited in texts as *JGL.*

11 The Dawes Act allotted land and awarded citizenship to members of tribal nations willing to reside "separate and apart from any tribe of Indians" (182). *Dawes Act, 1887,* Appendix A of D. S. Otis, *The Dawes Act and the Allotment of Indian Lands,* ed. Francis Paul Prucha (Norman, Okla.: University of Oklahoma Press, 1973), pp. 177–84.

12 According to Macpherson, the individual is (naturally) free to enter *voluntarily* into relations with other individuals and with society at large. In thus conceptualizing the person, legislators in the early nation excluded those from cultures with different conceptions of property from personhood. It is, moreover, the inalienability of the person that these cases conceptually problematize. In *Johnson v. McIntosh,* property cannot be alienated because it is not really owned, which deconstructs a self-ownership rooted in the inalienability of the person. (See Macpherson, pp. 23–26.)

G. Edward White similarly makes a distinction between African Americans and indigenes that turns on their different relations to property. He traces an evolving policy to expropriate tribal property that is similar to mine and notes that the justices' conflicting positions "functioned to exclude from discourse a third ideological point of view, that of cultural relativism"; however, he does not sufficiently consider the *representational* threat that obscures the possibility of attending to cultural relativism (*The Marshall Court and Cultural Change, 1815–35: The History of the Supreme Court of the United States,* p. 706).

13 Frantz Fanon, *Black Skins, White Masks,* trans. Charles Lam Markmann (New York: Grove Press, 1967), p. 161n.

14 For a fuller discussion of the emergence of Cherokee nationalism and the nationalists' conflict with the separatist traditionalists, see William G. McLoughlin, *Cherokees and Missionaries, 1789–1839* (New Haven: Yale University Press, 1984).

15 Letters from Thomas L. McKenney to James Barbour on, respectively, Nov. 29, 1827, and Feb. 20, 1827. Cited in McLoughlin, *Cherokees and Missionaries.*

16 "Of Mimicry and Men: The Ambivalence of Colonial Discourse," *October* 28 (Spring 1984): 125–33, 127. Future references in text are cited as MM. The Cherokee function as the colonized in Bhabha's formulation, returning "the look of surveillance as the displacing gaze of the disciplined, where the observer becomes the observed and 'partial' representation rearticulates the whole notion of *identity* and alienates it from essence" (129). Needless to say, the structural contingency of an act of mimicry at least complicates the possibility for critique. In the case of the Cherokee, the mimicry helped to promote dissent in the Cherokee nation and expedited removal. Nevertheless, the response of the United States government attests to the threat of mimicry.

17 Kettner, *The Development of American Citizenship,* pp. 146–47.

18 Lydia Maria Child, *Hobomok & Other Writings on Indians* (New Brunswick: Rutgers University Press, 1986), p. 136. Future references cited as *Hob.*

19 *Worcester v. Georgia. United States Reports,* vol. 31, pp. 350–403; p. 393. Future references in the text are cited as *WG.*

20 Emmet Starr, *Starr's History of the Cherokee Nation*, ed. Jack Gregory and Rennard Strickland (Fayetteville, Ark.: Indian Heritage Association, 1967), pp. 55–56.

21 It is interesting to note, in this context, that the Cherokee Constitution excludes descendants of Africans, including offspring of miscegenation, from "the rights and privileges of [the] nation."

22 I have taken the phrase "categorical authority" used in this context from Jacques Derrida, who argues that the obscured origins of the law obfuscate the positivist sources of its categorical authority. "Devant la loi," trans. Avital Ronell, *Kafka and the Contemporary Critical Performance: Centenary Readings*, ed. Alan Udoff (Bloomington: Indiana University Press), pp. 128–49.

23 Richard Ellis's *The Union at Risk* (New York: Oxford University Press, 1987) offers insight into how the Nullification Crisis influenced the resolution of *Worcester*. Jackson, already no friend to the Cherokee, was ironically supported in his position by Calhoun's skillful maneuvering to identify South Carolina's position with Georgia's. The fate of the Union prompted all parties except the Cherokee (that is, the government, the Georgia legislature, the Marshall Court, and even Worcester himself) to modify their stances. This outcome ensured the Cherokee's subsequent removal from Georgia.

24 Don E. Fehrenbacher explains the context of this "official" opinion in *Slavery, Law and Politics* (New York: Oxford University Press, 1981). Taney offers a long, partisan, and sometimes inaccurate opinion on contradictory aspects of the case (for example, his jurisdictional and territorial rulings may be in conflict). As a result, several of the concurring opinions do not seem fully to concur; nevertheless, the court's majority concurrence designates Taney's opinion as the "official opinion" of the Court. Fehrenbacher presents convincing evidence that Taney rewrote (and significantly augmented) his opinion in response to Curtis's lengthy and impressive dissenting opinion; the Court records are, therefore, not what was actually heard at the trial (and consented to by the concurring justices).

25 Walter Benn Michaels, in "The Vanishing American," *American Literary History* 2, no. 2 (Summer 1990): 220–41, traces the logical culmination of this process in the official policies through which, by the twentieth century, Indians were viewed as potential citizens and, with the Citizenship Act of 1924, declared citizens. He explains the symbolic process by which "Indians" were appropriated as "American" ancestors and had their identity reconceived as a cultural inheritance. I read Taney's contrast between tribal nations and descendants of Africans as an early indicator of the direction of this process.

26 Taney goes on to cite directly the first two paragraphs of the Declaration of Independence both to contrast policy toward indigenes and African Americans and to preempt the abolitionist appeal to the language of the Declaration.

27 *Downes v. Bidwell, United States Lawyer's Edition 179–82*, 1089–1146, pp. 1116 and 1139. Even the October 17, 1899, platform of the American Anti-Imperialist League, while "regretting that the blood of the Filipinos is on American hands," is explicitly more troubled by "the betrayal of American institutions at home." Cited in Carl Schurz, *Papers, Correspondence and Political Speeches*, ed. Frederic Bancroft, vol. 6 (New York: G. P. Putnam's Sons, 1913), pp. 77–79.

In a discussion of the relationship between popular historical romances and United States imperialism, Amy Kaplan shows how disembodied national power allows for an economic expansion that is not based on territorial expansion. "Romancing the Empire: The Embodiment of American Masculinity in the Popular Historical Novel of the 1890s," *American Literary History* 2, no. 4 (Winter 1990): 659–90. The "disembodied shade" of a territory thus (un)incorporated threatens to bring such strategies to consciousness.

28 The quoted phrase is from W. E. B. Du Bois's *Souls of Black Folk*. He refers to cultural observations so (ominously) obvious that they must be repressed.

Gauri Viswanathan

The Naming of Yale College

British Imperialism and American

Higher Education

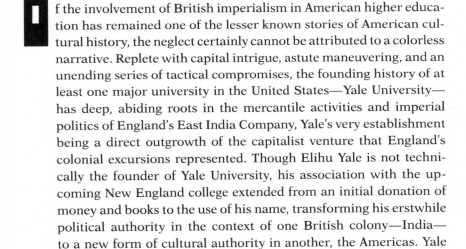f the involvement of British imperialism in American higher educa-
tion has remained one of the lesser known stories of American cul-
tural history, the neglect certainly cannot be attributed to a colorless
narrative. Replete with capital intrigue, astute maneuvering, and an
unending series of tactical compromises, the founding history of at
least one major university in the United States—Yale University—
has deep, abiding roots in the mercantile activities and imperial
politics of England's East India Company, Yale's very establishment
being a direct outgrowth of the capitalist venture that England's
colonial excursions represented. Though Elihu Yale is not technically the founder of Yale University, his association with the up-
coming New England college extended from an initial donation of
money and books to the use of his name, transforming his erstwhile
political authority in the context of one British colony—India—
to a new form of cultural authority in another, the Americas. Yale
College, as surrogate heir to the childless but wealthy English merchant, inherited a patrimony that united the destinies of American
higher education with the fruits of England's empire-building.

This essay seeks to elucidate that connection and flesh out the
details of Yale's years in India; simultaneously, in tracing the founding of American institutions of higher learning to British imperial
wealth, it also seeks to illuminate the conditions enabling the transition from British mercantilism, in its precentralized administrative phase, to full-blown imperialism and the circulation of colonial

wealth into a global economy that made possible the birth of institutions like Yale College.

Though Yale University is named after Elihu Yale, the idea for its establishment in 1676 did not originate with him but with a party of American Dissenters in Connecticut, whose chief representatives in subsequent years were Cotton Mather and Jeremy Dummer. Struggling to maintain an independent college impervious to royal control, while at the same time ensuring that there were adequate finances, the early Puritan founders sought avenues of access to wealthy merchants in England who might be prevailed upon to part with their money for the cause of higher learning in the American colonies. In the course of their far-flung search, the London "nabob" Elihu Yale, then living in Queen Square amid the "magnificent Oriental plunder of his Madras days,"[1] came to the attention of the Connecticut Dissenters, who made no attempt to hide the fact that their interest in Elihu Yale was purely mercenary: here was a man who was well known to have made a huge fortune through his twenty-eight years in India first as a clerk with the East India Company and then as governor of Madras. Furthermore, Elihu Yale was bereft of male issue and, in seeking an heir to bequeath his vast fortune, had a patrimony that was available for the asking. In shrewdly assessing that Yale might look favorably on the fledgling New England college because of his earlier—albeit tenuous—familial connections with the American colony, the Dissenters adopted a strategy of inflating cultural continuities between England and America (presented as analogous to family connections), to the point that these emerged as a set of reciprocal obligations and responsibilities that overrode ideological and religious differences between the Puritans in America and the Anglicans in England.

A small Dissenting institution turning to a staunch Church of England supporter like Elihu Yale is only one of many strange twists in a history that abounds in anomalies. The American colonists' representation of a continuum of shared identities between England and America extended to the paradoxical depiction of dissent as an affirmation of a universal religion, whose dissemination was compulsorily urged by the cultural imperatives of empire. The ties of dependency on the mother country for scarce economic resources, which forced the American colonists to turn to wealthy merchants in England for support, even while the college they sought to create was dedicated to principles entirely contrary to the mainstream religious doctrines, forced an unconvincing and strained reconciliation of starkly opposed ideological positions that smoothed over the historically asymmetrical relations between the English "center" and the American "periphery." The American Dissenters, in the seemingly subordinate position of "the colonized" but eager to establish their own independent intellectual centers of religious authority, secured exactly what they wished from Elihu Yale by presenting themselves to him as potential Church of England converts—a role that suggested a possible openness to opposed doctrines but, at the same time, reserved the privilege of agency to themselves.

But while pragmatic considerations might explain why the American colonists were driven to approach a man who was diametrically opposed to them doctrinally to be their potential benefactor, far more perplexing is the question of why Yale would want to support a college founded on entirely different principles from those he held. A fervid Anglican, he had already parted with a substantial portion of the wealth accumulated in India to promote the missionary activities of the Society for the Propagation of the Gospel both in England and abroad. Yale's eventual acquiescence to the Dissenters' pleas for money is less a sign of the whittling away of ideological differences between them than the result of Cotton Mather's carefully orchestrated strategy of appealing simultaneously to two important sides of Yale: to the devout Anglican's sense of English Protestantism as a universal missionary religion that, by definition, ought to leap to the challenge of winning over those dissenting from its premises (be those individuals "heathens" in the East Indies or unregenerate Christians in the American colonies); and to the heirless nabob's patriarchal ambition to perpetuate himself in apt symbols of posterity.

Given Yale's past career in the East India Company, where he had ample opportunity to develop an ethics of moral relativism that permitted him, as Yale University historian Edwin Oviatt remarked, to "squeeze that portion of mankind nearest him for his riches,"[2] his easygoing attitude to principle and dogma is not surprising. Indeed, Cotton Mather directly alluded to Yale's prior history in nothing less than the most laudatory terms: "There are those in these parts of western *India*, who have had the satisfaction to know something of what you have done and gained in the *eastern*, and they take delight in the story"[3] (emphasis in original). Mather's rhetoric played around a remapping of the sites of cultural authority: by forging a common identity between the American colonies (presented as "western India") and the East Indies, Mather reinforced the idea of England as the controlling center of both halves of the empire, reaffirming Yale's firm belief in the imminent triumph of a universal Anglicanism. The notion of England as the "center" is at once a cultural

construction of a universalizing discourse that links geographically disparate areas like India and America in a world economic system brought
into being by increasing colonial expansion, and a mode of representing
the British empire itself as situated between cultural extremities brought
into homogeneous unity by the commanding hand of imperial control.
Mather's description of America as "western India," of course, not only
plays on the original error upon which America was colonized as the "discovery" of India but also insists on perpetuating the error by urging the
essential interchangeability of India and America. But significantly, this
interchangeability is presented in the language of surrogacy. That Mather
deliberately chooses to efface the name of America altogether, even while
America is refitted into the geographical space referred to by the designation "western India," suggests the powerful surrogate functions that
renaming performs, enabling the collapsing of disparate colonized regions of the empire into a collective unity with the family name of "India."
In one effective stroke territorial distinctions dissolve, discrete colonization fades archaically into exotic discovery of a seamless, generic "India,"
and America emerges as India's colonial sibling.

But perhaps Mather's real stroke of genius was his unctuous promise
to Yale to name the college after him in return for his benevolence. The
language of surrogate parenthood and procreation that fills Mather's letter established a far deeper link between the man and the institution than
one of mere "benefactor" and "recipient":

> Sir, though you have your felicities in your family, which I pray God continue
> and multiply, yet certainly, if what is forming at New Haven might wear the
> name of YALE COLLEGE, it would be better than *a name of sons and daugh-
> ters.* And your munificence might easily obtain for you such a commemora-
> tion and perpetuation of your valuable name, as would indeed be much better
> than an Egyptian pyramid. (emphasis in the original)[4]

In a subsequent letter to the governor of Boston, confirming Yale's donation, Mather pursued the procreative imagery even further by boasting that

> what he now does is very little in proportion to what he will do, when once he
> finds, *by the name of it, that it may claim an adoption with him.* Yale College
> cannot fail of Mr. Yale's generous and growing bounty. I confess, that it was a
> great and inexcusable presumption in me, *to make myself so far the godfather
> of the beloved infant as to propose a name for it.* (emphasis added)[5]

If, as Mather suggests, the naming of institutions after oneself replaces biological reproduction as a more long-lasting way of ensuring posterity, his pragmatic plan to induce Yale to make a financial commitment by promising a college named after him was motivated by more than considerations of expediency: in a far-reaching way, the lure of conferring paternity through naming resonated in Yale's colonial past. In the psychodrama of the British presence in India, as in other colonies of the empire, the loss of children in the unfamiliar climate of the tropics brought out the deepest insecurity in the British male colonizer, his apparent power and authority in the military and political sphere undermined by his inability to ensure the continuity of his biological line. The compulsive urge to name towns, streets, buildings, and other sites after themselves or their deceased children marks a persistent tendency by European colonizers to bestow their paternity on the colonial landscape as a gesture of ultimate conquest.[6] The life of Elihu Yale vividly illustrates this impetus to surmount the possible extinction of the family line by reproducing its name elsewhere. The loss of his only son in Madras (as well as another son born in an illegitimate union with a Portuguese Jewish woman) marked a turning point in Yale's life: his best-known biographer maintains that Yale turned autocratic and imperious soon after the death of his son David, and even goes so far as to say that "if the Governor had been the Elihu Yale of his early married life, or of his accession to the supreme power as he was before his son died and his wife went back to England, it is not likely that he would have forced measures through against the opposition of practically all the members of his Council."[7] Not surprisingly, one of Yale's first actions after purchasing a fort near Madras in a private deal with a Hindu ruler was to rename it after his deceased son David. Therefore, when Cotton Mather described to Elihu Yale the naming of Yale College as a conquest of death itself (even sons and daughters cannot extend a man's life the way institutions can, he reminds Yale), he succeeded in striking exactly the right chord of an assured futurity in the aging, wealthy merchant of Queen Square, London.

The power of naming resonates with what Edward Said has described as the process of filiation and affiliation. If, as Said suggests, the failure to reproduce biologically (and to engender filiative relationships) induces a transition to the "compensatory order" of affiliation (i.e., to an institution, a culture, a political program, a religious creed), the new relationships promoted by naming as a form of affiliation attempt to recreate, if not perfect, the relationships that would normally prevail in filiative contexts, but now in the realms of culture and society rather than nature. Said's analysis of early twentieth-century high modernism is particularly useful—and relevant to my reading of Yale—in shedding light on the connections between the modern thrust toward affiliative relationships and what Said calls "the antinomies and atomizations of reified existence in the modern capitalist world-order."[8] While Said locates his analysis within the shifts in literary forms produced by an enervated and fragmented cultural consciousness in the era of modern capitalism, it is possible to situate such shifts even more specifically in the transition to global capitalism marked by the growth of institutions—political, cultural, and economic—supplanting the hierarchical, familial relationships engendered in a precapitalist order.

For instance, educational history records the development of schools and colleges to perform the work of training and disciplining young minds traditionally carried out by the family (particularly by the father) as an outcome of the new relationships engendered by the breakup of the old feudal order. Betokening the rise of the bourgeoisie, the infusion of new wealth into the social system through the increase of material production and the securing of global markets in the first phase of colonial acquisitions promoted the growth of cultural and educational institutions as sites of further investment of accumulated capital, but now taking the form of *cultural* capital. If the new economic order posed the danger of loosening family ties, with the school replacing the home as the source of instruction, the pressure to assure some measure of continuity between the institution and the family accentuated the comparable functions performed by both. Patrilineal naming offered one means of guaranteeing at least a discursive continuity: the practice of naming institutions after individuals rather than after descriptive abstractions emulates biological organicism, even as it gestures toward the survival of the institution beyond the limited lifespan of the individual.

If the rise of the English East India Company and other European trading companies can be taken to represent the early phase of modern capitalism, the complex process by which imperial wealth circulated in the global economy required not the filiative bonds of old but *affiliation*—the metaphorical translation of biological reproduction into institutional growth. The customary passing down of property and wealth from father to child, in a vertical line of descent, broadens to include a horizontal movement of capital toward the affiliative order of institutions—the new repositories of cultural capital that replicate the functions of the family in disseminating values, principle, and dogma. The role of imparting knowl-

edge and value, which binds the institution to the family, not only obscures the material foundations of institutional development under colonialism but also diffuses and *renames* economic growth as various forms
of cultural advancement. "Naming" is the link between the two states
of filiation and affiliation: a real historical breakthrough occurs when a
patronym can be passed down as easily from a man to an institution as
from a father to his sons or daughters, circumventing almost entirely the
role of the woman in the reproductive process.

In its calculated subordination of nature to culture, Cotton Mather's
letter to Elihu Yale induces precisely this breakthrough, with its profound
implications for the flow of personal wealth into a larger social system beyond the biological family. It is not without significance that Yale College
emerges as a possible beneficiary of Elihu Yale's fortune only after Yale
unceremoniously dropped his closest male relative, then living in North
Haven, as his legal heir. The affiliative relationships contracted by naming revise the laws of inheritance based exclusively on biological ties, and
the wealth of empire, instead of being attenuated by a depleted family
line, secures a fresh lease of life through the reproductive mechanism of
institutional and cultural investment. The extraordinary importance of
Cotton Mather's letter lies in its pushing Elihu Yale to make the necessary leap from nature to culture—a leap that reveals the deepest links
between Yale's missionary zeal and his patriarchal desire, and simultaneously effaces the moral discrepancy between the exploitative sources
of Yale's wealth and his "noble" objectives of disseminating principles
of knowledge and religion by establishing institutions of higher learning
founded on that wealth. Faced with the threat of reduction or extinction,
Yale's political authority in one part of the empire is guaranteed a respectable measure of *cultural* authority in another arena of empire, and it is
largely to Cotton Mather's adeptness in managing this transition that the
founding of Yale College must be credited.

Indeed, such refigurations of the whole concept of authority suggest
an even greater level of specificity about "naming" in the empire beyond
a more generalized theory that considers the development of affiliative
forms in relation to the rise of modernism and capitalism. If affiliation
functions as a "compensatory order" for failed biological reproduction,
the cultural authority that Yale's imperial wealth established for itself in
America exists in a similar relation to the failed political and military
authority he once wielded in India, not only as compensation, however,
but also as reenactment and enlargement. Yale spent his years in India
in intense competition with his distant superiors in England to be more

than a mere agent of the East India Company's trading activity and usurp the complete reins of power in the administration of Madras. His various actions, including the purchasing of territory without prior permission from the company, entering into independent contracts with Madras merchants in the name of the East India Company, and arresting and trying English soldiers and Madras citizens alike on his own private authority, all paint the picture of a man driven by personal ambition and desire to create his own little empire within an empire. His appropriative instinct was most marked in his pronounced tendency to name whatever he made his own after himself or related emblems of his power, not only in India but also back in England. While he renamed an illegally purchased fort near Madras after his dead son David, he named a church that he founded in London after the Madras settlement he had once ruled over virtually as his own private fiefdom. The Church of St. George the Martyr, which still stands in Queen Square not far from where Yale spent the remaining years of his life, received substantial contributions from Yale for its construction. The church took its name from the fact that its principal benefactor was the ex-governor of Fort St. George, the company settlement in Madras. This ability of names to travel was not unusual: if in the colonies the British obsessively named streets, towns, buildings, and other places after themselves or fellow Englishmen in a self-commemorative spirit, when they returned to England they often gave names to buildings and monuments evocative of their own presence in the colonies. That the colonial moment was able to stretch itself out in two directions in this manner attests to the power of naming as a form of appropriation and possession paralleling—indeed, even perpetuating—acts of territorial acquisition.

Mather's combined appeals to Yale's missionary leanings and patriarchal desire succeeded beyond his most ambitious hopes. Initially, Yale resisted making outright monetary contributions and sent only a limited collection of books, mainly on religious subjects and personally selected by him to emphasize Anglican precepts. Edwin Oviatt notes that some Yale College rectors and tutors actually returned to the Episcopal church by their studies in the books Elihu Yale donated. One prominent person who turned Anglican was the tutor Samuel Johnson, who later became the first president of King's College (Columbia University). From his new position at King's College, Johnson attacked the narrow Congregationalism of Yale College, which made it difficult for awakened Episcopalians like himself to continue teaching there, and praised Elihu Yale, the "Church of England pillar," for his inspired gift.[9] Johnson gave a strongly Anglican tone to Columbia and attracted like-minded Anglican converts to pursue their teaching and studies there, which contributed in no small measure to furthering Elihu Yale's dream of bringing Dissenters back into the mainstream of English Protestantism. The histories of at least two American universities—Yale and Columbia—were thus directly affected by Elihu Yale's munificence, to whose religious zeal and proselytizing ambition they must trace their intellectual genealogies.

The donation of books by Elihu Yale to the New England college did not cease there, however, and it was soon followed by a large shipment of textiles—muslins, poplins, silks, calico—and other assorted merchandise that could be turned into hard cash in the Boston market. As soon as this valuable shipment arrived from England in September 1718, just a few days before the commencement exercises were to take place, the hastily assembled trustees met to change the name of the college in honor of Elihu Yale, amidst the euphoria that this initial gift would be merely the precursor to a "succession of solid and lasting benefits." In a comical sequence that gave the word "commencement" a wholly new meaning, the old commencement program with the name "Collegiate School" was destroyed and hastily replaced by another, which dramatically bore, for the first time, the new name of "Yale College."

Of course, much of the merchandise at the center of all this celebration had been brought by Yale from India to sell in England at very high profits for himself. Some of these goods found their way into London's main auction houses, which Elihu Yale is said to have introduced in 1700.[10] Sidetracked to Connecticut, where the merchandise netted the new college well over eight hundred pounds (the largest private donation to the college for the next hundred years and more), these goods established the closest links between Yale College and the spoils of British imperialism, the plundering careers of East India Company men merging, almost as if by destiny, with the pragmatic aspirations of colonial America's new brood of educators and theologians.

When Cotton Mather claimed to take pleasure in the story of Yale's career in India, he was doing more than expressing a sycophantic sentiment designed to secure his desired funds. Yale's life in India was indeed one of a remarkable rise to the highest position in the East India Company administration of Madras by a man who came out to India as a lowly paid clerk. The enormous political authority that Yale wielded during his tenure as governor was matched only by the prodigious wealth that he managed to accrue during and before that period. What could have turned out to be a disastrous end for Yale, when he was disgraced by financial scandals and charges of authoritarian misconduct, was redeemed by his timely departure for England after twenty-eight years in India—a move that enabled him not only to take his accumulated wealth along with him but also to recreate a new legend back in England. This new mythology muted the tale of a man whose political ascendancy was sternly clipped by his superiors in London, even as it accentuated the aspects of religious zeal that drove Yale to revive the power that he had enjoyed in India by promoting institutions like churches, charity schools, and assembly places in England and, later, Yale College in America. Though he led a seemingly retired and inactive life in England, Elihu Yale's driving ambition to reenact the authority he wielded as governor of Madras took different forms in different arenas of the British Empire. His history of cantankerous independence and rebellion against the centralized command post in London reveals Yale's apparent need to establish areas of private dominion, and it acted as a prelude to his growing interest in "adopting" an institution like Yale College and claiming it as his own, at least in name.

Like so many of his young contemporaries, Elihu Yale found a berth in the East India Company through the canny exertions of his merchant father. Elihu Yale served his apprenticeship at the company's office on Leadenhall Street, where, as his biographer Hiram Bingham writes, he would have had to "pass daily under the striking facade, with its gigantic representation of the high stern of a great caravel, decorated with an elaborate mural painting of the three ships under full sail taken from the company's coat of arms, which masked the top floor. This was surmounted by a vivid effigy of a merchant prince, in the costume of the early Stuarts, flanked by two fierce leviathans resembling dolphins, but intended to represent the armorial sea lions."[11] The iconography of expansion and imperial ambition that this description evokes framed the experience of most young men beginning their careers in the East India Company, instilling in them through a cluster of vivid symbols a lust for lucre in the guise of national aggrandizement. The directors of the stockholding company, with whom Elihu Yale in later years as governor would have many difficult and hostile dealings, approved his assignment to India as a "writer," and in 1671 the twenty-one-year-old Elihu headed out to make his fortune in what Bingham aptly terms the "new world of old India."[12]

The world that Elihu Yale entered is so much a part of the early mythologies of British empire-building—a frontier world where noble Englishmen had to fend off daily attacks on English fortifications by savage "natives" and protect English trading interests from the conniving schemes of ruthless Indian rulers (all of which have suggestive parallels with the mythologies of frontier America)—that the mundane reality of the day-to-day operations of the East India Company, involving the unloading of cargo, the storage and transportation of goods to other factories in the English settlements, and the securing of contracts with Indian merchants for the distribution and sale of these goods does not find a place in the popular memory of how colonial influence spread and developed into a vast administrative structure of political governance.

At the time that Yale landed in India, Fort St. George—one of the earliest British settlements in India, established in 1639 on a piece of land in Madras six miles long and a mile across—was literally a garrison enclosure fortified with guns and soldiers. Fort St. George recreated a cultural world as far removed from the town surrounding it (which, without any pretense at euphemism, the British named "Black Town") as England was from India. New company clerks like Yale noted the contrasts between the houses of the townspeople, which were described as "very mean, being only dirt and thatch," and the "handsome mansions" of the British settlement, whose stately Italian porticos were framed by elegant rows of trees.[13] Whether such descriptions by British commentators were wishful recreations of an imagined domestic landscape or accurately represented how they saw their new world, they certainly suggested the cultural bifurcation that marked the earliest British presence in India and defined how the first East India Company "exiles" (as they called themselves) psychically experienced the challenge of their new careers in the East. Indeed, one of the first things Elihu Yale did when he assumed governorship of Madras was to give the streets sturdily English names like York Street, James Street, Charles Street, Church Street, etc.

In contrast to the company agents' attempt to reproduce English settings, their relation with the parent corporation could not have been more distant. The company viewed their activities with suspicion; in turn, the agents found their directors irrelevant and obstructive. The tensions between the London directors and the company agents in India echo similar rifts between England and its American colonies, but unlike America, where the conflicts led to the first political stirrings of nationalism in the "new world,"[14] in India the beleaguerment and harassment by the London office that the company agents were forced to cope with as a daily reality led them to express their independence, not by consolidating politically, but by extending themselves into activities normally undertaken by the East India Company—but now under their own private authority. Whereas in America revolt acquired a distinctly political dimension of mobilization and consolidation, in India under the English East India Company rebellion by frustrated (and often personally ambitious) company servants was too fragmented and dispersed to assume a political tone, but rather took the form of *reproduction*, on an individual basis, of areas of enterprise officially falling under the provenance of the parent company's operations. Indeed, the more harassing the measures from the London directors, the more pronounced was the tendency by company agents like Yale to set up little private enclaves of their own within the larger English settlement. In failing to achieve resolution through outright revolt, the tensions between Yale and his company superiors were often worked out through the former's re-formation of the company's mercantile activities in the private domain, and when even that too was thwarted in India by directors endowed with the power to dismiss or transfer their agents, the reproduction of parallel institutions of private maneuver continued elsewhere in different arenas of the British empire. The birth of Yale College can be considered one such outcome, along with the establishment of a chain of charity schools, churches, and assembly places with which Elihu Yale was associated for much of his life.

This impetus toward institution-building as a means of combating the company hegemony by its own agents in India took several forms in several arenas, but the two most striking expressions are the ecclesiastical and the entrepreneurial. The construction of the church of St. Mary's in Fort St. George in 1678—the "first Anglican church east of the Suez," proclaims the sign outside the church which still performs services today—was begun entirely on the intiative of company servants, including Elihu Yale, who voluntarily subscribed to the new religious establishment without any official support from the company. The fact that these individuals in the Fort St. George establishment made direct connections with the Church of England and completely bypassed the company as an intermediate body reveals the extent to which company agents were already constructing a parallel society with parallel institutions for themselves, which established closer cultural links with England outside the narrow hierarchized world of the East India Company. Streynsham Master, the original founder of St. Mary's Church, who was also governor of Madras from 1678 to 1681, has been described as "a man who did not disobey orders but acted without them,"[15] and the description accurately captures the dual tensions of subordination and independence characterizing the relationship of company agents to the London office. Master's single-minded determination to construct St. Mary's Church, as well as to reorganize the Fort St. George garrison and establish a new court of judicature in St. Mary's, brought him into inevitable conflict with the court of directors, who issued orders in 1681 to dismiss him from his office as governor of Madras.

Entrepreneurial expressions of independence by company servants, on the other hand, involved establishing close ties with Indian merchants and rulers of princely states. Far more than their superiors in the company establishment, factors and writers like Elihu Yale had a greater maneuverability in Indian territory and were able to penetrate effectively into interior provinces by engaging the assistance of local intermediaries, who often turned out to be their partners in a private trade running parallel to the East India Company's mercantile activities. In securing prior access to both goods and trading partners, company agents enjoyed the privilege of setting up the first English settlements or "factories" on their own, presumably in the name of the East India Company, but virtually run by themselves as local feudatories, often in paid alliance with Hindu or Mughal rulers. Elihu Yale's acquisition of a private fort from Rama Raja is the most outstanding instance of such territorial entrepreneurship, which did not even care to operate under the banner of the company: that it led to his ultimate disgrace and dismissal from office is perhaps less important than the fact that such acts of private expansionism were tolerated for so long by the company. The peculiar irony of this form of "revolt" by the company agents is that the London office could not squelch it, not because it lacked the power or the will, but because such private activities served to enhance the sphere of influence of the English in India: demoting or transferring recalcitrant agents was the extent of the punishment that could be meted out to them, even as the gains they made possible were solidly secured for the company.

As a "writer," Elihu Yale initially did not have a place on the council of Fort St. George, but his dutiful learning of Indian languages from the time of his arrival in Madras brought him to the attention of his superiors, who selected him to negotiate with the khan of Chingleput to set up a factory (or tradepost) in his province. Yale introduced a flamboyant style of negotiation that impressed both his local superiors and the court of directors in London for its demonstrable results in securing contracts with Indian merchants. Impeccably well-dressed and finely mannered, Yale garnished his personal grooming with handsome gift-giving (mostly at company expense, complained the London office), which always cleverly managed to stop short of ritualistic excess; his favorable reception by the khan did not go unnoticed by the more powerful members of the council in Fort St. George, who saw him as a useful broker between the English trading company and native authorities, his own nonmembership in the council obviously rendering him a less threatening presence than might have otherwise been the case. Yale's fondness for pomp and ceremony was encouraged by the council, who recognized his taste for the splendor of an "Oriental potentate" as a valuable trait in dealing with what they regarded as a ritual-bound society. But as with so many of the establishment's quixotic policies, the company's promotion of certain types of behavior in their agents as useful in doing trade with Indians was tempered by their condemnation of those same traits as signs of an arrogant and presumptuous temperament. The company's anxiety about its authoritative status as a corporate body remained in tension with its desire for exclusive contracts with Indian merchants and eventual elimination of foreign competition, and company servants found themselves condemned by the very policies that their superiors introduced to encourage their initiative.[16]

A significant turning point for young clerks like Elihu Yale, who earned abysmally low wages in the East India Company (for example, at the start of his career Yale earned ten pounds a year), was a resolution issued by the directors in London legalizing private trade by its agents in India. Initially, the resolution was passed in order to lower the discontent of company agents and increase their personal incentive to seek new markets, and indeed the promise of unlimited profits for lowly paid company servants in the sale of lucrative items like precious gems and Indian spices back in England contributed immeasurably to the East India Company's rapid growth as a major trading company. But the sanctioned activities of company servants in private trade also generated suspicion in the directors' minds that their agents hoarded the best items procured in various contracts for themselves and left the dregs for the company.

The key to Yale's success was his easy and chameleonlike maneuverability in the "native" population, a fact that was recognized by the East India Company as both a valuable and potentially dangerous trait— dangerous because it gave Yale a daring independence and private authority that a more distant position would perhaps not have conferred. Yale established valuable contacts with Indian merchants, and a certain Gopal Pundit became his most important link to the world of Madras commerce, securing him access to members of professional castes whose skills in specific trades, such as weaving and dyeing, could be harnessed to the objectives of mass manufacture and distribution of goods for English consumption. Yale's successful negotiations with Indian merchants and his securing of numerous contracts to set up factories in different provinces brought him to the attention of Sir Josia Child, then chair of the East India Company, who was so highly impressed by the enterprising young man that the thirty-eight-year-old Yale, who was acting governor of Madras while then Governor Gyfford made a tour of inspection of the factories on the Bay of Bengal, was asked to replace Gyfford altogether in July 1687.

Yale's subsequent career is steeped in controversy, with some historians and biographers of this period painting him as a martyr who was continually tested by the London office and could not be held directly responsible for repressive actions enjoined by his superiors. The image of Yale as a reluctant enforcer of English regulations contradicts the manner of his swift rise to governorship as it emerges in the official Fort St. George records,[17] for Yale's own uncompromising stand on collecting taxes from the inhabitants of "Black Town," or present-day Madras, even before he was made governor, reveals an authoritarian streak that did not require nurture from the parent company. The "taxes" that the English East India Company collected were a form of protection money designed to contribute to the building of fortifications around the city. The tensions between the inhabitants of Madras and the company officials stemmed from the formers' charge that, under the pretense of protection, the British were seeking to generate increased revenues for the maintenance of the East India Company—a motive made transparent in the collection of taxes on the basis of the value of a townsman's property and house. Through such coercive practices, it was evident that the English had set themselves up as landlords and rent collectors long before they had any kind of political or military authority in Madras supposedly in the name of providing adequate security against the attacks of rival trading companies. What many Madras inhabitants initially saw as a harmless contribution to the expenses of the garrison soon came to be recognized as a subtle but palpable attempt by the English to exert economic tyranny over those who had been stripped of rights to trade (many Indian merchants had signed over trading rights to the English settlement, obviously not out of ignorance but in the expectation that they would secure favors from the British later) and no longer had the income to maintain their own homes and property. The only condition on which they could continue to own their property was by subsidizing the East India Company. Or, as Elihu Yale bluntly told the townspeople in a specially assembled gathering, if they were not willing to pay the British, they were free to sell their homes and go elsewhere. Yale's ruthless repression of the townspeople's revolt was topped by a paternalistic reprimand to them about their civic responsibility in generating revenues to defray "overhead" costs.[18]

The success of Elihu Yale's unrestrained method of enforcing the regular payment of taxes encouraged the London directors to implement even stronger measures to punish those Madras citizens who defaulted. Throughout the period of Yale's tenure there were sporadic incidents of revolt against the company's collection of rent for the houses in town. A riot that nearly turned into a full-scale insurrection in 1686 was mercilessly quelled by the soldiers of the garrison. An ultimatum was later issued to the heads of several castes that if they failed to submit themselves before sunset to Yale, begging pardon for their revolt against the government and vowing obeisance to the company regulations enjoining a "contribution" toward the protection of the garrison, their houses would be decimated the following day, their property sold, and their families banished from the town.[19]

Yale's sternness applied equally to the soldiers of his garrison. While he was himself hugely fond of ceremony, he would not tolerate any of his subordinates to attire themselves in fashionable gear and once imprisoned a soldier for daring to sport a ceremonial umbrella. He was known to hang English "pirates" in public to present a chilling reminder to his men of the fate befalling those caught pilfering company goods.[20] One of the most infamous of Yale's actions was his hanging of a stable boy for running away on a company's horse.

Admiring biographers like Hiram Bingham in his 1939 study are quick to whitewash Elihu Yale of all wrongdoing and see his actions in the groom episode, for instance, as the just response of a civil servant to mutiny in the ranks, which, if allowed to go unchecked, would have netted Indian chieftains and princes as well into widespread rebellion against the English. A paranoia of revolt underwrites Bingham's resistance to the perspective of the mutineers, and Yale's image as a just ruler emerges relatively untarnished in his account, which is less concerned with Elihu Yale as British imperialist than with Yale as founding father of a great American university. The fact that the two roles played by Yale were not mutually exclusive and less stringently polarized than would appear—that indeed his authoritarian conduct in one setting reasserted itself as self-aggrandizement through institution-building in another, and that both are part of the same process of colonial "development"—would have required Bingham to see Yale's life and career as an ongoing narrative of self-enlargement in different locations that took on different forms at different times.

In contrast to Bingham's account, a different perspective on Yale's life, which attempts to restore the vital links between the two roles played by Elihu Yale, is provided by the English novelist Fanny Penny. The story of Yale's downfall is the subject of her 1922 novel *Diamonds*, which, though embellished by exotic details and romantic intrigue, is based on a remarkably close reading of the East India Company records. The novel complements Penny's more straightforward *History of Fort St. George* (1900) with an imaginative treatment of the complex world of the East India Company servant. Penny creates the character of a wide-eyed, innocent young English girl at Fort St. George through whom is refracted a range of possible ethical responses to the morality of British imperialism. The novel paints an unheroic and grim picture of the British trading company as an assemblage of self-interested men with little or no loyalty to the parent company. In its depiction of the rapacious English at Fort St. George, Fanny Penny's novel is continuous with the standard historical accounts of the early years of the British in India, though the novel dramatizes more vividly than do any other accounts of the same period the rank collusion between the Company merchant and the so-called interlopers and pirates (largely Dutch and Portuguese, but also including independent Englishmen and even Mughal and Hindu functionaries) who plied the high seas—the self-same marauders purportedly against whom the English built fortifications and extracted "protection" money from the townspeople for that purpose. The narrator of Penny's novel observes that "the interloper was the friend of every man who served the company; without his assistance it was impossible for the merchant to put together the wealth which should enable him to return to England and enjoy the fruits of his exile" (15).

Diamonds interweaves into a narrative of intrigue the whispered rumors and self-imposed silences of the constricted circle of the English at Fort St. George. One English character, Mrs. Bridger, attempts to name the unmentionable when she murmurs to her husband about Yale, " 'There was a time when the President himself—.' Her husband raised a warning finger and checked the word on her lips. He desired to live in peace with the authorities of Fort St. George. That peace must not be imperilled by the chattering of a woman." He advises his wife that " 'where men in power are concerned, a short memory is best,' " to which she readily assents with her own mangled version of moral relativism: " 'We are all driven to it when we first come out. There is no harm in it'" (16). The novel self-consciously foregrounds Elihu Yale's bequest to Yale College in a past history of repression, exploitation, and untrammeled desire for power by Yale.

Hiram Bingham's image of Yale as a helpless subordinate victimized by more powerful superiors runs contrary to a series of episodes indicative of Yale's own unwavering determination to assert his authority independently of orders from London—a view that is advanced not only by Fanny Penny's novel but by the records and histories of Fort St. George under the English East India Company, which Penny herself had assiduously studied.[21] The ambivalence of the court of directors' attitude to Yale, who was encouraged to act sternly but aroused alarm when he did so in his own capacity, must certainly be traced to the successful enlargement of the ambit of English mercantile activities by the very man who contributed toward such expansion as an act of personal aggrandizement. Yale's address to the Madras inhabitants coercing their obedience had a strongly patriarchal tone, which clearly established his absolute authority in a Fort St. George that displaced England as controlling center. Refusing to accept his role as one of mere medium for transmitting orders and policies issued by the London office (in much the same way that he later would have resisted seeing himself as acting out Cotton Mather's ambitions), Yale believed with absolute certitude that he had been invested with the power to be the final point of reference—indeed, the "progenitor," to stretch a metaphor—in a chain of command.

As Fanny Penny's literary representation shrewdly suggests, uncovering an element missing from Bingham's hagiography, Yale's adept movement in "native" society may have created the illusion of a man who was adaptable to all modes and circumstances, but the manner of his governance suggested that his penetration into the many sectors of indigenous society was motivated by a single-minded drive to incorporate disparate provinces into the structures of continuous English rule, with himself as a type of feudal chieftain on the "Oriental model."

This ready adaptability to difference, in order to reduce it to a governable form of identity, was an impetus that was not entirely unrelated to Yale's later willingness to support the Dissenters in America, who were diametrically opposed to him ideologically, in the belief that he would be able to bring them within a common religious fold. Yale's plan of religious and educational reform in America was virtually an extension of the activities of mercantile development, fortune-making, contractual negotiations, and territorial enlargement that he had begun in India: even in Madras Yale's role as agent and later governor went alongside his active participation in the Anglican life of St. Mary's Church, which he had helped found with his voluntary subscription and officiated over as vestry-man and treasurer. Indeed, apart from his personal annexation of the renamed Fort St. David, St. Mary's Church offers the closest link between Yale's driving ambition to channel money into the creation of separate institutions for the advancement of a religious creed given short shrift by the company—and through which Yale expressed an authority inde-pendent of the company's—and the later founding of Yale College. (The connections between St. Mary's Church in Madras and Yale University in New Haven are nowhere more vividly illustrated than in a commemo-rative plaque donated to St. Mary's by Yale University's Class of 1924, headed by former American ambassador to India Chester Bowles, on the 250th anniversary of the "naming of Yale College." Bowles and his class-mates chose to honor Elihu Yale—and Yale University—by making their presentation to a church that saw "lasting improvements" as a result of Elihu Yale's "dedicated service.")[22]

As Elihu Yale's political power increased, so too did his wealth. Much of his early wealth came from his marrying a woman with a considerable fortune, which he liberally used as capital to consolidate his own as-sets, but it also grew increasingly by his entering into questionable deals with both local and foreign merchants. The ambivalence of the London directors toward Yale's private transactions again highlights the strange paralysis they experienced in the face of his ever-increasing sphere of influence and control, especially since his ability to generate personal wealth was translated into tangible results for the East India Company by way of exclusive contracts and territorial gains. For instance, Yale's spectacularly fraudulent deception of the king of Siam over a period of years, through which he managed to amass a huge fortune, did not evoke more than a mild reprimand from the London directors, even though the event when uncovered provided an excuse to other European trading powers to stake their claims for exclusive rights to trade with Siam. Yale had quietly but steadily acquired a reputation as a diamond merchant (hence the title of Fanny Penny's novel) and entered into a private deal with the king of Siam to procure several priceless rubies for which he was paid a handsome sum of money. The gems that Yale sold the Siamese agents in Madras were later found to be worthless when examined by the king's jewel experts in Ayuthaya. The king's complaint that he had vastly overpaid Yale for mere pieces of glass went unheeded by the directors in London, from whom Yale managed to secure enough support to ward off charges of corruption and fraud. Yale's self-defense focused on the countercharge that the whole episode was manufactured by England's Dutch rivals to discredit him so that they could secure their own trade with Siam. Yale's argument so roused the Company's persistent anxiety about eliminating its foreign competition that it was prepared to overlook Yale's "indiscretions" and accepted his personal fortune-gathering as a necessary means of augmenting the East India Company's sphere of influence beyond India to include such regions as Siam, where Dutch and Portuguese trading companies provided stiff competition.[23]

Despite Yale's support from the company directors on the Siam episode, however, mistrust between the two grew as Yale's personal wealth accumulated and his streak of independence expressed itself in increasingly defiant and (to the company) unacceptable ways.[24] By 1691 Yale had amassed an unbelievably huge fortune equivalent to $5,000,000, and the methods he used to acquire so much money in such a short time came under sharp scrutiny.

Yale's difficulties with the directors multiplied in 1690 when, without consulting either his superiors in England or the council in Fort St. George, he sent his brother Thomas to buy a fort at Tevnapatam, which he renamed Fort St. David after his recently deceased son,[25] in a private transaction that drew on company funds.[26] The story of Yale's ultimate dismissal involved many players and subplots, but his flamboyant venture into unauthorized territorial acquisitions led the directors to fear, for the first time, that he had designs to set up an independent state presided over by himself as autocratic ruler, the clearest evidence of which was his channeling of the civil and military resources of the English trade settlement into the construction of his own personal fortification at the rechristened Fort St. David. This virtual declaration of independence by Yale brought about a crisis in his relations with the directors. With the purchase of the fort Yale's breakaway spirit expressed itself beyond a point of return to an attitude of subordination to the directors' will.[27] In it also converge a host of developing themes that retrace the trajectory of Yale's life and career in India: of territorial acquisition and institution-building in his own name; bestowing his paternity on the lands he acquired to compensate for the truncation of his own biological line; reinvesting the wealth produced by commercial activity into the construction of new personal fortifications; and establishing an autonomous domain which, though defiantly resistant to the company's hegemony, reproduced the essential form of the company's organization. Fort St. David, which Yale hoped to make more truly his own than any son he could have fathered, was intended to be an exact replica of Fort St. George in every respect but one: it was to be a combined private garrison enclosure and civil society ruled entirely by Yale and also a point of contact for the burgeoning trade that Yale had carved out for himself in alliance with Indian merchants.[28]

Even though Yale's private annexation of Fort St. David was eventually annulled by an order from the directors, who belatedly brought full charges against him, the seeds of desire for self-enlargement were too firmly planted in Yale by then to be vanquished by his dismissal from public office. In a revealing letter to the council, Yale complains of the company's refusal to take notice of his authority "as if I were a cypher and had no share in the government."[29] Yale's failure to secure an outpost of his own in India for the ultimate exercise of his authority, independent of the controlling hand of the company, marked the beginning of a series of attempts to seek that location where such extensions of the self into institutions were possible through a rechanneling of his accumulated wealth into public "development." Yale's obsessive involvement with the building of churches and charity schools on his return to London from India was not merely an outgrowth of his devout Anglicanism but, to an extent, a subtle continuation of his failed Fort St. David enterprise. It is indeed also possible to see his munificence to Yale College as a way of both fulfilling (by reproducing) and displacing the forms of authority and power that he claimed for himself as governor of Madras but was thwarted from realizing. After all, there was far more affinity between Yale and the American Dissenters than either may have realized: both were caught in relations of subordination to and independence from English colonial power, and both were constantly forced into drawing on resources from the parent state to set up a private domain of their own which would be impervious to the controlling influence of English ruling power.

In 1692 Yale was relieved of his duties as governor and president of the Madras council, though he continued to reside at Fort St. George until 1699 when he returned to England to spend his remaining years as a wealthy nabob at Queen Square, London. Despite the protracted official questioning of his financial dealings which precipitated his dismissal, Yale nonetheless managed to take most of his wealth gained in India back to England, and the politically disgraced Yale gave way in the English public memory to another image that embodied the most thrilling success tale of all: that of a wealthy East India Company merchant returning to England after twenty-eight years, laden with a shipload of valuable cargo that included spices, textiles, precious stones, and leather goods—plundered items that Yale was later to sell for more than two hundred percent beyond the prime cost. Part of that shipload, we have seen, ended up in Connecticut with the compliments of Elihu Yale, a gift from the spoils of empire that would lay the foundation stone for a distinguished American university.

Notes

I am grateful to Amy Kaplan for her detailed and thoughtful comments.

1 Edwin Oviatt, *The Beginnings of Yale 1701–1726* (New Haven: Yale University Press, 1916), p. 291.

2 Oviatt, p. 378.

3 Quoted in Hiram Bingham, *Elihu Yale: The American Nabob of Queen Square* (New York: Dodd, Mead, 1939), p. 322.

4 Letter of Cotton Mather to Elihu Yale, January 14, 1718; in Franklin B. Dexter, *Documentary History of Yale University 1701–1745* (New Haven: Yale University Press, 1916), p. 164.

5 Letter of Cotton Mather to Gurdon Saltonstall, August 25, 1718.

6 One particular story about renaming during the British period has become part of the folklore of Madras, and I am fully persuaded that the tale is too good to be apocryphal. The story as I have heard it goes as follows: In a mood of self-commemoration an early administrator of Madras, Lord Hamilton, named a bridge in Madras after himself. Because the short vowel 'a' does not exist in the Tamil language, the Madras inhabitants had trouble pronouncing the name 'Hamilton' properly and it came out as 'Hummulton.' When spoken fast, 'Hummulton' is very close to the Tamil word for barber. Nearly a century later, a British colonial surveyor, unaware of the Lord Hamilton renaming, attempted to do an inventory of all the bridges and other public structures in Madras and give English equivalents to Indian names wherever possible in an attempt to standardize names of streets, bridges, monuments, etc. When he asked a nearby Madras laborer the name of the bridge in question, he was told that it was called 'Hummutton' Bridge. Turning to his interpreter for the translation of this strange-sounding word, the surveyor was told that it meant 'barber' in Tamil. The surveyor dutifully recorded the name of the bridge in its English translation as 'Barber's Bridge'—the name by which it is still known today. The metamorphosis of the distinguished Lord Hamilton, seeking posterity in bridge-naming, into a commonplace barber by which his name is now known, is one of the delightful postcolonial rewritings of history that plays on the double entendres of multiple linguistic registers.

7 Bingham, p. 273.

8 Edward W. Said, *The World, The Text, and the Critic* (Cambridge, Mass.: Harvard University Press, 1983), p. 19.

9 Oviatt, p. 412.

10 *The Yale Family, or the Descendants of David Yale with Genealogical Notices of Each Family* (New Haven: Storer and Stone, 1850), p. 30. See also a catalog in the British Museum entitled *For Sale by Auction: A Catalogue of Divers Rich and Valuable Effects, Being a Collection of Elihu Yale* (London: 1722).

11 Bingham, p. 14.

12 Bingham, p. 15.

13 Bingham, p. 18.

14 This idea is forcefully advanced by Benedict Anderson in *Imagined Communities* (London: Verso, 1983), pp. 50–65. I am grateful to Amy Kaplan for suggesting this comparison.

15 W. H. Warren and N. Barlow, *St. Mary's Church, Fort St. George, Madras* (1905; rpt. Madras: Church of South India), p. 13.

16 At least one economic historian has argued that the East India Company was not unilaterally driven by a production-motive. Ramakrishna Mukherjee, in *The Rise and Fall of the East India Company* (New York: Monthly Review Press, 1974), argues that seventeenth-century English merchants were less interested in production than in making money as intermediaries between producers and consumers. This may partly explain the near-schizophrenic behavior of the directors of the company, who seemed continually to be sending mixed messages to their agents about goods for trade.

17 My observation is based on a reading of the 1686–87 volumes of the Tamil Nadu Archives (Madras Records Office), *Madras Public Consultations*.

18 *Madras Public Consultations* (1686), vol. 11: Order issued by the council of Fort St. George, August 12, 1686.

19 *Madras Public Consultations* (1686), vol. 11: Letter of Elihu Yale to council of Fort St. George, September 6, 1686.

20 *Madras Public Consultations* (1690), vol. 16: Letter of Elihu Yale condemning pirate and Alexander Peirson's subsequent voluntary confession, winning him pardon, October 20, 1690.

21 See Penny's *Fort St. George, Madras: A Short History of Our First Possession in India* (London: S. Sonnenschein, 1900).

22 The plaque currently stands in the southwest corner of St. Mary's, along with a huge portrait of Elihu Yale and a memorial from the gravestone of Yale's son David.

23 The 1688 volume of *Madras Public Consultations* provides elaborate accounts of the Siam episode.

24 A letter to Yale from the council used the most caustic language to express the general disenchantment with Yale's independence: "Most of your actions have often been either without our advice and knowledge or contrary to our approbations. From there and many of your regular proceedings no other conclusion can be made, than that you designe present destruction (?) to the place and the Rt. Hon. Comp. affaires, wherefore we desire your Hon. to satisfye us in writing, from whence it is you desire the power you daily exercise, which is so opposite to the Comp. orders, and so far exceeding their 'limits.' You continue acting singly with Comp. business without consulting with us." *Madras Public Consultations* (1691), vol. 17: Letter to Elihu Yale from John Cheney, William Fraser, Thomas Gray, January 6, 1691.

25 Yale's son David died two years before the fort was fully acquired. The momentous impact of the loss of his only son on Yale reverberates not only in his obsessive urge to name the newly purchased fort after David, but also in the memorials to the deceased boy which are still preserved in St. Mary's Church, the church that Elihu helped build and was closely associated with until his departure from India. Over the child's burial place in a plot of land slightly removed from the church area was constructed an imposing three-tiered structure resembling a combined church spire and pagoda. A simple but moving black marble tablet rests at its base with the following words engraved on it: "Hic jacet David filius honorobilis Elihu Yale Praesidentis et Gubernatoris Castelli St. Georgii et civitatis Madrasiae natus fuit 15 Maii 1684 et obit 25 Januarii anno 1688."

26 *Madras Public Consultations* (1690), vol. 16: Copy of letter to be given by Soundee Bollogoo and signed by Rama Raja king of the Chingee County for the purchase of Tevnapatam fort, July 15, 1690.

27 This is very evident in the stinging letter Yale wrote in response to the "scurrilous" charges leveled by his superiors. Yale asks why they are harassing him when they "were unanimously resolved to leave me to act by myself." *Madras Public Consultations* (1691), vol. 17; Letter of Elihu Yale to the Council, January 9, 1691.

28 See *Madras Public Consultations* (1690), vol. 16: Letter of Elihu Yale to Samuel Owen for the reloading of company goods at Madraspatam aboard the ship *Recovery* for Fort St. David, August 20, 1690; and commission and instruction to William Hattslee, deputy governor of Fort St. David or Tevnapatam, September 10, 1690, where Yale fully spells out his plans to rechannel company goods to Fort St. David for the rebuilding of an entire military and political society.

29 *Madras Public Consultations* (1691), vol. 17: Letter of Elihu Yale to the council of Fort St. George, January 9, 1691.

Eric Cheyfitz

Savage Law

The Plot Against American Indians in *Johnson and Graham's Lessee v. M'Intosh* and *The Pioneers*

[T]he laws alone remove us from the condition of the savages.
—Cooper, *The Pioneers* [1]

estern imperialism, and perhaps this is true of all imperialisms, founds its program on the disappearance of the "other." This of course necessitates the construction of others as an absolutely oppositional, completely homogeneous, and ultimately superfluous figure, rather than as figures in a possible dialogue of equals, figures with which one is implicated. It is the work of an imperial culture to accomplish this construction over and against resistance to this work, whether this resistance takes the form of the kind of deconstruction practiced by Montaigne in "Of the Cannibals," which eviscerates the word *cannibal* in order to expose the range of its irony; or of the kind of destruction practiced by the Cibecue Apaches in their jokes about white men, which replaces the Anglo-American stereotype of the Indian-as-other, with a liberating Apache parody of Europeans as those others who create stereotypes.[2] In fact the forms of this construction of the other are one form of the disappearance of others, which can take on many forms between the poles of death and assimilation.

I want to read in what follows an important moment in the construction of the other in the culture of U.S. imperialism, a moment that, as far as I know, has not been read before, and so has remained both silent and invisible, a silence and invisibility that are the very structure of those ghostly constructions of the other that U.S. imperialism conjures. This is the moment when, in 1823, the genre of the Western (the drama of cowboys and Indians) and the edifice of federal Indian law first appear as distinct yet, as I will argue, interlocking and inseparable institutions. Two texts constitute this moment: James Fenimore Cooper's *The Pioneers* and the Supreme Court decision, articulated by Chief Justice John Marshall, in *Johnson and Graham's Lessee v. M'Intosh.* [3]

The *Johnson* decision was the second Supreme Court ruling in Indian matters and a preamble to the famous Cherokee cases of 1831 and 1832 that limited the sovereignty of Indian peoples to that of "domestic dependent nations." The importance of this decision is that it translated Indian notions of native peoples' relation to their lands into the language of Anglo-American property law—that language where "title" is the supreme term—not so that Indians could be empowered in that language, but so that ultimate power over their lands, the historical inalienability of which constituted their cultures, could be "legally" transferred to the federal government. In short, *Johnson v. M'Intosh* translates Indian lands into the terms of title so that title over these lands can be claimed by the government; and in doing this, it becomes the cornerstone of the establishment of federal Indian law.

In *Johnson*, the government based, and still bases I would emphasize, its claim on a particular legal fiction, a particular historical narrative, that goes under the title of the "doctrine of discovery":

> On the discovery of this immense continent, the great nations of Europe were eager to appropriate to themselves so much of it as they could respectively acquire. Its vast extent offered an ample field to the ambition and enterprise of all; and the character and religion of its inhabitants afforded an apology for considering them as a people over whom the superior genius of Europe might claim an ascendency. The potentates of the old world found no difficulty in convincing themselves that they made ample compensation to the inhabitants of the new, by bestowing on them civilization and Christianity, in exchange for unlimited independence. But, as they were all in pursuit of nearly the same object, it was necessary, in order to avoid conflicting settlements, and consequent war with each other, to establish a principle which all should acknowledge as the law by which the right of acquisition, which they all asserted, should be regulated as between themselves. The principle was that discovery gave title to the government by whose subjects, or by whose authority, it was made, against all other European governments, which title might be consummated by possession. . . .
>
> In the establishment of these relations, the rights of the original inhabitants were, in no instance, entirely disregarded; but were necessarily, to a

considerable extent, impaired. They were admitted to be the rightful occupants of the soil, with a legal as well as just claim to retain possession of it, and to use it according to their own discretion; but their rights to complete sovereignty, as independent nations, were necessarily diminished, and their power to dispose of the soil at their own will, to whomsoever they pleased, was denied by the original fundamental principle that discovery gave exclusive title to those who made it. . . .

The history of America, from its discovery to the present day, proves, we think, the universal recognition of these principles. (572–74)

This "history of America" is, of course, generated by the same "principles" that it "proves": the principles of Western law, which are, precisely, those of *property* with its foundation in the notion of *title*. This history, then, is based on a totally self-reflexive, or self-serving, logic, the limits of which are the term *property*. Delivering the opinion of the Court, Marshall, in his position as a representative of a particular Western nation, is necessarily compelled to assert the inviolability of a nation's property law within the confines of its borders and in relation to any conquered peoples, even if "this restriction may be opposed to natural right, and to the usages of civilized nations" (591, see also 572). But we can understand how universal Anglo-American thinking takes the notion of "property" to be when, in the report of the "facts" of the *Johnson* case, presented prior to the opinion, we read the case's view of traditional Native American society:

> That from time immemorial, and always up to the present time, all the Indian tribes, or nations of North America . . . held their respective lands and territories each in common, the individuals of each tribe or nation holding the lands and territories of such tribe in common with each other, and there being among them no separate property in the soil; and that their sole method of selling, granting and conveying their lands, whether to governments or individuals, always has been, from time immemorial, and now is, for certain chiefs of the tribe selling, to represent the whole tribe in every part of the transaction; to make the contract and execute the deed on behalf of the whole tribe; to receive for it the consideration, whether in money or commodities, or both; and, finally, to divide such consideration among the individuals of the tribe; and that the authority of the chiefs, so acting for the whole tribe, is attested by the presence and assent of the individuals composing the tribe, or some of them, and by the receipt by the individuals composing the tribe, of their respective shares of the price, and in no other manner. (549–50)

When, at the end of the fifteenth century, Europeans began to invade what they would name the Americas, it was characteristic of kinship-based cultures, of which Native American cultures form various kinds, that they did hold their land "in common." But this "holding . . . in common" did not constitute a common *property* in the soil, as the *Johnson* case assumes. For the *traditional* commonality of kinship cultures is not, as the case portrays it, a Western commonality, composed of "individuals," who by virtue of being individuals can agree, through an elected representative, to alienate their common holding in the land and then divide the price individually. In traditional Native American cultures there are persons, but no "individuals." For in these cultures identity is conceived of as exclusively mutual, rather than, as in the West, mutually exclusive. Thus, traditionally, by which I mean prior or in resistance to the Anglo-American imposition of governmental forms, Indian governance is consensual not representative. That is, no person or persons can act *for* the whole, conceived of as a majority (a numerical preponderance made possible by the notion of separable entities termed "individuals"), because each person is inseparably a part of the whole. That is, each person's consent is necessary to constitute the whole, which is thus absolute not relative. So, in traditional kinship-based cultures, it is only the whole that can act in the name of the whole. And because there is no notion of individuality in these cultures (a notion we should not confuse with autonomy), there, traditionally, is no notion of property. For the idea of property depends on the possibility of an individual relation to the land (as the basis of wealth), either in the name of a single person or a group, such as a corporation, acting as a single person, in which this person, precisely because he or she or it is an "individual," is "free" to alienate this land in a market economy. Or we could reverse the proposition and say: there is no individuality without property, so inseparable are the two terms in the mixed material and metaphysical traditions of the West. Locke's formulation of primal individuality—"every man has a property in his own person"—succinctly states this inseparability, which is alien to Native American cultures.[4]

The "time immemorial" of the *Johnson* case is not, then, the time of any Native American culture. It is Western time forced on Native American cultures in the forms of the treaty and the law, which demanded that these cultures accept the terms of *property/individualism/representation* or die fighting for another set of terms. Native American resistance to the force of property—a resistance that persists into the present moment in continuing demands for tribal sovereignty based on a renewal of the treaty relationship[5]—has had to maneuver within the confines of Anglo-American legal forms.

The apotheosis of the force of these forms was the General Allotment, or Dawes, Act of 1887. In 1871 Congress had ended the treaty as a form of negotiation with the Indians. This marked a radical diminishment in the perception of Indian sovereignty by the United States government; for the form of the treaty, no matter how compromised it was by discrepancies between Anglo-American and Native American power, was still a sign of Indian sovereignty. The Dawes Act, which authorized the president to individualize tribal lands, that is, convert them totally to property, attacked the basis of this sovereignty, Indian identity itself, constituted, as it was and is, by a particular communal relationship to the land that I have tried to figure from my alien position and that, for polemical reasons, I have risked idealizing with my use of "traditional" in my schematization of kinship-based cultures. The rhetoric supporting the Dawes Act was, in Western terms, humanitarian: its stated intent was to "civilize" the Indians by turning them into American property holders. Its effects, which continue past its reversal in the Indian Reorganization Act of 1934 into the present moment, were to allow a massive grab of Indian lands by whites and to force most of the tribal population into deep poverty: "Between the passage of the Dawes Allotment Act in 1887 and the reversal of the allotment policy in the 1934 Indian Reorganization Act, the Indian estate dwindled from 138 to 52 million acres. . . . By 1934, the government had allotted 118 out of 213 reservations and brought over three-fourths of the Indians under the provisions of the Dawes Act."[6]

The Dawes Act tries to fulfill the logic of the history that writes and is written by *Johnson*. This history is Western history, with an Anglo-American slant. For it is specifically the history of the transmission of "legal" power over Indian lands in the Americas from the British crown to the United States government. *Johnson* implicitly emphasizes the authoritative continuity of this history by focusing on selected dates and the written documents that give these dates their force in the tradition that these documents inscribe, a tradition that takes no account of any autonomous Native American historical perspectives.

This history begins on May 23, 1609, when James I chartered the Virginia Company of London and granted to them "under certain reservations and limitations" the land previously named the colony of Virginia by the British, a vast tract of land occupying four hundred miles of seacoast and extending inland as far west as the Mississippi River (543–44).

In 1624, the next date mentioned in the historical summary that *Johnson* articulates, the Virginia Company was legally dissolved and the colony reverted to royal control "with the same territorial limits" (545).

In 1756 the French and Indian War began because France had invaded the western territory of Virginia and had taken "possession of certain parts of it, with the consent of the several tribes or nations of Indians possessing and owning them" (546). *Johnson* identifies the Indians only in their relation to the two European contestants and their desires in this war and in doing so radically simplifies shifting and complex alliances between Indians and Europeans; nor does *Johnson* mention the decisive part the Iroquois played in the British victory.[7]

On February 10, 1763, the "war was terminated by a definitive treaty of peace between Great Britain and France, and their allies" (546), the various Indian peoples involved, which gave Great Britain virtual control over North America. And "on the 7th of October, 1763, the King of Great Britain made and published a proclamation, for the better regulation of the countries ceded to Great Britain by that treaty. . . . By that proclamation, the crown reserved under its own dominion and protection, for the use of the Indians, 'all the land and territories lying to the westward of the sources of the rivers which fall into the sea from the west and north-west' and strictly forbade all British subjects from making any purchases or settlements, or taking possession of the reserved lands" (549, 594). This proclamation is crucial to the decision of the *Johnson* case; for the Court cites it as one of the "facts" that prove the continuity of title to Indian lands from the British Crown to its legitimate successor, the United States government. Stated in the proclamation as the positive protection of Indian lands from the incursions of individuals, this protection is provided by the device of the Crown itself claiming ultimate title to those lands, an ironic form of protection at best. The local history that ultimately generates the *Johnson* case occurs in the aftermath of the French and Indian War and can be understood as one of its microcosmic results that leads to the macrocosmic consequences of the case itself.

This local history is constituted by two land sales that took place in the western territories of Virginia in 1773 and 1775. Prior to the sales "sole and absolute ownership and possession of the country in question" (549) resided respectively with the Illinois, or Kaskaskias, and the Piankeshaw, or Wabash, Indians. The purchasers of the Indian lands were two groups of British subjects, with some overlapping membership in the groups, who, in accordance with the proclamation of 1763, must have had the sanction of the British government in order to make the purchases. The Indians were paid, respectively, $24,000 and $31,000 for their lands. The *Johnson* case notes that in both sales "the whole transaction was open, public and fair, and the deed fully explained to the grantors and other Indians by the sworn interpreters of the government, and fully understood by the grantors and other Indians, before it was executed" (554; see also 558). This formal language that assures legality is, as we have read, based on the legal fiction that "from time immemorial" Indians through their *representatives* had been selling the common *property* of their land and dividing the price *individually*. This fiction necessarily excludes problems of translation as well as the question of why these Indians would be selling large tracts of their lands in the first place, a question based on the cultural fact (also excluded by the fiction) that Indians could not sell their lands because these lands were never property, except, of course, under the compulsion of Western law. We can assume that the compulsion operating in this instance was due to the fact that the Kaskaskias and the Piankeshaw had been "allied" with the French and so had lost power in the French defeat and the subsequent consolidation of British power in the area. *Johnson* does take note of such an alliance in the case of the Kaskaskias, who, it is remarked, had signed a peace treaty with the British and the Iroquois (549).

The English buyers, however, "were prevented by the war of the American revolution" from taking "actual possession" (562) of the lands (in English common law "actual possession" is necessary to consummate title). And at the end of the war, in 1783, "the State of Virginia" transferred its title to its western lands (including those of the *Johnson* sale) taken from the British during the war and still "defined and prescribed by the letters patent of May 23rd, 1609" (559), to the U.S. government.

The *Johnson* case reports that "from the year 1781 till the year 1816" the original purchasers "petitioned the Congress of the United States to acknowledge and confirm their title to those lands . . . but without success" (562). Then in 1818 the U.S. government sold 11,560 acres of the land, now "situated within the state of Illinois" and "contained within" the lands of the 1775 sale to William M'Intosh (560). M'Intosh was subsequently sued for title by the lessee of Joshua Johnson and Thomas J. Graham, heirs of one of the original buyers in the 1775 sale and citizens of the United States. The District Court of Illinois found for M'Intosh, and this finding was upheld by the Marshall Court in 1823. The finding reads simply: "A title to lands, under grants to private individuals, made by Indian tribes or nations northwest of the river Ohio, in 1773, and 1775, cannot be recognized in the courts of the United States" (543).

The lawyers for the plaintiffs in the case argued in effect that Indian tribes held title to their lands and could transfer that title to individuals (562–67). The lawyers for the defendant argued that "the settled law, as laid down by the tribunals of civilized states, denied the right of the Indians to be considered as independent communities, having a permanent property in the soil, capable of alienation to private individuals. They remain in a state of nature, and have never been admitted into the general society of nations" (567).

Both sides, I want to emphasize without simply collapsing the two arguments, operated strictly within the terms of *property*, and within a history, governed by these terms, where the end was the alienation of Indian lands. The Marshall Court, in upholding the lower court decision and extending it to cover the relationship of all Indian peoples to their lands, operated, as we have read, within the same history. Let us note that this history is a history composed of written documents—charters, acts, treaties, deeds, and laws—in which *property* plots the narrative, property as a form of writing and writing as a form of property. And it is this writing that translates the oral histories of Native American peoples into its terms so that their voices become part of a master narrative, a legal fiction, that dispossesses them. Vine Deloria, Jr., give us an example of this translation process, which Native Americans continue to resist:

> There was also a great oral tradition among many tribes concerning the provisions of the treaties and their meaning. Fathers and grandfathers would pass along almost verbatim the words of the treaty commissioners which explained what the various articles and phrases of the treaties were supposed to mean. Courts had declared that this oral tradition could not be used by Indians in cases that involved treaties, and that only the writings and minutes taken by the government secretaries and officers would qualify, since they were considered "disinterested parties."[8]

Within this written history of property, it is only Christians who could have "discovered" the land they named "America," because the Indians, as Marshall notes in delivering the opinion of the Court, were not legally there: "So far as respected the authority of the crown, no distinction was taken between vacant lands and lands occupied by the Indians" (596). In this history Indians appear to disappear, either into the environment itself (they are assimilated into nature) or into the individualized figure of the property-holder.

The opposition that governs this history is a classic one: that between the "civilized" and the "savage." But this opposition is itself governed by the notion of *property*, in a specific way. For in the Western tradition that produces this opposition, the civilized is garbed in the figure of the farmer, who "settles" the land and in doing so converts it to property, whereas the savage is garbed in the figure of the hunter, who, to quote from the summary of M'Intosh's defense, "could have acquired no proprietary interest in the vast tracts of territory which they [the Indians] wandered over; and their right to the lands on which they hunted could not be considered as superior to that which is acquired to the sea by fishing in it" (569–70). What we should note at this point is a contradiction that nevertheless works quite cogently to dispossess the Indians of their lands. When it is necessary to justify such dispossession in microcosmic historical focus, Indians are admitted to the terms of property so that dispossession can be "legalized" as land sales. In macrocosmic focus, on the other hand, Indians, as "savages," or hunters, are excluded from the terms of property, so that the conquest of America, which will force Indians into a position where they must sell their lands, can be justified in terms of a particular "moral" economy, where farmers, because they are bringing "civilization" to the "wilderness," have a right to displace hunters, who are projected in this economy as no more than a part of that resistant wilderness itself.

The opposition savage/civilized, hunter/farmer, is a sheer fiction of the history of property under consideration. The fur trade is one crucial instance of the intermixing of Native American and European hunting economies. And it was Indian agriculture that enabled the survival of the colonists at Jamestown. We might expect that by 1823 Anglo-Americans would be well aware of the delusory shape of this opposition. Nevertheless, the Court, even with the Cherokee example of adapting near at hand, used it in *Johnson* to rationalize the dispossession of the Indians:

> But the tribes of Indians inhabiting this country were fierce savages, whose occupation was war, and whose subsistence was drawn chiefly from the forest. To leave them in possession of their country was to leave the country a wilderness; to govern them as a distinct people was impossible, because they were as brave and as high spirited as they were fierce, and were ready to repel by arms every attempt on their independence. (590)

I suspect that the Court's deployment of the opposition savage/civilized, which is representative of the era, is not cynical. Rather, it is propelled as a belief by a need to repress a truly threatening opposition, threatening because it is not morally reassuring or delusory but questions the ethics and the efficiency of the dominant economic/social system. I refer here to the opposition kinship/property that Montaigne read as the moral reversal of the opposition savage/civilized,[9] or kinship/capitalism, to state the form of the opposition most powerful in the Marshall Court's time and our own. Indian kinship economies, which, I want to make clear, I understand not as precapitalist but as anticapitalistic, constitute a powerful *and continuing* critique of the waste of an expansive, acquisitive capitalism that Marshall's United States with half a continent left to conquer and the dream of empire boiling in its brain could not *afford* to entertain. The loss in social vision was and is incalculable.

Given the critical focus on *The Pioneers* as a central text about law and property in the United States, I find it surprising that, as far as I know, no one has read the novel in relation to *Johnson*. I take this critical oversight as a mark of the same limits that bound the history that we have read in *Johnson*, the limits of *property/individualism/representation.* The critical tradition has read *The Pioneers* univocally within the context of these limits, thus ruling out consideration of the histories of kinship-based cultures in North America and their crucial relationship to this other history, almost as if Indians and Indian history in the Leatherstocking Tales were merely a rhetorical ornament to an essentially European content. This kind of reading produces hallucinations.

John P. McWilliams, to take a representative example, reads *The Pioneers* as a conflict between "Leatherstocking [who] exemplifies the just man in a Lockean State of Nature, [and] Judge Temple [who] must bring institutional justice to the State of Civilization." The Judge represents "gentlemen who relied upon property contracts, man-made law, and votes to build a good society at demonstrable expense to natural liberty," while Leatherstocking exemplifies "the individualist who, relying upon himself and the wilderness around him, pursued without qualification the laws of Nature's God." In its decontextualization of the law, this conflict is academic, not least of all because the person of property and the individualist are not opposed in American life; rather, they are ideological partners. Following David Noble, Brook Thomas has effectively deconstructed the Cooper/McWilliams opposition between the Judge and Natty, property and individualism, civilization and nature. But in doing so, he has remained resolutely within the terms of the opposition. That is, the legal history he articulates to enable his critique is a history of juridical conflicts *between white men*, specifically conflicts over property.[10]

But, from the perspective both contained in and repressed by *Johnson*, this history is enmeshed in and driven, indeed enabled, if you will, by a more compelling history: that of the conflict between Native Americans and Europeans over land. It is a history, as I have been arguing, of the violent translation by Europeans of the languages of Native American kinship systems into the terms of *property* and of Native American resistance to this translation. *The Pioneers* and *Johnson v. M'Intosh,* one a fiction about the law and one a legal fiction, work in what I will explain as *contradictory concert* to accomplish this translation. Reading this joint work, we can learn something about the way law and letters plot to construct the figure of the "other" in the liberal culture of U.S. imperialism in order to do the work of dispossession.

Both the legal fiction and the fiction about the law, as noted, were published in the same year. And both take up the same issue: the relation of Indian land to the Western institution of *property.* Near the middle of the novel, Judge Temple, the founder of the frontier settlement in New York where the action of the novel is located in 1793–94, is hostilely questioned by the romantic hero of the book, Edward Oliver Effingham (alias Oliver Edwards at this point), about the legitimacy of the Judge's title in relation to "Indian rights" to the land, rights represented throughout the novel by Natty Bumppo (*aka* Leatherstocking and Hawkeye) and his Indian companion, Chingachgook (*aka* Mohegan, John Mohegan, and Indian John), the classic duo that gives Cooper's Leatherstocking Tales the focus that made them so influential in determining the shape of the Western as a genre. The Judge's response to the contentious questions of Edwards, who appears to be an Indian at this point in the plot (an appearance to which we will return), finds its specific history in *Johnson:* "for the Indian title was extinguished so far back as the close of the old war; and if it had not been at all, I hold under the patents of the Royal Governors, confirmed by an act of our own State Legislature, and no court in the country can affect my title" (237).

Cooper's narrator represents Judge Temple as an authority of and on the law, just as Cooper represents this narrator, through its omniscient voice, as an authority on European/Indian political history, on northeastern Native American ethnohistory, and as an expert translator of Indian languages. My initial point is that *The Pioneers* asked and asks its readers to take this authority seriously,[11] just as seriously as the *Johnson* case asks its readers to take its authority, though the political effects of the two fictions have obvious differences that can correspond to the difference that Althusser posits between the "Repressive State Apparatus" and the "Ideological State Apparatus."[12] And yet the nostalgic coupling of Natty and Chingachgook, the white man and the "good" Indian—in this case a Delaware—and the equally nostalgic conflict between Natty/Chingachgook and the "Mingoes,"[13] or Iroquois, who represent the "bad" Indians in Cooper's Leatherstocking saga, are produced by a radically reductive ethnohistory that produces a fantastic rewriting of the history of the French and Indian War. In order to allow this coupling and conflict, Cooper must rewrite the history of the alliances that determined the outcome of the French and Indian War, the onto-historical context for the Leatherstocking Tales. For within the logic of the nostalgic opposition "good" Indian/"bad" Indian, the "good" Indians must fight on the side of the "good guys," who, in Cooper's story of the development of the United States, which is the overriding story of the Tales, are necessarily the English and their descendants. Thus, we have his fiction that the Iroquois (who, as he well knew, fought, by and large, on the side of the English and were crucial in the English victory over the French) allied themselves with the French, while the Delaware (who, by and large, were in the French camp until 1758, when their allegiance through the mediation of the Iroquois shifted to the English)[14] allied themselves exclusively with the English and against the Iroquois.

This incredible revisionary history appears to be generated by Cooper's reductive and partisan understanding, through his reading of the Reverend John Heckewelder (a Moravian missionary to the Delaware and a partisan of their culture), of the complex political relationship between the Iroquois and the Delaware (though he knew no Indian languages, Cooper's reading of Heckwelder seems to have given him a certain belief of expertise in this area as well).[15] And in *The Pioneers*, we can read that this reductive understanding is itself founded on a reductive ethnohistory of the native peoples of the northeastern and mid-Atlantic states that conforms to the simple opposition Delaware v. Iroquois: "Before the Europeans, or, to use a more significant term, the Christians, dispossessed the original owners of the soil, all that section of the country, which contains the New England States, and those of the Middle which lie east of the mountains, was occupied by two great nations of Indians, from whom had descended numberless tribes" (83). A Western idea of genealogy produces a Western fiction of Native American history that generates a Western fiction of Indian political relationships that becomes the structure for a fantastic rewriting of the French and Indian War, in which the "good" Indians, the Delaware, *must* fight univocally on the side of the "good guys." And the good guys, as noted, are necessarily the English, because they, in a patriarchal genealogical fiction, are the "fathers" of the people of the United States. In this fiction, in a way that is analogous to the writing of Indians and Indian history in *Johnson*, Indians and Indian history become no more than rhetorical embellishments in a story of Anglo-American triumph, a story that, as we will read, is the story, as in *Johnson*, of the triumph of property. In this story, as is suggested by their rhetorical deployment, Indians do not matter, except as they are used to organize desired affect in the European reader. Thus, it is implied, they are essentially superfluous in a history that would have been the same without them.

A master narrative is at work here in which the United States is the site of an homogeneous people of Western European origin. The scene of nineteenth-century pastoral unity that opens *The Pioneers* and is its tele- ology, in which "under the dominion of mild laws . . . every man feels a direct interest in the prosperity of a commonwealth, of which he knows himself to form a part" (15–16), is a figure for this narrative, where ide- ology supersedes accuracy or, better perhaps, fairness, in race, as well as gender and class terms. It is a narrative in which Indians appear to disappear. Chingachgook is not only the last of the Mohegans, who are confused by Cooper, following Heckewelder, with the Delaware.[16] Within the ideological dimensions of the master narrative, he figures the last Indian altogether. His self-willed death by fire at the end of *The Pioneers* marks a narrative moment of Anglo-American wishful thinking about all Indians as it masks in suicide Anglo-American homicide of Native Ameri- cans. This moment is typically recorded as a nostalgic lament for the *inevitable* "vanishing" of all Native American peoples, as a helplessness before the inevitable, as if it were part of an irreversible evolutionary process rather than political: "What can I do? what can my father do?" pleads Elizabeth Temple, daughter of the Judge. "'Should we offer the old man [Mohegan] a home and a maintenance, his habits would compel him to refuse us. Neither, were we so silly as to wish such a thing, could we convert these clearings and farms, again, into hunting-grounds, as the Leather-stocking would wish to see them'" (280). As in the *Johnson* case, the Temple rationale for dispossessing the Indians is based on the opposi- tion hunter/farmer, and the text of Elizabeth Temple, acting here as *porte parole* for the Judge, is the text of Judge John Marshall that we have read.

Both *Johnson* and *The Pioneers* work in concert to produce a history that rationalizes or legitimates in the name of *property* the dispossession of Native Americans even as it admits this dispossession. This joint work is forceful because it is accomplished through shared discursive prac- tices contained in the word *property*, rather than through some conscious collaborative effort, some "conspiracy." But this concerted effort, I want to argue now, is most concerted, most forceful, when these two fictions work in contradiction, when, that is, the fiction of Indian title that drives the plot of *The Pioneers* is contradicted by the fiction of Indian title that *Johnson* plots as law.

In a passage late in the novel where Judge Temple argues once again "the validity" of white "claims" to Indian lands against the accusation of Oliver Edwards, the jurist prefaces his argument by focusing on a claim that sustains *The Pioneers* traditional plot of concealed identity:

> "Oliver Edwards, thou forgettest in whose presence thou standest. I have heard, young man, that thou claimest descent from the native owners of the soil; but surely thy education has given to thee no effect, if it has not taught thee the validity of the claims that have transferred the title to the whites. These lands are mine by the very grants of thy ancestry, if thou art so descended; and I appeal to Heaven, for a testimony of the uses I have put them to." (345)

These two claims—Oliver's to an Indian identity and white claims to the land—are inseparable, both within the plot of the novel and within the cultural plot that the novel helps plot.

Until the very end of the novel, when his "real," or legal, identity is revealed, the other characters identify Oliver as an Indian: a "half-breed," as Richard Jones—the Judge's cousin and sheriff of the county—puts it, who, because of this addition of Indian "blood," "can never be weaned from the savage ways" (217). This identification comes about because of Edwards's close association with Natty and Mohegan, community familiars, coupled with his mysterious origin: the stranger appears out of the woods at the beginning of the novel with Leatherstocking and lives with him and Chingachgook the shared life of a hunter, as opposed to the settled life of the property-holding Judge. More specifically, the community starts to suspect that Edwards is an Indian from the moment when Chingachgook refers to him as "Young Eagle," who "has the blood of a Delaware chief in his veins" (138).

From his first appearance in the novel, where he is wounded by the Judge in a hunting accident, Edwards manifests what appears to be an unaccountable, because apparently motiveless, hostility toward the Judge. At first only the wound seems to explain the anger, but it is really no explanation, not only because the injury was accidental, but also because of its mildness and the fact that Judge Temple is more than generous in compensation, taking Oliver home, treating his wound, and then providing him with permanent residence and employment as his secretary. From the moment of the revelation of the wound, in fact, the Judge extends virtual kinship to the stranger: "all shall be done at my expence, and thou shalt live with me until thy wound is healed—aye, and for ever afterwards" (25). However, when Oliver assumes his Indian identity, which he does by simply letting the words of Indian John stand, his anger assumes an apparent ground: that of Indian dispossession by whites. And Judge Temple becomes the logical target of this anger because he is the largest landholder in the area, having purchased in New York "extensive possessions, at, comparatively, low prices" (36) of lands confiscated from Loyalists during the American Revolution. Until the very end of the novel, as we have read in two representative passages, Oliver Edwards speaks as an Indian defender of "Indian rights" to land, who, in taking this position, compels Judge Temple to speak as the defender of white "title." Epitomizing the legal history that *Johnson* elaborates, Judge Temple defends his title over and against the Indians' "natural," or prior, rights. In this defense, I want to emphasize, Judge Temple specifies in a passage we have read that his title to the lands is legitimate because he can trace it from "the patents of the Royal Governors, confirmed by an act of our own State Legislature," even if Indian title had not been "extinguished." In the language that will grow out of *Johnson*, the Judge holds his lands under the "doctrine of discovery."

But at the end of *The Pioneers* the opposition between "Young Eagle" and the Judge, between Indian and white, that has sustained the debate over land rights collapses, when it is revealed that Oliver Edwards is the son and heir of Judge Temple's former silent business partner, Colonel Edward Effingham, who has just drowned in a shipwreck. Taking opposing sides in the Revolution—Temple, the American; Effingham, the British—the friends necessarily parted company. In this division, Temple, with Effingham's consent, retained the assets of the business and subsequently purchased Effingham's estates in the land deals that he made after the Revolution. As the Judge's will reveals to young Effingham in "clear, distinct, manly, and even eloquent language" (443), Temple has been holding the property of Colonel Effingham in trust for the Colonel's son, whereas young Effingham has believed up until this moment that the Judge used the Revolution as an excuse to break faith with his father and amalgamate all the Effingham estate to himself. As in *Johnson* it is the Revolution that brings the question of ownership of Indian lands into focus through legal conflict.

At the same time that the Judge is revealing his good intentions to young Effingham so that the former Oliver Edwards can himself be "the judge" (439) of the Judge, the young man is revealing the origin of his Indian identity to the Judge. So, Oliver explains, his grandfather, Major Oliver Effingham, who "reared" Leatherstocking in his own family, saved the life of Chingachgook, who "induced the Delawares to grant [their land] to him, when they admitted him as an honorary member of their tribe." To this narrative, the Judge responds: "This, then, is thy Indian blood?"

> "I have no other," said Edwards, smiling;—"Major Effingham was adopted as the son of Mohegan, who at that time was the greatest man in his nation; and my father, who visited those people when a boy, received the name of Eagle from them, on account of the shape of his face, as I understand. They have extended his title to me. I have no other Indian blood or breeding; though I have seen the hour, Judge Temple, when I could wish that such had been my lineage and education." (441)

But that "hour," the hour of Young Eagle's anger, is past. For that anger, which dissipates in the revelation of the Judge's will, was not, finally, based in the fact of white dispossession of the Indians of their lands, but in the belief that the Judge dispossessed Oliver of his *property*. In this revelation, Indian claims are merely an allegory for the claims of an individual white man; the claims of kinship are merely an allegory for the claims of property. This allegorization of Indians for the purpose of telling stories about property, a rhetorical strategy that drives the narrative of the *Johnson* case as well, is made possible by a classic Western rhetorical division: that between the proper, or literal, and the figurative, in which the proper, like property, is a privileged place, so privileged that it tends to take on the status of the "natural," particularly in the nineteenth century with the rise of biology as a science and the concomitant naturalization of the category of "race."[17]

Because of this rhetorical division, which we understand is the effect of a set of discursive practices not limited to those of rhetoric but including those of law, anthropology and the sciences as well, Oliver Edwards is able to slip off his Indian identity, to reduce it to the merely figurative, or contingent, in order to reveal his "real," or "natural," white identity. We understand that this "natural" identity is merely literal, that is, written, a particular figure of speech itself, but one carrying the legal power to erase its own figurativeness within the culture in which it develops. From a Native American perspective, if such a perspective were not under erasure in *The Pioneers*, Oliver Edwards would remain an Indian. For it is the function of kinship-based societies to extend the terms of family to everyone in the culture, so that no similar division is made between the literal and the figurative, the natural and the cultural.

From the moment Young Eagle reveals his white identity, his legal inscription in the Judge's world of wills and deeds, *The Pioneers* moves quickly toward its happy ending: the marriage of Edward Oliver Effingham to the Judge's daughter, which is possible now that young Effingham has assumed his proper race and class. This proper marriage implies the consolidation of Temple and Effingham property in the establishment of Edward in another legal relationship to the Judge, that of son-in-law (a relationship that gives Effingham ultimate control over all the property because of the legal control that husbands had over wives' wealth). *The Pioneers*, which can define the genre of the traditional Western for us, is a romance of *property*, contained within the term itself in precisely the same ways as the *Johnson* case.

Or we might say that *The Pioneers* and the traditional Westerns that follow it romance the *Johnson* case, thus making its ideology available to a wide audience. For who reads the law, except lawyers and judges and, if they can, those who are immediately affected by it? *The Pioneers* romances the *Johnson* case by contradicting it in a certain way. For if Young Eagle receives title to his lands through the Judge, whose title, as we have read, is legitimated by the same history inscribed in *Johnson*, this title gains its original sanction, according to the narrative of how young Effingham received the "title" of Young Eagle, directly from an Indian "grant" to his grandfather.[18] This grant from Indians to individuals is, of course, illegal in the history that *Johnson* legitimates. But it is based on the same fiction that circumscribes both romance and law: the fiction that Indians, like individuals, have always already operated within a system where the alienation of land is the norm; the fiction that all land everywhere is always already *property* and all people individuals.

In making Effingham the direct heir of the Indians by virtue of his Indian title, Young Eagle, Cooper's romance seems to reassure its readers at the end that the Indians alienated their land willingly, even as at the beginning it speaks of the "dispossess[ion] of the original owners of the soil." This reassurance parallels the formula found in Indian land transactions that we have read in *Johnson:* "the whole transaction was open, public and fair, and the deed fully explained to the grantors and other Indians by the sworn interpreters of the government, and fully understood by the grantors and other Indians before it was executed." Certainly in these ways, both novel and legal formula romance the real force of dispossession that the Supreme Court's decision is based on and will generate. And just as the Court is basing its decision on the unassimilability of "savages," Cooper's romance seems to be telling its readers, through the figures of Young Eagle and Hawkeye, that the best Indians are white men anyway. Standing over Chingachgook's grave, Young Eagle proclaims the most deadly legal fiction, the master narrative of universal "man," where death finds its double in assimilation: "He was the last of his people who continued to inhabit this country; and it may be said of him, that his faults were those of an Indian, and his virtues those of man" (452).

Notes

1 James Fenimore Cooper, *The Pioneers, or the Sources of the Susquehanna: A Descriptive Tale* (1823; rpt. in Donald A. Ringe's Penguin edition, 1988, which is taken from the SUNY edition of Cooper's works, edited by James Franklin Beard). I would like to thank Darlene Evans for suggesting the title of this essay; and Bruce Levy, Dennis Foster, Amy Kaplan, and Michael Holahan for suggestions that helped in its revision.

2 I have elaborated my reading of Montaigne in *The Poetics of Imperialism: Translation and Colonization from "The Tempest" to "Tarzan"* (New York: Oxford University Press, 1991) pp. 142–57. My comments on the Cibecue Apache are based on my reading of Keith H. Basso, *Portraits of "The White Man": Linguistic Play and Cultural Symbols Among the Western Apache* (1979; New York: Cambridge University Press, 1980).

3 Henry Wheaton, *Reports of Cases Argued and Adjudged in the Supreme Court of the United States*, vol. 8 (New York: R. Donaldson, 1823), pp. 543–605.

4 John Locke, *The Second Treatise of Government*, ed. Thomas P. Peardon (1690; New York: Bobbs-Merrill, 1952), 5.27.

5 For a history of this resistance see Vine Deloria, Jr., *Behind the Trail of Broken Treaties: An Indian Declaration of Independence* (Austin: University of Texas Press, 1985). Of interest as well is Ward Churchill's article in *Z Magazine* (October 1991), "American Indian Self-Governance: Fact, Fantasy, and Prospects."

6 Janet A. McDonnell, *The Dispossession of the American Indian, 1887–1934* (Bloomington: Indiana University Press, 1991), pp. vii, 10.

7 For an excellent and concise description and analysis of the alliances that were constitutive of the Iroquois "confederacy" and the Covenant Chain, see Francis Jennings, "Iroquois Alliances in American History," in *The History and Culture of Iroquois Diplomacy: An Interdisciplinary Guide to the Treaties of the Six Nations and Their League*, ed. Jennings et al. (Syracuse: Syracuse University Press, 1985), pp. 37–65.

8 Deloria, *Behind the Trail of Broken Treaties*, p. 52.

9 For this reading of Montaigne, see Cheyfitz, *The Poetics of Imperialism*, pp. 142–57.

10 John P. McWilliams, Jr., "Innocent Criminal or Criminal Innocence: The Trial in American Fiction," in *Law and American Literature: A Collection of Essays*, ed. Carl S. Smith, John P. McWilliams, Jr., and Maxwell Bloomfield (New York: Alfred A. Knopf, 1983), p. 57. Brook Thomas, *Cross-Examinations of Law and Literature* (Cambridge: Cambridge University Press, 1987).

11 I have written about Cooper's representation of authority in these matters in "Literally White, Figuratively Red: The Frontier of Translation in *The Pioneers*," *James Fenimore Cooper: New Critical Essays*, ed. Robert Clark (Totowa: Barnes & Noble, 1985), pp. 55–95 (see in particular notes 2 and 7).

12 Louis Althusser, "Ideology and Ideological State Apparatuses," in *Essays on Ideology* (London: Verso, 1984; the essay was first published in French in 1970). The difference for Althusser between the Repressive State Apparatus and the Ideological State Apparatuses is that the former "functions massively and predominantly *by repression* (including physical repression), while functioning secondarily by ideology," while the latter "function massively and predominantly *by ideology*, but they also function secondarily by repression, even if ultimately, but only ultimately, this is very attenuated and concealed, even symbolic" (19). The difference between the two apparatuses, then, provides for a crucial area of overlap, in terms of both repression and ideology.

13 Historically, the Mingos were a disaffected group of young Mohawks, who, apparently, separated from the tribe and thus the Iroquois "confederacy" and moved into the Ohio valley in the early 1730s, when the "confederacy" was suffering setbacks at the hands of both English and French. See Francis Jennings, *The Ambiguous Iroquois Empire: The Covenant Chain Confederation of Indian Tribes with English Colonies from its Beginnings to the Lancaster Treaty of 1744* (New York: Norton, 1984), p. 308. This position in the Ohio valley, if they remained there, would probably have aligned the Mingos with the French in the Seven Years' War. My research to date has not been able to pursue them. But whether he was aware of it or not, Cooper is using a small part, a very small part indeed, to represent the whole, when he makes Mingos a synonym for Iroquois.

14 Jennings, "Iroquois Alliances in American History," pp. 54–55.

15 As we have known for a long time, Cooper's ethnology and ethnohistory come predominantly from the Rev. John Heckewelder's *History, Manners, and Customs of the Indian Nations, Who Once Inhabited Pennsylvania and the Neighboring States*, which was first published in 1819. For an elaboration of Cooper's narrator's pose as a translator of Indian languages, see my essay, "Literally White, Figuratively Red."

16 For an explanation of this confusion, see Gregory Lansing Paine, "The Indians of the Leather-Stocking Tales," *Studies in Philology* 23 (1926): 33–35.

17 My book *The Poetics of Imperialism* focuses on the politics of the rhetorical division between the proper and the figurative as it has manifested itself historically in the West from classical times to the present. In my essay on *The Pioneers*, "Literally White, Figuratively Red," I discuss this politics in relation to the plot of Cooper's novel.

18 At an early stage of the narrative we are told that the Effingham lands "had been originally granted to old Major Effingham, by the 'King's letters patent'" (97). This explanation, which brings the lands under the legal system that *Johnson* elaborates, never comes up again and is superseded by the romance of Indian title that ends the novel and makes America a gift from Indians to Europeans.

Bill Brown

Science Fiction, the World's Fair, and

the Prosthetics of Empire,

1910–1915

et me begin in the future, after World War I, with the publication of Edgar Rice Burroughs's sixth Martian novel. *The Master Mind of Mars* (1927) presents itself as a manuscript written by Ulysses Paxton and sent to Burroughs to add to his "as yet unappreciated contributions to the scientific literature of the world."[1] On the battlefield, this captain's legs have been "blown away from midway between the hips and knees." He shrinks "more from the thought of going maimed through life" than from the thought of death (360). But with his eyes focused on the Red Planet, Paxton is able to "throw off the hideous bonds of [his] mutilated flesh" and finds himself on Mars, standing "naked upon two good legs" (361). Re-membering the war-torn body, science fiction here performs a magic act of prosthetics.

But while the prosthetic fantasy empowers the hero to transcend his disintegrating body, the novel takes as its central task the injunction against any scientific production of such transcendence. A modern Frankenstein, the Master Mind of Mars, Ras Thavas, having developed a technology to preserve bodies and to transfer brains, furnishes his clientele with corporeal youth, and the resulting traffic in bodies provokes a kind of somatic chaos: "Two men, each possessing the body of the other," sit beside "an old and wicked empress whose fair body belong[s] to a youthful damsel," who sits beside "a great white ape dominated by half the brain of a human being" (476).

I want to read this scene—the penultimate moment in the text, before Paxton sets everything aright, returning bodies to their rightful owners, owners to their rightful bodies—as an irruption of what science fiction generally works to exclude. This is a moment of prosthetic excess wherein characters are non-self-identical; bodies become opaque; gender, sexual, and species codes verge toward incoherence; and the very notion of "prosthesis" has been undone by the availability not of artificial parts, but of whole, natural bodies. Put briefly, the scene appears to literalize, all at once, modernist subjectivity, consumer culture's promise of re-embodiment, and modernity's ideal of absolute interchangeability. If, as Alfred Sohn-Rethel has argued, abstract thought and the modern division of intellectual and manual labor have their material origin in the act of exchange, the "abstractness operating in exchange," then the novel here displays intellectual labor's consummate return to that beginning— a moment when thought has thought its way back to exchanging the body itself.[2] It is a world in which the body, with all its cultural inscriptions, can be comfortably discarded.

Now, let me turn to the past.

The Artificial Race

"If I had the making of men," Kirby speculates, on a tour of the inferno in *Life in the Iron Mills* (1861), "these men who do the lowest part of the world's work should be machines,—nothing more,—hands. It would be a kindness."[3] Making men instead of iron, this mill owner's son would, let us say, make men of iron, insensate and unconscious, never suffering from the filth, poverty, and physical deformity that Rebecca Harding Davis describes. What Edward Ellis describes, in *The Steam-Man of the Prairies* (1868), is a strong version of Kirby's "kindness," a vision in which an iron man compensates for human deformity. The "engineer" who has invented the Steam-Man and manages "the monster with rare skill" is a "deformed boy," Johnny, "hump-backed, dwarfed, but with an amiable disposition."[4] While his father's death in a boiler explosion exhibits one generation's struggle with technology, the son's command of technology makes him, as his mother says, "like Alexander, sighing for more worlds to conquer" (19). And like Alexander, Johnny eventually sets out on a conquest, accompanied not just by his machine but also by his sidekick, a frontiersman who is "strong, hardy, bronze . . . powered in all that goes to make up the physical man" (21). Still, it is not this "physical man," but the machine, and thus the boy its operator, who succeeds in repulsing both bears and Indians.

The machine, in this mechanized conquest of the indigenous race,

Figure 1. The Steam-Man.

is itself racially coded: the Steam-Man's face is "made of iron, painted a black color, with a pair of fearful eyes, and a tremendous grinning mouth" (12); in multiple editions of the novel he is illustrated variously, but invariably he is an enormous black man (figure 1). Thus, in its occasional moments of breakdown, a kind of technological frenzy, the Steam-Man may be said to embody the threat of the slave's (or the recently freed slaves') violent recalcitrance in the way that, as Andreas Huyssen has argued, the machine-woman of Lang's *Metropolis* comes to embody the threat of female sexual excess.[5] More simply, while this technology releases Johnny from the able/disabled somatic binary, it does so only by racializing the mind/body and capital/labor binaries. Which is to say that the novel emancipates man from his body but incarcerates the machine within the American system of somatic semiosis.

This codification makes immediate sense, of course, according to the Aristotelian logic with which George Fitzhugh and others defended slavery before the war: for if the "natural slave" is he "who is able to execute with his body what another contrives," then any American machine "naturally" appears as an American slave, which means: a black American.[6] The novel, participating in this logic, exemplifies Critical Theory's point that technology, far from being dependent on scientific neutrality, is and has been an objectification of divisions within society—in this case, an objectified preservation of divisions that have been politically (if not socially) overcome. As in the important quip made by Fanny Fern in 1853—"If Mrs. Adam wasn't the first sewing machine, then I'll stop guessing"—"the machine" names not an object but a social relation.[7] And in the industrializing postwar South, the relations of the slave system were soon to become the paradigm for making sense of technological culture: in Henry Grady's vision for the "New South," he explains that the planter who once bought a slave will now buy "a piece of machinery."[8]

In 1868 a disabled boy invents a powerful black man that fights off the violent Indian. This narrative, with its vaguely contemporary setting, could be read as allegorizing a host of postwar conflicts and as occupying a crucial place in the Fiedler history of the American (male) novel, obsessed with an interracial, cross-generational, and homosocial bond that, in this case, even characterizes man's relation to machinery.[9] But I want to emphasize something else: the way the novel responds not, for instance, to the loss of slave labor, but to the notorious loss of limbs suffered by Civil War soldiers. For *The Steam-Man of the Prairies*, on its way to answering one question about the labor force, legitimizes prosthetic technology, normalizing the (white) individual's difference from, and artificial completion of, his body. While the narrator of *Life in the Iron Mills* pleads that the reader understand how the central laborer, Hugh Wolfe, longs "to *be*— something, he knows not what,—other than he is," a longing artistically expressed in his creation of the Korl Woman (25), in Ellis's novel, Johnny, with his creation of the Steam-Man, can more simply achieve that otherness. He can emancipate himself from somatic self-identity. Borrowing the Jamesian formula, we can say: his body is *his*, but not *him*.[10]

The Steam-Man, expressing an era's conviction that, as Ronald Takaki says, the machine would become "a replacement for the human body" (149), also enacts the midcentury American coding of prosthesis that we find, for example, in the work of Oliver Wendell Holmes.[11] Writing in 1863 on the advances of prosthetic technology, lamenting how "the limbs of our friends and countrymen are part of the melancholy harvest which War is sweeping down," Holmes celebrates the famous Palmer leg that, along with the accounts of human locomotion provided by the recent development of instantaneous photography, prompts him to modernize the traditional image of man as a machine, but not without figuring that machine as a slave system: "The foot's fingers are the slaves in the republic of the body." Moreover, even when he goes on to describe the beauty of the "well-shaped, intelligent, docile limb," he equates it with the "beauty and firmness which moulded the soft outlines of the Indian girl and the White Captive in the studio of [Palmer's] namesake in Albany." The reference here—to the statuary of Erastus Dow Palmer—establishes the limb as female and as either "racially" distinct or captive. Reconstructions of the body ultimately inspire Holmes to produce a celebration of American technology that rhetorically reconstructs the nation, that establishes the power of this nation despite its present ills, and that envisions further national progress once "we recover from the social and political convulsion . . . and eliminate the *materies morbi.*" But this celebration, like the dime novel, reinscribes, within the prosthetically completed body, the very conditions that led to war.[12]

What I've been describing is the way the inaugural American science fiction novel can only restore a postbellum body by restoring antebellum race relations.[13] But it should be added that by establishing a race for machines *The Steam-Man* unveils a mechanics of race wherein "race" appears not as a biological property but as an effect of power. The text thus provides some purchase on the way technological advances could, in contrast, threaten the existing order. As Takaki argues, "the hope for industrial 'progress,'" which necessitated the industrial proletarization of the free slave, stood in obvious tension with "the desire for racial dependency and order" (211). The novel clearly inverts that dependency and makes a muck of that order. It stages a master/slave dialectic wherein mastery depends not just on the compliance of the slave but on the slave's becoming a compliant extension of the master's body. The inventor may never find himself, like Frankenstein, a slave of his creature, but his heroism depends on his hybridity—on being both white and black, both man and machine, both less and more than human.

And this can help to account for the fact that the book's first lesson—where the body was (ploughing fields, hauling rocks, fighting Indians) there the machine will be—is no longer taught during the sudden proliferation of science fiction from 1910 to 1915. In the foreword to Burroughs's *The Princess of Mars* (1912), serialized shortly before *Tarzan*, the hero, John Carter, is an "athletic man," "a splendid specimen of manhood, standing a good two inches over six feet, broad of shoulder and narrow of hip."[14] In the first pages of George Allan England's *Darkness at Dawn* trilogy (1912–14), the engineer, Allan Stern, wakes up from a millennium-long suspended animation having "kept the resilient force of vigorous manhood"; the "self-contained, courteous, yet unapproachable engineer

[has] disappeared" to reveal "just a man, a young man, thewed with the vigor of his plenitude."[15] Even in the most technologically oriented of novels, Hugo Gernsback's *Ralph 124C 41+* (serialized in 1911 in *Modern Electronics*, the country's first radio magazine, produced by Gernsback himself), the inventor exhibits the antithesis of Johnny's dwarfed and deformed body. *Ralph*, generally considered America's first "modern" science fiction novel, is generally admired for its prescient display of inventions: microfilm, radar, television, electric lights for the outdoor stadium. In the first episode of this *romance of the year 2660*, Ralph, living in New York, manages to communicate with a woman living in Switzerland and to save her from an avalanche, thanks to his technological imagination. But if this hero, "one of the greatest living scientists of the day," transcends the limits of his body (as he must in order to be the hero that he is), nonetheless his body is not displaced by, but corresponds to, his powers of invention: on the first page of the novel we discover a "big man," "a physique much larger than that of the average man of his times."[16] Body and mind metaphorize one another. Ralph's body is his, and it's *him*.

Johnny's frontier companion in *The Steam-Man* embodies a prior, pioneer mode of American success, which the crippled boy can share because of the subsequent division of mental and manual labor. Ralph's instrumentalization of reason may epitomize that division, but the equation of body and mind disavows it. For all its display of mechanical wizardry, the novel reaffirms that residual mode and cuts off what we might call the "prosthetic possibility," the very idea that machines can complete the human. All told, the science fiction of Gernsback, Burroughs, and England proclaims a myth of social and technological progress only while it proclaims a myth of no progress, as though to combat what Veblen called the "cultural incidence of the machine process," a mechanization of the everyday, and what Jean-Joseph Goux refers to as "technological sociality," wherein agency and the auto-centered subject no longer coincide.[17] These novels do not simply re-individualize agency by heroizing the engineer over and against the "incorporation of America"; they theatricalize the American male body according to the paradigm that Susan Jeffords has taught us to call the "remasculinization of America."[18] And to sustain this body, they resort, for all their futurism, to an imperialist narrative paradigm that had become recognizably outmoded in the first decade of the century, with the creation of the Panama Canal Zone, what we might call a prosthetic extension of American—not a "natural" expression of westward expansiveness, but the mechanical institution of hemispheric domination, the technological and technocratic control over the global flow of goods.[19] In turn, of course, preserving the vitality and innate difference of this body becomes the means of naturalizing American global power.

American Body Parts

In 1908, employing early trick photography, the Vitagraph company produced a comedy, *The Thieving Hand*, which must also be one of the first American horror films. After a one-armed pencil vendor buys an eerily animate artificial limb, he discovers that the arm and hand are obsessively, frantically pickpocketing passersby without his volition. Unable to control the hand, the vendor sells it to a pawn shop, from which the limb crawls back and reattaches itself to his body. When he is ultimately jailed for his unconscious crimes, the limb finds its rightful owner, a thief, and the thieving body becomes whole again.[20]

This prosthetic nightmare quickly locates us in the realm of the uncanny—more particularly, in the early parts of Freud's famous essay (1914) where he refers to the paper by Jentsch (1906) that suggests that uncanniness is prompted by automata and our more general doubts about "whether a lifeless object might not be in fact animate." To this, Jentsch adds "the uncanny effect of epileptic fits, and of manifestations of insanity, because these excite in the spectator the impression of automatic, mechanical processes at work behind the ordinary appearance of mental activity." While these last comments approach an (uncanny) account of Freud's own metapsychology, Freud himself focuses on the way dismembered limbs "have something peculiarly uncanny about them, especially when . . . they prove capable of independent activity in addition."[21] Following Freud, of course, we soon face castration anxiety. (Following Lacan, we more slowly face, in such events as war's dismemberment of the soldier, an unveiling of that "massive cultural disavowal of the lack upon which [male subjectivity] rests.")[22] But the automata in Jentsch's discussion and the autonomous limb in the film achieve a more remarkable uncanniness if we take a detour through the Marx of the *Grundrisse*, where he describes the transposition of "living labor" into the activity of the machine, capital's most explicit assimilation of "living labour into itself 'as though love possessed its body.'" In this personification of capital (the perpetual flip side of Marx's burgeoning antihumanism), it is capital's desire that becomes the ground for rethinking anxieties about the human body. Within the system of machinery, labor suffers its final "metamorphosis," wherein the machine "is itself the virtuoso," wherein "workers themselves can be no more than the conscious limbs of the automaton."[23]

This is meant to suggest that just as the somatic comedy of *The Thieving Hand* anticipates that of Chaplin's *Modern Times*, so too it expresses the somatic ramifications of mechanized production. In other words, within Freud's *heimlich/unheimlich* dynamic, *The Thieving Hand* is uncanny because the conscious limb is in fact so familiar—familiar because of the worker's translation into a limb and because of the fate of his limbs.

By the end of the nineteenth century, the celebration of modern prosthetics could hardly ignore the fact that modernization itself posed the most formidable threat to the body's parts: while "our war has long passed," one writer commented in 1895, the "electric motor and steam engine continue to make as many cripples as did the missiles of war."[24] Moreover, the very success of mechanized industry and the growth of scientific management had disintegrated the human body at the site of production. Frank Gilbreth's *Concrete System* (1908) and *Bricklaying System* (1909) successfully enumerated the distinct movements that comprised the worker's accomplishments, and, in his subsequent cyclographic studies of motion, he managed, as Siegfried Giedion explains, to separate motion from "its conjunction with the human body."[25] If, as Giedion suggests, the mechanical imagination begins by isolating the human hand, then the first decades of the twentieth century hypostasize that beginning—in Taylor's scientific management, Gilbreth's studies of motion, and Ford's assembly line. As Lefebvre has argued (historicizing the "fragmentation of the body" outside its relation to language), Taylorism extends "the division of labor into the very bodies of workers," rendering them "a mere collection of unconnected parts."[26] Human labor is analytically and materially reduced to the operation of the body part, and the individual human functions only as a part, the "conscious limb," within the machine system. The uncanny hand embodies both the worker's limb and the worker himself.

The science fiction of this period occasionally manifests another version of this uncanniness. In Burroughs's account of Mars, the green Martians possess an extra set of limbs (used either as legs or as arms), there are hounds with ten legs, and the general proliferation of limbs might be read as the converse of the modern limb's destruction. John Carter's body compensates for this uncanniness and for the fate of the body within modern production, and even Taylor himself, in his most famous work, momentarily adopts a similar strategy. While he offers *The Principles of Scientific Management* (1911) as a response to Roosevelt's question of "increasing our national efficiency," he recognizes that the ideal of efficiency alone will hardly do. Against the anticipated complaint that this ideal will transform the worker into a mere "automaton," he insists that the life of the "frontiersman" was in its intensity of focus fairly well comparable.[27] The "frontier" appears as a rhetorical antidote to machine culture. In Gernsback's novel, Ralph the inventor comes to recognize that he himself functions only as "a tool, a tool to advance science, to benefit humanity. He belonged, not to himself, but to his Government" (41). And his former sense of success as a "tool" is undone by his feeling for Alice, "an emotion he had never experienced before" (65). Having once lectured that love is "nothing but a perfumed animal instinct," he ends up missing his lectures because of the instinctual distraction (140).[28] His genius ultimately serves neither the government nor humanity but his own mission to save the woman he loves from the villainous foreigner, a Martian. A story of inventions becomes a story about instincts and about bodies, the man's strong body and the woman's weak body. Like Freud, let us say, Gernsback hastily introduces sexual relations as a way to displace any inquiry into relations of production.

The very title of Gernsback's novel, *Ralph 124C 41+*, marks the quantification of human being on which scientific management and mass production depend. But the novel's subtitle—*a romance*—names its own rescue mission, saving Ralph from the process of abstraction. In this respect, the text's two titles crystallize and neutralize the bifurcated fate of the American body in the closing decades of the previous century. In texts like "The Physical Proportions of the Typical Man" (1887), D. A. Sargent (who had become director of the Gymnasium at Harvard in 1879) explains how he devised "a uniform system of measurements" to provide "anthropometric data" and some "standards by which to judge symmetry and strength," inventing such devices as the "dynameter," the "spirometer," and the "manometer" to test the strength of lungs, chests, triceps, backs, and legs.[29] Sargent's somatic calculus standardizes a technology that can detail the "standard body," normalizing the body by inventing a fragmented "normalcy." But this disintegration of the body has as its complement the vision of an imperialist American body that will recuperate the nation. For the *Chicago Tribune*, William Matthews, rendering the benefits of physical culture for "Getting On in the World" (1871), points to England's "splendid empires," her "victories on the field, in the mart, in the study" as the inevitable result of English "physical ability." "When the sweeping work the Germans made of it in their late war with France is called to mind," another commentator asks, "does it not look as if there was good ground for the assumption so freely made, that it was the superior physique of the Germans which did the business?"[30] This more familiar body, wherein the nation's and the individual's health converge (as in Roosevelt's "The Strenuous Life"), appears not just as a "reorientation" within American culture, but as the expression of international, imperialist envy.[31] Only an imperializing nation could attain the same corporeal coherence as the human body in the era when "coherence" could not be said to characterize that body. And it is this imperialist physique, more so than any technology, that science fiction stages as the proper embodiment of American success. Rather, that body appears to assimilate mechanical triumph not as a machine-body, but as a eugenic body, an "innately" superior "moral, mental, and physical nature" that can express all forms of power.[32]

If the genre of the novel satisfies what Timothy Brennan, thinking alongside Benedict Anderson, terms the "the national longing for form" by "objectifying the 'one, yet many' of national life and by mimicking the structure of the nation, a clearly bounded jumble of languages and styles," then we might say that the subgenre of science fiction satisfies the imperialist longing for form, infinitely extending those boundaries while containing and taxonomizing the metropolitan jumble.[33] If the inter-imperialist rivalry of World War I was predicated by the world's unification—the transcendence of spatial barriers effected by travel and communication systems, the emergence of mass culture, and a burgeoning capitalist world-economy—then the very spatial collapse recounted by science fiction makes the novels' inter-imperialist rivalry and metropolitan interracial conflict appear wholly predictable.[34] If we recognize the period of 1880 to 1925 as the "take off period of globalization," as Roland Robertson suggests, we can respect science fiction as the genre that projects the "aerial" and the "interplanetary" as the point of view from which the globe—the newly produced and miniaturized globe—becomes perceptible.[35] Additionally, we can argue that the genre discursively reproduces the American naturalist and ethnographic spectacles (at world's fairs and natural history museums) that depended on the modern imperial/metropolitan network as a mode of collection.[36]

The point, then, is that American science fiction, in its moment of modern emergence, attempts to synchronize the modernity of the American imperialist trajectory with an imperialist body from the previous century. This body emerges during a transition from the theatricalization of the American male that took place during the Spanish-American War—epitomized by Roosevelt's Rough Riders—to the theatricalization

17)-9359-President Roosevelt running an American steam-shovel at Cule-bra Cut, Panama Canal. Copyright 1906 by Underwood & Underwood. U-9884.

Figure 2. Roosevelt in Panama. (*Library of Congress*)

of American machinery in World War I.[37] This body emerges when American technology, as epitomized by the Panama Canal, appears as the new mechanical mode of American international triumph, when Roosevelt is famously photographed not on top of a horse but sitting at the controls of the Bucyrus shovel at Pedro Miguel, the startlingly white American in control of, but miniaturized by, the gargantuan, dark prosthetic machine (figure 2). In relation to such an image, science fiction depicts not just an obsolescent "strenuousness" with which American extra-continental expansion was originally configured, but also a body so magnificent it will not be reduced to the miniature.

For all its conventionality, the genre finds itself in a dialectical relation to the rise of modernism, a dialectic revolving around an axis called "modernization." Strongly summarized, revisionist accounts have shown us that modernism can be understood as the aesthetic of globalization. *Ralph 142C 41+*, Burroughs's Martian and Pellucidar novels, and England's trilogy appeared in the period (1910–15) when, as Lefebvre says, "a certain space was shattered" (25), the inaugural phase of what David Harvey calls "time-space compression" (265)—the result not just of the industrial subjugation of the world's spaces, but also of Ford's spatialization of time in the factory and of such material developments as radio, film, and aerial photography. It is hardly surprising, then, to find William Carlos Williams writing that Gertrude Stein's "pages have become like the United States viewed from an airplane."[38] For Harvey, among others, "modernism" appears as "a response to a crisis in the experience of space and time," an effort to represent time through the fragmentation of space (267). For Lefebvre, "Picasso's space herald[s] the space of modernity," and it does so "in parallel with imperialism" (302). And Jameson, reading *Howards End* (1910), argues that modernist "style" can be understood as a set of "formal symptoms" of the "representational dilemmas of the new imperial world system," namely the ("necessary") occlusion of the relation between the life of the metropolis and the life of the colonized subject.[39]

Of course, science fiction, expressly recounting that relation and describing a technology that shatters space—from Stern's biplane, binoculars, and astronomical observatory to Ralph's aerocabs and space ships to Carter's flyers—exhibits no such formal symptoms. But its obsessive exhibition of a perfected, eugenic American body should be understood as the converse, diegetic symptom of technology's disintegration of the body *and* of technology's erasure of the body from the new mode of American expansion. While the genre fetishizes this body, projecting onto it the potency of that mode, it more crucially establishes this body as a transcendent, metasocial guarantee of wholeness, of totality—the sign of a globalization that does not incur or provoke rival processes of fragmentation.

Hercules

This recovery of an anachronistic corporeality, beneath and beyond technology, can be traced in other cultural surfaces as well—notably the World's Fair that took place during World War I, the San Francisco Panama-Pacific Exposition of 1915 that celebrated the completion of the Panama Canal. The St. Louis World's Fair of 1904, a celebration of the Louisiana Purchase, was in fact America's first extracontinental imperialist pageant, and it displayed the country's new colonial possession with six Philippine villages, the dog-eating Igorots prompting especial excitement. That kind of ethnographic display, which we can trace back at least as far as William Clarke's Western museum (established in St. Louis in 1816), also took place in San Francisco. But another connection between the fairs, rather between some of the events they celebrate, strikes me as the more pertinent means of gaining access to the problematic of imperial prosthesis. In the Spanish-American War, the *Oregon's* difficulty making its way from Puget Sound to Santiago provoked the kind of governmental and popular enthusiasm for the engineering project that helped Roosevelt accomplish what had been an international ambition since the sixteenth century, when Charles V imagined a canal, an ambition made practicable once Humboldt, in the early nineteenth century, had completed his studies of the isthmus. Needless to add, the transisthmian transport of treasures back to Europe (and the transport of California gold to the East) had long transformed the region into an imperialist vortex, especially after the midcentury completion of the transisthmian railroad. Following the bankruptcy of the private French endeavor and Great Britain's capitulation to U.S. interests in 1901, the Hay-Herrán treaty with Colombia in 1903 secured U.S. privilege to build the canal. The Colombia government's failure to ratify the treaty provoked Panamanian independence (an intermittent struggle since 1838), swift American intervention, Roosevelt's instant recognition of the revolutionary government, and the U.S. government's purchase of the New Panama Canal Company's property.[40] Just as the young Herbert Hoover, in his role as publicist for the San Francisco fair, thought of California itself as expressing "the last great conflict of these [northern and southern] races for the land," the completion of the canal itself was thought of as resolving an international conflict with clear U.S. hemispheric domination.[41] But this resolution, it should be emphasized, depended foremost on capital investment, the diplomatic system (however scandalous), labor management, and technological know-how—not on the sort of manliness that supposedly characterized the triumph over Spain. With the support of the United States, Panama's revolution had succeeded without casualties; work on the canal succeeded as a triumph of American artifice.

A celebration of this triumph—the complex excavation and the lock and dam construction that had taken more than ten years to complete— the fair, in the tradition of world expositions, also boasted a decade's "inspiring" inventions: "'Wireless,' 'radium,' 'automobile,' 'aeroplane,' 'Diesel engine,' 'high tension current,'" as one list began.[42] Besides the aviation acrobatics, two particular feats were singled out for special attention: President Wilson's switching the fair "on" from Arlington, Virginia ("an ethereal impulse spanned the continent in an instant") and the transcontinental "telephony," allowing fairgoers to hear the headlines, the weather report, and phonograph music from New York.[43] Almost unimaginably novel, these instances of time-space compression at once mechanically extend the human body and effectively disembody presidential power and the human voice. But accompanying this triumphant invisibility was a new cult of the visible, enacted through the cinematic image. Reporters were struck by the degree to which film (including a movie about building the transcontinental telephone line) had come to permeate a world exhibition. The "publicity experts," as Geddes Smith argued, "have not lost sight of the fact that this is the first great exposition since the popularization of moving pictures"; these included foreign, federal, and state advertising, as well as films at the Ford, Heinz, and U.S. Steel exhibits that displayed the inner workings of their plants and the happiness of their workers. As another commentator suggested, motion pictures had "become the servant of industry no less than they are the handmaid of drama."[44]

But if "moving pictures," "aeroplanes," and transcontinental "telephony" inspired admiration, it was the mechanized, $500,000 reproduction of the Panama Canal itself, exhibited in the "Zone" (San Francisco's version of Chicago's Midway), that inspired something like awe (figures 3 and 4). One "of the most remarkable reproductions ever seen," the canal left viewers agreeing with "the advertisements" that said, now "'you do not need to visit the Canal itself.'"[45] This sort of hyperreality achieved by the diversion—no one needed to see the real canal to know that they did not really need to see it—may well have resulted from its prefiguration of aerial cinematography, its anticipation of the visual experience that inventions at the fair were beginning to produce within the everyday: "one can almost imagine he is taking an aeroplane trip over the Isthmus of Panama. A birdseye view of the entire country is obtained as the moving platform slowly conveys one over the five-acre tract of land upon which has been constructed this clever piece of engineering work."[46] More exactly, the simulacrum makes authoritative sense because the fully mechanized mode of display corresponds to the newly mechanized mode of empire: machines represent machines. And as a gigantic miniature, showing the machinery at work, it could help appease the fear that the machinery of the canal was simply "too gigantic to be workable"; it could, like any miniature, present a transcendence that erases history and causality; and it could establish the proper power relation between spectator and spectacle, with the commodified image mimicking the commodified territorial possession that the Canal Zone itself had

Figure 3. Postcard of the fair's Panama Canal.

Figure 4. Postcard of the fair's Panama Canal.

become.[47] The exhibit's production of an aerialized, globalizing point of view had already been suggested by a Philadelphia *Inquirer* cartoonist in 1906, representing Roosevelt's "personal observation" of the canal site: rather than portraying any personal contact with officials or workers, as countless photographs did, the cartoon suspends the presidential figure

Figure 5. "Inspecting the Ditch," Philadelphia *Inquirer*, 1906. (Reprinted by Albert Shaw, *A Cartoon History of Roosevelt's Career* [New York, 1910]).

above the canal, and afar from it, attaining visual contact with Panama via the telescope and remaining in contact with Taft via "wireless messages." The Bull Moose here hovers as the prosthetically empowered emperor (figure 5).

On the one hand, the exhibit mechanically perfects what Mary Louise Pratt has described as "the face of the country" topos that characterized travel writing from the beginning of the nineteenth century: the landscape appears to present itself to an agentless beholder; travelers appear to be "a collective moving eye on which the sights/sites register."[48] On the other hand, the reality effect of the model canal recalls the faked newsreel footage of the Spanish-American War and the San Francisco Earthquake, the latter employing an elaborate model. More significantly, for the "crowds" whose numbers swelled as Easterners canceled their trips to an embattled Europe, the exhibit develops a territorializing, even militarized optical formation, producing a new truth effect that is akin to what Paul Virilio has termed the "logistics of military perception," crystallized by the European war. Over and against the local panoramas provided by the Eiffel

Figure 6. Postcard of the Aeroscope.

Tower, the Ferris Wheel, and San Francisco's own Aeroscope (figure 6), the canal exhibit provides "aerial aim" at Central America. For Virilio, "cinema and aviation seemed to form a single moment. By 1914 aviation was ceasing to be strictly a means of flying and breaking records. . . . [I]t was becoming one way, or perhaps even the ultimate way of *seeing*."[49] As a diversion at the fair, "The Panama Canal" mediates between a residual and an emergent, prosthetic mode of imperialist perception.

We can return now to *Ralph 124C 41+* and recognize that, despite Gernsback's involvement with radio, the novel concerns itself foremost with technologized visualization. In Ralph's house, a 650-foot glass cylinder, he works in the top floor, looking out on the passing "transoceanic" and "trans-continental" airliners, sharing their perspective on New York (40). In both the aerocabs and his space ship, the scientist achieves the *seeing* Virilio describes. Inventions of the day, such as the *Subatlantic Tube*, establish global connection (in this case, between New York and Brest, France), but the Telephot, a television phone, establishes

Ralph's visual contact with the rest of the world, just as his *Tele-Theater* (relying on "composite Telephot plates" to project a "perfect" full-scale illusion) brings live opera into his home, connecting the voice with the face (86). In this case, the aerialized world picture finds its complement in the close-up. For Ralph, "personal observation" is both distant and immediate; the "ultimate way of seeing" is to see the city and the world in miniature and from above, *and* to see the people of the world face to face. The prostheticized, aerial point of view does not erase the full-scale image of the human.

Despite the fair's display of technological marvels (and despite the fact that a hydroelectrical magnate, Charles C. Moore, served as chairman of the Panama Exposition Company), the official poster for the fair, Perham Nahl's "The Thirteenth Labor of Hercules," displays nothing technological (figure 7). Instead, it shows a muscled, naked, Michelangelesque hero forcing apart a pastoral Culebra Cut to create the canal—or, as Frank Todd, the fair's official historian, phrased it, "thrusting apart the continental barrier at Panama to let the world through to the Pacific and incidentally to the . . . Exposition, whose fair domes and pinnacles rise mistily beyond."[50] If such engineering marvels as the Crystal Palace and the Eiffel Tower were emblems of "progress," here it is instead a transcendental hero who emblematizes "power." And while colossal women (like Liberty, Columbia, and the Republic) typically symbolize the American nation, the male colossus now symbolizes the mechanical, international triumph.[51] The poster produces an antithetical point of view from that produced by the model canal exhibition: a terrestrial (even subterrestrial) enlargement inverts the aerial miniaturization; the gigantic body becomes the visual alternative to the miniature machinery of the Zone that operated "without" human bodies. This classical body subsumes the work of the 30–40,000 "white and negro workmen," primarily West Indians, employed to construct the canal (Todd, 18). It aestheticizes labor into the abstraction of "the thirteenth labor." But it simultaneously concretizes labor, rearticulating what Marx called the "many-sided play of the muscles" that is lost within a mechanized labor system.[52] Above all, it occults the mechanical achievement by refiguring the decade-long canal construction as the gesture of the individual, who is *whole* without being *part* of a labor, technological, or military force—without being a "tool of the government." While Todd admired the poster, it occasioned his complaint that the "literary language" used to describe the fair had become a "sheer mispresentation," concealing "the real wonders of the work" (Todd, 20).[53]

Figure 7. The Hercules poster, from Frank Morton Todd's *The Story of the Exposition.*
(San Francisco, 1921)

According to the Theweleit paradigm, work on the canal might be understood as part of the era's regulation of bodily (and psychic) flows and the "transcendence of a female/nature."[54] But Hercules, here, as a symbol of that construction (and despite a genital reading that the poster readily prompts), would seem instead to allegorize capital, or "the capitalist machine," in more strict accordance with Deleuze and Guattari's anti-oedipal romance. By this I mean that the poster figures not regulation, but a moment of deterritorialization—an opening up of borders, a facilitation of the flow of energy, money, and goods—before capital's "ancillary apparatuses, such as government bureaucracies and the forces of law and order, do their most to reterritorialize [that opening], absorbing in the process a larger and larger share of surplus value."[55] American history, read as this romance, might posit the completion of the Canal Zone with its military fortification and then the reproduction of the Zone within the Fair's Zone as premiere moments of reterritorializing mastery in which the territorializing gaze itself is finally offered for sale. For critics of the fair, wondering if "the exposition is anything more than a department store in costume," it was especially lamentable that the fair was meant to "Exploit the World," that "human achievement" had been put up "in individual packages for the world to come and take."[56] In the case of the model canal, moreover, the fair exploited the world by selling it the American production of "the world," and the world's access to the world. It is in this sense that, even if we no longer accept the simplicity of Marx's claim that the ideas of the ruling class are always the ruling ideas, we are still confronted, in the fairs that were funded by the nation's millionaires, with specific sites ruled by those ideas—or, more precisely, with "international exhibitions" where those ideas are deployed as and consumable as *internationality itself*.

While the official poster for the fair thus embodies both abstract and concrete labor, both deterritorialization and reterritorialization, it also embodies a dialectic of the national and international that characterizes the history of both the fair's and the canal's representation. On the one hand, the poster seems locatable in a national imaginary, wherein the nation endures a perpetual mirror-stage, requiring that its actual heterogeneity be integrated in the sight of a single body that appears (like Roosevelt, like the imperialist body) as the nation's own coherent (male) corporeality. On the other hand, this classical body denationalizes the engineering achievement, representing it as an international (natural and supernatural) event rather than as a complicated nationalist and imperialist project, fraught by counternationalisms, senate debates, political corruption, and mud slides. Describing the "monumental contrast" between the war and the exhibition, one report explained that each "is in its way an unexampled exhibition of war," one "a war between different races of mankind," the other "a war waged by the whole human race" against the forces of nature.[57] The fair itself, the guidebooks maintained, is "the celebration, not of San Francisco, not of the Pacific Coast, not merely of the United States, but of the whole world"; it is the celebration of "a race of people in the making" that can be traced back to Athens, Pericles, and Themistocles. At the same time, the fair represents, very specifically, "a Great American Achievement."[58]

Ironic as this internationalist nationalism may seem, given that the Klan revived in 1915 and that both anti-German and anti-Jewish sentiment had been provoked by the war, such accounts of the fair simply replay the accounts of the country's intervention in Colombia, understood as the "consummation of five centuries of effort to find or make a direct westerly route from Europe to the Orient."[59] As Roosevelt himself described the events in 1913, "the enterprise was recognized everywhere as responding to an international need"; the support of Panama, equated with the support of the canal, fulfilled responsibilities not just to the United States, but "to the civilized world which imperatively demanded that there should be no further delay in beginning the work."[60] Familiar as this internationalist nationalism has now become—ratified by World War I and revoiced ceaselessly during the Gulf Crisis—it should be recognized as a significant break from the "manifest destiny" that "propelled" the United States to California: for the country is now said to serve, and to embody the will of, something like the "world." The point is not, as it was in the Philippines, to help the natives, but to help all the peoples of the globe. Familiarly, Frank Todd, summarizing the history of the canal in his history of the fair, traces that history back to Balboa and argues that the transisthmian route is "in a very large sense, the gift of the United States to the world, America's contribution to world harmony." Nonetheless, his subsequent chapter begins by quoting G. W. Goethals, chairman and chief engineer of the commission, who explains that "our primary purpose in building the Canal was not commercial but military: to make sure that no battleship of ours would ever have to sail around South America" (Todd, 18, 20). Just as the body inevitably reappears, giganticized, in the machine-body dialectic of the fair and science fiction, so too, in the world-nation dialectic, the nation finally asserts its priority over any global flow. Goethals asserts a distinction between military aggression and economic gain as a way to assert a distinction between the national and the international.

"Modernity" was sequestered in the fair's Joy Zone or architecturally contained by "Spanish Gothic" buildings such as the Palace of Machines, and "modernism" was confined to the fine art exhibit. Guidebooks for the fair, carefully explicating such *outdoor* friezes and statues as "Natural Selection" and the "Survival of the Fittest," were stumped by the "ultramodern experience" of futurist canvases.[61] But it is not quite the work of the futurists, but Duchamp's *Nude Descending a Staircase*, exhibited at the Armory show two years earlier, that strikes me as the appropriate analogical antithesis to "The Thirteenth Labor of Hercules." For if we read Duchamp's painting not just as the reflection of modern "fragmentation," but as a composite of the photographic studies performed by Marey, Eakins, and Muybridge (from which both scientific management and film emerge), then Hercules, the classical embodiment of technological progress, can be read as nostalgically resuturing this technologized and scientized body.

The center of the exhibition's celebration of technology was the Court of Ages, constituted by a cluster of buildings displaying scientific and mechanical progress: the Palaces of Transportation, Manufacture, Varied Industries, Mines and Metallurgy, and Machinery. For the center of the court, Robert Aiken designed a fountain, from the center of which rose a sculpture, "Destiny": on either side of upright human figures lay, in the sculptor's own words, "a symbolized Destiny in the shape of two enormous arms and hands, giving life with the one and taking with the other."[62] To the degree that "Destiny" participated in the fair's general Herculean theme, to the degree that it (metaphorically) signifies "man the tool-user" and (synecdochically) the whole of Hercules, it accomplishes the same work of displacement and occlusion as the poster itself. But of course Aiken's statue has also fragmented the body and autonomized the body's parts, in such a way that, like *The Thieving Hand*, it may be said to manifest, rather than occlude, the corporeal designs of Taylorization and the effects of machinery on the human. The statue overcomes historical disjunction in its deployment of classicism, but it marks an experiential disjunction that Jameson, for one, associates with modernism: "an objective fragmentation of the so-called outside world" stands as the precondition for the "coming into existence of hitherto unimaginable levels of abstraction," crucially exemplified, in his account, by impressionism, the isolation of perception "as a semi-autonomous activity."[63] In this respect, Michael Fried's redescription of the "impressionist" project—where Crane and Norris, for instance, isolate not seeing, but *writing*, and metaphorize the act of writing in the representation of human disfigurement—could be recognized as an account of the writers' *own* disfigurement, the autonomization of the hand (and its relation to the pen and page). Such a recognition would be buttressed by Friedrich Kittler's account of how the typewriter, circa 1900, disintegrates the writing process, differentiating the physicality of writing from itself, distancing the eye from the hand, the hand from the page.[64] And it is as though, at the Panama-Pacific Exposition, this version of the body-machine, part-whole dialectic were also recognized and resolved in Underwood's contribution to the fair: a fourteen-ton typewriter, each key the size of a chair, generally photographed with visitors sitting on the keys. The (fully functioning) machine functions as a monumental synecdochic completion of "Destiny," reintegrating the human body at the site of technology. The whole body comes to signify (indeed, to act as) the body part, the finger.

Plotting Race in the Post-Prosthetic Empire

In 1910 an article in *Scientific American,* trying to think beyond the way the "similarity between living organisms and machines" had been traditionally described, explained "certain peculiarities of machines by reference to facts which are well known and familiar in connection with living creatures," such as the "theory of the origin of species."[65] Unwittingly, the essay intimates a world where machines, Marx's virtuosos, assume a life of their own, obeying their own evolutionary laws without regard for the human. In contrast, it was the more traditional law of survival that the statuary throughout the San Francisco fair made explicit. And at the fair's Race Betterment Conference, organized by David Starr Jordan, eugenicists modernized the study of race to assert more precisely the specifically human law of survival. Revisions to the Binet scale promised to measure racial intelligence scientifically; the new cephalic index became, for influential figures like Madison Grant, the "best method of determining race."[66] These formed the literal component of what Walter Benn Michaels has termed a "new technology for identifying white people" that appeared in the aftermath of *Plessy v. Ferguson,* wherein the correspondence of color and race was undone.[67] And that technology appeared in the aftermath of modern production's effective obliteration of racial characteristics, corresponding to what Kracauer called the "obliteration of national characteristics."[68] The issue is not just, in Taylor's formulation, that "an intelligent gorilla" could, scientifically managed, perform more efficiently than any self-managed worker (40)—a comment that actually returns us to the violation of the species barrier—but also that the autonomized body part, like abstract human motion, like abstract labor, is not available as a site for racial inscription. In a sense, it is just such a problem, intensified by a mechanized mode of production, that *The Steam-Man* foresaw and forestalled by representing machinery as a whole body, and as a black body.[69] Of course, Taylor's conceptualization of the worker as a machine that is part of a machine was meant to transcend ideological and class conflict. But for the eugenicists, racial conflict was the only way to make industrial progress make sense. For Jordan, efficiency, like aggression, could account for Anglo-American expansion into "lands scantily occupied by barbarous races."[70]

Yet, in the face of the universalizing claims of modernity, science fiction works toward replacing the "or" in Jordan's "peoples more efficient or aggressive" with an underscored "*and*" to stabilize social hierarchies with reference to instinct.[71] And the genre itself preserves the equation between physiognomy and race to clarify racial conflict, without which the imperial body could not exhibit its aggressive instinct, without which that body would be non-narratable. The scopic regime of *Ralph 124C 41+*, I want to emphasize now, allows its hero to see, via the Telephot, the faces of the villains who will launch the melodrama: Fernand, with his eyes too close together and his cunning mouth; and the Martian, instantly recognizable, with his "great black horse eyes in the long, melancholy face" and his "elongated slightly pointed ears." The latter's intractable sexual appetite, typically Martian, provokes him to circumvent the law against "the intermarriage of Martians and Terrestrials" (45). He abducts Alice. Ralph, his own sexual appetite just discovered, finally rescues her. The somatic semiosis with which the novel produces race and its attendant sexuality is a semiosis that is everywhere contested. Fernand employs a "Cloak of Invisibility"; Ralph himself projects an artificial comet to confuse the Martian; and science in the year 2660 challenges most notions of physicality (as does science in 1915 when it discovers, for instance, that "if our eyes were sensitive to ultraviolet light only, all men would be negroes, so far as color is concerned").[72] But in Ralph's hands, technology finally exposes "true" physicality. The Martian, within the future metropolis, appears as an embodiment of what Huston Baker has called the "black phallus"—"a symbol of the unconstrained force that white men contradictorily envy and seek to destroy."[73] The novel assures its readers that even in the unimaginable future that phallus will still exist, visibly, in relation to which American white masculinity can perpetually reconstitute itself.

Regarding the historical moment of the text's production, we can argue that its racism, its insistence on racial conflict, works to undermine the nationalized and racialized division of labor exemplified by work on the Panama Canal, where, let us say, the American mind managed West Indian hands. More generally, this conflict works to upend a set of dualisms—abstract/concrete, mind/body, culture/nature—that characterize what Nancy Harstock has called "abstract masculinity"; in other words, the text offers an oxymoronic, idealized, "concrete" masculinity.[74] That ideal, presented as an embodied global power, most explicitly appears in England's *Darkness and Dawn* trilogy, an extended American example of what Patrick Brantlinger has termed "invasion scare-scare stories, in which the outward movement of imperialist adventure is reversed."[75] *Darkness and Dawn* (1912) records the perils of an engineer and a stenographer who wake up in a New York skyscraper to find themselves the last two humans alive in a world that has been destroyed by an "Epic of Death." They are soon attacked by "demoniac hordes" of black, ape-like creatures with a "trace of the Mongol," and Allan Stern, believing himself to be "the only white man living in the twenty-eighth century," must defend himself and the woman he grows to love against racial extinction (108, 103). Facing a world "gone to pieces the way Liberia and Haiti and Santo Domingo once did when white rule ceased," Stern nurtures his "deep-seated love for the memory of the race" (112, 113). Finally, in the last of the novels, *The Afterglow*, he establishes a new social system among the other survivors (the so-called "Folk") where people are free because of the proliferation of scientific thought and the introduction of the English language, that "magnificent language, so rich and pure," its purity mirroring the racial purity achieved once Stern achieves "the extermination of the Horde" (645). But only in relation to that horde, only in the face of civilization's demise, does Allan Stern retrieve the ideals of "labor and exploration" and transform himself from the "man of science and cold fact" into a man who can feel the "atavistic passions" and the aggression that racial conflict provokes. The engineer's piloting skill makes "man and biplane [seem] almost one organism" (458), the prosthetic ideal, but the novel vigorously differentiates the human organism from machine culture. While *The Steam-Man* technologically restores a postwar body by rearticulating antebellum race relations, *The Afterglow* restores a post-technological body by reformulating the conditions of original conquest. Stern recognizes, as the novel comes to a close, that the "reconquest of the entire continent" remains to be accomplished, that indeed there is still the "whole world to reconquer" (665, 664).

The trilogy thus shares the traditional image of empire as, in Amy Kaplan's words, "the site for recuperating a primitive corporeality" (664) —in this case, a site in which being-with-others conditions the self's recognition of its bodily self, an arena of conflict in which the eugenic body makes sense. But more specifically, reconquest, racial conquest, becomes the condition for transcending the division between mental and manual labor, for reestablishing labor as the ground of American selfhood, and for marking an engineer's globalizing power with his body. It is hardly surprising, then, that Burroughs's Pellucidar series, beginning with *At the Earth's Core* (1914) and *Pellucidar* (1915), redivides mental and manual labor between generations and inverts the division provided by *The Steam-Man*. Abner Perry, a middle-aged amateur inventor, brings technology to the primitive peoples living underground. But it is the young David Innes, son of a mine owner, who performs a set of herculean labors, combats a host of underworld creatures, and finds himself elected emperor. In the earth's hollow center, the new empire is governed by the young American physique. Reading Burroughs's science fiction as a way to complete the other half of that project we now call "taking Tarzan seriously"—the "attempt to imagine the primitive as a source of empowerment"—amounts to imagining science and technology as insufficiently empowering.[76]

By the time that modern art was "marked by Americanism," by the time that Americanism and Taylorism had become synonymous and international,[77] and by the time that the canal marked American expansion as a technological accomplishment, only extreme temporal or geographic displacement could support that imagination. Burroughs's Martian novels explicitly thematize this displacement as the attempt to find a place for the anachronistic body. *The Princess of Mars* describes Carter as a Virginian who fought in the Civil War and then found himself a captain "in the cavalry of an army which no longer existed." He has ventured west and become a successful prospector, and from there he is mysteriously projected to Mars, this planet of war becoming the new site for American aggression (9–10). His strength and prowess enable him to resolve the conflict between the red and green races of Mars, to liberate the greenmen from their despotic ruler, to become a war lord, and to defend the princess he loves from repeated assault. He discovers, with the sort of certainty only dreamt of at the Race Betterment Conference, that the red and green races of Mars can be traced back to one "very dark, almost black" race and one "reddish yellow race" (62). And it is the threat of interracial abduction that he must prevent, saving the almost humanoid Martian princess from the sexual assault of a bestial green jeddack. While, in Owen Wister's *Virginian* (1902), the southern hero refashions southern chivalry and heroism within the confines of a Wyoming ranching economy, Burroughs's Virginian reclaims the full romance of the South, but only by moving beyond the boundaries of the nation and of the world. Like Dixon's *The Clansmen* (1905), *The Princess of Mars* depicts a white southern male reestablishing racial order, but for Burroughs this is no new birth of a nation. Rather, the genre recognizes that only beyond the modern nation, and beyond modernity's internation, will the recognizable American reappear.

At the close of *The Master Mind of Mars*, when that mind has been defeated by the American body, Ulysses Paxton finally meets John Carter. The soldier from the war where, as one analyst puts it, "the machine gun sealed the fate of horsed cavalry" meets the cavalryman from a war that first accelerated American mass production.[78] They recognize one another not just as humans, not just as speakers of English, but as Americans: "A countryman?" John Carter asks; "Yes, an American," Paxton replies (492). Nationality itself becomes all but physiognomically recognizable, overcoming what Benedict Anderson has articulated as the difference between nationalism, "which dreams in terms of historical destinies," and racism's will-to-ahistoricity (136–40).[79] But these national bodies appear only where the nation itself has disappeared; the national body is saved as the nation's expense. *The Master Mind*, which I originally described as a prosthetic fantasy, can finally help us, like *The Steam-Man*, to redescribe the emergence of modern science fiction in America. For despite the genre's depiction of a postprosthetic empire, the genre is of course fundamentally prosthetic, imaginatively repairing the damaged body, the fragmented body, the separated head and hand. The monumental male these texts produce is a body without scars, a body on which history is not written but erased, a body without memory, a national body with no nation. In this respect, the pulp market of the period should itself be defined as a traffic in bodies, or, far more precisely, the traffic in one body, circulating the same eugenic body, making it available for a reader's imaginary inhabitation. These days, since all the demythifications of science have hardly arrested technology's demythification of the human, it's no surprise to read that the recent and "intense fascination with the fate of the body" may well result from the fact that "the body no longer exists."[80] My remarks have certainly reflected that interest. But they've been meant to suggest that this nonexistence has a material history, which one idea of re-embodied empire, contesting the modernization of American global power, struggled to efface.

Notes

I consider these remarks part of an ongoing account of modernity, entitled *American Body Parts, 1910–1915*. The paper was presented at the University of Chicago's Committee on Critical Practice and at Chicago's Humanities Institute, and it has benefited from both subsequent discussions. In particular, I've tried to clarify or elaborate points in response to the generous comments made by Doug Brewster, James K. Chandler, Miriam Hansen, Jay Shleusener, and D. E. Young. Finally, I'd like to thank Peter Sattler for his indefatigable assistance in helping me pursue the research, and Stephen Longmeier for his photographic work.

1 Edgar Rice Burroughs, *Three Martian Novels* (New York: Dover, 1962), p. 364. Further references will be provided in the text.

2 Alfred Sohn-Rethel, *Intellectual and Manual Labour: A Critique of Epistemology*, trans. Martin Sohn-Rethel (Atlantic Highlands, N.J.: Humanities Press, 1978).

3 *Life in the Iron Mills and Other Stories*, ed. Tillie Olsen (New York: Feminist Press, 1985), p. 34. Further references will be provided in the text.

4 Edward Ellis, *The Huge Hunter; or, The Steam Man of the Prairies* (1868? [originally published under the title *The Steam Man of the Prairies*]; New York: Beadle and Adams, 1885), p. 18. The narrator goes on to explain, with the logic of Emersonian compensation, that "if nature afflicts in one direction she frequently makes amends in another direction" (p. 18). Further references will be provided in the text. For an overview of the literary reaction to American technology, see John Kasson, *Civilizing the Machine: Technology and Republican Values in America* (New York: Penguin, 1976).

5 Andreas Huyssen, *After the Great Divide* (Bloomington: Indiana University Press, 1986), pp. 65–81.

6 George Fitzhugh, *Cannibals All! or, Slaves Without Masters*, ed. C. Vann Woodward (Cambridge: Harvard University Press, 1960), p. 160.

7 Fanny Fern, "The Sewing Machine," *The Meridian Anthology of Early American Women Writers*, ed. Katherine M. Rogers (New York: Meridian Books, 1991), p. 408. For discussions of the Frankfurt School account of technology and instrumental reason, see Albrecht Wellmer, *Critical Theory of Society*, trans. John Cumming (New York: Herder and Herder, 1971); Jurgen Habermas, *Toward a Rational Society*, trans. Jeremy J. Shapiro (Boston: Beacon Press, 1970); and Stanley Aronowitz, *Science as Power* (Minneapolis: University of Minnesota Press, 1988).

8 Quoted by Ronald Takaki, *Iron Cages: Race and Culture in 19th-Century*

America (New York: Oxford University Press, 1990), p. 202. Further references to Takaki will be provided in the text.

9 Leslie A. Fiedler, *Love and Death in the American Novel* (New York: Stein and Day, 1982).

10 At the outset of his chapter on "The Consciousness of Self," James asks, "And our bodies themselves, are they simply ours, or are they *us.*" *The Principles of Psychology,* vol. 1, *The Works of William James,* ed. Frederick H. Burkhardt (Cambridge: Harvard University Press, 1981), vol. 1, p. 279.

11 For some sense of the proliferation of the industry, see the "Patent Claims" section of *Scientific American* for the war years. For an account of surgical practice during the war, see Stewart Brooks, *Civil War Medicine* (Springfield, Ill.: Charles C. Thomas, 1966).

12 Oliver Wendell Holmes, "The Human Wheel, Its Spokes and Felloes," *Atlantic Monthly* 11, no. 67 (May 1863): 567–80. For a full description of Frank B. Palmer's artificial leg, see *Science and Mechanism: Illustrated by Example in the New York Exhibition 1853–54,* ed. C. R. Goodrich (New York: G.P. Putnam, 1854), p. 147.

13 While *The Steam-Man* is generally regarded as the first science fiction *novel* in America, many stories, by Poe, Hawthorne, and Melville, among others, had already introduced science fiction into the American literary field. H. Bruce Franklin's interpretive anthology, *Future Perfect* (New York: Oxford, 1966), remains the best introduction to the genre in nineteenth-century America.

14 *A Princess of Mars and A Fighting Man of Mars* (New York: Dover, 1964), p. 5. Further references will be provided in the text.

15 *Darkness and Dawn* (Westport, Conn.: Hyperion Press, 1974), pp. 10, 17. Further references will be provided in the text.

16 *Ralph 124C 41+: A Romance of the Year 2660* (New York: Frederick Fell, 1950), p. 25. Further references will be provided in the text.

17 Veblen is specifically addressing the "disciplinary effect which [the] movement for standardization and mechanical equivalence has upon the human material." Thorstein Veblen, *The Theory of Business Enterprise* (1904; New York: Mentor, 1958), chap. 9. Jean-Joseph Goux, *Symbolic Economies,* trans. Jennifer Curtiss Gage (Ithaca, N.Y.: Cornell University Press, 1990), p. 196.

18 Susan Jeffords, *The Remasculinization of America: Gender and the Vietnam War* (Bloomington: Indiana University Press, 1989). On the romance of the engineer, see Cecelia Tichi, *Shifting Gears: Technology, Literature, Culture in Modernist America* (Chapel Hill: University of North Carolina Press, 1987), pp. 97–170. For a discussion of the way this romance becomes a part of the "critical technology" of the thirties, see Andrew Ross, *Strange Weather* (London: Verso, 1991), pp. 101–35. On the rise of the American corporate vision, see Alan Trachtenberg, *The Incorporation of America: Culture and Society in the Gilded Age* (New York: Hill and Wang, 1982).

19 My understanding of the Canal Zone as an expressly artificial addition to the nation derives from my reading of the "Convention Between the United States and the Republic of Panama for the Construction of a Ship Canal to Connect the Waters of the Atlantic and Pacific Oceans," proclaimed in 1904. Article II, for instance, grants the United States not just "in perpetuity the use, occupation and control" of the zone established for "the construction, maintenance, operation, sanitation and protection of said Canal," but further "the use, occupation and control of any other lands and waters outside of the zone above described which may be necessary and convenient" to accomplish those same tasks. In other words, the U.S. government could effectively assume control of the newly independent nation, but solely in order to sustain its engineering product. *U.S. Department of State Papers Relating to the Foreign Relations of the United States* (Washington: Government Printing Office, 1905), p. 54.

20 For a brief account of the film, see Jon Gartenberg, "The Thieving Hand," *Before Hollywood: Turn-of-the-Century Film from American Archives* (New York: American Federation of Arts, 1986), p. 131.

21 *The Standard Edition of the Complete Psychological Works of Sigmund Freud*, trans. James Strachey (London: Hogarth, 1955), vol. 17, pp. 226, 244.

22 See Kaja Silverman's analysis of the post-WW II film, *The Best Years of Our Lives*, in "Historical Trauma and Male Subjectivity," *Psychoanalysis and Cinema*, ed. E. Ann Kaplan (London: Routledge, 1990), pp. 110–27.

23 *Karl Marx: Selected Writings*, ed. David McLellan (New York: Oxford University Press, 1977), pp. 379, 373.

24 "Improved Artificial Limbs," *Scientific American* 72 (January 26, 1895): 52. See as well "The Manufacture of Artificial Limbs," *Scientific American* 73 (August 3, 1895): 1.

25 Siegfried Giedion, *Mechanization Takes Command* (1948; New York: Norton, 1969), p. 103. And see David F. Noble, *Science by Design: Science, Technology, and the Rise of Corporate Capitalism* (New York: Knopf, 1977), pp. 69–83.

26 Henri Lefebvre, *The Production of Space*, trans. Donald Nicholson-Smith (Oxford: Basil Blackwell, 1991), p. 204. Further references will be provided in the text.

27 *The Principles of Scientific Management* (New York: Norton, 1967), pp. 5, 125. Further references will be provided in the text.

28 We can understand one particular invention of Ralph's, allowing him to read while he sleeps, not only as compensating for human limitation, but also as rationalizing the unconscious, especially if we understand the text that he reads, *The Odyssey*, as an ancient account of the triumph of "regulative reason." See Max Horkheimer and Theodor W. Adorno, *Dialectic of Enlightenment*, trans. John Cumming (New York: Continuum, 1982), pp. 43–80.

29 D. A. Sargent, "The Physical Proportions of the Typical Man" (1887), *The Out of Door Library: Athletic Sports* (New York: Charles Scribner's Sons, 1897), pp. 13–26.

30 William Matthews, "Physical Culture" (1871), reprinted in *Getting On in the World; or, Hints on Success in Life* (Chicago: S.C. Griggs, 1877), p. 58; William Blaikie, *How to Get Strong and Stay So* (1879; New York: Harper and Brothers, 1883), p. 27.

31 See John Higham, "The Reorientation of American Culture in the 1890s," *Writing American History: Essays on Modern Scholarship* (Bloomington: University of Indiana Press, 1973), pp. 73–100. England and Germany stood as the contemporaneous exemplars of somatic nationality's success, Ancient Greece as the historical ideal. France and America joined in the hope of regenerating nations by regenerating bodies to the point where, as Robert Nye suggests, Pierre de Coubertin's organization of the modern Olympics in 1896, part of the French "explosion of physical activity," must be considered "nothing less" than the most obvious manifestation of a desire for "the regeneration of the French race itself." "Degeneration and the Medical Model of Cultural Crisis in the French *Belle Epoque*," *Political Symbolism in Modern Europe: Essays in Honor of George L. Mosse*, ed. Seymour Drescher, et al. (New Brunswick: Transaction Books, 1982), p. 33. Interimperialist rivalry helped solidify the national "race" (the French "race," the German "race"), and the Darwinian and Spencerian models of evolution, on the one hand, the Helmholtzian theory of energy on the other, authorized "the scientific basis" for a transformation from "moral" to "physical" models of degeneracy in both Europe and America. See, in the same volume, Anson Robinbach, "The Body Without Fatigue: A Nineteenth-Century Utopia," pp. 42–62, now reprinted in *The Human Motor: Energy, Fatigue, and the Origins of Modernity* (New York: Basic Books, 1990). And see Tim Armstrong, "The Electrification of the Body at the Turn of the Century," *Textual Practice* 5, no. 3 (Winter 1991): 303–25.

32 This understanding of the eugenic body is borrowed from "An Introduction to Eugenics," by Roswell H. Johnson, the introduction to his essay on "The Evolution of Man and Its Control," *Popular Science Monthly* 76 (January 1910): 49.

33 Timothy Brennan, "The National Longing for Form," *Nation and Narration*, ed. Homi Bhabha (London: Routledge, 1990), p. 49. Benedict Anderson, *Imagined Communities: Reflections on the Origin and Spread of Nationalism* (London: Verso, 1983), pp. 28–40. Further references to Anderson will be provided in the text.

34 David Harvey, *The Condition of Postmodernity* (Oxford: Basil Blackwell, 1989), pp. 260–83. In Lefebvre's version of the argument, the Great War "was the first sign that a world market was at last becoming established, and the earliest figure of the 'world'" (p. 302).

35 Roland Robertson, "Mapping the Global Condition: Globalization as the Central Concept," *Theory and Society* 7, nos. 2–3 (June 1990): 19.

36 See Donna Haraway, "Teddy Bear Patriarchy: Taxidermy in the Garden of Eden, New York City, 1908–1936," in this volume, and Robert W. Rydell, *All the World's a Fair: Visions of Empire at American International Expositions, 1876–1916* (Chicago: University of Chicago Press, 1984).

37 For a discussion of the spectacle of masculinity during the Spanish-American War and in the romances of the period, see Amy Kaplan, "Romancing the Empire: The Embodiment of American Masculinity in the Popular Historical Novel of the 1890s," *American Literary History* 2, no. 4 (Winter 1990): 659–90. Further references will be provided in the text.

38 Williams Carlos Williams, *Selected Essays* (New York: New Directions, 1954), pp. 116, 119.

39 Fredric Jameson, "Modernism and Imperialism," *Nationalism, Colonialism, and Literature* (Minneapolis: University of Minnesota Press, 1990), pp. 43–66.

40 With a timing that bespeaks the U.S. interference, the navy and marines arrived *as* the uprising began. For a brief account of the revolution, see Lawrence O. Ealy, *Yanqui Politics and the Isthmian Canal* (University Park, Pa.: Pennsylvania State University Press, 1971), pp. 59–70. For a full account of the canal's history, see David McCullough, *The Path Between the Seas: The Creation of the Panama Canal, 1870–1914* (New York: Simon and Schuster, 1977). For an account of American involvements in Panama, see Walter LaFeber, *The Panama Canal: The Crisis in Historical Perspective* (New York: Oxford, 1979).

41 Quoted by Rydell, p. 211.

42 French Strother, "The Panama-Pacific International Exposition," *World's Work* 30, no. 3 (July 1915): 350–51.

43 Strother, p. 353.

44 Geddes Smith, "A Shop Window of Civilization," *Independent* 82, no. 3473 (June 28, 1915): 535; Strother, p. 354. Movie producers also made use of the fair, and Lewis Selznick promoted the exposition with films shown across North America. See Rydell, pp. 231–32, who quotes D. W. Griffith (as reported by the *San Francisco Chronicle*) hoping to perpetuate the fair "in photography," "something stupendous . . . a film drama that will mark another leap forward as great as that of 'The Birth of a Nation.'" The Griffith film that merged out of his delight in the fair was, as Miriam Hansen argues, *Intolerance*. See *From Babel to Babylon* (Cambridge: Harvard University Press, 1991), pp. 237–38.

45 "The Spectator at the World's Fair," *Outlook* 109 (April 14, 1915): 897.

46 *The Red Book of Views of the Panama-Pacific International Exposition* (San Francisco: Official Exposition View Book Publisher, 1915), n.p.

47 "Is the Mechanism of the Panama Canal Locks Too Gigantic to be Workable?" *Current Opinion* 57, no. 2 (August 1914): 11–12. On the miniature, see Susan Stewart, *On Longing: Narratives of the Miniature, the Gigantic, the Souvenir, the Collection* (Baltimore: Johns Hopkins University Press, 1984), p. 60.

48 Mary Louise Pratt, *Imperial Eyes: Travel Writing and Transculturation* (New York: Routledge, 1992), p. 59.

49 Paul Virilio, *War and Cinema: The Logistics of Perception*, trans. Patrick Camiller (London: Verso, 1989), pp. 1–30. On the films of the war and the earthquake, see Raymond Fielding, *The American Newsreel, 1911–1967*, chaps. 2–3.

50 Frank Morton Todd, *The Story of the Exposition: Being the Official History* *of the International Celebration Held at San Francisco in 1915 to Commemorate the Discovery of the Pacific Ocean and the Construction of the Panal Canal*, 5 vols. (New York: G. P. Putnam's Sons, 1921), vol. 3, p. 20. Further references will be provided in the text.

51 See Martha Banta, *Imaging American Women: Idea and Ideals in Cultural History* (New York: Columbia University Press, 1987), pp. 499–552.

52 *Capital* (New York: International Publishers, 1967), vol. 1, p. 398.

53 One literary use of the figure of Hercules, however, Rubén Darío's 1903 poem "To Roosevelt," conflating the president and the nation as the *fuerte cazador*, naming America's intervention a "conspiracy of Hercules" inspired by greed, managed to reveal exactly what the poster veils. The poem is quoted by Ramsey Clark, "We Never Heard the Truth," *The U.S. Invasion of Panama: The Truth Behind Operation 'Just Cause'*, prepared by the Independent Commission of Inquiry on the U.S. Invasion of Panama (Boston: South End Press, 1991), p. 11.

54 Mark Seltzer provides such an understanding of the canal in *Bodies and Machines* (New York: Routledge, 1992), p. 164. Seltzer's general discussion of the "body-machine complex" explores a different archive and asserts different conclusions from the present essay, but it is a crucial account of the problematics of American technology in the early twentieth century.

55 Gilles Deleuze and Félix Guattari, *Anti-Oedipus: Capitalism and Schizophrenia*, trans. Robert Hurley et al. (Minneapolis: University of Minnesota Press, 1983), p. 34.

56 Geddes Smith, p. 534.

57 "The European War and the Panama-Pacific Exposition—A Monumental Contrast," *Current Opinion* 58, no. 5 (May 1915): 315.

58 *On the Shores of the Pacific: Opening of the Panama Canal—1915* (San Francisco, 1915?), n.p.

59 Forbes Lindsay, *Panama and the Canal Today: An Historical Account* (1911; Boston: L.C. Page, 1926), p. 1. And see Frank A. Gause and Charles Carl Carr, *The Story of Panama: The New Route To India* (1912; New York: Arno Press, 1970), chap. 1.

60 *Theodore Roosevelt—An Autobiography* (1913; New York: Da Capo, 1985), p. 534.

61 Rose V. S. Berry, *The Dream City, Its Art in Story and Symbolism* (San Francisco: Walter N. Brunt, 1915), p. 288. For discussions of the art at the fair, see Elizabeth N. Armstrong, "Hercules and the Muses: Public Art of the Fair," and George Starr, "Truth Unveiled: The Panama-Pacific International Exposition and Its Interpreters," both collected in Burton Benedict, *The Anthropology of World's Fairs: San Francisco's Panama Pacific International Exposition of 1915* (Berkeley: Scolar Press, 1983).

62 *The Blue Book: A Comprehensive Souvenir Book of the Panama Pacific International Exposition at San Francisco* (San Francisco: Robert A. Reid, Official Publishers of View Books, 1915), p. 43.

63 Fredric Jameson, *The Political Unconscious: Narrative as a Socially Symbolic Act* (Ithaca, N.Y.: Cornell University Press, 1981), pp. 229–30.

64 Michael Fried, "Almayer's Face: On 'Impressionism' in Conrad, Crane, and Norris," *Critical Inquiry* 17 (Autumn 1990): 193–236. Friedrich A. Kittler, *Discourse/Networks 1800/1900*, trans. Michael Meteer and Chris Cullen (Stanford: Stanford University Press, 1990), pp. 177–205.

65 Whilhelm Ostwald, "Machines and Living Creatures, Lifeless and Living Transformers of Energy," *Scientific American Supplement* 1803 (July 23, 1910): 55. The article is a translation from the German.

66 Madison Grant, *The Passing of the Great Race, or The Racial Basis of European History* (New York: Charles Scribner's Sons, 1916), p. 17. The Binet scale was soon used to test the racial intelligence of WW I soldiers. See Thomas F. Gossett, *Race: The History of an Idea in America* (New York: Schocken Books, 1963), pp. 365–69.

67 Walter Benn Michaels, "The Souls of White Folk," in *Literature and the Body: Essays on Populations and Persons,* ed. Elaine Scarry (Baltimore: Johns Hopkins University Press, 1988), p. 193.

68 Siegfried Kracauer, "The Mass Ornament" (1927), trans. Barbara Correll and Jack Zipes, *New German Critique* 5 (Spring 1975): 69.

69 And in a sense, when the train has been remetaphorized as an "octopus," rather than as an "iron horse," the rhetorical possibilities for identifying technology as an individual, rather than as a system, have disappeared.

70 David Starr Jordan, "Biological Effects of Race Movements," *Popular Science Monthly* 87 (September 1915): 267.

71 As Immanuel Wallerstein has argued with respect to contemporary world culture, "racism/sexism" inevitably appears as a way to combat universalization. "Culture as the Ideological Battleground of the Modern World-System," *Theory, Culture, and Society* 7, nos. 2–3 (June 1990): 39.

72 Gustave Michaud and Fidel Tristan, "Black and White Men in Invisible Light," *Scientific American* (July 27, 1912): 72.

73 Houston A. Baker, Jr., "To Move Without Moving: Creativity and Commerce in Ralph Ellison's Trueblood Episode," in *Black Literature and Literary Theory,* ed. Henry Louis Gates, Jr. (London: Methuen, 1984), p. 230.

74 Nancy C. M. Harstock, *Money, Sex, and Power: Toward a Feminist Historical Materialism* (Boston: Northeastern University Press, 1983), p. 241.

75 Patrick Brantlinger, *Rule of Darkness: British Imperialism, 1830–1914* (Ithaca, N.Y.: Cornell University Press, 1988), p. 233. His chief examples are *War of the Worlds* and *Dracula.*

76 Marianna Torgovnick, *Gone Primitive: Savage Intellects, Modern Lives* (Chicago: University of Chicago Press, 1990), pp. 42–72.

77 Peter Wollen, "Cinema/Americanism/the Robot," *Modernity and Mass Culture,* ed. James Naremore and Patrick Brantlinger (Bloomington: Indiana University Press, 1991), pp. 42–69. Also see, on the "Americanization of Labor Power," Rabinbach, *The Human Motor,* pp. 238–70.

78 Chris C. Demchak, *Military Organizations, Complex Machines: Modernization in the U.S. Armed Services* (Ithaca, N.Y.: Cornell University Press, 1991), p. 37.

79 On the conflation of national and racial identities, see Michaels, pp. 188–92, and Michael Rogin, *Ronald Reagan, the Movie* (Berkeley: University of California Press, 1987), pp. 192–98.

80 Arthur and Marilouise Kroker, "Theses on the Disappearing Body in the Hyper-Modern Condition," *Body Invaders: Panic Sex in America,* ed. Arthur and Marilouise Kroker (New York: St. Martin's, 1987), p. 10. In the same apocalyptic, Baudrillardian vein they introduce another collection of essays, *The Hysterical Male* (New York: St. Martin's Press, 1991) with the observation that "post-male power . . . leaves behind male subjectivity as a hysterical photographic negative of itself" (ix). A great deal of attention has been paid to recent science fiction, novels and films as a point of access to postmodernism. For one account that focuses on the issue of the body, see J. P. Tellotte, "The Tremulous Public Body: Robots, Change, and the Science Fiction Film," *Journal of Popular Film and Television* 19, no. 1 (Spring 1991): 14–23. Most significantly, Donna Haraway, thinking through recent feminist science fiction, articulates a politics of the feminist cyborg, "a kind of disassembled and reassembled, postmodern collective and personal self" that recognizes how, in the era of biotechnological revolution, "organisms have ceased to exist as objects of knowledge," how human-being, and being itself, have become frenziedly technological. "A Cyborg Manifesto: Science, Technology, and Socialist-Feminism in the Late Twentieth Century," *Simians, Cyborgs, and Women: The Reinvention of Nature* (New York: Routledge, 1991), pp. 149–81.

Richard Slotkin

Buffalo Bill's "Wild West" and

the Mythologization of the

American Empire

uffalo Bill's Wild West" was for more than thirty years (1883–1916) one of the largest, most popular, and successful businesses in the field of commercial entertainment. The Wild West was not only a major influence on American ideas about the frontier past at the turn of the century, it was a highly influential overseas advertisement for the United States during the period of massive European emigration. It toured all of North America and Europe, and its creator William F. Cody became an international celebrity, on terms of friendship with European royalty and heads of state, as well as with the leadership of the American military establishment. With its hundreds of animals, human performers, musicians, and workmen, its boxcars filled with equipment and supplies, it was nearly as large and difficult to deploy as a brigade of cavalry; and since it went everywhere by railroad (or steamship) it was far more mobile. The staff of the Imperial German army was said to have studied Buffalo Bill's methods for loading and unloading trains in planning their own railroad operations.[1]

William F. Cody or "Buffalo Bill" was the creator, leading manager, and until the turn of the century the chief attraction of the Wild West. Over the years he worked with a series of partners, whose ideas and decisions also influenced the development of the enterprise, and who often assumed a greater share of control over the design of the production. But it was Cody and his idea that provided the most coherent and continuous line of development. Certainly Cody himself was primarily responsible for establishing the Wild

West's commitment to historical authenticity and to its mission of historical education.[2]

The management of Cody's enterprise declared it improper to speak of their performance as a "Wild West Show." From its inception in 1882 it was called "The Wild West," (or "Buffalo Bill's Wild West") a name which identified it as a "place" rather than a mere display or entertainment. A "Salutatory" notice was added to the Program of the 1886 Wild West and appeared in every Program thereafter, which declared:

> It is the aim of the management of Buffalo Bill's Wild West to do more than present an exacting and realistic entertainment for public amusement. Their object is to PICTURE TO THE EYE, by the aid of historical characters and living animals, a series of animated scenes and episodes, which had their existence in fact, of the wonderful pioneer and frontier life of the Wild West of America.

The Wild West was organized around a series of spectacles, which purported to reenact scenes exemplifying different "Epochs" of American history: "Beginning with the Primeval Forest, peopled by the Indian and Wild Beasts only, the story of the gradual civilization of a vast continent is depicted." The first "Epoch" displayed the Wild West's Plains Indian dancers, but represented them as typical of the woodland Indians who greeted the colonists on the Atlantic shore (a tableau depicting either the Pilgrims at Plymouth Rock or John Smith and Pocahontas). The historical program then cut abruptly to the settlement of the Great Plains, displaying life on a Cattle Ranch, a grand "Buffalo Hunt," and Indian attacks on a settler's cabin and the "Deadwood Stage." Between these episodes were displays of "Cowboy Fun," of trick riding and roping, and spectacular feats of marksmanship by featured performers like Annie Oakley ("Little Sure Shot") and Buffalo Bill himself.

The historical rationale of the Wild West was carefully described in the elaborate Program; but all visitors, whether or not they purchased the Program, were admonished that "Attention to the Orator [announcer] will materially assist the spectator in his grasp of the leading episodes." The seriousness and authenticity of the historical program was vouched for by letters of recommendation from leading military officers, published in the Program, and by the use of figures publicly recognized as actual participants in the making of history: "The hardships, daring, and frontier skill of the participants" was "a guarantee of the faithful reproduction of scenes in which they had actual experience." Over the years Buffalo

Bill managed to engage such figures as Sitting Bull and Geronimo as performers, as well as a great number of Indians who had fought against
the cavalry (some within a year of their surrender) and regular units of the
U.S. Cavalry to perform opposite them. But the center of the Wild West,
as both premier performer and veteran of historical reality, was Buffalo
Bill himself: "The central figure in these pictures is that of THE HON. W.
F. CODY (Buffalo Bill), to whose sagacity, skill, energy, and courage . . .
the settlers of the West owe so much for the reclamation of the prairie
from the savage Indian and wild animals, who so long opposed the march
of civilization."[3]

It is the most extraordinary tribute to the skill of the Wild West's management that its performances were not only accepted as entertainment,
but were received with some seriousness as exercises in public education. The leading figures of American military history, from the Civil War
through the Plains Indian wars, testified in print to the Wild West's accuracy and to its value as an inculcator of patriotism. Brick Pomeroy, a
journalist quoted in the 1893 Program, used the newly minted jargon of
the educational profession to praise Buffalo Bill with the wish that "there
were more progressive educators like William Cody in this world." He
thought the show ought to be called "Wild West Reality" because it had
"more of real life, of genuine interest, of positive education [than] all of
this imaginary Romeo and Juliet business."[4]

But despite its battery of authentications, the Wild West writes "history" by conflating it with mythology. The reenactments were not recreations, but reductions of complex events into "typical scenes," based on
the formulas of popular literary mythology: the "Forest Primeval" epoch
reads colonial history in Fenimore Cooper's terms; the Plains episodes in
terms drawn from the dime novel. If the Wild West was a "place" rather
than a "show," then its landscape was a mythic space, in which past and
present, fiction and reality could coexist; a space in which history, translated into myth, was reenacted as ritual. Moreover, these rituals did more
than manipulate historical materials and illustrate an interpretation of
American history: in several rather complex ways, the Wild West and
its principals managed not only to comment on historical events, but to
become actors themselves.

Until 1869 William F. Cody had been a minor actor on the stage of
Western history, a frontier jack of all trades—teamster, trapper, Civil War
soldier, Pony Express rider, stagecoach driver, meat hunter for the Kansas
Pacific railroad, hunting guide, and army scout. The upsurge of inter-

est in the Plains that accompanied construction of the transcontinental railroads brought numerous tourists to the region, along with journalists, gentlemen-hunters in search of big game, and dime novelists looking for material. Cody was already well known as a guide when—without his knowledge or consent—"Ned Buntline" made him the hero of a dime novel (1869) and a stage melodrama (1871).[5] In 1871 James Gordon Bennett, Jr., editor and publisher of the New York *Herald*, hired Cody as a guide on one of the more elaborate celebrity hunting trips of the era; the next year General Sheridan named Cody to guide the hunting party of the Russian Grand Duke Alexis, then on a state visit. Both expeditions received extensive press coverage, and Bennett sought to exploit Cody's new fame by inviting him to New York. The visit was a turning point in Cody's career. In New York he took control of the commodity of his fame by forming a partnership with Ned Buntline for the production of Buffalo Bill dime novels and stage melodramas.[6]

Between 1872 and 1876 Cody alternated between his career as scout for the cavalry and his business as star of a series of melodramas in the East. His theatrical enterprises prospered, so that by 1873 he was able to form his own "Buffalo Bill Combination" with Wild Bill Hickok and "Texas Jack" Omohundro. The plays themselves were trivial, and the acting amateurish, but the success of the "Combination" was evidence of the public's deep and uncritical enthusiasm for "the West," which could best be addressed through a combination of dime-novel plots and characters with "authentic" costumes and personages identified with "the real thing."[7]

Cody's continuing engagement with the Plains wars strengthened his claims of authenticity, and in 1876 provided him with a windfall of public celebrity. The outbreak of war with the Sioux and Northern Cheyenne had been expected since the failure in 1875 of government attempts to compel the sale of the Black Hills, and preparations for three major expeditions into "hostile" territory began in the winter of 1875–76. Cody's service as Chief of Scouts had been solicited by General Carr, but theatrical engagements prevented him from accepting until the spring campaign had begun. On the 11th of June Cody announced from the stage in Wilmington, Delaware, that he was abandoning "playacting" for "the real thing," and within the week had joined the 5th (now commanded by Merritt) in southern Wyoming. On July 7 the command learned of Custer's disastrous defeat at the Little Big Horn (June 25). Ten days later a battalion of the 5th caught up with a band of off-reservation Cheyenne. In a rapid sequence of ambush and counterambush, Cody and his scouts engaged a small party of Cheyenne outriders. Cody singled out and killed a young warrior named Yellow Hand; then, as the troopers swept toward him, walked to the corpse, scalped it, and waved his trophy in the air.[8]

This scene became the core of the Buffalo Bill legend and the basis of his national celebrity. Before the year was over he would be hailed in the national press as the man who took "The First Scalp for Custer."[9] But the chief mythologizer of the event was Cody himself. That winter he would star in *The Red Right Hand; or, The First Scalp for Custer,* a melodrama in which the "duel" with Yellow Hand becomes the climax of a captivity-rescue scenario. (The story also appeared as a dime novel.) Moreover, it appears that Cody approached the event itself with just such a performance in mind. On the morning of July 17, knowing that the proximity of the Indians made battle probable, Cody abandoned his usual buckskin clothing for one of his stage costumes, "a brilliant Mexican *vaquero* outfit of black velvet slashed with scarlet and trimmed with silver buttons and lace"—the sort of costume that dime novel illustration had led the public to suppose was the proper dress of the wild Westerner. He was preparing for that moment when he would stand before his audience, wearing the figurative laurels of the day's battle and the *vaquero* suit, able to declare with truth that he stood before them in a plainsman's authentic garb, indeed the very clothes he had worn when he took "The First Scalp for Custer." In that one gesture he would make "history" and fictive convention serve as mutually authenticating devices: the truth of his deeds "historicizes" the costume, while the costume's conventionality allows the audience—which knows the West only through such images—to recognize it as genuine.[10]

Here the Buffalo Bill signature appears clearly in its characteristic confusion of the theatrical and the historical or political. The deed itself is unquestionably real—blood was shed, a battle won—but the event is framed by fiction from start to finish, and its larger meaning is determined by its transformation into myth and its ritual reenactment in the theater.

After 1882 the "Wild West" replaced the theater as Buffalo Bill's most important myth-making enterprise. The "Wild West" began as part of the July 4th, 1882, celebration in Cody's hometown of North Platte, Nebraska. Its primary features were rodeolike displays of cowboy skills—feats of marksmanship, riding and roping, horse races—framed by an elaborate parade. To this base were added elements that would appeal to the larger audience, which had been drawn to the Buffalo Bill Combination: scenes "typical" of Western life, developed around a standard melodramatic narrative scheme like the captivity/rescue. Many of these scenes were drawn from Buffalo Bill dime novels: the attack on the Deadwood Stage, the Pony Express display, the raid on the settler's cabin, the "Grand Buffalo Hunt on the Plains." As in the "Combination," authentic historical celebrities were recruited to lend credibility and exploit public curiosity: Major North and his Pawnee battalion were early favorites, Sitting Bull appeared in 1884–85, and métis veterans of the Riel Rebellion in Canada (1886). In later years the Wild West would feature appearances by Rain-in-the-Face ("the Indian who killed Custer"), Chief Joseph of the Nez Perce, Jack Red Cloud (son of a famous Sioux chief), and assorted sheriffs and outlaws whose exploits had attracted the attention of the newspapers.

In 1886 the Wild West program was reorganized and publicized as "America's National Entertainment," an exemplification of the entire course of American history. The different scenes were now presented as typifications of the stages of frontier history, although their content remained virtually unchanged. The emphasis on the Wild West as an exemplification of American history may also have been a response to the prospect of the company's first European tour (1887–89). The appeal of the Wild West could only be enhanced by representing it as a kind of cultural embassy from the New World to the Old: an exhibition of all the exotic American types that had piqued European imaginations since Cooper, if not since Columbus.[11]

Cody's stage persona was now given a more elaborate definition designed to present him as the archetype of the American frontier hero. Buffalo Bill is presented in the 1886 program as "the representative man of the frontiersmen of the past." He is "full of self-reliance," acquires scientific knowledge through the necessary operations of his native curiosity and engagement with Nature. The history of the West is, in effect, his "lengthened shadow": "His history, in fact, would be almost a history of the middle West, and, though younger, equalling in term of service and personal adventure Kit Carson, Old Jim Bridger, California Joe, Wild Bill, and the rest of his dead and gone associates." (It is worth noting that with the exception of Bridger, all of these figures were as well or better known as dime novel heroes than as historical personages.) "Young, sturdy, a remarkable specimen of manly beauty, with the brain to conceive and the nerve to execute, Buffalo Bill *par excellence* is the exemplar of the strong and unique traits that characterize *a true American frontiersman*."

Like Hawkeye, Cody is of plebeian and agrarian origins, which teach him the values of democracy and hard work. As "a child of the plains" he inevitably becomes acquainted with the wilderness and with the strife endemic to a border region. These "accident[s] of birth and early association" bring him (like Hawkeye) into intimate knowledge of the wilderness and the "implacable Indian foe." But where Hawkeye is disabled by this knowledge from living a civilized life, Cody's experience prepares him "to hold positions of trust, and without his knowing or intending it made him nationally famous." Cody is able to overcome Hawkeye's limitations because he possesses an innately superior moral character, whose powers go beyond the primitive virtues of loyalty, truthfulness, and honor. Cody's virtues are those of the manager and commander as well as the soldier. Though "full of self-reliance" he also possesses "the moral qualities associated with a good captain of a ship." His incipient gentility is attested by the certified "gentlemen" of the officer corps, particularly Generals Carr and Merritt, who praise him as "a natural gentleman in his manners as well as character." Sherman figuratively ennobles Cody as "King of them all [i.e., the army's scouts]." As Cody aged and prospered, the Wild West programs would present him as a patriarchal figure, of fully achieved gentility, a natural aristocrat able and worthy to socialize with royalty.[12]

In 1886 a reenactment of "Custer's Last Fight" was added to the Wild West's repertoire, and it eventually became not only the most spectacular of the "Epochs" but the center of a reorganized program. Unlike the "Deadwood Stage" and "Settler's Cabin" scenes, "Custer's Last Fight" referred to a struggle which was not yet concluded. Geromimo was still on the warpath, and most of the Indians who had fought Custer were still alive, living uneasily on the reservation; and Sitting Bull, widely regarded as the mastermind who had defeated Custer, was still regarded as a dangerous man.

Cody's presumption in addressing "history" so directly was of course defended by his insistence that the recreation was authentic. A visitor to his tent noted that he had only three books in his working library, a scrapbook of newspaper clippings, a manual of infantry drill and tactics, and Frederick Whittaker's 1876 illustrated biography of Custer. He dressed his cowboys as cavalrymen and gave them proper drill; the Indians he hired were Sioux and Cheyenne and included veterans of the Custer fight. But the "script" which these "genuine" performers played out ended in melodrama, with Cody's appearance on the stricken field before a transparency bearing the motto, "Too Late." The suggestion that Cody might have saved the Boy General had he only arrived in time was pure "dime novel": Cody never approached the battlefield in 1876 and had had no knowledge of (or concern with) Custer's column until July 7.[13]

Cody was of course well aware that his representation of historical events was inaccurate, to say the least. But he seems to have been sincere in his belief that the Wild West offered something like a poetic truth in its representation of the frontier. His "truth" had two aspects, the pictorial and the moral. Within the boundaries of good showmanship he strove for the greatest accuracy of detail because he wished to memorialize a period of his own life (and a regional life style) which he loved and from which time increasingly estranged him. This concern pervades both his public and private writing and shows as well in the care and consideration with which he treated his Indian performers and the wild animals used in the Wild West.

But the "moral truth" of the frontier experience, which the Wild West emphasized, was its exemplification of the principle that violence and savage war were the necessary instruments of American progress. Even the displays of marksmanship by Buffalo Bill and Annie Oakley are framed by the Program's essay on "The Rifle as an Aid to Civilization":

> [While it is] a trite saying that 'the pen is mightier than the sword,' it is equally true that the bullet is the pioneer of civilization, for it has gone hand in hand with the axe that cleared the forest, and with the family Bible and school book. Deadly as has been its mission in one sense, it has been merciful in another; for without the rifle ball we of America would not be to-day in the possession of a free and united country, and mighty in our strength.[14]

Cody's sense of the Wild West's educational and ideological mission was sharpened during the European tours he undertook between 1887 and 1892.[15] He was therefore well prepared for the opportunity presented by the World's Columbian Exposition to place the Wild West in a strategic and profitable situation. His success is attested by the achievement of over a million dollars in profit from the 1893 season.[16]

The show itself was larger and more spectacular than anything seen in America before, and Cody undertook an elaborate schedule of promotional activities to arouse and maintain public interest in the Wild West. The Program was far more elaborate in its framing of the Wild West's historical significance: the reenactment of the "Last Stand" would feature performers on both sides who had been actual participants in the battle; and other survivors, and even Mrs. Custer herself, were "consulted" in preparing the performance.[17] Cody himself now appeared as a hero whose authenticity as "representative man" was attested in two different worlds. Wild West posters and publicity blazoned his triumphs before "The Crowned Heads of Europe," his success as an exemplar and promoter of American values and national prestige on the world stage.

In addition, his reputation as a genuine Indian fighter had been recently refreshed by his service during the Ghost Dance troubles of 1890, first as a would-be peacemaker between his friends Sitting Bull and General Miles, then (after the massacre of Ghost Dancers at Wounded Knee) as a member of Miles's staff.[18]

Cody exploited his connection with Wounded Knee in advertising posters which alternately showed him overseeing the making of the Peace Treaty and charging into a village to rescue White captives. He also reconstructed on the Wild West's grounds the cabin in which Sitting Bull lived at the time of his assassination, where Cody staged a ceremony of reconciliation between cavalry and Indian veterans of the two battles of the Little Big Horn and Wounded Knee. The Crow scout "Curly," famed as the last man to see Custer alive, shook hands with Rain-in-the-Face, the Sioux who had been (unjustly) immortalized by Longfellow as the man who killed Custer, then cut out his heart and ate it. These ceremonies of reconciliation transfer to the Indian wars a species of public ritual previously associated with the reunion on Civil War battlefields of veterans of the Blue and Gray. Of course, the Indian war ceremony occurs not on the "real" battleground of the West, but on the fictive "battleground" of Buffalo Bill's Wild West. Nonetheless, the ideological import of the gesture was seriously intended. Cody framed the ceremony with a set of overt appeals for reconciliation between Whites and Indians. The Program now represented the "savages" as "The Former Foe—Present Friend—the *American*."[19]

This shift in the role assigned to the Indians signaled a change in the historical scenario enacted by the Wild West. In its original appearance, "Custer's Last Fight" had concluded the Wild West's first half and was followed by scenes displaying the peaceful life and labor of the ranch and mining camp.[20] In the new program, the "Last Fight" was the last act in the Wild West and served as an elegy for the *entire* period of American pioneering. What followed it was a vision of America assuming a new role on the world stage, as leader of the imperial powers: the parade of the "Congress of Rough Riders of the World."

The term "Rough Riders" had been applied to Western horsemen in dime novels before 1880, and Cody had adopted it during the European tours to characterize his White American horsemen. But the appeal of the "Last Fight" sequence had led the partners to increase the representation of military drill in the show. Military drill and trick-riding teams had been a regular feature of American fairs and circuses since the antebellum period; and such teams, drawn from regular army units, performed in European nations as well. Cody had obtained the services of such units in the countries visited by the Wild West between 1887 and 1892; and he brought a selection of them back to the States to provide an exotic and appropriately international note for the Columbian Exposition edition of "America's National Entertainment." These units were added to the American cowboys and cavalrymen to form the "Congress of the Rough Riders of the World," whose grand parades opened and closed each performance and whose displays of horsemanship became featured acts between the historical scenes.[21]

But the full "Congress" included other kinds of horsemen as well. Beside each American or European unit rode representative horsemen of the nonwhite tribesmen recently conquered by the imperial powers. At the head of this "Congress" rode Buffalo Bill, identified in the Program and by his precedence not merely as "Prince of the Border Men" or "King of the Scouts," but as "King of all the Rough Riders of the World. His preeminence was not merely personal but national, signifying the American assumption of a leading role in world affairs.[22]

The display of horseback skill by the Rough Riders was partly a development of the intervals of "Cowboy Fun" that had previously punctuated the staged "epochs." But the intensity with which the "Wild West" now pursued its historical program soon invested even these performances with ideological symbolism. If the "Custer's Last Fight" reenactment was the funeral rite of the old frontier, then the Rough Rider contests and pageants were the ritual games that looked to the beginning of a new age. This suggestion was given substance in the greatly expanded text of the 1893 Program. All of the standard features of earlier programs were reprinted, but new essays were added, including one by Colonel T. A. Dodge, which declared that the warfare of the future would primarily engage civilized nations with barbarian races and that therefore the American Indian-fighting cavalry would become the "pattern of the cavalry of the future." Cody's abortive embassy to Sitting Bull on the eve of Wounded Knee becomes the basis for an assertion that Buffalo Bill's mission offers a model for international diplomacy, which might well be applied to the approaching Franco-German crisis over Alsace-Lorraine.[23]

Buffalo Bill's potential as a force for "universal peace" is attested by the ease with which he can move from the "red wastes" to the "great cities of Europe" and from the mixture of military skill or power and peacemaking wisdom he brings to both settings. In moving rapidly between Dakota and Europe in 1890–91, Buffalo Bill had had a unique opportunity to contrast the might of industrial civilization with the lowest ebb of savagery, and (the Program suggests) a similar experience is available to the visitor who passes freely between the Wild West and the White City of the Columbian Exposition. But as the essay explores the meaning of this juxtaposition, an ideological ambivalence appears in the historical role assigned to violence. On the one hand, the contrast between Wild West and White City teaches us that the war-making spirit is an attribute of man in the "savage" state and that civilization requires the substitution of peace for war. But though war is denigrated as an end of civilization, it is exalted as a means to peace.[24]

The basic thesis of this historical argument is essentially the same as that of Theodore Roosevelt's advocacy of American imperialism in "Expansion and Peace" (1899): that "peace" can only be imposed on the "barbarian races" of the world by the armed force of a superior race. The history of the frontier has been one of Social-Darwinian racial warfare. It was inevitable that the Red man's "once happy empire" be "brought thoroughly and efficiently under the control of our civilization, or (possibly more candidly confessed) under the Anglo-Saxon's commercial necessities."

> [T]he practical view of the non-industrious use of nature's cornucopia of world-needed resources and the inevitable law of the *survival of the fittest* must "bring the flattering unction to the soul" of those—to whom the music of light, work, and progress, is the charm, the gauge of existence's worth, and to which the listless must harken, the indolent attend, the weak imbibe strength from—whose ranks the red man must join, and advancing with whose steps march cheerily to the tune of honest toil, industrious peace, and placid fireside prosperity.[25]

The Wild West's reenactments of the scenes of "savage war" were recognized as rituals designed to revive in overcivilized moderns the militant virtues of their frontier ancestors. A reporter for the Chicago *Inter-Ocean* declared that the 1893 performances of the "Deadwood Stage" and "Last Fight" scenes made him aware of "the aboriginal ancestor" that remains "in us after all the long generations of attempted civilization and education." David A. Curtis, writing in the *Criterion* in 1899, notes that the spectacle of "struggle and slaughter" produces effects like those of Roosevelt's "Strenuous Life": it awakens "the hidden savage," the "ineradicable trace of savage instinct" that lurks in the blood of all the great fighting races; it "stirs the thinnest blood and brightens the dullest eye" in the genteel Anglo-Saxon audience. The only "lack is that this . . . fighting is not real."[26]

As if anticipating Curtis's regret that its bloodshed was not "real," the publicity of the Wild West after 1893 asserted more strenuously than ever its claim to "realism" of detail. And it linked that claim to a more assertive statement of its educational mission. The copy attached to the Wild West's world's-record billboard of 1898–99 offered the clearest and most assertive definition yet of the Wild West's educational purpose. The billboard invited the viewer to "LOOK UPON THIS PICTURE," and behold "the VARIOUS EPOCHS of AMERICAN HISTORY, from the primitive days of savagery up to the memorable charge of San Juan hill," all reproduced with "remarkable fidelity." This epic image and performance is not merely a "show" but:

AN OBJECT LESSON

Differing as it does from all other exhibitions, BUFFALO BILL'S WILD WEST and CONGRESS OF ROUGH RIDERS OF THE WORLD stands as a living monument of historic and educational magnificence. Its distinctive feature lies in its sense of realism, bold dash and reckless abandon which only arises from brave and noble inspiration. It is not a "show" in any sense of the word, but it is a series of original, genuine and instructive object lessons in which the participants repeat the heroic parts they have played in actual life upon the plains, in the wilderness, mountain fastness and in the dread and dangerous scenes of savage and cruel warfare. It is the only amusement enterprise of any kind recognized, endorsed and contributed to by Governments, Armies and Nations; and it lives longest in the hearts of those who have seen it most often, since it always contains and conveys intensely inspiring ideas and motives, while its programme is a succession of pleasant surprises and thrilling incidents.[27]

The function of realistic presentation is first to memorialize the real past in a "living monument," preserving not only the details of past heroism but also the moral truth, that such "bold dash" can only arise "from brave and noble inspiration." Having memorialized true history, the Wild West's next task is to translate history into useful instruction, conveying to the public "intensely inspiring ideas and motives." Whatever these ideas may be, they are of a kind that is "endorsed and contributed to" by the official apparatus of the modern nation-state, for the Wild West's ultimate distinction is that it is the only "amusement enterprise" to be "recognized" by "Governments, Armies and Nations"—as if the fictive "place" that was the Wild West had achieved something like diplomatic recognition.

The Wild West's conflation of the frontier myth and the new ideology of imperialism was fully achieved in 1899 when "Custer's Last Fight" was replaced by the "Battle of San Juan Hill," celebrating the heroism of Theodore Roosevelt—whose First Volunteer Cavalry regiment was best known by its nickname of "The Rough Riders."

By incorporating Roosevelt in the Wild West, Cody would seem to have conferred the very honor Roosevelt sought through his energetic hunting, soldiering, and writing about the West: a place in the pantheon of frontier heroes whose founder is Daniel Boone and whose latest demigod is Buffalo Bill. But Roosevelt somewhat ungenerously denied his own real indebtedness to the Wild West for the regimental sobriquet of "Rough Riders." The 1899 Wild West Program reprints an exchange of letters between Cody and Roosevelt, in which the latter denies having borrowed the name from Cody's Congress, asserts that it was spontaneously bestowed by local citizens, and that Roosevelt himself was unaware of its reference. This (as Cody rather modestly points out) was hardly credible, given the fame of the Wild West (which Roosevelt had certainly attended) and the presence of some of the show's cowboys and Indians among Roosevelt's recruits. Roosevelt offered a mollifying compliment to the effect that, however it had come about, he was proud to share the name with those "free fearless equestrians, now marshalled under the leadership of the greatest horseman of all."[28]

This exchange of names between the agents of real-world imperialism and the mythmakers of the Wild West defines a significant cultural and political relationship. In performances, programs, and posters "San Juan Hill" was substituted for "Custer's Last Fight." It was the climactic act of the Wild West performances in 1899, where it was hailed as a battle equal in significance to Lexington and Concord, opening a new phase of America's history. The colossal 108-sheet billboard poster that advertised the 1899 Wild West restated the point in panoramic iconography: the poster illustrations recapitulated the historical "epochs" from "Attack on the Settler's Cabin" at the extreme left to "San Juan Hill" at the extreme right; and the whole was flanked with "bookends" of text that proclaimed the Wild West as "An Object Lesson" in American history. This substitution of an imperial triumph carried off in "Wild West" style, for a ritual reenactment of the catastrophe that symbolized the end of the old frontier, completes the Wild West's evolution from a memorialization of the past to a celebration of the imperial future.

By the terms of this exchange, the categories of myth shape the terms in which the imperial project will be conceived, justified, and executed; and the imperial achievement is then reabsorbed into the mythological system, which is itself modified by the incorporation of the new material.

One effect is clearly that of glorifying the "imperialization" of the American republic. But the use of Wild West imagery also has the effect of "democratizing" the imperial project—or rather, of investing it with a style and imagery that powerfully (if spuriously) suggests its "democratic" character. The point is visualized in an 1898 Wild West poster, "Art Perpetuating Fame," which compares Buffalo Bill with Napoleon Bonaparte as "The Man on Horseback of 1796" and "The Man on Horseback of 1898." At the center of the poster is the black-cloaked figure of an old woman sitting before an easel: the French portrait painter Rosa Bonheur, who had painted well-known equestrian portraits of both the Emperor Napoleon and Buffalo Bill. The two men sit on white horses, facing away from the center. Napoleon (on the left) is in uniform, but appears paunchy, and looks sidelong out of the frame; Buffalo Bill is slightly more frontal, appears young and trim, has an erect seat, and wears civilian clothes. The identification of the two as "Men on Horseback" associates them not only as soldiers, but as embodiments of the military principle in civil politics: the tag-phrase comes from French politics in the Dreyfus-case era, to identify the conservative glorification of the army, and hopes for a military assumption of civil power. The American version of this political type is youthful rather than decrepit and "civilian" rather than military; his triumphs (the caption tells us) are peaceful rather than violent (i.e., Wild West show tours vs. military conquests). If Buffalo Bill is America's "Man on Horseback," then the American empire will be a peaceful and republican one, animated by youthful energy rather than depressed by tyrannical conservatism.[29]

Cody's version of the charge of Roosevelt's Rough Riders of course featured "the very heroes and horses who were a part of what they portray" and invited comparison with the Last Stand by describing the attack as a forlorn-hope assault against superior numbers. But those who followed "Roosevelt and the flag" reverse the Custer scenario, triumphing over the lurking Spaniards. It is also characteristic of Cody that he emphasizes the ethnic and racial diversity of the soldiers, "white, red, and black" who followed Roosevelt. In this too the showman's generosity exceeds the politician's: Roosevelt does not emphasize the Indian presence in the regiment and denigrates the contributions of the black regular infantry regiment that charged beside the Rough Riders.[30]

Both the historical program of the Wild West and its intricate play with racial categories were transformed by its identification with imperialism. In subsequent years the military elements of the show—the cavalry drills, the display of new model artillery and Gatling guns (a feature of the San Juan Hill attack)—began to eclipse traditional Western elements like "Cowboy Fun." The racialist ideology implicit in the 1893 "Race of Races" is more sharply defined. In the 1893 Program the nonwhite riders had been identified by nationality, in 1894 as "primitive riders", and in 1898 their competition (always one of the first five acts) was described in terms suggestive of Social Darwinism as "The Race of Races."[31]

Percival Pollard, writing in the *Criterion*, found that the outbreak of the war with Spain made the familiar scenes of the Wild West seem "freighted with a newer meaning." If the Spaniards doubted we were "a manly race . . . they might do themselves good by viewing Buffalo Bill and his cohorts." Wartime performances of the Wild West were announced in terms that deliberately echoed war news: the headline "City Capitulated" was used for both the surrender of Santiago and the announcement of a Wild West box-office triumph. In an interview given to the New York *World* in April 1898, Cody proposed a "Wild West" approach to the coming war: "Buffalo Bill Writes On 'How I Could Drive the Spaniards from Cuba with 30,000 Indians,'" assisted by such chieftains of the "noble but dying race" as Geronimo and Jack Red Cloud. Wild West performers were sought out for pro-war quotations, and Buffalo Bill made the show an instrument of propaganda by developing acts featuring Cuban and Filipino insurgents. However, these "savages" of the new frontier presented some of the same ideological difficulties as the old. When the Filipinos rebelled against an American takeover of the islands in 1899, the Filipinos in the Wild West became objects of hostility. Buffalo Bill himself was identified as "an avowed expansionist" and was quoted as declaring that the American Indian "Outranks the Filipino in the Matter of Common Honesty." His assertion that "Their Fighting Tactics are Almost Identical" affirmed the polemical position taken by Roosevelt and other expansionists, that the Filipinos were "savages" like the "Apache." In a reversion to mythic origins, they were replaced in the San Juan Hill reenactment by the Wild West's Indians.

In 1901 San Juan Hill was replaced by a more recent imperial adventure, "The Battle of Tien-Tsin," reenacting the capture of that city by the Allied army that suppressed China's Boxer Rebellion and rescued the "captives" in the Peking Legation Quarter. In this performance, the Indians assumed the role of the Boxers, and the Wild West's soldiers and cowboys represented all of white civilization, storming the citadel from which flew "the Royal Standard of Paganism . . . proudly defiant of the Christian world," to place there "the Banners of civilization." After running "Tien-Tsin" in 1901–2, Cody reprised "San Juan Hill" in 1903–4, taking advantage of (and perhaps assisting) Roosevelt's run for reelection.[32]

It is appropriate that each should have benefited materially from the other's activities because their contributions to American culture were complementary and mutually reinforcing. The Wild West's casting of its cowboys and Indians as Rough Riders and Cubans, Allies and Boxers, makes literal and visible the central tenet of Roosevelt's racialist myth of progress: that the struggle between Red Men and White on the American frontier is the archetype and precedent for the worldwide struggle between "progressive" and "savage" or "regressive" races that shaped the modern world. The Wild West performed as myth and ritual the doctrines of progressive imperialism that Roosevelt promulgated as ideology. By dramatizing the imperial frontier as the logical extension of the continental frontier, Cody lent mythological support to Roosevelt's contention that there was no contradiction between the traditions of American democracy and the imperial enterprise—that empire was merely the continuation of Wild West democracy "by other means."

Notes

1 Don Russell, *The Wild West: A History of Wild West Shows* (Fort Worth: Amon Carter Museum, 1961), chaps. 1–2, esp. p. 40.

2 Russell, *The Lives and Legends of Buffalo Bill* (Norman: University of Oklahoma Press, 1960), chap. 20, and pp. 300–302, 370.

3 John M. Burke, "Salutatory," *Buffalo Bill's Wild West*, 1886 and 1887 (hereinafter *BBWW*, [date]). All citations from Wild West programs are from copies in the Western History Department, Denver Public Library. I am grateful to Eleanor M. Gehres and the library staff for their assistance.

4 Pomeroy quoted in "Hon. W. F. Cody—'Buffalo Bill,' " a biographical sketch which included sections on Cody as "A Legislator" and "As an Educator." The sketch and its appendices appear virtually unchanged in most Wild West Programs to 1900. See "Letters of Commendation from Prominent Military Men," *BBWW*, 1886, and *BBWW*, 1887, which adds letters from European royalty and American notables.

5 Russell, *Lives and Legends*, pp. 149–55, 181–84.

6 Ibid., pp. 181–84 and chaps. 11–13. On the grand duke's hunting party see Richard Slotkin, *The Fatal Environment: The Myth of the Frontier in the Age of Industrialization, 1800–1890* (New York: Atheneum, 1985), pp. 407–9.

7 Russell, *Lives and Legends*, chap. 15.

8 Russell, *Lives and Legends*, chap. 17.

9 *New York Herald*, July 23, 1876. p. 1; Charles King, *Campaigning with Crook and Stories of Army Life* (New York: Harper and Bros., 1890), esp. pp. 36–43.

10 Russell, *Lives and Legends*, pp. 230–32; on his use of the "relics" of Yellow Hand, ibid., p. 254; *New York Herald*, August 11, 1876, p. 3.

11 Russell, *Lives and Legends*, chaps. 21–22, and *Wild West Shows*, pp. 1–42; Sarah J. Blackstone, *Buckskins, Bullets, and Business* (New York: Greenwood Press, 1986), chaps. 2, 3, 5.

12 "Hon. W. F. Cody—'Buffalo Bill,'" *BBWW*, 1886.

13 On Cody's appropriation of the Last Stand see Russell, *Wild West Shows*, p. 25; Elizabeth B. Custer, *Tenting on the Plains; or, General Custer in Kansas and Texas* (New York: Charles L. Webster, 1887), pp. 46–47. Compare also the poster "Buffalo Bill to the Rescue" (Rennert, *100 Posters*, p. 68) with the illustrations of "The Battle of the Washita" in George Armstrong Custer, *My Life on the Plains; or, Personal Experiences with Indians* (Norman: University of Oklahoma Press, 1962). Cody's "Last Fight" was much imitated by competing shows: see Russell, *Wild West Shows*, pp. 31–32, 45.

14 "The Rifle . . . ," *BBWW 1886, 1893.*

15 Russell, *Lives and Legends*, chap. 23; Ray Allen Billington, *Land of Savagery, Land of Promise: The European Image of the American Frontier* (New York: W. W. Norton, 1981), pp. 48–56, 328–29. Although he returned for a brief American tour in 1888, his main purpose was to recruit more Indian performers and replenish his livestock; and the program for this tour omitted the more spectacular "epochs" he had mounted in Europe.

16 On the Columbian Exposition, esp. its racialism, see Alan Trachtenberg, *The Incorporation of America: Culture and Society in the Gilded Age* (New York: Hill & Wang, 1982), chap. 7; R. Reid Badger, *The Great American Fair: The World's Columbian Exposition and American Culture* (Chicago: Nelson-Hall, 1979), pp. 105–7; Robert W. Rydell, "The World's Columbian Exposition of 1893: Racist Underpinnings of a Utopian Artifact," *Journal of American Culture* (1978), pp. 253–75.

17 Russell, *Lives and Legends*, chap. 26. Cody published a newspaper to report on his activities and publicize his promotional schemes. See *Cody Scrapbooks*, vol. 2, esp. pp. 3, 8, 12, 21, 35, 37, 97–100, 102–7, in Denver Public Library.

18 Russell, *Lives and Legends*, chap. 25; Stanley Vestal, *Sitting Bull, Champion of the Sioux* (Norman: University of Oklahoma, 1957), chap. 26.

19 *BBWW*, 1893, pp. 10, 31–34, 49–50; Cody Scrapbooks, Denver Public Library, vol. 2, pp. 3, 8, 12, 21, 35, 37, 97–100, 102, 107.

20 *BBWW,* 1887.

21 Russell, *Lives and Legends*, p. 370, identifies John M. Burke as the originator of the idea.

22 *BBWW,* 1887, refers to "American Rough Riders." *BBWW*, 1893, "Programme" and "Salutatory," pp. 2, 4. See also Russell, *Lives and Legends*, pp. 370–

85, and *Wild West Shows,* pp. 61–72. See also posters of the parade, Rennert, *100 Posters,* "A Perfect Illustration . . . ," and "The Maze" pp. 104, 101.

23 *BBWW,* 1893, Dodge on p. 36; Cody and Wounded Knee, pp. 32–36, 38–45, 49–53; Alsace on pp. 60–61.

24 "A Factor of International Amity—Carnot," poster of 1893, in Rennert, *100 Posters,* p. 106.

25 *BBWW,* 1893, pp. 60–62. It is worth noting that the Wild West's is a "kinder, gentler" version of the Roosevelt thesis in that it envisions the integration of Native Americans into American life. This relatively liberal position on racial politics is a consistent one for Cody, who incorporated both Native Americans and African Americans as "American soldiers" in his imperial pageants.

26 "At the Fair," Chicago *Inter-Ocean,* Sept. 12, 1893, p. 3; David A. Curtis, "The Wild West and What it Lacks," *Criterion,* Cody Scrapbook, vol. 7, p. 183.

27 Rennert, *100 Posters,* rear end paper.

28 *BBWW,* 1899, pp. 32–36.

29 Rennert, *100 Posters,* p. 64. The image of Cody in this poster is far more youthful than that in the Bonheur portrait, p. 63.

30 Cody and Saulsbury attempted to mount a "Black" Wild West in 1895, which toured the South as "Black America," but the experiment was a failure. Russell, *Wild West Shows,* p. 60. Cody also included African-American troopers of the 9th and 10th Cavalry in his San Juan Hill re-enactment (*BBWW,* 1899, p. vi) and treated their exploits as comparable to those of the White Rough Riders. Cody's relatively liberal treatment of this aspect of the race question contrasts with Roosevelt's account of the battle, which denigrates the achievements and character of the Negro regiments. Compare Roosevelt's attitudes toward the African-American troops who fought with his Rough Riders, Thomas G. Dyer, *Theodore Roosevelt and the Idea of Race* (Baton Rouge: Louisiana State University Press, 1980), pp. 100–101. On Cody's treatment of Indians see Vine Deloria, Jr., "The Indians," *Buffalo Bill and the Wild West,* pp. 45–56; Blackstone, *Buckskins,* pp. 85–88.

31 Rennert, *100 Posters,* "The Race of Races [1895]," p. 65; "Wild Rivalries of Savage, Barbarous and Civilized Races [1898]." It has been argued that the "Race of Races" and the imperialist theme was not Cody's idea, and certainly his control of the Wild West program was weakened after 1895. However, he remained the Wild West's featured performer, and his public statements affiliated him with the imperialist cause, though according to Russell, "his heart was not really in it," *Lives and Legends,* p. 417.

32 Cody Scrapbooks, vol. 7, pp. iii, vii, xx, xxiv–xxv, 54–55, 65, 69, 73, 95, 97, 104, 107. *BBWW,* 1901, "Programme." See also the parallel depictions of frontier and imperial heroes in magazines published by Cody's associates, esp. *The Rough Rider* 1, no. 1 (1900): p. 6; 3, no. 4 (1901): cover and p. 2; *Frontier Guide* 2, no. 3 (1901).

Borderline Negotiations of Race, Gender, and Nation

Vicente L. Rafael

White Love

Surveillance and Nationalist Resistance in

the U.S. Colonization of the Philippines

Benevolent Bondage

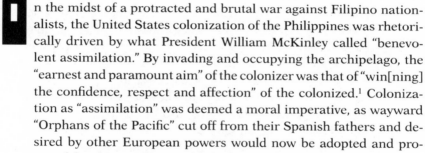n the midst of a protracted and brutal war against Filipino nationalists, the United States colonization of the Philippines was rhetorically driven by what President William McKinley called "benevolent assimilation." By invading and occupying the archipelago, the "earnest and paramount aim" of the colonizer was that of "win[ning] the confidence, respect and affection" of the colonized.[1] Colonization as "assimilation" was deemed a moral imperative, as wayward "Orphans of the Pacific" cut off from their Spanish fathers and desired by other European powers would now be adopted and protected by the compassionate embrace of the United States. As a father is bound to guide his son, Americans were charged with the development of native others. Neither exploitive nor enslaving, colonization entailed the cultivation of "the felicity and perfection of the Philippine people" through the "uninterrupted devotion" to those "noble ideals which constitute the higher civilization of mankind."[2] Because colonization is about civilizing love and the love of civilization, it cannot but be absolutely distinct from the disruptive criminality of conquest. The allegory of benevolent assimilation effaces the violence of conquest by construing colonial rule as the most precious gift that "the most civilized people" can render to those still caught in a state of barbarous disorder.

But instead of returning their love, Filipino "insurgents" seemed intent on making war. "Why these hostilities?" the Schurman Commission asked. "What do the best Filipinos want?" By demanding their independence which they had wrested from Spain, Filipinos appeared to have "misinterpreted" the "pure aims and purposes of the American government and people" and instead attacked American forces.[3] In resisting, the Filipinos were being unreasonable. As with errant children, they needed to be disciplined, according to McKinley, "with firmness if need be, but without severity so far as may be possible." Thus a crucial part of the "high mission" of colonization was the need to "maintain the strong arm of authority to repress disturbances and to overcome all obstacles to the bestowal of the blessing of a good and stable government upon the people of the Philippine Islands under the free flag of the United States."[4]

A certain approach to violence therefore underwrote the allegory of benevolent assimilation. The measured use of force was deemed consistent with the tutelary aims of colonization: that of making native inhabitants desire what colonial authority desired for them. The mandate to institute "democratic aspirations, sentiments, and ideals"[5] brought with it the need to enforce discipline and constant surveillance among the colonized population. Filipinos were called upon to accept the "supremacy of the United States . . . and those who resist it can accomplish no end other than [their] own ruin."[6] Thus was benevolent assimilation predicated on the simultaneous deployment and disavowal of violence. As such, U.S. officials like Secretary of State Elihu Root could state without any hint of irony that a war which claimed thousands of Filipino lives and led to the torture of numerous others was also "accompanied by the self-control, patience, [and] magnanimity" on the part of the American troops and "characterized by humanity and kindness to the prisoner and non-combattant."[7]

The allegory of benevolent assimilation thus foresaw the possibility, if not the inevitability of colonialism's end. But equally important, it also insisted on a single, unassailable way for determining the means to that end. While colonial rule may be a transitional stage to self-rule, the "self" that rules itself can only emerge by way of an intimate relationship with a colonial master who sets the standards and practices of discipline to mold the conduct of the colonial subject. The culmination of colonial rule, self-government, can thus be achieved only when the subject has learned to colonize itself. In this way can benevolent assimilation indefinitely defer its own completion, in that the condition for self-rule, self-mastery, can be made identical to the workings of colonial rule, the mastery of the other that resides within the boundaries of the self. White love holds out the promise of fathering, as it were, a "civilized people" capable in time of asserting its own "character." But it also demands the indefinite submission to a program of discipline and re-formation requiring the constant supervision of a sovereign master.[8]

How was it possible to sustain the fiction of benevolent assimilation, fostered by American official discourse and eventually accepted with varying degrees of alacrity by Filipino collaborators, that colonial rule amounted to democratic tutelage? I want to suggest that the link between benevolence and discipline was constructed through the practice of surveillance. Through continuous and discrete observations, the targets of benevolent assimilation could be identified, apprehended, and delivered for disciplinary subjugation. In the early period of American colonization, one of the most instructive documents relating to the workings of surveillance is the four-volume *Census of the Philippine Islands,* begun in 1903 and published in 1905.[9] In what follows, I want to consider the various ways by which the census functioned as an apparatus for producing a colonial order coextensive with the representation of its subjects. The census was part of a series of interlocking mechanisms designed to reform "natives" as colonial subjects requiring constant supervision by the penetrating but invisible gaze of benevolent tutelage. Whether it was in the area of public order or public health, education or elections, incarceration or commerce, surveillance sustained the articulation of colonial rule on both the ideological and practical levels. By rendering visible the subjects of colonization, surveillance set the limits of their identities within the borders of the colonial state.[10]

It is, however, important to stress that the census's salience as a discursive practice can best be understood in relation to the continuing crisis unleashed by the Filipino-American war. As such, I attempt in the latter part of this essay to juxtapose the census with one of the most popular forms of nationalist discourses among Filipinos during this period: vernacular plays whose performances were deemed "seditious" and ultimately banned by the American colonial regime.

Historically coincident with the taking of the colonial census, performances of the nationalist dramas between 1899–1905 sought to contest the means with which to delineate and authorize the difference between "Filipino" and "American" and, as I shall suggest, between "men" and "women" at a time of catastrophic changes when an American colonial state was yet to be stabilized amid the ruins of Spanish imperial hegemony and the collective memory of Filipino revolutionary victory over Spain. Seen in their historical conjuncture, the census and the plays were struggles over the representation of crisis as much as they were responses to the crisis over the representation of the "Philippines" growing out of the violence of nationalist revolution and imperialist intervention.

Surveying Subjects

Census reports are curious texts. They contain no single author, for standing behind them is not a person but the state apparatus made up of a veritable army of enumerators, clerks, and statisticians managed by a hierarchy of supervisors and directors. It is not therefore the case that a census has no author, but that the bureaucratic nature of its writing renders its authorship and authority dispersed and anonymous. Consequently, while the workings and the results of census reports are never completely visible to an individual, censuses can claim to see everything that can be individuated, that is, counted, tabulated, and classified. No single reader can exhaust the entirety of a census report, just as no single reading can comprehend its "meaning" insofar as its myriad tables and graphs of statistical data escape total recall. Compiled in a mechanical fashion, census reports exceed narrative synopsis. The power—which is to say the persuasiveness—of a census to convey what appears to be an objective representation of the world lies, in part, from its remarkable capacity to picture in unambiguous, quantitative terms the totality of the world's multiplicity. Thus the value of census reports to the colonial (and perhaps to any modern) state: they represent the state's ability to represent and so govern itself. In enumerating and classifying the resources and population of the state, censuses render visible the entire field of colonial intervention.

As the first Philippine census under American rule, the 1903 report was conceived as both a confirmation of and a means for consolidating the "pacification" of the archipelago. The Congressional Act of 1902 made the cessation of the "insurrection" a precondition for conducting the census. The creation of a Census Bureau under the direction of General Joseph P. Sanger (who had supervised earlier census reports for Puerto Rico and Cuba) was thus a way of officially asserting that the war was over. It was left to the victor to make an inventory of its new possessions. One reason for doing so was to set the conditions for holding elections within two years of the census's publication for Filipino representatives to the colonial legislature, to be known as the Philippine Assembly. Such a legislature was designed to consolidate the practice of Filipino collaboration, thereby rendering more efficient and cost effective the running of the colonial state while containing all remaining nationalist challenges to American hegemony. Collaboration was seen thus as an index to the success of tutelage, the measure of the Filipinos' recognition of their subordination to and desire for white authority. "The taking of the census," Governor General Taft wrote, "will therefore form a test of the capacity of the Filipinos to discharge a most important function of government. . . . The census is to be taken solely for the benefit of the Filipino people, . . . [and] they should lend their unanimous support to the successful taking of the census" (Census, 1: 20).

Calling for Filipino collaboration both as local supervisors and enumerators as well as objects of enumeration and supervision, the census would also serve as a kind of "test" of the natives' ability to perform a task. Discipline was called for by the census: that was why it could serve both the practical and ideological route to self-government in the future. As an instrument of white love, it was meant to give Filipinos an opportunity to perform before the solicitous gaze of American tutors. The census would be an exercise, as it were, in "character-building" where the capacity to count was coterminous with the ability to be accountable to a colonial hierarchy. Not only would the census provide the empirical grounds for shaping the direction of colonial legislation and facilitating the influx of American capital investments in the archipelago. As with the colonial legislature, it would also serve as a stage upon which Filipinos were to be represented as well as represent themselves as subjects of a colonial order: disciplined agents actively assuming their role in their own subjugation and maturation.

The American project of a centrally organized and nationally coordinated census superseded that of their Spanish predecessors. For its census data, the Spanish colonial state had relied mainly on the irregular and far from comprehensive records kept by parish priests of their local flocks. In addition, Spanish efforts at more systematic census gathering met with enormous resistance from the people inasmuch as they were geared primarily for the levying of taxes and the conscription of labor (Census, 1: 13). By contrast, the American census of the Philippines was suppose to elevate not exploit the populace. Thus did the Census Bureau lay great stress in seeking Filipino cooperation in order to neutralize popular reticence. Conducting the census was of a piece with American attempts at co-opting Filipinos from all classes. With appointments to the colonial judiciary beginning in 1899, the Philippine Constabulary (by 1901), municipal offices, and subordinate positions in the colonial civil service, Filipinos were drawn into a pattern of collaboration with the colonial state.[11] There were practical and pedagogical reasons for using Filipino personnel, particularly members of the provincial and municipal elites, for conducting the census. To do so was, as Census Chief General Sanger put it, "to identify them with the census and to test their capacity to perform duties never undertaken before, and which this country are supposed to require at least average intelligence" (Census, 1: 13).

Altogether, 7,502 Filipinos were employed, forty of whom were women. As with surrendering insurgents, local supervisors and enumerators were required to take an oath of allegiance to the government of the United States and received instructions on how to manage the canvassing of their districts. To supplement the ranks of American and Filipino supervisors, the Census Bureau also pressed into service all provincial and municipal officials, as well as American officers of the army and the Philippine Constabulary (Census, 1: 16, 18–19, 36).

The gathering of census data was an enormous undertaking involving the mobilization of a vast army of clerks and statisticians in the colonial capital and the deployment of enumerators across as much of the archipelago as possible. Although President Theodore Roosevelt had declared the Filipino-American war officially at an end by July 1902, guerrilla resistance continued in many parts of the country. In provinces such as Albay, Sorsogon, Bulacan, and Rizal, census takers were challenged by the guerrillas, now referred to under the criminal sign of "ladrones" or bandits by the colonial government. The enumeration of the population necessitated their pacification.[12] Constabulary forces often intervened to suppress the guerrillas and secure the areas to be canvassed. In parts of Mindanao, a "show of force" by the colonial army was usually necessary to gain access to sources of local information while in other parts of the country, local elites were pressed into providing information on and arranging for the surrender of local "ladrones" (Census, 1: 22–23).

The census thus illustrates the indispensable link between the policing of colonial borders and the annexation of local populations into the space of colonial knowledge. Census workers, white and native alike, labored under the watchful eyes of a hierarchy of supervisors even as they kept their eyes out for "insurgents." They surveyed the populace and were themselves surveyed by the state. In this sense, the census functioned as a machine for totalizing observation. Through the collection and classification of statistical data, it kept watch over the population, mapping their social location and transcribing them as discrete objects of information and reformation. And through the bureaucratization of surveillance underwritten by the organized deployment of violence, the census differentially disciplined those who managed as well as those who were targeted by its operations.

In order to better understand the manner by which surveillance promotes assimilation, that is, how it lays the discursive circuits that run between benevolence and discipline, I want to look in more detail at the mechanism for gathering census data. Two forms were utilized: a schedule for enumerating and classifying the people in a given area and a keyboard punch card for identifying each individual in relation to a set of categories indicated in the schedule. One served as an index for the other. Where the schedule sheets were designed to divide and distribute a person's identity into a series of delimited categories, the punch cards were meant to reconstitute him or her as the referent of a specific set of signs (Census, 2: 9–14).

The schedule sheet was written in Spanish for the sake of the Filipino enumerators unfamiliar with English. A facsimile of the schedule in English translation appears in the Census Report (figure 1). It consists of a series of vertically arranged categories such as "location," "name," "relationship," "Personal Description," "Race," "Age," "Sex," "Marital Status," "Occupation," and so forth for the "civilized" (i.e., Christian) population and a simpler, more abbreviated series for the "wild" (i.e., non-Christian) peoples. Enumerated on the sheet, one can imagine one's existence flattened out and neatly spread as a set of numbers across a table. It is as if becoming a subject of the colonial state entailed taking on a different kind of particularity. Plotted on a grid, one's identity becomes sheer surface and extension, abstracted from any historical specificity. Put differently, the census schedule projects a "profile" of colonial society by divorcing identity from biography. Where biography entails the articulation of the subject as an agent of its own history, the schedule positions its subjects as a series of aggregates locatable on a table of isolated and equivalent values.

Through the schedule, the census sought to transcribe the person into a series of numbers grafted on to a closed set of categories. However, in tabulating the results of the schedule, the census also sought to reconstitute the subject as an individuated and therefore *retrievable* item within the vast repositories of the colonial archive. Such was done through what amounted to a massive filing system in the form of the keyboard punch cards. These cards were designed for the electronic tabulation of population tables similar to what had been used for the twelfth United States census of 1900. Each card contained an array of numbers and letters

Census of the Philippine Islands taken under the direction of the United States Philippine Commission.

Supervisor's district, No. ——.
Enumeration district, No. ——.
Municipality, ——; barrio, ——; institution, ——.
Enumerated by me on the —— day of ——, 19—.   , Enumerator.

Province, ——.
Judicial district, ——.
Sheet No. —.   Page 1.

SCHEDULE No. 1.—POPULATION.

LOCATION.				Name of each person who resides with this family or in this house.	RELA-TIONSHIP.	PERSONAL DESCRIPTION.					NA-TIONALITY.	CITI-ZEN-SHIP.	OCCUPA-TION.	EDUCATION.				OWNERSHIP OF HOMES.				
In cities or pueblos.		Number of the house in the order of visitation.	Number of the family in the order of visitation.		Relationship of each person to the head of the family.	Color.	Sex.	Age at the last birthday.	Whether married or single, widowed or divorced.	Insane, deaf, dumb, blind.	Country of birth of this person.	Filipino, American, Spaniard, Chinese, Japanese, etc.	Occupation, trade, profession of each person of 10 or more years of age.	Months of school attendance during the past school year.	Prima-ry.		Superior.	Is the occupant of the house the proprietor of the house, or land, or of both, or of neither?	Which is rented, the land or the house?	What is the monthly rent?	Is the house of nipa or of more durable materials?
Street.	Number of the house.														Can read.	Can write.					
a	b	1	2	3	4	5	6	7	8	9	10	11	12	13	14	15	16	17	18	19	20

Census of the Philippine Islands taken under the direction of the United States Philippine Commission, 1903.

[Special statistics for non-Christian tribes of the Philippines.]

SCHEDULE No. 7.—POPULATION, SCHOOLS, AGRICULTURE.

Supervisor's district, No. ——.
Municipality of ——.
Enumerated by me this —— day of ——, 1903. ——, Enumerator.

Province of ——.
Judicial district ——.

PUEBLO OR RANCHERÍA.	Tribe.	INHABITANTS.								SCHOOLS.						AGRICULTURE.												OTHER INDUSTRIAL PRODUCTS.				
		Of more than 15 years of age.		Under 15 years of age.		Total.		Births in 1902.	Deaths in 1902.	Total number.	Teachers.		Pupils.		What is the approximate average of the inhabitants who can read and write?	Total area cultivated.	Products cultivated.					Number of domestic animals.								
		Males.	Females.	Males.	Females.	Males.	Females.				Males.	Females.	Males.	Females.																	
1	2	3	4	5	6	7	8	9	10	11	12	13	14	15	16	17	18	19	20	21	22	23	24	25	26	27	28	29	30	31	32

NOTICE.—When it is not possible to answer a question even approximately, write "Ign." instead of "Ignorado." The box headings of columns 18 to 32 have been left blank and should be filled out in accordance with the information collected. There should only be written down the products cultivated or harvested, such as hemp, tobacco, copra, vegetables, gutta-percha, etc. The names of these should be written in the box headings, and the quantities cultivated and harvested during the year 1902 should be written down in the columns underneath the numbers indicating the columns. If there are more products than the number of columns of the box headings, paste on an extra piece of paper and write down on this the quantities of the latter. The same method should be observed in connection with domestic animals, such as carabao, horses, sheep, cattle, fowls, etc. In columns 28 to 32 write down any other industries of the pueblo, such as pottery, textiles, cutlery, mats, hats, etc., and take notice of the instructions regarding agriculture and domestic animals given above.

Figure 1. Schedule sheet, Census of the Philippine Islands (1903).

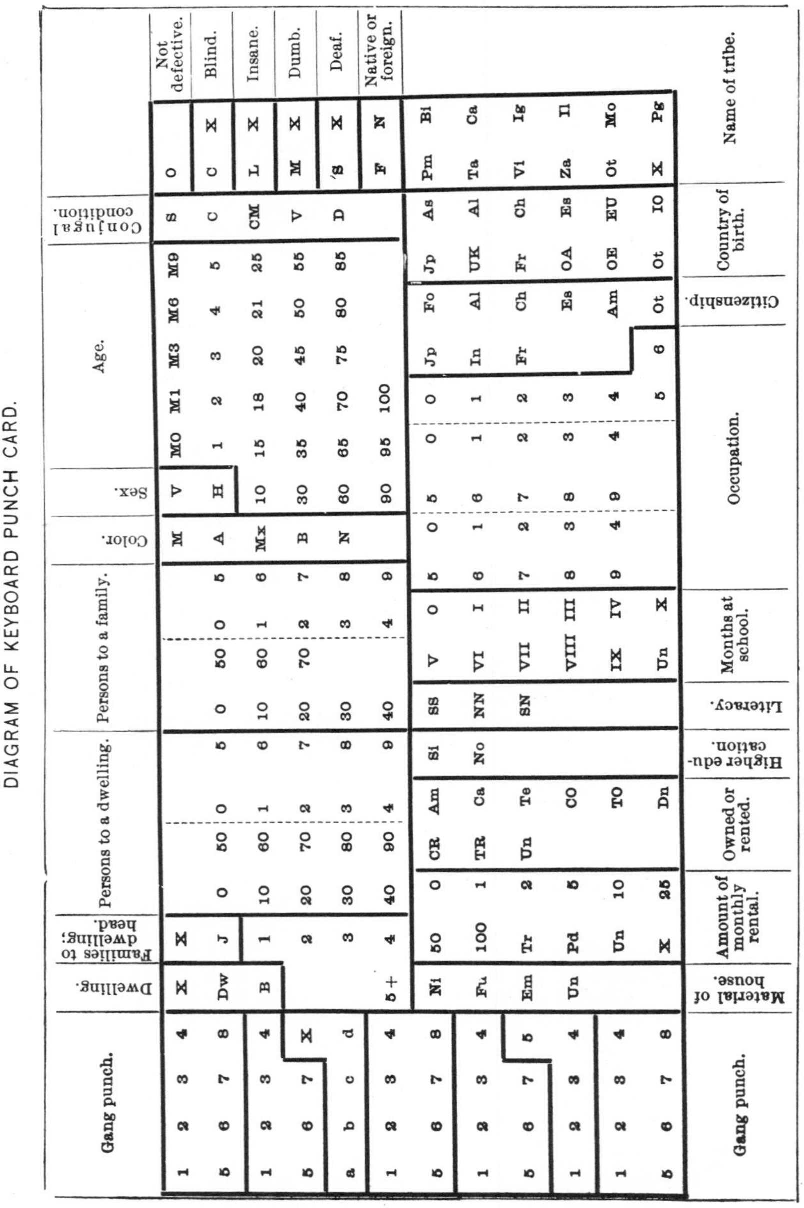

DIAGRAM OF KEYBOARD PUNCH CARD.

Figure 2. Keyboard punch card, *Census of the Philippine Islands*.

which corresponded to the data on the schedule sheets. In addition, a numbering system tied the cards to the name of a specific person and the area where she or he was counted (figure 2). By punching the appropriate holes—for instance, "B" for *blanco* (white), "M" for *moreno* (brown), "A" for *amarillo* (yellow), or "V" for *varon* (male), "H" for *hembra* (female)— the cards functioned to index a range of information regarding an individual's race, sex, age, occupation, and so forth. "By means of the gang punched holes and the numbers," declared the census, "any one of the approximately 7,000,000 cards corresponding to the population of the Philippines could be identified and the correctness of the punching verified" (Census, 2: 13).

The cards moved in the opposite but complementary direction as the schedules, citing the individual as the possessor of a range of qualities rather than as a collection of numbers attached to a set of categories. The schedules itemized the individual's characteristics, whereas the cards individualized the items in the schedule. In this sense, the census worked like an archive, where surveillance functioned as a system for cross-referencing "characters" with "characteristics." On the one hand, the census sought to constitute a "population" by enumerating the totality of heterogeneous peoples and recording them into a grid of reified categories. On the other hand, it sought to affix to each member of the population an essentialized, regulated, and therefore retrievable identity. "The fiction of the census is that everyone is in it, and that everyone has one and only one extremely clear place." [13]

The census could serve as an infinitely expandable repository for accumulating all that could be quantified and empirically known in the colony to the extent that it provided the grammar for classifying its objects of knowledge as subjects of a colonial order. As with the practice of enumeration, this grammar of classification was far from disinterested. Rather it was crucial in imaging the terms of colonial society as, above all, a racial hierarchy. It is to the census's construction of this hierarchy that I wish to turn next.

Recoding Race

White love for "little brown brothers," as Taft had referred to Filipinos, was predicated on white supremacy enforced through practices of discipline and maintained by a network of surveillance. General Sanger in his introduction to the census of 1903 remarked how Filipinos would, in the course of time, become good citizens in that already some of them had proved themselves to be "excellent soldiers" capable of following the orders of their white officers. Similarly, census workers under white supervision had showed the natives' potential for performing complex state functions. With appropriate training, there was no reason why the rest of the population could not become a disciplined people.

> Under the guidance of a free, just and generous government, the establishment of more rapid and frequent means of communication, whereby they could be brought into more frequent contact with each other, and with the general spread of education, the tribal distinctions which now exist will gradually disappear and the Filipino will become a numerous and homogeneous English-speaking race, exceeding in intelligence and capacity all other peoples of the Tropics. (Census 1: 40)

The above passage is instructive in the way it encapsulates the benevolent-disciplinary trajectory of colonial policy in general and the census in particular. Sanger reiterates the possibility, indeed the desirability of molding colonial subjects into a single people, here conceived as an "homogeneous English-speaking race." Predictably, homogenization can only come after a process of tutelage, one aimed at superseding if not suppressing existing "tribal distinctions." To do so, however, the general outlines of those distinctions need to be surveyed and accounted for. To transform the native races into *a* people, their differences had to be produced and reassembled.

The population tables of the census divide the inhabitants of the Philippines into two broad categories, "civilized" and "wild." Their difference, however, initially had less to do with their material culture than with their religious characteristics owing to the uneven impact of Spanish colonial rule. Those who were "civilized" were seen to adhere to a common Christian culture, while those who were "wild" were either Muslim or animist, but clearly outside of the Christian order. The former who comprised the majority of the archipelago's inhabitants owed their civilized state, the census assumed, to the effects of Spanish rule. The latter who had steadfastly resisted Spanish conquest, whether "pagan" headhunters in the mountains, nomadic forest dwellers, or Muslim peoples in the south, were thought to live in "stages between almost complete savagery and dawning civilization" (Census, 1: 22–23).

It is important to note, however, that the distinction between "civilized" and "wild" peoples is regarded in the census to be relative and transitional. "Wild" peoples owed their "barbarous state to the historical failure of Spain to conquer them, a condition which a more vigorous American regime would remedy. Indeed, colonial accounts are filled with glowing reports regarding the "wildmen" as ideal colonial subjects. Because they were free from the "corrupting" influence of Catholic Spain and lowland mestizo elites, wild men were seen to be far more receptive to the firm, straight-talking, tough love of white men. Hence could wild men be more easily disciplined through such tasks as massive road constructions that would link the lowlands with the mountains, mining explorations for American-owned companies, American-style athletic competitions staged for visiting colonial dignitaries, and the policing of the wild country from warring tribes to secure the safety of colonial hill stations and outposts. Wild men were ripe candidates for tutelage to the extent that they seemed most susceptible to subjugation.

Conversely, "civilized" Filipinos were more recalcitrant, even resistant to the call of benevolent assimilation. As "insurgents" fighting to assert their sovereignty after having defeated the Spanish army declared a Republic, framed a constitution, organized a cabinet, and convened a Congress by 1899, they were deemed dangerously ambitious and inherently deceptive. By their conduct in the war, these Filipinos had showed themselves to be "wild" and "barbarous." And when they chose to collaborate with the Americans, they remained shifty, opportunistic, and often lazy. Spanish colonization and the Catholic religion had done no more than imprint the natives with the outward signs of civilization. Inwardly, they remained inadequate to the task of civilizing themselves.

One of the most commonly cited traits of Filipinos in colonial sources that suggested to the Americans (and other Western writers before them) the former's semicivilized state was their supposed penchant for mimicry. Incapable of original thought, they could excel only in copying their colonial and class superiors. Sanger's remarks on the ability of Filipino soldiers to follow orders under competent white officers seemed to ratify this belief. The census repeatedly quotes passages from various colonial sources and travel accounts from the late sixteenth century to the early twentieth that retail this notion of native mimicry. Typical were the comments of Major Frank S. Bourns, army surgeon and, at one point, chief of the Bureau of Health:

> The race is quick to learn and has a fairly good natural ability, but such a class will have to be educated before great responsibility can be placed in its hands. . . . My idea [is that] if [Filipinos] associated with . . . a sufficient

number of Americans who are honorable and upright in their dealings, there would be a very strong tendency on their part to do as their colleagues do. They are natural imitators; it is a racial characteristic. (Census, 1: 505. See also pp. 494, 497, 499, 500–502, 507–8)

As "natural imitators," Filipinos perforce depend on external stimuli to shape their internal disposition. Merely reactive rather than reflective, they existed in immediate and sensuous relationship to their surroundings rather than as self-conscious agents of their own transformation. If they had committed "atrocious crimes" during the war, according to Governor General Taft, it was only because they were imitating the actions of their mestizo leaders (who in turn were imitating the actions of their Spanish masters.) Taft, like Bourns, accounts for this tendency of the Filipinos to blindly follow their racial superiors to the fact that "they are an oriental race. . . . Like all Orientals, they are a suspicious people, but when their confidence is won, they follow with a trust that is complete" (Census, 1: 530).

Mimicry on the part of the natives is construed as a sign of inferiority borne out of racial difference. But precisely for this reason, as Taft states, it is also an invitation to white supervision: "[The Filipinos] are merely in a state of Christian pupilage. They are imitative. They are glad to be educated, glad to study some languages other than their own, glad to follow European and American ideals" (Census, 1: 530). Just as the untainted state of the "wild" peoples provided white men the opportunity to display their manly love, the "civilized" but imitative, corrupted peoples of a hybrid Oriental-Christian culture called for the studious and diligent care of white tutors and commanders.

Wildness and civility were thus, at certain conceptual levels of colonial discourse, interchangeable terms. In mapping population differences, the census also projected their future reconfiguration. Such was possible because the religious difference between the "wild" and the "civilized" peoples was subsumed by larger considerations of color and race. Regardless of whether they were "Christian" or "non-Christian," marked or unmarked by European influences prior to American rule, both types were seen to display "great homogeneity" with regard to their "brown" color, to live in "tribes" with regard to their sociolinguistic organization, and to be "Malays," a species of "Orientals" with regard to their race (Census, 1: 411–12; 2: 42–54). Thus is the census able to imagine "civilized" and "wild" peoples existing side by side on the same map of the Philippines (Census, 2: 50–51). While their separate locations are indicated by the various colors of the map, one gets an acute sense of how their borders were encompassed and flattened out on the same homogeneous surface by the surveying eye of the state. Their identity as "wild" or "civilized" peoples was thus relative to their place on the colonial geobody, just as their distinct characteristics came into focus with reference to the assimilative gaze of white benevolence. The census not only mapped the structure of racial difference; it also established the privilege of a particular race to determine the borders of those differences.

This racial privilege was endowed with a genealogy. In the section entitled "History of the Population," then chief of the Bureau of Non-Christian Tribes David Barrows writes about the peopling of the archipelago in terms of waves of migrations of different "races" from the outside. In doing so, he reiterates the speculations of other colonial accounts regarding the prehistory of the Philippines—speculations which, since the archaeological advances of the 1960s, have been definitively discredited. My interest in pointing out the census's use of the wave migration theory has less to do with disproving its accuracy than with pointing out how its currency in official discourse grew out of the colonial concern with racializing Philippine history.

The original inhabitants of the islands were supposedly the Negritos, or Aetas, "aboriginal black dwarfs" whose origins, according to Barrows, remain shrouded in mystery. With their shorter stature, dark skin, "wooly hair," nomadic existence in the forests, and austere material culture, they seemed to Barrows and other American writers to be so racially distinct as to be historically removed from the rest of the population. "They probably approach as nearly to the conception of primitive man as any people thus far discovered." The "aboriginal" Negritos were then said to succumb to a succession of more culturally sophisticated and physically better endowed "Malays," at times referred to as "Indonesians," from the south. Arriving in large boats, they conquered the islands, pushing the aboriginal populations to the forests while occasionally intermarrying with them. Later migratory waves brought even stronger "Malays," some in possession of an Islamic faith acquired from Arabs, driving the older "Malays" into the mountains. The spread of Muslim Malays, however, was checked by the arrival of the Catholic Spaniards in the sixteenth century, marking the break between prehistorical and properly historical epochs in the Philippines. The Spanish conquest also led to an influx of a "Chinese element" into the population, as traders settled and intermarried with the Malays, giving rise to a small but economically and socially significant mestizo population (Census, 1: 411–17, 454, 532).[14]

This narrative of the peopling of the archipelago imagines the Philippines to have been a tabula rasa settled by successive waves of colonizers. As such, the racial and "tribal" diversity of the population can be explained in temporal terms as the inevitable retreat of darker skinned, more savage inhabitants in the face of advancing groups of lighter skinned, more civilized and physically superior conquerors. Indeed, the epochal break from the prehistorical to the properly historical era occurs only with the arrival of the Spaniards. Racial differences result then from a long history of colonization culminating, presumably, in the arrival of the strongest, most progressive, and lightest skinned colonizer to date: white Americans. The effect of racializing both the social structure and cultural history of the Philippines is to position the population in a derivative relationship to the outside. It is as if the country was naturally destined for conquest just as the United States was manifestly destined to colonize it. The historical recounting of the population, like its statistical accounting, renders colonial subjects visible from a transcendent, posthistorical vantage point, one occupied by what we might designate as the white gaze. Spatially, it is a gaze that surveys and catalogs other races while remaining unmarked and unseen itself; temporally, it is that which sees the receding past of nonwhite others from the perspective of its own irresistible future.

The privileged poise of seeing a regulated and well-policed future already prefigured in the heterogeneous and disorderly past comes across with special clarity in the photographs of Filipinos which appear in the Census Report. "Typical" examples of "wild" and "civilized" peoples are featured in the photographs in the first volume, along with pictures of native enumerators and their local supervisors. Set off from the textual and statistical sections of the census, the photographs are arranged to form an album of colonial subjectivities. Dressed in their "tribal" attires for the camera's lens, images of their bodies are wrenched from their historical and social contexts. In their frozen state, they suggest the appearance of specimens undergoing different stages of tutelage. At the lowest extreme, the scantily clad "Negritos" hunched over the ground, with tangled hair and minstrel-like grins, are made to appear farthest removed from the civilizing touch of colonial rule (figure 3). Head-hunting Igorottes, those putative descendants of the first wave of Malay conquerors, along with Muslim "Malays" appear more erect, even regal, decked out in their tribal ornaments signifying their more advanced state (figure 4). Closest to civilization are the Western-clad census workers. Set against the background of American flags, their appearance suggests well-

Figure 3. "Negritos" (Aetas), *Census of the Philippine Islands* (1903).

disciplined bodies, while the portraits of local supervisors identified by name and area of responsibility produce images of bourgeois respectability assimilated into the state machinery (figures 5 and 6).

Within the context of the census's racializing discourse, such photographs constitute the visual complement to the statistical tables, a distinct but related way of seeing native subjects as objects of knowledge and reform. Where statistical tabulations abstract native identities into faceless numbers, the photographs give a kind of composite face to the statistics. Shadowed by the notion of "typicality"—which I take to be the reduction of cultural differences into an ordered range of variations and a set of representative figures—these photographs form part of the same enumerative and classificatory optic of colonial knowledge.

Photographs of "wild" and "civilized" Filipinos are reproduced not only in the Census Report but in various official documents of the colonial archive. Many of them were taken by government officials themselves, most prominently Dean C. Worcester, as part of their regular trips to survey the peoples and conditions of the country. Within a colonial context, these photographs make a claim analogous to that of the census: that while a diverse collection of "tribes" may exist in the archipelago, they can be encoded within the same racial hierarchy and enclosed within a single

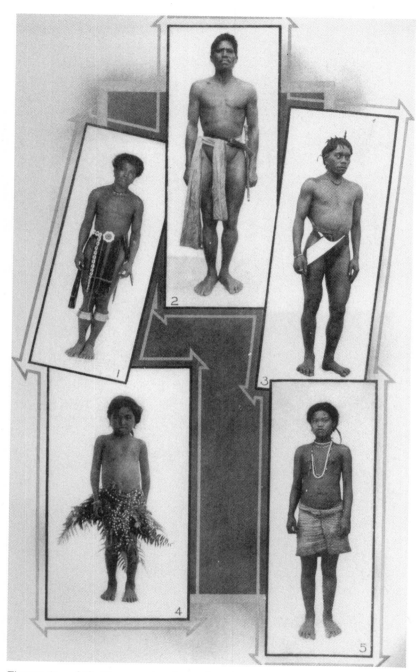

Figures 4a and 4b. Photographs of non-Christian "wild" peoples.

(4b)

Figure 5. "Civilized" peoples.

visual field. Constructed as examples and exemplars of native "types," photographic images of colonial subjects map cultural differences within the same representational grid. That is to say, they bear the marks of a colonizing gaze which, in remaining discrete and dispersed, is able to arrogate to itself the privilege to rank and assess the comparative value of the native inhabitants and their world. They image the subjects of colonialism as objects of transitional significance whose present is bound to fade into the past as they are wholly annexed to the civilizing embrace of the future. Mementos of conquest, such photographs serve as dioramas of benevolent assimilation. Like the census tables and graphs, they work to erase the traces of violence at the origins of American rule and instead pay tribute to the technologies of surveillance and classification that maintain the disciplinary devotions of white rule.[15]

Short-circuiting Surveillance:
The Tagalog "Seditious" Plays

Were there other ways of reading benevolent assimilation that went against the grain of the census? Did alternative styles of envisioning the

Figure 6. Portraits of Filipino supervisors.

"Philippines" exist that put in question the racializing narratives of the Philippine past along with the disciplinary prescriptions for its present and future?

At about the same time the census was being conducted and published between 1903 and 1905, a series of nationalist plays in the Tagalog vernacular were being performed in and around Manila. Written and performed by largely urban, working-class artists, some of whom had been active in both the revolution against Spain and the war against the United States, these plays were extraordinarily popular among both working-class audiences and members of the nationalist elite critical of American rule. Occupying the same historical terrain as the colonial census, nationalist melodramas point not so much to the internal contradictions of the census as to the limits of the census's discursive reach. While the census serves as an important foundation in the construction of a larger colonial archive—an archive which would come to include transcribed and translated examples of Tagalog "seditious" plays as part of the colonial court records—nationalist dramas performed a history whose meanings eluded the imperial logic of benevolent assimilation and the surveying gaze of the archive.

Under the Sedition Law, the colonial Supreme Court banned these nationalist dramas, claiming that they tended to "incite the people of the Philippine Islands to open and armed resistance to the constituted authorities" and "inculcate a spirit of hatred and enmity against the American people and the Government of the United States in the Philippines." Forced to perform underground in order to evade the constant scrutiny of the Philippine Constabulary and a paranoid white press, playwrights and casts were frequently arrested, fined, and imprisoned. Through such coercion, the colonial government managed to curtail and finally extinguish the production of nationlist plays after 1905. By the opening of the Philippine Assembly, the lower house of a colonial legislature monopolized by Filipino elites in 1907, nationalist discourse had been drained of much of its oppositional edge as the movements for independence came under the disciplinary tutelage of the colonial state.[16]

American anxiety over these nationalist dramas had to do with the extent of their popularity among the Filipinos. Playing to crowded houses in Manila, such dramas also attracted "every man, woman and child" in outlying barrios. It was not uncommon for the audience to "cheer on its feet, rabid with fury and frenzy for three hours" after a performance, as one American account nervously wrote. "When the seditious plays appeared, the people rose to it as one man, recognized that it told their story and patronized them liberally" [sic] (Riggs, xi, 45, 57). In order to evade colonial surveillance, theatrical groups relied on such tactics as publicizing the plays under different titles, staging impromptu songs and speeches advocating Philippine sovereignty, and dressing the cast in costumes which, when brought into formation on stage, momentarily created an image of the outlawed Philippine flag. They used visual props such as the rising red sun, symbolic of the revolutionary organization, the Katipunan, that had led the revolution against Spain, and structured their stories as allegories of romance and kinship to invoke recollections of recent events and to provoke sympathy (*damay*) with the sufferings of the "motherland" (*Inangbayan*). Through the characters, the playwrights staged debates about the present and the future of the nation, crafting lengthy soliloquies and pointed exchanges which questioned American pronouncements of benevolent assimilation and critiqued the practice of Filipino collaboration. Indeed, colonialism and collaboration were seen in the plays as mutually reinforcing, working to "enslave" (*alipinin*) the population and disrupt the affective ties that constituted the borders of the national community.

Drawing their formal coherence from the melodramatic conventions of nineteenth-century vernacular genres (e.g., *komedya* and *Moro-moro*), the plots of nationalist dramas served as screens for projecting profoundly felt and widely shared social experiences of revolution, colonial occupation, war, and the intense longing for "freedom" (*Kalayaan*).[17] These plots usually revolved around the relationship between a female beloved and her male lover-protector or between a mother and her children. One personified the nation and freedom, while the other stood for the patriot and the people. Their relationship is invariably threatened by a male foreign intruder harboring designs on the woman-nation. He is aided by a local collaborator who, in betraying his siblings and parents, substitutes the love of nation for the lust after money. Together, they abduct the woman-nation, thereby precipitating a crisis of filiation. Encouraged by their motherland, the male-patriot and his supporters battle both foreigner and collaborator in order to regain the freedom of the beloved nation. Extended calls to mourn (*damay*) those who had perished in the fighting are issued by the motherland (*Inangbayan*). She appeals to her sons and daughters to recall the sacrifices of those who had died, thereby turning death into an occasion to celebrate the bonds that unite them. Although the endings of the plays may vary in their details, they all envision in one form or another the spectacular reunification of the beloved nation, whether in the present or in the future, with her lover-patriot returning from imprisonment or from death itself to lead the people to victory against foreigners and collaborators alike.

Whereas the allegory of benevolent assimilation regarded colonial politics as the melodrama of white love for brown brothers, the stories of "seditious" plays used melodramas as a political language for expressing the love of nation. We can see how language is politicized in the plays by looking at the conventions of naming the different characters. The usual practice of playwrights was to use common nouns and adjectives to denote each character and to have each character signify a particular concept or social entity as gleaned from the plays' dramatis personae. For example, in Juan Abad's *Tanikalang Guinto* ("The Golden Chain"), Liwanag (literally "light," signifying "Freedom") is betrothed to K'ulayaw ("Defender," standing for the patriot), son of Dalita ("suffering," connoting the captive condition of the motherland). Liwanag, however, is desired by Maimbot ("avarice," that is, the American colonial government) who enlists the aid of the collaborator Nag-tapon ("throws," or "wastes away"). Nag-tapon accepts money from Maimbot and thus betrays his brother, K'ulayaw, and his mother, Dalita (Riggs, 497–542).

Similarly, in Juan Matapang Cruz's *Hindi Pa Aco Patay* ("I Am Not Yet Dead"), Macamcam ("avaricious," again, the American colonial state), son of Maimbot ("greedy," the United States government) seeks by force and deception to wed Karangalan ("dignity," "respect," connoting the natural resources of the country), daughter of Pinagsakitan ("she who suffers," the motherland). Macamcam and Maimbot employ the services of the son of Pinagsakitan, Ualang-hinayang ("shameless one," the Filipino collaborator) who, in exchange for money, helps to engineer the abduction of Karangalan. However, Karangalan's lover, Tangulan ("protector," the Filipino patriot), nephew of Katuiran ("reason," "justice," signifying Filipino rights), attempts to rescue her by challenging Macamcam to a duel. Macamcam seems momentarily victorious, and everyone believes that Tangulan is dead. But as the wedding between Macamcam and Karangalan is about to take place, Tangulan suddenly appears on the stage, declaring to the wild applause of the audience, "I am not yet dead!" (Riggs, 543–606).

In one of the most famous "seditious" dramas, *Kahapon, Ngayon, at Bukas* ("Yesterday, Today, and Tomorrow") by the prolific writer Aurelio Tolentino, Philippine history is depicted not as the successive waves of conquests described in the Census Report, but as the progression of anticolonial struggles against foreign invaders and local collaborators. In act 1, "Yesterday," Inangbayan ("motherland") rallies her people, led by the defender Tagailog (literally, "from the water," a reference to the Tagalogs) to defend their land, Balintawak (a reference to the site where the revolution of 1896 against Spain began) against the incursions of the "Chinese" despot, Batang Hari ("child-king," perhaps a reference to the seventeenth-century "Chinese" pirate, Limahong, who had threatened to invade the Spanish colony). Batang Hari is aided by the machinations of the collaborator Asalhayop ("behaves like an animal"). In act 2, "Today," Tagailog escapes from prison by killing the collaborator Dahumpalay ("venomous snake"), concealing his identity and rallying his fellow Tagalogs to rescue Inangbayan, then in the process of being buried alive by Matanglawin ("hawkeye," the Spanish colonial government), his wife Dilatnabulag ("sighted but unable to see," Spain herself), and Halimaw ("monster," the Spanish friar). Finally, in act 3, "Tomorrow," Tagailog presses a condescending Malaynatin ("one who we don't really know," the American government) to live up to its promise of granting independence to the people. Inangbayan also pleads with Malaynatin's wife, Bagongsibol ("fresh spring," the American nation), to convince her husband to accede to Tagailog's demands. The latter prepares an army to attack Malaynatin should he renege on his promise. But such a plan proves unnecessary, as Bagonsibol finally succumbs to the entreaties of the children of Inangbayan and gives the country its independence. "Tomorrow" ends in a hopeful note with everyone celebrating the new freedom of Inangbayan (Riggs, 607–51).

The American writer Arthur Stanley Riggs, who had compiled an extensive dossier on these plays for the colonial government, remarks on the practice of using common words to denote the names of characters:

> Such names . . . are to the native mind filled with the keenest suggestion, and the artful connotation of the playwright in thus making the very names of his mimes tell more than their set speeches has had a tremendous effect. Everytime the common nouns were employed in the body of the text, the audience saw not only the characteristic properties suggested by them, but also swiftly imagined the particular characters to which the names belonged. . . . The result was a quick, lively and entire confidence established between author, players, and audience impossible to obtain in any other way. (Riggs, 122)

In nationalist dramas, mimicry acquires a value different from that assigned to it by colonial sources in relation to native "characteristics." Characters on stage mime the qualities suggested by their names with the active and complicitous understanding of the playwrights and audiences. In this case, mimicry becomes a sign of acute, even ironic, self-consciousness geared toward acting out historical narratives that ran counter to official versions. Common names are invested with new meanings and remade by characters into emblems of collective experiences.

They become hieroglyphs, as it were, for recalling the nation's history and redrawing its moral boundaries. In this sense, the commonality of words becomes proper not only to the individual character on stage but to the particular vernacular community from and to which that character addresses her- or himself.

The practice of naming in nationalist melodramas bears comparison to the representational conventions of the Census Report. As we have seen, the population was designated as the aggregate of quantitatively visible entities within a closed set of categories. Reifying identities into schedules, cards, and photographic specimens of the "typical," the census consigned both naming and their interpretation to a bureaucratic apparatus. Translatable into numbers and locatable on a grid, names were regarded as part of an ensemble of objectifying devices with which to regulate and supervise the relationship between knower and known, state and subjects, white and nonwhite peoples.

By contrast, nationalist dramas turned common names into new sites for public life, rendering their referents readily accessible to actors, audiences, and authors who shared the same vernacular. The practice of naming was therefore a way of establishing an imagined continuity between communication and community. Thus could names speak more than their characters inasmuch as they provided not merely a way of marking one from the other on stage; they also opened up a space from which to address all those who considered themselves affiliated with the nation. Where colonial archives characterize and classify in order to render their subjects available for discipline, nationalist melodramas resignify the vernacular so as to reclaim the capacity of a people to nominate themselves as agents in and interpreters of their experiences.

The narrative of those collective experiences was shaped by a thematics of kinship ties. As with many island Southeast Asian societies, Filipino relations are bilaterally reckoned. Individuals trace their links equally on both the mother's and father's lines. Bilateral kinship descent allows for the cultivation of extended families through both ritual and extraritual means. Historically, such ties tended to be idealized along the lines of an economy of reciprocal obligations, that is, through conventions of deference, respect, and expectations of mutual caring between parent and children, older and younger siblings, husbands and wives, lovers and beloved, landlords and tenants, masters and servants, and any other configuration of superordinate and subordinate relations. Reciprocal obligations are in a sense the "grammar" of kinship ties, determining the lines of filiation and affiliation between self and other as simultaneously personal (face to face) and political (hierarchic and subject to conflict and change). Put differently, kinship is a way of conceiving the fatedness of self and other to a social order predicated on the circulation of mutual indebtedness. In a sense then, to acknowledge one's kin is to imagine the limits of one's social experience.[18]

By mapping the national community onto the extended family—and conversely, by imaging colonization and collaboration as the disruption of that family, the subversion of an economy of reciprocal indebtedness—nationalist dramas reenact the relationship between the personal and the political. As melodramas, they regard kinship as the terrain of conflicts and alliances that bear simultaneously on the private and public spheres—indeed, that call attention to their mutual constitution. To get a sense of how the plays dramatize the link between the personal and political, I want to take a look at the ways by which they engender the image of a nation by placing gender itself in motion.

As we had occasion to see earlier, the discourse of benevolent assimilation was predicated on a racial hierarchy which surveyed as it sought to discipline colonial subjects. However, the census also differentiated the population as "males" and "females," coordinating gender distinctions with race, age, occupation, cause of death, disability, and the like. Worth noting is the fact that while racial difference was conceived of in spatial and temporal terms as organized by and subordinate to whiteness, gender distinctions are posed without commentary, as if they were wholly natural. Indeed, the category of "gender" is not used at all, but rather that of "sex," so that the distinction between men and women appears to be universal and beyond any sort of social convention.

The extent to which gender appears unproblematic in the census is, I think, an indication of the overwhelmingly masculine construction of colonial discourse. There is never any doubt in official sources that white love is paternal and that the task of colonial administration, though it employed women as teachers in public schools and nurses in public health programs, is by and large men's work. Colonial politics was thus conceived of as a homosocial affair involving the tutelary bonding between white fathers and their male native-mestizo apprentices. To be coded "female" of whatever "race" was in effect to be consigned to a marginal position in the public sphere of colonial society. "Gender" was thus conflated with "sex" as the representation of sexual difference was naturalized in relation to the paternalism of the colonial state. Just as racial difference was organized from the vantage point of whiteness, sexual difference was structured from the masculine perspective of the state. To be classified as "male" or "female" meant becoming visible as such to the gaze of white fathers.[19]

Nationalist melodramas, by contrast, do not contain a discourse on race. Whatever hostile references these plays may have to "foreigners," such characters are never distinguished by color or race but in terms of behavior and language. Hence, characters standing for the American colonial government are depicted as loud and disrespectful, given to excessive drinking and crude behavior (as Filipinos often witnessed American soldiers do during the war), and untrustworthy by virtue of having reneged on past obligations. Indeed, in Tolentino's play, the "foreigners" representing "America" are even more complex, depicted in a sympathetic light as potentially responsive to the rights of Filipinos. The occasional reference to "Chinese" invaders may reflect a sense of anti-Sinicism cultivated by Spanish colonial policies in the past, but these "Chinese" remain so vaguely drawn and unracialized as to be tokens in a larger discourse about nationalist resistance to colonial rule.

"Race" as a trope for difference and power is thus remarkably absent in these plays. What seems crucial in drawing social distinctions, however, is gender. The importance of gender is apparent in the names and plots of the dramas. Figures for the beloved nation (e.g., Inangbayan, Pinagsakitan, Karangalan, and Dalita) and the desired freedom (Liwanag, Bituin, Malaya) are invariably cast as "woman" (*babae*). Those who desire her, whether patriot-protectors or colonialist and collaborators, are always cast as "men" (*lalaki*). It is as if these dramas triangulate social desire, casting nationhood in terms of the masculine struggle over a feminized object. The relationship between the nation and the nationalists and colonizers alike is thereby mediated by gender stereotypes. While men act—they threaten or protect, abduct or rescue, wage war and make peace—women react and watch the spectacle of men seeking them out.

Yet in the text of the plays, these gender stereotypes appear provisional and shifting. In attributing a "gender" to the characters, the plays also problematize the meaning of those roles particularly under severe conditions of revolutionary upheaval and colonial dislocation. In *Hindi Pa Aco Patay*, for example, Karangalan calls out to Tangulan to rescue her from Macamcam. Nonetheless, it is she who ends up rescuing him in the forest by shooting a predatory bird symbolizing the Philippine Constabulary. It is also from her that we hear the most incisive critique of collaboration as mere enslavement to money and the most resonant refutation of American assessments regarding the "unfitness" of Filipinos for self-government. *Luhang Tagalog* ("Tagalog Tears"), an earlier play by Tolentino, features the character Bituin ("star," signifying independence) who protects her husband from the murderous designs of his collaborationist father. She also counsels the mothers and wives of those going off

to war, offers a trenchant critique of war as an arena of masculine privilege, and eloquently exposes the link between benevolent assimilation
and colonial subjugation (Riggs, 352–422). As the suffering motherland
(Busilak in Tomas Remigio's *Malaya* ["Freedom"], Pinagsakitan in *Hindi
Pa Aco Patay,* and Inangbayan in *Kahapon, Ngayon at Bukas*), women do
not serve as passive spectators to their own rescue. Rather, they initiate
the call to struggle by putting forth the need to remember the dead. They
invoke the importance of mourning (*damay*) which, because it rekindles
ties between the living and the dead, the past and the future, constitutes
the historical and affective boundaries of the national community.

Women personify the beloved nation waiting to be rescued; yet they
also generate the conditions that make their rescue both possible and
desirable. As nurturing mothers and vulnerable lovers, the woman-nation
also takes up arms, plans battles, and demands accountability from characters and audiences alike. They are objects of masculine contention, but
they are also active interlocutors in the debate over the future disposition
of their body politic.

Part of what renders woman's position so complex is the remarkable fact that fathers are either marginal or absent in these plays. The
"foreigners" who covet the woman-nation are constructed as illegitimate
or unacceptable fathers. Collaborators are often depicted as less than
human, almost animal because of their association with money. Patriot-
protectors, as lovers, are not yet husbands and tend to occupy shifting
positions as characters in need of defense as much as they seek to defend
the nation. When taken together, these masculine roles have the effect
of deferring the emergence of any kind of paternal hegemony within
the world of the nationalist dramas. Just as the relationship between the
nation and its people crystallizes in opposition to the "avaricious" and
monopolizing intentions of the colonial state, so it would seem that the
gender differences between women and men do not coalesce around a
paternal figure of authority. Instead these differences come up against
and before the persistent figure of the motherland. Such is not to say that
men and women were equal; only that the inequality inherent in gender
formations was put in question, cast as provisional and conditional on
specific historical circumstances. Gender in these plays does not come
across as a series of fixed and natural categories, but as a set of negotiable
positions in the articulation of nationhood. In the absence of a symbolic
father that would serve as a point of reference in the gendering of social
relations at a time of intense turmoil and uncertainty, it is conceivable
that the association between "woman" and "nation" in the dramas did not
simply reproduce gender stereotypes; it also suggested alternative roles,

empowering women to speak and to act in the defense of the body politic against the designs of colonizing others. Small wonder then that, as Riggs wrote, "the women are as ardent theatre-goers, even in times of political stress, as their husbands, brothers and sons" (Riggs, 46).

These nationalist dramas suggest that the imaging of "nation" as "woman" did not invariably translate into a reified gender hierarchy. Rather, the ambiguous construction of gender categories in the plays arose from the specificity of Filipino notions of kinship historically articulated in relation to the turbulence of war, the revolutionary expectations of "freedom" (*Kalayaan*), and the absence of a stable patriarchal state between 1899 and 1905. What makes the plays significant is that by imagining the nation as woman, they also projected a notion of the nation as *distinct* from the state. And such was imaginable precisely at a particular historical moment when the structures of authority—colonial as well as familial—were up for grabs. Thus did nationalist plays implicitly put forth a discourse on gender that allowed for a certain play on the meanings of "men" and "women." The unresolved status of gender roles (where, for example, a display of utter weakness rather than confident mastery can be a "male" attribute as much as it is a "female") underlines, once again, the differences between the representational operations of the census and the plays. Where the former was organized around the production of a stable state apparatus that would rule paternally over a racialized and gendered people, the latter were far more concerned with imaging the nation as an extended family predicated less on a patriarchal principle of authority as on a general economy of reciprocal obligations freed from the violence of colonial rule.

Unlike the census, then, nationalist plays did not seek to represent the population as implacably bound to gender and racial categories subject to the continuous gaze of white benevolence. Their "seditiousness" consisted precisely in providing alternative sources of knowledge and power—sources into which colonial agents were assimilated, but as figures disruptive of reciprocal obligations. As melodramas, they depicted social desires in motion, thereby reintroducing a deep sense of contingency into the narrative of recent events on the levels of language and gender. For where white love prescribed manly discipline, the love of nation postulated a different kind of bondage, one where a network of surveillance gave way to a spectacular commerce in tears. I quote as a concluding example Aurelio Tolentino's dedication of his play *Luhang Tagalog* ("Tagalog Tears") to the "motherland":

Weeping without ceasing for your children,
    And weeping always for your sorrows,
I have taken care to write this piece
    So that my tears should flow
    Together with the tears from your eyes.
To you I offer this: it is so very fragile
    because it is from me;
    Still accept this
For I have nothing more valuable to give. (Riggs, 352)

Notes

I want to thank the following for their comments and criticisms of earlier versions of this essay: Benedict Anderson, Don Brennies, Oscar Campomanes, Doreen Fernandez, Amy Kaplan, George Lipsitz, Resil Mojares, Ambeth Ocampo, Michael Salman, and Don Siegel.

1 United States, Adjutant General of the Army, *Correspondences Relating to the War with Spain*, vol. 2, p. 859. For related documents, see also "Instructions of the President to the First Philippine Commission," January 20, 1899, in the Appendix of Dean C. Worcester, *The Philippines: Past and Present*, 2 vols. (New York: McMillan, 1914), vol. 2, p. 975; and United States, 56th Congress, Document No. 138, *Report of the Philippine Commission*, 2 vols. (Washington: Government Printing Office, 1900), vol. 1, pp. 3–4.

2 *Report of the Philippine Commission*, 1900, vol. 1, p. 4.

3 Ibid.

4 McKinley, in United States, Adjutant General of the Army, *Correspondences Relating to the War with Spain*, vol. 2, p. 859.

5 *Report to the Philippine Commission*, 1900, vol. 1, p. 4.

6 Ibid., p. 5.

7 Elihu Root, Letter addressed to the Army of the United States, July 4, 1902, in United States, Adjutant General of the Army, *Correspondences Relating to the War with Spain*, 2 vols. (Washington: Government Printing Office, 1902), pp. 1352–1353. The indispensable collection of Filipino and American documents relating to the war can be found in John R.M. Taylor, *The Philippine Insurrection Against the United States*, originally completed in 1906 but not published until 1971 (Pasay: Eugenio Lopez Foundation), 5 vols., with an introduction by Renato Constantino.

8 Woodrow Wilson, for example, writes with reference to the Philippines that "self-government is a form of character. It follows upon the long discipline which gives a people self-possession, self-mastery, and the habit of order and peace . . . the steadiness of self-control and political mastery. And these things cannot be had without long discipline. . . . No people can be 'given' the self-control of maturity. Only a long apprenticeship of obedience can secure them the precious possession."

Constitutional Government in the United States (New York: Columbia University Press, 1921 [originally published 1908]), pp. 52–53.

Self-government like self-mastery is thus non-negotiable. It is not the product of a social contract among equals but the result of sustained disciplinary measures requiring the colonized to submit unstintingly to a pedagogy of repression and mastery. For while the Filipinos—not yet a "people"—possess disparate "characteristics," they lack the "character" with which to synthesize and control these. Such is the premise of benevolent assimilation.

For a more recent example of the continuing currency of these notions of benevolent assimilation, see Stanley Karnow's Pulitzer Prize book, *In Our Image: America's Empire in the Philippines* (New York: Ballantine Books, 1989). And for a trenchant critique of this book, see Michael Salman, "In Our Orientalist Imagination: Historiography and the Culture of Colonialism in the U.S.," in *Radical History Review* 50 (Spring 1991), pp. 221–32.

9 United States, Bureau of the Census, *Census of the Philippine Islands*, 4 vols. (Washington: Government Printing Office, 1905). References to this work will hereinafter appear in the main body of the text.

10 See for example the important writings of Reynaldo Ileto, *Pasyon and Revolution: Popular Movements in the Philippines, 1840–1910* (Quezon City: Ateneo de Manila University Press, 1979), esp. chaps. 5 and 6, and "Cholera and the Origins of the American Sanitary Order in the Philippines," in David Arnold, ed., *Imperial Medicine and Indigenous Societies* (Manchester: Manchester University Press, 1988), pp. 125–48. See also Warwick Anderson, "Medicine and Colonial Discourse," in *Critical Inquiry* 18, no. 3 (Spring 1992); Rodney Sullivan, "Cholera and Colonialism in the Philippines, 1899–1903," in Roy Macleod and Milton Lewis, eds., *Disease, Medicine and Empire* (New York: Routledge, 1988), pp. 284–300; and the excellent work of Michael Salman, "The United States and the End of Slavery in the Philippines, 1898–1914: A Study of Imperialism, Ideology, and Social Change," (Ph.D. diss., Stanford University, 1993); and "'Nothing Without Labor:' Labor, Discipline, and Independence in the Philippines under United States Colonial Rule, 1898–1914," unpublished paper, December 28, 1990.

The continuum among an ideology of benevolence, practices and institutions of discipline, and networks of surveillance—in short, of knowledge and power— may be inferred from a careful reading of the writings of such revisionist scholars as Glenn May, *Social Engineering the Philippines* (Connecticut: Greenwood Press, 1980); Peter Stanley, *A Nation in the Making: The Philippines and the United States, 1899–1921* (Cambridge: Harvard University Press, 1974); the essays in Ruby Paredes, ed., *Philippine Colonial Democracy* (Quezon City: Ateneo de Manila University Press, 1989); and Michael Cullinane, "Ilustrado Politics: The Response of the Filipino Educated Elite to American Colonial Rule, 1898–1907" (Ph.D. diss., University of Michigan, 1989), to mention only a few. Much of what follows in my discussion of American colonialism is in part informed by the works of Michel Foucault, especially *Discipline and Punish: The Birth of the Prison*, trans. Alan Sheridan (New York: Vintage, 1979). Also useful are the essays collected in *The*

Foucault Effect: Studies in Governmentality, ed. Graham Burchell, Colin Gordon, and Peter Miller (Chicago: University of Chicago Press, 1991); and Paul Rabinow's lucid "Introduction" in *The Foucault Reader* (New York: Pantheon Books, 1984), pp. 3–29.

11 See Norman G. Owen, ed., *Compadre Colonialism: Philippine-American Relations, 1889–1946* (Ann Arbor: Michigan Papers in South and Southeast Asian Studies, no. 3, 1971); Bonifacio Salamanca, *The Filipino Reaction to American Rule, 1901–1913* (Norwich, Conn.: Shoestring Press, 1968); Onofre D. Corpuz, *The Bureaucracy in the Philippines* (Quezon City: University of the Philippines Institute of Public Administration, 1957), and *The Roots of the Filipino Nation,* 2 vols. (Quezon City: Aklahi Foundation, 1989), chap. 21; Stanley, *A Nation in the Making,* chaps. 3–6; Cullinane, "Illustrado Politics," and the essays in Paredes, ed., *Philippine Colonial Democracy* are all incisive and detailed studies into the dynamics of Filipino collaboration.

12 See Ileto, *Pasyon and Revolution,* chaps. 5 and 6; and "Orators and the Crowd: Philippine Independence Politics, 1910–1914," in Stanley, ed., *Reappraising an Empire,* pp. 85–113. See also David Sturtevant, *Popular Uprisings in the Philippines, 1840–1940* (Ithaca: Cornell University Press, 1976).

13 Benedict Anderson, *Imagined Communities: Reflections on the Origins and Spread of Nationalism,* rev. ed. (London: Verso Press, 1991), p. 166. I am indebted to Anderson's astute remarks on colonial censuses and maps for my own understanding of the census of 1903. I have also profited considerably from the fine essay by Alan Sekula on the intertwined history of photography and statistics in the conceptualization of populations as domains of state intervention, "The Body and the Archive," in *October* 39 (Winter 1986): 3–64.

14 See also United States, Bureau of Insular Affairs, *A Pronouncing Gazetteer and Geographical Dictionary of the Philippine Islands* (Washington: Government Printing Office, 1902), pp. 63–67; William Cameron Forbes, *The Philippine Islands,* 2 vols. (Boston: Houghton Mifflin, 1928), vol. 1, pp. 586–90. For a concise review of current archaeological evidence that decisively disputes the wave migration theory, see William Henry Scott, *Prehispanic Source Materials for the Study of Philippine History,* rev. ed. (Quezon City: New Day Publishers, 1984), pp. 31–32, 143–44. For a recent critique of American colonial anthropology, see Renato Rosaldo, "Imperialist Nostalgia," in his book *Culture and Truth: The Remaking of Social Analysis* (Boston: Beacon Press, 1989), pp. 68–87.

15 The image of the census—indeed of the entirety of colonial government reports—as a series of dioramas in an imperialist museum of native history was suggested to me by Donna Haraway's brilliant essay, "Teddy Bear Patriarchy: Taxidermy in the Garden of Eden, New York City, 1908–1936," reprinted in this volume.

16 The citations from the colonial Supreme Court appear in Arthur Stanley Riggs, *The Filipino Drama (1905)* (Manila: Ministry of Human Settlements, Intramuros Administration, 1981), p. xi. This text contains both the original Tagalog texts of the seditious dramas as well as their English translation, accompanied by the author's instructive, even if at times hysterical ramblings, on the threats posed by such plays to the American regime. Hereinafter, references to this volume appear in the main text.

Other useful background materials on the nationalist plays can be found in Cullinane, "Ilustrado Politics," pp. 173–83; and E. Arsenio Manuel, *Dictionary of Philippine Biography* (Quezon City: Filipiniana Publications, 1970), vol. 2, pp. 371–83; Amelia Lapena-Bonifacio, *The "Seditious" Tagalog Playwrights: Early American Occupation* (Manila: Zarzuela Foundation of the Philippines, 1972). Also helpful in understanding the larger historical setting of the nationalist dramas are Doreen Fernandez, *The Iloilo Zarzuela* (Quezon City: Ateneo de Manila University Press, 1978); Edna Z. Manlapaz, ed., *Aurelio Tolentino: Selected Writings* (Quezon City: University of the Philippines Press, 1975); and Resil Mojares, *Origins and Rise of the Filipino Novel: A Generic Study of the Novel until 1940* (Quezon City: University of the Philippines Press, 1983).

17 See Ileto's nuanced discussion of how popular notions of "freedom" (*kalayaan*, from the root word *layaw*, a condition of perfect reciprocity usually associated with the child's relationship with its mother) varied considerably from American and Filipino elite understandings of "independence" as originating from the actions of the state in *Pasyon and Revolution*, chap. 5; and in "Orators and the Crowd," in Stanley, *Reappraising an Empire*, pp. 85–113.

18 For a more detailed discussion of notions of reciprocal indebtedness in Tagalog society, see Vicente L. Rafael, *Contracting Colonialism: Translation and Christian Conversion in Tagalog Society Under Early Spanish Rule* (Durham: Duke University Press, 1993), chaps. 3–4, and "Patronage and Pornography: Ideology and Spectatorship in the Early Marcos Years," in *Comparative Studies in Society and History* 32, no. 2 (April 1990): 282–304.

19 My remarks on the intersection of race, gender, and sexuality in this particular colonial setting are preliminary and for that reason, unsatisfactory. The colonial articulation of gender (and race) in the Philippines is undoubtedly more complex than what I've just sketched above, and it is a complexity that I am at present trying to unpack. In fact, where Philippine studies is concerned, it is these complex relations among race, gender, sexuality, and class that remain acutely understudied.

In the case of nationalist discourse, I have sought to outline not so much the patriarchal basis of nationalism as its tendency to produce a desire for patriarchy in the face of colonial fathers (e.g., Spanish friars) deemed illegitimate and degenerate. See Vicente L. Rafael, "Nationalism, Imagery and the Filipino Intelligentsia of the Nineteenth Century," in *Critical Inquiry* 16 (Spring 1990): 591–611. For a regional overview and comparative case studies of the intersection of gender categories with the construction of local notions of power, see the illuminating essays in Jane Atkinson and Shelly Errington, eds., *Power and Difference: Gender in Island Southeast Asia* (Stanford: Stanford University Press, 1990).

Amy Kaplan

Black and Blue on

San Juan Hill

hat Virginia Woolf wrote of books, that they "continue each other," can also be said of wars: wars continue each other.[1] Wars generate and accumulate symbolic value by reenacting, reinterpreting, and transposing the cultural meaning of prior wars. The Spanish-American War of 1898 can be understood to have continued the Civil War in an imperial national discourse of the United States at the turn of the century. Politicians and journalists represented the war with Spain as a nostalgic recuperation of the heroism of an earlier generation and as a purgative final battle, healing the wounds and divisiveness of their internecine war while completing its goals of national reunification. While the hundred-day brevity of the later conflict counteracted the interminable length of the earlier one, the international war also promised to reunify the nation by bringing together the North and the South against a common external enemy. Moreover, new battlefields abroad reputedly restored health and vigor to the male body, so massively dismembered in the war between the states. In fact, the vitality of the male body became the symbolic medium for national restoration, as manliness figured the common ground between previously warring factions. And all this, staged on the remote islands of Cuba and the Philippines, leaving the American landscape unscathed. No wonder John Hays called it a "splendid little war."

Yet to continue the Civil War as the final destination on what has been called the "road to reunion," the Spanish-American War had to collapse and undo the thirty-year history separating the two conflicts by waging an ideological battle against Reconstruction, the prior "continuation" of the Civil War. The conflicted legacy of Reconstruction disrupted this unilinear narrative of continuity. Representations of the later war can thus be seen doing battle on two related fronts: the international struggle with Spain and its colonies aspiring for national independence and the domestic struggle with African Americans fighting to achieve civil rights during Reconstruction. External and internal fronts met to pose the question of the position of African Americans in relation both to the union reconfigured by the Spanish-American War and to the newly colonized subjects acquired by that war. Would these subjects be assimilated into a post-Reconstruction model of race relations at home and would the empire abroad facilitate the subjugation of blacks as colonized subjects at home? Would African Americans position themselves in a relation to American nationhood that reinforced or resisted their assimilation into the role of either imperialized or imperialist?

The representation of empire at the turn of the century could function both as an external catalyst and as a medium for resolution of domestic racial conflict. This complex interaction underlies one of the most enduring cultural icons of the Spanish-American War: the battle for San Juan Hill. The charge up San Juan Hill can easily be debunked or demystified, and it has been since the earliest reports of the war: it was not heroic, but a military fiasco; not a massive orderly charge, but a straggling line of desperate soldiers, pitilessly exposed to enemy fire; not even the romantic San Juan Hill, but the more mundane "Kettle Hill" (itself an apocryphal name). But more useful than demystifying is to understand how the battle of San Juan Hill was produced as an icon precisely because it processed, contained, and crystallized multivalent and contradictory political meanings into a monumental frieze.

No American has remained more visible and virile in the iconography of San Juan Hill than Theodore Roosevelt leading his Rough Riders. In Richard Harding Davis's words, "he was without doubt, the most conspicuous figure in the charge . . . mounted high on horseback, and charging the rifle-pits at a gallop and quite alone, [he] made you feel that you would like to cheer."[2] In contrast to his own conspicuousness, Roosevelt, in his account of the battle (which first appeared in *Scribner's* in April 1899 and later in *The Rough Riders*), calls attention to how "astonishing what a limited area of vision and experience one has in the hurly-burly of a battle."[3] In fact, so limited was his vision that he only killed one Spanish soldier—whom he could see point-blank—and that, not surprisingly, with a revolver from the sunken battleship *Maine* (given to him by a brother-in-law in the navy).

In marked contrast to this blurred vision is the remarkable clarity with which Roosevelt notes the presence of black American soldiers "completely intermingled" with his own troops. "Such mixing," he explains, "was inevitable in making repeated charges through thick jungle," but was in need of "reforming" under his command (135). As the American troops entrench themselves on the top of San Juan Hill, Roosevelt's narrative retrenches along racial lines. The battle concludes without a cathartic shoot-out with Spanish soldiers, but instead with a sustained confrontation with African American soldiers that caps the horizontal narrative throughout the report of the threatening intermingling of blacks and whites. An emblem of this threat comes into focus when the color sergeant of the black Tenth Regiment ends up bearing his own colors and those of the white Third Regiment as well (whose flag bearer was killed).

Toward the end of the battle, Roosevelt notes that neither white regulars nor volunteers were weakening, in contrast to the "strain of the colored infantrymen" whose white officers had been killed—and who were left as masterless men in vague affiliation with Roosevelt's troops. When the black soldiers start to drift to the rear to join their own regiment or transport the wounded, Roosevelt perceives them as "depleting my line" and confronts them violently and theatrically: "So I jumped up, and walking a few yards to the rear, drew my revolver, halted the retreating soldiers, and called out to them that I appreciated the gallantry with which they had fought and would be sorry to hurt them, but that I should shoot the first man, who on any pretense whatever went to the rear" (138). When he vows to keep his word, all of his men watched with "utmost interest"; his "cow-punchers, hunters, and miners solemnly nodded their heads and commented in chorus, exactly as if in a comic opera, 'He always does, he always does!'" (138–39). Roosevelt claims that his show worked when the black soldiers, the "'smoked Yankees'—as the Spaniards called them," played their own minstrel parts. They "flashed their white teeth at one another, as they broke into broad grins, and I had no more trouble with them" (139). Roosevelt concludes this confrontation with a paean to racial harmony and national unity: "they seem[ed] to accept me as one of their officers" and the Rough Riders, with their "strong color prejudice, grew to accept them with hearty good-will as comrades, and were entirely willing, in their own phrase, 'to drink out of the same canteen'" (139). At this point in the narrative, with racial trenches dug deeply and national unity thus affirmed, Roosevelt can return to the battle in a roll call that names and praises the gallantry of the individual Rough Riders, as though their individual integrity has been protected by his confrontation with African American troops.

This showdown on San Juan Hill, which serves as both the climax to and digression from the narrative of the battle, raises several interesting questions. Why did the presence of African American soldiers loom so large to Roosevelt as to disrupt the uphill trajectory against the Spanish, with a counternarrative of sidelong glances to the racial intermixing of American soldiers? Why did the potential absence of the African Americans in returning to their regiments, appear even more threatening? In addition, why is the scene at once so startlingly violent and yet so comically theatrical?

There is a familiar trope in war fiction and journalism of dislocation and loss of vision on the battlefield, in response to which a visual anchor must be found—a comrade, a flag, a feature of the landscape—to reorient the soldier and reader. For Roosevelt, black and white intermingling provides both an emblem of this chaos as well as a familiar footing or anchor.[4] Roosevelt's confrontation with the black troops reestablishes the reassuring order of the domestic color line in a foreign terrain, as their heightened visibility displaces and compensates for the occluded vision of the Cuban political landscape. Intermixing is not the only challenge to Roosevelt's order posed by black soldiers in blue uniforms. Their presence raises the white fear of armed insurrection and of national self-representation, which African American soldiers pursued in their printed rebuttals of Roosevelt's account. This double threat of revolt and representation resonated with the claims of the Cuban revolutionaries whom the American soldiers were sent both to liberate and to subdue. This scene of domestic racial confrontation in *The Rough Riders* cannot be separated from its international context of shifting alliances and conflicts between the Americans and the Cubans.

To analyze this scene in *The Rough Riders*, it is necessary to understand how American journalism was remapping the political coordinates of the Cuban battlefield, how reports were implicitly working to supplant Cuban counternarratives scripted by a prior long revolutionary struggle against Spain. A repeated theme that emerges from the reports of the Cuban battlefield is the contrast between the invisibility of both the Spanish enemy and the Cuban allies and the almost suicidal conspicuousness of the American troops. Soldiers and reporters repeat the refrain: "I didn't catch sight of a single Spaniard, not a one," a lack of visibility which comes to signify their cowardly lack of manliness (as they are often compared to "red Indians"). As many reporters commented, in contrast to the Spanish who hid behind trenches, their Cuban guerillas who sniped from behind tree tops—and the Cuban insurgents who cowered behind their American liberators, the American soldiers marched out into clear view.

They offered an inviting target made even more obvious by their outdated smoking guns, in contrast to the Spanish modern smokeless weapons. In addition, reporters noted the large lumbering observation balloon sent up ahead of the troops, which proved not only impotent in surveying enemy positions, but even worse, drew dramatic attention to the position of the Americans and turned them into open targets.[5]

The lack of overarching surveillance of the enemy presented a problem for representation as well as for military strategy, as one photographer for *Harper's Weekly* explained: "Although I was thus on the first firing line, and many men were wounded and killed all about me, as you will see by my photographs. . . . I found it impossible to make any actual 'battle scenes,' for many reasons—the distance at which the fighting is conducted, the area which is covered, but chiefly the long grasses and thickly wooded country."[6] This absence of a "scene," a context for the wounded bodies, is due to more than the hindrance of the landscape, but to a kind of political myopia. Whereas Elaine Scarry has argued that wounded bodies in warfare give meaning to an otherwise abstract political conflict, I would suggest the inverse here; the spotlight on wounded bodies effaces the political context by fetishizing those bodies as the only meaningful focal point.[7] In other words, the conspicuousness of American bodies and the corresponding invisibility of all other combatants had to be produced ideologically as subject positions, not just perceived as military positions. The positions were plotted in part by a narrative that effaced the prior history of the Cuban war against Spain and located the U.S. entry into the war as the point of historical origin.

Although the exposure of the American soldier was lamented as strategically suicidal, it had the important ideological effect of defining American masculinity itself. Report after report praises officers for needlessly yet gallantly standing up in full view under fire, and the charge is portrayed as a kind of grandstanding conspicuousness of sheer bodies hurling themselves up the hill against impregnable trenches. Pictorial representations depict the battle from the point of view of the artist looking up the hill behind the troops and drawing their backs. But a figure usually breaks this perspective by turning around frontally to the spectator, even when he is shooting ahead of him. Rather than directing his focus to confront the enemy, he turns to pose for an audience at home.[8]

The spectacle of the American male body remaps the coordinates of the battlefield to wrest away political agency from the Cubans on both sides of the conflict, a process put in motion as soon as the Americans land in Cuba. Roosevelt's first impression of the insurgents was as a "crew of as utter tatterdemalions as human eyes ever looked on, armed with every kind of rifle in all stages of dilapidation" (71). Their appearance provides evidence for him and many others not of the prior history of the dire material context in which the Cuban insurgents had been fighting their three-year war of independence, but of the fact "that they would be no use in serious fighting, but it was hoped that they might be of service in scouting" (71). When the battle begins, however, Roosevelt is disappointed, but not surprised, to find that the Cuban guide at the head of the column ran away at the first sign of fighting. He contrasts this figure with two Americans who remained, "who though non-combatants—newspaper correspondents—showed as much gallantry as any soldier in the field" (82). The replacement of Cuban scouts with American newspaper reporters is apt; better guides in remapping the coordinates of the battlefield to foreground the spectacle of American manhood, they supplant the Cuban map of the entangled political terrain that antedated U.S. intervention. This triangulation of the soldier with the journalist and domestic audience recuperates an image of American masculinity by denying masculinity and political agency to the Cubans, who were in the midst of a long revolutionary process, which is made to disappear.

This displacement can be seen quite starkly in Stephen Crane's aptly titled "Vivid Story of San Juan Hill" published in the *New York World*.[9] (Crane himself was said by Davis to have engaged in this theatrical visibility by exposing himself to fire atop the hill until Davis embarrassed him by calling attention to his self-dramatizing conspicuousness.)[10] Crane represents the charge as a sporting event, referring to the absent audience who "would give an arm to get the thrill of patriotic insanity that coursed through us" and referring as well to the international audience of foreign attachés who were shocked and impressed by such foolish gallantry (158). In a populist note, Crane also represents the charge as a "grand popular movement" led by the "gallantry of the American private soldier" whose officers were left behind (155). Yet when the Americans reach the top of the hill to entrench themselves for the night, Crane abruptly interrupts his narrative and shifts directions from the upward battle for Santiago to the horizontal struggle with America's allies, the Cuban insurgents. "It becomes necessary to speak of the men's opinion of the Cubans," pauses Crane. "To put it shortly, both officers and privates have the most lively contempt for the Cubans" (163). Class divisions within the American army between privates and officers—which Crane previously celebrated—are healed in their common contempt for their allies.

Crane's article never returns to the continuation of the battle but instead backtracks to review the same events in terms of Cuban nonparticipation. While the Americans "sprinkled a thousand bodies in the grass," not a single Cuban was visible. Once an "efficient body," the insurgents have now become "no more useless body of men anywhere," demoralized and emasculated by American aid (163). While the Americans fight, the Cubans are only interested in feeding their bodies with U.S. rations. Thus the end of the narrative charge up San Juan Hill for Crane is neither the conquest of Santiago nor combat with Spanish soldiers, but the appropriation of the Cuban uprising as an American popular movement and the displacement of lazy, inefficient, hungry Cuban bodies with the spectacle of aggressive American manhood.

The physical absence of Cubans from the battlefield of San Juan Hill was due to the U.S. political decision to exclude the Cuban command from military operations and consequently from deciding on their future in the peace settlement with Spain. Yet the journalistic representations of the Cubans as cowardly, undisciplined, and unsoldierly—in short, unmanly—blames them for their disappearance from the scene. Even Crane's depiction of Cubans and Americans fighting side by side in an earlier battle undermines their alliance by turning the Cubans into a backdrop or foil against which the erect "strong figures" of the Americans are composed. In contrast to the "businesslike" marines, for example, the Cubans are described as "a hard-bitten, under-sized lot, most of them Negroes, and with the stoop and gait of men who had at one time labored at the soil. They were in short peasants—hardy, tireless, uncomplaining peasants—and they viewed in utter calm these early morning preparations for battle."[11] While these peasants show no capacity to reflect on their position, "contrary to the Cubans, the bronze faces of the Americans were not stolid at all" (135). When they fight, Crane comments on the "rock-like beautiful poise" of the marines taking aim, which "one noticed the more on account of the Cubans who used the Lee as if it were a squirt gun." In the midst of fighting, "toiling, sweating marines" stand out against "shrill jumping Cubans" (138). Finally, when a Cuban is hit, he is described as "a great hulking Negro" who "seemed in no pain; it seemed as if he were senseless before he fell." And when a fellow soldier carries him, they appear not as comrades in arms, but "the procession that moved off resembled a grotesque wheelbarrow" (138). Thus while the overt narrative trajectory of these reports pits Americans against Spaniards, the detailed representation pits American bodies against Cuban ones to disaffiliate them as allies. Whether stolid or hysterical the Cubans relinquish control to the Americans and become a passive yardstick for measuring

American prowess. By the end of the battle for San Juan Hill, Crane sees the dependency of the Cuban on the American as a de facto abdication of his right to independence: "If he stupidly drowsily remains out of these fights, what weight is his voice to have later in the final adjustments?" The Cubans themselves are "the worst thing for the cause of an independent Cuba that could possibly exist" (164).

In a battle showcasing American masculinity, the Cubans forfeit their identity as men in the eyes of Americans: "the more our commanding officers see of the Cubans the less they appear to think of them as soldiers or as men."[12] The pivot for this differentiation is often linked to their racial identity, as another reporter notes, "I have seen degradation in Negro slaves, but never have I seen such degradation as a Cuban exhibits in everything that means manhood."[13] It is a short leap from their absence from the front line to their insufficiency as men, to their racial identity as "Negro" (which visually looms large for Crane), to the impossibility of their nationhood, as one correspondent concludes: "I ask where is the Cuban nation. There is no Cuba. There is no Cuban people. There are no freemen here to whom we could deliver this marvelous land."[14]

We can now counterpose the climax of Crane's narrative atop San Juan Hill—the disaffiliation from the Cubans—to that of Roosevelt's— the discipline of African American troops. In both cases, the narrative shifts from conflict with an external enemy, Spain, to internal struggles with reputed allies. These breaks signal a disruption not only in political alliances but also in the links among representations of national, racial, and gendered identities. If Crane's narrative renders Cubans invisible as military political agents, in what ways might Roosevelt displace them with the heightened visibility of African American troops in need of control? Roosevelt, after all, claims that he forced the "smoked Yankees" not to run away as the Cubans did, but to stay and be men under his command. Yet if Cubans are dismissed as unmanly and incapable of nationhood partly on the basis of racial identity, how might the presence of black soldiers in blue uniforms reinforce, undermine, or further complicate this dismissal? And what does their presence mean for the constitution of American nationhood in the male body? What then is the relationship between the forced abdication of Cubans from the military and political battlefield and the field of representation and the forced placement of African American soldiers in the front line under Roosevelt's command?

To answer these questions, we must consider the fact that Roosevelt does not simply relate a tale of battle but implicitly engages in unspoken debate with counternarratives in several overlapping contexts. Though published less than a year after the war, Roosevelt's narrative was involved in a struggle over writing the history of that war, a struggle in part against an African American narrative that had gained some currency. For a brief moment after the war, black regiments were acknowledged for their heroism by the black and white press, homecoming parades, and congressional medals, all of which bolstered the case for African American commissioned officers.[15] Accounts of several battles took on legendary stature, in which the Tenth Cavalry preceded the Rough Riders up San Juan Hill by cutting through barbed wire, rescued the Rough Riders from a Spanish ambush, and launched the charge with the shout of a black trooper. While African American newspapers repeatedly lambasted the white press for never mentioning the names of individual black soldiers and for ignoring their contributions, Roosevelt's account raised special outrage for its blatant distortions of those accomplishments which had entered the public limelight. African American soldiers and correspondents responded to Roosevelt's account and the white press coverage in general as a national conflict over the public narration of history, a conflict with as vital political consequences at home as the international war abroad; as John R. Conn underscored in the ending of his letter on the battle to *The Evening Star*, "the sword rested while the pen fought."[16] Presley Holliday, a member of the Tenth Cavalry on San Juan Hill, ended his detailed rebuttal of Roosevelt's account in a letter to the *New York Age*: "I could give many other incidents of our men's devotion to duty, of their determination to stay until death, but what's the use? Colonel Roosevelt has said they shirked, and the reading public will take the Colonel at his word."[17] Holliday thus situates Roosevelt's account in a rigged contest over public words, in which Roosevelt's narrative overrides the words with which Holliday ends his letter: "No officers, no soldiers."[18]

One political stake in this struggle was the campaign for the appointment of African American commissioned soldiers, which the military successes of the black regiments were used to bolster. Roosevelt's account explicitly contributed to the argument against black officers, which he based on common stereotypes: the natural servitude of blacks, their lack of discipline, and their incapacity for self-governance. Describing his "mixed force" on the San Juan heights, including black infantrymen without white officers, Roosevelt insists at length that the troops are "peculiarly dependent on their white officers" (137); in contrast to both the white regulars and his own Rough Riders, who could fight on their own once their officers were killed, "with the colored troops," he asserted, "there should always be some of their own officers" (137). After the showdown with the "smoked Yankees," he praises the white officers of the Ninth and Tenth, under whose leadership "the colored troops did as well as any soldiers could possibly do" (139). Roosevelt's threat to shoot those troops thus forces them into this submissive role to prove his point retrospectively, since in fact many of the white officers were either killed or lagged behind and the black soldiers did indeed fight independently. The initiative taken by white privates ahead of their officers, which Crane praised as a popular movement, Roosevelt finds threatening in black privates. They must have conjured up the specter of armed blacks out of control, of racial intermixing as political insurrection.

In establishing himself as their accepted officer, Roosevelt implicitly linked the political fate of African Americans at home to that of Cubans abroad. The same argument about the need for white officers to discipline black soldiers was made about the need for the United States government to discipline the Cubans by radically circumscribing their status as a nation through the conditions of the Platt Amendment. Furthermore, the Cubans' perceived racial identity (as Negro) bolstered the argument about their incapacity for self-government—the power to represent themselves. Filipinos were similarly portrayed as stereotypically "Negroid" in popular writing and political cartoons. This interchangeability of colonized subjects marked by homologous racial identity, however, became a contested signifier, open to conflicting political interpretations. Southern Democrats deployed their belief in the unfitness of inferior races—at home and abroad—for self-government as an argument against colonial annexation of the Philippines, so as not to include more nonwhites in the·republic.[19] Yet this negative identification of Cubans, African Americans, and Filipinos as "colored" found contradictory political interpretations among African Americans. It was used by some—both at home and in the battlefield—as an argument on behalf of the efficacy of incorporating African Americans into the imperial project because of their natural ability to mediate between the United States and its colonies. It was transformed by others into an adamant political position against American imperialism. Many editorials in the black press took the side of their "brown brothers" and decried the exportation of post-Reconstruction disfranchisement, Jim Crow laws, and the resurgence of violence and virulent racism to the new outposts of empire. Du Bois's well-known prophetic statement from *The Souls of Black Folk*, "The problem of the twentieth century is the problem of the color-line,—the relation of the darker to the lighter races of men in Asia and Africa, in America and the islands of the sea," originally addressed this international link at the first Pan-African Conference of 1900.[20]

Thus when Roosevelt published his account almost a year after the battle, the events on San Juan Hill were less important than their refraction through the lenses of their consequences: the postwar debates about the viability of American imperialism and the fitness of nonwhites at home and abroad for self-government. His account was published during the U.S. war waged against Filipino nationalists, who he viewed as no more capable of nationhood than were black troops capable of fighting alone. While confronting and subordinating African Americans within the national body, Roosevelt was simultaneously making a place for newly colonized subjects in the disembodied American empire. He was also inscribing a special relation between white manhood and American nationhood. The use of "smoked Yankees" implicitly defines "real Yankees" as "Anglo-Saxon" and contributes to the popular understanding of that term as both a biological racial category and a political historical category, denoting the exclusive originating power and present capacity for self-government.

It would be historically inaccurate and theoretically simplistic to collapse the relations of imperial America to Filipinos, Cubans, and African Americans into a monolithic model of colonized and colonizer. Such a model not only assumes a false coherence in the identity of the colonizer, but also ignores the historical and global differences among colonized subjects. Roosevelt, for instance, was both identifying African Americans and differentiating them from the imagined unassimilable Cubans and Filipinos. If the latter could be relegated to a national limbo, denied both self-government and incorporation into the American republic, the former posed more of a problem for the Republican Roosevelt, who had to represent African Americans within the national body, a problem magnified by their presence in uniform abroad.

In its unsettling intermixture of races, the imperial battlefield may have mirrored to Roosevelt the domestic urban site he had recently left as police commissioner of New York City, and he would have brought his experience with non-Anglo-Saxon immigrants from the city to bear on the heights of San Juan Hill. In a revealing letter to Frederick Jackson Turner, Roosevelt complained of his lack of time to work on his history of the West because of his duties as police commissioner.[21] His "duties" at that time included a controversial and ultimately unsuccessful effort to enforce the excise tax and blue laws in a struggle against Tammany Hall which would have shut down saloons on Sunday and regulated drinking laws in the immigrant community—especially German and Irish. For Roosevelt these laws would have accomplished what the frontier did according to Turner: create individual Americans. Blue laws would have contributed to the Americanization of immigrants by denying their autonomous cultural practices revolving around the beer garden or the pub. In disciplining African American troops on San Juan Hill, Roosevelt was exercising the regulatory power of Americanization that eluded his grasp on the streets of New York. (Politically he would have viewed Tammany Hall as a formidable opposition and African Americans as traditional clients of the Republican Party.) Roosevelt's narrative on San Juan Hill disciplines African American troops in a subordinated integration to deny them the autonomy and equality they sought within the army in the agitation for their own officers. They are forced into the body politic at gun point, Americanized by keeping their place—in the line of fire and in the color line.

In Presley Holliday's rebuttal of Roosevelt, he explains that the African American soldiers who broke the line found racial "intermingling" threatening because it already embodied the hierarchical social order Roosevelt was trying to assert:

> It is a well know fact, that in this country most persons of color feel out of place when they are by force compelled to mingle with white persons, especially strangers. . . . [S]ome of our men (and these were all recruits with less than six months' service) felt so much out of place that when firing lulled, often showed their desire to be with their commands. . . . White soldiers do not as a rule, share this feeling with colored soldiers. The fact that a white man knows how well he can make a place for himself among colored people need not be discussed here.[22]

What Holliday leaves undiscussed points to the violent effort in making this "place" for the white man by taming the threats of autonomous black agency. Roosevelt was trying to incorporate and to Americanize black soldiers in a racially "mixed lot" by forcing them to stay within the national line of defense, as he was reasserting the color line at the same time to forge the bond of national unity. According to him, only by remaining in line, under white command, could black troops achieve entry into the ranks of American nationhood.

In positioning African Americans in a nationalist hierarchy, Roosevelt was also constructing what Holliday calls the unique place of the white man among nonwhites, to protect the special connection between white manhood and American nationhood. The designation "smoked

Yankees" aligns the volunteer Rough Riders, often derided in the press for their theatrical playacting, with the white regulars, professional soldiers, against the black regulars of the Tenth Cavalry, who had gained the nickname Buffalo Soldiers for their own fighting in Indian wars. The visual image of "smoked Yankees" suggests whites fighting in blackface and implicitly relegates these professional soldiers to the role of comic actors, impersonated shells with no agency of their own. Roosevelt's fear that the amateur Rough Riders would not be taken seriously as soldiers is projected onto the theatrical image of the grinning blackface soldiers.[23] In this realignment, which makes black regulars dependent on white volunteers, Roosevelt also defends the virile image of the Rough Riders from the stories circulating about black troops rescuing them from ambush or abetting their charge. Such narratives would severely compromise the image of the Rough Riders' autonomy—cowboys on a new frontier—as well as their role as chivalric liberators of the Cubans; in fact, they would then play the passive feminized role of the rescued to the active male role of the black troops.

The role of the chivalric rescuer, used so pervasively in imperial discourse, was indeed subject to contested meanings, for African American soldiers not only deployed the chivalric mode in writing of their military experience in relation to the Cubans, or to their fellow soldiers, but they also brought that image back home to the South. Reports from soldiers encamped in the South take a chivalric relation to local African Americans; they cut down trees where blacks had been lynched, protect local communities from white brutality, and overstep Jim Crow laws with the force of their numbers, arms, and authority of their blue uniforms. In the contest over the uses of chivalry, Roosevelt can be seen as attempting to rescue the chivalric mode itself from black counternarratives and preserve it as an exclusively Anglo-Saxon possession. In Cuba, Roosevelt may have rediscovered the Western frontier he abandoned in the city; yet the nostalgia motivating the Rough Riders to act like cowboys and seek new Indians in a Wild West abroad is realized not in confrontation with the Spanish or even the Cubans, but with African Americans in a foreign terrain that threatens to "intermix" black and white. Only after his confrontation with "smoked Yankees" does Roosevelt turn to summarizing his account of the battle, naming his individual Rough Riders and their gallant deeds as though he has rescued their subjectivity as soldiers from the threat of a kind of male miscegenation.

Roosevelt's protection of the white male subject contributes to the purgative discourse with which this essay opens, of the Spanish-American

War as the final antidote to Reconstruction, healing the conflicts of the Civil War by bringing together blue and grey on distant shores. The Rough Riders have been understood as a unifying cultural symbol—between North and South, West and East, working class and patrician, and this unity is grounded in the notion of manliness, in the physicality of the male body that transcends or underlies social difference. In the words of a popular poem about the Rough Riders,

> Let them know there in the ditches
> Blood-stained by the swells in the van
> And know that a chap may have riches
> And still be a man.[24]

Common graves, common streams of blood, bodies strewn in the Cuban grasses all sanctify a democracy of manhood to which some were even willing to add African Americans, as an officer of a black regiment stated: "White regiments, black regiments, regulars and Rough Riders, representing the young manhood of the North and South, fought shoulder to shoulder, unmindful of race or color, unmindful of whether commanded by an ex-Confederate or not and mindful only of their common duty as Americans."[25] Roosevelt's confrontation on San Juan Hill baldly exposes the ground of hierarchy and violence in which this national unity is embedded.

Although white and black regiments could be seen to merge in their "common duty as Americans," black and white male bodies have different symbolic resonances, a different signifying function in the political landscape. One of the rationales for organizing federal regiments of African American volunteers (when many individual states balked at organizing militias) was the Lamarckian argument that they were immune to the diseases of the tropical environment. These troops actually came to be known as the Immune Regiments, as though they were physically closer to the terrain, more like "natives" than like white Americans. This attribution allowed them to be assigned the most loathsome duties, but also positioned them ideologically. Immune, they could serve as a buffer between the white soldiers and the contagious environment and allow the spectacle of the restored white male body to emerge unscathed by the physical and political landscape. This recuperation was especially important given the pervasive presence at home of dismembered veterans of the Civil War and, more immediately, given the fact that more men died of dysentery, malaria, and food poisoning from army rations in Cuba than they did of fighting in the Spanish-American War. The presence of the black body immersed in yet invulnerable to the physical contagions of the imperial battlefield works to elevate the figure of the white male to a level of political abstraction, but makes him dependent on that same embodied presence.

The foundations for the construction of the white male body as a figure for American nationhood lie in the subjugation of black male bodies. We can trace this process in the following passage by Richard Harding Davis, from an early stage of the battle for San Juan Hill (Davis was outspoken in his support of African American soldiers and their contribution to the war effort and in his harsh criticism of the United States command in its inept conduct of the war):

> I came across Lieutenant Roberts of the Tenth Cavalry, lying under the roots of a tree beside the stream with three of his colored troopers stretched around him. He was shot through the intestines, and each of the three men with him was shot in the arm or leg. They had been overlooked or forgotten, and we stumbled upon them only by the accident of losing our way. They had no knowledge as to how the battle was going or where their comrades were, or where the enemy was. At any moment, for all they knew, the Spaniards might break through the bushes about them. It was a most lonely picture, the young lieutenant, half naked, and wet with his own blood, sitting upright beside the empty stream, and his three followers crouching at his feet like three faithful watch-dogs, each wearing his red badge of courage, with his black skin tanned to a haggard gray, and with his eyes fixed patiently on the white lips of his officer. When the white soldiers with me offered to carry him back to the dressing station, the negroes resented it stiffly. "If the Lieutenant had been able to move, we would have carried him away long ago," said the sergeant, quite overlooking the fact that his arm was shattered. "Oh, don't bother the surgeons about me," Roberts added, cheerfully. "They must be very busy. I can wait."[26]

On the surface, this is a tableau of national consolidation between whites and blacks, bonded by shared wounds and self-sacrifice. In fact, the bloody wounds, imaged through Crane's popular novel, bleach everyone one shade whiter. The troopers turn less black, a "haggard grey," while the lieutenant turns even whiter, with his "white lips." Yet this tableau reinscribes the racial hierarchy out of which national unity is forged, not only in the explicit racist images of the blacks as "watch-dogs" or the fact that they, in contrast to the white officer, remain unnamed, but in the way in which the heroic white body is intimately constructed out of black bodies in several hybrid configurations. In describing immobilized bodies, Davis vividly invokes and quells the implicit sexual threat of racial "intermingling," which Roosevelt confronts in the upheaval of the battle. From one angle, they appear as one grotesque body—white on top and black on the bottom: the upright white lieutenant wounded in the middle is the torso and the black troopers form the limbs or lower body. They are joined by their common wounds, a symbolic castration. From another angle, these figures are ambiguously sexualized and gendered, with the lieutenant an upright phallus and the black privates a separate male or female body, crouched ready to receive him. From still another perspective, the black soldiers act as chivalric knights protecting their lady as they gaze lovingly at his lips. When they resent the interference of the white soldiers, threatening to touch their officer, they "stiffen" and thereby assert their virility, forgetting their symbolic castration, not only their wounded limbs, but their social inability to touch him, their racial difference. The African American soldiers here, wounded on the periphery of their own bodies, stand at the periphery of the body politic, or at the bottom of a representational hierarchy. They pledge their allegiance to, their affiliation with their white officer, while he is capable of a higher allegiance to the cause, which he displays in his cheerful, "don't mind me." They represent their officer, their master, while he represents the whole nation, America. The upright white male body, rooted in his black counterparts, also differentiates them, as he becomes a mediator between the crouched black masses—the unnamed soldiers—and the nation, which they cannot represent directly.

Thus Davis's tableau of unity on San Juan Hill has the same violently differentiating effect as Roosevelt's more overtly violent form of post-Reconstruction politics. In fact, Davis may assume a natural servitude on the part of African Americans, while Roosevelt implicitly acknowledges the threat of their agency and claim to national representation. Davis sheds light on the debate about African American officers who threaten not only to take on leadership roles and bear weapons, but also to represent the nation directly, unmediated through their allegiance to white officers. The challenge of black officers to white authority lies in their capacity to represent more than their own blackness subsumed into a white nation, but to represent American nationhood in a foreign terrain. Just as Roosevelt and others supported the black troops as long as they were led and represented by white officers, there is a hierarchy of representation underwriting these images of unity, whereby the white male alone in the wilderness of empire on San Juan Hill comes to displace, appropriate, and incorporate the agency of nonwhites both in the empire and at home.

Black troops in blue on San Juan Hill, however, threaten to destabilize this hierarchy by occupying a range of possible positions. The specter of armed African American soldiers may threaten betrayal of the United States empire through their realignment with outside forces or may challenge the internal coherence of that empire by demanding participation and representation as equals. In both cases, many black soldiers in the aftermath of the Cuban campaign preferred to be sent to fight the war in the Philippines—and, in a few well publicized cases, switched sides— rather than face the racism encircling the army encampments of the South. Black in blue raises the white fear that the imperial war meant to heal the rifts of the Civil War may continue to heighten that conflict by recasting it as a global race war. The threat of black soldiers in blue uniforms, like that of the "colored" color bearer, lies in their direct representation of American nationhood in lands defined as inhabited by those unfit for self-government, those who cannot represent themselves, and who are thus in need of the discipline of the American Empire.

Notes

This essay has benefited from the responses to earlier versions by colleagues at Columbia University, Stanford University, U.C. Irvine, UCLA, and Mount Holyoke.

1 Virginia Woolf, *A Room of One's Own, and Three Guineas* (London: Chatto & Windus, 1984), p. 75.

2 Richard Harding Davis, *The Cuban and Porto Rican Campaigns* (New York: Scribner's, 1898), p. 217.

3 Theodore Roosevelt, *The Rough Riders: A History of the First United States Volunteer Cavalry* (New York: Scribner's, 1899), p. 133. Subsequent references cited parenthetically in text.

4 I am grateful to Robert Ferguson for pointing out this trope.

5 Each of these features can be found in accounts of the battle by Crane and Davis cited below; many more examples are brought together in Charles H. Brown, *The Correspondents' War: Journalists in the Spanish American War* (New York: Scribner's, 1967), chap. 15.

6 James Burton, "Photography Under Fire," *Harper's Weekly*, August 6, 1898, p. 774.

7 Elaine Scarry, "The Structure of War: The Juxtaposition of Injured Bodies and Unanchored Issues" in *The Body in Pain: The Making and the Unmaking of the World* (New York: Oxford University Press, 1985), pp. 60–157.

8 For a pictorial example see the illustration by H. L. V. Parkhurst, "The Charge at San Juan Hill," in Roosevelt, p. 132.

9 Stephen Crane, "Stephen Crane's Vivid Story of the Battle of San Juan," *New York World*, July 14, 1898. Reprinted in Fredson Bowers and James B. Colvert, eds., *Stephen Crane: Reports of War* (Charlottesville: University of Virginia Press, 1971), pp. 154–65. Subsequent references cited parenthetically in text.

10 Brown, p. 363.

11 Crane, "The Red Badge of Courage Was His Wig-Wag Flag," in Bowers and Colvert, p. 135.

12 George Kennan, quoted in Louis A. Pérez, *Cuba Between Empires, 1878–1902* (Pittsburgh: University of Pittsburgh Press, 1983), p. 204.

13 *New York Times*, August 9, 1898, p. 2.

14 *New York Times*, August 7, 1898, p. 2.

15 Willard Gatewood, *Black Americans and the White Man's Burden, 1898–1903* (Chicago: University of Illinois Press, 1975), pp. 41–65.

16 Willard Gatewood, ed., *'Smoked Yankees' and the Struggle for Empire: Letters from Negro Soldiers, 1898–1902* (1971; reprint, Fayetteville: University of Arkansas Press, 1987), p. 71.

17 Gatewood, *'Smoked Yankees'*, p. 96.

18 In his *A New Negro for a New Century*, which depends heavily on the demonstration of black military heroism, Booker T. Washington not only reprints Holliday's rebuttal of Roosevelt (pp. 54–62), but also reprints an earlier election speech of Roosevelt against himself, in which he praises the heroism of the Tenth and their harmony with the Rough Riders at a political rally in Harlem (pp. 50–52) (1900; reprint, Miami, Fl.: Mnemosyne Publishing, 1969).

19 Christopher Lasch, "The Anti-Imperialists, the Philippines, and the Inequality of Man," *Journal of Southern History* 25 (August 1958): 319–31. See also Walter Benn Michaels, "Anti-Imperial Americanism," in this volume.

20 For this wide range of views see both books by Gatewood, and George Marks, ed., *The Black Press Views American Imperialism, 1898–1900* (New York: Arno Press, 1971); W. E. B. Du Bois, *The Souls of Black Folk* (1903; reprint, New York: Vintage, New American Library, 1990), p. 221.

21 *The Letters of Theodore Roosevelt*, ed. Elting Morison et. al. (Cambridge: Harvard University Press, 1951), vol. 1, p. 564. I am grateful to Danny Czitrom for pointing out this Turner correspondence in the context of urban conflicts.

22 Gatewood, *'Smoked Yankees'*, pp. 95–96.

23 In *A New Negro*, Washington speculated that Roosevelt was anxious about having his Rough Riders linked with black troops by the press, who were most interested in how both the "colored" troops and Roosevelt's flamboyant volunteers would perform under fire.

24 Quoted in G. Edward White, *The Eastern Establishment and the Western Experience: The West of Frederic Remington, Theodore Roosevelt, and Owen Wister* (New Haven: Yale University Press, 1968), p. 155.

25 Lieutenant John J. Pershing cited in Frank Freidel, *The Splendid Little War* (Boston: Little, Brown and Company, 1958), p. 173.

26 Davis, *The Cuban and Porto Rican Campaigns*, pp. 210–11.

Donna Haraway

Teddy Bear Patriarchy

Taxidermy in the Garden of Eden,

New York City, 1908–1936

Nature teaches law and order and respect for property. If these people cannot go to the country, then the Museum must bring nature to the city.[1]

I started my thoughts on the legend of Romulus and Remus who had been suckled by a wolf and founded Rome, but in the jungle I had my little Lord Greystoke suckled by an ape.[2]

I. The Akeley African Hall and the Theodore Roosevelt Memorial in the American Museum of Natural History: Experience

n the heart of New York City stands Central Park—the urban garden designed by Frederick Law Olmsted to heal the over-wrought or decadent city dweller with a prophylactic dose of nature. Immediately across from the park the Theodore Roosevelt Memorial presides as the central building of the American Museum of Natural History, a monumental reproduction of the Garden of Eden. In the Garden, Western Man may begin again the first journey, the first birth from within the sanctuary of nature. An institution founded just after the Civil War and dedicated to popular education and scientific research, the American Museum of Natural History is the place to undertake this genesis, this regeneration. Passing through the Museum's Roosevelt Memorial atrium into the African Hall, opened in 1936, the ordinary citizen may enter a privileged space and time: the Age of Mammals in the heart of Africa, scene of the origin of our species.[3] A hope is implicit in every architectural detail: in immediate vision of the origin, perhaps the future can be fixed. By saving the beginnings, the end can be achieved and the present can be transcended. African Hall offers a unique communion with nature at its highest and yet most vulnerable moment, the moment of the interface of the Age of Mammals with the Age of Man. This communion is offered through the sense of vision by the craft of taxidermy.

Restoration of the origin, the task of genetic hygiene, is achieved in Carl Akeley's African Hall by an art that began for him in the 1880s with the crude stuffing of P. T. Barnum's elephant, Jumbo, who had been run down by a railroad train, the emblem of the Industrial Revolution. The end of his task came in the 1920s, with his exquisite mounting of the Giant of Karisimbi, the lone silverback male gorilla that dominates the diorama depicting the site of Akeley's own grave in the mountainous rain forest of the Congo, today's Zaire. So it could inhabit Akeley's monument to the purity of nature, this gorilla was killed in 1921, the same year the Museum hosted the Second International Congress of Eugenics. From the dead body of the primate, Akeley crafted something finer than the living organism; he achieved its true end, a new genesis. Decadence—the threat of the city, civilization, machine—was stayed in the politics of eugenics and the art of taxidermy. And the Museum fulfilled its scientific purpose of conservation, of preservation, of the production of permanence. Life was transfigured in the principal civic arena of Western political theory—the natural body of man.[4]

Behind every mounted animal, bronze sculpture, or photograph lies a profusion of objects and social interactions among people and other animals, which in the end can be recomposed to tell a biography embracing major themes for the twentieth-century United States. But the recomposition produces a story that is reticent, even mute, about Africa. H. F. Osborn, president of the American Museum from 1908 to 1933, thought Akeley was Africa's biographer. This essay will argue that Akeley is America's biographer, or rather a biographer of part of North America. Akeley thought in African Hall the visitor would experience nature at its moment of highest perfection. He did not dream that he crafted the means to experience a history of race, sex, and class in New York City that reached to Nairobi. He thought he was telling the unified truth of natural history. His story will be recomposed to tell a tale of the commerce of power and knowledge in white and male supremacist monopoly capitalism, fondly named Teddy Bear Patriarchy.[5]

To enter the Theodore Roosevelt Memorial, the visitor must pass by a James Earle Fraser equestrian statue of Teddy majestically mounted as a father and protector between two "primitive" men, an American Indian and an African, both standing and dressed as "savages." The facade of the memorial, funded by the State of New York and awarded to the American Museum of Natural History on the basis of its competitive application in 1923, is classical, with four Ionic columns fifty-four feet high topped by statues of the great explorers Boone, Audubon, Lewis, and Clark. Reminiscent of coins, bas-relief seals of the United States and of the Liberty Bell are stamped on the front panels. Inscribed across the top are the words TRUTH, KNOWLEDGE, VISION and the dedication to Roosevelt as "a great leader of the youth of America, in energy and fortitude in the faith of our fathers, in defense of the rights of the people, in the love and conservation of nature and of the best in life and in man." Youth, paternal solicitude, virile defense of democracy, and intense emotional connection to nature are the unmistakable themes.[6]

The building presents itself in many visible faces. It is at once a Greek temple, a bank, a scientific research institution, a popular museum, a neoclassical theatre. One is entering a space that sacralizes democracy, Protestant Christianity, adventure, science, and commerce. It is impossible not to feel entering this building that a drama will be enacted inside. Experience in this public monument will be intensely personal; this structure is one of North America's spaces for joining the duality of self and community.

Just inside the portals, the visitor enters the first sacred space where transformation of consciousness and moral state will begin.[7] The walls are inscribed with Roosevelt's words under the headings Nature, Youth, Manhood, the State. The seeker begins in Nature: "There are no words that can tell the hidden spirit of the wilderness, that can reveal its mystery. . . . The nation behaves well if it treats its natural resources as assets which it must turn over to the next generation increased and not impaired in value." Nature is mystery and resource, a critical union in the history of civilization. The visitor—necessarily a boy in moral state, no matter what accidents of biology or social gender might have pertained prior to the excursion to the museum—progresses through Youth: "I want to see you game boys . . . and gentle and tender. . . . Courage, hard work, self mastery, and intelligent effort are essential to a successful life." Youth mirrors Nature, its pair across the room. The next stage is Manhood: "Only those are fit to live who do not fear to die and none are fit to die who have shrunk from the joy of life and the duty of life." Opposite is its spiritual pair, the State: "Aggressive fighting for the right is the noblest sport the world affords. . . . If I must choose between righteousness and peace, I choose righteousness." The walls of the atrium are full of murals depicting Roosevelt's life, the perfect illustration of his words. His life is inscribed in stone in a peculiarly literal way appropriate to this museum. One sees the man hunting big game in Africa, conducting diplomacy in the Philippines and China, helping boy and girl scouts, receiving academic honors, and presiding over the Panama Canal ("The land divided, the world united").

Finally, in the atrium also are the striking life-size bronze sculptures by Carl Akeley of the Nandi spearmen of East Africa on a lion hunt. These African men and the lion they kill symbolize for Akeley the essence of the hunt, of what would later be named "man the hunter." In discussing the lion spearers, Akeley always referred to them as men. In every other circumstance he referred to adult male Africans as boys. Roosevelt, the modern sportsman, and the "primitive" Nandi share in the spiritual truth of manhood. The noble sculptures express Akeley's great love for Roosevelt, his friend and hunting companion in Africa in 1910 for the killing of one of the elephants which Akeley mounted for the museum. Akeley said he would follow Roosevelt anywhere because of his "sincerity and integrity."[8]

In the museum shop in the atrium in the 1980s, one may purchase *T.R.: Champion of the Strenuous Life*, a photographic biography of the twenty-sixth president. Every aspect of the fulfillment of manhood is depicted within; even death is labeled "The Great Adventure." One learns that after his defeat in the presidential campaign of 1912, Roosevelt undertook the exploration of the Amazonian tributary, the River of Doubt, under the auspices of the American Museum of Natural History and the Brazilian government. It was a perfect trip. The explorers nearly died, the river had never before been seen by white men, and the great stream, no longer doubtful, was renamed Rio Roosevelt by the Brazilian state. In the picture biography, which includes a print of the adventurers paddling their primitive dugout canoe (one assumes before starvation and jungle fever attenuated the ardor of the photographer in this desolate land), the former president of a great industrial power explains his return to the wilderness: "I had to go. It was my last chance to be a boy."[9]

The joining of life and death in these icons of Roosevelt's journeys and in the architecture of his stony memorial announces the central moral truth of this museum. This is the effective truth of manhood, the state conferred on the visitor who successfully passes through the trial of the museum. The body can be transcended. This is the lesson Simone de Beauvoir so painfully remembered in *The Second Sex;* man is the sex which risks life and in so doing achieves his existence. In the upside down world of Teddy Bear Patriarchy, it is in the craft of killing that life is constructed, not in the accident of personal, material birth. Roosevelt is clearly the perfect locus genii and patron saint for the museum and its task of regeneration of a miscellaneous, incoherent urban public threatened with genetic and social decadence, threatened with the prolific bodies of the new immigrants, threatened with the failure of manhood.[10]

The Akeley African Hall itself is simultaneously a very strange place and an ordinary experience for literally millions of North Americans over more than five decades. The types of display in this hall spread all over the country, and even the world, partly due to the craftspeople Akeley himself trained. In the 1980s sacrilege is perhaps more evident than liminal experience of nature. What is the experience of New York streetwise kids wired to Walkman radios and passing the Friday afternoon cocktail bar by the lion diorama? These are the kids who came to the museum to see the high tech Nature-Max films. But soon, for those not physically wired into the communication system of the late twentieth century, another time begins to take form. The African Hall was meant to be a time machine, and it is.[11] The individual is entering the Age of Mammals. But one is entering alone, each individual soul, as part of no stable prior community and without confidence in the substance of one's body, in order to be received into a saved community. One begins in the threatening chaos of the industrial city, part of a horde, but here one will come to belong, to find substance. No matter how many people crowd the great hall, the experience is of individual communion with nature. The sacrament will be enacted for each worshipper; here is no nature constituted from statistical reality and a probability calculus. This is not a random world, populated by late twentieth-century cyborgs, for whom the threat of decadence is a nostalgic memory of a dim organic past, but the moment of origin where nature and culture, private and public, profane and sacred meet—a moment of incarnation in the encounter of man and animal.

The Hall is darkened, lit only from the display cases which line the sides of the spacious room. In the center of the Hall is a group of elephants so life-like that a moment's fantasy suffices for awakening a premonition of their movement, perhaps an angry charge at one's personal intrusion. The elephants stand like a high altar in the nave of a great cathedral. That impression is strengthened by one's growing consciousness of the dioramas that line both sides of the Main Hall, as well as the sides of the spacious gallery above. Lit from within, the dioramas contain detailed and life-like groups of large African mammals—game for the wealthy New York hunters who financed this experience; they are called habitat groups and are the culmination of the taxidermist's art. Called by Akeley a "peephole into the jungle," [12] each diorama presents itself as a side altar, a stage, an unspoiled garden in nature, a hearth for home and family. As an altar, each diorama tells a part of the story of salvation history; each has its special emblems indicating particular virtues. Above all, inviting the visitor to share in its revelation, each tells the truth. Each offers a vision. Each is a window onto knowledge.

A diorama is eminently a story, a part of natural history. The story is told in the pages of nature, read by the naked eye. The animals in the habitat groups are captured in a photographer's vision and a sculptor's vision. They are actors in a morality play on the stage of nature, and the eye is the critical organ. Each diorama contains a small group of animals in the foreground, in the midst of exact reproductions of plants, insects, rocks, soil. Paintings reminiscent of Hollywood movie set art curve in back of the group and up to the ceiling, creating a great panoramic vision of a scene on the African continent. Each painting is minutely appropriate to the particular animals in the foreground. Among the twenty-eight dioramas in the Hall, all the major geographic areas of the African continent and most of the large mammals are represented.

Gradually, the viewer begins to articulate the content of the story. Most groups are made up of only a few animals, usually including a large and vigilant male, a female or two, and one baby. Perhaps there are some other animals—a male adolescent maybe, never an aged or deformed beast. The animals in the group form a developmental series, such that the group can represent the essence of the species as a dynamic, living whole. The principles of organicism (i.e., of the laws of organic form) rule the composition. [13] There is no need for the multiplication of specimens because the series is a true biography. Each animal is an organism, and the group is an organism. Each organism is a vital moment in the narrative of natural history, condensing the flow of time into the harmony of developmental form. The groups are peaceful, composed, illuminated—in "brightest Africa." Each group forms a community structured by a natural division of function; the whole animal in the whole group is nature's truth. The physiological division of labor that has informed the history of biology is embodied in these habitat groups, which tell of communities and families, peacefully and hierarchically ordered. Sexual specialization of function—the organic bodily and social sexual division of labor—is unobtrusively ubiquitous, unquestionable, right. The African buffalo, the white and black rhinos, the lion, the zebra, the mountain nyala, the okapi, the lesser koodo all find their place in the differentiated and developmental harmony of nature. The racial division of labor, the familial progress from youthful native to adult white man, was announced at the steps leading to the building itself; Akeley's original plan for African Hall included bas-relief sculptures of all the "primitive" tribes of Africa complementing the other stories of natural wild life in the Hall. Organic hierarchies are embodied in every organ in the articulation of natural order in the museum.[14]

But there is a curious note in the story; it begins to dominate as scene after scene draws the visitor into itself through the eyes of the animals in the tableaux.[15] Each diorama has at least one animal that catches the viewer's gaze and holds it in communion. The animal is vigilant, ready to sound an alarm at the intrusion of man, but ready also to hold forever the gaze of meeting, the moment of truth, the original encounter. The moment seems fragile, the animals about to disappear, the communion about to break; the Hall threatens to dissolve into the chaos of the Age of Man. But it does not. The gaze holds, and the wary animal heals those who will look. There is no impediment to this vision. There is no mediation, nothing between the viewer and the animal. The glass front of the diorama forbids the body's entry, but the gaze invites his visual penetration. The animal is frozen in a moment of supreme life, and man is transfixed. No merely living organism could accomplish this act. The specular commerce between man and animal at the interface of two evolutionary ages is completed. The animals in the dioramas have transcended mortal life and hold their pose forever, with muscles tensed, noses aquiver, veins in the face and delicate ankles and folds in the supple skin all prominent. No visitor to a merely physical Africa could see these animals. This is a spiritual vision made possible only by their death and literal re-presentation. Only then could the essence of their life be present. Only then could the hygiene of nature cure the sick vision of civilized man. Taxidermy fulfills the fatal desire to represent, to be whole; it is a politics of reproduction.

There is one diorama that stands out from all the others, the gorilla group. It is not simply that this group is one of the four large corner displays. There is something special in the painting with the steaming volcano in the background and Lake Kivu below, in the pose of the enigmatic large silverback rising above the group in a chest-beating gesture of alarm and an unforgettable gaze in spite of the handicap of glass eyes. Here the painter's art was particularly successful in conveying the sense of limitless vision, of a panorama without end around the focal lush green garden. This is the scene that Akeley longed to return to. It is where he died, feeling he was at home as in no other place on earth. It is where he first killed a gorilla and felt the enchantment of a perfect garden. After his first visit in 1921, he was motivated to convince the Belgian government to make of this area the first African national park to ensure an absolute sanctuary for the gorilla in the future. But the viewer does not know these things when he sees the five animals in a naturalistic setting. It is plain that he is looking at a natural family of close human relatives, but that is not the essence of this diorama. The viewer sees that the elephants, the lion, the rhino, and the water hole group—with its peaceful panorama of all the grassland species, including the carnivores, caught in a moment outside the Fall—all these have been a kind of preparation, not so much for the gorilla group, as for the Giant of Karisimbi. This double for man stands in a unique personal individuality, his fixed face molded forever from the death mask cast from his corpse by a taxidermist in the Kivu Mountains. Here is natural man, immediately known. His image may be purchased on a picture post card at the desk in the Roosevelt atrium (figure 1).

It would have been inappropriate to meet the gorilla anywhere else but on the mountain. Frankenstein and his monster had Mont Blanc for their encounter; Akeley and the gorilla first saw each other on the lush volcanoes of central Africa. The glance proved deadly for them both, just as the exchange between Victor Frankenstein and his creature froze each of them into a dialectic of immolation. But Frankenstein tasted the bitter failure of his fatherhood in his own and his creature's death; Akeley resurrected his creature and his authorship in both the sanctuary of Parc Albert and the African Hall of the American Museum of Natural History. Mary Shelley's story may be read as a dissection of the deadly logic of birthing in patriarchy at the dawn of the age of biology; her tale is a nightmare about the crushing failure of the project of man. But the taxidermist labored to restore manhood at the interface of the Age of Mammals and the Age of Man. Akeley achieved the fulfillment of a sportsman in Teddy Bear Patriarchy—he died a father to the game, and their sepulcher is named after him, the Akeley African Hall.

The gorilla was the highest quarry of Akeley's life as artist, scientist, and hunter, but why? He said himself (through his ghostwriter, the invisible Dorothy Greene—is she ever absent?), "To me the gorilla made a much more interesting quarry than lions, elephants, or any other African game, for the gorilla is still comparatively unknown." [16] But so was the

Figure 1. The Giant of Karisimbi. (Courtesy of the American Museum of Natural History, no. 315077, photo: Charles H. Coles and Thane Bierwert)

colobus monkey or any of a long list of animals. What qualities did it take to make an animal "game"? One answer is similarity to man, the ultimate quarry, a worthy opponent. The ideal quarry is the "other," the natural self. That is one reason Frankenstein needed to hunt down his creature. The obscurity of the gorilla was deepened and made sacred by this question, the title of Akeley's chapter urging scientific research in the new

Parc Albert, "Is the gorilla almost a man?" Hunter, scientist, and artist all sought the gorilla for his revelation about the nature and future of manhood. Akeley compared and contrasted his quest for the gorilla with the French-American's, Paul du Chaillu, the first white man to kill a gorilla, in 1855, eight years after it was "discovered." Du Chaillu's account of the encounter stands as the classic portrayal of a depraved and vicious beast killed in the heroic, dangerous encounter. Akeley disbelieved du Chaillu and told his own readers how many times du Chaillu's publishers made him rewrite until the beast was fierce enough. Frankenstein plugged up his ears rather than listen to his awful son claim a gentle and peace-loving soul. Akeley was certain he would find a noble and peaceful beast; so he brought his guns, cameras, and white women into the garden to hunt, wondering what distance measured courage in the face of a charging alter-ego.

Like du Chaillu, Akeley first came upon a sign of the animal, a footprint, or in Akeley's case a handprint, before meeting face to face. "I'll never forget it. In that mud hole were the marks of four great knuckles where the gorilla had placed his hand on the ground. There is no other track like this in the world—there is no other hand in the world so large. . . . As I looked at that track I lost the faith on which I had brought my party to Africa. Instinctively I took my gun from the gun boy."[17] Later, Akeley told that the handprint, not the face, gave him his greatest thrill. In the hand the trace of kinship writ large and terrible struck the craftsman.

But then, on the first day out from camp in the gorilla country, Akeley did meet a gorilla face to face, the creature he had sought for decades, prevented from earlier success by mauling elephants, stingy millionaires, and world war. Within minutes of his first glimpse of the features of the face of an animal he longed more than anything to see, Akeley had killed him, not in the face of a charge, but through a dense forest screen within which the animal hid, rushed, and shook branches. Surely, the taxidermist did not want to risk losing his specimen, for perhaps there would be no more. He knew the Prince of Sweden was just then leaving Africa after having shot fourteen of the great apes in the same region. The animals must be wary of new hunters; collecting might be very difficult.

Whatever the exact logic that ruled the first shot, precisely placed into the aorta, the task that followed was arduous indeed—skinning the animal and transporting various remains back to camp. The corpse had nearly miraculously lodged itself against the trunk of a tree above a deep chasm. As a result of Herculean labors, which included casting the death mask pictured in *Lions, Gorillas, and their Neighbors*,[18] Akeley was ready for his next gorilla hunt on the second day after shooting the first ape. The pace he was setting himself was grueling, dangerous for a man ominously weakened by tropical fevers. "But science is a jealous mistress and takes little account of a man's feelings."[19] The second quest resulted in two missed males, a dead female, and her frightened baby speared by the porters and guides. Akeley and his party had killed or attempted to kill every ape they had seen since arriving in the area.

On his third day out, Akeley took his cameras and ordered his guides to lead toward easier country. With a baby, female, and male, he could do a group even if he got no more specimens. Now it was time to hunt with the camera.[20] "Almost before I knew it I was turning the crank of the camera on two gorillas in full view with a beautiful setting behind them. I do not think at the time I appreciated the fact that I was doing a thing that had never been done before."[21] But the photogenic baby and mother and the accompanying small group of other gorillas had become boring after two hundred feet of film, so Akeley provoked an action shot by standing up. That was interesting for a bit. "So finally, feeling that I had about all I could expect from that band, I picked out one that I thought to be an immature male. I shot and killed it and found, much to my regret, that it was a female. As it turned out, however, she was such a splendid large specimen that the feeling of regret was considerably lessened."[22]

Akeley commented on his satisfaction with the triumphs of his gun and camera and decided it was time to ask the rest of the party waiting in a camp below to come up to hunt gorillas. He was getting considerably sicker and feared he would not fulfill his promise to his friends to give them gorilla. His whole purpose in taking white women into gorilla country depended on meeting this commitment: "As a naturalist interested in preserving wild life, I was glad to do anything that might make killing animals less attractive."[23] The best thing to reduce the potency of game for heroic hunting is to demonstrate that inexperienced women could safely do the same thing. Science had already penetrated; women could follow.

Two days of hunting resulted in Herbert Bradley's shooting a large silver back, the one Akeley compared to Jack Dempsey and mounted as the lone male of Karisimbi in African Hall. It was now possible to admit another level of feeling: "As he lay at the base of the tree, it took all one's scientific ardour to keep from feeling like a murderer. He was a magnificent creature with the face of an amiable giant who would do no harm except perhaps in self defense or in defense of his family."[24] If he had succeeded in his aborted hunt, Victor Frankenstein could have spoken those lines.

The photograph in the American Museum film archive of Carl Akeley, Herbert Bradley, and Mary Hastings Bradley holding up the gorilla head and corpse to be recorded by the camera is an unforgettable image. The face of the dead giant looks like Bosch's conception of pain, and the lower jaw hangs slack, held up by Akeley's hand. The body looks bloated and utterly heavy. Mary Bradley gazes smilingly at the faces of the male hunters, her own eyes averted from the camera. Akeley and Herbert Bradley look directly at the camera in an unshuttered acceptance of their act. Two Africans, a young boy and a young man, perch in a tree above the scene, one looking at the camera, one at the hunting party. The contrast of this scene of death with the diorama framing the giant of Karisimbi mounted in New York is total; the animal came to life again, this time immortal.

Akeley felt he was in the most beautiful spot on earth and decided the scene of the death of Bradley's gorilla must be painted for the gorilla group in African Hall. There was no more need to kill after another day's observation of a multi-male, multi-female group; instead, the last capture was with the camera. "So the guns were put behind and the camera pushed forward and we had the extreme satisfaction of seeing the band of gorillas disappear over the crest of the opposite ridge none the worse for having met with white men that morning. It was a wonderful finish to a wonderful gorilla hunt."[25] Once domination is complete, conservation is urgent. But perhaps preservation comes too late.

What followed was the return to the United States and active work for an absolute gorilla sanctuary providing facilities for scientific research. Akeley feared the gorilla would be driven to extinction before it was adequately known to science.[26] His health weakened but his spirit at its height, Akeley lived to return to Kivu to prepare paintings and other material for the gorilla group diorama. Between 1921 and 1926, he mounted his precious gorilla specimens, producing that extraordinary silver back whose gaze dominates African Hall. When he did return to Kivu in 1926, he was so exhausted from his exertions to reach his goal that he died on November 17, 1926, almost immediately after he and his party arrived on the slopes of Mt. Mikeno, "in the land of his dreams."[27]

Akeley's was a literal science dedicated to the prevention of decadence, of biological decay. His grave was built in the heart of the rain forest on the volcano, where "all the free wild things of the forest have perpetual sanctuary."[28] Mary Jobe Akeley directed the digging of an eight foot vault in lava gravel and rock. The hole was lined with closely set wooden beams. The coffin was crafted on the site out of solid native mahogany and lined with heavy galvanized steel salvaged from the boxes used to pack specimens to protect them from insect and other damage. Then the coffin was upholstered with camp blankets. A slab of cement ten by twelve feet and five inches thick was poured on top of the grave and inscribed with the name and date of death of the father of the game. The cement had been carried on porters' backs all the way from the nearest source in Kibale, Uganda. The men apparently ditched the first heavy load in the face of the difficult trails; they were sent back for a second effort. An eight-foot stockade fence was built around the grave to deter buffalo and elephant from desecrating the site. "Dersheid, Raddatz, Bill and I worked five days and five nights to give him the best home we could build, and he was buried as I think he would have liked with a simple reading service and a prayer."[29] The grave was inviolate, and the reincarnation of the natural self would be immortal in African Hall. In 1979, "grave robbers, Zairoise poachers, violated the site and carried off [Akeley's] skeleton."[30]

II. Carl E. Akeley (1864–1926), the Gun, the Camera, and the Hunt for Truth: Biography

For this untruthful picture Akeley substitutes a real gorilla.[31]

Of the two I was the savage and the aggressor.[32]

Carl Akeley's boss at the American Museum, H. F. Osborn, characterized the taxidermist as a sculptor and a biographer of African life. Akeley sought to craft a true life, a unique life. The life of Africa became his life, his telos. But it is not possible to tell his life from a single point of view. There is a polyphony of stories, and they do not harmonize. Each source for telling the story of Akeley's life speaks in an authoritative mode, but the historian felt compelled to compare the versions, and then to cast Akeley's story in an ironic mode, the register most avoided by her subject. Akeley wanted to present an immediate vision; I would like to dissect and make visible layer after layer of mediation. I want to show the reader how the experience of the diorama grew from the safari in specific times and places, how the camera and the gun together are the conduits for the spiritual commerce of man and nature, how biography is woven into and from a social and political tissue. I want to show how the stunning animals of Akeley's achieved dream in African Hall are the product of particular technologies, that is, the techniques of effecting meanings. Technologies are concretized moments of human possibility. Marx called them dead labor, needing the animation of living labor. True enough. Akeley's grave was built in the heart of the rain forest on the volcano, but the relations of life and death in technologies of enforced meaning, or realist representation, are not so straightforward, even for early twentieth-century organic beings, much less for ourselves, late twentieth-century cyborgs, reading stories about the dead craftsman and the obsolete craft of resurrection.[33]

Life Stories

According to the available plots in U.S. history, it is necessary that Carl Akeley was born on a farm in New York State of poor, but vigorous old (white) American stock. The moment of his birth was also necessary, 1864, near the end of the Civil War. The time was an end and a beginning for so much in North America, including the history of biology and the structure of wealth and social class. His boyhood was spent in hard farm labor, in which he learned self-reliance and skill with tools and machines. From the beginning he passed long hours alone watching and hunting the wildlife of New York. By the age of thirteen, aroused by a borrowed book on the subject, Akeley was committed to the vocation of taxidermy. His vocation's bibliogenesis was also ordained by the plot. At that age (or age sixteen in some versions), he had a business card printed up. No Yankee boy could miss the connection of life's purpose with business, although young Carl scarcely believed he could make his living at such a craft. He took lessons in painting, so that he might provide realistic backgrounds for the birds he ceaselessly mounted. From the beginning Akeley's life had a single focus: the capturing and representation of the nature he saw. On this point all the versions of Akeley's life concur.

After the crops were in, at the age of nineteen, Akeley set off from his father's farm "to get a wider field for my efforts."[34] First he tried to get a job with a local painter and interior decorator whose hobby was taxidermy, but this man, David Bruce, directed the young man to an institution which changed his life—Ward's Natural Science Establishment in Rochester, where Akeley would spend four years and form a friendship pregnant with consequences for the nascent science of ecology as it came to be practiced in museum exhibition. Ward's provided mounted specimens and natural history collections for practically all the museums in the nation. Several important men in the history of biology and museology in the United States passed through this curious institution, including Akeley's friend, William Morton Wheeler. Wheeler completed his eminent career in entymology at Harvard, a founder of the science of animal ecology (which he called ethology—the science of the character of nature) and a mentor in the philosophy of science and of society to the great organicists and conservative social philosophers in Harvard's biological and medical establishment.[35] Wheeler was then a young Milwaukee naturalist steeped in German "kultur" who began tutoring the rustic Akeley for entry into Yale's Sheffield Scientific School. However, eleven hours of taxidermy in the day and long hours of study proved too much; so higher education was postponed, later permanently in order to follow the truer vocation of reading nature's book directly.

Akeley was sorely disappointed at Ward's because business imperatives allowed no room for improvement of the craft of taxidermy. He felt animals were "upholstered." He developed his own skill and technique in spite of the lack of encouragement, and the lack of money, and got a chance for public recognition when P. T. Barnum's famous elephant was run down by a locomotive in Canada in 1885. Barnum did not want to forego the fame and profit from continuing to display the giant (who had died trying to save a baby elephant, we are told), so Akeley and a companion were dispatched to Canada from Rochester to save the situation. Six butchers from a nearby town helped with the rapidly rotting carcass; and what the young Akeley learned about very large mammal taxidermy from this experience laid the foundation for his later revolutionary innovations in producing light, strong, life-like pachyderms. The popular press followed the monumental mounting, and the day Jumbo was launched in his own railroad car into his postmortem career, half the population of Rochester witnessed the resurrection. The first big period of trial was over for the young taxidermist.[36]

In 1885 Wheeler had returned to Milwaukee to teach high school and soon took up a curatorship in the Milwaukee Museum of Natural History. Wheeler urged his friend to follow, hoping to continue his tutoring and to secure Akeley commissions for specimens from the museum. At this time, museums did not generally have their own taxidermy departments, although the years around 1890 were a period of flowering of taxidermic technique in Britain and the United States. Akeley opened his business shop on the Wheeler family property, and he and the naturalist spent long hours discussing natural history, finding themselves in agreement both about museum display and about the character of nature. The most important credo for them both was the need to develop scientific knowledge of the whole animal in the whole group in nature— that is, they were committed organicists. Wheeler soon became director of the Milwaukee museum and gave Akeley significant support. Akeley had conceived the idea for habitat groups and wished to mount a series illustrating the fur-bearing animals of Wisconsin. His completed muskrat group (1889), minus the painted backgrounds, was probably the first mammalian habitat group anywhere.

As a result of a recommendation from Wheeler, in 1894 the British Museum invited Akeley to practice his trade in that world-famous institution. On the way to London, Akeley visited the Field Museum in Chicago, met Daniel Giraud Elliot and accepted his offer of preparing the large collection of specimens the museum had bought from Ward's. In 1896 Akeley made his first collecting expedition to Africa, to British Somaliland, a trip that opened a whole new world to him. This was the first of five safaris to Africa, each escalating his sense of the purity of the continent's vanishing wild life and the conviction that the meaning of his life was its preservation through transforming taxidermy into an art. He was again in Africa for the Field Museum in 1905, with his explorer/adventurer/author wife, Delia, to collect elephants in British East Africa. On this trip Akeley escaped with his life after killing a leopard in hand-to-fang combat.

In Chicago, Akeley spent four years largely at his own expense preparing the justly famous Four Seasons deer dioramas depicting typical scenes in every detail. In 1908, at the invitation of the new president, H. F. Osborn, who was anxious to mark his office with the discovery of major new scientific laws and departures in museum exhibition and public education, Akeley moved to New York and the American Museum of Natural History in hope of preparing a major collection of large African mammals. From 1909 to 1911 Akeley and Delia collected in British East Africa, a trip marked by a hunt with Theodore Roosevelt and his son Kermit, who were collecting for the Washington National Museum. The safari was brought to a limping conclusion by Carl's being mauled by an elephant, thus delaying fulfillment of his dream of collecting gorillas. His plan for the African Hall took shape by 1911 and ruled his behavior thereafter. He spent World War I as a civilian assistant engineer to the Mechanical and Devices Section of the Army. He is said to have refused a commission in order to keep his freedom to speak freely to anyone in the hierarchy.

During the war, his mechanical genius had full scope, resulting in several patents in his name. The theme of Akeley the inventor recurs constantly in his life story. Included in his roster of inventions, several of which involved subsequent business development, were a motion picture camera, a cement gun, and several stages of new taxidermic processes, particularly methods of making manikins to go under the animal skins and methods of making highly naturalistic foliage.

With the close of war, Akeley focused all his energy on getting backing for the African Hall. He needed more than a million dollars. Lecture tours, articles and a book, and endless promotion brought him into touch with the major wealthy sportsmen of the state, but sufficient financial commitment eluded him. In 1921, financing half the expense himself, Akeley left for Africa again, this time accompanied by a married couple, their five-year-old daughter, their governess, and Akeley's adult niece whom he had promised to take hunting in Africa. Akeley felt bringing women and children to hunt gorillas was the definitive proof of his theme of brightest Africa, where the animals were noble in defense of their families, but never wantonly ferocious. On this trip, he collected five gorillas, with the help of the Bradleys, once again nearly died from jungle fevers, and returned to New York determined to achieve permanent conservation for the gorillas in the Belgian Congo. In 1924 he married the explorer/adventurer/author Mary L. Jobe, who accompanied him on his last adventure, the Akeley-Eastman-Pomeroy African Hall Expedition, that collected for ten dioramas of the Great Hall. George Eastman, of Eastman Kodak fortunes, and Daniel Pomeroy, the benefactors, accompanied the taxidermist-hunter to collect specimens for their bequests. Eastman, then seventy-one years old, went with his own physician and commanded his own railroad train for part of the excursion.

En route to Africa the Akeleys were received by the conservationist and war hero King of Belgium, Albert. He was the son of the infamous Leopold II, whose personal rapacious control of the Congo for profit was wrested away and given to the Belgian government by other European powers in 1908. Leopold II had financed Henry Stanley's explorations of the Congo. Akeley is pictured in his biographies in the line of the great explorers from Stanley and Livingstone, but also as the man who witnessed and indeed helped birth a new bright Africa. Albert, who had been led to his views on national parks by a visit to Yosemite, confirmed plans for the Parc Albert and gave the Akeleys a commission to prepare topographical maps and descriptions of the area in cooperation with the Belgian naturalist, Jean Derscheid. There was no room for a great park for the Belgians in Europe, so naturally one was established in the Congo, which was to include protection for the Pygmies who lived within park boundaries. The park was to provide sanctuary for natural primitives, as well as to foster scientific study by establishing permanent research facilities within park boundaries. After ten months of collecting, Carl and Mary Jobe set off for the Kivu forest and the heart of remaining unspoiled Africa. Their purpose this time was not to collect gorillas, but to observe the apes, collect plants, and obtain paintings for the gorilla diorama. Carl Akeley died in November 1926, of fever a few days after arriving at the site of his 1921 encampment, the most beautiful spot in all of Africa for him. His wife and the other members of the expedition buried him on Mt. Mikeno "in ground the hand of man can never alter or profane."[37]

Taxidermy: From Upholstery to Epiphany

Transplanted Africa stands before him—a result of Akeley's dream.[38]

The vision Carl Akeley had seen was one of jungle peace. It was this that he needed to preserve permanently for the world. His quest to embody this vision alone justified to himself his hunting, turned it into a tool of science and art, the scalpel that revealed the harmony of an organic, articulate world. Let us follow Akeley briefly through his technical contributions to taxidermy in order to grasp more fully the stories he needed to tell about the biography of Africa, the life history of nature, that is, the natural history of life. Akeley and others have summarized many times in print how his labors transformed taxidermy from the stuffing of animals into an art capable of embodying truth, so this recapitulation will select only those themes essential to my story.[39]

It is a simple tale: Taxidermy was made into the servant of the "real." Akeley's vocation, and his achievement, was the production of an organized craft for eliciting unambiguous experience of organic perfection. Literally, Akeley "typified" nature, made nature true to type. Taxidermy was about the single story, about nature's unity, the unblemished type specimen. Taxidermy became the art most suited to the epistemological and aesthetic stance of realism. The power of this stance is in its magical effects: what is so painfully constructed appears effortlessly, spontaneously found, discovered, simply there if one will only look. Realism does not appear to be a point of view, but appears as a "peephole into the jungle" where peace may be witnessed. Epiphany comes as a gift, not as the fruit of merit and toil, soiled by the hand of man. Realistic art at its most deeply magical issues in revelation. This art repays labor with transcendence. Small wonder that artistic realism and biological science were twin brothers in the founding of the civic order of nature at the American

Museum of Natural History. Both were suckled by nature, as Romulus and Remus. It is also natural that taxidermy and biology depend fundamentally upon vision in a hierarchy of the senses; they are tools for the construction, discovery of form.

Akeley's eight years in Milwaukee from 1886 to 1894 were crucial for his working out techniques that served him well the rest of his life. The culmination of that period was a head of a male Virginia deer he entered in the first Sportsman's Show, held in New York City in 1895. The judge in that national competition, in which Akeley's entry placed first, was Theodore Roosevelt, whom Akeley did not meet until they befriended each other on safari in Africa in 1906. The head, entitled "The Challenge," displayed a buck "in the full frenzy of his virility as he gave the defiant roar of the rutting season—the call to fierce combat."[40] Jungle peace was not a passive affair, nor one unmarked by gender.

The head was done in a period of experimentation leading to the production in Chicago of four habitat groups of deer displayed in the four seasons. In crafting those groups over four years, Akeley worked out his manikin method, clay modeling, plaster casting, vegetation molding techniques, and early organized production system. He hired women and men workers by the hour to turn out the thousands of individual leaves needed to clothe the trees in the scenes. Background canvases were painted by Charles Abel Corwin, from studies done in the Michigan Iron Mountains where the animals were collected. Akeley patented his vegetation process, but gave rights for its use free of charge to the Field Museum in Chicago; he did not patent his innovative methods of producing light, strong papier-mâché manikins from exact clay models and plaster casts, but allowed free worldwide use of his techniques. Cooperation in museum development was a fundamental value for this taxidermist, who did not make much money at his craft and whose inventions were a significant part of his economic survival. "Four Seasons" was installed in the Field Museum in 1902.[41]

Akeley continued to make improvements in his taxidermic technique throughout his life, and he taught several other key workers, including James Lipsitt Clark, who was the director of Arts, Preparation, and Installation at the American Museum in the years after Akeley's death when African Hall was actually constructed. While Akeley worked long hours alone, it would be a mistake to imagine taxidermy as he helped to develop its practice to be a solitary art. Taxidermy requires a complex system of coordination and division of labor, beginning in the field during the hunting of the animals and culminating in the presentation of a finished diorama allowing solitary, individual communion with nature. A minimum list of workers on one of Akeley's projects must include fellow taxidermists, other collectors, artists, anatomists, and "accessory men."[42] Pictures of work in the taxidermy studios of the American Museum show men (males, usually white) tanning hides, working on large clay models of sizeable mammals (including elephants) or on plaster casts, assembling skeleton and wood frames, consulting scale models of the planned display, doing carpentry, making vegetation, sketching, etc. Clark reports that during the years between 1926 and 1936 when African Hall opened, still unfinished, the staff of the project usually employed about forty-five men. Painting the backgrounds was itself a major artistic specialization, and the artists based their final panoramas on numerous studies done at the site of collection. In the field, the entire operation rested on the organization of the safari, a complex social institution where race, sex, and class came together intensely. The safari will be discussed more fully below, but now it is useful to note that skinning a large animal could employ fifty workers for several hours. Photographs, moving picture records, death masks of the animals, extensive anatomical measurements, initial treatment of skins, and sketches all occupied the field workers. It would not be an exaggeration to claim that the production of a modern diorama involved the work of hundreds of people in a social system embracing the major structures of skill and authority on a worldwide scale.

How can such a system produce a unified biography of nature? How is it possible to refer to *Akeley's* African Hall when it was constructed after he died? On an ideological level, the answer to these simple questions is connected to the ruling conception of organicism, an organic hierarchy, conceived as nature's principle of organization. Clark stressed the importance of "artistic composition" and described the process as a "recreation" of nature based on the principles of organic form. This process required a base of "personal experience," ideally in the form of presence in Africa, at the site of the animal's life and death. Technical crafts are always imagined to be subordinated by the ruling artistic idea, itself rooted authoritatively in nature's own life. "Such things must be felt, must be absorbed and assimilated, and then in turn, with understanding and enthusiasm, given out by the creator. . . . Therefore, our groups are very often conceived in the very lair of the animals."[43]

The credos of realism and organicism are closely connected; both are systematizations of organization by a hierarchical division of labor, perceived as natural and therefore productive of unity. Unity must be authored in the Judeo-Christian myth system, and just as nature has an

Author, so does the organism or the realistic diorama. In this myth system, the author must be imagined with the aspects of mind, in relation to the body which executes. Akeley was intent on avoiding *lying* in his work; his craft was to tell the truth of nature. There was only one way to achieve such truth—the rule of mind rooted in the claim to experience. All the work must be done by men who did their collecting and studies on the spot because "[o]therwise, the exhibit is a lie and it would be nothing short of a crime to place it in one of the leading educational institutions of the country."[44] A single mind infused collective experience: "If an exhibition hall is to approach its ideal, its plan must be that of a master mind, while in actuality it is the product of the correlation of many minds and hands."[45] Training a school of workers was an absolutely fundamental part of Akeley's practice of taxidermy; on his success rested the possibility of telling the truth. But above all, this sense of telling a true story rested on the selection of individual animals, the formation of groups of typical specimens.

What does it mean to claim a diorama tells a unified story, a biography essential to nature? What was the meaning of "typical" for Akeley and his contemporaries in the biological departments of the American Museum of Natural History? What are the contents of these stories and what must one *do* to see these contents? To answer these questions, we must follow Carl Akeley into the field and watch him select an animal to mount. Akeley's concentration on finding the typical specimen, group, or scene cannot be overemphasized. But how could he know what was typical or that such a state of being existed? This problem has been fundamental in the history of biology; one effort at solution is embodied in African Hall. Three hunts illustrate Akeley's meanings of typical.

First, the concept includes the notion of perfection. The large bull giraffe in the water hole group in African Hall was the object of a hunt over many days in 1921. Several animals were passed over because they were too small or not colored beautifully enough. Remembering record trophies from late nineteenth-century hunters undermined satisfaction with a modern, smaller specimen taken from the depleted herds of vanishing African nature. When at last the bull was spotted and taken as the result of great skill and daring, the minute details of its preservation and recreation were lovingly described.

Similarly, in 1910–11, the hunt for a large bull elephant provided the central drama of the safari for the entire two years. An animal with asymmetrical tusks was rejected, despite his imposing size. Character, as well as mere physical appearance, was important in judging an animal to be perfect. Cowardice would disqualify the most lovely and properly proportioned beast. Ideally, the killing itself had to be accomplished as a sportsmanlike act. Perfection was heightened if the hunt were a meeting of equals. So there was a hierarchy of game according to species: lions, elephants, and giraffes far outranked wild asses or antelope. The gorilla was the supreme achievement, almost a definition of perfection in the heart of the garden at the moment of origin. Perfection inhered in the animal itself, but the fullest meanings of perfection inhered in the meeting of animal and man, the moment of perfect vision. Taxidermy was the craft of remembering this perfect experience. Realism was a supreme achievement of the art of memory, a rhetorical achievement crucial to the foundations of Western science.[46]

There is one other essential quality for the typical animal in its perfect expression: it must be an adult male. Akeley describes hunting many fine cows or lionesses, and he cared for their hides and other details of reconstruction with all his skill. But never was it necessary to take weeks and risk the success of the entire enterprise to find the perfect female. There existed an image of an animal which was somehow the gorilla or *the* elephant incarnate. That particular tone of perfection could only be heard in the male mode. It was a compound of physical and spiritual quality judged truthfully by the artist-scientist in the fullness of direct experience. Perfection was marked by exact quantitative measurement, but even more by virile vitality known by the hunter-scientist from visual communion. Perfection was known by natural kinship; type, kind, and kin mutually defined each other.

But Akeley hunted for a series or a group, not just for individuals. How did he know when to stop the hunt? Two groups give his criterion of wholeness, the gorilla group collected in 1921 and the original group of four elephants mounted by Akeley himself after the 1910–11 safari. At one point in his hunt for specimens, Akeley shot a gorilla, believing it to be a female, but found it to be a young male. He was disturbed because he wished to kill as few animals as possible, and he believed the natural family of the gorilla did not contain more than one male. When he later saw a group made up of several males and females, he stopped his hunt with relief, confident that he could tell the truth from his existing specimens. Similarly, the photograph of Akeley's original group of four elephants unmistakably shows a perfect family. The reproductive group had the epistemological and moral status of truth tellers. It was nature's biographical unit.

Akeley wanted to be an artist and a scientist. He gave up his early plan of obtaining a degree from Yale Sheffield Scientific School and then of becoming a professional sculptor. Instead, he combined art and science in taxidermy. Since that art required that he also be a sculptor, he told some of his stories in bronzes as well as in dioramas. His criteria were similar; Akeley had many stories to tell, but they all expressed the same fundamental vision of a vanishing, threatened scene.[47] In his determination to sculpt "typical" Nandi lion spearmen, Akeley used as models extensive photographs, drawings, and "selected types of American negroes which he was using to make sure of perfect figures."[48] The variety of nature had a purpose—to lead to discovery of the highest type of each species of wild life, including human beings outside "civilization."

Besides sculpture and taxidermy, Akeley perfected another narrative tool, photography. All of his story-telling instruments relied primarily on vision. Each tool was capable of telling his truth, but each caught and held slightly different manifestations of natural history. As a visual art, taxidermy occupied for Akeley a middle ground between sculpture and photography. In a sense, both sculpture and photography were subordinate means to accomplishing the final taxidermic scene. But from another point of view, photography represented the future and sculpture the past. Let us follow Akeley into his practice of photography in the critical years suspended between the manual touch of sculpture, which produced knowledge of life in the fraternal discourses of organicist biology and realist art, and the virtual touch of the camera, which has dominated our understanding of nature since World War II. The nineteenth century produced the masterpieces of animal bronzes inhabiting the world's museums. Akeley's early twentieth-century taxidermy, seemingly so solid and material, may be seen as a brief frozen temporal section in the incarnation of art and science, before the camera technically could pervert his single dream into the polymorphous and absurdly intimate filmic reality we now take for granted.[49] Critics accuse Akeley's taxidermy and the American Museum's expensive policy of building the great display halls in the years before World War II of being armature against the future, of having literally locked in stone one historical moment's way of seeing, while calling this vision the whole.[50] But Akeley was a leader technically and spiritually in the perfection of the camera's eye. Taxidermy was not armed against the filmic future, but froze one frame of a far more intense visual communion to be consummated in virtual images. Akeley helped produce the armature—and armament—that would advance into the future.

Photography: Hunting With the Camera

Guns have metamorphosed into cameras in this earnest comedy, the ecology safari, because nature has ceased to be what it had always been—what people needed protection from. Now nature—tamed, endangered, mortal—needs to be protected from people. When we are afraid, we shoot. But when we are nostalgic, we take pictures.[51]

This essay has repeatedly claimed Akeley and his peers feared the disappearance of their world, of their social world in the new immigrations after 1890 and the resulting dissolution of the old imagined hygienic, pre-industrial America. Civilization appeared to be a disease in the form of technological progress and the vast accumulation of wealth in the practice of monopoly capitalism by the very wealthy sportsmen who were trustees of the museum and the backers of Akeley's African Hall. The leaders of the American Museum were afraid for their health; that is, their manhood was endangered. Theodore Roosevelt knew the prophylaxis for this specific historical malaise: the true man is the true sportsman. Any human being, regardless of race, class, and gender, could spiritually participate in the moral status of healthy manhood in democracy, even if only a few (Anglo-Saxon, male, heterosexual, Protestant, physically robust, and economically comfortable) could express manhood's highest forms. From about 1890 to the 1930s, the Museum was a vast public education and research program for producing experience potent to induce the state of manhood. The Museum, in turn, was the ideological and material product of the sporting life. As Mary Jobe Akeley realized, "[the true sportsman] loves the game as if he were the father of it."[52] Akeley believed that in the end, the highest expression of sportsmanship was hunting with the camera: "Moreover, according to any true conception of sport—the use of skill, daring, and endurance in overcoming difficulties—camera hunting takes twice the man that gun hunting takes."[53] The true father of the game loves nature with the camera; it takes twice the man, and the children are in his perfect image. The eye is infinitely more potent than the gun. Both put a woman to shame—reproductively.

At the time of Akeley's first collecting safari in 1896, cameras were a nearly useless encumbrance, incapable of capturing the goal of the hunt— life. According to Akeley, the first notable camera hunters in Africa appeared around 1902.[54] The early books were based on still photographs; moving picture wild life photography owes much to Akeley's own camera and did not achieve anything before the 1920s. On his 1910–11 safari to east Africa, Akeley had the best available equipment and tried to film the Nandi lion spearing. His failure due to inadequate cameras, described with great emotional intensity, led him during the next five years to design the Akeley camera, which was used extensively by the Army Signal Corps during World War I. Akeley formed the Akeley Camera Company to develop his invention, which received its civilian christening by filming Man-O'-War win the Kentucky Derby in 1920. The camera's innovative telephoto lens caught the Dempsey-Carpentier heavyweight battle. Awarded the John Price Wetherhill Medal at the Franklin Institute in 1926 for his invention, Akeley succeeded that year in filming to his satisfaction African lion spearing, on the same safari on which Rochester's George Eastman, of Eastman-Kodak fortunes, was both cosponsor and hunter-collector.[55] Recall that Akeley's first taste of his own camera in the field was in 1921 in the Kivu forest. Within a few days, Akeley shot his first gorillas with both gun and camera, in the experiences he saw as the culmination of his life.

The ambiguity of the gun and camera runs throughout Akeley's work. He is a transitional figure from the Western image of darkest to lightest Africa, from nature worthy of manly fear to nature in need of motherly nurture. The woman/scientist/mother of orphaned apes popularized by the National Geographic Society's magazine and films in the 1970s was still half a century away.[56] With Akeley, manhood tested itself against fear, even as the lust for the image of jungle peace held the finger on the gun long enough to take the picture and even as the intellectual and mythic certainty grew that the savage beast in the jungle was human, in particular, industrial human. Even at the literal level of physical appearance, "[t]o one familiar with the old types of camera the Akeley resembled a machine gun quite as much as it resembled a camera."[57] Akeley said he set out to design a camera "that you can aim . . . with about the same ease that you can point a pistol."[58] He enjoyed retelling the apocryphal story of seven Germans in World War I mistakenly surrendering to one American in France when they found themselves faced by an Akeley. "The fundamental difference between the Akeley motion-picture camera and the others is a panoramic device which enables one to swing it all about, much as one would swing a swivel gun, following the natural line of vision."[59] Akeley semi-joked in knowing puns on the penetrating and deadly invasiveness of the camera, naming one of his image machines "The Gorilla." "'The Gorilla' had taken 300 feet of film of the animal that had never heretofore been taken alive in its native wilds by any camera. . . . I was satisfied— more satisfied than a man ever should be—but I revelled in the feeling."[60]

The taxidermist, certain of the essential peacefulness of the gorilla, wondered how close he should let a charging male get before neglecting the camera for the gun. "I hope that I shall have the courage to allow an apparently charging gorilla to come within a reasonable distance before shooting. I hesitate to say just what I consider a reasonable distance at the present moment. I shall feel very gratified if I can get a photograph at twenty feet. I should be proud of my nerve if I were able to show a photograph of him at ten feet, but I do not expect to do this unless I am at the moment a victim of suicidal mania."[61] Akeley wrote these words before he had ever seen a wild gorilla. What was the boundary of courage; how much did nature or man need protecting? What if the gorilla never charged, even when provoked? What if the gorilla were a coward (or a female)? Who, precisely, was threatened in the drama of natural history in the early decades of monopoly capitalism's presence in Africa and America?

Aware of a disturbing potential of the camera, Akeley set himself against faking. He stuffed Barnum's Jumbo, but he wanted no part of the great circus magnate's cultivation of the American popular art form, the hoax.[62] But hoax luxuriated in early wild life photography (and anthropological photography). In particular, Akeley saw unscrupulous men manipulate nature to tell the story of a fierce and savage Africa; this was the story which would sell in the motion picture emporia across America. Taxidermy had always threatened to lapse from art into deception, from life to upholstered death as a poor sportsman's trophy. Photography too was full of philistines who could debase the entire undertaking of nature work, the Museum's term for its educational work in the early decades of the twentieth century. The Museum was for public entertainment (the point that kept its Presbyterian trustees resisting Sunday opening in the 1880s despite that day's fine potential for educating the new Catholic immigrants, who worked a six-day week); but entertainment only had value if it communicated the truth. Therefore, Akeley encouraged an association between the American Museum and the wildlife photographers, Martin and Osa Johnson, who seemed willing and able to produce popular motion pictures telling the story of jungle peace. Johnson claimed in his 1923 prospectus to the American Museum, "The camera cannot be deceived . . . [therefore, it has] enormous scientific value."[63]

Entertainment was complexly interwoven with science, art, hunting, and education. Barnum's humbug tested the cleverness, the scientific acumen, of the observer in a republic where each citizen could find out the nakedness of the emperor and the sham of his rationality. This democracy of reason was always a bit dangerous. There is a tradition of active participation in the eye of science in America which makes the stories of nature always ready to erupt into popular politics. Natural history can be—and has sometimes been—a means for millennial expectation and disorderly action. Akeley himself is an excellent example of a self-made man who made use of the mythic resources of the independent man's honest vision, the appeal to experience, the testimony of one's own eyes. He saw the Giant of Karisimbi. The camera, an eminently democratic machine, has been crucial to the crafting of stories in biology; but its control has always eluded the professional and the moralist, the official scientist. But in Martin Johnson, Akeley hoped he had the man who would tame specular entertainment for the social uplift promised by science.

In 1906 Martin Johnson shipped out with Jack London on the *Snark* for a two-year voyage in the South Seas. The *Snark* was the photographer's *Beagle*. Its name could hardly have been better chosen for the ship that carried the two adventurers whose books and films complemented *Tarzan* for recording the dilemma of manhood in the early twentieth century. Lewis Carroll's *The Hunting of the Snark* contains the lines that capture Johnson's and London's—and Akeley's—Darwinian revelation:

> In one moment I've seen what has hitherto been
> Enveloped in absolute mystery,
> And without extra charge I will give you at large
> A lesson in Natural History.[64]

From 1908 to 1913 Johnson ran five motion picture houses in Kansas. In the same period and after, he and Osa traveled in the still mysterious and potent places, filming "native life": Melanesia, Polynesia, Malekula, Borneo, Kenya Colony. In 1922 Martin and Osa sought Carl Akeley's opinion of their just completed film *Trailing African Wild Animals*. Akeley was delighted, and the result was the Museum's setting up a special corporation to fund the Johnsons on a five-year film safari in Africa. The Johnsons' plans included making two short films, including one on "African Babies." "It will show elephant babies, lion babies, zebra babies, giraffe babies, and black babies . . . showing the play of wild animals and the maternal care that is so strange and interesting a feature of wildlife."[65] The human life of Africa was repeatedly consigned to the Age of Mammals, prior to the Age of Man. That was its only claim to protection, and of course the ultimate justification for domination. Here was a record of jungle peace.

The Johnsons planned a big animal feature film as the capstone of the safari. The museum lauded both the commercial and educational values;

Osborn commented that the "double message of such photography is, first, that it brings the aesthetic and ethical influence of nature within the reach of millions of people . . . [and] second, it spreads the idea that our generation has no right to destroy what future generations may enjoy."[66] It was perfect that the Johnson film safari overlapped with the Akeley-Eastman-Pomeroy expedition. The Akeleys spent several days helping the Johnsons film lion spearing in Tanganyika, finally capturing on film this endangered apotheosis of primitive manhood. Johnson was confident that their approach of combining truth and beauty without hoax would ultimately be commercially superior, as well as scientifically accurate. "[T]here is no limit to the money it can make. . . . My past training, my knowledge of showmanship, mixed with the scientific knowledge I have absorbed lately, and the wonderful photographic equipment . . . make me certain that this Big Feature is going to be the biggest money maker ever placed on the market, as there is no doubt it will be the last big Africa Feature made, and it will be so spectacular that there will be no danger of another film of like nature competing with it. For these reasons it will produce an income as long as we live."[67] Africa had always promised gold.

The "naked eye" science advocated by the American Museum was perfect for the camera, ultimately so superior to the gun for the possession, production, preservation, consumption, surveillance, appreciation, and control of nature. The ideology of realism essential to Akeley's aesthetic was part of his effort to touch, to see, to bridge the yawning gaps in the endangered self. To make an exact image is to insure against disappearance, to cannibalize life until it is safely and permanently a specular image, a ghost. It arrested decay. That is why nature photography is so beautiful and so religious—and such a powerful hint of an apocalyptic future. Akeley's aesthetic combined the instrumental and contemplative into a photographic technology providing a transfusion for a steadily depleted sense of reality. The image and the real mutually define each other, as all of reality in late capitalist culture lusts to become an image for its own security. Reality is assured, insured, by the image, and there is no limit to the amount of money that can be made. The camera is superior to the gun for the control of time; and Akeley's dioramas with their photographic vision, sculptor's touch, and taxidermic solidity were about the end of time.[68]

III. Telling Stories

The synthetic story told above has three major sources and several minor ones. Telling the life synthetically masks the tones and versions which emerge from listening to these sources. The single biography, the ideological achieved unity of African Hall, can be brought to the edge of an imagined heteroglossic novel which has not yet been written. A polyphonic natural history waits for its sustaining social history. In order to probe more deeply into the tissue of meanings and mediations making the specific structure of experience possible for the viewer of the dioramas of African Hall—and of the Giant of Karisimbi—I would like to tease apart the sources for one major event of Akeley's life, the elephant mauling in British East Africa in 1910. This event can function as a germ for expanding my story of the structure and function of biography in the construction of a twentieth-century primate order, with its specific and polymorphous hierarchies of race, sex, and class. With an ear for the tones of audience, historical moment, social interests and intentions of authors, and the material-physical appearance of sources, I would like to consider in greater detail the question of story-telling. In particular, whose stories appear and disappear in the web of social practices that constitute Teddy Bear Patriarchy? Questions of authorized writing enforced by publishing practices and of labor that never issues in acknowledged authorship (never father of the game) make up my story.[69]

Authors and Versions

> She didn't write it.
> She wrote it but she shouldn't have.
> She wrote it, but look what she wrote about.[70]

Carl Akeley's book, *In Brightest Africa*, appears on the surface to be written by Carl Akeley. But we learn from Mary Jobe Akeley, a prolific author, that the taxidermist "hated to wield a pen."[71] She elaborates that the publishers, Doubleday and Page (the men, not the company), were enthralled by Carl's stories told in their homes at dinner and so "determined to extract a book from him." So one evening after dinner Arthur W. Page "stationed a stenographer behind a screen, and without Carl's knowledge, she recorded everything he said while the guests lingered before the fire." The editing of this material is then ascribed to Doubleday and

Page, but the author is named as Carl. The stenographer is an unnamed hand. These notes gave rise to articles in a journal called *World's Work*, but a book was still not forthcoming from the taxidermist. Then Akeley discovered a newspaper account of his Kivu journey that he greatly liked; the piece had been written by Dorothy S. Greene while she worked for the director of the American Museum. Akeley hired her as his secretary, to record his stories while he talked with other explorers or scientists or lectured to raise funds for African Hall. "She unobtrusively jotted down material which could be used in a book."[72] Who wrote *In Brightest Africa?* In the answer to that question resides a world of motivated history of the relation of mind and body in Western authorship.

The physical appearance of the books is itself an eloquent story. The stamp of approval from men like H. F. Osborn in the dignified prefaces, the presence of handsome photographs, a publishing house that catered to wealthy hunters: all compose the authority of the books. The frontspieces are like Orthodox icons; the entire story can be read from them. In *Lions, Gorillas and their Neighbors*, the book prepared for young people, the frontspiece shows an elderly Carl Akeley in his studio gazing intently into the eyes of the plaster death mask of the first gorilla he ever saw. Maturity in the encounter with nature is announced. *The Wilderness Lives Again*, the biography that resurrected Carl through his wife's vicarious authorship, displays in the front a young Carl, arm and hand bandaged heavily, standing outside a tent beside a dead leopard suspended by her hind legs. The caption reads: "Carl Akeley, when still in his twenties, choked this wounded infuriated leopard to death with his naked hands as it attacked him with intent to kill."

Let us turn to Carl Akeley's story of his encounter with the elephant which mauled him. The tale occurs in a chapter of Akeley's book called "Elephant Friends and Foes." Several moral lessons pervade the chapter, prominently those of human ignorance of the great animals—partly because hunters are only after ivory and trophies, so that their knowledge is only of tracking and killing, not of the animals' lives—and of Akeley's difference because of his special closeness to nature embodied in the magnificent elephants. On this safari, Akeley witnessed two elephants help a wounded comrade escape from the scene of slaughter, inspiring one of the taxidermist's bronzes. But also in this chapter, the reader sees an earthy Akeley, not above making a table to seat eight people out of elephant ears from a specimen which nearly killed him and Delia, despite each of them shooting into his head about thirteen times. In this chapter, the taxidermist is hunting as an equal with his wife. He does not hide stories which might seem a bit seedy or full of personal bravado; yet his "natural nobility" pervaded all these anecdotes, particularly for an audience of potential donors to African Hall, who might quite likely find themselves shooting big game in Africa.

His near-fatal encounter with an elephant occurred when Akeley had gone off without Delia to get photographs, taking "four days' rations, gun boys, porters, camera men, and so forth—about fifteen men in all."[73] He was tracking an elephant whose trail was very fresh, when he suddenly became aware that the animal was bearing down on him directly:

> I have no knowledge of how the warning came. . . . I only know that as I picked up my gun and wheeled about I tried to shove the safety catch forward. It refused to budge. . . . My next mental record is of a tusk right at my chest. I grabbed it with my left hand, the other one with my right hand, and swinging in between them went to the ground on my back. This swinging in between the tusks was purely automatic. It was the result of many a time on the trails imagining myself caught by an elephant's rush and planning what to do, and a very profitable planning too; for I am convinced that if a man imagines such a crisis and plans what he would do, he will, when the occasion occurs, automatically do what he planned. . . . He drove his tusks into the ground on either side of me. . . . When he surged down on me, his big tusks evidently struck something in the ground that stopped them. . . . He seems to have thought me dead for he left me—by some good fortune not stepping on me—and charged off after the boys.[74]

Akeley follows this cool description full of counsel about planning for life's big moments with remarks about what elephants are reputed to do in other charges and with remarks about the behavior of his party. "I never got much information out of the boys as to what did happen, for they were not proud of their part in the adventure. . . . It is reasonable to assume that they had scattered through [the area which the elephant thoroughly trampled] like a covey of quail."[75]

Akeley tells that he lay unconscious and untouched for hours because his men felt he was dead, and they came from groups which refused ever to touch a dead man. When he came to, he shouted and got attention. He relates that word had been sent to Mrs. Akeley at base camp, who valiantly mounted a rescue party in the middle of the night against the wishes of her guides (because of the dangers of night travel through the bush), whom she pursued into their huts to force their cooperation. She sent word to the nearest government post to dispatch a doctor and arrived at the scene of the injury by dawn. Akeley attributed his recovery to her prompt arrival, but more to the subsequent speedy arrival of a neophyte

Scottish doctor, who sped through the jungle to help the injured man partly out of his ignorance of the foolishness of hurrying to help anyone mauled by an elephant—such men simply didn't survive to pay for one's haste. The more seasoned government official, the chief medical officer, arrived considerably later.

The remainder of the chapter recounts Akeley's chat with other old hands in Africa about their experiences surviving elephant attacks. The tone is reasoned, scientific, focused on the behavior and character of those interesting aspects of elephant behavior. The constant moral of the chapter emerges again in the conclusion:

> But although the elephant is a terrible fighter in his own defense when at- tacked by man, that is not his chief characteristic. The things that stick in my mind are his sagacity, his versatility, and a certain comradeship which I have never noticed to the same degree in other animals. . . . I like to think back to the day I saw the group of baby elephants playing with a great ball of baked dirt. . . . I think, too, of the extraordinary fact that I have never heard or seen African elephants fighting each other. They have no enemy but man and are at peace amongst themselves. It is my friend the elephant that I hope to per- petuate in the central group in Roosevelt African Hall. . . . In this, which we hope will be an everlasting monument to the Africa that was, the Africa that is fast disappearing, I hope to place the elephant on a pedestal in the centre of the hall—the rightful place for the first among them.[76]

Akeley's interests are constantly in the perpetuation, conservation, and dignity of nature in which man is the enemy, the intruder, the dealer of death. His own exploits in the hunt stand in ironic juxtaposition only if the reader refuses to discern their true meaning—the tales of a pure man whose danger in pursuit of a noble cause brings him into communion with the beasts he kills, with nature. This nature is a worthy brother of man, a worthy foil for his manhood. Akeley's elephant is profoundly male, singular, and representative of the possibility of nobility. The mauling was an exciting tale, with parts for many actors, including Delia, but the brush with death and the details of rescue are told with the cool humor of a man ready for his end dealt by such a noble friend and brother, his best enemy, the object of his scientific curiosity. The putative behavior of the "boys" underlines the confrontation between white manhood and the noble beast. Casual and institutional racism only heightens the experi- ence of the life story of the single adult man. The action in Akeley's stories focuses on the center of the stage, on the meeting of the singular man and animal. The entourage is inaudible, invisible, except for comic relief and anecdotes about native life. In Akeley's rendering, empowered by class and race, white woman stands without much comment in a similar moral position as white man—a hunter, an adult.

Mary L. Jobe Akeley published her biography of her husband, *The Wilderness Lives Again,* in 1940, four years after the Akeley African Hall opened to the public, his dream assured. Her purpose was no longer to raise money and tell stories to other hunters, but to promote conservation and fulfill her life's purpose—accomplishing her husband's life work. Her biography of Carl should be taken literally. She presents herself as the inspired scribe for her husband's story. Through her vicarious authorship and through African Hall and the Parc Albert, not only the Wilderness, but Akeley himself, whose meaning was the wilderness, lives again. Mary L. Jobe had not always lived for a husband. In the years before her marriage she had completed no fewer than ten expeditions to explore British Columbian wilderness. She recounts the scene at Carl's death when she accepted his commission for her, that she would live thereafter to fulfill his work. The entire book is suffused with her joy in this task. Her self-construction as the other is breathtaking in its ecstasy. The story of the elephant mauling undergoes interesting emendations to facilitate her accomplishment. One must read this book with attention because Carl's words from his field diaries and publications are quoted at great length with no typographical differentiation from the rest of the text. At no point does the wife give a source for the husband's words; they may be from conversation, lectures, anywhere. It does not matter, because the two are one flesh. The stories of Carl and Mary Jobe blend imperceptibly—until the reader starts comparing other versions of the "same" incidents, even the ones written apparently in the direct words of the true, if absent, author-husband.

The key emendation is an absence. The entire biography of Carl Akeley by Mary Jobe Akeley does not mention the name or presence of Delia. Her role in the rescue is taken by the Kikuyu man Wimbia Gikungu, called Bill, Akeley's gun bearer and native companion on several safaris. Bill is credited with rousing the recalcitrant guides and notifying the government post, thus bringing on the Scotsman posthaste.[77] The long quotation from Carl in which the whole story is told simply lacks mention of his previous wife.

Mary Jobe tells a sequel to the mauling not in Akeley's published stories, and apparently taken from his field diaries or lectures. Because it is not uncommon for a man to lose his nerve after an elephant mauling and decline to hunt elephants again, it was necessary for Akeley to face elephants as soon as possible. Again, the first thing to notice is an absence. It is never questioned that such courage *should* be regained. But the actual story does not ennoble Akeley. He tracked an elephant before he was really healthy, needing his "boys" to carry a chair on the trail for him to sit on as he tired, and the elephant was wounded from unsportsmanlike hasty shots and not found before it died. Akeley's nobility is saved in this story by noting his humility: "The boys helped me back to camp. I felt perfectly certain that we would find him dead in the morning. The whole thing had been stupid and unsportsmanlike."[78]

Before leaving Mary Jobe Akeley's version for Delia Akeley's tale, one more aspect of the Canadian Northwest explorer deserves note. She is pictured as Carl's companion and soul mate, but not really as his co-adventurer and buddy hunter—with one exception. Mary Jobe fired two shots in Africa, and killed a magnificent male lion: "an hour later we came upon a fine old lion, a splendid beast, Carl said, and good enough for me to shoot. And so I shot. . . . The lion measured nine feet six inches from top to tip, carried a dark and splendid mane; and because of its size, age, and rugged personality, Carl considered it a valuable specimen; but I was chiefly concerned that I fulfilled Carl's expectations and had killed the lion cleanly and without assistance."[79] Mary Jobe's authority as a biographer does not depend on her being a hunter, but there is no question that her status was enhanced by this most desirable transforming experience. In this act, her moral status approached that of the sportsman, a critical condition for communion with nature in the life of the American Museum of Natural History.

Delia Akeley pictures herself as a joyous and unrepentant hunter, but her husband has some warts, at least by the publication of *Jungle Portraits* in 1930. It is hard to believe her stories; she simply does not have the authorial moral status of the artist/hunter/scientist, Carl Akeley, or his socially sure second wife, who met easily with kings and commanded his safari for a major scientific institution after his death. There are some very interesting presences in Delia's tales which help highlight the kind of biography African Hall was to tell, and the kind that was to be suppressed. Experience in African Hall leads to transcendence, to the perfect type, to the heightened moment beyond mere life. First, let us look at Delia's story of the rescue. Bill appears in Delia's story, and he behaves well. But her own heroism in confronting the superstitions of the "boys" and in saving her endangered husband is, of course, the central tale in the chapter "Jungle Rescue": "Examining and cleansing Mr. Akeley's wounds were my first consideration. . . . The fact that his wounds were cared for so promptly prevented infection, and without doubt saved his life. . . .

The following day Dr. Phillips, a young Scottish medical missionary, arrived."[80]

But why did Delia tell this story at all, aside from an easily imagined pain at developments in her family life and a desire to set her role on record? Whatever her personal motivation, Delia had a biographical purpose quite at odds with the official histories; she was intent on showing mediations in the form of fallible people behind the experience of natural history museums. In the opening lines of "Jungle Rescue" Delia considers at some length issues of sickness and injury for the early collectors and explorers; she remarks pointedly on insects, weariness, and failure. All this is contrasted with the experience provided the current (1930) traveler, the tourist, or indeed, even the museum visitor. She does have an interest in picturing the devoted and unremarked wife of the single-minded explorers who kept camp in the jungle and house at home. Her purpose in telling the reader that she managed Carl's safaris, that there were very material mediations in the quest for manhood and natural truth, is patent. And then there is her pique at all the attention for her scientist-husband: "The thrilling story of the accident and his miraculous escape from a frightful death has been told many times by himself from the lecture platform. But a personal account of my equally thrilling night journey to his rescue through one of the densest, elephant-infested forests on the African continent is not nearly so well known."[81] It is hard to conjure the picture of Carl Akeley talking about elephant-infested forests! This is not the wife who devotes herself to his authorship of wilderness. Indeed, she repeatedly refers to darkest Africa throughout the book.

There are other instances of Delia's insisting on her glory at the expense of the official nobility of her husband. The reader of Delia's book discovers Carl Akeley frequently sick in his tent, an invalid dangerously close to death whose courageous wife hunts not only for food for the camp, but also for scientific specimens so that he may hasten out of this dangerous continent before it claims him. One learns again that in the elephant hunt following the mauling, Carl was searching to restore his endangered "morale." His wife was his companion in what is portrayed as a dangerous hunt terminating in a thrilling kill marked by a dangerous charge. Delia tells the story so that one cannot know who fired the fatal shot, but "fatigue and a desire to be sure of his shot made Mr. Akeley slow in getting his gun in position."[82] She includes in her chapter an extraordinary photograph of a dashing Carl Akeley smoking a pipe and lounging on top of the body of a large fallen elephant; her caption reads, "Carl Akeley and the first elephant he shot after settling the question of his morale." She concludes her narrative, "Although years have passed since that morning when I stood with my invalid husband on the edge of the vast bush-covered swamp looking for an elephant in the fog, I can see it all as clearly as if it happened yesterday. . . . [I]t is this vision which comes to my mind when I think of the monumental group of elephants which Mr. Akeley and I risked so much to obtain for the New York Natural History Museum."[83]

But hunting in the Museum's archive for that photograph of Akeley lounging astride his kill reveals something curious and perhaps more revealing than Delia's compromising and compromised story. Delia was lying about that elephant, as the photos which accompany hers in the archive demonstrate. But the lie reveals another truth. The photos in the archive suggest a version of reality, a biography of Africa, which the Museum and its official representataives never wanted displayed in their Halls or educational publications. A reader will not find that particular photograph of Akeley in any other publication than Delia's, and even in the 1980s, archive staff are said to be leery of allowing republication of this particular photograph. The images from the photo archive upstairs haunt the mind's eye as the viewer stands before the elephant group in African Hall.

It is clear that this particular elephant with the lounging Carl could not have been killed on the occasion Delia described. The cast of accompanying characters is wrong. Another picture clearly taken on the same occasion shows the white hunter, the Scotsman Richard John Cunninghame, hired by Akeley in 1909 to teach him how to hunt elephants, lounging with Delia on the same carcass. The museum archive labels the photo "Mrs. Akeley's first elephant." It is hard not to order the separate photos in the folder into a series, hard not to tell a story. So the next snapshot shows the separated and still slightly bloody tusks of the elephant held in a gothic arch over a pleased, informal Delia. She is standing confidently under the arch, each arm reaching out to grasp a curve of the elephantine structure. But the real support for the ivory is elsewhere. Cut off at the edge of the picture are four black arms; the hands come from the framing peripheral space to encircle the tusks arching over the triumphant white woman. The Museum archive labels this photo "Mrs. Akeley's ivory." The next and last photograph shows a smiling Cunninghame solemnly annointing Mrs. Akeley's forehead with the pulp from the tusk of the deceased elephant. She stands with her head bowed under the ivory arch, now supported by a single, solemn African man. The Museum's spare comment reads, "The Christening" (figure 2).

Figure 2. The christening. (Courtesy of the American Museum of Natural History, no. 211526, photo: Carl E. Akeley)

This then is also an image of an origin, a sacrament, a mark on the soul signing a spiritual transformation effected by the act of first killing. It is a sacred moment in the life of the hunter, a rebirth in the blood of the sacrifice, of conquered nature. This elephant stands a fixed witness in the Akeley African Hall to this image of an intimate touch shown by the camera's eye, which here captured an iconic moment where race, sex, and nature met for the Western hunter. In this garden, the camera captured a retelling of a Christian story of origins, a secularized Christian sacrament in a baptism of blood from the victim whose death brought spiritual adulthood, that is, the status of hunter, the status of the fully human being who is reborn in risking life, in killing. Versions of this story recur again and again in the history of American approaches to the sciences of animal life, especially primate life. One version is the biography of white manhood in Africa told in Akeley African Hall. With Delia, the story is near parody; with Carl it is near epiphany. His was authorized to achieve a fusion of science and art. Delia, by far the more prolific author, who neither had nor was a ghostwriter, was erased—by divorce and by duplicity.

Safari: A Life of Africa

> Now with few exceptions our Kivu savages, lower in the scale of intelligence than any others I had seen in Equatorial Africa, proved kindly men. . . . How deeply their sympathy affected me! As I think of them, I am reminded of the only playmate and companion of my early childhood, a collie dog.[84]

The Great Halls of the American Museum of Natural History simply would not exist without the labor of Africans (or South Americans or the Irish and Negroes in North America). The Akeleys would be the first to acknowledge this fact; but they would always claim the principle of organization came from the white safari managers, the scientist-collector and his camp-managing wife, the elements of mind overseeing the principle of execution. From the safari of 1895, dependent upon foot travel and the strong backs of "natives," to the motor safaris of the 1920s, the everyday survival of Euro-Americans in the field depended upon the knowledge, good sense, hard work, and enforced subordination of people the white folk insisted on seeing as perpetual children or even as wildlife. If a black person accomplished some exceptional feat of intelligence or daring, the explanation was that he or she (though no examples of such a woman appear in the texts examined in this essay) was inspired, literally moved, by the spirit of the master. As Mary Jobe put it in her un-self-conscious colonial voice, "It was as if the spirit of his master had descended upon him, activating him to transcendent effort."[85] This explanation was all the more powerful if the body of the master was literally, physically far removed, by death or trans-Atlantic residence. Aristotle was as present in the safari as he was in the taxidermic studios in New York or in the physiological bodies of organisms. Labor was not authorized as action, as mind, or as form.

Both Carl and Mary Jobe Akeley's books provide important insight into the organization of the safari over the thirty-year span of Akeley's hunting life. The photographs of usually solemn African people in a semicircle around the core of white personnel, with the cars, cameras, and abundant baggage in the background, are eloquent about race, sex, and colonialism. The chapters discuss the problems of cooks, the tasks of a headman, the profusion of languages which no white person on the journey spoke, numbers of porters (about thirty for most of the 1926 trip, many more in 1895) and problems in keeping them, the contradictory cooperation of local African leaders (often called "sultans"), the difficulty of providing white people coffee and brandy in an unspoiled wilderness, the hierarchy of pay scales and food rations for safari personnel, the behavior of gun bearers, and the punishment for perceived misdeeds. The chapters portray a social organism, properly ordered by the principles of organic form: hierarchical division of labor called cooperation and coordination. The safari was an icon of the whole enterprise in its logic of mind and body, in its scientific marking of the body for functional efficiency.[86] The Africans were inscribed with their role by the Western construction of race; they were literally written into the script of the story of life—and written out of authorship.[87]

Very few of the black personnel appear with individual biographies in the safari literature, but there are exceptions, object lessons or type life histories. Africans were imagined as either "spoiled" or "unspoiled," like the nature they signified. Spoiled nature could not relieve decadence, the malaise of the imperialist and city dweller, but only presented evidence of decay's contagion, the germ of civilization, the infection which was obliterating the Age of Mammals. And with the end of that time came the end of the essence of manhood, hunting. But unspoiled Africans, like the Kivu forest itself, were solid evidence of the resources for restoring manhood in the healthy activity of sportsmanlike hunting. It is worth studying one of these individual biographies to glean a hint of some of the complexity of the relation of master and servant in the pursuit of science on the safari. The life story is told from the point of view of the white person; Wimbia Gikungu, the Kikuyu known as Bill who joined Carl Akeley in British East Africa in 1905 at thirteen years of age, did not write my sources. He was not the author of his body, but he was the Akeley's favorite "native."

Bill began as an assistant to Delia Akeley's tent boy, but is portrayed as rapidly learning everything there was to know about the safari through his unflagging industry and desire to please. He was said to have extraordinary intelligence and spirit, but suffered chronic difficulty with some authority and from inability to save his earnings. "He has an independence that frequently gets him into trouble. He does not like to take orders from any one of his own color."[88] He served with Akeley safaris in 1905, 1909–11, and 1926, increasing in authority and power over the years until there was no African whom Carl Akeley respected more for his trail knowledge and judgment. Akeley speaks of him sometimes as a man, but usually as a boy, like all other male Africans. Bill got into some kind of trouble serving on the Roosevelt safari, having been recommended by Akeley. Roosevelt dismissed him and had him blacklisted. Nonetheless,

Akeley immediately rehired him, assuming he had had some largely innocent (i.e., not directed against a white person) eruption of his distaste for authority.[89]

Akeley describes three occasions on which he "punished" Ginkungu; these episodes are condensed manifestations of Akeley's assumed paternal role. Once Bill refused to give the keys for Carl's trunk to other white people when they asked, "saying that he must have an order from his own Bwana. It was cheek, and he had to be punished; the punishment was not severe, but coming from me it went hard with him and I had to give him a fatherly talk to prevent his running away."[90] Four years later, the Kikuyu shot at an elephant he believed was charging Akeley without the latter's seeing it. Akeley had seen the animal, but did not know his "gun boy" did not know. Akeley spontaneously slapped Ginkungu "because he had broken one of the first rules of the game, which is that a black boy must never shoot without orders, unless his master is down and at the mercy of a beast." Akeley realized his mistake, and "my apologies were prompt and as humble as the dignity of a white man would permit."[91] The African could not be permitted to hunt independently with a gun in the presence of a white man. The entire logic of restoring threatened white manhood depended on that rule. Hunting was magic; Bill's well-meaning (and well-placed) shot was pollution, a usurpation of maturity. Finally, Akeley had Ginkungu put in jail during the 1909–11 safari when "Bill" actively declined to submit when Carl "found it necessary to take him in hand for mild punishment" for another refusal of a white man's orders about baggage.[92] The African caught up with the safari weeks later after spending two weeks in jail. The white man's paternal solicitude could be quite a problem.

Repeatedly, Akeley relied on Ginkungu's abilities and knowledge. Always, his performance was attributed to his loyalty for the master. Collecting the ivory of a wounded elephant, organizing the rescue after the elephant mauling, assisting Mary Jobe Akeley about Carl's death—these deeds were the manifestations of subordinate love. There is no hint that Ginkungu might have had other motives—perhaps including a nonsubservient pity for a white widow in the rain forest, pleasure in his superb skills, complex political dealings with other African groups, or even a superior hatred for his masters. Attributing intentions to "Bill" is without shadow of doubt; the African played his role in the safari script as the never quite tamed, permanently good boy. Bill was believed to be visible; other Africans largely remained invisible. The willed blindness of the white lover of nature remained characteristic of the scientists who went to the Garden to study primates, to study origins, until cracks began to show in this consciousness around 1970.

IV. The American Museum of Natural History and the Social Construction of Scientific Knowledge: Institution

"Speak to the Earth and It Shall Teach Thee."[93]
"Every specimen is a permanent fact."[94]

From 1890 to 1930, the "Nature Movement" was at its height in the United States. Ambivalence about "civilization" is an old theme in U.S. history, and this ambivalence was never higher than after the Civil War, and during the early decades of monopoly capital formation.[95] Civilization, obviously, refers to a complex pattern of domination of people and everybody (everything) else, often ascribed to technology—fantasized as "the Machine." Nature is such a potent symbol of innocence partly because "she" is imagined to be without technology, to be the object of vision, and so a source of both health and purity. Man is not in nature partly because he is not seen, is not the spectacle. A constitutive meaning of masculine gender for us is to be the unseen, the eye (I), the author. Indeed that is part of the structure of experience in the museum, one of the reasons one has, willy nilly, the moral status of a young boy undergoing initiation through visual experience. Is anyone surprised that psychologists find twentieth-century U.S. boys excel in dissecting visual fields? The museum is a visual technology. It works through desire for communion, not separation, and one of its products is gender. Who needs infancy in the nuclear family when we have rebirth in the ritual spaces of Teddy Bear Patriarchy?

Obviously, this essay is premised on the inversion of a causal relation of technology to the social relations of domination: the social relations of domination, I am arguing, are frozen into the hardware and logics of technology. Nature is, in "fact," constructed as a technology through social praxis. And dioramas are meaning-machines. Machines are time slices into the social organisms that made them. Machines are maps of power, arrested moments of social relations that in turn threaten to govern the living. The owners of the great machines of monopoly capital—the so-called means of production—were, with excellent reason, at the forefront of nature work—because it was one of the means of production of race, gender, and class. For them, "naked eye science" could give direct vision of social peace and progress despite the appearances of class war and decadence. They required a science "instaurating" jungle peace, with its promise of restored manhood, complete with a transcendent ethic of hunting; and so they bought it.

This scientific discourse on origins was not cheap; and the servants of science, human and animal, were not tame. The relations of knowledge and power at the American Museum of Natural History are not caught by telling a tale of the great capitalists in the sky conspiring to obscure the truth. Quite the opposite, the tale must be of committed Progressives struggling to dispel darkness through research, education, and reform. The great capitalists were not in the sky; they were in the field, armed with the *Gospel of Wealth*. They were also often armed with an elephant gun and an Akeley camera.[96] This entire essay has been about the "social construction of knowledge." There is no boundary between the "inside" and "outside" of science, such that in one universe social relations appear, but in the other the history of ideas proceeds. Sciences are woven of social relations throughout their tissues. The concept of social relations must include the entire complex of interactions among people, as individuals and in groups of various sizes; objects, including books, buildings, and rocks; and animals, including apes and elephants.[97]

But in this section of Teddy Bear Patriarchy, I want to explore one band in the spectrum of social relations—the philanthropic activities of men in the American Museum of Natural History which fostered exhibition (including public education and scientific collecting), conservation, and eugenics. These activities are the optic tectum of naked eye science, that is, the neural organs of integration and interpretation. This essay has moved from the immediacy of experience, through the mediations of biography and story-telling; we now must look at a synthesis of social construction.

But first a word on decadence, the threat against which exhibition, conservation, and eugenics were all directed as coordinated medical interventions, as prophylaxis for an endangered body politic. The museum was a medical technology, a hygienic intervention, and the pathology was a potentially fatal organic sickness of the individual and collective body. Decadence was a venereal disease proper to the organs of social and personal reproduction: sex, race, and class. From the point of view of Teddy Bear Patriarchy, race suicide was a clinical manifestation whose mechanism was the differential reproductive rates of Anglo-Saxon vs. "non-white" immigrant women. Class war, a pathological antagonism of functionally related groups in society, seemed imminent. A burning question in the last decades of the nineteenth century concerned the energetic economy of middle-class women undertaking higher education: was their health, reproductive capacity and nutritive function, imperiled; were they unsexed by diverting the limited store of organic energy to their heads at crucial organic moments? Nature was threatened by the machine in the garden; the proper interface of the Age of Man and the Age of Mammals could perhaps preserve the potency of the vision of nature and so restore the energy of man. These are strange concerns for the cyborgs of the late twentieth century, whose preoccupation with stress and its baroque technicist, code-implicated pathologies makes decadence seem quaint. Infection and decay have been incorporated into coding errors signified by acronyms—AIDS. But for white, middle-class Americans before World War II decadence mattered. Lung disease (remember Teddy Roosevelt's asthma and alcoholic brother, not to mention America's version of *Magic Mountain*), sexual disease (what was not a sexual disease, when leprosy, masturbation, and Charlotte Perkins Gilman's need to write all qualified?), and social disease (like strikes and feminism) all disclosed ontologically and epistemologically similar disorders of the relations of nature and culture. Decadence threatened in two interconnected ways, both related to functioning, energy-limited productive systems. The machine (remember the iconic power of the railroad) and its fierce artificiality threatened to consume and exhaust man. And the sexual economy of man seemed vulnerable on the one hand to exhaustion and on the other to submergence in unruly and primitive excess. The trustees and officers of the museum were charged with the task of promoting public health in these circumstances.

Exhibition

The American Museum of Natural History was (and is) a "private" institution, as private could only be defined in the United States. In Europe the natural history museums were organs of the state, intimately connected to the fates of national politics.[98] Kennedy's history of the American Museum stresses how intimately connected the development of all the U.S. natural history museums was with the origins of the great class of capitalists after the Civil War. The social fate of that class was also the fate of the museum; its rearrangements and weaknesses in the 1930s were reproduced in crises in the museum, ideologically and organizationally. Philanthropy from the hands of the Rockefellers was mediated by a very complex machinery for the allocation of funds and determination of worthy recipients. The American Museum was not buffered in that way from intimate reliance on the personal beneficence of a few wealthy men. The American Museum is a particularly transparent window for spying on the wealthy in their ideal incarnation, for they made dioramas of themselves.

The great scientific collecting expeditions from the American Museum began in 1888 and stretched to the 1930s. By 1910 they had resulted in gaining for the Museum a major scientific reputation in selected fields, especially paleontology, ornithology, and mammalogy. The Museum in 1910 boasted nine scientific departments and twenty-five scientists. Anthropology also benefited, and the largest collecting expedition ever mounted by the Museum was the 1890s Jessup North Pacific Expedition so important to Franz Boas's career.[99] The sponsors of the Museum liked a science that stored facts safely; they liked the public popularity of the new exhibitions. Many people among the white, Protestant middle and upper classes in the United States were committed to nature, camping, and the outdoor life; Teddy Roosevelt embodied their politics and their ethos. Theodore Roosevelt's father was one of the incorporators of the Museum in 1868. His son, Kermit, was a trustee during the building of African Hall. Others in that cohort of trustees were J. P. Morgan, William K. Vanderbilt, Henry W. Sage, H. F. Osborn, Daniel Pomeroy, E. Roland Harriman, Childs Frick, John D. Rockefeller III, and Madison Grant. These are leaders of movements for eugenics, conservation, and the rational management of capitalist society. They are patrons of science.

The first Great Hall of dioramas was Frank Chapman's Hall of North American Birds, opened in 1903. Akeley was hired to enhance the museum's ability to prepare the fascinating African game, especially elephants; and he conceived the African Hall idea on his first collecting trip for the American Museum. Osborn hoped for—and got—a North American and Asian Mammal Hall after the African one. The younger trustees in the 1920s formed an African Big Game Club that invited wealthy sportsmen to join in contributing specimens and money to African Hall. The 1920s were prosperous for these men, and they gave generously. Thirty to forty expeditions in some years were mounted in the 1920s to get the unknown facts of nature. There were over one hundred expeditions in the field for the American Museum in that decade.[100]

There was also a significant expansion of the Museum's educational endeavors. Over one million children per year in New York were looking at "nature cabinets" put together by the Museum. Radio talks, magazine articles, and books covered the Museum's popular activities, which appeared in many ways to be a science for the people, like that of the *National Geographic*, which taught republican Americans their responsibilities in empire after 1898. Significantly, both *Natural History*, the Museum's publication, and *National Geographic* relied heavily on photographs.[101] There was a big building program from 1909 to 1929; and the Annual Report of the Museum for 1921 quoted the estimate by its director that 2,452,662 (any significant decimal places?!) people were reached by the Museum and its education extension program, including the nature cabinets and food exhibits circulating through the city public health department.

Osborn summarized the fond hopes of educators like himself in his claim that children who pass through the Museum's halls "become more reverent, more truthful, and more interested in the simple and natural laws of their being and better citizens of the future through each visit." He maintained also that the book of nature, written only in facts, was proof against the failing of other books: "The French and Russian anarchies were based in books and in oratory in defiance of every law of nature.[102] Osborn went beyond pious hopes and constructed a Hall of the Age of Man to make the moral lessons of racial hierarchy and progress explicit, lest they be missed in gazing at elephants.[103] He countered those who criticized the Halls and educational work as too expensive, requiring too much time that would be better spent on science itself. "The exhibits in these Halls have been criticized only by those who speak without knowledge. They all tend to demonstrate the slow upward ascent and struggle of man from the lower to the higher stages, physically, morally, intellectually, and spiritually. Reverently and carefully examined, they put man upwards towards a higher and better future and away from the purely animal stage of life."[104] This is the Gospel of Wealth, reverently examined.

Prophylaxis

Two other undertakings in this period at the American Museum require comment: eugenics and conservation. They were closely linked in philosophy and in personnel at the Museum, and they tied in closely with exhibition and research. For example, the notorious author of *The Passing of the Great Race*, Madison Grant, was a successful corporation lawyer, a trustee of the American Museum, an organizer of support for the North

American Hall, a cofounder of the California Save-the-Redwoods League, activist for making Mt. McKinley and adjacent lands a national park, and the powerful secretary of the New York Zoological Society. His preservation of nature and germ plasm all seemed the same sort of work. Grant was not a quack or an extremist. He represented a band of Progressive opinion, one terrified of the consequences of unregulated monopoly capitalism, including failure to regulate the importation of nonwhite (which included Jewish and southern European) working classes who invariably had more prolific women than the "old American stock." The role of the Museum in establishing Parc Albert in the Belgian Congo has already been noted. Powerful men in the American scientific establishment were involved in that significant venture in international scientific cooperation: John C. Merriam of the Carnegie Institution of Washington, George Vincent of the Rockefeller Foundation, Osborn at the American Museum. The first significant user of the sanctuary would be sent by the founder of primatology in America, Robert Yerkes, for a study of the psychobiology of wild gorillas. Yerkes was a leader in the movements for social hygiene, the category in which eugenics and conservation also fit. It was all in the service of science.

The Second International Congress of Eugenics was held at the American Museum of Natural History in 1921 while Akeley was in the field collecting gorillas and initiating plans for Parc Albert. Osborn, an ardent eugenicist, believed that it was "[p]erhaps the most important scientific meeting ever held in the Museum." All the leading U.S. universities and state institutions sent representatives, and there were many eminent foreign delegates. The proceedings were collected in a volume plainly titled "Eugenics in Family, Race, and State." The Congress had a special fruit savored by Osborn. "The section of the exhibit bearing on immigration was then sent to Washington by the Committee on Immigration of the Congress, members of which made several visits to the Museum to study the exhibit. The press was at first inclined to treat the work of the Congress lightly . . . but as the sound and patriotic series of addresses and papers on heredity, the Family, the Race and the State succeeded one another, the influence of the Congress grew and found its way into news and editorial columns of the entire press of the United States." Immigration restriction laws, to protect the Race, the only race needing a capital letter, from "submergence by the influx of other races,"[105] were passed by the United States Congress in 1923.

The 1930s were a hiatus for the Museum. Not only did the Depression lead to reduced contributions, but basic ideologies and politics shifted, making the formations discussed in this essay less relevant to the American ruling classes, although the Museum remained popular with New York's people way beyond the 1930s and eugenics sterilization laws have remained on the books into the late twentieth century. The changes were not abrupt; but even the racial doctrines so openly championed by the Museum were publicly criticized in the 1940s, though not until then. Conservation was pursued with different political and spiritual justifications. A different biology was being born, more in the hands of the Rockefeller Foundation and in a different social womb. The issue would be molecular biology and other forms of post-organismic cyborg biology. The threat of decadence gave way to the catastrophes of the obsolescence of man (and of all organic nature) and the disease of stress, realities announced vigorously after World War II. Different forms of capitalist patriarchy and racism would emerge, embodied as always in a retooled nature. Decadence is a disease of organisms; obsolescence and stress are conditions of technological systems. Hygiene would give way to systems engineering as the basis of medical, religious, political, and scientific story-telling practices.

To summarize the themes of Teddy Bear Patriarchy, let us compare the three public activities of the Museum, all dedicated to preserving a threatened manhood. They were exhibition, eugenics, and conservation. Exhibition has been described here at greatest length; it was a practice to produce permanence, to arrest decay. Eugenics was a movement to preserve hereditary stock, to assure racial purity, to prevent race suicide. Conservation was a policy to preserve resources, not only for industry, but also for moral formation, for the achievement of manhood. All three activities were a prescription to cure or prevent decadence, the dread disease of imperialist, capitalist, and white culture. All three activities were considered forms of education and forms of science; they were also very close to religious practice and certainly shared qualities, as well as professional interest, of medical practice. These three activities were all about preservation, purity, social order, health, and the transcendence of death, personal and collective. They attempted to insure preservation without fixation and paralysis, in the face of extraordinary change in the relations of sex, race, and class.

The leaders of the American Museum of Natural History would insist that they were trying to know and to save nature, reality. And the real was one. The explicit ontology was holism, organicism. There was also an aesthetic appropriate to exhibition, conservation, and eugenics from 1890 to 1930: realism. But in the 1920s the surrealists knew that behind the day lay the night of sexual terror, disembodiment, failure of order; in short, castration and impotence of the seminal body which had spoken all the important words for centuries, the great white father, the white hunter in the heart of Africa.[106] And the strongest evidence presented in this essay for the correctness of their judgment has been a literal reading of the realist, organicist artifacts and practices of the American Museum of Natural History. Their practice and mine have been literal, dead literal.

Notes

The staff in the archives of the American Museum of Natural History have earned a special thanks for courtesy and competence. Friends and colleagues who have generously commented on drafts of Teddy Bear include the members of the 1984 Feminist Theory seminar of the History of Consciousness Board at the University of California Santa Cruz, and Jim Clifford, Barbara Epstein, Sandra Harding, Val Hartouni, Nancy Hartsock, Rusten Hogness, Jaye Miller, Dorothy Stein, and Adrienne Zihlman. Robert Filomeno helped with library research at a crucial time. Wendy Graham of *Social Text* was a wonderful editor. Alexander, Sojourner, and Moses were unfailingly patient. This essay first appeared in *Social Text* 11 (Winter 1984–85).

1 Henry Fairfield Osborn, Report to the Trustees, American Museum of Natural History, May 1908, and in John Michael Kennedy, *Philanthropy and Science in New York City: The American Museum of Natural History, 1868–1968* (Ph.D. diss., Yale University, 1968), pp. 69–130, 347 (hereinafter Kennedy). The American Museum is hereafter AMNH.

2 Edgar Rice Burroughs in Irwin Porges, *Edgar Rice Burroughs: The Man Who Created Tarzan* (Provo, Utah: Brigham Young University, 1975), p. 129.

3 Osborn believed *Homo sapiens* arose in Asia, and important Museum expeditions into the Gobi desert in the 1920s were mounted in an attempt to prove this position. However, Africa still had special meaning as the core of primitive nature, and so as origin in the sense of potential restoration, a reservoir of original conditions where "true primitives" survived. Africa was not established as the scene of the original emergence of our species until well after the 1930s.

4 The body as generative political construction has been a major theme in feminist theory. See Nancy Hartsock, *Money, Sex, and Power* (New York: Longman, 1982): D. J. Haraway, "Animal Sociology and a Natural Economy of the Body Politic," *Signs* 4 (1978): 21–60; and for reflections on meanings of citizenship in this essay, *Social Research* (Winter 1974), essays from the New School for Social Research "Conference on the Meaning of Citizenship."

5 The Deauvereaux or Hotel Colorado in Glenwood Springs, Colo., contains a plaque with one version of the origin of the Teddy Bear, emblem of Theodore

Roosevelt: T. R. returned empty-handed from a hunting trip to the hotel, and so a hotel maid created a little stuffed bear and gave it to him. Word spread, and the Bear was manufactured in Germany shortly thereafter. Another version has T. R. sparing the life of a bear cub, with the stuffed version commemorating his kindness. It is a pleasure to compose an essay in feminist theory on the subject of stuffed animals.

6 Visual communion, a form of erotic fusion connected with themes of heroic action, especially death, is built into modern scientific ideologies. Its role in masculinist epistemology in science, with its politics of rebirth, is at least as crucial as ideologies of separation and objectivism. Feminist theory so far has paid more attention to gendered subject/object splitting and not enough to love in specular domination's construction of nature and her sisters. See Evelyn Fox Keller, *Gender and Science* (New Haven: Yale University Press, 1985); Carolyn Merchant, *Death of Nature* (New York: Harper and Row, 1980); and Sandra Harding and Merrill Hintikka, eds., *Discovering Reality: Feminist Perspectives on Epistemology, Metaphysics, Methodology and Philosophy of Science* (Dordrecht: Reidel, 1983), esp. E. F. Keller and C. R. Grontkowski, "The Mind's Eye."

7 I am indebted to William Pietz's 1983 UCSC slide lecture on the Chicago Field Museum for an analysis of museums as scenes of ritual transformation.

8 Carl E. Akeley, *In Brightest Africa* (New York: Doubleday, Page, 1923), p. 162. Hereinafter IBA.

9 William Davison Johnson, *T.R.: Champion of the Strenuous Life* (New York: Touchstone of Simon and Schuster, 1981); T. Roosevelt, *Theodore Roosevelt's America*, Farida Wiley, ed. (Devin, 1955); P. R. Cutright, *Theodore Roosevelt the Naturalist* (New York: Harper and Row, 1956).

10 It is hardly irrelevant to the symbolism of fear of the new immigrants that it is women who had all the frightening babies. It is also hardly irrelevant to the lives of the women who had to respond to the realities of immigrant life in a racist society. Linda Gordon, *Woman's Body, Woman's Right* (New York: Grossman, 1976); James Reed, *From Private Vice to Public Virtue* (New York: Basic Books, 1978); Carole McCann, "Politics of Birth Control and Feminist Political Options in the 1920s," ms., History of Consciousness, UCSC; John Higham, *Strangers in the Land* (Greenwood reprint of 1963 ed.). Roosevelt popularized the term "race suicide" in a 1905 speech.

11 The construction of nature, the primitive, the other through an allochronic discourse that works by temporal distancing is explored in Johannes Fabian, *Time and the Other* (New York: Columbia University Press, 1983). "[G]eopolitics has its ideological foundation in chronopolitics," p. 144. "Woman" is also constructed outside shared or coeval time, as well as outside historical time.

12 Akeley to Osborn, March 29, 1911, in Kennedy, p. 186. The change from African Hall's dioramas to the radically decontextualized boutique displays of more recent AMNH practice is at least evidence for relaxed anxiety about decadence.

13 James Clark, "The Image of Africa," in *The Complete Book of African Hall* (New York: AMNH, 1936), pp. 69–73 for principles of composition; special issues on African Hall, *The Mentor*, January 1926, and *Natural History*, January 1936.

14 Malvina Hoffman's bronzes of African men and women in this hall, as well as her heads of Africans at the entrance to the hall, are extraordinary testimony to a crafted human beauty in Akeley's temple of nature. They hardly tell a story of natural primitives. On Osborn's failed effort to enlist Hoffman in his projects, see Charlotte Porter (Smithsonian), "The Rise to Parnassus: Henry Fairfield Osborn and the Hall of the Age of Man," unpublished ms. Joshua Taylor, "Malvina Hoffman," *American Art and Antiques* 2 (July/Aug. 1979): 96–103.

15 I am indebted to James Clifford's sharp eye for this perception. He and I read the dioramas together in New York City in March 1982. For a method of reading evolutionary texts as narrative, see Misia L. Landau, *The Anthropogenic: Paleontological Writing as a Genre of Literature* (Ph.D. diss., Yale University, 1981), and "Human Evolution as Narrative," *American Scientist* 72 (May/June 1984): 262–68.

16 IBA, p. 190.

17 IBA, p. 203.

18 Carl E. Akeley and Mary L. Jobe Akeley, *Lions, Gorillas, and their Neighbors* (New York: Dodd and Mead, 1922), hereinafter LGN.

19 IBA, p. 211. The jealous mistress trope is a ubiquitous element of the heterosexist gender anxieties pervading scientists' writing about their endeavors. See esp. Keller, *Gender and Science*.

20 William Nesbit, *How to Hunt with the Camera* (New York: Dutton, 1926); G. A. Guggisberg, *Early Wildlife Photographers* (New York: Talpinger, 1977); Colin Allison, *The Trophy Hunters* (Harrisburg, Pa.: Stackpole, 1981); J. L. Cloudsley-Thompson, *Animal Twilight: Man and Game in Eastern Africa* (Dufour, 1967).

21 IBA, p. 221.

22 IBA, p. 222.

23 IBA, p. 226. For the white woman's account of this trip, see Mary Hastings Bradley, *On the Gorilla Trail* (New York: Appelton, 1922).

24 IBA, p. 230.

25 IBA, p. 235.

26 IBA, p. 248. Scientific knowledge canceled death; only death before knowledge was final, an abortive act in the natural history of progress.

27 Mary L. Jobe Akeley, *Carl Akeley's Africa* (New York: Dodd and Mead, 1929), chap. 15. Hereinafter CAA.

28 Mary Lee Jobe Akeley, *The Wilderness Lives Again: Carl Akeley and the Great Adventure* (New York: Dodd and Mead, 1940), p. 341. Hereafter WLA.

29 CAA, p. 189–90.

30 Dian Fossey, *Gorillas in the Mist* (Boston: Houghton-Mifflin, 1983), p. 3.

31 Osborn in IBA, p. xii.

32 IBA, p. 216.

33 Cyborgs are cybernetic organisms whose birth should be sought in social reality and science fiction from the 1950s. For considerations of cyborg existence, see D. J. Haraway, *Simians, Cyborgs and Women: The Reinvention of Nature* (New York: Routledge, 1991).

34 IBA, p. 1.

35 Cynthia Russett, *The Concept of Equilibrium in American Social Thought* (New Haven: Yale University Press, 1966); Mary Alice Evans and Howard Ensign Evans, *William Morton Wheeler, Biologist* (Cambridge: Harvard University Press, 1970); William Morton Wheeler, *Essays in Philosophical Biology* (Cambridge: Harvard University Press). For organicism in the history of ecology and primatology, see D. J. Haraway, "Signs of Dominance: From a Physiology to a Cybernetics of Primate Society," *Studies in History of Biology* 6 (1983): 129–219.

36 WLA, chap. 3; IBA, chap. 1.

37 WLA, p. 340.

38 Clark, *Complete Book of African Hall*, p. 73.

39 IBA, chaps. 2 and 10; WLA, chaps. 6 and 10; Clark.

40 WLA, p. 38.

41 Virtually simultaneously in New York, Frank Chapman of the Department of Mammalogy and Ornithology was working on North American bird habitat groups, which were installed for the public in a large hall in 1903, one of the first evidences of a generous policy by the trustees from about 1890 to 1930. From the mid-1880s, British Museum workers innovated methods for mounting birds, including making extremely lifelike vegetation. The American Museum founded its own department of taxidermy in 1885 and hired two London taxidermists, the brother and sister Henry Minturn and Mrs. E. S. Mogridge, to teach how to mount the groups. Joel Asaph Abel, Head of Mammalology and Ornithology, was able to hire Frank Chapman in 1887; Chapman is a major figure in the history of American ornithology and had an important role to play in the initiation of field primatology in the 1930s. Bird groups done at the American Museum from about 1886 on were very popular with the public and induced major changes in the fortunes of the Museum. "Wealthy sportsmen, in particular, began to give to the museum." This turning point is critical in the history of the conservation movement in the United States, which will be discussed further below. Significantly because of the scientific activity of the staff of the Department of Mammalogy and Ornithology, the scientific reputation of the American Museum improved dramatically in the last years of the nineteenth century. Kennedy, pp. 97–104; Frank M. Chapman, *Autobiography of a Bird Lover* (New York: 1933); pamphlet of Chicago Field Columbia Museum, 1902, "The Four Seasons"; "The Work of Carl E. Akeley in the Field Museum of Natural History" (Chicago: Field Museum, 1927).

42 The term is Mary Jobe Akeley's, WLA, p. 217.

43 Clark, p. 71.

44 IBA, p. 265.

45 IBA, p. 261.

46 Fabian, chap. 4, "The Other and the Eye," in *Time and the Other*.

47 IBA, chap. 10.

48 Martin Johnson, "Camera Safaris," in *Complete Book of African Hall*, p. 47.

49 See Jane Goodall in *Among the Wild Chimpanzees* (National Geographic Society Film, 1984); David Attenborough, *Life on Earth* (Boston and Toronto: Little, Brown, 1979) and BBC TV series of the same name; and for astonishing pictures of human mother, baby, and wild elephant intimacy, Iain and Oria Douglas-Hamilton, *Among the Elephants* (New York: Viking, 1975).

50 Kennedy, p. 204.

51 Susan Sontag, *On Photography* (New York: Delta, 1977), p. 15.

52 CAA, p. 116.

53 IBA, p. 155.

54 IBA, chap. 8; Edward North Burton, *Two African Trips*, 1902; C. G. Schillings, *With Flashlight and Rifle*, 1905; A. Radclyffe Dugmore, *Camera Adventures in the African Wilds*, 1910.

55 CAA, p. 127–30; WLA, p. 115.

56 Jane Goodall, "My Life among the Wild Chimpanzees," *National Geographic*, August 1963, pp. 272–308; Dian Fossey, "Making Friends with Mountain Gorillas," *National Geographic*, January 1970, pp. 48–67; Birute Galdikas-Brindamour, "Orangutans, Indonesia's 'People of the Forest,'" *National Geographic*, October 1975, pp. 444–73, and "Living with the Great Orange Apes," *National Geographic*, June 1980, pp. 830–53.

57 IBA, p. 166.

58 IBA, p. 166.

59 IBA, p. 167.

60 IBA, p. 223–24. Akeley recognized the utility of his camera to anthropologists, who could (and would) use the telephoto feature "in making motion pictures of natives of uncivilized countries without their knowledge." IBA, p. 166. The photo archive of the American Museum of Natural History is a wonderful and disturbing source of early anthropological photography. These images should be systematically compared with the contemporary safari material.

61 IBA, p. 197.

62 Neil Harris, *Humbug: The Art of P. T. Barnum* (Boston: Little, Brown, 1973); Herman Melville, *The Confidence Man*, first published 1857.

63 October, 1923, prospectus, AMNH archives; Martin Johnson, "Camera Safaris," *The Complete Book of African Hall*, 1936; CAA, p. 129; July 26, 1923, Akeley memorandum on Martin Johnson Film Expedition and additional material from 1923 AMNH archive, microfilm 1114a and 1114b. See Martin Johnson, *Through the South Seas with Jack London* (Dodd and Mead); *Cannibal Land* (Houghton Mifflin); *Trailing African Wild Animals* (Century); and the films *Simba*, made on the Eastman-Pomeroy expedition, and *Trailing African Wild Animals*.

64 Lewis Carroll, "The Hunting of the Snark," in *Alice in Wonderland*, Norton Critical Edition, p. 225.

65 October 1923, prospectus to the AMNH, archives microfilm 1114a.

66 October 1923, Osborn endorsement, AMNH archive microfilm 1114a.

67 Martin Johnson, July 26, 1923, prospectus draft, microfilm 1114a. The expectation that a film made in the middle 1920s would be the last wild life extravaganza is breathtaking in retrospect. But this serious hope is a wonderful statement of the belief that nature did exist in essentially one form and could be captured in one vision, if only the technology of the eye were adequate. The film made by the Johnsons was *Simba*.

68 Much of this paragraph is a response to Sontag, *On Photography*. On the fears and need for mirrors of the American mythical self-made man, see J. G. Barker-Benfield, *The Horrors of the Half Known Life* (New York: Harper and Row, 1976) and Susan Griffin, *Woman and Nature* (New York: Harper and Row, 1978).

69 The principal sources for this section are correspondence, annual reports, photographic archives, and artifacts in the AMNH: IBA; Mary Jobe Akeley's biography of her husband, WLA; Mary Jobe and Carl Akeley's articles in *The World's Work;* LGN; and Delia Akeley's adventure book, *Jungle Portraits* (New York: Macmillan, 1930). Delia is Delia Denning, Delia Akeley, Delia A. Howe. See N.Y. *Times*, 23 May, 1970, p. 23. The buoyant racism in the books and articles of this contemporary of Margaret Mead makes Mary Jobe and Carl look cautious.

70 Joanna Russ, *How to Suppress Women's Writing* (Austin: Texas University Press, 1983), p. 76. For a superb discussion of the world in which Delia and Mary Jobe worked, see Margaret W. Rossiter, *Women Scientists in America: Struggles and Strategies to 1940* (Baltimore: Johns Hopkins University Press, 1982).

71 WLA, p. 222.

72 WLA, p. 223.

73 IBA, p. 45.

74 IBA, pp. 48–49.

75 IBA, p. 49.

76 IBA, pp. 54–55.

77 WLA, chap. 9.

78 WLA, p. 126.

79 WLA, p. 303.

80 JP, p. 249.

81 JP, p. 233.

82 JP, p. 93.

83 JP, pp. 90, 95.

84 CAA, p. 200.

85 CAA, p. 199.

86 The literature examining functionalism in scientific discourse is large, but critical to this essay are: Alfred Sohn Rethel, *Intellectual and Manual Labor* (London: Macmillan, 1978); Bob Young, "Science *Is* Social Relations," *Radical Science Journal* 5 (1977): 65–129; Hilary Rose, "Hand, Brain, and Heart: A Feminist Epistemology for the Natural Sciences," *Signs* 9 (1983): 73–90.

87 CAA, chap. 5; WLA, chap. 15; IBA, chap. 7.

88 IBA, p. 143.

89 IBA, p. 144.

90 IBA, p. 134. "Father to the game" obviously included the highest game of all in the history of colonialism—the submission of man.

91 WLA, p. 132.

92 IBA, p. 144.

93 *Job* 12:8, engraved on a plaque at the entrance to the Earth History Hall, AMNH.

94 H. F. Osborn, 54th Annual Report to the Trustees, p. 2, AMNH archives.

95 Leo Marx, *The Machine in the Garden* (London, Oxford, New York: Oxford University Press, 1964); Roderick Nash, *Wilderness and the American Mind*, 3d rev. ed. (New Haven: Yale University Press, 1982); Roderick Nash, "The Exporting and Importing of Nature: Nature-Appreciation as a Commodity 1850–1980," *Perspectives in American History* 12 (1979): 517–60.

96 One capitalist in the field with Akeley was George Eastman, an object lesson in the monopoly capitalist's greater fear of decadence than of death. I am claiming that realism is an aesthetics proper to anxiety about decadence, but what kind of realism is celebrated in a literature describing a septuagenarian Eastman getting a close-up photograph at 20 feet of a charging rhino, directing his white hunter when to shoot the gun, while his personal physician looks on? "With this adventure Mr. Eastman began to enjoy Africa thoroughly . . ." WLA, p. 270.

97 Bruno Latour, *Les microbes. Guerre et paix suivi de irreductions* (Paris: Metairie, 1984), pp. 171–265; Bruno Latour and Steve Woolgar, *Laboratory Life: The Social Construction of Scientific Facts* (Beverly Hills and London: Sage, 1979), esp. on inscription devices and "phenomenotechnique"; Karin Knorr-Cetina and Michael Mulkay, eds., *Science Observed* (Beverly Hills, London, New Delhi: Sage, 1983).

98 Camille Limoges and his collaborators at L'Institut d'histoire et de socio-politique des sciences, Université de Montréal, provide the most complete analysis of the Paris natural history museums from the early nineteenth century. Gerald Holton and William A. Blanpied, eds., *Science and Its Public: The Changing Relation* (Dordrecht: Reidel, 1976).

99 Kennedy, p. 141ff. Osborn presided over considerable disbursements to the Department of Anthropology, despite his own opinion that anthropology was largely "the gossip of natives." Osborn was more inclined to favor the skeletons of dinosaurs and mammals, and he is responsible for building one of the world's finest paleontology collections. H. F. Osborn, *Fifty-two Years of Research, Observation, and Publication* (New York: AMNH, 1930).

100 Kennedy, p. 192.

101 Philip Pauly, "The World and All That Is in It," *American Quarterly*, 31, no. 4 (1979): 517–32.

102 Osborn, "The American Museum and Citizenship," 53rd Annual Report, 1922, p. 2. AMNH archives.

103 Osborn, *The Hall of the Age of Man,* AMNH Guide Leaflet Series, no. 52.

104 Osborn, "Citizenship," 54th Annual Report, p. 2.

105 Osborn, 53rd Annual Report, 1921, pp. 31–32. Ethel Tobach of the AMNH helped me interpret and find material on social networks, eugenics, racism, and sexism at the Museum. The organizing meetings for the Galton Society were held in Osborn's home.

106 Joseph Conrad, esp. *Heart of Darkness,* is crucial to this aspect of my story, especially for exploring complexities of language and desire. See also Fredric Jameson, "Romance and Reification: Plot Construction and Ideological Closure in Joseph Conrad," *The Political Unconscious* (Ithaca: Cornell University Press, 1981).

José David Saldívar

Américo Paredes and

Decolonization

One of the last models of "city and country" is the system we know as imperialism.—Raymond Williams, *The Country and the City* (1973)

t is well these days to be explicit about one's location and positionality as a writer, critic, and cultural worker. I work these days at a relatively new branch of the University of California, located at the university and beach town of Santa Cruz—seventy-five miles to the south of San Francisco. At Santa Cruz, I am on the Steering Committee for the Center for Cultural Studies, a research organization now entering its fifth year of operation. While the center has some real connections with the legendary Cultural Studies Centers in Britain—Kobena Mercer and Stephen Heath (who studied with Raymond Williams and/or Stuart Hall) actively participate in its operation—our Cultural Studies Center also aspires for local and homegrown sources for its priorities in popular cultures, issues of resistance and hegemony, and its engagement with the new social movements and the political arts. My own interests, for example, lie in exploring recent research from an influential area of interculture: borderland culture, what Lawrence Herzog[1] calls the emergence of a new "transfrontier" social space situated along the two-thousand-mile-long *frontera* between the United States and Mexico. In other words, I am interested in analyzing whether or not borderland cultures depart from "interior" zones. Do they develop patterns and interests different from the centers of power in Washington, D.C., and Mexico City? Are the borderlands new political and artistic heterotopias?

To begin answering a few of these questions, I will dwell for the most part in this chapter on the experimental anthropological and anti-imperialist literary work of Américo Paredes, who was honored in 1989 by the National Endowment for the Humanities as one of the first recipients of the Frankle Prize for lifetime achievement in the arts, and who in 1990 was one of the first Chicano inductees to the *Orden de Águila Azteca* by the Mexican government for the preservation of Mexican culture in the United States. For the purposes of this study, moreover, Paredes's cultural work, *"With His Pistol in His Hand": A Border Ballad and Its Hero* (1958), *George Washington Gómez: A Mexicotexan Novel* (1990), and *Between Two Worlds* (1991), has a more specific meaning as well.[2] As I suggested in *The Dialectics of Our America* (1991), Paredes's antidisciplinary border project underscores the ways in which the dominant Anglocentric discourse suppresses regional differences.[3] In matters of cultural description, Paredes shows that what is striking (in this Anglocentric context) is the steady discrimination of certain regions as in this limited sense "regional," which can only hold if certain *other regions* are not seen in this way. This discrimination is a function, he suggests, of centralization; a form of what Raymond Williams called the "city-country" opposition.[4] It is clearly connected with the distinction between "metropolitan" (core) and "provincial" (peripheral) cultures, which became significant from the sixteenth century. Because Paredes's early and late cultural work represents the complex self-fashionings brought about by borderland conflict, they also constitute needed insights into the boundary disputes between and among academic disciplines as well as geographical territories. Paredes's bold deterritorializations thus serve as both tactical political strategies specifically designed to counter Anglocentric hegemony in border disputes as well as interdisciplinary fantasms designed to transgress rigidly "border patrolled" discursive boundaries.

Seen in this light, Paredes occupies a unique position among borderland writers today. No contemporary figure of the proto-Chicano Movement generation has so extensive an oeuvre to their credit. The range of this work, moreover, is probably unprecedented in either the United States or Latin America, including ethnographies on the people of Greater Mexico, literary criticism, analysis of ballads, collections of folktales, semantic inquiry, poetry, film scripts, short stories, and novels. Yet until recently sustained discussion of Paredes's work has been relatively wanting. Despite its increasing authority and influence in the field of Chicano Studies, there has so far been no attempt to analyze the border-defying work as a whole. The immense variety of Paredes's writing, crossing academic boundaries and confounding disciplinary expectations, has no doubt been one of the reasons for this quiet. It wasn't until the 1980s that the first assessment came, with the appearance in 1986 of two essays "Mexican Ballads, Chicano Epic: History, Social Dramas and Poetic Persuasions" and "The Return of the Mexican Ballad"[5] by José E. Limón, an anthropologist and former pupil of Paredes. Almost simultaneously, Paredes for his part addressed himself to major definitions and representations of spatial materialism and the politics of cultural identity, with the publication of *George Washington Gómez,* a novel he started writing in 1936, completed in 1940, but did not publish until the exemplary postmodern year of 1990. Due to the pressures of everyday life, Paredes let the novel sit for almost fifty years.[6] Thematizing the culture of conflict and empire along the border between the United States and Mexico, Paredes's text shows how the patterns of conflict since Polk's expansionist policies in the 1840s had become by the early twentieth century firmly set up in the knowable communities along the border.

Perhaps more than anyone else's, Paredes's influence (like Raymond Williams's in his border country of Wales/England) is felt in Chicano cultural studies. He taught us especially that intellectual work cannot and should not stop at the borders of single texts, folksongs, or single, monological disciplines. In such "founding texts" as *"With His Pistol in His Hand": A Border Ballad and Its Hero* (1958), *Folktales of Mexico* (1970), *A Texas-Mexican "Cancionero": Folksongs of the Lower Border* (1976), "The Folk Base of Chicano Literature" (1979), *George Washington Gómez: A Mexicotexan Novel* (1990), and *Between Two Worlds* (1991) "border culture" is a term and site that transgresses various disciplines and theoretical boundaries: folklore, ethnography, musicology, history, and literary "theory." Let me hasten to add that to these *transfrontera* texts, scholars will need to include two new books by Paredes: *Folklore and Culture on the Texas-Mexican Border* (1993), a collection of essays, and *Uncle Remus con Chile* (1992), an encyclopedic book of border jokes, jests, and vernacular narratives.[7]

Throughout these interventions, Paredes's focus on people's history, culture, and social class arrangements is powerfully personal and at times indulges in textual experimentation.[8] *"With His Pistol in His Hand"* tells the story about the hegemonic border and the history of his ancestors in south Texas. Like many postcolonial Chicano/a writers, Paredes declares that he is not an immigrant. Neither his ancestors in the 1750s in Nuevo Santander nor he years later moved from the borderlands; instead U.S. military aggression transformed the Río Grande Valley from an organic class society (where a certain social order and relations made sense to a people) into a barbed wired and segregated society.[9]

After discussing how the border was imposed on south Texas, Paredes focused on how Chicanos used *corridos* (ballads of border conflict) to counter Anglocentric hegemony. As literary scholar Ramón Saldívar puts it, "the nineteenth- and twentieth-century *corridos* served the symbolic function of empirical events (functioning as a substitute for history writing) and of creating counterfactual worlds of lived experience (functioning as a substitute for fiction writing)."[10] To be sure, Paredes saw his project as participating in the cultural conversations of the Southwest borderlands, where border culture is a serious contest of codes and representations. More specifically, *With His Pistol in His Hand*" inaugurates a Chicano artistic and intellectual response to the white supremacist scholars of the 1930s and 1940s such as Walter Prescott Webb and his followers who represented in their texts a popular, romanticized history. At the same time, it must be emphasized that Paredes's book contested the nationalist and chauvinistic new interdisciplinary project of American Studies. For Paredes the consensus rhetoric of American Studies with its emphasis upon the motto "*e pluribus unum*" had to be negated and supplemented with a more sophisticated sense of "culture" as a site of social struggle.[11]

To dramatize his sense of culture as a site of social contestation, Paredes's focus on *corridos* is "antisubjectivist" because in ballads of border conflict like "El Corrido de Gregorio Cortez" he located the sources of meaning not in individual subjectivities, but in social relations, communication, and cultural politics. While the *corrido* certainly points to border men such as Gregorio Cortez (who resisted arrest by Sheriff Morris and who defended himself "con la pistola en su mano,") the subject in this *corrido* is meant to stand not as an individual but as an epic-like construction of the south Texas society that interpellated him. As is well known, Cortez's fate, for Paredes, cannot be distinguished from communal fate.[12]

Paredes's *"With His Pistol in His Hand"* concludes by bemoaning the "fall" of the *corrido* proper and its containment as a form of symbolic social resistance. "The period of 1836 to the late 1930's," he writes, "embraces the life span of the corrido of the Lower Border" (p. 132). The Civil War, the English-speaking invasion of the borderlands, and the French invasion of Mexico, however, "complicated the clash of peoples along the Border" (132). Additionally, after the 1930s, with the commercialization of popular music by both the Mexican and American mass cultural music industry, and with the dissolution and fragmentation of formerly organic Texas Mexican ranching communities by way of the effects of "world system" agribusiness and the green revolution, the need for alternative symbolic forms to express resistance became all the greater. Paredes himself acknowledges the fall of the *corrido* after it entered its "decadent" phase when he turns to another form of social resistance, namely, the Chicano novel. The transfiguration of the *corrido* hero and the decline of the utopian *corrido* epoch in south Texas is the subject of Paredes's historical bildungsroman, *George Washington Gómez,* written during the Great Depression. Indeed we can say without exaggeration that Paredes's novel is very precisely about the large and small dislocations in space that must occur before, at the novel's end, the hero George G. Gómez can completely assimilate. And that place itself is precisely located by Paredes at the center of competing local, national, and international interests, spanning the hemisphere. Formally, Paredes represents the Great Depression in south Texas—what he calls "La Chilla" (the Squeal)—as a structure of expansion and contraction. That is, he introduces the formal structure upon which many of the novel's sections will be patterned, for he gives the reader a generalized view of the plight of Mexican American men and women, followed by a close-up of his representative characters, the García and Gómez. This formal literary pattern, of course, echoes the structural features of one of the most sensational social protest novels of the period, namely, John Steinbeck's *The Grapes of Wrath.* [13] Central to *George Washington Gómez,* then, is Paredes's preoccupation with cultural identity, representation, and the politics of location, for Mexican American identity is not as transparent as we have been taught to think.

Paredes's *George Washington Gómez* is set in the midst of south Texas borderland conflict: the 1915 uprising by Border seditionists (Los sediciosos) from south Texas and northern Mexico and their thorough suppression by the U.S. Calvary and Texas Rangers. Inspired by the "Plan de San Diego" manifesto, this document called for a coalition of Mexicans with (Amer)Indians, blacks, and Asians, and the utopian creation of a Spanish-speaking republic of the Southwest. Led by Luis de la Rosa and Aniceto Pizaña, the seditionists fought the dominant powers, including the U.S. Army, up and down the Río Grande. Paredes's narrative thus recreates the mood of life on the border in the first three decades of the twentieth century, a historical moment when the resistance of borderers such as Gregorio Cortez are quickly fading into the past. Brownsville, Texas, the site of numerous incidents of cultural resistance, is represented by the author as "Jonesville-On-the-Grande," a place under occupation by the conquering U.S. army based at "Fort Jones." *George Washington Gómez* thus specifically sets itself in the period just after the last great resistance by Texas Mexicans on the border seeking to regain land lost by their parents and grandparents to Anglo-Americans and their Texas Rangers.

George Washington Gómez literally begins with the birth of a new type of border hero in the midst of these "border troubles." The protagonist's father, Gumersindo, along with an Anglo doctor, makes his way through mesquite and Texas Ranger roadblocks to aid María in the birth of their third child. "A good Mexican," Gumersindo is determined from the start to raise a son named after "the great North American . . . who was a general and fought the soldiers of the king" (16). But why does Paredes trace his hero's cultural genealogy to the leader of both revolutionary and republican America? Does he want to suggest that his character's rhetoric of descent (simultaneously a rhetoric of ascent and consent) is central to the dynamics of cohesion in America? Will his brown hero's future lead a new republic replete with mythic past and "manifest" destiny? Hybrid and heteroglot that it is, *George Washington Gómez* reexamines—ironically as the title suggests—the decline of the *corrido's* heroic age and the rise of ethnogenesis on the border. Anticipating Stuart Hall's notion of cultural identity "as a production . . . always in process, and always constituted within, not outside, representation,"[14] Paredes suggests that your name becomes you because you retroactively become what you are named.

Like José Martí's cultural deconstruction in "Nuestra América" (1891) of the name America, Paredes begins the novel by thematizing the ritual naming of Gumersindo's and María's son: "[María] looked at him tenderly. And what shall we name him? she wondered aloud" (16). In response to her question, her husband, mother, and brother all suggest names, each symbolic of the alternative possibilities for the hero's "manifest" destiny: "Crisósforo," a "grandiose" name, is offered by the boy's proud father but is quickly ridiculed by the signifyin[g] Feliciano as sounding too ridiculously close to the Spanish word, *fósforo*. Next the grandmother offers a safe, Catholic name, José Ángel, but she is quickly overruled by Gumersindo's blunt "Ángel! . . . It would ruin him for life." Names alluding to Mexican and Chicano revolutionaries, Venustiano Carranza and "Cleto" Pizaña, and even the father's own name Gumersindo, alas, are momentarily considered but dismissed. María finally settles the ritual process by saying: "I would like my son. . . . She faltered and reddened. I would like him to have a great man's name. Because he's going to grow up to be a great man who will help his people" (16). Searching for the names of "great men" that the *norteamericanos* had produced over the years, Gumersindo thinks out loud: "I remember Wachinton. Jorge Wachinton." Unable to pronounce the foreigner's name, the grandmother hilariously calls out: "Guálinto." And thus the hero is named. This hybrid clash of cultural identities, of course, will be the very ground for the larger cultural clashes in the novel.

"Born a foreigner in his native land" and "fated to a life controlled by others" (15), George Washington (Guálinto) Gómez's Americanization will be fraught with contradiction. In ideological terms, what Paredes offers us in his Mexicotexan bildungsroman is an ongoing thematization of the child's traditional organic community and the forces of the new dominant culture. Life in the border site of Jonesville-On-the-Grande is made concrete in the opening chapters by the brutal suppression of Chicanos by the Texas Rangers, and by the symbolic competing names of the hero: Guálinto (an Amerindian-sounding name like Cuahútemoc) and George Washington.

When Gumersindo is gunned down by the Rangers, he makes his brother-in-law Feliciano promise him "never to tell his son" (31) how he had died at the hands of the *rinches,* for he "wanted his son to have no hatred in his heart" (31). While raised by Feliciano and María to be "a leader of his people," Guálinto acculturates through stages, acquiring through his schoolteachers "an Angloamerican self" (147). Although he is able to negotiate his proliferating subject positions quite well and he eventually realizes that there isn't "one single Guálinto Gómez" (147), at the novel's end, Paredes's protagonist graduates from high school, attends the University of Texas, marries a white ethnographer, Ellen Dell (whose father was once a Ranger), legally changes his name to George G. Gómez, and becomes a "spy" for the U.S. army during World War II. Claiming that he is a lawyer for a multinational plant that is expanding in the global borderlands, he returns to south Texas as a first lieutenant in counterintelligence whose new job is "border security." Yet it is precisely at this stage in the hero's constructing a solid bourgeois identity that we realize Paredes's cultural deconstruction, for his recommendation in the narrative is not to solve the crisis of the hero's identity politics but proliferate and intensify the crisis by having George's "I" dissimulated through a recurring fantasy and daydream:

> He would imagine he was living in his great-grandfather's time, when the Americans first began to encroach on the northern provinces of the new Republic of Mexico. Reacting against the central government's inefficiency and

corruption, he would organize *rancheros* into a fighting militia. . . . He would discover the revolver before Samuel Colt, as well as the hand grenade and a modern style of portable mortar. In his daydream he built a modern arms factory at Laredo, doing it all in great detail, until he had an enormous, well-trained army that included Irishmen and escaped American Negro slaves. Finally, he would defeat not only the army of the United States but its navy as well. He would reconquer all the territory west of the Mississippi River and recover Florida as well.

At that point he would end up with a feeling of emptiness, of futility. . . . He always awoke with a feeling of irritation. Why? he would ask himself. Why do I keep on fighting battles that were won and lost a long time ago? Lost and won by me too? They have no meaning now. (282)

This passage is neither the best nor the worst of Paredes's text. Rather it shows dramatically the many complicated pressures working within the novel. The nuanced consciousness of Anglocentric expansionism into the borderlands, beginning with the Texas Wars of Independence in 1835–36 and continuing with Polk's chauvinist war with Mexico in 1846–48, is a necessary accompaniment. At the same time, there is the remarkable critique of Mexican party politics and the corrupt presidency of Antonio López de Santa Anna that inevitably played a decisive role during the war, for as historian Richard Griswold del Castillo points out the struggle between various groups produced "chronic instability" that in turn made it impossible for Mexican forces to match up against U.S. forces.[15] If global imperialism, as Edward Said notes, can be "said to have begun in the late 1870s, with the scramble for Africa,"[16] Paredes's novel suggests that the homemade American kind began earlier. The importance of 1835–48 for Guálinto, of course, is that this period marks the emergence of U.S. empire. Additionally, 1848 has a particular meaning for him because not only had Mexico been defeated (yielding the spoils of Texas, California, and New Mexico) and the Oregon Territory appropriated but because U.S. imperialism had created a group of second-class citizens within the belly of the beast.

These considerations, I think, suddenly provide a fascinating expanded dimension to *George Washington Gómez,* for a good deal more can be said about what Amy Kaplan[17] has called the double discourse of imperialism—nationhood and manhood—and how Paredes's novel can provide access to the repressed political context of American imperialism. While Guálinto's conscious connections are to people and places in south Texas, his latent dreamwork reveals that there are *other* connections of which he has faint glimmerings that nonetheless demand his attention, particularly his plan to build an "arms factory" at Laredo and to put together "an enormous army that included Irishmen and escaped American Negro slaves." Like the small group of Whig party members who opposed the 1846 war, Guálinto suspects that the war itself was a plot to strengthen the position of the slave owners. In other words, Polk used the war as an opportunity to expand the slavocracy. It is, therefore, hardly surprising that Guálinto dreams of armed solidarity with escaped African American slaves.

If Judith Butler (using the psychoanalytical work of Jean Laplanche and J. B. Pontalis) is correct that there is "no subject who has a fantasy, but only fantasy as the scene of the subject's fragmentation,"[18] Paredes demonstrates in this scene how the political "phantasmatic" of the border-lands continually haunts and contests the borders which circumscribe George's construction of a stable identity. What are the possibilities for social change, Paredes suggests, in the face of capitalist hegemony whose powers of co-optation are so great that they manage to turn desire against itself, colonizing the unconscious?

With George G. Gómez we are far removed from the utopian collective concerns of border heroes like Gregorio Cortez. Paredes, however, in recreating the "border troubles" in his narrative opens the stage for the Chicano novel thirty years before the so-called Chicano Renaissance of letters in the 1960s. His focus, moreover, on *corridos* and on folklore and musical performance in his numerous writings forces us to look at folklore and pop culture as equally powerful, creative, and influential areas of counter-discourses. Paredes, indeed, dwells in his writings on the role of folklore as an instrument of the culture of conflict because it wages struggle itself in the forms of songs, legends, *dichos*, and proverbs. As anthropologist Richard Bauman argues, Paredes' "work is an exemplary vindication of that premise on which the best of folklore and anthropology is built: that a deep, detailed, nuanced understanding of the local will inspire a more global vision."[19]

Paredes's novel (written in the late 1930s) is—as I have been suggesting—a nicely problematic parable for comparative cultural studies in the 1990s. It specifically relates among other things the encounter of the ethnographic field-worker with the native inhabitants of south Texas. In other words, Paredes begins to open up the question of how cultural analysis constitutes its objects—societies, traditions, knowable communities, subjectivities, and so on. Near the novel's end, he asks the following "postcolonial" questions about historical/anthropological fieldwork: Who is being observed? What are the political locations involved? How is one group's core another's periphery? Paredes deconstructs the ethnographic encounter in south Texas by sardonically describing the traveling culture collector, K. Hank Harvey:

> [H]e was considered the foremost of authorities on the Mexicans of Texas. Hank Harvey had been born in New York City some sixty years before. He had gone to grade school there and then worked in a delicatessen to make some money so he could come down to his dreamland, Texas. . . . After he had come to Texas with only a few years of schooling, he resolved to become an authority on Texas history and folklore. In a few years he had read every book there was on the early history of Texas, it was said, and his fellow Texans accepted him as the Historical Oracle of the State. There was a slight hitch, it is true. Most early history books were written in Spanish, and K. Hank didn't know the language. However, nobody mentioned this, and it didn't detract from Harvey's glory. (271)

The striking part of this passage is Paredes's attempt to demystify the authority of the executive historical ethnographer and to open to discussion what James Clifford calls "ethnography's hierarchy and the complex negotiation of discourses in power-charged, unequal situations."[20] If thinking of the observer as neither an innocent nor omniscient is striking, Paredes shakes things up a bit more by representing Harvey as a monological scholar incapable of fully inscribing his "native" subjects. Eventually Harvey learns a "few words of Spanish which he introduced into all of his later writings, somewhat indiscriminately," and his fame as a historian and folklorist grows "too big even for the vast Texas," and soon he becomes a "national and then an international figure" (271). Paredes's wry description of Harvey, however, becomes full of rage, for Harvey's scholarly project occurs alongside a peculiar sense of mission—what used to be called the white man's burden:

> K. Hank Harvey filled a very urgent need; men like him were badly in demand in Texas. They were needed to point out the local color, and in the process make the general public see that starving Mexicans were not an ugly, pitiful sight but something very picturesque and quaint, something tourists from the North would pay to come and see. By this same process bloody murders became charming adventure stories, and men one would have considered uncouth and ignorant became true originals. (271–72)

For Paredes, what has come to be called the Spanish borderlands by ethnographic historians such as K. Hank Harvey is in fact an invention, an imperialist historical formation, an enactment, a political paradox, an ongoing (mis)translation. To be sure, Harvey functions in the novel as a symbol for scholars such as Charles F. Lummis (*The Land of Poco Tiempo*) and J. Frank Dobie (*Flavor of Texas*) who claimed to have "discovered" and invented the Spanish Southwest for the Anglo-American popular readership. As Héctor Calderón writes, "In a span of nine years, from 1891 to 1900, Lummis published eleven books, changing what was a physical and cultural desert into a land internationally known for its seductive natural and cultural attractions."[21] Dobie, like Lummis, was instrumental in constructing disciplinary folklore societies in the Southwest and was the first to teach a course on the culture of the Southwest at the University of Texas at Austin. Paredes thus pegs the Harveys of the Southwest as representing the "Mexicans of south Texas" in the mode of what anthropologist Renato Rosaldo called "imperialist nostalgia,"[22] that longing on the part of imperialist agents such as missionaries, ethnographers, government officials, and others for the indigenous forms of life that they often had a hand in destroying. In this discourse, Paredes describes the Spanish borderlands as the site where men like Harvey can be real authorities, where they can lament the closing of the frontier.

When Harvey is invited by the local white administrators to give the keynote address at Guálinto's graduation from Jonesville High, Paredes's hero, along with the majority of Chicanos in the audience "shift[ing] nervously in their seats," have to listen to the speaker's discourse of empire: "We're here to honor this bunch of fine young people, citizens of this great state of Texas, who are going out into the world. May they never forget the names of Sam Houston, James Bowie, and Davey Crockett. May they remember the Alamo wherever they go." Oblivious to the fact that for his brown audience history really hurts, he ends his tale of empire by saying:

> Whenever our forefathers rose on their hindlegs and demanded independence . . . , when they arose with a mighty shout and forever erased Mexican cruelty and tyranny from the fair land, when they defeated bloody Santa Anna and his murderous cohorts at the heroic battle of San Jacinto, they set an example which younger, weaker generations would do well to follow. Girls and boys, I give you the world; it is at your feet as young Americans. (274)

At a time when a well-financed and increasingly powerful group of intellectuals and journalists are attempting to reverse the democratic processes that have lately made the university more representative, I think that Paredes's critique of U.S. empire and white supremacy at the novel's end requires attention. Though the recent assaults on multiculturalism and feminism in U.S. education arise from present rather than past conditions, the antidemocratic narrowing of culture in the university bears the imprint of the past Paredes so clearly describes.[23]

Lurking behind the title of Paredes's novel, there is the haunting cultural symbology of George Washington, who in his Farewell Address proclaimed: "The name of American must always exalt [your] just pride . . . more than any appellation derived from local discriminations. With slight shades of difference, you have the same Religion, Manners, Habits, and political principle."[24] For Américo Paredes, however, "the name of American" was an interpretative fiction. Doing the work of the dominant culture, Washington's address, like the rest of the classic American literary canon, interprets away differences between the religions, manners, habits, and political principles of the people from Our America. As Bercovitch suggests, "the name of American worked not only to displace the very real (and deepening) differences within the country, but equally—within the country's reigning liberal constituency—to display differences of all kinds of proof of a victorious pluralism."[25] Paredes thus presents a counterdiscourse to the homemade discourses of U.S. imperialism: he articulates the experiences, the aspirations, and the vision of a people suffering colonial/postcolonial rule from the inside. What distinguishes him from his Anglocentric contemporaries lies not in his intellectual or aesthetic judgment but in the depth of his extraordinary understanding of the dynamics of empire.

From this perspective, Paredes is a writer who belongs to a pan-American tradition not usually considered his, that of the (anti)(post)-colonial intellectual bringing before the reader's eyes the upheaval of an anti-imperialist imagination in the borderlands. If this is not a customary way of seeing Paredes, his poetry written during the 1930s and 1940s—published in *Between Two Worlds* (1991)—can shed light on a lyrical poet situated between innovative vernacular verse and traditional poetic forms such as the sonnet. As Ramón Saldívar suggests, "*Between Two Worlds* . . . could arguably be called the historical divide between the modern and the postmodern, represent[ing] the bifurcated, interstitial . . . quality of the kind of writing that has come to be called 'border writing.'"[26]

Without doubt, the theme of liberation comes out in this volume, a strong postcolonial theme that is already present in the works of Paredes's pan-American heirs such as Langston Hughes, Aimé Césaire, Nicolás Guillén, and Luisa Espinel.[27] This resistance literature, of course, developed quite consciously out of a desire to distance the "native" intellectual from the European and (more recently) the Anglo-American master.

Let me hasten to add that if there is something more tangible that ties Paredes to the imagination of anti-imperialist writing, it is the primacy in many of his poems of "spatial geographical violence" (what Edward Said simply calls another name for imperialism) through which south Texas is chartered, explored, mapped out, and brought under the Anglocentric empire's control. As Paredes suggests in his explicitly vernacular poem written in protest against the state's centennial celebration in 1935, "The Mexican-Texan": "He no gotta country, he no gotta flag / He no gotta voice / all got is the han' / To work like the burro; he no gotta lan' . . ." (26–27). For Paredes, the history of the south Texas borderlands is inaugurated by the loss of local place, whose geographical and cultural identity must be searched for and recovered through the poetic imagination.

Many of the poems, therefore, attempt to map, invent, and chart a territorial space that derives historically from the deprivations of the present. This border poetry, we might say, is explicitly *cartographic,* anticipating the postmodern geographies of space dramatized in the deterritorialized border writings of Arturo Islas, Gloria Anzaldúa, and Alberto Ríos.[28] Of the many striking examples of this cartographic mapping is the poem entitled "The Rio Grande":

I was born beside your waters,
and since very young I knew
That my soul had hidden currents
That my soul resembled you.

. . . .

We shall wander through the country
Where your banks in green are clad,
Past the shanties of rancheros
By the ruins of old Bagdad. (15–16)

With the Rio Grande's "swirls" and "counter-currents," with its contested territoriality, there comes in the poetry a whole set of assertions, recoveries, and devastated locations and "ruins" and "shanties"; all of them quite literally flowing on this poetically projected riverscape, wandering down "by the margin of the sea" (16). Certainly Paredes's allusion to the "ruins of old Bagdad" signals his concern with the colonial past of south Texas, evoking the "orientalized" mystery of crumbled empires and the emergence of new ones. The eighteenth-century *ranchero* economy is now gone, and the poet is in the midst of Anglocentric capital agribusiness formations of the early twentieth century.

If Paredes's *Between Two Worlds* participates in producing a poetry of decolonization, in insisting on historical alternatives to U.S. empire (he indeed searches for a more congenial revolutionary history in Nicaragua in the poem entitled "A César Augusto Sandino"), his volume also antici- pates the changing borderland subjectivities implicit in the poetry of the Chicano Movement period, reconstructing a new narrative for his people, and, more importantly, interweaving vernacular "folkloric" verse such as the *copla, décima, son,* and *danzón* with the "high art" sonnet form. As one reads Paredes's poetry of the early 1930s, there is an uncanny resem- blance to the engagement and pan-American project of creating a poetry with "color" as the Cuban poet Nicolás Guillén sardonically put it in his famous prologue to *Sóngoro cosongo* (1931)[29].

To be sure, to write a *mestizo* or an "ethnic" sonnet is no simple matter, for as Gustavo Pérez Firmat suggests, "to write an [ethnic] son- net . . . is to transculturate [one] of the 'whitest' literary forms, [a genre] whose whiteness extends even to [its] conventional content."[30] Paredes's achievement as a poet is not only to add geographical violence and car- tographic spatiality to his work, but also add "local color" to the outlines of traditional Old World literary conventions and figures. As we will see, his use of the sonnet (*sonnetta*) in *Between Two Worlds* is not only nu- anced but varied. Like Guillén he employs consonance, at other times assonance. Topically, the sonnets in the volume also deal with a range of subjects, from a haunting Llorona-like woman to moonlight nights on the Rio Grande.

While many of the poems not only demonstrate the young poet's debt to Guillén and Hughes (Paredes's long onomatopoetic work entitled "Africa" with its obsession with drums could easily have come straight out of Guillén's *Motivos de son*), the poetry also owes much to the *modernista* poetics of Rubén Darío. A representative early poem is entitled "Agua- fuerte estival."

El sol de la tarde, cual viejo lascivo
acaricia su cuerpo
con luz moribundo—ella exhala un suspiro

Sus ojos confusos
no miran de lleno
su cuerpo desnudo,

muslos sonrosados,
cadenas redondas
y seno elevado
tiemblan como

una llama peridida
entre rojas tinieblas.

Y por el campo de sus ojos
pasan en estampida
los centauros. (71)

[The afternoon sun, like a lascivious man / caresses your body / with mori-
bund light—she exhales a sigh / in front of the grand mirror. Its confused
eyes / do not see / your body / pink muscles / round hips / and full breasts /
trembling like a lost flame / in the twilight of leaves. / And in the center of your
clear eyes / the centaurs passing.]

The mature author of *"With His Pistol in His Hand"* is nowhere to be found
in these adolescent verses. The one local note is the passing reference
to the south Texas "sol de la tarde." The woman in the poem, moreover,
is a construction of commonplaces that probably goes as far back as to
Petrarch. "Aguafuerte estival," in this light, thematizes the poet's debt to
the well-established tradition of the Italian sonnet and its well-known
patriarchal conception of "woman."

Using "Aguafuerte estival" as a sign for Paredes's youthful poetry, let
us study another poem entitled "Flute Song."

Why was I ever born
Heir to a people's sorrow
Wishing this day were done
And yet fearful for the morrow.

Why was I ever born
Proud of my southern race,
If I must seek my sun
In an Anglo-Saxon face.

Wail, wail, oh flutes your dismal tune,
The agony of our new birth;
Better perhaps had I never known
That you lived upon the earth. (24)

Although there are affinities between this poem and the previous poem
(both rely heavily on a constellation of literary commonplaces), "Flute
song," like Mahmud Darwish's Palestinian poetry of half a century later,
renders a "people's sorrow" under military occupation and highlights the
persistence of an antithetical geopolitical space where the "southern race"
"must seek my sun / In an Anglo-Saxon" North.[31] One feels in reading
poems like "Flute Song" and "The Rio Grande" not just the disappoint-

ments of life brought on by Anglo-American empire but of a haunting beauty and nostalgia of the "shanties of rancheros" that mark the poetic landscape.

Like all poets of decolonization, then, Paredes struggles to symbolize his local (border) culture and to begin deviating from the Old World order that animates many of his early sonnets. Many of the poems, however, attempt to focus on the poet's and his people's genealogy. Paredes's "Moonlight on the Rio Grande" even attempts to transculturate his verse by injecting into its very rhythms and structures a brown and working-class ancestry.[32]

> The moon is so bright it dazzles me
> To look her in the eye,
> She lies like a round, bright pebble
> On the dark-blue velvet sky,
> She hangs like a giant pebble
> In the star-incrusted sky.
>
> The Rio Grande is bent and brown
> And slow, like an aged peon,
> But silver the lazy wavelets
> Which the bright moon shines upon,
> As bright as the little silver bells
> On the round hat of a peon. (28)

The transculturation of the Rio Grande into a "bent and brown" "peon" entails important alterations in the rest of the poems, for once Paredes replaces conventional poetic topoi from the Old World landscape to south Texas ones, his verses begin to acquire a profoundly creative and hybrid dimension. Thus, the vernacular musical verses such as "Coplas," "Tango Negro," "Guitarreros," and "Boleros," together with his sonnets dramatize the apparent poetic "betweenness" announced in the title of the book. On a more careful reading, however, Paredes's *décimas, coplas, tangos* and *danzones*—border songs "in miscellaneous forms" (p. 139)—as he later noted in *"With His Pistol in His Hand"* and the Old World sonnet (which was initially a musical form—*sonnetto*) demonstrate that the Old World and New World forms may in fact be distant kin. As a speculative reading may suggest, the border *danzón* and the Italian *sonnetto* might very well disrupt the "betweenness" of these poetic worlds. We might say—following Pérez Firmat's logic—that for Paredes the *danzón* is south Texas's native *sonnetto*, and the *sonnetto* is the Italian *danzón*.

Without doubt, the role of music in the poems discussed above makes them perfectly compatible with Paredes's more renowned vernacular poetry, foreshadowing his mature interests in border music (the *corrido*) and folklore. If anything, my focus on the poems in the anti-imperialist *Between Two Worlds* is simply to demonstrate that the young poet's work in "Flute Songs" and "Moonlight on the Rio Grande" do not lack what José Limón calls "focused imagery" and "complex poetic arguments."[33] Quite the contrary, the poems in the collection border on being "ethnic" verses of decolonization, for even when Paredes begins from a set of Italian and *modernista* commonplaces, he transculturates them by giving the forms a brown sensibility all his own.

I want to conclude with an informal description of the immediate context for my own view of cultural studies and what it may mean for this project on the "cultures of U.S. imperialism." My work will continue to be influenced more by concepts of the social spaces of everyday life than by debates about multiculturalism in the academy. This is partly the result of the way that Raymond Williams's *transfrontera* fiction from *Border Country* (1960) to his two-volume *People of the Black Mountains* (1989 and 1990)[34] leads me to think about postmodern geographies and spatial stories. As liminal heterotopias, Williams's (like Paredes's) literary work forces us to recognize that the stories of borders and geographical spaces and countries and cities are intimately bound together.

For these reasons, my favorite founding texts for my version of cultural studies in the borderlands are Paredes's and Williams's splendid series of spatial narratives. Of course, it would not be too farfetched to claim that my essay privileges the discursive space of "in betweenness" that many postcolonial intellectuals now claim as our own—spaces in which our histories are fragmented, our cultures hybridized and ruptured, and our identifications phantasmatic and displaced. These splitting wounds, as Homi Bhabha writes, "are wounds of my body [but] also a form of revolt."[35]

Notes

This essay was completed during my tenure in 1991–92 as a visiting faculty at the Stanford Center for Chicano Research, Stanford University. I wish to thank Amy Kaplan, Donald Pease, and Ramón Saldívar—all of whom helped in the preparation of this essay.

1 Lawrence Herzog, *Where North Meets South: Cities, Space, and Politics on*

the U.S.-Mexico Border (Austin: Center for Mexican American Studies and University of Texas Press, 1990).

2 See the following by Américo Paredes: *"With His Pistol in His Hand": A Border Ballad and Its Hero* (Austin: University of Texas Press, 1958); *George Washington Gómez: A Mexicotexan Novel:* (Houston: Arte Público Press, 1990); and *Between Two Worlds* (Houston: Arte Público Press, 1991). All page references to these texts will be cited parenthetically in the text.

3 José David Saldívar, *The Dialectics of Our America: Genealogy, Cultural Critique, and Literary History* (Durham: Duke University Press, 1991), especially pp. 49–84.

4 Raymond Williams, *The Country and the City* (New York: Oxford University Press, 1973).

5 See José E. Limón's "Mexican Ballads, Chicano Epic: History, Social Dramas and Poetic Persuasions," SCCR Working Paper 14, Stanford University, 1986, and "The Return of the Mexican Ballad: Américo Paredes and His Anthropological Text as Persuasive Political Performance," SCCR Working Paper 16, Stanford University, 1986.

6 Unpublished interview with Ramón Saldívar, July 1991.

7 See Américo Paredes, *Folktales of Mexico* (Chicago: University of Chicago Press, 1970); *A Texas-Mexican "Cancionero": Folksongs of the Lower Border* (Urbana: University of Illinois Press, 1976); "The Folk Base of Chicano Literature" in *Modern Chicano Writers: A Collection of Critical Essays,* ed. Joseph Sommers and Tomás Ybarra Frausto (Englewood Cliffs, N.J.: Prentice Hall, 1979), pp. 4–17; *Uncle Remus con Chile* (Houston: Arte Público Press, 1992); and *Folklore and Culture on the Texas-Mexican Border,* ed. and intro. Richard Bauman (Austin: Center for Mexican American Studies and University of Texas Press, 1993).

8 See José E. Limón's groundbreaking study of Américo Paredes's ethnographic textual experimentations in *Mexican Ballads, Chicano Poems: History and Influence in Mexican-American Social Poetics* (Berkeley: University of California Press, 1992).

9 For a full analysis of racial segregation in south Texas, see David Montejano, *Anglos and Mexicans in the Making of Texas, 1836–1986* (Austin: University of Texas Press, 1987).

10 Ramón Saldívar, *Chicano Narrative: The Dialectics of Difference* (Madison: University of Wisconsin Press, 1990), p. 48.

11 While the American Studies movement was a necessary response to the formalist practices of New Criticism in the United States, it was not and has not been an oppositional movement.

12 For a superb discussion of *corrido* subjectivity, see Ramón Saldívar, *Chicano Narrative: The Dialectics of Difference* (Madison: University of Wisconsin Press, 1990), especially chapter 2, "The Folk Base of Chicano Narrative," pp. 26–46. See also José David Saldívar, "Chicano Border Narratives as Cultural Critique,"

in *Criticism in the Borderlands: Studies in Chicano Literature, Culture, and Ideology*, ed. Héctor Calderón and José David Saldívar (Durham: Duke University Press, 1991), pp. 167–80.

13 For a splendid reading of John Steinbeck's *The Grapes of Wrath*, see Louis Owens, *John Steinbeck's Re-Vision of America* (Athens: University of Georgia Press, 1985).

14 Stuart Hall, "Cultural Identity and Diaspora," in *Identity: Community, Cultural, Difference*, ed. Jonathan Rutherford (London: Lawrence and Wishart, 1990), p. 222.

15 See Richard Griswold Del Castillo, *The Treaty of Guadalupe Hidalgo: A Legacy of Conflict* (Norman: University of Oklahoma Press, 1990), pp. 6–7.

16 See Edward W. Said, "Yeats and Decolonization," in *Nationalism, Colonialism, And Literature*, ed. and intro. Seanus Deane (Minneapolis: University of Minnesota Press, 1990), p. 70.

17 See Amy Kaplan's "Romancing the Empire: The Embodiment of American Masculinity in the Popular Historical Novel of the 1890s," *American Literary History* 2, no. 4 (Winter 1990): pp. 659–90.

18 See Judith Butler, "The Force of Fantasy: Feminism, Mapplethorpe, and Discursive Excess," *Differences: A Journal of Feminist Cultural Studies* 2, no. 2 (1990): p. 110.

19 See Richard Bauman's admirable "Introduction" to Américo Paredes's *Folklore and Culture on the Texas-Mexican Border*, p. xii.

20 See James Clifford's "Traveling Cultures," in *Cultural Studies*, ed. Lawrence Grossberg, Cary Nelson, and Paula Treichler (New York: Routledge, 1992), p. 100.

21 See Héctor Calderón and José David Saldívar, "Editors' Introduction," in *Criticism in the Borderlands: Studies in Chicano Literature, Culture, and Ideology*, ed. Héctor Calderón and José David Saldívar (Durham: Duke University Press, 1991), p. 3.

22 See Renato Rosaldo, *Culture and Truth: The Remaking of Social Analysis* (Boston: Beacon Press, 1989), pp. 68–90.

23 For a critique of the assumptions and values that produce judgments such as "America is our common ground," see Stanley Fish, "The Common Touch," in *The Politics of Liberal Education*, ed. Darryl J. Gless and Barbara Herrnstein Smith (Durham: Duke University Press, 1992), pp. 241–66.

24 Quoted in Sacvan Bercovitch, *The Office of the Scarlet Letter* (Baltimore: Johns Hopkins University Press, 1991), p. xv.

25 Ibid., p. xv.

26 Ramón Saldívar, "The Borders of Modernity: Amérco Paredes's *Between Two Worlds* and the End of Modernism," unpublished manuscript, p. 5.

27 For comparative readings of U.S. and Latin American poetry, see Vera Kutzinski, *Against the American Grain: Myth and History in William Carlos Williams, Jay Wright, and Nicolás Guillén* (Baltimore: Johns Hopkins University Press,

1987). Luisa Espiñel, as Paredes acknowledges in a long footnote in the volume, popularized the *son* in the Southwest borderlands when she toured "the U.S. with a program of Southwest Mexican songs in the mid-1930s, which she called 'Songs My Mother Taught Me,' " p. 140.

28 See José David Saldívar, *Border Matters: Sites of Cultural Contestation* (Berkeley: University of California Press, forthcoming).

29 See Nicolás Guillén, *Obras Poética 1920–1972*, 2 vols., ed. Ángel Augier (Havana: Editorial de Arte y Literatura, 1974).

30 See Gustavo Pérez Firmat's "Nicolas Guillén between the *Son* and the Sonnet," *Callaloo* 10, no. 2 (1987): p. 319.

31 See Mahmud Darwish, *Victims of a Map*, trans. A. al-Udhari (London: Al Saqi Books, 1984).

32 "Transculturation" was coined in the 1940s by Cuban sociologist Fernando Ortiz in a pioneering study of Afro-Cuban culture, *Contrapunteo Cubano* (Caracas: Bibiliotheca Ayacucho, 1978). Ortiz proposed the term to replace the paired concepts of acculturation and deculturation that described the transference of culture in reductive fashion from within the interests of the metropolis. Of relevance here is Mary Louise Pratt's *Imperial Eyes: Travel Writing and Transculturation* (London: Routledge, 1992). According to Pratt, "Ethnographers have used [the term transculturation] to describe how subordinated or marginal groups select and invent from materials transmitted to them by a dominant or metropolitan culture," p. 6.

33 See Limón, *Mexican Ballads, Chicano Poems*, p. 58.

34 See Raymond Williams, *"Border Trilogy": Border Country* (London: Chatto & Windus, 1960); *Second Generation* (London: Chatto & Windus, 1964); and *The Fight for Manod* (London: Chatto & Windus, 1979). See also his postmodernist novel about Wales, *People of the Black Mountains*, 2 vols. (London: Chatto & Windus, 1989, 1990).

35 Homi Bhabha, "Postcolonial Authority and Postmodern Guilt," in *Cultural Studies*, ed. Lawrence Grossberg, Cary Nelson, and Paula Treichler (New York: Routledge, 1992), p. 66.

Vicente M. Diaz

Pious Sites

Chamorro Culture Between Spanish Catholicism and

American Liberal Individualism

Invocation

hamorro cultural history is etched in the topography and architecture of the land.[1] Go to Agana, the capital of the island of Guam, and stand directly in front of the basilica. As the seat of the Archdiocese of Agana, the basilica edifies the Spanish Catholic legacy in the Marianas archipelago. Directly before you towers a statue of a praying Santa Marian Kamalen, the physical manifestation of the Blessed Virgin Mary to the Chamorro people of Guam.

To your left stands a life-size statue of Padre Diego Luis de Sanvitores, the Spanish Jesuit who was killed as he tried to establish the Catholic mission among the Chamorro people here in the seventeenth century. In a move that certified the authenticity (and the heroism) of his martyrdom, the Vatican beatified the now "Blessed" Diego in 1985 and in so doing placed him well on the road to becoming a patron saint of the Marianas.

To your right there is a revolving statue of Santo Papa, a commemoration of Pope John Paul II's historic visit to Guam in 1981. It is under John Paul II that the Sacred Congregation for the Causes of Saints—the Vatican assembly before which appear formal causes for beatification and canonization—has been nicknamed the "saint factory."[2]

You stand before the Virgin Mother, a Blessed Father of the

Marianas mission to the left, a spiritual (and mobile) descendant of St. Peter to the right, and you turn around.

You turn around and you face the Guam Legislature Building—home, if you will, of the island's civic Sons and Daughters.

Creed

Chamorro cultural history traverses the line between church and state, as symbolized in the proximity of these particular sacred and secular buildings and monuments in that particular spot on the island. But the politics of Chamorro cultural history, too, are etched in transactions on the topography and architecture of the land, transactions that recall troubled entanglements among indigenous and exogenous ideas and practices, transactions that trouble, too, national and cultural boundaries.

In her pioneering study *Daughters of the Island: Contemporary Chamorro Women Organizers on Guam,* Chamorro scholar and organizer Laura Souder argues that the key agents in this political terrain are Chamorro women organizers who, as primary caretakers of *custumbren Chamorro,* must also be seen as the "makers and shapers of Guam history."[3] Friendly with Souder's thesis, I will explore in this article some of the peculiar and troubling ways in which other folks and other ideas, both indigenous and exogenous, also participate in the making and shaping of cultural histories that comprise custumbren Chamorro, or what is sometimes understood as "traditional" Chamorro culture. Chamorro Catholics—men and women, fathers and mothers, sons and daughters—in capacities as clergy and lay people, as politicians and as everyday folk, and, often enough, in the forms of anonymous individuals, also participate in this political history through what I call the local "construction sites" of piety. But I suggest that these local structures of Chamorro faith and moral behavior neither stay rooted in their apparent localities nor neatly contain their congregations. There are, in other words, what might be called transnational and transcultural characteristics to these local structures; their hybrid and fluid features recall the messy entanglement among Chamorro, Spanish Catholic, Liberal American, and increasingly Japanese-based economic legacies.

This essay focuses on two events in the late twentieth century: a suicide by a former governor of Guam and an anti-abortion law passed by the Guam legislature. These two events embody the cultural and historical transactions that appear in the "singular" effort to canonize Blessed Diego and that more generally constitute the complexity of the Marianas mission history. The suicide, the anti-abortion legislation, and the bid to canonize Blessed Diego all concern historical constructions and reconstructions of Chamorro identities as they negotiate with foreign ideas and practices. Here, they build on certain sacred Catholic and American-liberal ideas of life, death, and the vitality of good identities and communities. Their hybrid nature also reveals a certain "ambivalent" character of Guam's colonial and countercolonial legacy.[4] The ambivalence describes not only the simultaneity of oppression and liberation that constitutes colonial discourse, but also the various social layers in which such an ambivalent colonial legacy articulates itself. The ambivalent character of Guam's colonial history features (at the very least) a two-way flow of power that constrains but also furnishes possible modes (and often competing levels) of indigenous expression and survival insofar as the layered expressions are themselves constituted in a two-way process of historical and political action and reaction between the colonizer and the colonized. I will return to these themes after my representation of the two events that have rocked the island (and others elsewhere) in recent times.

The First Testimony

Hours before he was to depart the island to serve time in a federal correctional facility, former Governor of Guam Ricardo ("Ricky") J. Bordallo parked his Suzuki Samurai jeep at the grassy edge of Chief Kepuha Park in Agana. The ex-governor approached a larger-than-life statue of *magalahe as Kepuha*—the seventeenth-century Chamorro chief who welcomed the Spanish Jesuit missionaries to the island.[5] Behind and beneath Kepuha, Bordallo placed several placards and a Guam flag. The ex-governor then drew a .38 calibre pistol to his head and shot himself. Bordallo was pronounced dead hours later at the nearby U.S. Naval Hospital.

On one of his placards were words familiar to students of American history: "My only regret is that I have but one life to give to my people." On another: "Adios, Todos taotao Guam. Goodbye everyone. May we all meet again some day. May God bless you all . . . Ricky Bordallo."

The Second Testimony

On March 20, only a few weeks after Bordallo's state funeral and Christian burial, the Guam attorney general's office charged Ms. Janet Benshoof, director of the Reproductive Freedom Project of the American Civil Liberties Union, with soliciting abortions. The criminal charges were filed only hours after a speech Benshoof made the day after Governor Joseph Ada signed the "stiffest" abortion law passed in the United States to date.[6] Insisted Ada, "I am not taking this action . . . to affect anyone's life in the fifty states. I believe that this is a community issue and a community concern, first and foremost."[7]

Unanimously approved by the Guam legislature—twenty of twenty-one senators are Catholic (almost half are women)—the law prohibits all abortions except when the mother's life is endangered. In that event, a legal abortion requires the approval of two physicians and a final review by a committee appointed by the Medical Licensure Board. In a televised interview during the legislative hearings prior to the vote, Archbishop Anthony Apuron activated the Roman Catholic church's pro-life position with a threat to excommunicate any senator who voted against the bill.

Benshoof came to Guam to lobby against the bill, which she had labeled "a Pearl Harbor for Women."[8] In her speech to the (predominantly white) Guam Press Club and for which she was charged with solicitation, Benshoof told women that they could get legal abortions in Hawaii and provided the Honolulu address and telephone number of the organization Planned Parenthood.[9] In what is now a test case, Benshoof and the ACLU have challenged the constitutionality of the law on the basis that it violated rights to privacy, speech, due process, and abortion as upheld in the 1973 Supreme Court decision in *Roe vs. Wade* (1973). The Guam judge before whom Benshoof was to be arraigned disqualified himself for religious reasons. On March 23, Federal Judge Alex Munson issued a temporary restraining order which was made permanent on August 23.[10]

Benshoof had been alerted to the passage of the antiabortion bill by local attorney Anita Arriola, one of a handful of islanders who testified against the bill. Ms. Arriola is the daughter of Senator Elizabeth Arriola, who authored the bill. Of her daughter's position, the senator remarked that "it hurts me personally, although I respect it." The younger Arriola contended that "the silence out here is so oppressive."[11]

Vicente M. Diaz

Moment of Silence

next to of course god america i
love you land of the pilgrims' and so forth oh
say can you see by the dawn's early my
country 'tis of centuries come and go
and are no more what of it we should worry
in every language even deafanddumb
thy sons acclaim your glorious name by gorry
by jingo by gee by gosh by gum
why talk of beauty what could be more beautiful than these heroic happy dead
who rushed like lions to the roaring slaughter
they did not stop to think they died instead
then shall the voice of liberty be mute?

He spoke. And drank rapidly a glass of water

e.e. cummings[12]

Homily

Filiated with the majority of voters, I too expressed publicly my political view with a vote for Ricky Bordallo during the 1982 gubernatorial election in the American territory of Guam. Regarded as a "charismatic champion of Chamorro rights by his supporters, and as a volatile, romantic dreamer by his opponents," the one-time prisoner of a Japanese concentration camp literally concretized many of his dreams during his two terms (1974–78 and 1982–86) as governor.[13] In addition to attempting to institute an agricultural green revolution designed to combat seventy years of dependence on American imported products, Bordallo also embarked upon numerous island beautification programs designed specifically to instill in Chamorros pride in themselves and in their island. Among the numerous edifices initiated by the "Builder," as one reporter called Bordallo, was the Chief Kepuha Memorial Park in Agana.

Upon his second inauguration in 1982, Bordallo resumed his public service and took an especially active role in the political status and autonomy debates that had begun openly to challenge American patronage.[14] As chair of the Commission on Self-Determination and creator of the draft Commonwealth Act (to replace Guam's "unincorporated territory" status) Bordallo prepared to navigate through a relatively hostile

U.S. Congress a controversial measure that included provisions for Chamorro self-determination and local control of immigration—provisions that appear to violate the Constitution of the United States.[15] In 1986, while campaigning for a third term, Bordallo was indicted on eleven counts of corruption. Calling the indictment a "political persecution through federal prosecution," Bordallo believed "with my whole heart and soul that this entire investigation reek[ed] of colonialism and even racism."[16]

While the governor's suicide shocked and angered many of us, his supporters and opponents alike eulogized him as one of the island's greatest political leaders. Delivering the official eulogy, Superior Court Judge B. J. Cruz situated Bordallo "in the tradition of (Kepuha) and other brave soldiers" whose "ultimate sacrifice of [their] own live[s] would be necessary in defense of liberty, freedom, dignity and self-respect." He continued: "With his sacrifice, and one shot which he hoped would be heard around the country, he reached the American people. But, more important, he would have wanted his supreme sacrifice to rekindle the consciousness of his people."[17]

Whether or not his one shot reached the American people, Bordallo's life and death, according to Joe T. San Agustin, speaker of the legislature, was likened to the planting of a "fervent political seed in his people." "The people are now asserting their rights," warned San Agustin, and the United States had better "reevaluate its policies toward the territory."[18] The local community reacted to Bordallo's "shot" with shock and anger. In the ensuing days, amidst death threats to various federal and military personnel stationed on the island, Guam's six-foot-tall replica of the famed Statue of Liberty was found decapitated.

During preparations for Bordallo's state funeral, the propriety of a Christian burial was questioned. There was also confusion and ambivalence surrounding the former governor's suicide. Had he lost hope? Did he "chicken out"? Was this a supreme form of self-aggrandizement? Was he trying to punish his federal and local political opponents through guilt? Given the church's view of death as the possibility for everlasting life, the ambivalence meant even more: Did Bordallo lose faith? In approving the Christian burial, Archbishop Apuron explained that since Vatican II, people who commit suicide are nevertheless "given the benefit of the doubt as long as they remain Catholics to the very end."[19] To the best of the archbishop's knowledge, Ricky had never recanted his faith.

In a pastoral message read ten days later at every mass in every village parish, the Archbishop clarified the church's stance on suicide in general, and on Bordallo's in particular, "in light of the best that theology, philosophy, and psychology has to offer." The pastoral letter also indicated that to the Catholic church, suicide is an "abhorrent" and "unnecessary wastage of what belongs to God, for life is a gift bestowed on us by a gracious Creator." And although suicide "may carry some personal or political meaning, it fails to carry the ultimate meaning of life for a Christian." Amidst the flurry of interpretations, Archbishop Apuron provided the narrative's closure: "Suicide is never to be equated with martyrdom, never to be glorified or honored or judged as an acceptable solution; it should not even be dignified with the word 'sacrifice.'" The primary meaning of a Christian life then, as the observant community knows, is to acknowledge its status as a gift from God. To acknowledge this would appear to defer to the Catholic church's interpretation of the event. Following Apuron's interpretation, to commit suicide is to commit a "grievous offense against God, the Creator and Lord of Life," and to commit "a sin of despair in not allowing the Holy Spirit to open up new possibilities for the human future."[20]

Earlier in his political career, Ricky Bordallo had invoked other Chamorro Catholic possibilities for the human future. And other spirits. At the 1986 dedication of another controversial edifice—the new Adelup Governor's Office ("Ofisinan Magalahe")—Bordallo defended his latest addition to "public landmarks that house the spirit of the Chamorro people" thus: "[Adelup] is a monument which allows us to cross over that cultural gap which has been widening to a point where our heritage was being threatened with extinction. It allows the people to cross over the past so that we may cross back over into a better future. Adelup links us with one another."[21] Chief Kepuha Park ranks among such landmarks that house the spirit of the Chamorro people, and I believe that Bordallo could not have chosen a more appropriate site from which to cross, in a heroic and salvific drama, the widening gap that threatens a Chamorro cultural past in order to rekindle a Chamorro spirit of revolution. For Kepuha, the chief who welcomed Blessed Diego in 1668, is a subject of another *widely* complex Chamorro Catholic ambivalence. Understood as the protector of the mission by modern Chamorro Catholics (indeed by Catholic and secular historians of the Marianas alike), Kepuha is also quietly and privately scorned for having sold out to foreign agents. Kepuha is contrasted with other contemporaries such as Matapang, chief of Tumhon, who assassinated Blessed Diego, or Hurao, another defender of Chamorro rights. It is as if Bordallo, a Chamorro rights champion and a dreamer, saw in the Kepuha memorial a way to fuse the power of Christian and nationalist martyrdom with the iconic representation of a proud ancient Chamorro society.[22] His "suicide" at this particular spot had less to do with simply wanting to mobilize an anti-American sentiment (Bordallo could never have condoned the "vandalism" of Ms. Liberty) than with imagining (in a hybridization of "traditional" Chamorro, Spanish Catholic, and American ideas) a way to "link" *spatially and temporally* the enduring spirits of Chamorro people with one another for a "better future."

One way to understand this political profusion (or con-fusion) of spirits is to turn to a seventeenth-century French Jesuit whose *History of the Marianas* endures as a canonical text in postcontact Chamorro historiography and cultural studies. Writing in 1700, Fr. Pierre Le Gobien reveals a (noble?) savage discourse that, in general, depicts the Chamorros as nature-, nation-, liberty-loving creatures whom the Spanish fathers were duty-bound to save. For instance, Le Gobien asserts: "Before the Spaniards appeared in these islands, the inhabitants lived in complete *freedom*. They had no laws except those that each individual imposed upon himself," and "the free and simple life they lead without worry, without dependence, without chagrin, and without inquietude gives the health that is unknown in Europe."[23] (10; emphasis added).

Le Gobien is also the most generous among the historians of the region in that he provides the Chamorros with scripts—that is, with things to say. For example, Kepuha says to Blessed Diego in 1668: "You please us, Fathers, and you bring us good news which will cause joy to our entire nation, for we have wanted you here for a long time."[24] The enthusiasm and pleasure inscribed in Kepuha's reception of Blessed Diego is read by Le Gobien as a sign of Kepuha's attraction to Catholic spirituality. I bracket for the moment other possible reasons why church historians might attribute such anticipation and desire to key indigenous actors and suggest, as others have, that native longings for Christianity also had (have) less to do with Catholic spirituality than with an anticipation of the temporal and political opportunities that come with the establishment of a mission station in one's own locality.[25] Still I don't wish to draw so neat a distinction between temporal and spiritual political yearnings.

As far as Le Gobien was concerned, Kepuha and other recent converts on the island were not only good Christians, they were exemplary. Kepuha and other "new Christians" exemplified virtue "of which the first centuries of the Church would be proud." Kepuha "preserved with care the grace received in Baptism" and "lived thereafter for many years in the exact practice of Christian virtues." But beyond these heroic, one might say "saintly" traits, what most distinguished Kepuha, according to Le Gobien, was the fact that his death "edified the new Church and [so] was of great consolation to Blessed Diego":

> [Kepuha's] death helped to destroy an ancient superstition. It was the custom of the Chamorros to bury their dead in caves designated for this purpose and their obstinacy in this matter was very strong. They did not want to be separated from their ancestors[;] they said it was their duty to be united to them after death. Father Sanvitores resolved to abolish this custom so contrary to the laws of Christianity. Thus he decided to bury [Kepuha] in the Church with all the honor due to persons of distinguished merit. The relatives of the deceased were opposed to this plan, claiming that he must be buried in the tomb of his ancestors. Father Sanvitores won out and held a funeral that pleased the Chamorros.[26]

Blessed Diego's victory over the manner of Kepuha's burial is seen to necessitate the destruction of native *supersticiones* surrounding the fate of spirits of the dead. This was the materiality, the stuff which, according to Le Gobien and Blessed Diego, was used in the "edification" of the new church. But this should not surprise us. Saints—exemplary models and heavenly intercessors whose lives were filled with heroic virtues or crowned with martyred deaths—not only constitute an intimate cornerstone in the maintenance of the "one, holy, catholic, and apostolic church" (as Catholics would profess); their very lifestories would themselves be built sometimes upon, sometimes against a plethora of non-Christian (read pagan) customs and practices surrounding life and death. Peter Brown, for instance, reminds us that the cult of saints emerged from the historical appropriation of Roman tombs and cemeteries.[27] But Le Gobien himself also relates another curious observation: the Chamorros themselves are said to be "pleased" at Sanvitores's victory, that is, at Kepuha's Christian burial. Now, does this apparent pleasure—much like the pleasure Kepuha is earlier said to have expressed in welcoming Sanvitores—instead signify church desire? Do these longings serve to justify the mission's presence? Allay possible guilt of intrusion? Or might the Chamorros of this particular hamlet have actually spied in that ritual something else of value? What else, other than the demise of local customs, other than the discarding of native spiritual belief and its attendant temporal favors, might Kepuha's acceptance of Christian life, death, and his Christian burial have signaled for the Chamorros of this particular locality?

Vicente Rafael reminds us that spirits have miasmic tendencies.[28] Did

Bordallo seek such spirits in his desire to rekindle a Chamorro political consciousness? Can Chamorro political consciousness be understood as restless spirits? Might Kepuha's Christian burial have multiplied the possibilities of Chamorro mortal and spiritual relations? Is that what Bordallo also alludes to when he bade a temporary farewell in anticipation of a reunion with his cultural kin? Could the edification of the Catholic church on Guam have been premised less on the destruction of native spirits as Le Gobien and Blessed Diego understood than on a strategic fusion *and* separation of local and foreign spirits and their material (political) value for mortals?[29] Where do such spirits dwell today?

Bordallo obviously chose the Kepuha memorial as his self-sacrificial altar for its political value. As an icon of an historical intimacy between the Chamorro people and the Spanish Catholic church, the Kepuha memorial would simultaneously draw upon and implicate both traditions and their shared histories in a co-implicated struggle against another equally enduring regime, the American colonial order in the Pacific. His mimicry of Nathan Hale, whose inflammatory cry of regret fired a fabled American revolution, attests to this co-implication. A builder to the end, Bordallo sought to edify and direct a durable and fiery Chamorro consciousness against foreign tyranny and local opponents in a live enactment of the religious and secular narratives of martyrdom and self-sacrifice for God and country/island. This he sought in the presence of the Chamorro "edification" of the Catholic church as memorialized in Chief Kepuha's ennobled statue. But did it work? We are reminded, once again, that spirits are restless. Their destinations, like their origins, are uncertain. The day after Bordallo's death, island resident Andrea Manglona joined other supporters in decorating the site with wreaths and votive candles. She said: "Ricky needs the light to find his way. He is lost in the dark. It is essential the candles be lighted so he can find his way to God. Bordallo is in darkness because he took his life before it was God's time for him to die."[30]

The abhorrent practice of taking away a gift of life from God, in the late twentieth-century Guam and elsewhere, is not restricted to practices of suicide or martyrdom. The idea of life as a gift from God, as well as the idea that the gift comes into being at the moment of biological conception, anchors both the anti-abortion legislation on Guam and a persistent Chamorro view of the family as sanctuary of "traditional culture." This particular historical convergence is troubling, at best.

In an editorial entitled "Guam's Grotesque Muddle," the *Los Angeles Times* recognized the serious consequences of Guam's new abortion law for an American democracy.[31] Initially tempted to dismiss the "con-stitutional drama . . . as a theater of the absurd," the editorial warned that "when the first legal action taken under the island's restrictive new anti-abortion statute seeks not to halt termination of a pregnancy but to prohibit speech, it becomes clear that what's in progress is comedy too dark for laughs." What the editorial realizes to be dark and not funny is the fact that Ms. Benshoof of the ACLU was charged with solicitation for having advised pregnant women to leave the island and obtain abortions in Honolulu. The editorial's final paragraph in full:

> Cooler heads will sort out the grotesque muddle created on Guam, but not before the right to privacy established in Roe vs. Wade and delicate questions of free speech are put to a burdensome and dangerous test. If there is any value to this distasteful exercise, it is that it reminds us again that a woman's right to decide her fate in the private sanctuary of her own conscience and the right of any person to speak his or her mind are threads inextricably inter-woven in the fabric of individual liberty. Pull one such thread away and the entire fabric frays to rags, leaving *us all* to shiver in the cold wind of tyranny. (Emphases added.)

Enraged at so distasteful a law and at the forms of its political opposi-tion on Guam and on the "mainland," I find myself at a loss as to which particular thread to pull and which group of "us" I want to make shiver. I should begin with my own firm conviction that a fetus is a living human being, in spite of a rather narrow American "pro-life" rhetoric that at-tempts to monopolize the value of human life and prescribe its divergent practices.[32] Sometime in the early 1970s the *Pacific Voice*—the weekly newspaper published by the Archdiocese of Agana—featured an inter-view with a "Mrs. Fulana" (a localized version of "Jane Doe") that had a deep effect on me. Mrs. Fulana appeared, for all intents and purposes, a typical local housewife, with ten children, who remained active in local parish activities. In her interview, Mrs. Fulana recounts a moment of an-guish that took place years earlier in the examination room of a local medical clinic. Against her religious conviction and her own conscience, and in light of the financial difficulties posed by the number of children she and her husband had already been *blessed* with, Mrs. Fulana had gone ahead and scheduled an abortion. Her terror peaked as the doctor ap-proached. At the last second she dashed out of the room and clinic in tears. Of course, smiled Mrs. Fulana, the child that was born has brought "many tears of joy to our family."

Yet, while moved by this story, I remain deeply disturbed at the passage of so restrictive a law, and at the anti-abortion movement on the mainland in general. For, as a certain tradition of feminist intellectual practice helps us understand, the anti-abortion rhetoric has the debilitating effect of treating women's bodies as "hostile environments" on which the state can then justifiably intervene on behalf of a presumed innocent fetus. Such a "politics of surrogacy" serves to criminalize women who are seen to jeopardize an unborn's life. Moreover, the pro-life rhetoric equates the troubled issue of terminating pregnancies with a "pro-death" stance. In spite of myself, I am frightened by a politics of surrogacy which not only treats women who abort pregnancies as murderers, but which also assumes that individual women are unable to judge and act morally on the question of their pregnancy. It is as if the ways we've come to define ourselves and our (ethnic, gendered/sexual, national, and religious) identities have spawned peculiar conceptions of women's bodies. Or have particular conceptions of women's bodies spawned our very moral identities? [33]

Jennifer Terry argues that the "reproductive rights" issue in the United States—the pitting of women's rights to their bodies against fetus rights through a politics of surrogacy—reveals the limits of liberal individualism in American politics. She describes the situation as a "collision course of a [liberal rights] pluralism that grants rights to the fetus over and against the rights of pregnant women" (39). If this is so, then what is the status of liberty as it becomes displaced and is pitted against other political claims on the island of Guam? How are these confrontations congealed in the anti-abortion law and whose jurisdiction was clearly local? Janet Benshoof's remarkable depiction of the legislation as "a Pearl Harbor for women," and her own heroic and salvific presumption to liberate local women (and protect mainland women), articulates an ignorance of and insensitivity to the history of a people who suffered unspeakable losses under Japanese invasion and occupation during World War II for no other reason than America's prior claim to sovereignty over that Pacific region since the turn of the century.

Beyond the insult, and the racism (for its lumping together of perceived Asiatic peoples), there is a kind of hypocrisy in the ACLU's failure to address other civil liberties on the island. Duty-bound to individual liberty (in a way reminiscent of the earlier Jesuits' heartfelt responsibility to save the ignorant Chamorros *from* liberty) the ACLU and Benshoof are mute on the vexed question of Chamorro self-determination. Is Benshoof not aware that the indigenous movement draws, in part, from a global history of postwar "Third World" decolonization efforts which were themselves modeled, in part, on the very claims to the universality of liberal rights that structured their colonial master's regimes and groups such as the ACLU? Souder speaks to this precise point when she describes the Chamorro bid for sovereignty as "the *inalienable right* of Chamorros to continue to be Chamorro, speak Chamorro, and live a Chamorro way of life." Nonetheless, the ACLU's apparent inability to address the question of self-determination while defending individual liberties is further complicated by Governor Ada's view that the legislation is not meant to affect anyone's life in the fifty states. The legislation, to recall the governor's insistence, is primarily a local concern. Yet the history of American colonization, and the territorial incorporation of the island of Guam within it, simply proves the governor wrong. Local matters have national stakes and vice versa. To say the least. Guam is and isn't as much a part of America as America is and isn't a part of Guam.

Still, the racism, the hypocrisy, and the testimony to the limits of liberal individualism—despite the latter's persistence as the only "available political language" in the (contiguous or otherwise) U.S. marketplace—are also to be found in the *Los Angeles Times* editorial passage.[34] Recall the passage's final warning of the danger this (Guamanian) "comedy too dark for laughs" poses for "the fabric of individual liberty." Chilled, the editors write, "pull one such thread [freedom of speech] away and the entire fabric frays to rags, leaving us all to shiver in the cold wind of tyranny."[35]

If I may continue to muddle an already grotesque muddle, to brave the winds of tyranny, I will pull what Edward Said calls an "orientalist" thread in the editorial which resonates with Ms. Benshoof's equation of the local anti-abortion bill with an infamous Japanese surprise attack on American(ized) Hawaiian soil.[36] Since I am coded dark, male, and therefore potentially scary in white America, I begin to pale when I recognize the editorial's coloration of this event in the Far East also as shaded (and as a theater of surveillance and an object of a gaze) and as monstrous. But beyond trafficking in negative stereotypes (and why should being dark be negative?), orientalist discourse presumes the inability of certain (typically non-Western) peoples to represent their historical and political realities.[37] Like the politics of surrogacy that anchors the "pro-life" movement (that is, where the state is legitimized as the legal guardian for fetuses through the marginalization and negation of women's historical agency), the orientalist opening line defers to a Euro-American political center for the conflict's proper resolution. The opening line of the passage is cautious, but confident: the ugly muddle "created on Guam" *will* be sorted out by cooler heads who must first "put to a burdensome and dangerous test" the "delicate question of free speech" and the "right to privacy established in Roe vs. Wade" (emphasis added). The confidence takes comfort in the view that calm, white lawyers will figure this one out on the mainland.

But to characterize the muddle as a distant creation, to locate it comfortably far away, is to fail amazingly to historicize the imperial conditions on which the American Constitution has come to preside in the region and the inability of a constitutionally insured American democracy to address the tyranny of its colonial reaches in the Pacific ocean region. Why does the American flag fly over Guam? Does the Constitution follow the flag? And how did the turn-of-the-century Supreme Court "Insular Cases" which classified Guam as an "unincorporated territory" justify and legalize the holding of foreign (now domestic) territories?[38] Is this why local Guam legislation could now directly threaten American women thousands of miles from Guam's shores? In an editorial for the Gannett News Service, DeWayne Wickham writes, "Once an outpost of American democracy, Guam is now leading the assault on the civil liberties of U.S. citizens."[39] For Wickham, the abortion law and the archbishop's participation in the process "ensures for Guam a central role in a period of American history that threatens to be more divisive than the Civil War."

The specific threads in jeopardy are named by the editorial as "a woman's right to decide her fate in the private sanctuary of her own conscience and the right of any person to speak his or her own mind."[40] But why these, and not other rights? Do Chamorros have the right to decide their fate in the private sanctuary of their own conscience and the right to speak their own minds? And why stop here? In both the editorial and my own appropriation there persist yet other threads, for instance, in the invocation of sacred notions of "conscience" and a "sanctuary" that sanctify the secular space of the privacy of one's "own mind." As "conscience" in Christian theology has been understood to be the "sanctuary" of the "soul," for which the church would serve as protectress, so too has the "mind" served as the private space for whose protection a state would legitimize its presence in civil society. The political limits of this last analogy recall another recurring thread in my commentary: under what and whose conditions is something perceived in need of protection also to be given a woman's body? And under what and whose conditions is a woman's body figured as something in need of protection? But if the Constitution of the United States—that veritable guarantor of liberty—

be not applicable to Guam, then what recourse or protection would other Chamorro and non-Chamorro women have who do want to terminate unwanted pregnancies?

If these engendered histories of the sacred and the secular, of the private and the public, of the near and the distant, spill out of the boundaries of the editorial's concern for individual liberty and freedom, then such multiple meanings are only compounded in the vehicle of an anti-abortion measure on the island of Guam. To reduce the event to the political opposition of life vs. choice, or to (dark) religious fanaticism vs. rational (white) civility, as structured in the ACLU's and the editorial's narratives, is to ignore the many local and global threads that bind this and other singular, historic events on Guam, and the specific and complex ways by which past and present Chamorros have sought to use such threads.

I will end this commentary with a glance at a particular set of relations surrounding the abortion debate on Guam. For the context within which a lawmaking Chamorro Mother Elizabeth is pitted against lawyer-daughter Anita Arriola illustrates the propensity of the anti-abortion debate on Guam to disturb its reigning categories of description.

Transubstantiation

In her analysis of the makers and shapers of Guam history, Laura Souder contends that Chamorro women manifest "the dialectic between the colonizers and the colonized, between tradition and modernity."[41] Through their powerful traditions of formal and informal organizing—especially around issues that threaten the family—local women have been active in the making of custumbren Chamorro as it encountered over four hundred years of Spanish, Japanese, and American (and then Japanese again?) rule. For Souder, custumbren Chamorro is in fact a "pool of syncretic cultural traits," an amalgamation of Chamorro, Spanish, and American ways (8). Yet, while custumbren Chamorro is described in terms of a hybridity, it does not preclude the existence of a specifically distinct Chamorro heritage. The view that "we have no real history outside of our relations with western powers" is, for Souder, "erroneous" (227). Grappling with the question "how American is Guam?" Souder notes that "being Chamorro is first and foremost being of Chamorro blood or *haga'*. For some this is a "birthright" (40). Souder asserts that while Chamorros "do not deny that our racial mixture precludes a purist argument . . . the historical record does document [the persistence] of a racial strain that has survived to the present day" (40).

Haga' pronounced slightly differently, also means "daughter" (5). For Souder, *Hagan haga'*, or "blood daughter," becomes the privileged site of the transmission and preservation of custumbren Chamorro. The regulation of blood and language constitutes the "dialectic between the colonizer and the colonized" that Souder earlier saw manifest in Chamorro women organizers. That dialectic consisted in the "transmission and the [maintenance] of Chamorro traditions in conjunction with this adaptive form of racial continuity despite the implementation of genocidal policies since contact" (40).

To Souder, Senator Elizabeth Arriola is a "prototypical Chamorro woman organizer" on an island whose women have traditionally held "positions of authority in proportionately greater numbers" than women "from most contemporary societies in the Third World" (3). Mrs. Arriola fits Souder's (computer-tabulated) "composite portrait" of typical Chamorro woman organizers:

> She is likely to be a middle-age married woman with more than the average number of children. . . . A fluent speaker of both English and Chamorro, she nevertheless prefers Chamorro as it is the language of her childhood and the one most used by family members and friends. While she practices Chamorro traditions actively, she is quite concerned that her children's generation is losing touch with cultural values embodied in the extended family and the Chamorro language.

> The prototypical Chamorro woman organizer is a well-educated professional who has remained active in the labor force throughout her adult life. She is an active community volunteer who spent nascent years as an organizer working with church related groups . . . (16)

Most importantly, the prototypical Chamorro woman organizer embodies what Souder calls "the contradictory images that characterize Chamorro women":

> They are women in transition. They were born and reared at a time when Guam's population was culturally homogeneous, yet they have lived a substantial portion of their adult lives in the last two decades [1970s and 1980s]. They have witnessed unprecedented change in values, customs, and family life. Having experienced firsthand the lifestyle and traditions characteristic of Guam prior to modernization [for Souder, the 1960s], their cultural perspectives differ considerably from those of their children. These women have their feet planted in two worlds, so to speak. They have attempted to bridge

the gap between the domestic and public spheres [institutionalized during the "American era" since 1898] in their efforts to serve their community. (17)

With her feet planted in (at least) two worlds, Senator Arriola epitomizes that already familiar desire to "bridge the gap between domestic and public spheres" (173) of the family and political life, of custumbren Chamorro and the "homogenizing effects of modernization on the traditional cultures" (215). For it is precisely around the debilitating effects of modern America on the Chamorro Catholic family—here in the specific form of the threat of organized crime in an attempt to legalize gambling on Guam—that prompted Arriola's entry into island-wide politics in the late 1970s. In her interview with Souder, Arriola confesses: "I remembered vividly when the Bishop [late Archbishop Felixberto Flores] called and asked if I would be willing to co-chair the campaign. And of course at the time I said, oh my gosh this is a big thing. It's too much, too big. But then, I think knowing in my own heart that I felt very strongly against [gambling], I just was very glad. . . . I knew then and there that it was going to be the Christian Mothers that was going to be the core of the organization" (172). Fearing the arrival of organized crime through legalized gambling, Arriola helped organize a "battalion of crusading mothers to urge their own families, relatives, neighbors and friends to vote against [the measure] at the public referendum in April 1977" (172). It was this "groundswell of support" (to "resolve a problem which [the women] defined as threatening to their families and to the community") that defeated the bill (173). Arriola and the other Christian mothers defeated an opposition that was composed of island businessmen and politicians who wielded "a substantial budget and a consulting firm whose track record included legislation that legalized gambling in Atlantic City, New Jersey" (176). From parish hall politics to island-wide politics, Mrs. Arriola had already distinguished herself in the Guam legislature as a guardian of "the family." Her authorship of the anti-abortion bill follows that political trajectory.

In a chapter in which she surveys their representation in the historical record, Souder reveals the paradox of how Chamorro women have not only evaded but also appropriated foreign (and local) male regimes. In a section entitled "Motherhood," Souder argues that through deep matrifocal and matrilineal traditions, Chamorro mothers "have been figures of power and authority throughout history" (51). Though Chamorro matrilineality has been lost, matrifocality—Chamorro motherhood, or better known as *Si Nana*—preceded and continues to exceed local male,

Spanish Catholic, and American civil attempts to domesticate Chamorro women through sacred and secular institutions of matrimony (51). Si Nana, too, was at stake when many Chamorro women resisted both Blessed Diego's attempts to institutionalize the Sacrament of Matrimony in 1668, and the Chamorro men's "fondness" for the introduced practice when they realized how "obedient, diligent and 'circumspect' the wives of the first converts were in relation to their husbands" (50). Si Nana was at stake, again, in the seventeenth century when certain Chamorro women "practiced abortion as an act of defiance against Spanish (Catholic) domination" (71). Souder continues: "Notwithstanding the drastic reduction in their numbers, some women apparently chose to terminate pregnancies rather than give birth to children whose 'freedom' would be denied" (71). Larry Lawcock reminds us that even a half century after the Spanish Chamorro wars, that is, by the mid-eighteenth century, women who had abortions were still "whipped and sentenced to forced labor."[42] And in a way, motherhood was also at stake in a Spanish Catholic order that historically sought to articulate a Spanish *Madre Patria* through the offices of *Padres*.[43] In similar ways, motherhood (via fathers' rights) was at stake when civil marriage was instituted by the American Naval establishment in 1899. Patriarchy was further consolidated under the guise of "local autonomy" when the U.S. Congress passed the Guam Organic Act in 1950 which established the government of Guam. Part III, Title I of the new Guam Code was enacted in 1953:

1. The marriage of a female has the legal effect of changing her last or family name to that of her husband.
2. The husband may choose any reasonable place or mode of living, and if the wife does not conform thereto, it is desertion.
3. The husband is the head of the family.

All three provisions have since been amended. Women may take "whatever names they choose at marriage," and female members of the legislature have also been active in proposing other amendments to "make Guam's marital laws more equitable for both spouses."[44]

Equally committed to the protection of other family members, Senator-Chamorro Mother Elizabeth Arriola was compelled to sponsor the now infamous anti-abortion legislation. With the banning of abortion as "the main goal of her political career," Senator Arriola explains, "I look out my window and the trees are alive. How much more a human being! We have to take care of the unborn."[45]

Communion

If the rights of the unborn and the rights of women are on a collision course in the United States, I suggest that the abortion muddle on Guam in the postwar years describes a kind of supercollider. But the collision course here involves less the bombardment of a universally bounded nuclear family than deeply entrenched histories of how families and identities within families on the island have been engendered in colonial and countercolonial histories. For also at stake in the anti-abortion debate on Guam is the sanctity of the Chamorro family as it has been constructed and reconstructed by island women in the historical intercourses between indigenous, Spanish Catholic, and liberal American ideals. The political opposition embodied in what can be called Arriola vs. Arriola had been predicted by Souder. "It is highly probable," she writes, "that the daughters of these organizers will have different views. When Chamorro women begin to define their sense of worth in terms of personal autonomy, another major turning point in the Chamorro female experience will have occurred."[46]

As if to signal such a turning point, the younger Anita Arriola speaks out against her mother's legislation when she proclaims that "the silence out here is so oppressive."[47] This Hagan Haga', and others in her generation, to be sure, have big stakes in a constitutionally backed set of civil liberties. Through their voices for choices, a significant and vocal facet of Chamorro cultural survival continues to articulate itself but through a liberal discourse of rights as guaranteed (as of this date) in an American-backed Constitution. In doing so, however, the Chamorro pro-choice proponents also echo that other loud call for Chamorro "self-determination" and sovereignty that also, ironically enough, informs the "right to (Chamorro) life" narratives informed by custumbren Chamorro. For, as we might recall Souder's definition, Chamorro sovereignty consists of "the inalienable right of Chamorros to continue to be Chamorro, speak Chamorro, and live a Chamorro way of life."

The political opposition between mother and daughter—not a light matter in the island of Guam ("It hurts me personally," admits the elder Arriola)—is itself enabled through a deeper bonding between the two. If she is pained by her own daughter's apparent public rebellion, the elder Arriola also "respects" the public value of her and her daughter's own personal opinions. Situated between Spanish, American, and local male stakes in those histories, the two Chamorro women have learned to respect, in different ways, the public articulation of private opinions. The respect defers, in both cases, to the sanctity of the Chamorro family, to peace in the home. Meeting with her mother and seven siblings before "speaking publicly," Arriola noted that "everybody agreed that if my mother and I don't attack each other personally, we could each express our views politically."[48]

I suggest, however, that in these narratives lies something of a common kinship that extends beyond the biological contingencies between mother, daughter, and siblings. There is something thicker than blood that binds the Chamorro family especially as it is guarded, protected by Chamorro mothers and daughters. The two Hagan Haga'—though opposed in the surrogate political arena of the American judicial system— here conspire in the historical task of groping for a political language in which indigenous female identities and desires could be articulated. The continuity of familia and forms of its expression are at stake here. From their respective corners, mother and daughter embrace oppositional narratives (pro-life and pro-choice respectively) whose own histories are themselves complicit in the continual colonization of the Chamorro families. This situation, actually a kind of political predicament, reveals something of the "ambivalence"—the simultaneous oppressive and liberatory tendency and possibility—which is characteristic of colonial discourse.[49] While the opposing narratives of choice and life are complicit in the colonization of the Chamorro people, and while their legal resolution in the U.S. Supreme Court itself ensures the American colonial regime on Guam, these oppositional narratives and their institutional settings themselves furnish the very possible languages under which Chamorro self-determination (in the ways we've seen defined in this chapter) can articulate its "own" desires. Given the mediated nature of indigenous political expression shared by mother and daughter, I will close this final discussion with a peek at exactly what and for whom Attorney Arriola speaks.

As attorney for Ms. Benshoof, Anita Arriola also legally speaks for the Guam Society of Obstetricians and Gynecologists, the Guam Nurses Association, an Episcopal Priest, three doctors, and one "Maria Doe" in the aforementioned class action suit against the government.[50] Of all these possible clients, I will dwell on the one of whose background we are supposed to know very little. "Maria Doe" was a pregnant local woman whose scheduled abortion was postponed due to the passage of the law. She fuses a typical local first name, in fact, Our Blessed Mother's namesake, with what is ostensibly a generic, typical American (whatever that is) surname, if only to secure her anonymity and (especially in such a

Catholic island as Guam) a safe place to speak. Though ensuring (in this particular legal contest/context) the desired anonymity and security, the name "Maria Doe" nevertheless openly calls into question not only the twin colonial regimes that have ruled the island in the last three hundred years, but also the predicament of expressing a local female identity and desire within the messiness of these entangled orders and local investments therein. The choice of that packed name is reminiscent of Bordallo's romantic/sarcastic invocation of Nathan Hale's cry of regret and the Bordallo supporter who, while placing devotional candles around the base of the Kepuha memorial, also brought irreverent attention to the status of her departed leader's restless spirit. Likewise, the mimicry in the choice of "Maria Doe's" name recalls the (layered) ambivalence of colonial and countercolonial narratives on Guam, as spied in the Bordallo and abortion cases. In its proper context, "Maria Doe" must speak through a surrogate officer, another local (Chamorro) woman lawyer who must herself speak through the apparatus of a legal system that historically denies indigenous expression in its own right (whatever that is too). As we have seen, the attorney and her client do this in opposition to kin (does Maria Doe wish to be anonymous so as not to embarrass her family on Guam?) who must themselves embrace political narratives (here pro-life) which also historically deny the indigenous expression they wish to continue in their fight (as we heard Senator Elizabeth Arriola and Governor Ada explain).

The mimicry and mockery that come from these (subaltern?) spaces raises, at least for me, certain political questions vis-à-vis ambivalent colonial legacies. Under these particular conditions, what recourse, other than discursive play, do we have in the project of decolonization?

Meditation

Bordallo's suicide and the local abortion muddle embody Chamorro cultural continuity as it constructs its survival among a host of intrusive ideas and institutions. Yet, these stories, these events, these political sites of history and culture, intersect in a complex and confusing grid of indigenous and exogenous ideas and practices (of man, woman, children, God and spirits) that serve as much to break down as to secure extant social and political structures on the island. Bordallo's suicide and the anti-abortion legislation, as we have seen, seem to pit indigenous Chamorro, Spanish Catholic, and American liberal individual beliefs and practices against each other, in ways that act to blur their own distinctions and identities. The terms Chamorro, Spanish Catholic, and American are thrown into question. On Guam they are troubled, and the more they are invoked in efforts of reconsolidation, the more troubled they become. But I would like to suggest that beyond providing a feel for the complex and the paradoxical, the two stories bring into focus a larger problematic, perhaps precisely for their refusal to remain in any neat categories of description and analyses. For in raising the question of the status of displaced (Chamorro, Spanish Catholic, and American) institutions and practices—the local topographies and architectures of piety—Bordallo's suicide and the anti-abortion legislation also summon the need to rethink critically reigning notions of history, politics, and culture as "located" on Guam and elsewhere.[51]

To what extent can piety be viewed as a site, a topography and architecture, of history and politics? And just what kind of site is this? Just as missionaries such as Blessed Diego felt compelled to go to faraway places to convert or to relocate what they thought were "lost" souls back to their presumed proper place under God, people from faraway places—such as the Chamorros from the Western Pacific—have sought to localize novel, powerful ideas and practices (such as Christianity) into indigenous ways of life. These processes built local homes. The effect of these cultural and historical transactions, or what Rafael has described as a multilayered and polydiscursive contractual relationship, was (is) a blurring of the distinctions between the participating identities even as these identities were themselves being forged or reinforced.[52] Elsewhere I have surveyed the official and popular stakes in the effort to make Blessed Diego a patron saint of the Mariana Islands.[53] With attention to the pious practices found in a displaced, relocated Catholic church, I ask whether these practices can themselves be viewed as sites, as topographies and architectures of "local" culture and history. Rafael shows us how Tagalog conversion to Catholicism concerned Spanish imperial and native desires to convert the foreign and the dangerous into the familiar, the pleasurable, and the valuable.[54] On Guam, I ask, What kinds of identities get built from the cultural and historical confrontations of traditional and novel ideas and practices—whether indigenous Chamorro, Spanish Catholic, or American liberal? And, What are the political implications of attempts to secure any one of these identities?

Like the effort to canonize Blessed Diego, the suicide and the anti-abortion bill involve an historical and political task of shuttling between indigenous and exogenous realities, between the inside and the outside of various cultures, and between local and global terrains, all of which have powerful but troubling consequences for all involved. For instance, the act of beatifying Sanvitores—of declaring him a Blessed and thus worthy of local veneration—rested on what we might call the theological and historical correctness of his martyrdom.[55] I have suggested that what it took to position this missionary as martyr—as agent of God in life and death—was a repositioning of his Chamorro adversary (one chief Matapang) as agent of the Devil in spite of the fact that Chamorro Catholics endorse the proceedings.[56] In this way we can see how a negative identity continues to be foisted upon indigenous sensibilities, especially when these native identities are understood to oppose Catholic doctrine. Yet, while the effort to canonize Blessed Diego can be shown to "work" the native to produce a saint, it is equally true that natives can be shown to work the saint to produce what might be called stronger "canons" of the self. Catholicism, with tools such as patron saints, has become one powerful form of Chamorro identity and tradition. In this way, we can begin to see how Chamorro cultural continuity makes a home within intrusive, foreign systems (such as fledgling Catholic regimes or the seventeenth-century Castilian order) that sought to reconsolidate themselves in imperial and evangelical imperatives among people (such as indigenous Chamorros) who also sought to reconsolidate their own notions of self and society. But while Roman Catholic desires and Chamorro interests can be shown mutually to work each other, they never do so equally. Nevertheless, pious processes of mutual but unequal appropriation on Guam continue to take place within a late twentieth-century political context that features a hybrid "self-determination" movement; a movement that increasingly calls into question American political and social patronage in the region even as it invokes its ideals. Has American liberal individualism and self-determination become the most recent home for Chamorro cultural continuity? Nonetheless, how can such a politicized history of mutual but unequal appropriations help us rethink reigning notions of culture, history, and politics as located in tiny, obscure places like Guam?

Benediction

(More than) Chamorro cultural history is etched in the topography and architecture of the land. Return to the Agana Basilica. Santa Marian

Kamalen before and above you, Santo Papa to the right, Blessed Diego to the left, the Guam legislature to the rear.

A National Public Radio reporter traveled to Guam recently to cover the anti-abortion controversy that has frightened many Americans on the "mainland."[57] In Agana the reporter suddenly realizes that the line between church and state on the island is traversed with as much ease as it takes to cross the narrow street that separates the Agana Basilica from the Guam Legislature. But for an *entangled* history of Spanish, American, and indigenous desire on Guam, the short passage between the Agana Basilica and the Guam Legislature itself traverses historical, geopolitical, *and* national boundaries.

A Post-script(ure): Prefigurations

During a recent return to Guam for a conference I had the pleasure of taking a few visitors on a sight-seeing jaunt around the island. Along Cross-Island Road in the south we pass graffiti on a wall. It reads: "Legalize Spiritual Development."

Legalize . . . Spiritual . . . Development.

Today the island is experiencing the most rapid economic growth in its history. It is a boomtown. More and more land-owning local families are "wining and dining" Japanese investors. In fact, the local community looks to the Japanese converted yen as an antidote to a century of dependence on the American dollar even while the Chamorro continue to celebrate annually the American liberation of the island from Japanese occupation during World War II. Indeed, the paradoxes and the contradictions surrounding the latest (re)entry of yet another set of stories, identities, communities, and buildings from beyond Guam's topography are sprayed, quite glaringly, on proverbial cross-island walls.

Notes

1 I thank James Clifford, Donna Haraway, Martha Duenas, Terry Teaiwa, Marita Sturken, and Haunani-Kay Trask for critical comments on earlier drafts. An earlier form of this essay was published as "Pious Stories: Chamorro Cultural History at the Crossroads of Church and State," in *Isla: A Journal of Micronesian Studies* 1, no. 1 (Rainy Season, 1992). My discussion is limited to the island of Guam, and to the Roman Catholic and American legacies with the Chamo-

rro people there. The specific relations on Guam (as opposed to on the Northern Mariana islands) and the Chamorro encounters with Spanish and American
Catholicism and liberalism do not exhaust the complexity of Chamorro cultural
history.

2 Alan Riding, "Vatican 'Saint Factory': Is It Working Too Hard?," *New York
Times*, 15 April 1989.

3 Laura M. Souder, *Daughters of the Island: Contemporary Chamorro Women
Organizers on Guam* (Agana, Guam: Micronesian Area Research Center, 1987) p. 3.

4 This is my rendition of the idea of colonial and countercolonial ambivalence developed by Homi Bhabha, "Of Mimicry and Man: The Ambivalence of
Colonial Discourse," *October* 28 (1984).

5 I prefer to use the name "Kepuha" rather than the more conventional "Quipuha" for an added irony found in the Chamorro orthography. In the vernacular,
the name "Kepuha"—the seventeenth-century chief who is said to have welcomed
the Catholic mission to Guam—is translated as "dare to overturn" (as in "dare to
overturn a canoe"); see Oscar L. Calvo, Monsignor, Interview, 13–18 January 1991,
Makati, Philippines. In favoring the use of "Kepuha" to the hispanicized (anglicized) "Quipuha," I myself dare to overturn histories and practices that would
themselves dare to obscure indigenous meaning systems. But then again, for the
majority of other names and places referred to here in this article, I defer to Hispanic and Anglo conventions in the tactical interest of communication and out of
sheer historical and cultural necessity.

6 Jane Gross, "Stiffest Restrictions on Abortion in U.S. Are Voted in Guam,"
New York Times 16 March 1990: 1A.

7 Nancy Yoshihara, "First Charges Filed to Test Strict Guam Abortion Law,"
Los Angeles Times 21 March 1990: A4.

8 Gross, p. 1.

9 Tamar Lewin, "First Test of Abortion Law in Guam," *New York Times*
21 March 1990: 1.

10 The case was upheld in the Ninth Circuit Court of Appeals in Honolulu,
Hawaii in April, 1992. Though Governor Ada and the Government of Guam had
appealed, the U.S. Supreme Court eventually decided not to hear the Guam case.

11 Gross, p. 10.

12 e.e. cummings, "Next to Of Course God," *100 Selected Poems* (New York:
Grove Press, 1954), p. 31.

13 Robert F. Rogers, "Guam's Quest for Political Identity," *Pacific Studies* 12,
no. 1 (1988): 60.

14 Laura Souder and Robert Underwood, eds., *Chamorro Self-Determination/
I direchon y taotao* (Agana, Guam: Chamorro Studies Association and Micronesian Area Research Center, 1987); and Hope Alvarez-Cristobal, "The Organization
of Peoples for Indigenous Rights: A Commitment Towards Self-Determination,"
Pacific Ties 13, no. 4 (1990): 10–24.

15 See Rogers.

16 Ron Ige, "Bordallo Known as Dreamer, Builder: Lived life of Triumph and Loss," *Pacific Daily News* 1 February 1990: 3.

17 Brian Perry, "Eulogy Addresses Bordallo's Suicide," *Pacific Daily News* 9 February 1990: 4.

18 Brian Perry, "Bordallo's Life, Death Contemplated," *Pacific Daily News* 10 February 1990: 10.

19 Henry Evan, "Christian Burial Not Prohibited," *Pacific Daily News* 2 February 1990: 5.

20 Anthony S. Apuron, Archbishop, "Pastoral Message on Suicide," *Pacific Daily News* 13 February 1990: 5.

21 Ige, p. 3.

22 Rafael argues that, among other things, it was a discursive reworking of Tagalog notions of death and life by Spanish Catholic teachings that furnished the vernacular for an incipient Tagalog nationalist movement during the late nineteenth century; see Vicente Rafael, *Contracting Colonialism: Translation and Christian Conversion in Tagalog Society under Early Spanish Rule* (Durham: Duke University Press, 1992). For a rich reading of memorials as occasions for historical narrativizing, see Marita Sturken, "Memory and Its Members," Qualifying Essay, University of California, Santa Cruz, 1990.

23 Paul V. Daly, trans. *History of the Marianas Islands* [By Charles Le Gobien, Paris: Pepie, 1700] (Agana: Nieves Flores Library, 1949), pp. 8, 10; emphasis added.

24 Daly, p. 24.

25 See David Hanlon, *Upon a Stone Altar: A History of the Island of Pohnpei to 1890* (Honolulu: University of Hawaii Press, 1988) p. 130; and Rafael, p. 166.

26 Daly, p. 27–28.

27 Peter Brown, *The Cult of Saints: Its Rise and Function in Latin Christianity* (Chicago: University of Chicago Press, 1981).

28 Vicente Rafael, "Imagination and Imagery: Philippine Nationalism in the Nineteenth Century," *Inscriptions* 5 (1989).

29 See Rafael, *Contracting Colonialism*, p. 166, for the distinction between discourses of syncretism and separation.

30 Christine Kohler, "Supporters Lighting Candles," *Pacific Daily News* 2 February 1990: 3.

31 Editorial, "Guam's Grotesque Muddle," *Los Angeles Times* 21 March 1990: B6.

32 For critiques of the "embryo-as-an-individual" viewpoint, see Charles A. Gardner, "Are Embryos People?," *San Jose Mercury News* 3 December 1989: 5; Jennifer Terry, "The Body Invaded: Medical Surveillance of Women as Reproducers," *Socialist Review* 19, no. 3 (1989), pp. 13–43; and Rosalind Pollack Petchesky, "Fetal Images: The Power of Visual Culture in the Politics of Reproduction," *Feminist Studies* 13, no. 2 (1985): 263–93.

33 My point of arrival in this line of questioning is inspired by recent attempts to reread the fate of bodies of non-Western and women of color by an emergent "third world" and "women of color" writers. For some examples, see Lata Mani, "The Construction of Women as Tradition in Early Nineteenth Century Bengal," *Cultural Critique* 7 (1987): 119–56; and Norma Alarcón, "Chicana's Feminist Literature: A Re-vision Through Malintzin / or Malintzin: Putting Flesh Back on the Object," in *This Bridge Called My Back: Writings by Radical Women of Color*, ed. Cherrie Moraga and Gloria Anzaldua (New York: Kitchen Table, Women of Color Press, 1981), pp. 182–92.

34 Terry, p. 39.

35 *Los Angeles Times*, B6.

36 Edward Said, *Orientalism* (New York: Vintage, 1979).

37 Lata Mani and Ruth Frankenberg, "The Challenge of Orientalism," *Economy and Society* 14, no. 2 (1985): 174–92.

38 Fredric Coudert, "The Evolution of the Doctrine of Territorial Incorporation," *Columbia Law Review* 26 (1926).

39 DeWayne Wickham, "Guam Going Down in History for Assault on Citizens' Rights," *Pacific Daily News* 21 March 1990: 24.

40 *Los Angeles Times*, B6.

41 Souder, *Daughters of the Island* 38, subsequent page references cited parenthetically in text.

42 Larry Lawcock, "Guam Women: A Hasty History," in *Women of Guam*, ed. Cecilia Bamba, Laura Souder, and Judy Tompkins (Agana, Guam: Guam Women's Conference, 1977), p. 10.

43 Rafael, "Imagination and Imagery."

44 Souder, *Daughters of the Island*, p. 51.

45 Gross, p. 10.

46 Souder, *Daughters of the Island*, p. 215.

47 Gross, p. 10.

48 Gross, p. 10.

49 Again, I borrow from Bhabha's notion of "ambivalence" of colonial discourse and "mimicry" as tactic.

50 Frale DeGuzman, "Abortion Law Put on Hold," *Pacific Daily News* 27 March 1990.

51 Stuart Hall maps out the breakdown of the local/global split in terms of the politics of ethnicity in "The Local and the Global: Globalization and Ethnicity," *Culture, Globalization and the World System*, ed. Anthony King, SUNY (Binghamton: MRTS, 1991): 19–39.

52 Vicente M. Diaz, "Restless Na(rra)tives," *Inscriptions* 5 (1989).

53 Vicente M. Diaz, *Repositioning the Missionary: The Beatification of Blessed Diego Luis de Sanvitores and Chamorro Cultural History* (Mangilao, Guam: Micronesian Area Research Center, forthcoming).

54 Rafael, *Contracting Colonialism*.

55 Fr. Juan Ledesma, *The Cause of the Beatification of Ven. Diego Luis de San-*

vitores, Apostle of the Marianas. Deposition on the Life and Martyrdom (Rome: The Sacred Congregation for the Causes of Saints, Historical Section 94, 1981).

56 Diaz, "Pious Stories."

57 Amy Goodman, "Guam: Territory in Turmoil," *On the Issues* (Winter 1990).

Christopher P. Wilson

Plotting the Border

John Reed, Pancho Villa, and *Insurgent Mexico*

or a brief moment in 1913–14, on the crest of Francisco Villa's stunning military victories during the second phase of the Mexican Revolution, American war correspondence became virtually pre-occupied with the question: "What Will Villa Do?" In the forecasts of interventionists, occupationists, and anti-imperialists alike, Villa—a self-educated peasant, anticleric, part-Indian, bandit, bigamist, murderer with a massive army—seemed an unlikely candidate for acceptance into the (North) American fold. During the years when famous correspondents could implicitly refer to "Central America" as a republic soon to be forged out of the "parcel" of "little states" by U.S. intervention, American reporters habitually cited the "savage" state of Villa and his followers—a label which, in the late-Victorian lexicon, meant animalistic, childlike, unable to repress emotions or think in the abstractions necessary for civilized governance. One journalist compared Villa to a tiger, adding that "he looked as one might imagine a robust representative of the lower regions" disguised to visit "a more civilized realm"; others compared Mexicans to plantation Negroes or "redskin[s] of the United States Reservations."[1]

Nevertheless, Villa did find himself cast in a scenario which some Americans could imagine. The occasion came when General Hugh Scott, in command of American troops to the North, greeted Villa with a copy of the U.S. *Rules of Land Warfare*.[2] To consecrate this scene, reporter George Marvin—writing for *The World's Work*—invoked (and modified) the presiding (dark) angel of imperial discourse, Rudyard Kipling. East is not West, Marvin intoned,

But there is neither North nor South, Border,
    nor Breed, nor Birth
When two strong men stand face to face, tho'
    they come from the ends of the earth!

Here Marvin elicited a repressed interventionist fantasy, a pincer movement: Villa riding up from the South, a Rooseveltian figure down from the North. As Nell Irvin Painter has suggested, Villa even looked like a Mexican Theodore Roosevelt. Marvin's magazine ran photographs with a caption which read: "Pictures of General Villa That Suggest the Rough-and-Ready Quality of His Leadership." And as the border disappeared, the once-exotic, Southern other collapsed into his "civilized" Northern self: Indian into cowboy, bandit into policeman.[3]

The fantasy, of course, only puts a different twist on a familiar story. It is hardly news that ostensible support for foreign nationalism can surreptitiously collude with imperialism's ends—a risk American war correspondents routinely run. Bound to American combatants by a mixture of envy, guilt, and replication (what Michael Herr calls the journalist's "personal movie") and ignoring natives on the margin; often apprenticing in crime reporting, and thus inured to seeing counterinsurgency merely as police action; tending, especially in the Victorian era, to discount guerilla warfare as an unmanly game of "hide-and-seek"—war correspondents habitually measure the legitimacy of a conflict by how effectively American troops wage it, contributing to a "Great Powers" cartography even in the conventions of the modern dateline ("from the far reaches of . . ."). If the late-Victorian era marks the juncture when what literary historians call "romance" became what diplomatic historians call "realism," then war correspondence—a romance of "fact"—may well trace the cultural inversion.[4]

Any attempt to reconstruct American war correspondence in the era of the "new" imperialism (1898–1914) must entertain the power of these conventions. Yet even granting their governance, I want to examine how extensive their domain was by taking a text, John Reed's *Insurgent Mexico* (1913–14), which presents itself both as a critique of conventional reporting and an affirmation of solidarity with Villa's cause. Reed's book offers a good test case, moreover, for adjudicating what James Clifford has identified as the conditions of domination and dialogue within cross-cultural transcription—here, the procedures of war reporting.[5] On the one hand Reed, having ridden with Villa and his followers for four months while on assignment for the liberal-socialist *Metropolitan* magazine and the *New*

York World, still draws praise (from U.S. and Latin American scholars) as having produced a firsthand, "participant observer's" account of Villa's insurgent agrarianism. On the other hand, it would be difficult to imagine a text more saturated with late-Victorian exoticism, originally delineated not in battle but in the halls of Harvard (and patterned after writers like Kipling himself).[6] Critical readings of Reed's work generally circumvent this problem by explicit appeal to the powers of "romance." If *Insurgent Mexico* is acknowledged as a quest by the Greenwich Village bohemian to recuperate his own masculine "phantasmic afterimage" in an exotic terrain—if his cross-cultural understanding is in doubt—scholars nevertheless argue Reed's book transcends these limitations and presents us with the "spirit" of the revolution.[7] This characterization is in fact exemplary of the historiography of war correspondence generally—which, to date, has been content to rehearse the logistical tensions and romantic exploits of battlefield reporting, deaf to its literary conventions, immune to the unsettling possibility that what is called "news" may only trace another "itinerary" of "silencing."[8]

Of course, we need to guard against our own claims to transcendence: the centripetal drives and limits of my own training in "American" Studies, for instance, often simply replay many of Reed's own. On the other hand, my initial sense is that neither the micropolitics of *this* revolution, nor the vacillation of official U.S. policy, support a view of Reed's reporting as yet another episode of a totalizing, epistemic violence commonly suggested by recent analyses of discourse in the imperial context. As a counterpoint to such potentially unilateral and seductively idealistic renderings, I want to explore the degree to which the social practice, determinate material constraints, and generic conventions of turn-of-the-century war correspondence constituted, in Todd Gitlin's formulation, a contested area of ideological and policy struggle in the given, specific time frame. Reed's reporting is surely a romantic "fable of rapport" exporting many mainstream conventions, yet it also was contested by Villa's own representations in a way that ultimately modified its policy position.[9]

Whether John Reed presented an "authentic" Pancho Villa will, no doubt, continue to be argued over by specialists in inter-American and Mexican history; recuperating Villa's voice is not my object here.[10] But by the same token, by assuming, a priori, that there *was* a single, rigid, and wholly hegemonic discursive convention governing American war correspondence (instead of what Benita Parry calls a "diversified map" distributing the native in multiple positions), we might unwittingly contribute to the crime we so often chastise, the writing out of the native subject(s).[11] Any full reading of Reed's reporting, that is, must include indigenous control over the information gathered and sent North. Therefore, by describing the map distributing Villa in mainstream American war correspondence; by suggesting a source like Villa mediated (or staged) his own interpretation, even interrogated his own romancing; by reading through *Insurgent Mexico*'s exoticism to the frictions in the project of American "correspondence"—we can begin to glimpse a more fluid discursive situation, a modestly collaborative but ultimately contested local knowledge sent, with mixed results, across the border.

At the turn of the century, the popularity of reporters like Richard Harding Davis, Julian Ralph, and Julius Chambers served to sanctify nineteenth-century conventions regarding war (or "special") correspondence blending local color and U.S. policy concerns. Successful reporters were mythologized as masculine, globe-trotting vagabonds. They were hybrids of Henry Stanley and the modern police reporter: news or headline "hunters," who habitually equated assignments with going *"en safari."* The genre began literally as "letters" from a foreign clime or military front, gradually becoming illustrated lectures commissioned by magazines or Sunday newspapers; here, reporters' exoticism was commonly cast in what Gitlin calls a "reformist key." Far from cultivating neutrality, Ralph wrote, you must write to "rhyme with your convictions." The lecture had two (necessarily segmented) audiences. As a "soldier of fortune"—Ralph called the correspondent a "knight of the pen" from our "free and enlightened land"—the reporter's worldly experience ostensibly baptized him as an American representative. Thus, when he pronounced on "civilized" conduct or drew the line between genuine revolution and merely lawless "banditry," he spoke *both* to American audiences and his own "foreign" interviewees themselves. When he recorded a country's natural wealth, not uncommonly he remarked that it was in the possession of "barbaric" stewardship from which it would have to be wrested away. Conversely, when freedom fighters abroad *were* compared to American heroes—a Cuban farmer to Nathan Hale, or Villa himself to General Grant—it was often merely as a prelude to interventionist argument (they need our help). Indeed, when war correspondents accompanied gun running or filibuster expeditions in advance of U.S. troop commitments, they offered their reporting explicitly as advance scouting for future U.S.-military operations.[12]

Of course, contradictions abounded in this specular practice. The democratic aura of the correspondent was undercut by the aristomilitary conventions of "news hunting," which implicitly targeted nonchivalric, "savage," or "beastly" enemies; insurgents did not always welcome the exportation of these lectures; "Great Power" plots often called for detailing a U.S. economic interest, while the conventions of exoticism usually meant repressing it. Nor should we confuse the romantic memoir with the day-to-day social practice of reporting itself. Then as now, the exotic dateline cliché of the "war-torn capital" disguised what was often, in practice, what trade pundits call "parachute" journalism (that is, after-the-fact arrival). Correspondents typically began their work as camp followers after a conflict had begun, transmitting official dispatches from headquarters, at most reporting on the battles, personalities, and sidelights of a military campaign. At its best, war correspondence might play off the news center (headquarters) and its margins, but rarely did it overstep an officially sanctioned radius. More commonly, reporters wrote about the implementation of strategy (how fighting men interpreted commands), about troop morale (essentially the same axis), or the contrasts between front and back lines. During the Mexican conflict, reporters' complaints were consequently confined to mundane matters like disrupted rail travel, downed telegraph lines, or the absence of visible military fronts (a continuing problem in reporting guerilla war). If (then as now) war correspondents worried about military censorship, even this complaint only identified the material and ideological tether on their own operations. Except for sporadic and usually unfulfilled threats, however, correspondents were given considerable latitude of movement, and thus it was no coincidence that Villa's Northern rebellion—that is, the wing closest to the U.S. border—came to center stage in the American press.[13]

Yet reporting on a geographically diverse and politically fluid Mexican insurgency did alter the rules subtly. In particular, the micropolitics of Villa's rebellion were not so easily decipherable to American eyes. In its peasant manifestations, the revolution in the North was grounded in long-standing disputes over land and water in villages and *haciendas*, disputes exacerbated by population growth, large-scale class exploitation and modernization spurred by foreign investment during the Díaz regime—the turning, as Friedrich Katz has put it, of a Mexican "frontier" into a "border" marked by U.S. investment.[14] However, the class base of Villa's movement was heterogeneous: many in Chihuahua who took up arms for Francisco Madero in 1910, and subsequently for Villa, were recruited from the *rancheros* who faced losses of land, or of autonomy, in the boom development of estates driven by the accelerating export economy;

other participants, meanwhile, rebelled only after evictions, drought, and other experiences of social instability. This diverse and quite local base posed obstacles for the reporter's traditional camp-following strategy: traveling with a mobile army, when war was waged *between* towns and *through* haciendas, could not easily engage the complex overlay of historical, current, personal, and class grievances. Among battlefield reporters, "coverage" of military action tended to "cover over"—see as *only* personal—the temporary, provisional settlement of local disputes that Villa, for one, made along the way.[15]

Villa, however, certainly dominated the mainstream American press coverage during 1913–14. But as mentioned earlier, correspondents measured his legitimacy with Anglocentric, urban, and racist yardsticks. Following the convention of separating political rebellion from criminality, "bandit" (or "brigand") was affixed to Villa virtually as a surname. The *New York Times* called him nothing more than a "gang" leader or "bully" who had been chased out of El Paso by a "man who was his master," the town's Irish mayor. ("I think I can best describe [Villa]," the *Times* man wrote, "as a man I would not care to meet in a lonely neighborhood on a dark night.") The *Review of Reviews* unhesitatingly identified Mexico as an American "police" beat—a designation which, incidentally, encoded invasive, preemptive action[16]—while the chaos of alliances led Richard Harding Davis to declare the revolution not even a war, but a "falling out among cattle-thieves." Villa's physical stature was always noted, classified by type as a "beast" or "primordial man" fit for modern "ethnology" and ascribed "primitive" characteristics like violent temper. According to one A. P. correspondent, Villa was essentially " 'unmoral' where matters of life and death were in question," thus unlike the "cooler-blooded Anglo-Saxon race." Conventionally Central American revolutionary (uncivil) temper was thought to be in the primitive's "Latin" (*sic*) "blood."[17] Mexico as a nation was described as a land of "buts" and "perhaps" and mañanas inaccessible to reason.

The empowering of the American lecturer was itself predicated on assumptions about the inarticulate state of "primitive" rebels. The brief flap over whether Villa would honor those *Rules of Land Warfare* epitomized the war correspondent's exportation of a "civilized" aristomilitary standard by which this "mentality" was tested. Yet Mexicans, reporters said, ostensibly could not think in the abstractions of military strategy; childlike peons saw the campaign as a "perpetual picnic" and fought, George Mason of *The Outlook* said, only for looting, revenge, hero worship—for patriotism only "of an unseeing . . . variety." More covertly, this infantilization served to measure how Mexican fighters might stand up to American troops, just as vivid retelling of wartime devastation often implicitly evaluated the ability of Mexico's financial infrastructure to rebound for investment. Yet while fact sheets and tables sometimes presented Mexico's natural resources, the extent of American economic interest was more commonly downplayed. Rather, Mexico was pressed back into a medieval past—Mexico was supposedly hundred of years behind the United States (and Villa "A Survivor from the Middle Ages")—its battles seen as between "slaves" and "princes." This historical exoticizing and sometimes feminizing of Mexico made it a precious object, unworthy of the Mexican forces who fought *over* it. Here Villa the "tiger" became a "scavenger," a brutal beast not owning or earning his keep, and Mexico a bull "pecked to death" in a domestic and international ring.[18]

Collaterally, the savage and supposedly inarticulate state of Mexicans was made interchangeable with the desert landscape, a site of "cyclonic passion," prickly politics, and yet often mysterious silence. Briton Herbert Whitaker wrote for *The Independent* that "[u]nder all his bombastic talk, the veneer of civilization we have imposed upon him, the Mexican is still a savage. . . . Fickle, irresponsible, treacherous, his purposes are as water, his intent is written on shifting sand" (490). In this vein, reporters often elided the voice of the insurgents—and, notably, Villa's advisers—by concluding a priori that "talk" was no route to "savage" intentions. Instead, correspondents invoked an historical-economic determinism—the longstanding battle between aristocrat and the "lower" masses—in order to portray the unreasonability and lack of agency among the competing elements of a class war. (Here, a kind of "worst of all possible times," a Dickensian counterpoint, worked to flatter the American middle-class reader.) Whitaker, for instance, insisted that the insurgency was fueled by fate, something boiling up from below (rather than, that is, the result of a high-republican, deliberative politics). Comparing Villa's uprising to the French Revolution, he says: "In the same way that long record of injustice can be washed out only by blood; and Villa, a peon himself, is merely the instrument of fate" (490). For such reasons—his Indian and lower class status, and his standing as only such an instrument—Villa was also seen as an unreliable ally; war correspondents typically reminded their readers that one assassin's bullet would bring anarchy in its wake.[19]

As dominant as the plots of these lectures were, it would be misleading to represent their contours—or their context—as static or fully determinative. Villa's physical stature, or even the label of "savage," for instance, was convertible to suggest brute heroism, noble savagery, or uncanny military instinct. Similarly convertible was Villa's standing as bandit: even the *New York Times*, before long, took to labeling him the Robin Hood of Mexico.[20] Meanwhile, American policy itself, now under Woodrow Wilson, vacillated, misrepresented its aims, and repeatedly shifted its support in midstream. The Wilson administration's desire (expressed through its *own* lectures) that "no one shall take advantage of Mexico" (RR, 176) after Díaz was deposed—the "noninterference" policy of "watchful waiting," "legalism" (regarding U.S. property), and nonrecognition of Huerta—concealed an extensive pattern of threatening, confidential agents, and geopolitical chess-playing, including the revoking of an arms embargo on Venustiano Carranza's behalf in February 1914, backing Villa by August, then turning back to Carranza.[21] If Carranza's "Constitutionalist" banner implicitly appealed to Wilsonianism, Villa's military victories, and the sheer size of his following, only appetized the conventional tastes of both interventionist liberals and camp-following correspondents—where political legitimacy was assumed to follow from military success.

The redistribution of Villa, therefore, was not executed only by American power liberals, though they led the way. Republican Rooseveltians cast him in the plot of a muckraking novel, with the plutocracy created by monopolistic American investment abroad as his antagonist. Mason, for instance, grew to distrust both the Mexican *arrivistes* and the American plutocracy they mimicked; his reports on Villa, which began with the racist dismissals cited above, shifted to endorsement in a few months. Now, Mason wrote that "[i]t must be admitted that the hatred of foreigners, and of Americans in particular, . . . is largely justified. A good many of the Americans here are the sort we do not want in America— plutocratic privilege-seekers or third-class mining-camp riffraff," all lost in a "morass of materialism." "To a large extent," Mason now wrote, "the people are only getting back what has been taken from them." Villa's distrust of military pomp also subverted the aristomilitary role drafted for him. George Marvin saw that the "authority [Villa] exercises is not artificial, a thing of titles and shoulder straps"; he could, Marvin said, be "a good deal more calm and mature in the crisis than some peace lovers north of the border." Again, one should not mistake these reporters as endorsing Villa's own goals. Yet in retrospect it is striking how *many* correspondents—Mason, Marvin, Whitaker, Edward Gibbons of the Chicago

Tribune, and of course John Reed—were, over time, drawn to Villa's possibilities, even if it meant dissenting from both American policy and their
editors' views.[22]

The interpretive grid American reporters brought to Mexico encountered a peasant leader, Francisco Villa, remarkably adept at news management; tellingly, *Insurgent Mexico* is one of the better accounts of this
encounter. If the book portrays Villa as indifferent or at best amused
by correspondents (75)—and implicitly excepts Reed himself—in fact, it
also shows Villa demonstrating marked skills in the "sly civility" of news
management, particularly by exploiting the camp-following habits of reporters, Reed included. Sensing that reporting might be a vehicle for his
own pitch to American audiences, Villa let Reed interview and accompany him repeatedly and issued a blanket safe-conduct, telegraph, and
reporting pass (still extant) for Reed's entire stay (190). Meanwhile Villa
established a special correspondents' train, conducted tours of his famous
hospital boxcar, and used the very symbol of border modernization (the
rail line) to control reporters' access to battle. To the horror of the *Times*
(in part to finance his operations without foreign assistance) Villa even
hired a film crew to record his exploits, a fact Reed mentions (193). Villa
had a train car painted, in Spanish, "The Chicago *Tribune*—Special Correspondent" while Edward Gibbons traveled with him.[23] The trajectory of
Insurgent Mexico itself reflects similar control. After being four days away
from a telegraph (63) in its early sections, Reed's narrative is soon contained *within* the linear railroad assault line of Villa. In one battle, Reed
is even forced to imagine the front (201) because he is kept from actually
witnessing it.

Armed with these logistics, Villa himself contributed to his increasingly romantic portraiture north of the border. If Reed pictures himself
as a "musketeer" (59), Villa had read Dumas in prison and "found great
consolation" in him. "Pancho Villa" was, after all, an outlaw's name he
(Doreteo Arango) had adopted from Mexican folk history. In addition,
Villa also reflected back Americans' bodily surveillance by dubbing (114)
Reed *chatito* (pug nose) and Mason *el largo* for his long legs; in another
moment, he wittily compared Reed to a lost donkey (205).[24] Reed, like
many observers, also saw the cautious and self-protective side of this guerilla leader who, unlike the passionate "Latin," avoided excessive drink
(110), and often slept away from camp so as to keep strategy to himself
until the last moment (99).

Villa likewise toyed with above-border placements by alternately honoring and then debunking aristomilitary codes handed down. Demonstrating his understanding of war correspondents' advance guard potential, in one instance he accused Reed's questions of trying to foment discord with Carranza—an accusation which had its effect—and promised to spank Reed (thereby reversing the typical infantilization) and send him back to the border (114). (As American reporters will, Reed kept asking Villa if he wanted to be president.) In Reed's account,[25] Villa the guerilla leader finds those *Rules of Land Warfare* hopelessly hypocritical (118). Comic, confrontational, and engaging all at once, Villa is experimental when it comes to military governance, reveres education (105), and scorns the pomp and circumstance of aristocratic military culture. Given a medal by Maderista officers, Villa scratches and yawns, "with some intense interior amusement, like a small boy in church" (96), then causes "the bubble of Empire" to be "pricked then and there with a great shout of laughter," pledging his "heart" to the revolution (97).

These sides to Villa were hardly Reed's incarnation: Villa's followers affirmed many of the details above in oral testimony and memoirs.[26] In one account, reconstructed by lawyer and aide-de-camp Martín Luis Guzmán as Villa's fictional autobiography, we see traces of the representation Villa and his followers may have hoped to re-interject, surely in its own domesticated and ambivalent forms, into American reporting. Furthermore, in the parts of interpolated narrative explicitly *un*changed from contemporary interviews, Villa does not come across as anything like a folk hero; rather, he presents himself as a peon become military man.[27] Villa emerges, in fact, as a man who admires the charity of the rich (38) and recalls that, while in prison, he had taught himself how to type and keep books, planning eventually to make good in business (79). Villa's class identifications aside, what also emerges is his tendency to reconstruct incidents of betrayed trust or nondeferential treatment as contexts or pretexts for political, personal, or military action. Starting with a family insult that led to his life as a bandit, then covering his time in a Del Verde mine (14), Villa continually emphasizes instances of personal abuse, like a landlord who harassed the sweetheart of a man he had exiled to the army (18). That is, Villa talks (literally, since these parts of the text were dictated in the 1910s) not so much of exploitation as of persecution, seduction, or humiliation (21). And Villa's deep respect for authority was matched only by his willingness to avenge himself upon its lapses.[28]

This paradox—which allowed Villa the revolutionary's skill of substituting his own authority for others'—is exemplified in Guzmán's recollection of Villa's comments on the Catholic church and the obligations of a godfather:

> "*Señor*, to contract the duties of godfather does not imply recognizing any laws in this world or any other. Men are compadres by virtue of the bonds of friendship and custom . . . because the duties that unite us with our fellowmen require it. . . . Most so-called religious men use religion to promote their own interests, not the things they preach, and so there are good priests and bad priests, and we must accept some and help them and prosecute and annihilate others. . . . I think they [for example, the Jesuits] deserve greater punishment than the worst bandits in the world, for the bandits to not deceive others in their conduct or pretend to be what they are not, while the Jesuits do, and by this deception they work very great hardships on the people." (284–85)

Naturally, this invocation of custom over doctrine, reversing the positions of law and bandit, easily blurred personal vendetta, insults to honor, and political rebellion. If more mundane than the Robin Hood superimposition, it did propose to "leverage up" a history of grievance from daily life. Recent revisionist scholarship of the broader revolution has in fact emphasized this connection. This was not so much an insurgency without a dominant ideological or doctrinal platform, as one in which the operative vocabularies converged local, familial, personal, and moral concerns. Mexican peasant rebellions consequently visualized their political future in *retrospective* terms harking back to a mythic "Golden era" which residually drew upon the interdependence of rural communities, military colonies, and banditry.[29] In both domesticated and annihilating manifestations, shepherded by Villa's own news management, traces of this moralistic, erratic, but still-vibrant golden era contested the exotic structure governing *Insurgent Mexico*.

At first reading, *Insurgent Mexico*'s Pancho Villa can easily seem little more than the intuitive poet/warrior figure envisioned in Reed's Harvard poetry and fiction; the book is in fact dedicated to Reed's Cambridge instructor and his injunction to "see the hidden beauty of the visible world." Reed's text seems to immerse itself in the exotic, referring to the "mask-like faces" (98) of Indians and their "stoicism" (150), to Villa as the "Mexican Robin Hood" (99), and to his generals as "superb" animals. Simple, premodern beings (114) "prior" to "civilization" (102), Mexicans are presented as "pure race" and without racism (235) themselves.[30] Like his peers, Reed presents the revolution as a medieval struggle, cleansing Mexican society of foreign actors and geopolitical intrigue; the harsh facts of modern economic life (vague references to "certain foreigners"

[244], Singer sewing machines [23], and the like) are kept sub rosa, as if keyed only to readers in the American left intelligentsia, but not to Reed's *World* audience. In Reed's exotic locale of "red porphyry mountains" or a "turquoise cup of sky" holding "an orange powder of clouds" (22), we might hardly recognize that, by some estimates, Americans owned, by 1910, over 40 percent of Mexican land (and other foreigners nearly another 25 percent), and well over half of silver, lead, and copper mines, oil, and rubber production.[31] Instead, Reed presents Mexico as an occasion for a contrapuntal "testing" in battle and a more pacific loss of self in the landscape. A "peace beyond anything I ever felt, wrapped me around," he writes. "It is almost impossible to get objective about the desert, you sink into it—become part of it" (37). "It is impossible to imagine how close to nature the peons live on these great haciendas," he adds. "Their very houses are built of the earth upon which they stand, baked by the sun. Their food is the corn they grow; their drink the water from the dwindled river, carried painfully upon their heads." But love runs freely, and "jealousy is a stabbing matter" (34). Understandably, most have read such passages—accentuated especially in the book's finale, "Mexican Nights"—as being as much about Reed's own romantic suppositions as the political context at hand.

Yet in truth, this more pacific zone only emerges because aristomilitary romance is in ruins early in the book, a transformation best signified by Reed's loss of coat and camera (76) in a life-threatening retreat. After this humiliating baptism, Reed's persona and practice deviated more decisively from conventional war correspondence idioms. During that retreat, he mocks the "unreal" feeling of being "Richard Harding Davis" having "an experience" and later utterly dismisses "soldiers of fortune" (128–29) as mercenary grandstanders. Likewise, Reed subsequently prefers folklore about Villa to American news reports, since the latter he deemed "prejudiced" (98–99); he presents class war as existing below and *above* the border (41); he portrays most of his fellow correspondents as a band of cowardly, jingoistic braggarts (207). In addition, Reed seems to chafe under Villa's tether: most at home with *la Tropa* in the book's early sections, even when Reed reports Torreon—the scoop he is credited with—he writes that long battles are "the most boring thing in the world" (202). As if resisting his profession's conventions and Villa's own plotting, *Insurgent Mexico*'s final sections mark a noticeable turn: accounts of looting by Villa's army (204); a discouraging interview with a nearly senile Carranza; and then "Mexican Nights," three community portraits far removed from battle.

Along the way, Reed's strategy shifts. While most reporters were interested in troop counts, Reed translates interviews with peons, and hardly infantilizes their commitment to battle. Rather, if most correspondents habitually detached Mexican words from intentions, Reed restores them. In particular, where Mason heard only "nonsense" songs and "Mother Goose" ditties, Reed's notebooks show that—drawing upon his Harvard training—he collected and translated Mexican *corridos*, which scholars like Américo Paredes and Ramón Saldívar have theorized presented an epic, transpersonal, and counterhegemonic narrative of communal resistance to imperial power. (In one, for instance—reversing the iconography of a Richard Harding Davis—the bull is the federal army and the matador is the constitutionalist army [53].) Indeed, if we reread Reed's exoticism in these lights, we see that it too begins to argue a covert case about peon resistance. When he raptuously writes "[i]t was a land to love—this Mexico—and a land to fight for" (53), he means to invoke a time-honored, if-too-unconscious loyalty on the part of the peon that takes the place of ideology and "political theory" (the words he uses, rather mockingly, in the very ending lines [256] of *Insurgent Mexico* itself). In fact, Reed theorized the power of the ballad form itself in precisely this manner: to work in a "diastole and systole" motion which called up unseen loyalties of a dispossessed heart.[32] Even Mexican days and "Nights" are figured contrapuntally, as oscillating "returns" to native "professions" (e.g., as vaqueros) (43) or festivities in the midst of battle. And in moving beyond the customary radius of "camp following," in turning to villages and haciendas, Reed is in fact *not* looking at "premodern" peasants, but peons close to the land because it has been returned to them *after* redispossession in the revolution. Reed presents the land, that is, as a lost precious object peons deserve to recover—a desire which provokes a combination of sporadic violence, sadness, despair, and even rebellion; it is an eternal, nearly hieroglyphic essence beneath the "visible" conflict which the revolution surfaces.[33] Thus, unlike his colleagues, Reed recognized the vital importance of how Villa carried out local governance in Chihuahua *during* the fighting—expropriating large haciendas, printing money, lowering food prices, establishing war relief and credit for peasants.[34] Villa personifies this reciprocal code: honoring his debts (101), remaining loyal to a fault (e.g., to a brutal lieutenant), pausing for the funeral of a fellow fighter (113).

In a way Reed's guerrilla or radical image belies, *Insurgent Mexico* is ultimately constructed much like a fragile, even elegiac, but highly strategic pastoral, playing off battle and desires for peace. This balance is built around Villa's *persona* but not confined to it. At the close of the section (II) bearing his name, Villa's dream—putatively, to disband his army, retire, and live in an industrial colony with his *compañeros*, and run a farm on the side—is given a one-page, quite lyrical coda, and is the pinnacle of the book (120). Villa the military man is turned good shepherd (and not unimportantly, Good Neighbor). Perhaps reading back from Villa's own mockery of aristomilitary conventions, Reed may have recognized that valorizing Villa as a military strategist alone might only have enhanced border anxieties or interventionist plots; similarly, conventional exoticism only appetized Wilsonian stewardship (and continued American exploitation). Thus the balancing act: while *Insurgent Mexico* certainly reverses the conventional field and praises Mexican bravery and honesty—and can hardly be said to soft-peddle Villa's brutality—quite a bit of emphasis also falls on *pacific* virtues: on a people who recite Benito Juarez's "[p]eace is the respect for the rights of others" (40), on *pacíficos* and troops who know war's fickleness all too well, even on revolutionaries who will probably do little more than scale down a customary rate of profit (233). That Reed's pastoralizing *was* strategic is suggested by several additional facts: Reed's delaying (as if answering Villa's charge) of the Carranza interview (section V), which virtually predicted the falling out with Villa; his excision of German and British interests, often the objects of U.S. anxiety; the fact that his *corridos*, contrary to custom, rarely antagonize the United States.[35]

Indeed, the final shaping of *Insurgent Mexico*—first a sketch at the border, then travels with *la Tropa* (I), through Villa (II), the battle train (III), and Mexican back lines (IV), to the Carranza interview (V), to three portraits of Mexican villages (VI)—is by and large a movement *back* in actual and mythic time, away from geopolitics and literally into the hills.[36] The book closes in a chapter called "Los Pastores," referring to a *pastorella* (miracle play) Reed witnessed. Reed opens with an exotic yet resisting landscape again, a *serrano* village:

> The romance of gold hangs over the mountains of northern Durango like an old perfume. There, it is rumored, was that mythical Ophir when the Aztecs and their mysterious predecessors drew the red gold that Cortez found in the treasury of Montezuma. Before the dawn of Mexican history the Indians scratched these barren hillsides with dull copper knives. You can still see traces of their workings. And after them, the Spaniards . . . a tiny colorful fringe of the most brilliant civilization in Europe flung itself among the canyons and high peaks of this desolate land. . . . The Spaniards enslaved the Indians of the region; . . . the Spanish overseers lived like princes.

> But they were a hardy race, these mountaineers. They were always re-belling. There is a legend of how the Spaniards . . . two hundred leagues from the seacoast, in the midst of an overwhelmingly hostile native race, attempted one night to leave the mountains. Fires sprang up on the high peaks, and the mountain villages throbbed to the sound of drums. Somewhere in the narrow defiles the Spaniards disappeared forever. And from that time, until certain foreigners secured mining concessions there, the place had an evil name. The authority of the Mexican government barely reached it. (244)[37]

But if "[h]ere is romance for you" (245), Reed also interjects that his villagers have little respect for the lost "traditions" of the *Conquistadores* (245); the play itself, supposed to be dramatized in the house of a rich man, is shifted instead to the adobe of a widow and peon. There, following the traditional plot, we hear of a shepherd couple, Arcadio and Laura, and a community divided by the deposed Satan's temptation of riches and power on the peaceful eve of the Christ child's arrival. Satan is dressed, fittingly, in the regalia of a Roman legionary (250). As if surfacing a hieroglyphic trace of Villa's own history, the play also shows a rich man who, paralleling Satan, unsuccessfully tries to tempt the young wife away from her shepherd by dwelling upon his poverty (251). The tempter is immediately recognized, by an audience prone to literalizing and personalizing (246), as *Huertista* (250). The *pastorella* is thus the pastoral counterforce to the more resisting *corrido*: Villa's pacific dream extends itself while Villa himself—the warrior—disappears; in his place arises a vision liable to subvert the border by suggesting which was the "Christian" nation in this struggle. In each of the final chapters, in fact, pacific virtues counterpoint insurgent ones—and the spirit evoked is not so much a "future" as a past of vacillating peace and violence. A battle report interrupts the play, but only for a moment (256).[38]

My point, therefore, is not that Reed's microcosmic portraits of these communities, interweaving stories of personal loyalty, grievances, and erratic honoring of rules—indeed very much threads within the unstable fabric of Villa's insurgency—were perfectly congruent with it (or, to use my initial pun, "corresponding"). Reed's revolution suppressed the non-agrarian, middle- and upper-class, *ranchero*, and intellectual elements; he made peon class-consciousness a form of unconsciousness, a ploy a longer look at, say, Emiliano Zapata would have contradicted. Nor was the "great moral" (246) of the *pastorella* equivalent to the "bonds of friendship and custom" Villa so pragmatically deployed *against* the *curas* (priests).[39] But if Reed's account was hardly documentarian and hardly nonpartisan, it was also not exempt from Villa's fashioning and the material conditions of the revolution itself. In fact, the policy context may put the text's internal contestations in perspective. *Insurgent Mexico* offered, in essence, a quite *strategic* pastoral—indeed, given Villa's own immediate policy goals, to a degree it offered itself as a propositionally *bilateral* text, a momentary flanking movement which challenged both the interventionist pincer fantasies and the "watchful waiting" of Wilsonian liberalism. Exported within persisting conventions of war correspondence, power and constitutional mimicry were, respectively, the presiding political and diplomatic litmus tests for Villa's legitimacy—standards which Reed and Villa both felt, if American interference ensued, would bring the revolution to an end. The book's final underscoring of the localized collectivity of village culture also countermanded the U.S. media's recurring tendency to anoint a singular (bourgeois) Moses—in this case, Carranza—to lead his people to the promised values of the United States.[40]

However, as a news narrative in the pastoral mode contested from without and within, *Insurgent Mexico* provided at best a temporary stay. Wilson was indeed briefly swayed to the camp of Villa—who himself would welcome American troops when they occupied Vera Cruz—yet the United States soon abandoned him. Reed, assumed to have gone "native" and lost the "objectivity" his Harvard classmate Walter Lippmann would soon advocate, was to be lectured *by* the president during what was supposed to be an interview. Most correspondents themselves soon were off to Europe, Reed to the other end of the class war in Colorado. And while the United States proceeded under the banner of Wilsonian nonintervention, in truth an interventionist plan, not unlike George Marvin's fantasy, soon took hold: the troops of Carranza, now to U.S. eyes the true "constitutionalist," were allowed by Wilson to cross the border at Eagle Pass, traverse Texas, New Mexico, and Arizona, and defeat Villa's wing in April 1915. After Villa's troops ransacked American border towns in revenge, a dead line was drawn in the middle of El Paso, separating Mexicans and Americans "till things quieted down." Villa was a bandit again for the infamous Punitive Expedition of General Pershing, and a "Brown Scare" ensued in Texas.[41] But however much we issue our own constitutional edicts, change the rules, or police "our" beat, reports of Villa and other bandits will continue, no doubt, to taunt the border.

Notes

The author would like to thank Vicente Diaz, Wai-chee Dimock, Richard Fox, Amy Kaplan, José David Saldívar, Jenny Sharpe, Adrian Trotman, and John Tutino for their reactions to earlier versions of this essay.

1 On "Central America," see Richard Harding Davis, *Three Gringos in Venezuela and Central America* (New York: Harper & Bros, 1903), esp. 145–48. On "lower regions" see N. C. Adossides, "Pancho Villa, Man and Soldier," *Review of Reviews* 49 (May 1914): 566–73; George Mason, "Going South with Carranza," *Outlook* 107 (May 2, 1914): 25.

2 In a contemporary version—U.S. War Department, Office of the Chief of Staff, *Rules of Land Warfare* (Washington: Government Printing Office, 1914)—the American military set forth rules governing "acceptable" armaments, the limits of military necessity in war, responsibilities to prisoners of war and civilians, and the like. One principle behind the "Unwritten Rules" of combat was "the principle of chivalry, which demands a certain amount of fairness in offense and defense" (13). Uniforms were required for belligerents; assassination and acts of revenge were ruled "criminal," not military, action.

3 George Marvin, "Villa," *World's Work* 28 (July 1914): 269–84; poem and caption, p. 272. For typical contemporary commentary, see Arthur Wallace Dunn, "Uncle Sam on Police Duty," *Review of Reviews* 43 (April 1911): 462–65; "Is Intervention Near?" *Review of Reviews* 49 (February 1914): 150; "The Mexican Chaos: A Poll of the Press," *Outlook* 103 (March 1, 1913): 473–76; *New York Times* editorials from: December 11, 1913, 10: 4; December 20, 1913, 12: 1; January 8, 1914, 10: 5; March 23, 1914, 10: 4; "Our Duty to Mexico," *The Nation* 96 (February 27, 1913): 196; "Prospects for Peace," *Independent* 78 (June 8, 1914): 439; "Villa, Bandit and Brute, May Be Mexican President," *New York Times*, December 14, 1913, 6, 3:1; "What Mexico Lacks," *Review of Reviews* 43 (April 1911): 403; "What Will Villa Do?" *Review of Reviews* 49 (February 1914): 152. For a defense of Mexican economic development, see Caspar Whitney, *What's the Matter with Mexico* (New York: Macmillan, 1916). Cf. also Nell Irvin Painter, *Standing at Armageddon* (New York: W.W. Norton, 1987). "Speak softly, and carry a big stick," of course, referred to "police actions," inspired by Roosevelt's tenure as New York City police commissioner.

4 Cf. Benita Parry, "Problems in Current Theories of Colonial Discourse," *Oxford Literary Review* 9 (1978): 35. "Unmanly" from Mary Sue Mander, "Pen and Sword: A Cultural History of the American War Correspondent, 1895–1945," University Microfilms, 1979, p. 32; Michael Herr, *Dispatches* (New York: Avon Books, 1978), p. 187 ff. "Outpost" iconography of dateline from Daniel C. Hallin, "Cartography, Community, and the Cold War" in Michael Schudson et al., *Reading the News* (New York: Pantheon, 1986), pp. 109–45. One *New York Times* correspondent was hardly atypical when, after interviewing Pancho Villa, he said he rode North and "back into civilization again." E. Alexander Powell, "A Visit to the Bandit-General Pancho Villa," *New York Times*, March 29, 1914, 6, 1:1. On "realism" in foreign policy see, for instance, Robert Dallek, *The American Style of Foreign Policy* (New York: Knopf, 1983), p. 34 ff.

5 Cited throughout is John Reed, *Insurgent Mexico* (New York: Penguin, 1983). The best reconstruction of this chronology is to be found in Robert A. Rosenstone's fine biography, *Romantic Revolutionary* (New York: Vintage Books, 1981), pp. 150–57. Hereinafter cited as "RR." On ethnographic authority, see James Clifford, *The Predicament of Culture* (Cambridge: Harvard University Press, 1988), esp. pp. 21–54. Gayatri Chavravorty Spivak's reservations about "dialogue," which Clifford calls a "constructive negotiation" between "conscious, politically significant subjects" (41), arise in *The Post-Colonial Critic: Interviews, Strategies, Dialogues*, ed. Sarah Harasym (New York: Routledge, 1990), p. 142. Contrast Edward Said, *Covering Islam* (New York: Pantheon, 1981), p. 142.

6 I have discussed Reed's Harvard work in my "Broadway Nights: John Reed and the City," *Prospects* (1989), pp. 273–94. One Harvard tale recounts the experience of an Egyptian priest who raises mowers, brickmakers, and meatsellers against a Pharoah. When the governor flees through the desert, he encounters the spirit of the insurgency—a song, Reed wrote, "Egypt had been trying to crush for a hundred moons." "The Pharaoh," *Harvard Monthly* 47 (January 1909): 156–60.

7 This emphasis probably began with Walter Lippmann's early praise, discussed in RR, pp. 166–67, and George Mason, "Reed, Villa, and the Village," *Outlook* 140 (May 6, 1925): 1–2. Since then Rosenstone's reading has dominated. See, for instance, David C. Duke, *John Reed* (Boston: Twayne, 1987), pp. 84–88; and Jim Tuck, *Pancho Villa and John Reed: Two Faces of Romantic Revolution* (Tucson: University of Arizona Press, 1984). See also Mexican journalist Renato Leduc's praise of Reed as a "master guerilla journalist" whose spirit was "forged" in these months in the (New York: International Publishers, 1969) edition of *IM*, pp. 17 and 25–27, and Adolfo Gilly, *The Mexican Revolution* (London: Verso, 1983), trans. Patrick Camiller. Cf. Chris Bongie, *Exotic Memories: Literature, Colonialism, and the Fin de Siecle* (Stanford: Stanford University Press, 1991), esp. pp. 1–32; Amy Kaplan, "Romancing the Empire," *American Literary History* 2 (Winter 1990): 659–89.

8 Among the few exceptions to this rule is Mander's work; on recent foreign correspondence, see also Mort Rosenblum, *Coups and Earthquakes: Reporting the World for America* (New York: Harper & Row, 1979). "Itinerary" from Spivak, p. 31.

9 For a critique of discourse analysis, see Parry, pp. 27–58; Alan Knight, *The Mexican Revolution*, 2 vols. (Cambridge: Cambridge University Press, 1986), esp. p. 163. Todd Gitlin in "News as Ideology and Contested Area: Toward a Theory of Hegemony, Crisis, and Opposition," *Socialist Review* 48 (November–December 1979): 11–54, later developed in *The Whole World is Watching* (Berkeley: University of California Press, 1980). See also David C. Bailey, "Revisionism and the Recent Historiography of the Mexican Revolution," *Hispanic American Historical Review* 58 (1978): 62–79, and W. Dirk Raat, *The Mexican Revolution: An Annotated Guide to Recent Scholarship* (Boston: G.K. Hall, 1982), xxiii–xxxviii. "Fable of rapport," "encounter," and "indigenous control" from Clifford, pp. 40–45.

10 As Jenny Sharpe has pointed out, proposals to recuperate "native" voices run the risk of reproducing the "ideological effect" (139) of colonialism itself through substituting the "educated colonial for the native as such." "Figures of Colonial Resistance," *Modern Fiction Studies* 35 (Spring 1989): 137–55.

11 Parry, p. 36. The idea that sources "make" news is commonplace within news criticism; see, for instance, Leon V. Sigal, "Sources Make the News," in Schudson, pp. 9–37. Compare Gitlin's notion of "contested" news space with Homi K. Bhabha's notion of the "splitting" and "agonistic" character to colonial power in "Signs Taken for Wonders: Questions of Ambivalence and Authority under a Tree Outside Delhi, May 1817," *Critical Inquiry* 12 (Autumn 1985): 144–65.

12 On idea of illustrated lectures, see the Gitlin essay, pp. 24 and 39. Jacob Riis, of course, compared himself to a war correspondent, implicitly in a holy war against "Street Arabs" and others: see *How the Other Half Lives* (New York: Dover, 1971), p. 61; Julian Ralph, *The Making of a Journalist* (New York: Harpers, 1903), pp. 23, 114, 115; *"en safari"* from Julius Chambers, *News Hunting on Three Continents* (London: John Lane, 1922), p. 141; Richard Harding Davis, *A Year from a Reporter's Notebook* (New York: Harper & Bros, 1898), pp. 97–134. Stanley explicitly mentioned in Richard Harding Davis, "The Work of a War Correspondent," *Outlook* 103 (March 29, 1913): 716–18. On stewardship, see Davis, *Three Gringos*, 147–48. On the Cuban figure, Davis in *Notebook*, p. 106; on Grant, Joseph Rogers Taylor, "'Pancho' Villa at First Hand," *The World's Work* 28 (July 1914): 267. Cf. Kaplan, pp. 664–65.

13 Here and throughout, for the notion of news writing as a "social practice," I have relied on Raymond Williams, *Marxism and Literature* (New York: Oxford, 1977), pp. 87, 158 ff. Term "parachute journalism" from Rosenblum, p. 11 and ff. On "camp following," see Phillip Knightley, *The First Casualty* (New York: Harcourt Brace Jovanovich, 1975), pp. 3–64, and Joseph J. Matthews, *Reporting the Wars* (Minneapolis: University of Minnesota Press, 1957), pp. 51–78. See also Thomas Millard, "The War Correspondent and His Future," *Scribner's* 37 (February 1905): 242–48, and Richard Harding Davis, "The War Correspondent," *Collier's* 48 (October 7, 1911): 21–22, 30. Tellingly, when Richard Harding Davis criticized censorship, he in fact pressed not for greater autonomy, but greater *integration* of war correspondents into war efforts, even arguing that correspondents be bivouacked with junior officers (Davis, *Collier's*, p. 30).

14 Dictator Porfirio Díaz had ruled Mexico for thirty-five years before resigning in 1911; his successor, Francisco Madero, had been executed by General Victoriano Huerta in a coup that sparked the revolution's "second" phase—led by Villa in the North, Emiliano Zapata in South, and Coahuila governor Venustiano Carranza, who named himself "first chief" of the rebellion. On its diverse social base, see esp. John Tutino, *From Insurrection to Revolution in Mexico* (Princeton: Princeton University Press, 1986), pp. 299–301; Knight, esp. 78–170; and on the political scene, Friedrich Katz, *The Secret War in Mexico* (Chicago: University of Chicago Press, 1981).

15 An interesting exception to the general focus on camp following was a woman reporter who wrote on refugees: Alice M. Williamson, "My Attempt to Be a War Correspondent," *McClure's* 43 (September 1914): 66–76.

16 This is often overlooked in accounts of the so-called Roosevelt Corollary to the Monroe Doctrine: in the nineteenth century, "most arrests occured as the result of police initiative, or, in other words, there was no complainant pressing the police to action." Eric H. Monkkonen, *Police in Urban America, 1860–1920* (Cambridge: Cambridge University Press, 1981), p. 103.

17 Quotations from *New York Times* editorial, "Villa, Bandit and Brute, May Be Mexican President," December 14, 1913, 6, 3:1; Powell, *passim;* "cattle thieves" from Davis, "When a War," p. 43; on "unmoral" state, see Taylor, p. 266. Anglo-Saxon blood cited in "What Mexico Lacks," p. 403; compare Davis, *Three Gringos,* p. 143. Reed, by contrast to the *Times's* hero, presents a border sheriff who is mocked as a faithful Owen Wister reader (17). Mason's reporting ran in a series: "The Army of Protection," *Outlook* 107 (July 18, 1914): 651–54; "Campaigning in Coahuila," *Outlook* 107 (June 20, 1914): 391–97; "Going South" and "The Mexican Man of the Hour," *Outlook* 107 (June 6, 1914): 292–306; "With Villa in Chihuahua," *Outlook* 107 (May 9, 1914): 74–78. See also his "Reed, Villa," pp. 1–2.

18 Mañana from Herbert Whitaker, "Villa—Bandit—Patriot," *Independent* 78 (June 8, 1914): 450. On the Edmonds flap, see Marvin, pp. 272–75. "Picnic" from "Childish Conquerors," p. 488; "unseeing" patriotism from "Going South," p. 23. On fighters, see "Mexican Man of the Hour," p. 302, or Whitaker, p. 490. See also "A Survivor from the Middle Ages," *New York Times,* March 23, 1914, 10: 4; scavenger image in Adossides, p. 567; on precious Mexico, see Davis, "When a War," p. 52, and Charles Macomb Flandrau, *Viva Mexico!* (New York: Appleton, 1914). On the mule image, see Richard Harding Davis, "When a War Is Not a War," *Scribner's* 56 (July 1914): 41–52.

19 "Cyclonic passion" from Whitaker, "Villa—Bandit—Patriot," p. 451; "shifting sand" and "desert cactus" from Whitaker, "Childish Conquerers," p. 490. For comparisons to revolutions of the Middle Ages, see Whitaker, "Childish Conquerers," p. 490, and Davis, "When A War," p. 52—where the "scavenger" and bullfight images also appear. On unreliability, see Mason, "Man of the Hour," p. 305, and Whitaker, "Villa—Bandit—Patriot," p. 452.

20 See Painter, pp. 289–91, and "Survivor from the Middle Ages," p. 4. One American border official did see Villa rob the rich and give to the poor: see the testimony of Clifford A. Perkins in Oscar J. Martínez, *Fragments of the Mexican Revolution: Personal Accounts from the Border* (Albuquerque: University of New Mexico Press, 1983), 112–13.

21 Even Wilson's ardent supporters have long acknowledged this failure of U.S. policy. See, for instance, Arthur S. Link, *Woodrow Wilson and the Progressive Era, 1910–1917* (New York: Harper and Row, 1954), pp. 107–44; contrast W. Dirk Raat, *Revoltosos: Mexico's Rebels in the United States, 1900–1923* (College Station: Texas A & M Press, 1981), pp. 253–69.

22 Mason, "Going South," p. 24; "With Villa," p. 75; "Going South," p. 23; Marvin, p. 276. Mason opposed *intervention* when the *Outlook* itself, under T. R.'s influence, came to favor *occupation;* Mason then turned to favoring Villa's dictatorship. On the *Outlook*'s stands, see v. 107 (July 11, 1914): 585–86; Mason in "Mexican Man of the Hour," p. 306, and "Campaigning," pp. 392–97. See also Floyd Gibbons, *Floyd Gibbons: Your Headline Hunter* (New York: Exposition Press, 1953), p. 55.

23 Whitaker in "Villa—Bandit—Patriot" depicts Villa as welcoming correspondents with him, so as to explain his views (452). Reed's pass is still in the John Reed Manuscripts, Houghton Library, Harvard University. Friedrich Katz points out this important distinction from Carranza's strategy, which was not to confiscate estates and to shift the burden of the financing the Revolution to foreign interests. "Villa: Reform Governor of Chihuahua," in *Essays on the Mexican Revolution,* ed. George Wolfskill and Douglas W. Richmond (Austin: University of Texas Press, 1979), p. 38. On the film crew, see the *New York Times* editorial, January 8, 1913, 10:5. Gibbons, pp. 55–57.

24 Martín Luis Guzmán, *Memoirs of Pancho Villa,* trans. Virginia H. Taylor (Austin: University of Texas Press, 1965), p. 79 ff. All further citations in text. "*El largo*" cited in Mason, "Campaigning," p. 397.

25 Not in others; compare Reed's account with that of Marvin, p. 272.

26 On mimicry, see Bhabha, p. 152. On Villa's passion for schools, see the interview of Dr. Alfonso de Gorari in Martínez, pp. 62–64; the testimony of Villa's widow, Soledad Seanez, in Jessie Peterson and Thelma Cox Knoles, eds., *Pancho Villa: Intimate Recollections by People Who Knew Him* (New York: Hastings House, 1977), pp. 249–58; and Carl A. Beers, in Peterson, pp. 259–66.

27 To a degree, this account compares with what John Beverly and others have called the *testimonio,* where "the relation of narrator and compiler in the production of a *testimonio* can function as an ideological figure or *ideologeme* for the possibility of a union of a radicalized intelligentsia and the poor and working classes of a country" (19). Beverly, "The Margin at the Center: On *Testimonio* (Testimonial Narrative)," *Modern Fiction Studies* 35 (Spring 1989): 11–28. See, however, Guzmán's comments on Villa, xii.

28 This character trait is the kernel of the larger trope of the memoir, the turning against his *jefe* (chief) Carranza—which the chief provoked; compare Guzmán, p. 98 ff, and Katz, *Secret War,* pp. 260–65. See Guzmán's comments on his reconstructions, ix–xi.

29 On this ethos, see Knight, pp. 158–63.

30 Cf. Wilson, "Broadway Nights," pp. 276–77. *Insurgent Mexico* says nothing, for instance, about Villa's persecution of Mexico's Chinese. For but one example, see, in Peterson, the interview with Cleofas Culleros, pp. 33–34.

31 Cf. Painter, pp. 284–85. That Reed knew is evident in his "What About Mexico," *The Masses* (June 1914), reprinted in *John Reed for the Masses,* ed. James C. Wilson (Jefferson, N. C.: McFarland, 1987), pp. 79–94.

32 Typescripts, apparently translations, are in the Harvard Collection. As to why Villa's peons fought, compare Reed's account with the interviews with Pedro González (22) and Severo Márquez (48) in Martínez. For a good account of the *corrido*, see Ramón Saldívar, *Chicano Narrative* (Madison: University of Wisconsin Press, 1990), pp. 26–42; on Reed's thinking, see "Broadway Nights," pp. 276–77. Mother Goose in "Mexican Man of the Hour," p. 304.

33 See again, "What Mexico Wants," pp. 82 and 84, on this point about articulation; compare Knight, pp. 160–61.

34 Reed does (115) prematurely credit Villa's unfulfilled promise of sixty-two and one-half acres to every male citizen in Chihuahua State. On the limits to Villa's egalitarianism, see esp. Katz, "Villa," pp. 25–45, and *Secret War*, p. 140 ff.

35 The book version presents Carranza as removed from the "real" revolution (243) and dismissive of Villa as an "'ignorant peon'" (252). On the delay of this interview, see RR, p. 164. Contrast my reading with Katz, *Secret War*, p. 142 ff, and Reed's *corridos* with the account given by Saldívar, pp. 27–35.

36 Contrast RR, which portrays Reed as "loafing" in "peaceful, sleepy towns drowsing in the sun and the lingering romance of lost Spanish gold mines" where "peons live without politics in a world where no such word as war or revolution is spoken" (168). For a recent rendering of the *serrano* theory, see esp. Knight; contrast Katz, *Secret War*, pp. 144–45. This case, drawn from Eric Hobsbawm's *Primitive Rebels* (New York: Praeger, 1963), Reed anticipates in "The Mexican Tangle," *Masses*, June 1916, reprinted in Wilson, *John Reed for the Masses*, p. 106.

37 Cf. Villa's own account of the Spaniards in Guzmán, p. 106.

38 I have read two variants of this play: M. R. Cole, trans., *Los Pastores: A Mexican Play of the Nativity* (Boston and New York: American Folk-Lore Society, 1907), and George C. Barker, trans., *The Shepherd's Play of the Prodigal Son (Coloquio de pastores del hijo pródigo)* (Berkeley: University of California Press, 1953).

39 On Zapata, see Arturo Warman, "The Political Project of Zapatismo," trans. Judith Brister, ed. Friedrich Katz, *Riot, Rebellion, and Revolution* (Princeton: Princeton University Press, 1988), pp. 21–337. Reed himself would vacillate on who best represented the "masses"; at the end of his stay, he in fact pleaded with his editor to send him south to Zapata (RR, 163).

40 "What About Mexico," p. 84. For the comparison to Moses, see Whitaker, "Villa—Bandit—Patriot," p. 451.

41 On Reed and Woodrow Wilson, see RR, p. 169 ff.; on Reed's reporting of the Ludow Massacre, see RR, pp. 170–79. On the "dead line," see El Paso's Fink in Peterson, 57. For a personal account of Villa's bitterness, see the interview with Severo Márquez in Martínez, p. 50. On the "Brown Scare" in El Paso, see Mario Garcia, *Desert Immigrants* (New Haven: Yale University Press, 1981).

Colonizing Resistance or Resisting Colonization?

Walter Benn Michaels

Anti-Imperial Americanism

Nation or Empire?

homas Nelson Page's *Red Rock* was published in 1898, the year in which the United States annexed Hawaii, went to war in Cuba, seized the Philippines from Spain, and emerged as an imperial power. Needless to say, *Red Rock*, written the year before these events took place and written about events that had themselves taken place some thirty years earlier, is unconcerned with Cuba or the Philippines. But it is not unconcerned with American imperialism; indeed, American imperialism, and above all the resistance to it, is its main subject. *Red Rock* tells the story of a conquered people, of how they survived under occupation, and of how they eventually "reconquered" what it sometimes refers to as their "country" and sometimes as their "section." It is, in short, an anti-imperialist novel.

In the years immediately after its publication, a good many other similarly anti-imperialist novels appeared, most notably Thomas Dixon's *The Leopard's Spots* (1902) and *The Clansman* (1905).[1] Like *Red Rock*, they are set in the Reconstruction South and make no mention of Cuba or the Philippines.[2] But they are nevertheless importantly marked by the anti-imperialist arguments that had been invoked against McKinley, in particular by the description of the campaign in the Philippines as "a war of conquest" and by the claim that the president had no authority to "govern any person anywhere outside the constitution"[3]: "The constitution," insisted Chicago reformer Edwin Burritt Smith, "makes no provision for the forcible intervention by our government in the affairs of a people who do not form an integral part of our union." More important still, "To the extent we permit our chosen representatives to exercise arbitrary powers, *whether at home or abroad*, we allow them to sap and destroy representative government itself" (emphasis mine).[4] McKinley's commitment to governing the Philippines "without constitutional restraint" was thus seen as an attack not merely upon Filipino rights but upon American rights, upon "the very principles for the maintenance of which our fathers pledged their lives." Hence Lincoln, in *The Clansman*, asserting that his first postwar "duty is to reestablish the Constitution as our supreme law over every inch of our soil" (43), denies that the Civil War was "a war of conquest" (44)[5] and refuses to establish martial law or to enforce "Negro suffrage" in North Carolina: "The Constitution," he says, "grants to the National Government no power to regulate suffrage, and makes no provision for the control of 'conquered' provinces" (42). And hence his radical Republican enemy Stoneman (Thaddeus Stevens) wishes to make the "Negro" "the ruler" and condemns the Constitution as "the creation, both in letter and spirit, of the slaveholders of the South" (43).

Thus, although the major anti-imperialist literature of the turn of the century made no mention of the major imperialist adventures of the turn of the century, it did not fail to address the issues raised by those adventures. Rather it understood those issues as having essentially to do with the nature of American self-government and American citizenship. "Nation or Empire?" was the question posed by the anti-imperialists.[6] The return to Reconstruction for the answer to this question placed anti-imperialism at the heart of an emerging discourse of American national, racial, and, eventually, cultural identity. Texts like *Red Rock,* I will argue, sought to avoid the perils of empire by avoiding the perils of nationhood first; for Page and for the plantation tradition more generally, the South was a "Region" rather than a political entity. In *Red Rock,* no government can quite be legitimate, and this refusal of legitimacy is connected with a comparative indifference to racial identity (signaled by a feudal identification with the Indian) and an insistence on the importance of the family. For Progressives like Dixon, however, citizenship in the "new nation," produced out of resistance to an "African" empire, became *essentially* racial; the legitimacy of the state (its identity as nation rather than empire) was guaranteed by its whiteness. (This is why in *Red Rock,* where whiteness doesn't yet have any real meaning, the state cannot be legitimated—the choice there is between the illegitimate government and the "tribe.") Then in the 1920s, as whiteness becomes a culture, the Indian and the family reappear, first as models for a nativist Americanism (Cather) and second as models for a pluralism of native cultures (La Farge, Yezierska). Indeed, with respect to the topic of this book, I will argue first that anti-imperialism promoted racial identity to an essential element of American

citizenship; second, that this promotion made possible, both as its negation and its extension, the emergence of a new cultural Americanism;
and, third, that this cultural Americanism emerged also as what we might
today call multiculturalism in the cultural pluralism of the 1920s.

In *Red Rock*, by what would come to be Progressive standards, no
one is American. *Red Rock* is set in the old South, in a "Region" without
a name, referred to as "'the old County,' or, 'the Red Rock section,' or
just, 'My country, sir.'" Its heroes are those "aristocrats" who, "subjected
to the humiliation" of Reconstruction, eventually "reconquered their section and preserved the civilization of the Anglo-Saxon" (viii). But where,
in Dixon, the resistance to Reconstruction will involve not just reconquer-
ing the "section" but nationalizing it, making Southern anti-imperialism
the basis for the new American nation, in Page the restoration of "the old
County" to "the rule of its own citizens" (506) is really meant to be just
that, a restoration; it's no accident that the "old patrician[s]" of the South
use china presented to their "ancestors by Charles the Second" (284). And
where, in Dixon, what Anglo-Saxon civilization will be saved from is "the
Negro," in *Red Rock* it is saved from ambitious "clerks" and "overseers."
"Anglo-Saxon" in Dixon will mean "white"; in *Red Rock* it means aristocratic. *Red Rock*'s clerks and overseers derisively refer to Page's heroes as
"Lords," but the point of the novel is to confirm this identification and to
insist on its patriarchal accessories. Thus, in contrast to the social threat
posed by the new class of ambitious white men, *Red Rock*'s blacks present
no real racial threat and stand instead as a kind of bulwark against the
new whites: "these quality-niggers," the scalawag overseer explains to the
carpetbagger clerk, "are just as stuck up as their masters" (129).

The "quality-nigger's" quality derives from membership in a quality
family, and it is the family that Page presents as the essential unit of Red
Rock society. During the war, slaves behave "more like clansmen" (43)
and after the war, they are insulted by the new offer of wages: "How much
does you pay Miss Bessie?" (91) Mammy Krenda asks her former master,
contemptuously analogizing the idea of his Mammy being paid by him
to the idea of his wife's being paid by him. In the context of the contemporary critique of marriage as a kind of prostitution (in, say, Charlotte
Gilman), this analogy made a feminist point; in *Red Rock*, however, its
purpose is to make it clear that Negroes are "member[s] of the family" (92)
and that, as such, they cannot be sold or bought—even from themselves.
The surest signs of the overseer's degeneracy are his desire to divorce his
wife and his history as a "nigger-trader," both understood as assaults on
the family.

The transformation in race relations envisioned by Dixon requires the destruction of this essentially multiracial family; it calls for the elimination of the old "Uncles" and "Aunts" of the plantation tradition and a general rewriting of the childhood intimacies with blacks that were supposed to enable white Southerners to understand and appreciate them better. In *The Leopard's Spots*, the lonely Charlie Gaston finds a "playmate and partner in work" in the "ragged little waif" Dick who attaches himself to the Gaston household and even helps to defend it against a "Negro uprising." In plantation versions of this story, Dick, sticking "doggedly to Charlie's heels" (99), would count as the loyal Negro in contrast to the new Negroes of Reconstruction and especially of the 1890s. In *The Leopard's Spots*, however, Dick disappears in the early 1870s only to reappear some twenty years later as rapist and murderer of a young white girl. Gaston's attempt to save him from being burned alive is represented here as a feeble and ineffectual deviation from his own white supremacist principles, and Dixon's account of the girl's death doubles the repudiation of the old attachments to blacks by refusing even to allow her to be buried by a black man. The girl's father spurns the grave dug by "old Uncle Reuben Worth" (376) ("the only negro present") and asks "a group of old soldier comrades" to dig him a new one. Comradeship with white soldiers severs the ties of affection with blacks. The transformation of the friendly little black boy into a savage murderer, a transformation that is revealed rather than explained by the novel since it takes place entirely off-stage, is made to stand, precisely because it is unexplained, as a revelation of the truth about blacks. In Dixon, the brutality of the new Negro exposes as a lie the fidelity of the old one.

But this exposure has positive consequences because it is only by means of this confrontation with the new Negro that new ties of affection among whites can be made available: "In a moment the white race had fused into a homogeneous mass of love, sympathy, hate and revenge. The rich and the poor, the learned and the ignorant, the banker and the blacksmith, the great and the small, they were all one now" (368). This "fusion" involves to some extent the blurring of lines that might in other contexts seem to divide whites racially among themselves; thus the speech that wins Gaston the gubernatorial nomination characterizes his fellow North Carolinians as descended, "by the lineal heritage of blood" (442), not only from the "Angle" and the "Saxon" but also from the "Roman," the "Spartan," and the "Celt." Out of several possible races, "fusion" creates one "white race." But, more important than the elision of potential ethnic differences is the elision of social and political ones. The revolt against

Reconstruction succeeds when rebellion against "black rule" melts the South's "furious political passions" into "harmonious unity" by collapsing Whigs and Democrats, Unionists and Secessionists, into a "White Man's Party" arrayed against "the Black Man's Party." And when, in the 1890s, faced with the new problem of the gap between rich and poor, the old alliance seems exhausted and unable to stand for anything except "the stupid reiteration of the old slogan of white supremacy" (197), the threat of the new Negro manages to make even the old slogan new too. Listening to Gaston offer as the only plank of the Democratic platform a proclamation that "the hour has now come in our history to eliminate the Negro from our life and reestablish for all time the government of our fathers" (433– 34), the veteran General Worth experiences both nostalgia for "the years of his own daring young manhood" and admiration for "this challenge of the modern world." The nostalgia is for the war and the struggle against Reconstruction—both of which Dixon understood as an attempt to unite the nation along racial lines; the admiration is for the renewal and extension of that attempt in the 1890s, the effort to make out of that united nation what Dixon calls a "State."[7]

The target against which Dixon's racial "fusion" is directed is the political "fusion" that successfully united Populists and Republicans against Democrats in the North Carolina elections of 1894 and 1896, and the point of Dixon's "fusion" is to eliminate political differences among whites by transforming them into racial differences between whites and blacks. Politics "is a religion," according to Charlie Gaston; the "Government is the organized virtue of the community" and "the State is . . . the only organ through which the whole people can search for righteousness" (281). What is being imagined here is something like the literal conditions of Progressive nonpartisanship, but what political theorists like Walter Lippmann and Herbert Croly hoped to find in bureaucratic technologies that would turn political issues (i.e., conflicts of political interest) into administrative issues (i.e., conflicts of expertise), Dixon finds in race. As long as there can be "but one issue, are you a White Man or a Negro?" (159), there can be no partisan divisions between citizens.[8] For the two parties, the Democratic "White Man's Party" and the Populist/Republican "Black Man's Party," represent not a division between citizens but the division between citizens and noncitizens.

It was "on account of the enfranchisement of the Negro," Gaston says, that "the people of the South had to go into politics" (280). The Negro left in slavery would have left the essentially prepolitical, prenational plantation intact. But—every crisis an opportunity—his enfranchisement brought Southerners into politics in the effort to make the South part of the nation. And now the effort to disfranchise him (an effort that succeeds in *The Leopard's Spots* and that succeeded also in the elections of 1898) makes possible the elevation of politics to a "search for righteousness." For the Progressive Croly's desire to "purify" politics (340) and Dixon's insistence on the "purity" (281) of the "State" both require that political differences be understood as moral ones. "The principle of democracy is virtue," wrote Croly in *The Promise of American Life* (1909); for democracy to succeed, the "citizen" must aspire to become a "saint."[9] The great triumphs of *The Leopard's Spots* are thus its translation of political fusion into racial "fusion," its representation of a debate between citizens as a debate over who can be a citizen, and its consequent identification of citizenship with "righteousness."

From this perspective, *Red Rock*, with its evocation of the prewar "family, black and white," and its suspicion of the "Government," represents a certain resistance both to the emergence of race as the crucial marker of identity and to the commitment to the state that the primacy of race makes possible. In Dixon, racial ties replace familial ones; the Klan, racially pure in a way that, as I have argued elsewhere, the family can never be, becomes the guarantor of racial identity—its white sheets are whiter than anyone's skin.[10] But in *Red Rock*, the Klan's sheets are disparaged as a "disguise" for "blackguards and sneaks" (352) and the familial "clan," in its biological and aristocratic purity, is multiracial. More striking still, *Red Rock's* repudiation of the Klan is articulated not as respect for the laws the Klan violates but as respect for the code of "honor" that is itself violated by the law. (Think of Judge Driscoll's horror in *Pudd'nhead Wilson* [1894] when he learns that Tom, instead of taking physical revenge for Count Luigi's "assault" on him, has "crawled to a court of law about it.")[11] In *Red Rock*, it is carpetbaggers who embody the law, walking about, literally, with copies of "The Statutes of the United States" clasped under their arms, whereas Southern gentlemen, black and white, are bound by "honor" not to betray each other to the "Government." In Dixon, however, both the forming of the Klan and its disbanding are attempts to replace blood and honor with law and order.

This is most obviously true in the last volume of the trilogy, *The Traitor*, which, although it is sometimes described as Dixon's attempt to back away from the positions he had taken so strongly in the first two volumes, is, in fact, an extension rather than a repudiation of them. Its hero, John Graham, is the leader of the Klan in North Carolina and so of the resistance to the "African Government," but as the Klan degenerates and becomes increasingly identified with "lawlessness," he will become increasingly reluctant to participate in its activities and will eventually seek to disband it. When he is nonetheless arrested for a murder (actually committed by a carpetbagger), he rejects the possibility of escape, proclaiming, "I'm done with lawlessness. . . . I've led a successful revolution . . . and now with silent lips I'll face my accusers" (266). But while it is true that rejection of escape is somewhat anomalous in Dixon, the rejection of lawlessness and the proclamation of the "successful revolution" suggest the ways in which *The Traitor* continues the commitments of its predecessors. For insofar as the real effort of these books is to replace an illegitimate ("African") state with a legitimate one, "lawlessness" can never be countenanced. Indeed, Graham's submission to and eventual redemption by authority is here contrasted to the refusal of authority embodied in the "African Government" itself. For that government, making the Klan illegal, suspending habeas corpus, proclaiming martial law in the South, and placing Graham's home "county of Independence under military government," stands "in violation of the Constitution" (330). And Graham's threat to take his case all the way to the Supreme Court, "the last bulwark of American liberties," produces a hasty pardon from those "little politicians" who finally "do not dare to allow the Supreme Court to overwhelm them with infamy." The point, then, is that Graham's is the true commitment to "the process of the law" (61) and to the Constitution that is both the ultimate law of the land and the originating document of the state.

In sum, anti-imperialism here becomes synonymous with a certain constitutionalism. Just as the enemy throughout the trilogy is the imperial "African," usurping the Constitution, the hero is inevitably a defender of the Constitution and a creature of the state. In Page the "clan" was saved from the state (loyal blacks supporting honorable whites against the corrupt administrators of the "Statutes"); in Dixon the state is saved by the Klan ("We have rescued our state from Negro rule," [53] Graham tells his fellow Klansmen). Or rather, since Dixon actually imagines no preexisting state to be saved from the empire by the Klan, the state is *constituted* or *prefigured* by the Klan, which offers racial identity as a kind of rehearsal for the collective identity required by the new modes of national citizenship. Making it white, Dixon distinguishes the nation from the family and chooses it over the empire, indeed, creates it out of resistance to the empire. His point, then, is not the defense of the white state but the creation of the state through whiteness.

Doing a Navajo Thing

Red Rock, the novel, is named for "Red Rock," the plantation, which gives its name also to the whole "region" that, otherwise, has no name and is called only "the old County" or "my country." I have suggested above that the refusal to give this "country" a name involves a refusal to understand it as part of a "nation," and even the etiology of the name "Red Rock"— the rock is supposed to have been made red by "the blood of the Indian chief" who killed the first settler's wife and was in turn killed by him— represents a kind of solidarity with those who, like the Confederacy, resist the imperial power of the United States. For if the "Lords" of Red Rock have always been "Indian-killer[s]" (that's what the first one was called and, at the end of the novel, that's what the last one is out West doing), they are also in a way Indians themselves: young Rupert is a "volunteer scout" (473), which is to say that although he fights Indians, he serves with that branch of the army that was made up mainly of Indians; and it is said of the Red Rock "aristocrats" generally that "they stick together like Indians," so that, the overseer complains to his carpetbagger ally, "if one of 'em got hurt, the whole tribe would come down on me like hornets" (206). To which the carpetbagger's reply, "We'll be more than a match for the whole tribe. Wait till I get in the Legislature; I'll pass some laws that will settle 'em," represents precisely the opposition (between family and state [as tribe and law]) that Dixonian or Progressive racism sought to overcome.

But if identification with the Indian could function at the turn of the century as a *refusal* of American identity, it would come to function by the early 1920s as an *assertion* of American identity. Perhaps the most powerful literary instance of this process is the production of Tom Outland as the descendant of Colorado cliff dwellers in Willa Cather's *The Professor's House* (1925), but Cather's earlier novel, *A Lost Lady* (1923), provides an even clearer outline of how the old regionalist resistance to the American state could begin to be transformed into the defense not of that state but, instead, of what might provisionally be called an American culture.[12] The Indian-identified "aristocratic" family that in Page resisted subsumption by the Progressive American "nation" in Cather provides the technology enabling an Americanism that will go beyond the merely national American citizenship offered by the state. But to provide this technology the family must itself be altered; it must in particular cease to be the site of a certain indifference to racial difference (the family "black and white") and must be made instead into the unequivocal source of racial difference.

In *A Lost Lady*, the family in question is Captain Forrester's, and Forrester himself is both a member of what Cather calls the "railroad aristocracy" (9) and—through his status as one of the "pioneers" whose "dreams" settled the West—an Indian. "All our great West has been developed from . . . dreams," Captain Forrester says, but his account of those dreams (and of the disappearance of the aristocratic pioneers) culminates in a "grunt" that Cather describes as "the lonely, defiant note that is so often heard in the voices of old Indians" (55). In one sense, of course, this identification is exceptionally misleading; after all, it was the pioneers and railroad men who made the Indians disappear. But in Cather, as in Page, killing Indians is no obstacle to being Indian, and the fact that the pioneers are now themselves a vanishing race only confirms the identification. The "Old West had been settled by dreamers, great-hearted adventurers . . . a courteous brotherhood," but it is now "at the mercy of men like Ivy Peters, who . . . never dared anything, never risked anything" (106). Ivy Peters makes his fortune by "cheat[ing] Indians" (124). ("He gets splendid land from the Indians some way, for next to nothing.") Which is to say also, by exploiting men like Captain Forrester. And in this he is like Forrester's own partners who, after their bank has failed, refuse to "come up to the scratch and pay their losses like gentlemen" (90). "In my day," the Captain's aristocratic lawyer exclaims, "the difference between a business man and a scoundrel was bigger than the difference between a white man and a nigger" (92). Now that the difference between businessmen and scoundrels is disappearing, the difference between white men and "niggers" must be preserved. The reason that Ivy Peters can't properly succeed Captain Forrester is that he's more like a "nigger" than he is like an Indian.

In *The Great Gatsby*, published two years after *A Lost Lady*, Gatsby's relation to Daisy seems, at least to Tom, a kind of miscegenation, a threat to the difference between white men and "niggers." Fitzgerald had read and admired *A Lost Lady* while working on *Gatsby* and subsequently wrote Cather a famous note, apologizing for what he described as an act of "apparent plagiarism," an unintentional similarity between descriptions of Mrs. Forrester and Daisy. How similar the descriptions actually are is a nice question but the connection—with respect to miscegenation— between the Captain's wife Marian and Daisy Buchanan is real enough. Though married to an aristocrat, Marian reveals herself, in sleeping with Ivy Peters, to be nothing but "a common woman" (170). What gets "betrayed" by this affair is not exactly the Captain, since he's dead, but the "quality" the Captain and Mrs. Forrester herself supposedly embodied.

This is what makes it, like Daisy's affair with Jimmy Gatz, a kind of misce-genation. Mrs. Forrester is untrue to something more than her husband: "she was not willing to immolate herself, like the widow of all these great men, and die with the pioneer period to which she belonged" (169). The great men, like Indians, had died rather than adjust to changing condi-tions; Mrs. Forrester "preferred life on any terms." She is like an Indian who has somehow consented to change; what she betrays is not so much a husband as a race.

The racial meaning of this betrayal is clarified by the substitution two years later in *The Professor's House* of the Jewish Louie Marsellus for the merely unscrupulous Ivy Peters (as well as by Gatsby's association with Meyer Wolfsheim and Brett Ashley's affair with Robert Cohn). Marian Forrester's affair with Ivy Peters counts as a kind of miscegenation, one might say, not because he's black but because he's a proto-Jew. At the same time, then, that *A Lost Lady* asserts the importance of the differ-ence between the "white man" and the "nigger," it also begins to rewrite that difference as the difference between an Indian and a Jew. And this rewriting can hardly be read as the adjustment of an older racist struc-ture to new racial tensions: for one thing, racial conflict between Indians and Jews was hardly a social phenomenon of even observable magnitude; and, for another, the older racist structure is not perpetuated with a new content, rather it is altered. For the new valorization of the Indian points toward an interest in an essentially *pre*-national (i.e., pre-Revolutionary or, in Dixonian terms, pre-Civil War) America, an interest that one finds everywhere in the 1920s from Cather to Calvin Coolidge (the end of *Gatsby* is, perhaps, the most obvious example) and that repudiates the political nationalism of the Progressives: Americanism would now be understood as something more than and different from the American citizenship that so many aliens had so easily achieved.

Indeed the substitution of the Jew for the "nigger" makes the point even more strongly. When, in Dixon, the outlaw remnants of the dis-banded Klan set out to raid "old Sam Nicaroshinski, the Jew storekeeper, and rob 'im ter-night," the act of robbery as such is a sure sign of the "new" Klan's renegade status, its identification with the "lawlessness" that in *The Traitor* is essentially "African." But robbing a Jew is even more damning, for if the Jew in the 1920s will be a problematic figure for the Klan, the Jew in Dixon is a fellow revolutionary: "A refugee from Poland, his instinctive sympathies had always been with the oppressed people of the South" (107). The Jew has a place in the anti-African revolutionary American state that he will not have in American culture. When Graham is led through the streets to be carried away to the penitentiary (in a chapter Dixon calls "The Day of Atonement"), it is Nicaroshinski who slips him a hundred dollars and whispers, "don't you vorry, me poy, ve'll puild a monumendt to you in de public squvare yedt" (328). In 1924, however, the Jew's "instinctive sympathies" make him not an anti-imperialist Southerner, but "a Jew." The Jew is "by primal instinct a Jew," according to Dr. H. W. Evans, the Imperial Wizard of the Klan; he is "a stranger to the emotion of patriotism as the Anglo-Saxon feels it."[13] Which does not mean that the Jew in relation to the Klan of 1924 occupies the position occupied by the black in relation to Dixon's Klan. On the contrary, not even the black occupies that position any longer. For the slogan of the Klan, as an Indiana colleague of Dr. Evans puts it, is "Difference Not Inferiority": the "implications" of "Ku Kluxism" are "not those of inferiority, but those of difference; and it cherishes no hostility to Catholic, Jews, Negroes or foreigners as such" (51).

It should not be thought, however, that the declared absence of "hostility" and commitment to difference represent any diminution of racism. After all, the numerous whippings and occasional lynchings carried out by the Klan in the early 1920s make it clear that a good deal of racial hostility continued to be felt. But, even setting these incidents aside, the commitment to difference itself represents a theoretical intensification of racism, an intensification that has nothing to do with feelings of tolerance or intolerance toward other races and everything to do with the conceptual apparatus of pluralist racism.[14] For insofar as the Dixonian commitment to a hierarchical ranking of the races survived into the 1920s, it was seen to require a common scale of measurement; thus Frank H. Hankins, a critic of pluralism, argued that, since racial identity consisted in a set of "distinctive hereditary traits" distributed within each race on a bell-shaped curve, there was, on the one hand, no "discontinuity" between the races and, on the other hand, no equality. There could be no discontinuity because all the traits of all the races could be plotted somewhere along the curve, hence racial differences were necessarily "not those of kind but those of degree; not those of quality but of quantity."[15] There could be no equality because if the distribution of traits in one race exactly matched the distribution in another, there would be no grounds for distinguishing between the two races. Hankins's denial that racial differences are differences "of kind" thus amounts to an insistence on racial inequality—if there are races, they must be unequal. And, by the same token, the pluralist denial of racial inequality amounts to an insistence that, since they can't be "of degree," racial differences must be "of kind." Pluralism requires the assertion of differences in "quality," not just "quantity." Where Hankins's commitment to white supremacy required that races be different from each other only insofar as one had more or less of what the others also had, the antisupremacist or pluralist commitment to difference without hierarchy made races essentially different rather than more or less like each other. It was only, in other words, the pluralist denial of hierarchy that made possible the escape from the common scale and the emergence of an unmeasurable and hence incomparable racial essence.

The transformation of the Progressive opposition between "white man" and "nigger" into the new opposition between Indian and Jew thus signals at least two changes in racist discourse: first, a change in the sense of what is being preferred and, second, a change in the sense of why it is being preferred.[16] In Progressive racism, Confederate comrades in arms offer the image of a racial entity that breaks the organic bonds of the (multiracial) family and substitutes for them the superorganic bonds of the white "State"; in the 1920s, the Indian embodies a racial entity that finds through the family a "heritage" or "culture" that transcends the (multiracial) state. In Progressive racism, the "nigger" is essentially inferior; the difference between races must be maintained so that the lower will not contaminate the higher. What emerges in the 1920s, however, is a racial pluralism: one prefers one's own race not because it is superior but because it is one's own.

It would be a mistake, however, to think that these changes took place neatly or all at once. As late as 1927, for example, the poet Stephen Vincent Benet could choose the Civil War as his subject for an American epic, and as late as 1928 the critic Henry Seidel Canby could praise Benet for being (along with Sinclair Lewis) the first American writer "concerned with the great theme of a national life."[17] Indeed, it was precisely Benet's treatment of the war that marked for Canby his originality. According to Canby, a true understanding of the Civil War had not been possible until the Great War because it took the Great War to make us see that the Civil War had been the first truly "modern" war, modern in the sense that it was "a people's war." Previous treatments of the war, Canby wrote, had been "content either with odes on the North and paeans on the South, or with local color sketches like Stephen Crane's *The Red Badge of Courage*" (x). In other words, from the standpoint of what Canby praises as the "intense nationalism" of *John Brown's Body*, previous treatments had been insufficiently *national*, devoted, almost as if the war had never taken place, to one side or the other ("odes on the North and paeans on the South") or, if not actually taking sides between the two regions, to the idea of regionalism itself (*The Red Badge of Courage* as "local color"). For Canby, then, Benet is the first truly national writer because he is the first to see what the Civil War created, the first to see the Civil War as the origin of the American nation.

There is, of course, an important sense in which this claim is obviously false: the whole point of the Civil War for a writer like Dixon was that, freeing racism from slavery, it dissolved the sectional differences between North and South and replaced them with the racial difference between black and white, thus making possible the trans-sectional, white nation. But there are important senses also in which Canby's sense of the novelty, if not exactly the originality, of *John Brown's Body* is appropriate. For one thing, it is true that the major writers of the Progressive period—Dreiser, Wharton, London—were comparatively indifferent to the question of American national identity: even in Dreiser's major work of the postwar period, *An American Tragedy*, "American" signifies a certain set of social and economic conditions rather than a political entity or cultural heritage. It is as if, during the period when industrial America was devoted to assimilating and "Americanizing" its immigrants as quickly and thoroughly as possible, only those confronted with what seemed to them the unassimilable "Negro" were compelled to produce an account of the constitutive boundaries of the American. It is from this standpoint that a book like *The Leopard's Spots*—without any literary merit or, for that matter, any real literary ambition—can count as a rehearsal for the major literary achievements of Cather, Fitzgerald, Hemingway, and others.

And for another thing, in addition to the fact that Benet's literary ambitions are closer to Cather's than to Dixon's, there are important differences between *John Brown's Body* and its nationalist predecessors. If, for Dixon (and even for Canby), the alternative to "American" is sectional—northern or southern, "local"—for Benet it is "foreign" ("This flesh was seeded from no foreign grain / But Pennsylvania and Kentucky wheat" [7]) or "alien" ("To strive at last, against an alien proof"). The "American thing" (5) in Benet is not the state that subsumes local differences and that (as embodied in the various Progressive projects of Americanization) converts aliens into Americans; it is the "native" ("As native as the shape of Navajo quivers" [3]) that insists on its difference from the "alien." Benet's nationalism, in other words, is a kind of (tolerant) nativism, committed not to turning the alien into an American but to distinguishing between the alien and the American. And this anti-Progressive, anti-Americanization shows up even in his treatment of racial difference: "Oh, black-skinned epic, epic with the black spear, / I cannot sing you, having too white a heart" (308). Canby says (amazingly) that Benet's "Negroes are the truest I know in American poetry" (xiv), but Benet's essentially pluralistic nationalism commits him more truly to denying that he can represent the Negro at all than to representing him well. The discovery of "the American thing" thus appears most certainly in the assertion of what the "American Muse" *can't* sing: the Negro, the alien. The inability of the American Muse to sing it is the proof that she's American.

It is, in other words, as nationalism turns into nativism that it becomes also a kind of pluralism. From the standpoint of the Indianized American, the "native," this must involve the repudiation of the "alien's" efforts at Americanization, where Americanization is understood no longer as the alien's attempt to become a citizen but instead as his attempt to join the family. Tom Outland could marry the Professor's daughter because Tom is already imagined by *The Professor's House* as his son (incestuous marriages bring no one into the family). But marriage to Louie Marsellus compromises the family; indeed, it compromises *two* families. The Jew is, by "deliberate election," "unassimilable," writes the Klan's Dr. Evans; "He rejects intermarriage" (14). A thoroughgoing pluralism would cast Louie Marsellus's father in the same position as the Professor, in opposition to a marriage that will eliminate differences rather than preserve them.

Of course, the self-appointed spokesman for the Jew here is the Imperial Wizard of the Ku Klux Klan and, when asked to comment on these remarks, Israel Zangwill, the author of *The Melting Pot*, disputed him, claiming that intermarriage of Jews with gentiles was frequent, more frequent than intermarriage of "protestants with Catholics" (32). But it's hardly as if nativist pluralism went unarticulated among Jews. Anzia Yezierska's *Bread Givers*, for example (published, like *Gatsby* and *The Professor's House*, in 1925), presents itself as a first-person narrative of the attempt to assimilate, almost as if a suitably reconfigured *Professor's House* had been written from the standpoint of a lower-class Louie Marsellus. But the central conflict is not between assimilating aliens and Americans who unjustly reject them, it is between Sara, whose desire to become one of the "real Americans"[18] is so intense that successful Americanization seems to her the equivalent of being "changed into a person" (237), and her father, whose embodiment of the Jewish "race" is so absolute that he seems to his family "an ancient prophet that had just stepped out of the Bible" (125). Insofar as Sara is like a "pioneer," compared by a sympathetic Dean at her "real American" college to his own "grandmother" contending with the "wilderness" (232), her father, Reb Smolinski, is an Indian: "In a world where all is changed, he alone remained unchanged—as tragically isolate as the rocks" (296). From this standpoint, from the Jewish as opposed to the American standpoint, Sara is less like Louie Marsellus than like the woman he marries, the Professor's daughter Rosamond; as Rosie betrays her family by marrying a Jew, Sara wants to marry "an American-born man" (66). And her father, Reb Smolinski, is like the Professor; indeed, to reproduce in *Bread Givers* not just the thematic but the *affective* structure of *The Professor's House*, one need only imagine it written from the point of view of Reb Smolinski, *The Rabbi's House*. But the goal here, of course, is not simply to find ways of mapping these two texts onto each other; it is to suggest instead (in part, through such a mapping) that the nativist's vanishing Indian could function simultaneously as the alien's vanishing Jew: assimilation could be repudiated from both sides.

The opposition between "Indian" and "Jew" is not in this way undone, it is just, like the *Bread Givers* imagined above, reconfigured. The Indian who in Cather (and elsewhere: see, for example, Zane Grey's *The Vanishing American* [1925] or Hart Crane's *The Bridge* [1930]) embodies the nativist American is made instead to embody the nativist ethnic and in both positions resists assimilation. This is made most explicit in Oliver La Farge's *Laughing Boy* (1929), where the Indians really are Indians and the "foreigners" or "aliens" are the Americans. La Farge's Slim Girl (like Grey's Carlisle Indian, Nophaie) has been sent to an American-run school and the Navajos think of her as no longer Navajo: "She is a school-girl. . . . She is not of the People any more, she is American."[19] But where *The Vanishing American* works to narrativize the opposition between Indian and American so that, by the text's end, the Indian can melt into the American, becoming not his antagonist but his ancestor, *Laughing Boy* insists on the antagonism. Nophaie marries an American but Slim Girl, having been seduced and prostituted by Americans, turns the act of prostitution into an act of war—when she returns from sleeping with her American, she has the "look," La Farge says, "of a man who has just killed and scalped a hated enemy" (88)—and seeks to restore herself to the Navajos by marrying one: "he was the means of returning to the good things of the Navajo, the good things of life" (109). Thus where the Indians in *The Vanishing American*, as in *The Professor's House*, are foundational for a distinctly *American* cultural identity, in *Laughing Boy*, they have become a culture of their own, no longer deployed in opposition to the ethnics but as one of them.

But the point embodied in Slim Girl involves more than insisting on the difference between Navajos and Americans by repudiating intermarriage between them. For while miscegenation counts in itself as the betrayal of the racial family, simply ceasing to sleep with Americans cannot restore Slim Girl to "the People." Navajo identity in *Laughing Boy* involves something more than biological fidelity to the Navajo race; to be a Navajo, in this text, is not only to be born a Navajo but to behave like a Navajo. Biology is an essential but not a sufficient condition of what here emerges as a specifically cultural identity, an identity that can be embraced or rejected. Thus Slim Girl's learning to weave, to ride, and to sleep out under the stars are represented by the text as her attempt to exercise a "right" (62) granted her by birth but requiring at the same time that she lay claim to it. *Laughing Boy* enacts, in other words, the project of becoming Navajo, a project made possible only by the fact that there's a sense in which Slim Girl isn't a Navajo and made fulfillable only by the fact that there's a sense in which she is.

Laughing Boy was written by an American who had done anthropological work among the Navajos, and La Farge's admiration for them is obvious throughout. But the particular ingenuity of the book is in its translation of the American anthropologist's affection for Navajo culture into what amounts to a Navajo affection for Navajo culture. That is, by provisionally depriving Slim Girl of her "heritage," La Farge is able not only to depict a heritage as essentially the kind of thing (unlike one's racial identity or one's social practices) that you can get separated from but also to make that thing potentially an object of affect. Thus when Slim Girl camps out, she takes pleasure not in the act of camping out as such and not even in her perception of the night as "beautiful with stars" but in her sense that "camping . . . was a part of her people's heritage. She was doing a Navajo thing" (99). What this involves is the representation of your culture not as the things you love to do but as the things you love to do because they are your culture. The drama of the schoolgirl's separation thus makes two points: that your cultural practices are yours even if you don't practice them—this is what it means for Slim Girl to have a "right" to weaving even when she can't weave—and that cultural practices are attractive to you insofar as they are yours—this is what it means for her to like "doing a Navajo thing."

The attractions of Navajo things thus consist in the fact of their being Navajo; authenticity becomes a crucial aesthetic concept. Laughing Boy's turquoise and silver jewelry, for example, is admired because it is "strong, pure stuff, real Northern Navajo work, untouched by European influence" (79). And the mark of its purity is that not only tourists but "other Indians" buy it. In *Laughing Boy,* Navajos are represented as a people with a powerful aesthetic sense, concerned above all with doing things "in a beautiful way" (64), and Laughing Boy himself is presented as desiring to make his every action beautiful: "He was thinking hard about what he was doing; he was putting forth every effort to make it good and beautiful" (63). But what the invocation of purity makes clear is that Navajo culture is the criterion as well as the instantiation of beauty; Navajo things are beautiful insofar as they are Navajo. This is, of course, a characteristically anthropological view but, again, it is part of the originality of *Laughing Boy* that it here appears as a Navajo view. The Navajos in *Laughing Boy* understand their behavior not as constituting their culture but as representing it. And this understanding, insofar as it makes possible a discrepancy between behavior and culture, also makes possible both the mistake of straying from your culture and the project of returning to it.

"He was the Old World. I was the New," Sara Smolinski says of her father and herself in *Bread Givers*. But the claim to belong to the New World by virtue of your distance from the Old was becoming obsolete as she spoke; even *Bread Givers* ends with Sara and her father reconciled. Furthermore, although Sara is compelled to recognize the "oneness of the flesh that's in him and me" (286), that oneness is not in itself sufficient for their reunion. This can only be effected through the medium of her new husband, Hugo, who is at once an American, an expert in English pronunciation, and a *"landsleute"* (277), from the same part of Poland. "We talked one language. We had sprung from one soil" (278). Through Hugo, Sara begins to experience her affection for her father as an affection for the old ways, and Hugo's desire to have her father teach him Hebrew ("An American young man, a principal, and wants to learn Hebrew?" [293]) makes explicit the emergence of ethnicity as something to be reclaimed (or repudiated) rather than simply embodied. To resume for a second the analogy with *The Professor's House*, Hugo plays the role of Tom Outland; his learning Hebrew from Reb Smolinsky will be like Tom's learning Latin on the Blue Mesa, an act of filial piety. Thus Hugo's willingness to accept Reb Smolinski into his home restores Sara to her father and reconstitutes the Jewish family, but with a difference: learning Hebrew, doing a Jewish thing, the family becomes a culture.

A Man Without a Past

"What is Africa to me?" is the initiating question of Countee Cullen's "Heritage," asked in a spirit of skepticism that the poem will seek to eliminate but that has nonetheless prompted Arthur Schlesinger, Jr., recently to cite "Heritage" as evidence of a traditional African American indifference to Africa.[20] Schlesinger presumably hasn't read past the poem's first ten lines but an essay that appears some hundred pages after "Heritage" in Alain Locke's *The New Negro* (1925) does provide some support for Schlesinger's anti-Afrocentrism. The Negro represents "a case of complete acculturation," Melville J. Herskovits wrote in "The Negro's Americanism."[21] Denying the idea of a "cultural genius" (356) that could be identified with any "innate" or racially "African" characteristics, Herskovits denies also that any of the "customs" of "ancestral Africa" have survived in America. Insofar as there is anything in Harlem different from the "white culture" that surrounds it, that difference can best be explained, Herskovits argues, as "a remnant from the peasant days in the South" (359). For "One three centuries removed / From the scenes his fathers loved," Herskovits's answer to the question "What is Africa to me?" is nothing: the Negro has become completely "Americanized," "Of the African culture, not a trace."

But in "Heritage," of course, that answer is not allowed to stand. For although the scenes the father loved are initially presented as "unremembered" by the son, the tendency to *forget* (as if Africa were too distant to matter) is immediately reinterpreted as a requirement to repress (as if Africa were too near to be forgotten): "One thing only I must do / Quench my pride and cool my blood / Lest I perish in their flood," "Lest the grave restore its dead" (250–51), lest an apparently lost ancestral Africa turn out not only to be present but to be a force as strong as or stronger than the Negro's Americanization. And this attempt to repress the African past is now presented as a failure, since the metaphor through which Africa is supposed to be kept out—"Though I cram against my ear / Both my thumbs and keep them there"—is in fact the technique through which it is discovered that Africa is already inside—"So I lie, who always hear . . . Great drums beating through the air." Trying not to hear the drums outside involves hearing instead the drums inside, the circulation of one's own "dark blood." Thus Africa is, in the end, triumphantly, not only "remembered" but repeated; in *The New Negro*, "Heritage" appears in a section entitled "The Negro Digs Up His Past."

In *The New Negro*, then, Herskovits's view of the Negro as completely assimilated was anomalous; and by 1941 (indeed, in his private correspondence, as early as 1927), Herskovits himself had come to see things very differently.[22] In 1925 he had argued that "All racial and social elements in our population who live here long enough become acculturated, Americanized in the truest sense of the words, eventually" (360), and that the Negro was no exception; in 1941, in *The Myth of the Negro Past*, he argued that the distinguishing traits of "Italians or Germans or Old Americans or Jews or Irish or Mexicans or Swedes" could not be understood "without a reference to a preceding cultural heritage" (299) and, again, that the Negro was no exception. What he had seen in 1925 as the Negro's likeness to other groups in becoming acculturated, he now saw as the Negro's likeness to other groups in *not* becoming acculturated.

The myth of the Negro past, in other words, was that he had none, that he was either completely a creature of the culture imposed upon him in slavery or that he had no culture at all and, insofar as Negroes were themselves brought to accept this view, Herskovits regarded them as the victims of cultural imperialism. *Native Son*'s (1940) Bigger Thomas, for example, is described by Richard Wright as "bereft of a culture." "The Negro," according to Wright, "possessed a rich and complex culture when he was brought to these alien shores," but it was "taken from" him.[23] Herskovits's argument in *The Myth of the Negro Past* was that it had *not* been taken from him and that the myth of the Negro's unique cultural "pliancy" was a function of "racial prejudice." His point, then, was to show both that the Negro did have a past and that, like other groups, he had clung to it. The "stereotype of the pliant Negro . . . which contrasts him to the Indian, who is held to have died rather than suffer enslavement" (90) is false, Herskovits claimed. The Indian who died to show his "cultural tenacity" now becomes the model not only for "Old Americans" like Tom Outland and old Jews like Reb Smolinski but for the newly historicized Negro whose "pre-American traditions" make him an ethnic like the others.

Precipitated out of the family "black and white" as the first American race, the Negro—filtered through the Indian—now becomes the last American culture. But here Herskovits is not simply catching up to the 1920s, he is advancing the argument. For cultural identity in the 1920s required, as we have seen, the anticipation of culture by race: to be a Navajo you have to do Navajo things, but you can't really count as doing Navajo things unless you already are a Navajo. For Herskovits, however (and here *The Myth of the Negro Past* is consistent with "The Negro's Americanism"), racial identity plays no role in the constitution of cultural identity; his "analysis is consistently held to the plane of learned behavior, so that whatever role innate endowment may play, it is not permitted to confuse the issues of the research" (14). Thus where Countee Cullen identified the African heritage genealogically, finding it in the body's "black blood," Herskovits saw the distinctive "Africanisms" of the body as "cultural" rather than "biological": his research assistant, Zora Neale Hurston, he noted, was "more White than Negro in her ancestry" but her "motor behavior" was "typically Negro."[24]

When Herskovits sought to prove that the Negro was not "a man without a past," then, the past he sought to give him was entirely cultural. The idea was to show that many aspects of contemporary Negro behavior could be traced back to African beliefs and practices and the point in doing this was to help the Negro toward a proper "appreciation of his past," for a "people that denies its past cannot escape being a prey to doubt of its value today" (32). When, in *Native Son*, Bigger goes to the double feature the movies he sees are *The Gay Woman* and *Trader Horn*. *The Gay Woman*, as Wright describes it, is about "rich white people," "dancing, golfing, swimming and spinning roulette wheels";[25] *Trader Horn* is about "black men and women, dancing free and wild, men and women who were adjusted to their soil and at home in their world" (36). *Trader Horn*, in Herskovits's terms, presents Bigger with the spectacle of an African culture that should be his—a display of those "distinctive" "motor habits" (148) that he is supposed to have brought with him from Africa. But it is a spectacle that Bigger himself cannot see. "He looked at *Trader Horn* unfold . . . and then gradually the African scene changed and was replaced by images in his own mind of white men and women dressed in black and white clothes, laughing, talking, drinking and dancing" (35–36). The white world from which he is shut out is more alluring than the African world with which Herskovits wishes to reconnect him. This, from the standpoint of Herskovits, is what it means to belong to a people that denies its past.

But Bigger's indifference may perhaps be more easily understood as a critique of Herskovits than as a failure to live up to his ideals, and what seems to Herskovits at best the Negro's inability to recognize his past and at worst his commitment to denying his past may be read instead as a question about why the past in question is his. For in his identification of the Negro "people" and, more particularly, in his characterization of African customs as part of that people's past, Herskovits turns out to lean more heavily on the concept of racial identity than his culturalist rhetoric suggests. Indeed, how else can an American Negro of the twentieth century be said to be denying his or her past in denying that his or her practices have their roots in Africa?[26]

In *Laughing Girl*, Slim Girl's *actual* past, the things she has herself done (her American education, her conversion to Christianity, her love affair with an American), are regarded as less crucial to her identity than her people's past, the things her mother and father used to do. "Her past" is "dead," Laughing Boy thinks, and, indeed, he himself represents to her "an axe with which to hew down the past" and "a light with which to see her way back to her people" (45). The way to beliefs she has never held and to customs she has never practiced can seem a way *back* in *Laughing Boy* because race provides the necessary (but, crucially, not sufficient) ground of Slim Girl's identity. Neither what she was born nor what she has done is sufficient to confer cultural identity; she can make herself a Navajo only by doubling Navajo birth with the doing of Navajo things. The discrepancy between Slim Girl's actual past and her people's past is thus the enabling condition for the appearance of cultural identity as a project, the project of lining up her practices with her genealogy. Herskovits, however, cannot afford such a discrepancy between what people do and what their ancestors did. Since his analysis is committed only to a genealogy of "learned behavior," a break in that genealogy (a failure actually to do yourself what your ancestors did) can only count as a complete rupture with the past; there can be no appeal to racial continuity.

Thus Herskovits is required to explain, for example, how the "retention of Africanisms" (133) was possible for house slaves and others "in close contact with whites." Such people, despite being thoroughly trained in white ways and encouraged in the "adoption of white values" (132), could "reabsorb Africanisms" during the periods when they were released from their duties and could mingle with field hands whose practices had been left relatively untouched or, even better, he suggests, with "newly arrived Africans" whose practices were completely untouched. Whatever the historical plausibility of this explanation, and even though the movement from retention to reabsorption suggests a certain slippage (if you were trained as a house slave, why would absorbing Africanisms count as reabsorbing them?), its theoretical purpose is clear: to guarantee an unbroken chain of (cultural) Africanisms and so avoid any appeal to "innate endowment."

In fact, however, the appearance of a break in the cultural chain only makes visible what must already be present for the "retention of Africanisms" to count as the acquisition of a "past." For the fact that some people before you did some things that you do does not in itself make what they did part of your past. To make what *they* did part of *your* past, there must be some prior assumption of identity between you and them, and this assumption is as racial in Herskovits as it is in Cullen or La Farge. The things the African Negro used to do count as the American Negro's past only because both the African and the American are "the Negro." Herskovits's antiracist culturalism can only be articulated though a commitment to racial identity.

"What is Africa to me?" The answer, if you are Herskovits's Negro, is "my past." Arthur Schlesinger, Jr., as I noted earlier, cites that question as an instance of the rejection by black Americans of the idea that their past is African. But, although he locates it in a different country, Schlesinger is no more skeptical than Herskovits about the "right" of black Americans "to seek an affirmative definition of their past" (30). In fact, Schlesinger simply represents the right wing of what is today a broad consensus on the importance of cultural identity. That consensus has its origin in the anti-imperialist promotion of racial identity to an essential aspect of American citizenship and although—beginning, at least, with Herskovits—it has presented itself as a critique rather than an extension of racial thinking, concepts like the "Negro past" are, I have suggested, irreducibly racial. In this respect, it is far from clear that today's debates over multiculturalism represent anything more than a reconfiguration of the essential terms of American nativism.[27]

Notes

I I characterize *The Leopard's Spots* and the other two novels in *The Trilogy of Reconstruction* (*The Clansman* [1905] and *The Traitor* [1907]) as anti-imperialist despite the fact that *The Leopard's Spots* describes the war in Cuba as a triumphant proclamation of "the advent of a giant democracy" (Dixon, *The Leopard's Spots* [New York, 1902], p. 407). (Subsequent references are to this edition and are cited in parentheses in the text.) The congressional resolution under which the United States went to war with Spain had explicitly abjured "sovereignty, jurisdiction, or control" over Cuba, and by 1902, the year in which *The Leopard's Spots* was published, the Platt Amendment had granted the Cubans complete independence. (For accounts of this process, see Ernest May, *Imperial Democracy* [New York, 1961] and Walter LaFeber, *The New Empire* [Ithaca, 1963].) Hence it was the invasion and annexation of the Philippines that served as the focus of American anti-imperialism—indeed, some anti-imperialists explicitly distinguished the "war for humanity against the Spanish in Cuba" from "the war for conquest against the Filipinos" (J. Laurence Laughlin speaking at the Chicago Liberty Meeting of April 30, 1899, reprinted in *The Anti-Imperialist Reader*, vol. 1, ed. Philip S. Foner and Richard C. Winchester [New York, 1984], pp. 290–91)—and it is the arguments against annexation of the Philippines that I describe below as playing a central role in Dixon's novels. These arguments tended to take two forms: first, racist assertions that Filipino self-government was the only way to avoid burdening the United States with what Mrs. Jefferson Davis called "fresh millions of foreign negroes," even "more ignorant and more degraded" (in *The Anti-Imperialist Reader*, 1: 236) than those at home, and, second, political appeals to the unconstitutionality and, more generally, antirepublican character of imperial acquisition. These latter arguments were sometimes antiracist but even when, as was more often the case, they displayed a certain amount of racial contempt for the Filipinos, that contempt was only incidental to the political point. If, then, anti-imperialist critiques were generally *either* racist *or* constitutional, one way of beginning to understand Dixon's contribution is by noting that in the *Trilogy*, the racial and constitutional arguments against imperial conquest are not only understood as equally important but also (for reasons I give below) as inextricably linked.

The need for something like the preceding paragraph was made clear to me by Amy Kaplan's and Michael Rogin's spirited objections to my characterization of Dixon's anti-imperialism. Although I don't imagine that my response will entirely meet those objections, I am grateful to Kaplan and Rogin for expressing them. This is, perhaps, also the opportunity to thank the other participants (especially Donald Pease) in the Dartmouth Conference on "Cultures of U.S. Imperialism" and to thank also Frances Ferguson and Michael Fried for their critical readings of an earlier draft.

2 Ernest Howard Crosby's *Captain Jinks, Hero* (1902, reprinted in *The Anti-Imperialist Reader*, vol. 2, ed. Philip S. Foner [New York, 1986], pp. 267–394) is virtually the only anti-imperialist text I know that deals explicitly with the events in the Phillippines, and *Captain Jinks* is more plausibly described as antimilitarist than as anti-imperialist since its primary concern is to burlesque as a "peculiar kind of insanity" the "preoccupation with uniforms and soldiers, and the readiness [of Jinks] to do anything a man in regimentals tells him to" (393).

3 "Platform of the Liberty Congress of Anti-Imperialists Adopted in Indianapolis, August 16," in *The Anti-Imperialist Reader*, vol. 1, ed. Philip S. Foner and Richard C. Winchester (New York, 1984), p. 309.

4 Edwin Burritt Smith, "Liberty or Despotism," in *The Anti-Imperialist Reader*, 1: 293.

5 The term "war of conquest" was employed so frequently in anti-imperialist descriptions of the invasion of the Philippines (by people like Bishop Spaulding and Carl Schurz as well as by the anonymous authors of the "Platform" quoted above) that it is difficult not to believe that Dixon intended his audience to hear their voices echoed in the voice of his Lincoln.

6 "We have come as a people to the parting of the ways. Which shall it be: Nation or Empire. . . . Let us look this imperialism squarely in the face and realize what it means. It means the surrender of American democracy. It means a menace to free American citizenship" (*Liberty Tract No. 12* [1900], reprinted in *Anti-Imperialist Reader*, 1: 306–7). This analysis of imperialism as a threat above all to *self*-government tends to be overlooked by those (like Lenin, for whom American anti-imperialists were "the last Mohicans of bourgeois democracy") who criticize what Robert L. Beisner [in *Twelve Against Empire*] has called the "impotence" of American anti-imperialism and who see them as essentially "conservative" (Beisner, *Twelve Against Empire* [Chicago, 1985], p. 222). If we understand American anti-imperialism as committed above all to the revisionary rescue of the concept of American citizenship described in this section, then we must also understand it to have been largely successful and, in its conceptual alliance with what Joel Williamson has called "radical" racism, hardly conservative.

7 On the Klan's nationalism and, especially, on the use made of Dixon by D. W. Griffith in *The Birth of a Nation*, see Michael Rogin, "The Sword Became a Flashing Vision" in *Ronald Reagan, The Movie* (Berkeley, 1987), pp. 190–235.

8 In fact, after winning the elections of 1894 and 1896, the fusionists were soundly defeated by the Democrats in 1898 and, after the disfranchisement of blacks in 1900, North Carolina followed Louisiana, Mississippi, and South Carolina into the ranks of the Solid Democratic South. Charles L. Flynn, Jr., has recently argued that because the southern Democracy (he is speaking of Georgia in particular but the argument can be generalized) was held together by "a conspiracy theory of national politics," Democrats were "unable to conceive of legitimate dissent outside of their party" ("Procrustean Bedfellows and Populists: An Alternative Hypothesis," in *Race, Class and Politics in Southern History: Essays in Honor of Robert F. Durden*, ed. Jeffrey J. Crow, Paul D. Escott, and Charles L. Flynn, Jr. [Baton Rouge, 1989], p. 102). Emphasizing the similarity of Populist and Democratic views in fundamental issues, his point is to revise C. Van Woodward's account of the destruction of radical Populism at the hands of conservative Democrats by suggesting that the ideological differences between the two groups were not as great as the more properly political ones; what the Democrats found most disturbing about the Populists, in effect, was that they were not Democrats. And Flynn traces this nonideological loyalty to the Democratic party back to the Reconstruction identification of Republicans as a "money aristocracy" out to plunder the South. His emphasis on the nonideological character of loyalty to the Democratic party seems to me powerfully suggestive, but I would also argue that it is crucial not to think of this loyalty as simply the continuation of provincial or sectional paranoia. For Progressives (Southern and national), the one-party state could be understood less as a relic of Reconstruction than as a harbinger of the disappearance of partisan politics altogether and of their replacement by (as in Colonel House's *Philip Dru, Administrator*) the "commission"-run, administered state.

9 Herbert Croly, *The Promise of American Life* (1909: reprinted, New York 1965), p. 454. Croly is quoting and endorsing Santayana, who is himself quoting Montesquieu.

10 Walter Benn Michaels, "The Souls of White Folk," in *Literature and the Body*, ed. Elaine Scarry (Baltimore, 1988), pp. 185–209.

11 Mark Twain, *Pudd'nhead Wilson and Those Extraordinary Twins*, ed. Sidney E. Berger (New York, 1980), p. 60.

12 For extended discussion of *The Professor's House* in relation both to the

Johnson Immigration Act of 1924 and the Indian Citizenship Act of the same year, see Walter Benn Michaels, "The Vanishing American," *American Literary History* (Summer 1990), pp. 220–41.

13 *Is the Ku Klux Klan Constructive or Destructive? A Debate Between Imperial Wizard Evans, Israel Zangwill and Others,* reported by Edward Price Bell, ed. E. Haldeman-Julius (Girard, Kansas, 1924), p. 14. Subsequent references are cited in parentheses in the text.

14 The most important recent (literary) critic of pluralism has been Werner Sollors, both in his *Beyond Ethnicity* and, especially, in "A Critique of Pure Pluralism" (*Reconstructing American Literary History* [Cambridge, 1986], pp. 250–79), where, citing Horace Kallen's 1924 description of the choice facing Americans as one between "Kultur Klux Klan" and "Cultural Pluralism," Sollors calls attention to the "notion of the eternal power of descent, birth, *natio,* and race" (260) that Kallen shares with his racist opponents. Students of cultural identity (especially the skeptical ones) owe Sollors a great debt. It is essential to see, however, that pluralism can no more be thought of as a simple extension of racism than it can be thought of as a repudiation of racism since, as I argue in the text, it produces a fundamental change in what racism is. And it's important also to note, as I've suggested in the closing pages of "The Vanishing American" and as I argue in the last section of this essay, that the substitution of culture for race (the idea that ethnic identity is culturally rather than genetically transmitted) can never, as long as cultural identity counts as anything more than a description, be complete.

15 Frank H. Hankins, *The Racial Basis of Civilization* (New York: 1926; revised edition, 1931), p. 293.

16 It signals also a narrowing of the category "white" and an expansion of "nigger": the Klan flogged a Greek for going out with a "white" woman, ordered all Syrians expelled from Macon, Georgia, and boycotted Italian storekeepers in Illinois (see David Chalmers, *Hooded Americanism: The History of the Ku Klux Klan* [Durham, 1987], p. 110 and *passim*).

17 Stephen Vincent Benet, *John Brown's Body,* intro. Henry Seidel Canby (Chicago, 1990), p. ix. Subsequent references are cited in parentheses in the text.

18 Anzia Yezierska, *Bread Givers* (New York, 1975), p. 210. Subsequent references are cited in parentheses in the text.

19 Oliver La Farge, *Laughing Boy* (New York, 1971), p. 33. Subsequent references are cited in parentheses in the text.

20 Arthur M. Schlesinger, Jr., *The Disuniting of America* (New York, 1991), p. 46. Subsequent references are cited in parentheses in the text.

21 *The New Negro,* ed. Alain Locke (New York, 1925), p. 360. Subsequent references both to Herskovits's essay and to Countee Cullen's poem "Heritage" (which originally appeared in *The New Negro*) are cited in parentheses in the text.

22 For an account of Herskovits's career, see Walter Jackson, "Melville Herskovits and the Search for Afro-American Culture," in *Malinowski, Rivers, Benedict and Others,* ed. G. W. Stocking, Jr. (Madison, 1986), pp. 95–126.

23 Richard Wright, "I Bite the Hand that Feeds Me," *Atlantic Monthly* (June 1940), pp. 827–28.

24 Quoted in Jackson, p. 107.

25 Richard Wright, *Native Son* (New York, 1966), p. 33. Subsequent references are cited in parentheses in the text.

26 Where Herskovits wished to attack the idea of racial identity by substituting for it the idea of historical identity, other writers have sought to *save* the idea of racial identity by redescribing it as historical identity. For a brilliant critique of this effort, one that has influenced my critique of cultural identity, see Kwame Anthony Appiah, "The Uncompleted Argument: Du Bois and the Illusion of Race," in *"Race," Writing, and Difference*, ed. and intro. Henry Louis Gates, Jr. (Chicago, 1985), pp. 21–37. It is unclear to me, however, to what extent Appiah's own "hermeneutic" conception of cultures as "communities of meaning, shading variously into each other in the rich structure of the social world" is meant to do the racial work that I criticize in the remainder of this section.

27 My point here is not to deny the differences between the various participants in the debate over multiculturalism or to suggest that they all have the same political interests or goals—if they did, there wouldn't be a *debate*. My point is rather that they all rely on the same notion of culture and that this notion of culture cannot do the prescriptive work it is asked to do without itself relying on a racial essentialism that virtually every participant in the debate repudiates. The reason everybody repudiates it is that we all feel a certain skepticism about whether very much can be said about people's beliefs and practices on the basis of their biological resemblance to other people of roughly the same size, shape, and color. But the reason that this repudiation doesn't in fact make the racial essentialism go away is that without racial essentialism we have no way of imagining a discrepancy between our culture on the one hand and our actual beliefs and practices on the other. And it is only this discrepancy that makes possible exemplary culturalist projects like recovering our culture, defending our culture, stealing someone else's culture, etc.

This is why anti-essentialist accounts of race (so-called), which insist that our racial identity is a function not of biology but of history or of culture, won't work. As Anthony Appiah has argued (in "The Uncompleted Argument: Du Bois and the Illusion of Race," *Critical Inquiry* 12, no.1 [Autumn 1985]), our racial identity can't be determined by the common history we share with others since, without some criterion of identity that is not itself historical, we have no way of determining the commonality of the history. We can't, for example, say that black Americans in the late twentieth century can be racially distinguished from white Americans in the late twentieth century by their history of enslavement, since the only thing that makes enslavement a part of the history of black Americans rather than white Americans is their blackness, is, in other words, the biological criterion of race that the historical criterion means to replace. So the appeal to history depends on rather than replaces the appeal to biology. There is no equivalent contradiction in thinking of race as culturally determined; there is, in other words, nothing contra-dictory in saying that "white" people are people who read Shakespeare (rather than Zora Neale Hurston), play baseball (rather than basketball), listen to Bach and heavy metal (rather than rap and Thelonious Monk), etc. But if racial identity is culturally determined in this way, then, of course, the culturalist phenomena mentioned above—losing your cultural identity, defending it, recapturing it—be-come impossible. For anyone who stopped reading Hurston and started reading Shakespeare would not have *lost* his cultural identity, he would just have *changed* it. And if he went back to reading Hurston, he would not have regained his cul-tural identity, he would just have changed it again. Culture, in other words, cannot provide a link between you and any practices other than the ones you actually practice; it cannot make things you never did or used to do more a part of your identity then the things you actually do. What can provide this link is race. Hence the appeal to culture, like the appeal to history, relies on the racial essentialism it sincerely professes to disdain.

From this standpoint, the interesting political question today is not the mean-ing of the debate over multiculturalism but the meaning of the agreement that makes the debate possible. It probably doesn't matter whether we read Shake-speare or Hurston; it probably does matter that our opposition to racial essential-ism is actually a commitment to racial essentialism.

Kenneth W. Warren

Appeals for (Mis)recognition

Theorizing the Diaspora

n 1920, some three years before he actually visited the African continent, Langston Hughes had implicitly theorized his connection to Africa in such poems as "The Negro Speaks of Rivers." Written on a train as Hughes traveled across the Mississippi river, the poem became a signature piece, its first line providing the title for one of the chapters of Hughes's autobiography *The Big Sea:*

> I've known rivers
> > I've known rivers ancient as the world and older
> > > than the flow of human blood in human veins.
>
> My soul has grown deep like the rivers.
>
> > I bathed in the Euphrates when dawns were young.
> > I built my hut near the Congo and it lulled me to sleep.
> > I looked upon the Nile and raised the pyramids above it.
> > I heard the singing of the Mississippi when Abe
> > > Lincoln went down to New Orleans, and I've seen
> > > its muddy bosom turn all golden in the sunset.
>
> I've known rivers;
> > Ancient, dusky rivers.
>
> My soul has grown deep like the rivers.[1]

To see the poem as a theory one has to see it as a claim of racial identity, of shared consciousness, of a Negro intersubjectivity in which old world and new world stand together in a mutual relationship that predates European civilization. The voice of Hughes's Negro, despite its movement across time from the "dawn of civilization" to the emancipation of enslaved black Americans, is presented as timeless. The poem creates "a unified image of . . . racial and spiritual antecedents" which has been deemed characteristic of African American thinking about the African mainland.[2] Emphasizing the African American's "original bonds with the ancestral continent," Hughes's "theory" sutures the new world and the old, thus positing the possibility of erasing the diaspora since the consciousness alluded to in the poem knows no separation: Africa is where its people are, and going to Africa is going to the self one already knows. Africa is not so much a discovery as a reconfirmation.

By reprinting his poem in *The Big Sea* Hughes suggests that his theory of African identity was subjected to a more or less empirical test when in 1923 he first visited Africa while serving as a mess-boy on a freighter. As Hughes narrates his voyage, he recalls that upon finally reaching "the great Africa of my dreams," he was forced to realize that "the Africans looked at me and would not believe I was a Negro" (11). They called Hughes a " 'white man,' " making Africa "the only place in the world where I've ever been called a white man" (103). This paradox opens Hughes's autobiography, a book which ends with the failure of the Harlem Renaissance and with Hughes heading to Haiti, rather than to Africa, because he "needed sun" (334).

Framed by voyages to Africa and the Caribbean, *The Big Sea* marks out the contradictions that often haunted attempts to realize black transatlantic political visions through the first forty years of the twentieth century. What I want to discuss here are not so much the overwhelming obstacles—the intellectual, political, economic, and military interventions of Western governments—that have impeded or undermined attempts to mobilize intercontinental black alliances against colonialism and imperialism, whether those attempts took the form of Marcus Garvey's United Negro Improvement Association or of W.E.B. Du Bois's call in *Darkwater* for the "building of a new African State."[3] Rather, using *The Big Sea* as a template, I would first like to explore the way that Hughes's biography illuminates the ambiguities that inhere in diasporic thought—ambiguities that make diasporic visions possible. Then I would like to address the way that those ambiguities encourage and frustrate both the desire to forge links between blacks in Africa and the West and the attempt to establish connections between black elites and masses in urban centers in the United States. If Hughes's poem proclaims the identity of the disparate peoples of the diaspora, his narrative confronts the difficulty of sustaining, from a new world perspective, the imaginative contemporaneity of Africa and the "West" and of black elites and masses.

Although "The Negro Speaks of Rivers" seeks to bring together the voices of the diaspora, the poem can make coincident only an African past and an African American present, leaving uninterrogated the relationship of Africans to black Americans in 1920.[4] Ancient Egypt in the poem is closer to blacks in the United States than is the Dakar or the Monrovia of the 1920s. Where Benedict Anderson has argued that nationalisms were launched largely upon the engine of print capitalism (the novel and the newspaper guaranteeing the simultaneity of experience that makes possible the imagined communities of nations),[5] Hughes tries to imagine an African transnationalism that dispenses with the technologies of print culture. As he embarks for Africa, Hughes throws his books, "all the books I had had at Columbia, and all the books I had lately bought to read," into the ocean (3).[6] Treating books as if they would be an impediment to his encounter with his idealized homeland, Hughes in "The Negro Speaks of Rivers" proffers the river itself, which is timeless and not marked by any date, as the shared text of the African imagination.

To be sure, the construction of pasts and traditions and the shedding of "foreign" influences are central features of nationalist visions. Here, however, Hughes's repudiation of written texts sets the stage for confounding the very project he is seeking to accomplish. To return again to Anderson's argument, the novel, the newspaper, and the "steady onward clocking of homogenous, empty time" denoted by the latter helped create an "imagined linkage" among disparate individuals, necessary for imagined communities. The newspaper guarantees the movement of time so that "if Mali disappears from the pages of *The New York Times* after two days of famine reportage, for months on end, readers do not for a moment imagine that Mali has disappeared or that famine has wiped out all its citizens. The novelistic format of the newspaper assures them that somewhere out there the character Mali moves along quietly, awaiting its next reappearance in the plot."[7] The series of rivers in "The Negro Speaks of Rivers," however, is really one continuing flow of water. Though it, too, assures us of Africa's continued existence, it does so only in terms of an endless extension of an "original bond." One never imagines that Mali ceases to exist; Africa is always there. Upon reencountering Mali, however, the voyager in Hughes's poetic vision also asserts that "time" has not meant anything to it or, for that matter, to any African geography. The Nile in "The Negro Speaks of Rivers" is the Nile of the pyramids. There is nothing new in Africa.

In fact, Africa is routinely imagined as the place about which, and from which, it is difficult to get the news. W. E. B. Du Bois, writing in his

1940 autobiography *Dusk of Dawn: An Essay Toward an Autobiography of a Race Concept* (and writing, not so coincidentally, about his trip to Liberia in 1923), observed that "The one great lack in Africa is communication—communication as represented by human contact, movement of goods, dissemination of knowledge. All these things we have. . . . [O]ur newspapers and magazines so overwhelm us with knowledge—knowledge of all sorts and kinds from particulars as to our neighbors' underwear to Einstein's mathematics—that one of the great and glorious joys of the African bush is to escape from 'news'"[8] The dateline that provides the pretext for simultaneous activity in the cultures of print capitalism would serve no purpose here. Africa is always imagined in retrospect— as the place one has come from—or in a retrospective prospect—as the home one is going to. In either case the contemporary "reality" of Africa and Africans is largely occluded by retrospective and prospective visions. Even when not fully occluded, African contemporaneity requires a reshuffling of temporal categories. "At the same time" acquires a different meaning when Du Bois attempts to place Africans and Westerners in the same temporal frame. "Primitive men," Du Bois writes, "are not following us afar, frantically waving and seeking our goals: primitive men are not behind us in some swift foot-race. Primitive men have already arrived. They are abreast, and in places ahead of us; in others behind. But all their curving advance line is contemporary, not prehistoric. They have used other paths and these paths have led them by scenes sometimes fairer, sometimes uglier than ours, but always toward the Pools of Happiness."[9] A version of the separate development argument, Du Bois's efforts to put Africa and the West on an equal temporal footing seems to require putting them on a "separate" temporal footing.

Upsetting Du Bois's harmonic diachrony, however, is the discovery that in having gotten at least some of the latest news, Africans are not only treading different paths, but intruding on Du Bois's own. Elsewhere in *Dusk of Dawn*, when describing the trouble he encountered while trying to establish the Pan-African Congress, Du Bois concedes that some communication was not difficult to get, even on the African continent: "News of [Marcus Garvey's] movement . . . [had] penetrated every corner of Africa."[10] Confirming Du Bois's observation, Hughes also observes that "the name of Marcus Garvey was known the length and breadth of the West Coast of Africa" (102). Moreover, not only had Africans heard of Garvey, they were willing to contest metropolitan readings of the news about him and to "read" Hughes and Du Bois in the light of the Garveyesque text. Hughes notes that many of the Africans he encountered regarded Garvey with a seriousness that he was no longer able to command in New York. "The Africans did not laugh at Marcus Garvey, as so many people laughed in New York. They hoped what they had heard about him was true—that he really would unify the black world, and free and exalt Africa" (102). African interpretations of Western news about Garvey were such that Du Bois was moved to complain that his own "Pan-African Congress was [often] confounded with the Garvey movement." As a result, Du Bois lamented that Garvey's problems reverberated beyond the sphere of his own organization, likewise subjecting Du Bois's enterprise to "suspicion and attack."[11]

Du Bois and Hughes discover that their own encounters with peoples from Africa were necessarily shaped by the Africans' prior encounters with those "presumably like them" (or with news about those presumably like them). Prior encounters and prior news mark the history of continued contact between Africa and African descendants in the West, a history which tends to get written out of imaginings such as those in "The Negro Speaks of Rivers" and which though acknowledged in *The Big Sea* does not become the basis of continued interactions. This elision both makes possible the misrecognitions that I will speak of shortly and points up how differences among black intellectuals and political leaders in the West (especially as these elites sought to legitimate themselves vis-á-vis the newly urbanized black masses) figure as central features of diasporic thinking.

Often described as a primitive, non-Western mass, the African Americans who began migrating to Northern cities during the early decades of the twentieth century presented to black writers and intellectuals a problem similar to that presented by the geographically distant inhabitants of Africa. In Richard Wright's *12 Million Black Voices*, another text contemporary with *The Big Sea*, Wright describes the migrating peasantry as a people whose "faces do not change . . . [whose] cheek bones remain as unaltered as the stony countenance of the Sphinx."[12] These masses read the newspapers, but take from these papers not an assurance that time moves on evenly throughout the world. Instead what they discover is that time moves for others and not for themselves: "We pick up the Chicago *Daily Tribune*, or the Cleveland *Plain Dealer*, or the Detroit *Free Press*, or the Philadelphia *Inquirer*, or the New York *Times*, and see that some former neighbor of ours, a Mr. and Mrs. Klein or Murphy or Potaci or Pierre or Cromwell or Stepanovich and their children—kids we once played with upon slag piles—are now living in the suburban areas, having swum upstream through the American waters of opportunity into the professional classes."[13] Wright's river, which he himself has successfully navigated, is not a river of memory but a river of progress. (In contrast to Hughes who hymns the Mississippi River as timeless, Wright sings the praises of the Ohio River as a threshold for the future—"it is a symbol, a line that runs through our hearts, dividing hope from despair, just as once it bisected the nation, dividing freedom from slavery" [205].) And like the immigrants he names in *Voices*, Wright has moved into the world defined by the newspaper, leaving behind those black Americans who "move slowly and speak slowly,"[14] and who in fact resemble Wright's father—"a black peasant who had gone to the city seeking life, but who had failed in the city . . . that same city which had lifted me in its burning arms and borne me toward alien and undreamed-of shores of knowing." The writer and the black peasant are "forever strangers, speaking a different language, living on vastly different planes of reality."[15] Written in the first-person plural as if to suggest that Wright's voice and that of the black laboring classes are one and the same, *12 Million Black Voices* nonetheless underscores the difference between Wright and his black brethren. If the first-person plural of *12 Million Black Voices* were to be realized, it would not be voiced by African Americans as they were, but as they were becoming. It would be uttered by those, who—unlike Wright's father—possessed the capacity to "mov[e] into the sphere of conscious history."[16]

While Hughes's account of the newly urbanized black peasantry departed dramatically from Wright's description of them as the backwater of racial progress, their visions share similar features. For Hughes, "the ordinary Negroes . . . who work hard for a living with their hands . . . [were] the people who keep on going" (208–9). The laboring folk who persisted in their country ways provided the guarantee of cultural continuity. Nonetheless these folk in Hughes's vision did not inhabit the same world as the black elites. In Harlem for example, time and experience are not at all homogenous for the different classes of blacks, but bifurcated: "The ordinary Negroes," Hughes observes, "hadn't heard of the Negro Renaissance" that had come to define the black literati (228). One had to have been an intellectual to have believed that the Harlem Renaissance had revolutionized the nation's racial hierarchy. According to Hughes, the renaissance had had a class-specific character to it, leaving the ordinary Negroes, like African blacks, in a different time frame.

What also functions in these narratives (other than temporal bifurcation) as a powerful organizing force is the emergence of the metropolis, not merely as the locus for trade but as the psychic map for renegotiating personal and group identity. The emergence of the urban center signals an initially subtle but ultimately decisive rewriting of points of origin—whether African homeland or rural small town—in terms of a telos of urbanization. This emergence did not necessarily mean, as Eric Hobsbawm points out, that the "urban poor were prepared to follow the lead of the frankly anti-traditionalist modernizers."[17] It signaled, rather, that these new urban masses were changing the world within which their "leaders" had traditionally operated.

When Booker T. Washington wrote *Up From Slavery* at the turn of the century, he could still lament urbanization as a false start for the development of black people. Troubled by the African Americans he saw in Washington, D. C., the Wizard of Tuskegee uttered the wish "that by some power of magic I might remove the great bulk of these people into the country districts and plant them upon the soil, upon the solid foundation of Mother Nature, where all nations and races that have ever succeeded have gotten their start—, a start that at first may be slow and toilsome, but one that is nevertheless real."[18] Though his wizardry was not equal to his wish, Washington's power as a Southern race leader was sufficient to impel a number of others to try to impede the black migration northward. "From Hampton Institute, Tuskegee, and elsewhere, Washingtonian spokesmen advised black southerners to stay on the farm."[19]

Washington's lament and efforts notwithstanding (he died in 1915), Northern cities by the 1920s had become the sites of the most up-to-date production of black identities which, it was assumed, would inspire emulation in those from the hinterlands. James Weldon Johnson's *Black Manhattan* (1930) in essence writes the history of African Americans as a journey to Harlem, with heroic figures from the black past—Harriet Tubman and Frederick Douglass—performing not merely as black Americans, but as prototypical New Yorkers. Of the latter, Johnson writes that "As long as there are American Negroes Frederick Douglass will be remembered, but he will be remembered and honoured chiefly for the prodigious things he accomplished as a Negro in New York."[20]

While it is undeniably true that a great deal of nostalgia for African American folk life attended the accelerated urbanization of the 1920s, it is important to see that such nostalgia did not necessarily bespeak a real desire to return to the countryside. The fact that Harlem itself, even during its 1920s heyday, was often the object of nostalgic longings indicates otherwise. These longings for return were rather a way of wondering whether "white" civilization on the one hand and black peasant culture on the other could be retrofitted with components taken from one another. If such an operation were plausible, then quite possibly an urbanized black intellectual elite would emerge not merely as the leadership cadre of blacks in the United States but as the vanguard of blacks worldwide. In the opinion of Antonio Gramsci, there was reason to welcome the "influence that these negro intellectuals could exercise on the backward masses of Africa."[21]

Whether uttered by Du Bois, Garvey, Gramsci, and others, optimism about the possibility of worldwide black leadership tended to assume that this process would proceed, at least for a time, along imperialist lines of power established between the West and Africa. In general, as Judith Stein points out, there was widespread agreement that jump-starting African modernity would require the "European . . . planning and efficiency" of the "new imperialism."[22] African American influence on the African continent would depend, according to Gramsci, largely on whether "American expansionism should use American negroes as its agents of conquest of the African market and the extension of American civilisation."[23] Striking similar notes, E. W. Blyden favor[ed] both English language and colonization as means for grafting "European progress wholesale on African conservatism and stagnation,"[24] and Marcus Garvey imagined the "trade relationship . . . in Africa, in the United States, in South and Central America and the West Indies" in such a way that the binding ties among black folk would have looked little different from those that linked American whites to African blacks. Had his enterprise succeeded, Garvey proclaimed, "we would have been removing raw materials from plantations of far-off Africa, from South and Central America, and the West Indies, to our factories in the United States."[25]

If the placement of Africa under direct control of European nation-states would make possible the capitalist transformation that African blacks, left to themselves, could not bring about, then all Western black elites need insist on was the ultimate right of blacks to rule in the stead of Europeans.[26] To be sure there were critical differences, real and imagined, between black and white imperialism. For example, the commission for the African State that Du Bois imagined in the 1920s was infused with socialist principles and urged that "there should be no violent tampering with the curiously efficient African institutions of local self-government through family and the tribe."[27] Nonetheless, though he was visiting Liberia under the auspices of the United States government, Du Bois clearly hoped that there was no chance of mistaking his intentions for those of untrustworthy white government officials. It should either have been possible for Liberians to recognize at a glance that Du Bois represented progressive rather than exploitative transatlantic relations or for

Du Bois to assure the Liberians that "the wishes and hopes of Negro Americans . . . [for] the advancement and integrity of Liberia [were] the sincere prayer[s] of America."[28]

If nothing else, Hughes's *The Big Sea* illustrates how uncertain was the likelihood of either possibility. Returning for the moment to the unwillingness of the Africans to regard Hughes as black, what Hughes receives from a Kru man from Liberia, presumably the Tom Pey who is mentioned elsewhere in the narrative, is an explanation which reveals that the refusal was more than a matter of color:

> "Here," he said, "on the West Coast, there are not many colored people— people of mixed blood—and those foreign colored men who are here come mostly as missionaries, to teach us something, since they think we know nothing. Or they come from the West Indies, as clerks and administrators in the colonial governments, to help carry out the white man's laws. So the Africans call them all *white* men."
>
> "But I am not white," I said.
>
> "You are not black either," the Kru man said simply. "There is a man of my color." And he pointed to George, the pantryman, who protested loudly.
>
> "Don't point at me," George said. "I'm from Lexington, Kentucky, U.S.A. And no African blood, nowhere."
>
> "You black," said the Kru man.
>
> "I can part my hair," said George, "and it ain't nappy."
>
> But to tell the truth, George shaved a part in his hair every other week, since the comb wouldn't work. The Kru man knew this, so they both laughed loudly, for George's face was as African as Africa. (103)

This comedy of misrecognition, in which Hughes who appeals for misrecognition as an African is misrecognized as white and George who appeals for misrecognition as a Kentuckian is misrecognized as African points up the conditions of the diasporan subject. Recognition can never preclude misrecognition because one can always be identified as other than what one claims to be. Hughes's appeal to be recognized by the Kru man as a fellow African opens up the possibility that he can be misrecognized as something other than African, as someone from a place outside of Africa, with interests distinct from those with whom he claims affinity. By Hughes's own admission the Kru man's misrecognition is correct. For example, in regard to his labor relations with the native people, Hughes, like "everybody else on board," had "an African boy to do my washing, my cleaning, and almost all my work" (7). Thus to be cognizant of oneself as a diasporan subject is always to be aware of oneself, no matter where one is, as from elsewhere, in the process of making a not quite legitimate appeal to be considered as if one were from here.

Even when Hughes "tell[s] the truth" about George's hair, he has not settled the matter. In light of the reasons that West Africans label colored people white, George would be no more African than Hughes. He is part of the crew on which Langston serves and which participates in the despoiling of the African towns where the ship docks. As if to depict graphically the ambiguity of diasporan identity, Hughes recalls a day when "crew-solidarity out weighed race" (116): During a fight against a multiracial crew from a British ship, "George and the Puerto Ricans and I yelled, too: 'Get them niggers! Get them limeys,'" forgetting that "we didn't like the word *nigger* applied to ourselves" (116).

The rather surprising ease with which racial solidarity is supplanted, even if only momentarily, by another group identification further indicates that the Kru man's suspicion about Hughes's claims of racial affinity are at least partially warranted. Had Hughes's critic been watching the altercation between the Malone and the British ship and overheard the epithets yelled by Hughes and his shipmates, he would have felt more than justified in labeling Hughes a white man. Nonetheless, Hughes's willingness to report this embarrassing episode suggests that a central concern of *The Big Sea* is not to hide, but to explore the various failures to secure black transatlantic aims. For example, Hughes dramatizes the failure of Garveyism by presenting "a colored tailor, a Garveyite who had long worshipped Africa from afar, and who had a theory of civilization all his own." An unmistakable air of ridicule pervades Hughes representation of the tailor's belief "that if he could just teach the Africans to wear proper clothes, coats and pants, they would be brought forward a long way toward the standards of our world" (8). In contrast to the sailors like Hughes who "carried nothing but ourselves" to the African continent, the Garveyite "carried with him on his journey numberless bolts of cloth, shears, and tailoring tools, and a trunk full of smart patterns" (8). The tailor's supplies, Hughes tells us, are of no use. Hughes goes on to claim that "years later, by accident, I ran into that same tailor in Washington and he said he had had no luck at all selling suits to Africans" (112).

Hughes's luck among the Africans in *The Big Sea*, however, is little better. If carrying copious supplies proves to be of no avail to the tailor's attempt to secure connections on the African continent, carrying nothing but oneself is shown to be equally ineffective for Hughes and his fellow black sailors, if their desire is to secure mutually beneficial relations. Hughes is rebuffed in his attempt to see the Omali dance because he is identified as "a white man." And when the penniless George spends the night with a woman on shore, it is only a Garveyesque manuever that saves him. Having been given a suit of clothes by the chief engineer, "George later gave the suit to a woman in Lagos with whom he stayed the night, because, in the morning he had no money to pay her, so she raised hell. Therefore, he gave her the suit" (110).

More curiously, when met with an African of mixed racial background named Edward, it is Hughes who rebuffs the attempted connection. Described as "a mulatto boy of perhaps sixteen or seventeen, whose skin was golden, not brown, or black" and "dressed in European clothing," Edward shows an extraordinary interest in England and the United States and "ask[s] if we had any English papers or magazines" (104). The boy's interest in the West derives largely from his isolation in his village where disapproval of his mother's relationship with a white man leaves Edward with "almost nobody to talk to" (104). Hughes, however, fails to provide the needed rescue. Studiously avoiding referring to Edward as an African, Hughes sympathizes with the young man's plight, but does not apparently assist him. Having thrown his books into the ocean, Hughes presumably has little to offer the young man except the news of the place he is trying to forget. Lonely and isolated, Edward is clearly seeking companionship and possibly passage out of Africa. He wishes to be a part of the world of print and print culture and to that end "had taken [Hughes's] address to write [him] in America" (105). The boy does write, but Hughes fails to respond, saying that he did not "know what to say" (105).

Hughes's failure to respond to Edward's letter—his inability to sustain a connection with the young man (Hughes does write a short story, "African Morning," based on the boy's troubles) marks a turning point in the narrative. The exploits of the sailors aboard the Malone grow more hostile to the coastal peoples. Having nothing to give in exchange for what one wants sets the stage for gross depredations by the Malone's crew. On one occasion Hughes's crew finds itself carrying British currency in a French colony, making it impossible for them to trade with the inhabitants: "The natives would not take the British money. They didn't know what it was. In fact, they thought it wasn't money at all, so we couldn't buy anything" (108). Like the rest of his crew, Hughes cannot conduct business. When, however, another boy in Hughes's crew discovers that United Cigar Coupons look passably like French francs, the crew is able to put this worthless currency into circulation so that they "bought up the town" (109). They go from being unable to buy anything to being able to buy everything, giving the peoples with whom they conduct business nothing of value in exchange. Then when two "African girls" row out to the Malone in order to sell sexual favors, they are exploited by crew. The "bo'sun" takes one of the girls for himself, and the other is raped repeatedly by the crew, who leave unanswered her cries for "Mon-nee! Mon-nee!" (108).

Hughes's text in no way endorses the Malone's more heinous exploits—Hughes goes to bed during the rape because he "couldn't bear to hear [the girl] crying," and when the African men in Burutu tell Hughes that "white strong men come to take our palm oil and ivory, our ebony and mahogany, to buy our women and bribe our chiefs" (108, 120), Hughes is deeply disturbed by a vision of a trade in African flesh that has not ended even in the twentieth century. Yet while registering Hughes's disgust with the actions of his shipmates, the autobiography mimics the Malone's desire to place distance between itself and its African transactions. For Hughes the text displays a desire to put distance between himself and the obligation that poems like "The Negro Speaks of Rivers" had implicitly assumed. These poems had attracted the attention of his wealthy white patron Charlotte Mason, whose preoccupation with a primitive vision of Africa threatened to fix Hughes in a rigid relationship with the continent. Wishing to create a museum of African art, she imagined, "little Negro children running in and out learning to respect themselves through the realization of those treasures. And . . . as the fire burned in me, I had the mystical vision of a great bridge reaching from Harlem to the heart of Africa, across which the Negro world, that our white United States had done everything to annihilate, should see the flaming pathway . . . and recover the treasure their people had had in the beginning of African life on the earth."[29] Hers is a vision that seeks to heal the separation constitutive of the diaspora, and it finds a welcome echo in Hughes's work.

In the light of her vision of a transatlantic highway, Mason insisted that Hughes continue to turn out poetry celebrating black "primitiveness." But as Hughes describes his decision in *The Big Sea*, he resisted her vision by adopting George's strategy of claiming an identity located in American geography: "She wanted me to be primitive and know and feel the intuitions of the primitive. But, unfortunately, I did not feel the rhythms of the primitive surging through me, and so I could not live and write as though I did. I was only an American Negro—who had loved the surface of Africa and the rhythms of Africa—but I was not Africa. I was Chicago and Kansas City and Broadway and Harlem. And I was not what she wanted me to be" (325). While Hughes could have objected to his patron's expectations by challenging her definition of Africa as the locale of the primitive (he might have, for example, told her of Tom Pey and of Edward), he chooses instead to locate himself within an American geography, an urban geography, reinvoking George's protest to the Kru man. However, while George's invocation of American geography was calculated simply as a denial of an African connection, Hughes uses the American claim to assert a specific political identity. He claims a class identification within the African-American social structure which sets him against the "upper class colored people consist[ing] largely of government workers, professors and teachers, doctors, lawyers, and resident politicians" (206), giving in the text a hint at the radical politics that had really upset Mason. Having written poems that subsume race within an interracial class identification, Hughes had precipitated a break with his patron.

But in *The Big Sea* even his embrace of a radical identity is more a strategy of disavowal than an assumption of another obligation. Poems which would have irked Mason, like "An Open Letter to the South" which laid claim to "the mines and the factories and the office towers/At Harlan, Richmond, Gastonia, Atlanta, New Orleans," are largely supplanted in the text by the urban geographies of lower-class black folk.[30] While Arnold Rampersad overstates the case in saying that in *The Big Sea* Hughes's "leftist opinions and involvements have vanished without a trace"[31]—Hughes reminds his readers that his poems had been called "proletarian" (272)— Hughes was indeed worried about his possible "estrange[ment] from the black masses." The problem, however, was not that "radicalism paid very poorly in America,"[32] but that poetry itself was not a mass art form, and Hughes's aesthetic called for him to be a poet of the people who was paid like a professional.

Although Hughes opens his text by throwing his books into the ocean, the desire that becomes most evident by the end of the narrative is the desire "to put into books" the "masses of our people" and to "mak[e] my living from writing." Correspondingly, Hughes ends *The Big Sea* with a gesture of retrieval: "Literature is a big sea full of many fish. I let down my nets and pulled" (335). The sea that Hughes imagines, however, is a sea full of fish and not fishermen. The masses have a story worth telling, but Hughes's narrative does not, indeed cannot, fully imagine them doing so. Nonetheless in expressing the desire to connect with others outside the pages of a book, Hughes's text utters the political desires of a literary elite to ground itself in a distinctly black, laboring class identity. This desire was not specious but stemmed from the fact that the expressive power of black literature in the West has derived from its necessary misrecognition as a world-changing force. *The Big Sea* censures the naive aspects of such misrecognitions by excoriating the millennial expectations of the Harlem literati. Nonetheless, Hughes's commitment to the laboring black masses and to the lingering shadow of Africa was itself evidence that Hughes could not entirely dispense with such misrecognitions himself. This is to say that the world that Hughes's text sought to imagine and represent was indeed undergoing dramatic changes, changes which his work could register and seek to keep abreast of, but which it could not itself affect or control. The well-rounded shape of Hughes's biography notwithstanding, what *The Big Sea*—even through its title—pointed up was that the diaspora is a thought whose closure cannot be seen by any one individual nor imagined by any single text. It both was and was not Garvey's *Black Star Line* and Du Bois's Pan-African Congress. It was and was not Tom Pey's refusal to countenance Hughes's face as African. It was and is, perhaps most of all, a desire to speak these contradictions in a single voice. Yet, as emblemized by Edward's unanswered letter to Langston Hughes, this voice could not be single but was, and is, poignantly dependent on getting an answer from invisible shores.

Notes

1 Langston Hughes, *The Big Sea* (New York: Hill and Wang, 1940), pp. 55–56. Further references appear parenthetically in text.

2 Abiola Irele, *The African Experience in Literature and Ideology* (Bloomington: Indiana University Press, 1970), p. 90.

3 W. E. B. Du Bois, "The Hands of Ethiopa," in *Writings* (New York: Library of America, 1986), p. 948.

4 Also see in this regard, "Afro-American Fragment," in *Selected Poems of Langston Hughes* (1959; New York: Vintage, 1990), p. 3.

5 Benedict Anderson, *Imagined Communities: Reflections on the Origin and Spread of Nationalism* (New York: Verso, 1983), pp. 28–49.

6 Hughes did, however, keep his copy of Walt Whitman's *Leaves of Grass*. See Arnold Rampersad, *The Life of Langston Hughes: vol. 1 1902–41, I, Too, Sing America* (New York: Oxford University Press, 1986), p. 72.

7 Anderson, p. 37.

8 W. E. B. Du Bois, *Dusk of Dawn: An Essay Toward an Autobiography of a Race Concept*, in *Writings*, p. 648.

9 Ibid., p. 647.

10 Ibid., p. 757.

11 Ibid., p. 757.

12 Richard Wright, *12 Million Black Voices,* photo direction by Edwin Rosskam (1941; New York: Thunder's Mouth Press, 1988), p. 102.

13 Ibid.

14 Ibid., 103.

15 Richard Wright, *Black Boy (American Hunger),* in *Later Works* (New York: Library of America, 1991), p. 35.

16 Ibid., p. 24.

17 Eric Hobsbawm, *The Age of Empire: 1875–1914* (New York: Vintage, 1987), p. 31.

18 Booker T. Washington, *Up From Slavery,* in *Three Negro Classics* (New York: Avon, 1965), p. 77.

19 James R. Grossman, *Land of Hope: Chicago, Black Southerners, and the Great Migration* (Chicago: University of Chicago Press, 1989), p. 57.

20 James Weldon Johnson, *Black Manhattan* (New York: Da Capo Press, 1930), p. 57.

21 Antonio Gramsci, "The Intellectuals," in *Selections from the Prison Notebooks,* ed. and trans. Quintin Howe and Geoffrey Nowell South (New York: International Publications, 1971), p. 21.

22 Judith Stein, *The World of Marcus Garvey: Race and Class in Modern Society* (Baton Rouge: Louisiana State University Press, 1986), p. 11.

23 Gramsci, p. 21.

24 Quoted in V. Y. Mudimbe, *The Invention of Africa: Gnosis, Philosophy, and the Order of Knowledge* (Bloomington: Indiana University Press, 1988), p. 103.

25 Marcus Garvey, "Autobiography," in *Marcus Garvey: Life and Lessons: A Centennial Companion to the Marcus Garvey and Universal Negro Improvement Association Papers,* ed. Robert A. Hill and Barbara Bair (Berkeley: University of California Press, 1987), p. 91.

26 Stein, p. 11.

27 Du Bois, "The Hands of Ethiopia," p. 949.

28 Du Bois, *Dusk of Dawn,* pp. 645–646.

29 Quoted in Rampersad, pp. 147–148.

30 Langston Hughes, "An Open Letter to the South," in *Voices of a Black Nation: Political Journalism in the Harlem Renaissance,* ed. Theodore G. Vincent (Trenton, N. J.: Africa World Press, 1973), p. 173.

31 Rampersad, p. 378.

32 Ibid., p. 375.

Doris Sommer

Resisting the Heat

Menchú, Morrison, and Incompetent Readers

> Melting everything else with resistless heat, and solving all lesser and definite distinctions in vast, indefinite spiritual, emotional power.—Walt Whitman, "Democratic Vistas"

ears of privileged literary training, understandably, add up to a kind of entitlement to know a book, possibly with the possessive and reproductive intimacy of Adam who knew Eve. As teachers and students we have until now welcomed resistance as a coy, teasing invitation to test and hone our mastery. We may pick up a book because we find it attractive—or because of mimetic desire through (for) a model reader, the real object of our murderous desire to displace her. Always, we assume in our enlightened secular habits that the books are happy to have our attention, like so many wallflowers lined up to be selected for a quick turn or an intimate tête-à-tête. If the book seems easy, if it allows possession without a struggle and cancels the promise of self-flattery for an expert reading, our hands may go limp at the covers. Easy come easy go.

The more difficult the book the better. Difficulty is a challenge, an opportunity to struggle and to win, to overcome resistance, uncover the codes, to get on top of it, to put one's finger on the mechanisms that produce pleasure and pain, and then to call it ours. We take up an unyielding book to conquer it and to feel grand, enriched by the appropriation and confident that our cunning is equal to the textual tease that had, after all, planned its own submission as the ultimate climax of reading. Books want to be understood, don't they, even when they are coy and evasive? Evasiveness and ambiguity are, as we know, familiar interpretive flags that readers erect on the books they leave behind. Feeling grand and guiltless, we proceed to the next conquest.

"I am only interested in what does not belong to me. Law of Man. Law of the Cannibal" is the gluttonous way Oswald de Andrade inflected this desire to conquer difference. Appropriation of the other is what our New World cultures feed on, according to the Brazilian modernist, as long as the other offers the spice of struggle. Cannibals reject the bland meat easily consumed, in this digestion of Montaigne's essay.[1] Europe, apparently, was also constituted by ingesting its others. And Andrade's point is, after all, that cannibalism is what makes us all human, or at least participants in an extended occidental culture nourished on novelty. Therefore, his provocations can stand in more clearly for other, more contrite, admissions of plunder.

But refusal need not be entirely coy, not simply a barrier to enhance desire for the chase. It is also a barricade against the rush of short-lived sentimental identification that oversteps restricted positions and lasts hardly longer than the reading. Refusal becomes the unaccountable remainder of voracious mastery, an indigestible residue of bones and bitter innards. It is a self-authorizing strategy that incites desire in order to chasten it.

Some books resist the competent reader, intentionally. Cool before the Whitmanian heat that would melt down differences, as if they obstructed democratic vistas, unyielding texts erect signposts of impassable terrain between reader and text. They raise questions of access or welcome to produce a kind of readerly "incompetence" that more reading will not overcome. I am not referring to the ultimate or universal impossibility to exhaust always ambiguous literature through interpretation. Ambiguity, unlike the resistance that interests me here, has been for some time a consecrated and flattering theme for professional readers. It blunts interpretive efforts and thereby invites more labor, so that ambiguity allows us to offset frustrated mastery with a liberating license to continue endlessly. Nor do I mean resistance as the kind of ideally empty or even bored refusal to narrate that Flaubert apparently pioneered when he would stop a story to contemplate some diegetically insignificant detail.[2]

The kind of incompetence I am advocating is obviously not what Alan Bloom and others lament as a failure of education, but rather a modest-making goal. It is the goal of respecting the distances and refusals that some texts have been broadcasting to our still deaf ears.[3] Here my language feels the lack of a transitive verb derived from "modesty." Its intransitivity may be no surprise for those of us who inhabit carefree, or careless, languages of criticism and who can easily name the contrary movement: to approach, explore, interpret, freely associate, understand, empathize, assimilate, conquer.

Neither the undecidability of interpretation nor the novel pauses over what is or is not relevant to tell; the issue is, rather, the rhetoric of selective, socially differentiated understanding. Announcing limited access is the point, not whether or not some information is really withheld. Resistance does not necessarily signal a genuine epistemological impasse; it is enough that the impasse is claimed in this ethico-aesthetic strategy to position the reader within limits. The question, finally, is not what "insiders" can know as opposed to "outsiders"; it is how those positions are being constructed as incommensurate or conflictive. And professional readers who may share some social space with a writer, enough to claim privileged understanding and explanatory powers, may miss, or hastily fill in, the constitutive gaps these texts would demarcate.

I want to call attention to the habitually overlooked markings that would construct this kind of incompetence, because privileged readers are unaccustomed to rebuffs, so unaccustomed and ill prepared that slights may go unattended.[4] As textual markers of inassimilable difference, these slights are critical for obvious political as well as aesthetic reasons. No less scandalous than Flaubert's narrative sidetracks, the refusals of familiarity should produce the kind of gaps between text and reader that Gérard Genette describes as shaped like literary figures.[5] But unfamiliarity with those figures means that readers may fail to notice them. And failing to notice means that our readerly vocabulary of conventions lags behind the literary production. Readers override restrictions they have never been taught to respect. The tautological result has been that, because signs of resistance lack a recognizable pattern for readers, they remain obscure and unexpected, as unremarked and invisible for privileged reading as ethnicity or gender can be for conservative politics. Anticipating resistance is one partial remedy. One purpose of this essay, then, is to build an expectation of calculated rebuff. A corollary purpose is to contribute, if only minimally, to a provisional vocabulary for the patterns and tropes of resistance. These would describe a strategic (not paradoxical) invitation to exclusion.

Sometimes the signs will be easy to read. But recognizing polite evasiveness or defensive distractions will take both practice and the sensitivity that comes along with expectation. Zora Neale Hurston gives this lesson to would-be collectors of Afro-American folklore and very possibly to readers of Afro-American literature as well.

> They are most reluctant at times to reveal that which the soul lives by. And the Negro, in spite of his open-faced laughter, his seeming acquiescence, is particularly evasive. You see, we are a polite people and we do not say to our questioner, "Get out of here!" We smile and tell him or her something that satisfies the white person because, knowing so little about us, he doesn't know what he is missing. The Indian resists curiosity by a stony silence. The Negro offers a feather-bed resistance. That is, we let the probe enter, but it never comes out. It gets smothered under a lot of laughter and pleasantries.
>
> The theory behind our tactics: "The white man is always trying to know into somebody else's business. All right. I'll set something outside the door of my mind for him to play with and handle. He can read my writing but he sho' can't read my mind. I'll put this play toy in his hand, and he will seize it and go away. Then I'll say my say and sing my song."[6]

The newly identified tropes may sound like so many textual defense mechanisms. And the label is hardly misplaced, as long as defense carries its military and strategic meanings. Hurston may be suggesting that the defense strategies work *because* they are unperceived and so do not provoke a dogged insistence to trespass. Like the Greek art of *metis* (transformation and transmutation) which Françoise Lionnet sees revived by writers such as Maya Angelou, this is "an aesthetics of the ruse that allows the weak to survive by escaping through duplicitous means the very system of power intent on destroying them."[7] Yet Hurston herself calls attention to the tactic, saying, in effect, that whites can never know blacks except through mediations, such as the book we are reading.[8] Is Hurston's own self-defensive move simply a self-serving promotion of her book? Is it a friendly caution against useless prying? Or is it a characteristically polite hint that the "knowledge" used by whites against blacks is hopelessly naive? If she is indeed saying that we cannot know all the while that she is telling us how we might go about it—"hitting a straight lick with a crooked stick," so typical of Eatonville, she says, and of her own notably evasive autobiography[9]—the only responsible reading would be to acknowledge the rhetorical maneuver that positions us as outsiders and therefore as ignorant. The purpose of announcing an epistemological dead end, I imagine, is to stop short our presumption that knowledge and the power it implies are attainable.

Outsider, it will be objected, is not a fixed or impermeable category. Frederick Douglass, for one, knew that and explained that different understandings of slavery resulted from unequal experiences, not from essential differences among blacks and whites. Presumably, emancipated blacks saw things differently from black slaves. The free human being, Douglass explained, "cannot see things in the same light with the slave, because he does not, and cannot, look from the same point from which the slave does."[10] Douglass also noted that he could hardly have commented on that experience if he were not already outside it.[11] Likewise, Hurston intimates that coming home to Eatonville with a "spy-glass of Anthropology" made her a bit exotic there.[12] And certainly Menchú suffers the irony of betraying norms of her community in order to preserve it, becoming an "outsider" in order to stay inside.

Remembering Douglass in this context suggests that responsible incompetence and degrees of readerly underachievement may teach us to remark the resistant signs of an older tradition of Afro-American literature that knew how to distance its "ideal" abolitionist readers. Writing often at the unrefusable request of white allies and supporters, slave narrators may logically have foregone uncooperative gestures. Yet many readers will recall how Harriet Jacobs interrupts her otherwise intimate confessions of *Incidents in the Life of a Slave Girl* (1861) to stop her white readers from presuming to judge her. You "whose purity has been sheltered from childhood, who have been free to choose the objects of your affection, whose homes are protected by law, do not judge the poor desolate slave girl too severely!"[13] And some readers may find it significant that Cuba's Juan Francisco Manzano changed his mind about what to write for abolitionist Domingo del Monte. The slave had agreed to record his memoirs for the man whose support could mean freedom for the author, but a second letter explained that candor about certain incidents would be impossible. One reason may have been the retaliation he feared in a still slavocratic country; another, as Sylvia Molloy notes, was the developing control that came with the project of self-authorship.[14] I want to speculate, though, that a third reason may have been some skepticism about the possibility of sharing the pain specific to slavery. Typically, the narrative locates a threshold and stops: "but let's leave to silence the rest of this painful scene."[15] Frederick Douglass's general point—about the locus of enunciation constituting knowledge—would surely evoke more remembered refusals to identify with readers, if only we had learned to recognize a rhetoric of refusal.

To notice the unstable boundaries between the self who writes and the other who reads is not to vitiate the opposition. It is merely to repeat what every military strategist knows: that the lines of battle change and the conflict continues. Subject positions, we know, are not fixed through time. But in the war of positions that reading so often is, historically specific positions matter.[16]If we are used to assuming the virtues of over-stepping the frontier between self and other, or to confusing deconstruc-tion with assimilation, we may need to consider the differential effects of liberal and universalist principles when the other is magnanimously absorbed into the greater self. This condescendingly generous gesture in, for example, Tzevan Todorov's *The Conquest of America* has characteris-tically evoked very different responses. One is guilt-ridden sympathy for the Aztecs (whose worldview and technology could not compete with the more realistic Spaniards). Another is outrage at the invidious compari-sons that lament the disaster by explaining its inevitability. Like Mexico's first Jesuit chroniclers and catechists, Todorov assumes that the catholic or universal self already inhabits the particularist pagan other and that history is a process of accommodations that need not be so violent.[17]

It may surprise some well-meaning readers to find that particular-ists are not always accommodating, that assimilation rhymes more with cultural annihilation than with progressive *Aufhebung*. The ecumenical gestures to reduce otherness to sameness suggest that difference is a superable problem rather than a source of pride or simply the way we are in the world.[18] Unyielding responses to the liberal embrace, the re-sponses that I am tracking here, range from offering up a surrogate self whose absorption is no real loss, the "feather-bed resistance" that Hurston described, to striking the pose of an intransigent, unaccommodating self from the place "competent" readers have associated with the other. This "strategically essentialist"[19] pose may not need to construct a stable, co-herent, speaking subject whom readers, after all, could then presume to know and to represent. The purpose of intransigence and refusal is to cast doubts on our capacity to know, without allowing incapacity to float into the comforting, unmanageable, mists of ambiguity. It is to say that some texts decline the intimately possessive knowledge that passes for love.

I remember Edward Said interrupting a question about the possibili-ties for curing the blindness he denounced in *Orientalism*. How should we achieve a better understanding of the Arab world, the sincere col-league was asking. "How we can avoid the mistakes, get closer to the truth, and . . ." Said interrupted to ask why Westerners suppose that the "Orient" wants to be understood correctly. Why did we assume that our interest in the "Orient" was reciprocated? Did we imagine that the desire was mutual or that we were irresistible? Could we consider, along with the dangerous spiral of knowledge and power decried in his book, the possibility that our interest was not returned? This possibility of nonrequited interest is one lesson to be learned from the kind of textual resistance I am describing here.

Rigoberta Menchú has been teaching it to me. It was her testimonial that tipped me off about the function of loud silences and publicly refused intimacy[20] (suggesting that interpretation may want to pursue Hurston's lead into anthropology). Menchú's quincentennial experience with Spanish-speaking conquerors of Guatemalan Indians had warned her not to share secrets with ill-prepared, and unreliable, readers who "cannot [and should not] know" them.[21] She uses the document as a screen, in the double sense of showing and covering up, allegedly hiding the largely "public" secrets, known to the Quichés and kept from us in a gesture of self-preservation. "They say that the Spaniards raped and destroyed the best of our ancestors' children . . . to honor them we must guard our secrets. And those secrets no one will discover except for us, the indigenous people" (Menchú, 50).[22] (See also 55, 60, 118, 131, 133, 155, 212, 275, 299.) The very last words of the testimonial are, "I continue to hide what I think no one else knows. Not even an anthropologist, nor any intellectual, no matter how many books he may have read, can know all our secrets" (377).[23] But the almost four hundred foregoing pages are full of information: about Rigoberta herself, her community, traditional practices, the armed struggle, strategic decisions.

Therefore, a reader may wonder what "cannot know" secrets means and why so much attention is being called to our insufficiency as readers. Does it mean that the knowledge is impossible or that it is forbidden? Is she saying that we are *incapable* of knowing or that we *ought* not to know? Her withholding, on this reading, is a calculated investment in diversification, much like the passages in Toni Morrison's *Beloved* where the story stops short, seems reluctant. Perhaps one woman's telling restraint can help to say something about another's.

Now Rigoberta's audible silence is apparently a response to an anthropologist's questioning. If she were not being interrogated, there would be no reason to refuse answers. And of course Morrison's display of reticence seems equally explicable by a familiar narrative logic that makes delayed information goad curiosity and build suspense. But this readerly reasoning doesn't really explain why Rigoberta's refusal to tell secrets remains on the page after the anthropologist's editing job is done nor why Morrison bothers to perform an insistent refusal of her genre's demand for intimacy, all the while divulging more and more un-kept secrets. Certain habits of reading may therefore overstep the trench that both performances dig between competency and satisfaction.

Some readers actually manage to embrace Rigoberta in an autobio-graphical reflex that presumes identification with the writer, despite her reluctance to be fully comprehended. The projections of presence and truth are hardly generous here. Instead, they allow for an unproblema-tized appropriation which disregards the text's insistence on the political value of keeping us at a distance. And I wonder whether Morrison's nar-rative evasions may give as little pause to her readers whose habit of processing suspended or guarded information as a simple technique for building intrigue misses Morrison's intriguing double bind: To tell Sethe's story and arouse sympathy for her is also to reveal so much pain that tell-ing threatens to reinscribe the terror and humiliation she escaped. "Paul D. had only begun, what he was telling her was only the begin-ning when her fingers on his knee, soft and reassuring, stopped him. Just as well. Just as well. Saying more might push them both to a place they couldn't get back from. He would keep the rest where it belonged: a tobacco tin buried in his chest where a red heart used to be" (72). (I am reminded also of a young German scholar who recently wondered out loud why we children of Jewish survivors prefer to elicit that "Just as well" from parents who stop telling war stories, as if it were difficult for him to intuit that the hunger for memory might be sated or even spoiled by unchildish recollections of a displaced persons' camp, recur-ring parental nightmares, occasional unsolicited details.) Yet not to tell would leave Sethe, Paul D., and an entire society of survivors without the history that binds them, leave them unwritten like the displaced postwar blacks who were "Silent, except for social courtesies, when they met one another[;] they neither described nor asked about the sorrow that drove them from one place to another" (53). It is Denver's broken silence, after all, that makes her mother available for the sympathy that effects a col-lective absolution. Morrison is both bound to tell and to claim she is not telling. "It was not a story to pass on," repeats the double-binding epilogue about this story just passed on to us. Morrison's novel makes us worry too, about how much can or should be known, as if the testimony and the fiction were both media for producing this readerly circumspection.

How else are we to take Rigoberta's, or Morrison's, protestations of silence as she/they continue(s) to talk? How to distinguish between one text's fact and the other's fiction? Are there really many secrets that Rigo-berta is not divulging, in which case her restraint would be "true" and real? Or is she consciously performing a kind of rhetorical seduction in which she lets the fringe of a hidden text show in order to tease us into thinking that the fabric must be extraordinarily complicated and beautiful, even though there may not be much more than fringe to show? Conversely, is fictional seduction all we get in *Beloved,* or are we enchanted with the help of disturbingly historical details that tease us into wanting more? If we happen not to be anthropologists or historians, how passionately interested do they imagine the reader to be in their secrets? Yet both narratives make this very assumption and therefore pique a curiosity that may not have preexisted their resistance. That is why it may be useful to notice that the refusal is performative; it constructs metaleptically the apparent cause of the refusal. Before Rigoberta denies us satisfaction, we are not aware of any desire to know her secrets. Before Morrison flaunts a historical fringe before us, we may not know how much historical fabric we need to recover.

This is to say that resistant texts are necessarily provocative too. They seem calculated to produce desire in order to restrain or to frustrate it. A challenge for Menchú or Morrison is, logically, how to be interesting without promising the dividends of ownership. It is to produce enough desire for refusal to be felt, because the objective here is to engage unfamiliar, perhaps unfriendly, readers, not to be ignored by them. And through a convenient metalepsis that René Girard should help us to notice,[24] refusal itself can produce desire. Their books will aggressively claim power, if only the power to exclude, to say no to master's (dividend bearing) interest. Before they can refuse attention, they have to elicit it. And they do so by a slight to our vanity. Smarting from the snub by the humble likes of a Guatemalan Indian or the Mexican washwoman in Elena Poniatowska's novel,[25] and from the reserve of the black novelist and a Chicano conservative like Richard Rodriguez,[26] we may wonder what kind of superiority in the other accounts for our interpretive demotion.

Their tactic is neither to chastise our egotism nor to implore our ethical self-effacement, as Emmanuel Levinas does in work briefly considered below. They do not insist or plead for recognition by creating individual subjectivities associated with empowered men, the way some feminists have done. A limitation or boomerang effect of all these strategies is that they assume the primacy of the privileged reader, the one who can chose to be modest or who can learn to share his fully human status with others. Instead, the writers I want to privilege here assume that their own positionality is primary and that access to it is limited. With telling asides about the reader's difference from the narrator, with truncated allusions and purposeful incomprehensibility, their texts refuse to flow. The readings they permit, between stop signs and warnings against trespassing, teach a faltering, self-doubting step too lame for conquest.

The lesson is directed aggressively at the reader. And it should make us suspicious of our habitual resistance to resistance from an apparently liberationist, feminist point of view. During decades of feminist campaigns for self-empowerment, we have learned to demand that books "break the silence." And yet I am arguing here that respect demands hearing silence and refusal without straining to get beyond them. Strategic silence may itself be the message. Long ago, Sor Juana Inés de la Cruz gave the same reading instructions to the bishop who demanded her silence. She complied, in a way, but insisted that the discreet hush of her reply should not be taken for acquiescence. "But as silence is a negative thing, though it explains a great deal through the very stress of not explaining, we must assign some meaning to it that we may understand what the silence is intended to say. So that of things one cannot say, it is needful to say at least that they cannot be said."[27] To listen for reluctance, we will have to resist the reflex that Adrienne Rich, among many others, celebrated in a classic statement of 1975. "[W]e are breaking silences long established, 'liberating ourselves from our secrets, . . . hearing each other into speech.' How do we listen? How do we make it possible for another to break her silence?"[28]

By this point in the women's movements (and of the present essay) a reader may wonder if all women are equally served by candid, open disclosure of information and feelings to an indiscriminate public. That would assume that we are all equally affected by information and intimacy. Does insisting on speaking up liberate some and violate others? This is one underdeveloped question in a white feminism that finds it hard to acknowledge hierarchy among women. For one glaring example, consider the insistence of the editors of *Autobiographical Essays by Native American Writers* in response to contributors who resist telling. "While our presentation of autobiographies of contemporary Native American writers may seem to testify to the congeniality of the autobiographical form to Indians today, the reality is finally much more complex. Thus, a contributor . . . movingly wrote in a covering letter: 'You should realize that focusing so intently on oneself like that and blithering on about your own life and thoughts is very bad form for Indians.'"[29] And though black women increasingly bring the literature and experience of Afro-American women more plainly into focus, as does Barbara Smith, they may well protest the pain and personal costs that the work incurs.[30]

In some resistant texts, silence is a willed omission of trauma, a defensive armor against humiliating or panic provoking memories. "Silent, except for social courtesies, when they met one another," Morrison writes of displaced blacks; "they neither described nor asked about the sorrow that drove them from one place to another."[31] And another passage of *Beloved* begins, "Everything in it [her past life] was painful or lost. She and Baby Suggs had agreed without saying so that it was unspeakable."[32] Harriet Jacobs had written to the New York *Tribune*, "But no, I will not tell you of my own suffering—no, it would harrow up my soul."[33] The unspoken agreement to force forgetting into a willed activity, the common understanding that to evoke a past degradation may diminish us (despite promises that confronting the past is liberating, promises probably made from outside of the horrific history), these necessarily recall for me some passages of Holocaust literature too. It thematizes silence in a way that points to the missing and gruesome details that are refused inscription. Consider, for one short example, Eleonora Lev's self-censuring reminiscence called "Don't Take Your Daughter to the Extermination Camp." "The thing I always try to keep secret from her—out of shame, out of fear of hurting—is the rabid dog, the drooling, worm-infested beast, eyes inflamed, who races about madly in a corner of my mind. . . . What do you do when you visit a gas chamber, what do you do? . . . For years you've been imagining, haven't you, that studying the technical details would help you understand, digest it, lance the inner abscess which fills with pus each time anew. Why did you imagine that?"[34] Instead, we might imagine another reason, besides the provocations of unrequited desire, for writers like Morrison and Menchú to protest silence. Perhaps they withhold secrets because we are so different and would understand them only imperfectly. Or should we not know them for ethical reasons, because our knowledge would lead to a preempting power. Like Nietzsche's meditation on the nature of rhetoric in general, the difference between cannot and should not is undecidable.[35] Because even if Rigoberta's own explicit rationale is the nonempirical, ethical reason about keeping powerful information from outsiders, she suggests another constraint. It is the degree of our foreignness, our cultural difference that would make her secrets incomprehensible to the outsider. This may be why Morrison takes so long to get to the point: "Sethe knew that the circle she was making around the room, him, the subject, would remain one. That she could never close in, pin it down for anybody who had to ask. If they didn't get it right off—she could never explain. Because the truth was simple. . . . she was squatting in the garden and when she saw them coming . . . if she thought anything, it was No. No. Nono. Nonono. Simple. She just flew" (163). We could never know the secrets, even if she told them, because we would inevitably force them into our framework. And Rigoberta complains, for example, that "Theologians have come who have seen and constructed a very different conception of the indigenous world" (42).

Guatemalan Indians have a long history of being read that way by outsiders who speak European languages. From the sixteenth century to the present, the Maya have been "Surviving Conquest," as a recent demographic analysis puts it. "Model villages are designed to serve similar purposes as colonial congregaciones—to function as the institutional means by which one culture seeks to reshape the ways and conventions of another, to operate as authoritarian mechanisms of resettlement, indoctrination, and control."[36] The less apprehension in/by Spanish, the better; it is the language that the enemy uses to conquer differences. For an Indian, to learn Spanish can amount to passing over to the other side, to the Ladinos, which simply means "Latin" or Spanish speakers.[37] One paradox that Rigoberta has to negotiate in her politics of cultural preservation is the possibility of becoming the enemy because she needs Spanish as the lingua franca in a country of twenty-two language groups. But Morrison is already at the far side of a more subtle negotiation for an internal distance, squarely inside an English language that had exiled and then eliminated competing others. "What Nan told her she had forgotten," Sethe remembers, "along with the language she told it in. The same language her ma'am spoke, and which would never come back. But the message—that was and had been there all along" (62). Rigoberta's analogous message of independence and resistance is also delivered in the displacing language, the only one that can make her an effective leader of a heterogeneous coalition of peasants and workers.[38] Binding herself to politics and bound to her people, Rigoberta doubles herself dangerously. To perform in Spanish, her father warns, "you would try to forget what we have in common" (162).[39] That's why he keeps her out of school where she would be Latinized, declassed, as she calls it (301). Being Indian is a fragile cultural-linguistic construction, not an indelibly "racial" given. No wonder that the Quiché marriage ceremony includes the couple's promise to raise children as Indians.[40] The danger, in other words, is as much assimilation as it is aggression. Whether the Ladinos are welcoming or murderous, they mean cultural extinction.

It is perfectly possible, and (personally) tragic for Rigoberta, to stop being an "Indian" because in this testimonial, in the coalition, and at forums such as the United Nations she constructs herself in Spanish; that is, she reads herself in a homogenizing code that eliminates by inclusion. It is a curiously different code from the English that effects no catholic subsumption but an internal displacement for Morrison, one that makes her telling both possible and impossible.[41]

My reason for posing the question of rhetorical strategy—whether Rigoberta's "secrets" are withheld information or tropes of refusal, whether Morrison is hiding or seeking communication—is to read appropriately and responsibly texts which ceaselessly call attention to their difference from the reader and to the danger of overstepping cultural limits. Personally, I prefer to think that Rigoberta's secrets are more "literary" than "real." Let me explain why. Reading her refusal of intimacy as a deliberate textual strategy, whether or not much data come between the producer and consumer of this text, makes the gesture more self-conscious and repeatable than it would be if she merely remained silent on particular issues. The gesture precisely is not silence but a resonant No. No. Nono. Calling attention to an unknowable subtext is a profound lesson, because it hopes to secure Rigoberta's cultural identity, yes, but also because it is an imitable trope. Not that a reader should want to compete with Rigoberta's text, but that s/he might well want to take a lead from it about participating in coordinated rather than centralized political engagements. The calculated result of Rigoberta's withholding from sympathetic readers is, paradoxically, to exclude us from her circle of intimates. She can neither have nor make ideal readers who dispense with explanations, because those who ideally understand Rigoberta, members of her own Quiché community, are not readers at all, neither in Spanish nor in English. And those of us who do read her are either intellectually or ethically unfit to know secrets. Likewise, if Sethe has to explain what she did, it is only to those who can never understand. But unlike Rigoberta's ritual distance from her Latinized neighbors, Morrison can hardly exclude Anglicized readers, if English is her code as much as theirs. So she includes us on her own terms. By the time Sethe finds explanations superfluous, the intimate circle of knowing readers has been drawn by the novel itself with narrative leads that have already insinuated the story in a way that makes readers complicitous, prepared to intuit the terrible efficacy of her sacrifice. Morrison seduces readers into a particular American code of feeling as masterfully as Whitman did when he called each reader his confidant, by the simple virtue of reading him. "This hour I tell things in confidence, / I might not tell everybody but I will tell you" ("Song of Myself," line 19). Just as masterful as this liberal supply of a demand for himself, but purposefully less enthralling, Morrison's appeal is cautious. Like Rigoberta's, it counts on our necessarily imperfect readings to produce a particular kind of distance akin to respect. So simple a lesson and so fundamental; it is to modestly acknowledge that Rigoberta refuses to be redeemed from difference, to remember that Morrison's text reinscribes it at the very moment when Sethe supplies the explanation she claims to be superfluous. "Anyone who had to ask" could never know, neither Paul D. nor the sensation-hungry reader.

Rigoberta's first person voice never quite spills over to the reader as it might in an autobiography. We are too foreign, and there is no pretense here of universal or essential human experience. That is why, at the end of a long narrative in which she has told us so much, Rigoberta reminds us that she has set limits. And our compassion for Sethe may fall short of comprehending her; our alliance may—and should—fall short of containment. In rhetorical terms, whose political consequences may be evident, there is a fundamental difference here between the *metaphor* of autobiography and heroic narrative in general, which assumes an identity by substituting one (superior) signifier for another (I for we, leader for follower, Christ for the faithful), and *metonymy,* a lateral move of identification through relationship, which acknowledges the possible differences among "us" as members of an alliance. As readers we are invited to be *with* the speaker rather than to replace her.

When Rigoberta talks about her*self* to *you,* she implies both the existing relationship to other representative selves in the community and potential relationships that extend her alliances through the text. She calls us in, interpellates us as readers who identify with the narrator's project and, by extension, with the political community to which she belongs. The appeal produces something different from mere admiration for the ego-ideal, of the type we might feel for an autobiographer who impresses us precisely with her difference from other women, different from the consequent yearning to be (like) her and so to deny her and our distinctiveness. Rather, the testimonial produces complicity. *Beloved* does this too, I think, by rendering Sethe's sacrifice imaginable, iterable, inevitable for her readers.

Finally, the undecidability of how to read Rigoberta—as telling or troping—is rather academic, because in either case she is evidently performing a defensive move in the midst of her seduction. Her testimonial is an invitation to a tête-à-tête, not a heart to heart. This should not necessarily be a disappointment; putting heads together is precisely what members of her community do every time they meet to discuss plans for a wedding or tactics for confronting the government. The respectful distance that we learn from Rigoberta's textual seduction is an extension of the same kind of respect for secrets learned repeatedly inside her own community.[42] Perhaps, then, our difference from that society, and from the thirty women who re-form as a community outside of Sethe's house, is one of degree; maybe we are not so much outsiders as marginals, allies in a possible coalition rather than members. We are not so much excluded from the Quiché world, or from *Beloved*'s, as we are kept at arm's length. Even if, or perhaps because, the reader cannot identify with the protagonist enough to imagine taking her place, the map of possible identifications through the text spreads out laterally, metonymically. And we can be called in to take minor, supporting roles.

The distance that silence performs can be strategic in more than self-protective ways. For Rigoberta, at least, it can be a cunning strategy for interpellating the reader as supporter, not leader, of a coordinated activity. Rigoberta's reservations, in other words, resist the murderous *Vertretung*, or substitutive representation, that Gayatri Spivak protests in elite writers.[43] Inassimilable books perform on a discursive tangent away from the elite self-criticism that moves in vicious circles, as Spivak aptly shows. The tangent provides a vantage point for rereading more than subaltern silence; it also promises to get beyond our habitual interpretive strategies by pointing to another ground, a ground that we cannot, or may not, occupy and that remains other. The strategically demure posture allows us to imagine, I want to speculate, a politics of coalition among differently constituted positionalities, rather than the identity or interchangeability of subjects as the basis for equality. And a political vision adventurous enough to imagine differences, yet modest enough to respect them, may be the most significant challenge posed by learning to read resistance.

This obstinacy to assimilation discriminates between the authorial community (which will not read Menchú and is not the sole reader of Morrison) and the authorial audience of perhaps predominantly curious outsiders. Richard Rodriguez is just as discriminating, even though readers have bypassed his dividing line: "You who read this act of contrition should know that by writing it I seek a kind of forgiveness—not yours. The forgiveness, rather, of those many persons whose absence from higher education permitted me to be classed a minority student. I wish that they would read this. I doubt they ever will."[44] The line is meant to distance those who would read in the presumptuous register of "If I were a . . ." failing to assimilate lessons about how positionality helps to constitute knowledge. Social asymmetry restricts travel from one position to the other, despite the fantasies of mutuality that motivate some studies of "multiculturalism," as if one's effort to understand an ethnically inflected text were somehow commensurate with the writer's decision to perform in an imperial language.[45] "Ideal" or target readers for resistant texts are, then, hardly the writer's coconspirators or allies who putatively share experiences and assumptions, as we have presumed in our critical vocabulary.[46] They are marked precisely as strangers, incapable of—or undesirable for—conspiratorial intimacy. Discrimination here assumes that differences in social positionality exist and that they effect (or require, for safety's sake) different degrees of understanding.[47] Written from clearly drawn positions on a chart where only the powerful center can mistake its specificity for universality, these "marginal" or "minority" texts draw boundaries around that arrogant space. They refuse to flatter the "competent" reader with touristic invitations to intimacy and produce instead what we can call the "Cordelia effect" of crippling authority by refusing to pander to it.[48] Unlike so many opportune books (at least since the time of the Inca Garcilaso de la Vega), which have parlayed the author's "exoticism" into classical norms—as a wager to confuse boundaries and win some space at the center—these uncooperative texts declare their intransigence. They locate traditionally privileged readers beyond an inviolable border. From there we can be "ideal," paradoxically, to the extent that we are excluded.

Of course readers have felt exclusion before, in esoteric traditions, for example, or in the elitism that made the other Garcilaso de la Vega and his baroque successors so intriguingly hard-to-get. And the skepticism about language's capacity to mean, in some literature, may promote games of interpretive hide and seek. But unlike elitist and esoteric forms of exclusion, which address a limited circle of initiated ideal readers, no initiation is possible into a resistant text. How could it be, when the authorial or target audience is constructed as outsider or antagonist to the author's world? Esoteric writing may set restrictions that are tantamount to demands for dedication, for the slow approach that constitutes a conversion before the object of knowledge can be achieved; and skeptical subterfuges of meaning may inscribe endless detours for the writer along with the reader. But resistant texts draw a radically different map of restrictions. It is not a labyrinth that can be negotiated once the guiding thread is found, or that one inhabits with good- or ill-humored resignation. Instead, it is a walled city that announces no trespassing at every gate. The unfamiliar appeal of the books that occupy me here is to reach out to privileged readers in order to keep us at arm's length.

As a final, and cautionary, reflection, I would like to consider Emmanuel Levinas's promising posture of philosophical modesty. Like Adorno who demoted knowledge to an unrealizable (if still worthy) goal, and unlike Foucault who guiltily accepted the complicity between knowledge and power,[49] Levinas refuses philosophy's desire to understand. For him, existing relationships need not reproduce themselves endlessly. They will dictate subjectivity only until the subject breaks with the ontological assumptions that produce discursive power. And the effort of Levinas's work "is directed toward apperceiving in discourse a non-allergic relation with alterity."[50]

In some important ways, Levinas's passionate voice is a most welcome discovery for me during these early stammerings about learning to acknowledge difference. He has been warning Western readers about the self-serving solipsism of a philosophical tradition (including its hermeneutical strains) that strives to overcome mystery with clarity. Ours is a culture that presumes to reduce the experience of self and other into a neat totality that fits ontological paradigms. If everything fits into the One, of which the ego is an expression, then the other logically fits inside the self with no remainder, no loose, particular, or incompatible features. It is the kind of ultimate fit—understood as a goal—that drives some universalist projects forward. "This primacy of the same was Socrates's teaching: to receive nothing of the Other but what is in me, as though from all eternity I was in possession of what comes to me from the outside—to receive nothing, or to be free."[51] Levinas takes this hubris of the subject of philosophy as the target of an ambitious dismantling campaign in order to reach back, according to Derrida, before Plato's neutralization and co-optation of the other in order to recognize that other as inaccessible alterity, mystery, divinity.

Although the lesson in modesty and respect is a profound one, and although Levinas casts himself as a voice in the wilderness whose appeals for ethical selflessness often pulse with passion, for this reader of Latin American literature discovering sentences like these was more an affirmation than a revelation: "If the other could be possessed, seized, and known, it would not be the other. To possess, to know, to grasp are all synonyms of power."[52] "The void that breaks the totality can be maintained against an inevitably totalizing and synoptic thought only if thought finds itself *faced* with an other refractory to categories."[53] But if I were to conjecture a chronological reversal of encounters, I must wonder if reading him first could have produced a humbling effect comparable to that of confronting resistant texts.

Levinas professes humility. He exhorts us to venerate the incomprehensible alterity of the face that we see and that sees us. Yet the message might have been lost on me because of the way his argument reaffirms what he patently strains to dislodge. The appeal seems wholly constructed from, and directed toward, the subject of philosophy, the construct he apparently diminishes by its confrontation with the unmanageable, infinitely and absolutely other. My concern follows the contours of Derrida's astute reading. He asks, to begin, how difference can be absolute? Doesn't the other assume a point of comparison with the self, and an inescapable negativity at that, despite Levinas's insistence that the terms are incommensurable and that the other is purely positive? Derrida's more general and characteristic critique, as it has often been his self-critique, is that Levinas cannot escape the language of philosophy as he philosophizes against it. By deploying phenomenological arguments against the tradition, Levinas is reaffirming it. "[T]he attempt to achieve an opening toward the beyond of philosophical discourse, by means of philosophical discourse, which can never be shaken off completely, cannot possibly succeed *within language*"; and language is, paradoxically, both the defeat and the necessary condition of violence.[54] There seems no point outside the tradition from which to launch a critique against it. Archimedes cannot move the world since he cannot stand on ground outside of it. And Levinas remains similarly in his own world, I am suggesting, because the alien ground on which the other stands remains invisible and largely imaginary for him; it is a ground he always already knows he cannot know. He achieves ignorance by contemplating the other as pure positivity (perhaps the construct of his own speculative powers), not as a response to the other's warnings.

The point is worth underlining. To the extent that Levinas acknowledges the enigma that confronts and limits his ability to know, he is the ideal "incompetent" reader I have been imagining for resistant texts. Speech does not fill the gaps between interlocutors; it continually marks their separation for Levinas; unlike vision, which appropriates the other into an interior totality, the space of discourse is exterior.[55] However, to the degree that the other here is "absolute" and incommensurable with the self, his enigma cannot be apprehended as a strategic resistance; instead it appears somehow beyond mundane struggle. To this extent, I wonder if Levinas may be missing some opportunities to listen. For Derrida, the contradiction (or paradox) derives from the "nonviolent urgency" of Levinas's ethics, which proposes "a language without phrase," while at the same time speech is privileged over sight as the safeguard for exteriority.

"Violence appears with *articulation*"; and yet righteousness is only possible through discourse. Derrida observes the hypocritical use of speech against speech: "The very elocution of nonviolent metaphysics is its first disavowal."[56] But the more troubling problem for me is that, unable himself to give up speech, through which he protests submissiveness, Levinas may in effect be suspending speech in the other, as if only the face were divinely nonviolent enough to keep silent. On the one hand, the face is characterized by the ability to speak;[57] but on the other hand, either it resists the speech of egotistic desire or Levinas resists listening.

It is one thing to read an inscrutable face and conclude that attempting to understand it would be a violation; it is another (but certainly related) thing to hear a foreign accent set the terms for respectful distance. In Levinas, different voices do not jar the subject. Even if "only the irruption of the Other permits access to the absolute and to the irreducible alterity of the other," that irruption is strangely muted.[58] Voices are subsumed in the unity of a foreign face, in this ethics where others are tantamount to the other. Nowhere do they produce the din that might make his Archimedean world vibrate and perhaps crack open. Levinas's subject of philosophy remains mesmerized before an unfathomable other, perhaps more because the subject chooses to humble himself than because of another's human effort to resist appropriation. And the ethical dissymmetry of a meek self—prostrate before the transcendent, divine other—may turn out to be the mirror image that reinscribes the older violent dissymmetry of the voracious subject before its objects of knowledge. Humility may not be the result of recognizing oneself as the other's other, as the potential object of another (symmetrical) desire.[59] Instead, it may be a willed gesture that presumes, of course, a greatness that can be humbled. And the generous self-limitation resembles nothing so much as what Jewish mystics called *tzimtzum* to describe God's loving self-diminishment in order to make room for his creation.

A break, a destabilizing irruption outside the self, is what I learned to miss in Levinas from having read profoundly fissured books, books that appeal to a privileged readership in order to resist us. Perhaps this is an unfair disappointment, if it derives from the paradox of writing self-effacingly. Levinas continues to write, to fill the pages with admirable humility and keeps filling more pages, taking more effort and attention. Philosophy continues to speak of the other, who must remain absent[60] But perhaps, also, the disappointment is in tune with Levinas's ethical imperative to acknowledge the other. When others speak, their appeal, I have been saying, is not an entreaty; it brooks no subordination nor expects empathy from the reader. Empathy, and the murderous mutuality it presumes, may be the enemy in this demand for respect.[61] By appeal I mean attractiveness, the books' capacity to engage and to play on our habits of carefree identification and appropriation. The deadly serious game is to stop us short. Sometimes I think that Rigoberta Menchú, Jesusa Palancares, the nameless narrator of *Balún Canán*,[62] and Richard Rodriguez write at length about their apparently private selves precisely to withhold the anticipated intimacy that would invite conquest. Their most provocative performance may be, then, the cold-shoulder impact on the reader, a sensation that makes us doubt their availability and our desirability. Noticing this effect probably allies me to reader-response critics, because the last instance of this approach is, allegedly, to locate the ways a text educates the reader by teaching her how to read.[63] More boldly, we might say that concern for readerly responses asks how texts constitute readers through the seductive education that make us social subjects; that is, how books intervene in the world.

When, in my last project, I asked how nineteenth-century foundational fictions intervened in Latin America, I could trace back from their galvanizing effects to their beguiling strategies of slipping allegorically between passion and patriotism.[64] There we could correctly assume that readers are invited as participant observers in the love affairs that generated countries. Identification with the frustrated lovers whose union could produce the modern state was precisely the desired effect on the tenuous citizenry of newly consolidated countries. It was a mirror effect that survived mass distribution to required readers who were told, in that dangerously democratic embrace of compulsory education, that their differences from the elite lovers did not really matter. My project, in other words, was to read foundations with a foundational theory that conjugated imagined communities with dreams of love. Rather than refuse the programmatic clarity of those novels in favor of deconstructive unravelings that can show how any text wavers and contradicts its apparent message, I chose to address the books in their own ideal terms.

But to read resistant fictions in *their* ideal terms needs a paradigm shift. How could a theory derived from narrative foundations of inclusive communities manage to read books that show and stretch the cracks at the base of society? To follow these defiant books, our critical vocabulary will strain after antifoundationalist terms. It will struggle because their characteristic rhetorical strategies have evidently seemed unremarkable. In the vicious circle of familiarity and predictability that I referred to above and that describes some hermeneutical habits, the unanticipated lessons these texts could teach seem hard to read. How can the books teach reading effectively, if our readerly training is precisely to ignore their lessons? There is so much that one must ignore anyway, especially in long works, that it would be rather easy to continue our inattention. If our training assumes that learning is a progression, that it is always learning something, how does interpretive reticence make sense? At our most modest we have been assuming, with the New Critics and then more radically with deconstruction, that ambiguity cannot be conquered. But distance from the object of desire? Confessed ignorance of that object? Prohibition against trespassing? We have yet to recognize those purposefully off-putting enticements.

Notes

I am grateful to Robert Gooding-Williams for his many astute criticisms and suggestions. Thanks also to George Yúdice and Amy Kaplan.

1 Oswald de Andrade, "Manifesto Antropofago" of 1928. "Cannibalist Manifesto," trans. Leslie Bary, *Latin American Literary Review* 19, no. 38 (July–December 1991): 35–47. I thank Heloisa Buarque de Hollanda for pointing this out.

2 Gérard Genette, *Figures of Literary Discourse*, trans. Alan Sheridan, chap. 9, "Flaubert's Silences" (New York: Columbia University Press, 1982), pp. 183–202.

3 In an apparently pioneering essay, Reed Way Dasenbrock argues that "the meaningfulness of multicultural works is in large measure a function of their unintelligibility." Therefore, and paradoxically, intelligibility cannot be considered the sole criterion for understanding of this literature. See his "Intelligibility and Meaningfulness in Multicultural Literature in English," *PMLA* 102, no. 1 (1987): 10–19, esp. 14. Quoted in Marta Sánchez, "Hispanic- and Anglo-American Discourse in Edward Rivera's *Family Installments*," *American Literary History* 1, no. 4 (Winter 1989): 853–71, esp. 858.

4 The success of literary figures depends in part on a reader's awareness of them. Genette, p. 54. See also Peter J. Rabinowitz, *Before Reading: Narrative Conventions and the Politics of Interpretation* (Ithaca: Cornell University Press, 1987), p. 27.

5 Genette, chap. 3, "Figures," pp. 45–60.

6 Zora Neale Hurston, *Mules and Men* (1935; Westport, Conn.: Negro University Press, 1969), p. 18.

7 Françoise Lionnet, *Autobiographical Voices: Race, Gender, Self-Portraiture* (Ithaca: Cornell University Press, 1989), p. 18.

8 For Edward Said, in "Representing the Colonized: Anthropology's Interlocutors," *Critical Inquiry* 15, no. 2 (Winter 1989): 205–25, divulging the mechanisms tends to vitiate them.

9 See Robert Hemenway, "Introduction" to Zora Neale Hurston, *Dust Tracks on a Road: An Autobiography* (1942; Urbana: University of Illinois Press, 1984). "She gauged her audience very carefully" (xvi). "The conventions of autobiography create the expectation that Zora will explain how she came to her position of prominence. Hurston's reaction to this convention is to avoid offering such an explanation of personal success, substituting instead an interpretation of black cultural life meant to deflect attention away from herself" (xviii–xix). "*Dust Tracks* fails as autobiography because it is a text deliberately less than its author's talents, a text diminished by her refusal to provide a second or third dimension to the flat surfaces of her adult image."

10 Charles T. Davis and Henry Louis Gates, Jr., eds., *The Slave's Narrative* (New York: Oxford University Press, 1985), p. xiii. The editors take Douglass's lead when they write that the genre "could no longer exist after slavery was abolished" (xxii).

11 See *The Narrative Life of Frederick Douglass* (1845), *The Classic Slave Narratives* (New York: Mentor, 1987), ed. and introd. Henry Louis Gates, Jr., pp. 243–331, esp. pp. 262–63, where he corrects white responses to the "sorrow songs."

12 *Mules and Men*, p. 17.

13 Harriet Jacob, *Incidents in the Life of a Slave Girl* (1861; New York: Harcourt Brace, 1973), intro. and notes by Walter Teller, p. 54.

14 See Sylvia Molloy, "From Serf to Self: The Autobiography of Juan Francisco Manzano," in *At Face Value: Autobiographical Writing in Spanish America* (Cambridge and New York: Cambridge University Press, 1991), pp. 36–54. "While the first letter gave full power to del Monte over Manzano's story, the second establishes a line between what has been promised to the critic . . . and what Manzano keeps for himself. The previous letter, marked by subservience, waived Manzano's rights to the text by 'giving' it to del Monte; the second letter, marked instead by resistance, has Manzano keep the text for himself" (43).

15 Susan Willis quotes this in "Crushed Geraniums: Juan Francisco Manzano and the Language of Slavery," in Charles T. Davis and Henry Louis Gates, Jr., eds., *The Slave's Narrative* (New York: Oxford University Press, 1985), pp. 199–224, esp. p. 208. Willis is disappointed with the stops and attributes them to a narrative convention that is "artificial" in the "full, vivid detail" of his story (209). Nevertheless, the silence that "occurs more than once and always at an extreme moment of torture" can be read as exercises of writerly control rather than as literary pretension.

16 I borrow the term loosely from Antonio Gramsci, for whom the war of position is a process of ideological disarticulation (of bourgeois hegemony) and re-articulation (of a workers' hegemonic bloc). It is the ideological struggle between the fundamental classes over elements that could serve either one, a struggle that precedes military confrontation. See his *Selections from the Prison Notebooks*, ed. and trans. Quintin Hoare and Geoffrey Nowell Smith (New York: International

Publishers, 1971), pp. 238–39. See also Chantal Mouffe, "Hegemony and Ideology in Gramsci," in *Gramsci & Marxist Theory*, ed. Chantal Mouffe (London: Routledge & Kegan Paul, 1979), pp. 168–204.

17 See review essay by Fernando Coronil, "Mastery by Signs, Signs of Mastery," *Plantation Society* 2, no. (December 1986): 201–7. Also Jose Piedra, "The Game of Critical Arrival," *Diacritics* (Spring 1989).

18 For the collusion between the apparently opposite projects of universalizing (saming) and subordination of the "other" (othering), see Naomi Schor, "This Essentialism Which Is Not One: Coming to Grips with Irigaray," *Differences* 1, no. 3 (Summer 1989), pp. 38–58.

19 For Spivak's formulation, see "Subaltern Studies: Deconstructing Historiography," in *In Other Words* (New York and London: Methuen, 1987), pp. 197–221, where she doesn't dismiss the essentialism; it's "a *strategic* use of positivistic essentialism in a scrupulously visible political interest" (205). Allying themselves with the subaltern is an "interventionist strategy" (207). For a more cautious consideration, "within a personalist culture" where essentialism can be smuggled in again to serve the powerful, see her interview with Ellen Rooney in the special issue of *Differences* devoted to *The Essential Difference: Another Look at Essentialism*, vol. 1, no. 2 (Summer 1989). "In a Word. Interview," pp. 124–156, esp. pp. 128–29. In the same issue, Diana Fuss, in "Reading Like a Feminist," pp. 77–92, anticipates some of Spivak's concerns. One thing is for subaltern to use essentialism, another is for the hegemonic group to use it. "The question of the permissibility . . . is therefore framed and determined by the subject-positions from which one speaks" (86).

20 Rigoberta Menchú, *I, Rigoberta Menchú: An Indian Woman In Guatemala*, ed. and intro. Elisabeth Burgos-Debray, trans. Ann Wright (London: Verso, 1984). The Spanish original is *Me llamo Rigoberta Menchú: Y asi me nacio la consciencia* (Habana: Casa de las Américas, 1983) "El indígena ha sido muy cuidadoso con muchos detalles de la misma comunidad" (42).

21 See Doris Sommer, "Rigoberta's Secrets," *Latin American Perspectives* Issue 70, vol. 18, no. 3 (Summer 1991): 32–50.

22 "Se dice que los españoles violaron a los mejores hijos de los antepasados, . . . y en honor a esas gentes más humildes nosotros tenemos que seguir guardando nuestros secretos. Y esos secretos nadie podrá descubrir más que nosotros los indígenas."

23 "Sigo ocultando lo que yo considero que nadie lo sabe, ni siquiera un antropólogo, ni un intelectual, por más que tenga muchos libros, no saben distinguir todos nuestros secretos."

24 René Girard, *Deceit, Desire and the Novel*.

25 Elena Poniatowska, *Hasta no verte Jesus mio* (Mexico: Era, 1968).

26 I am referring to Richard Rodriguez, *Hunger of Memory: The Education of Richard Rodriguez* (New York: Bantam Books, 1983).

27 Sor Juana Inés de la Cruz, *A Woman of Genius: The Intellectual Autobiography of Sor Juana Inés de la Cruz,* trans. Margaret Sayers Peden (Limerock, Conn.: Limerock Press, 1982), pp. 18–20.

28 Adrienne Rich, "Women and Honor: Some Notes on Lying (1975)," in *On Lies, Secrets, and Silence: Selected Prose 1966–1978* (New York: W. W. Norton, 1979), p. 185.

29 Brian Swann and Arnold Krupat, *I Tell You Now: Autobiographical Essays by Native American Writers* (Lincoln: University of Nebraska Press, 1987), p. ix.

30 Barbara Smith, "Toward a Black Feminist Criticism," in *But Some of Us Are Brave: Black Women's Studies,* ed. Gloria T. Hull, Patricia Bell Scott, and Barbara Smith (New York: Feminist Press, 1982), pp. 157–75, esp. p. 158. "It seems overwhelming to break such a massive silence. Even more numbing, however, is the realization that so many of the women who will read this have not yet noticed us missing either from their reading matter, their politics, or their lives."

31 Toni Morrison, *Beloved* (New York: New American Library, 1988), p. 53.

32 *Beloved,* p. 58.

33 Letter to New York *Tribune,* June 21, 1853. Quoted in Jean Fagan Yellin, "Text and Contexts of Harriet Jacobs's *Incidents in the Life of a Slave Girl Written by Herself,*" in Charles T. Davis and Henry Louis Gates, Jr., eds., *The Slave's Narrative* (New York: Oxford University Press, 1985), pp. 262–82, esp. p. 267.

34 *Tikkun* 2, no. 1, pp. 54–60, esp. pp. 55 and 59.

35 Friederick Nietzsche, A posthumous passage dating from the fall of 1887, quoted in Paul de Man, *Allegories of Reading* (New Haven: Yale University Press, 1979), pp. 119–20.

36 W. George Lovell, "Surviving Conquest: The Maya of Guatemala in Historical Perspective," *Latin American Research Review* 23, no. 2 (1988): 25–57, esp. 47.

37 "Mi papá los llamaba indígenas ladinizados . . . es que tienen ya la actitud del ladino, y del ladino malo" (66).

38 The cuc (Comité de Unidad Campesina).

39 "tratarías de olvidarte de lo que hay en común."

40 "Después piden perdón y piden ayuda a los padres, que los tienen que ayudar para siempre, para que sus hijos sean indígenas y que nunca pierdan jamás sus costumbres y, aunque haya pleitos, tristeza o hambre, sigan siendo indígenas" (131).

41 Rigoberta attributes her political doubts, for example, to the fact that she has strayed from the community. Nevertheless, she registers a hint of a "deconstructed" practice in which the traditional categorical rigidity is simultaneously revered and sacrificed. For the price of the destabilizing distance from her community she earns some political clarity. "I used to defend my ancestors down to the last detail. But I didn't really understand what I was doing, because we only understand when we speak with one another. . . . Ladinos with us, the Indians." (269)

42 "[E]l indígena siempre guarda un secreto. Ese secreto, a veces no es conveniente que los hijos lo sepan. No es porque sea inconveniente, sino porque no hay necesidad. . . . Son los niveles que respetamos en la comunidad" (155).

43 Gayatri Chakravorty Spivak, "Can the Subaltern Speak?" in *Marxism and the Interpretation of Culture*, ed. Cary Nelson and Lawrence Grossberg (Urbana: University of Illinois Press, 1988), pp. 271–316. She points out that the problem with "our efforts to give the subaltern a voice in history" has been the ways we essentialize that experience. To illustrate, a long discussion follows about the ironies of Sati, widow self-immolation, as it has been coded either in terms of British revulsion or through patriarchal nativism, never by the self-sacrificing women. Her conclusion here and at the very end of the essay (where we learn how easily a political suicide is explained away) is that, "There is no space from which the sexed subaltern subject can speak" (307). "The subaltern cannot speak," presumably because the insurgent act—such as the silent suicide—is necessarily misunderstood in its articulations. Insurgency has no codes; it exceeds language.

A disappointing deduction, to be sure, though the analysis of chosen texts is admirable. The disappointment is that it leaves so little room for the verbal insurgency of a war of positions. It assumes more than an unbreachable gap between elites and others; it assumes that language is already so heavy with meaning and so securely in the elite domain, that others' gaps and silences are smothered under the weight of anticipated articulations.

44 Rodriguez, p. 153.

45 Reed Way Dasenbrock presumes just that in "Intelligibility and Meaningfulness . . ."; that is, an equivalence and reciprocity between writer and reader, an interchangeability that allows for precisely the kinds of ultimate identification between self and other that override differences. "At the *tangi* and in the novel *Tangi*, we are on Maori ground, and, for a change, we have to do the accommodating and the adapting. As we do so, we experience the kind of shifting and adapting a Tama undergoes every day in his life" (17).

46 Peter J. Rabinowitz, *Before Reading: Narrative Conventions and the Politics of Interpretation* (Ithaca: Cornell University Press, 1987). He reviews the generally accepted notion of authorial audience as one the writer could have predicted. Not that all its readers are ideal, but they are "deformed" in ways he would have known and shared. They are "members of the same cultural community" (22, 26, 28).

47 For an earlier and very astute exploration of this inscribed difference, see Marta Sánchez, "Hispanic- and Anglo-American Discourse in Edward Rivera's *Family Installments*," *American Literary History* 1, no. 4 (Winter 1989): 853–71.

48 In George Steiner's pithy indictment, "Like murderous Cordelia, children know that silence can destroy another human being. Or like Kafka they remember that several have survived the songs of the Sirens, but none their silence." George Steiner, *After Babel: Aspects of Language and Translation* (London, New York: Oxford University Press, 1975), p. 35.

49 Michel Foucault, *Discipline and Punish* (1977), pp. 27–28. "[P]ower and knowledge directly imply one another; . . . there is no power relation without the correlative constitution of a field of knowledge, nor any knowledge that does not presuppose and constitute at the same time power relations." See Mailloux, p. 143.

50 Emmanuel Levinas, *Totality and Infinity: An Essay on Exteriority*, trans. Alphonso Lingis (Pittsburgh: Duquesne University Press, 1969), p. 47.

51 Levinas, p. 43.

52 Quoted in Jacques Derrida, "Violence and Metaphysics: An Essay on the Thought of Emmanuel Levinas," in *Writing and Difference*, trans. Alan Bass (Chicago: University of Chicago Press, 1978), pp. 79–153, esp. p. 91.

53 Levinas, p. 40.

54 Derrida, "Violence and Metaphysics," pp. 110, 117: "Speech is doubtless the first defeat of violence, but paradoxically, violence did not exist before the possibility of speech. The philosopher (man) *must* speak and write within this war of light."

55 Levinas, p. 295.

56 Derrida, p. 147.

57 Derrida, p. 113. "This text of the glance is *also* the text of speech. Therefore it can be called Face."

58 Derrida, p. 105.

59 See Derrida's comparison with Husserl, whose ethics begin precisely from the assumption of mutual alterity, pp. 128–33.

60 Again, Derrida remarks on this boomerang effect, p. 103.

61 I am apparently siding with Kant against Schopenhauer, according to Robert Gooding Williams, in their debate about the basis of ethics. For one it was respect for rational beings (the demand for respect constituting, it seems to me, a sign of rationality); for the other it was compassion.

62 Rosario Castellanos, *Balún Canán* (Mexico: FCE, 1956).

63 Steven Mailloux, *Rhetorical Power* (Ithaca: Cornell University Press, 1989), p. 49.

64 Doris Sommer, *Foundational Fictions: The National Romances of Latin America* (Berkeley: University of California Press, 1991).

Kevin Gaines

Black Americans' Racial Uplift Ideology as "Civilizing Mission"

Pauline E. Hopkins on Race and Imperialism

n its December 1904 issue, the Atlanta-based black periodical *Voice of the Negro* announced a forthcoming series of articles by Pauline E. Hopkins, the prolific novelist and journalist, on "The Dark Races of the Twentieth Century." Hopkins is best known for her historical novel of 1900, *Contending Forces,* [1] a fictional treatment of the contemporary crisis of race relations and political debates among black leadership in the United States. But in the next few years her writings tackled the politics of race within the international context of imperialism. She had produced a short story, "Talma Gordon," which discussed themes of miscegenation and expansion, and 1903 saw the appearance of a serialized novel, *Of One Blood*, which combined an inventive critique of racial and sexual oppression in the United States with an "Afrocentric" mystical tale of a hidden city beneath a pyramid inhabited by descendants of the ancient Ethiopians. Hopkins's nonfiction series on the "darker races" further pursued this linkage of domestic and global racial issues, addressing the rising Anglo-American racial nationalism that justified imperialist policies abroad while reinforcing white supremacy in the United States. [2]

Hopkins's series presents us with an opportunity to shed much needed light on the tortuous, complex history of the social construction of race in the United States. Our pursuit of a historical understanding of "race" through Hopkins's writings must be explicitly linked to the contemporary project to demystify lingering assumptions which posit race as a natural, absolute, and "God-given" basis for maintaining and justifying social inequities. My approach to race here follows recent scholarship[3] which questions past and present efforts to fix the definition of "race" and which rejects dubious psychocultural explanations which locate the phenomenon, for example, in "human nature." Instead, this literature interprets race as a constantly changing and contested field of discourse. Thus, as Evelyn Brooks Higginbotham has observed, "we must recognize race as providing sites of dialogic exchange and contestation, since race has constituted a discursive tool for both oppression and liberation."[4]

Hopkins's use of "race" cuts both ways, both resisting and replicating racist mythologies. She joined a tradition of black writers who argued for the recognition of ancient African contributions to world civilization, even as she was wont to replicate commonplace imperialist knowledge of "the primitive." Moreover, the concern for black women's oppression in the United States that animated much of her fiction receded in her *Voice of the Negro* articles, as Hopkins sought to refute racism by adopting a "scientific" Western ethnological persona. Her statements raise the question of what it meant at that time to attempt a "refutation" of racist discourse. Clearly, given the deferential posture of Hopkins and other black writers to the received terms of dominant racial ideologies, effective refutation was at best difficult.

The manner in which Hopkins advanced pan-African race ideals in the series, and in her novel *Of One Blood*, reflected her assent to the prevailing view of "race" as essentially a masculine ideal. In a departure from her previous work, Hopkins had exchanged the "feminine" form of domestic fiction, with its American setting and substantial female presence, for the "male" persona of a scientific expert on the darker races, claiming an influence within the male-dominated realm of imperial power. Hopkins's particular use of civilizationist and pan-African ideologies was rooted not only in the powerlessness facing all black writers seeking to enter the forbidden territory of public commentary on race. She also found it necessary to defer to the black community's assumptions of male leadership that tended to marginalize Hopkins's contributions as a black woman intellectual. As Hopkins wrote to the black nationalist journalist John E. Bruce, "being only a woman [I] have received very small notice" on matters of import to the race.[5]

Hopkins may well have regarded imperialism, with its pivotal issue of race, as a topic that might enhance her credibility as a spokesperson within a black leadership community that remained parochial on women's issues. At the same time, ideologies of "race," and the "problems" with which they were inevitably associated, confronted black writers at every turn. Fueled by imperialism, pejorative racial designations took on both domestic and global connotations, as they were applied in Hopkins's day not only to African descended peoples, but also to immigrant groups and colonial subjects.[6] Likewise, attempts to restrict Asian immigration gained force by alarmist fears of the "yellow peril." The triumphant spirit of empire led one British commentator to contemplate an Anglo-American imperial alliance: "Will the Twentieth Century unify the English-speaking race?" Such calls for a "Reunited Race" reflected the growing perception of a world polarized into two conflicting race groups, pitting the ruling "Anglo-Saxon" against all other races. This perception was shared by those who identified their interests with those of the "darker races," as seen in W. E. B. Du Bois's well-known observation in 1900 that "[t]he problem of the Twentieth Century is the color line." Appropriately, Hopkins observed that "the remarkable development of the imperialistic fever among governments, has caused a searching of the obscure corners of the globe even among untutored savages for world markets and . . . conquests." Thus, Hopkins claimed that "the time is ripe for a popular study of the science of ethnology."[7]

Ironically, Hopkins and many others found the fields of ethnology and anthropology, originally fertile fields of racist ideology, equally suited to undermining racism. But such resistance to racism was no easy course, no simple matter. Writers like Hopkins believed that claiming affinity with dominant notions of race and civilization would oppose racism. Their assimilationist perspective was crucial to their claim for the status of bourgeois professionalism, leadership, and expertise. Hopkins ventured such a claim for elite status through the Western-dominated pan-Africanism that she advanced in *Of One Blood*, in which its black American male protagonist is crowned king of an ancient Ethiopian civilization. This was a typical black American variation on the imperialist theme of the civilizing mission. Hopkins's elite, Western vision of African heathenism was meant to enhance black Americans' race pride, but at the expense of the autonomy of African peoples, whose cultures and histories remained a blank page for imaginary conquest.[8]

Hopkins's writing was part of a broader tendency among marginalized racial, religious, and gender minorities who used the idea of civilization at the turn of the century to give credence to their own aspirations to status, power, and influence. While the intellectual and cultural production of minorities played a crucial role in discrediting the most vulgar nineteenth-century theories of scientific racism,[9] what remained was a revised racial hierarchy drawn from the dominant evolutionary notion of "race development" measured on the scale of civilization. By 1910 the academy had claimed a professional interest in U.S. imperialism in these terms. A scholarly writer described the purpose of the new *Journal of Race Development* "as a forum for the discussion of problems which relate to the progress of races and states generally considered backward in their standards of civilization. . . . The necessity of understanding these countries better . . . is due in part to the increased importance of these lands in the political and economic life of the West." But instead of imperialism, this commentator spoke euphemistically of "the worldwide race problem," linking "the negro [sic] problem—a problem still unsolved" with the problems of foreign affairs posed by "primitive cultures" in the Pacific. The point here is that cruder racisms rooted in biological difference were augmented by a seemingly benign, but imperial, scholarly language of cultural relativism which had its genesis in the debates on expansion at the turn of the century. This language of civilizationist ideology was one that many blacks felt compelled to emulate even as they challenged its assumptions. Of course, blacks' qualified consent to this body of imperialist knowledge has more to do with its hegemony than its perceived validity or "truth."[10]

As Nell Painter has argued, "[f]or anyone concerned about the American race issue [at the turn of the century], the parallel between white supremacy at home and imperialism abroad was obvious."[11] For many black spokespersons, including Hopkins, imperialism brought into focus new terms and possibilities for resistance to racism. At the height of national and congressional debates on imperialism, anti-imperialists, black and white, pointed out the hypocrisy of civilizationist, missionary ideology as a rationale for colonization by force. At the first pan-African conference in London in 1900, W. E. B. Du Bois had challenged civilizationist rhetoric, which made imperial conquest more palatable for the consumption of domestic populations: "Let not the cloak of Christian Missionary enterprise be allowed in the future, as so often in the past, to hide the ruthless economic exploitation and political downfall of less developed nations."[12]

Like the rest of the country, black leadership was divided on the issue of imperialism; while many blacks vigorously denounced the racism and hypocrisy inherent in imperialist ideology, others preferred to view the participation of black soldiers in, for example, the wars in Cuba and the Philippines as proof of the race's loyalty and patriotism, the recognition of which might overcome domestic race prejudice. Imperialism, as the historian Willard Gatewood reminds us, was a hotly debated issue which among blacks raised to the surface enduring conflicts over racial and national identity.[13] Militant black anti-imperialism marked an exception to the prevailing strategy of racial uplift black leaders employed against racism through the 1890s. That strategy of racial uplift ideology was generally an expression of the material and political struggles of blacks during a devastating period of American history that one historian termed "the nadir" for black Americans.[14] In response to their waning political power in the post-Reconstruction New South, many elite blacks waged an ideological struggle to gain recognition from influential whites of their entitlement to citizenship status, an avowedly bourgeois agenda which blacks usually equated with "the race's" progress. Generally, prominent blacks defended themselves against racial stereotypes and voiced their aspirations to middle-class identity and leadership status by espousing an ethos within which they increasingly saw themselves obliged to act as privileged agents of progress and civilization for the disadvantaged black majority—hence the often used phrase "uplifting the race." The ethos of racial uplift was generally assimilationist in character, reiterating the so-called progressive era's stock assumptions of racial Darwinism and of "civilization" as the scale upon which individuals, races, and nations, as contemporaries routinely put it, were ranked. Because it shared many of the assumptions of an evangelical worldview, the rhetoric of racial uplift often resembled the imperialist notion of the "civilizing mission." In short, by claiming through uplift ideology the status of agents of civilization, blacks hoped to topple racial barriers and regain citizenship rights. Thus evangelical, missionary ideals found more secularized expression as the theme of uplift was commonly espoused, albeit for varying purposes, by most prominent black spokespersons of the day, including Frances E. W. Harper, W. E. B. Du Bois, Alexander Crummell, Booker T. Washington, and Anna Julia Cooper.[15]

However much imperialists invoked the "civilizing mission" to justify conquest, many black writers, including Hopkins, nonetheless saw value in civilizationist ideology—through its domestic application as uplift ideology—as a weapon against racism in the United States. "The quest for gentility despite the many obstacles erected by the white majority," Wilson J. Moses has observed, "is one of the important themes of Afro-American life in the Victorian age." For Hopkins and others, their options restricted by hostility, discrimination, and repression that very sense of gentility was sought in uplift and civilizationist ideology. What complicated matters for Hopkins was that uplift ideology also evoked an evangelical, New England abolitionist spirit that had animated much of her protest fiction, particularly *Contending Forces*. In any case, gentility, uplift, and evangelicalism were crucial to her sense of identity and bourgeois selfhood; to these attributes she sought to add, through her popular ethnological study of the "Darker Races," the authoritative guise of a scientific expert on races.[16]

Black commentators often invoked social Darwinism and imperial locutions when they described their domestic plight by portraying social relations between "stronger and weaker races" as having one of two possibilities: domination or uplift. In her 1892 novel *Iola Leroy*, Frances E. W. Harper dramatized this set of options in a debate between Dr. Gresham, a Northern white doctor, and Iola, Harper's black female protagonist. To Gresham's claim that blacks "learn to struggle, labor and achieve" against a "proud, domineering, aggressive" Anglo-Saxon race "impatient of a rival, and . . . [with] more capacity for dragging down a race than uplifting it," Iola countered that blacks would one day assume a higher level of civilization than that of "you Anglo-Saxons" who "will prove unworthy of your high vantage ground if you only use your superior ability to victimize feebler races and minister to a selfish greed of gold and a love of domination." Harper's novel sought to promote a moral vision of racial uplift ideology that revived the abolitionist, radical Republican legacy of the Reconstruction era. Her depiction of slavery's cruelty, remanding Iola into slavery despite her education, refinement, and near-white appearance, and tearing apart black families, was meant to strengthen the moral authority and resolve of educated blacks to devote themselves to service to their race, promoting literacy, temperance, thrift, and bourgeois morality. By placing the reunion of family members separated by slavery at the center of the novel's plot, Harper reinforced her theme of a natural, organic relationship between black elites and masses, figuring the race as a family transcending emerging class, cultural, and color differences. For Harper and other black writers, including Hopkins, this notion of uplift as an evangelical mission of mercy was the antithesis of Anglo-Saxon dominance and brutality. Indeed, in Harper's view, that a divine teleology of uplift would supplant conquest had already been demonstrated by the visitation of divine retribution on the slavocracy for its crimes.[17]

Harper and others with roots in evangelical reform movements, such as Hopkins, Anna Julia Cooper, Alexander Crummell, and later, W. E. B. Du Bois, helped lay the foundation for racial uplift ideology as a blueprint for professional social work and institution-building in the age of

Jim Crow. In the late nineteenth century, the education of former slaves was seen by philanthropists, educators, and church foreign missions societies as synonymous with efforts to bring Christianity and civilization to native Americans, Hawaiians, and "primitive" foreign peoples abroad, in Africa, India, China, and Japan.[18] As a product of Hampton Institute, founded by Samuel C. Armstrong, a missionary who, with his wife, had worked in Hawaii and among native Americans, Booker T. Washington usurped the evangelical spirit in a manner that eclipsed the radical Republicanism and protest of Harper, Hopkins, Cooper, and others. In his 1901 autobiography *Up From Slavery*, Washington advanced a more conservative version of uplift ideology, one that portrayed enslavement less harshly than did Harper and that depended for its content not only on evangelical missionary crusades, but also, on a none too subtle language of empire. Notwithstanding what he called the "cruelty and moral wrong" of enslavement, Washington asserted that American blacks who "went through the school of American slavery" were "materially, intellectually, morally and religiously" the most advanced "black people in any other portion of the globe." Pressing his point, Washington noted that those assimilated graduates of "the school of slavery are constantly returning to Africa as missionaries to enlighten those who remained in the fatherland." Along with his skillful use of the success myth, Washington manipulated civilizationist ideology and uplift ideals of self-help to monopolize the philanthropy of the business class with his laissez-faire philosophy and the Hampton-Tuskegee approach to industrial education for blacks. He portrayed his message, embodied by the school he founded, Tuskegee Institute in Alabama, as a beacon of enlightenment among benighted Southern blacks; Washington attributed blacks' pursuit of higher education and politics, those false idols of the Reconstruction period, to "generations in slavery, and before that, generations in the darkest heathenism." Throughout *Up From Slavery*, Washington spoke of black opposition—strikes or independent black voting—as the archaic, almost minstrel-like behavior of the undeveloped "Old Negro," who was "largely disappearing" to make way for a more responsible black leadership committed to a vision of uplift that, as Washington would have it, served the interests of both races and classes.[19]

Washington's use of civilizationist rhetoric was compelling, as it coincided with considerable missionary interest in Africa among elite black Americans, dating from the antebellum period. Indeed, it was at the 1895 Atlanta Exposition, where Washington made the speech that hastened his rise to national prominence, that black American missionaries, including Crummell, took part in the "Congress on Africa," which promoted missionary contacts between black Americans and Africans. Although Crummell eventually opposed Washington's accommodationist pact with business elites, philanthropists, and Southern politicians, his role in the congress echoed the Western portrayals of Africa as a "dark continent" of heathenism and backwardness that characterized the proceedings. Crummell's writings, like Washington's, indicate that blacks' internalizations of this image of African heathenism informed the domestic relation of "uplift" that presumably united the interests of black elites and masses. Since the 1870s, the missionary enterprise, with its image of a "pagan" Africa awaiting "regeneration" by its elite progeny, was central to some black Americans' attempts to demonstrate black progress in a racist society that barred most conventional routes to power and professional status. Within the domestic context, the analogous function charted by elite blacks' racial uplift ideology would serve a similar purpose. The imagined uplift of African peoples from their so-called degraded condition promised refuge, psychic and otherwise, from the desperate situation black Americans faced. According to a black historian of the 1880s, "[a] morning star of Hope for the millions in Africa who have yet learned nothing of Christianity, nor taken the first lessons of civilization, shines over the lowly cabins of their brothers in America."[20]

Washington's use of the evolutionary axiom that measured race development by civilizationist standards marked a decisive break from the earlier, more egalitarian notions of uplift exemplified by Harper and other abolitionists of all colors, a view which derived its character not only from the antislavery content of black folk religion, but also from the democratic reforms of the Reconstruction era. Before the onslaught on black political rights, and the rise of the wizard of Tuskegee, uplift had signified social advance, freedom, and full citizenship rights, which were regarded by many abolitionists as a natural right, bestowed by God, and protected by the civil rights amendments to the Constitution. Meanwhile, Washington, who counseled that blacks forsake politics for an indefinite period of time, aided a hostile climate for black opposition leaders. With whom, after all, did the power to declare blacks' "readiness" or entitlement to political rights ultimately rest? Within the repressive New South social and economic order of disfranchisement, political terror, debt slavery, and gerrymandering, Washington's application of the developmental ideology to black politics lent legitimacy to the notion that black reconstruction was a mistake not to be repeated.

Just as the finery of civilizationist ideology hid the nakedness of imperial conquest through its promises of bringing Christian enlightenment and moral progress to colonial subjects, so did Washington's autobiography bring a similar pacification of social conflicts in the South. Industrial education provided the answer to both labor agitation in the wake of Populist insurgency, as well as the solution, barring more violent measures, to the "Negro problem." Besides eclipsing the protest content of the vision of uplift embodied by Harper, Cooper, Hopkins, and others, Washington's emphasis on blacks' civilizing mission to Africa served perhaps the more crucial function of effacing the memory of the recent, often angry, contribution of black Americans to the vexed national debate on the fate of the Philippine independence movement in 1899. The war in the Philippines, and in Cuba before it, coincided with a wave of antiblack violence throughout the South, fueled by the racist rhetoric of imperialists and white supremacists in Congress. The domestic crisis heavily influenced black opinion on the Philippine question, as many angrily denounced Republican party expansionism and the rhetoric sustaining it. Washington's autobiography, and his subsequent efforts to secure controlling interests in many black newspapers (including the Boston-based *Colored American Magazine,* for which Hopkins was a contributing editor), indicate what was, for a time, a largely effective strategy of imposing an illusory consensus by suppressing black dissent.[21]

The period of expansion, from 1889 to 1901, saw almost 2,000 black men, women, and children lynched in the South. After blacks were elected to office in North Carolina in 1898, armed whites led by ex-Confederate Colonel A. M. Waddell seized power through a murderous rampage that destroyed not only the interracial political coalition but also the black newspaper in that city. Senator "Pitchfork" Ben Tillman of South Carolina (an anti-imperialist who believed contact with colonial subjects would bring whites' racial degeneration), where Fraser Baker, a black federal office appointee, was murdered by a white mob in 1898, offered his view of how the state prevented "black domination," declaring that "[w]e have scratched our heads to find out how we could eliminate the last one of them. We stuffed ballot boxes. We shot them. We are not ashamed of it." Such statements and deeds elicited biting sarcasm in the comment of one of many militant anti-imperialist black editorials that "maybe the Filipinos have caught wind of the way Indians and Negroes have been Christianized and civilized" in America. The Cleveland *Gazette* reported that Ida B. Wells, a leading member of the anti-Bookerite National Afro-American Council, spoke in 1898 before a Washington, D.C., gathering on "Mob Violence and Anarchy, North and South." Wells was said to urge blacks "to oppose expansion until the government was able to protect the Negro at home."[22] After black soldiers had served with distinction in the war for Cuba's independence, the poet Paul Laurence Dunbar summed up the national mood this way: "Negroes you may fight for us, but you may not vote for us. . . . You may be heroes in war, but you must be cravens in peace." At a mass meeting of blacks chaired by the lawyer Archibald H. Grimké in Boston, where black opposition to Washington was perhaps the most outspoken, an open letter of protest was addressed to President McKinley which read in part:

> We, sir, at this crisis and extremity in the life of our race in the South, and in this crisis and extremity of the republic as well, in the presence of the civilized world, cry to you to pause, if but for an hour, in pursuit of your national policy of "criminal aggression" abroad to consider the "criminal aggression" at home against humanity and American citizenship, which is in the full tide of successful conquest at the South, and the tremendous consequences to our civilization, and the durability of the Union itself, of this universal subversion of the supreme law of the land, of democratic institutions, and of the previous principle of the religion of Jesus in the social and civil life of the Southern people.[23]

Given the hopeless choice in the 1900 national election between McKinley's indifference to black concerns and the anti-imperialist, but overtly racist Democratic party led by William Jennings Bryan, many alienated black Republicans followed African Methodist Episcopal Zion Church Bishop Alexander Walters, who, after briefly weighing a third-party alternative, "held his nose" and voted for McKinley. While the months preceding the election marked the high tide of the linkage of anti-imperialism and domestic protest among blacks, W. E. B. Du Bois would revive the analogy in 1903 in challenging Washington's program of industrial education as the exclusive means of the "uplifting and civilization of black men in America." Du Bois denounced Washington's policy, indicative of a tendency "born of slavery and quickened and renewed to life by the crazy imperialism of the day, to regard human beings as among the material resources of a land to be trained with an eye single to future dividends."[24]

Hazel Carby, Ann duCille, Elizabeth Ammons, and other scholars have demonstrated the importance of Hopkins's historical fiction for its radical critique of domestic racial and sexual oppression. But in the series in *Voice of the Negro*, Hopkins backed away from the radicalism of her fiction which tackled what Carby has provocatively termed the "internal colonization" of black American men and women through the practices of lynching and rape in the United States.[25] This trend in Hopkins's writings illustrates black writers' dilemma of negotiating the obstacles imposed by domestic racism: isolation, powerlessness, negligible institutional supports and professional opportunities, and, finally, the confining terms of Western imperialist ideology. In her case, such obstacles contributed to her emphasis on a pan-Africanism based on a patriarchal notion of race, which further rendered her pursuit of a more autonomous, oppositional consciousness all the more difficult.

Hopkins was a prolific contributor to black literary magazines, which provided crucial outlets for the promotion of this middle-class racial uplift ideology. Organs of education and instruction, these genteel publications also served as testimonials to the ideals of uplift and black progress. Hopkins was a founder and executive editor of the *Colored American Magazine,* a nationwide periodical based in Boston, which sought to promote racial solidarity and self-improvement among its largely black readership. Gender issues were highly visible in her wide-ranging contributions to the magazine, which included nonfiction such as "Famous Women of the Negro Race," an account of the black women's club movement, and a historical sketch on "Toussaint L'Ouverture," the military commander of the Haitian Revolution. Given the tenuous social position of blacks, for whom uplift ideology represented all the cultural capital they had, even the constant espousal of race-conscious middle-class aspirations, ideology, and activism through popular history and fiction was not enough to financially sustain many black periodicals and newspapers. The precarious existence of such institutions restricted the range of expression. In 1904 Washington and his Tuskegee Machine purchased the *Colored American Magazine.* Not long afterward, in a move that hardly seemed coincidental, Hopkins left that journal, which had provided a crucial medium for her writings, to become a contributor to the *Voice of the Negro.*[26]

Throughout the course of her study, which diverged greatly from her previous subject matter, Hopkins's outlook was hardly immune to Western assumptions of racial hierarchy and cultural superiority, even as she was engaged in an antiracist project. Indeed, a dominant perspective on race and imperialism crowded the pages of the series, reserving little room for anti-imperialist statements. Hopkins brought together an idiosyncratic assortment of nineteenth-century racial ideologies and myths: the civilizing mission, ethnocentric discourses of Victorian anthropology, Biblical myths of the origin of races, and ethnological discussions cataloging the physical characteristics and customs of such South Pacific peoples as Samoans, Polynesians, New Guineans, and Malays.[27]

Generally, Hopkins's writings represented two distinct visions of imperialism: it took on a benign character—advancing Christianity, progress, and civilization—when Hopkins was discussing those South Pacific peoples whom she regarded as the most politically and culturally remote from Western Christian civilization. She seemed reluctant to declare an affinity, political or otherwise, with these "darker races." But the opposite was true of the relation she drew toward Japan, and particularly toward the "African race"; when discussing these groups, with whom she claimed solidarity, Hopkins more explicitly identified imperialism with a secular notion of domination and with a critique of Anglo-American ethnocentrism. Within her staunchly religious worldview, Hopkins ultimately regarded these particular "darker races" as messianic foes of Anglo-Saxon assumptions of "white supremacy" and dominance.

Thus, in the context of her ethnological series, Hopkins's view of race depended a great deal upon which "race" she was discussing. Reflecting the protean, irrational nature of much writing on race, a condition which clearly did not deter most commentators, racist and antiracist, from a confident air of scientific authority, Hopkins's views on race, despite their ostensibly scientific format, were too grounded in evangelical sentiment to constitute a consistent critique. As Sander Gilman and Nancy Stepan have noted, this strategy of employing religious ethics to advance a moral critique of scientific racism was common among black writers of the period.[28] Yet there were moments when Hopkins's religious outlook masked her antiracist intent. Thus, her discussion of the Philippines turned on her claim that its destiny was "To bring . . . the United States prominently before the civilized world in the character and promoter of human progress." If Hopkins is being sarcastic in this instance, such a reading is not supported by her apparent lack of interest in the rights of Filipinos. She preferred to speculate on the significance of race mixture among Filipinos and the African ancestry of the islands' Negritos. She stressed "progress" rather than the issue of rights, claiming that "[Manila] has improved greatly since its occupation by Americans," with its new public works and commercial enterprise. What impressed Hopkins most about the Filipino Negritos, as well as "the other dark races of Australasia," was her belief that they "are of the family of Ham." Here, the biologism of her claim of the African ancestry of South Pacific peoples supported an argument reiterated by contemporary advocates of "Afrocentricity": "[W]hy not allow that the theory of Ethiopia as the mother of science, art and literature is true?" Even though Hopkins claimed racial identity with the Negritos, she was more concerned with defending black peoples against the Aryanization of ancient history than granting Filipinos the right to self-government.[29]

Indeed, *Of One Blood* contains a pan-African theme then commonplace among black writers in its challenge to the putative "whiteness" of Hellenic civilization. These writers sought to make Western civilization a racially inclusive, universal category by calling attention to its origins in ancient African societies. Thus, the fantastic plot of Hopkins's novel resolves during an expedition led by a gadfly British professor which discovers a lost Ethiopian city, its descendants, and its supernatural technology advanced far beyond that of the West. In a pan-African racial reunion, the brilliant African American (though passing for white) doctor of the expedition, Reuel Briggs, is in turn recognized by the Ethiopians, governed by Candace, an interim female monarch, as Ergamenes, their long-absent heir to the throne. Accepting the throne, Reuel also reclaims his racial identity and takes charge of the historical destiny of the race. A fundamental condition of Briggs's ascension is that the Ethiopians exchange their vague spiritualism for Christianity, to which Briggs's Ethiopian adviser and prime minister readily assents on behalf of his people: "O Ergamenes, your belief shall be ours; we have no will but yours. Deign to teach your subjects." As with racial uplift ideology, potential tensions between authoritarian leadership and democratic consent are explained away; monarchism takes on the benevolent face of Christianity. The novel became not only an assertion of the racial destiny of what Hopkins called the "modern Ethiopian"; Reuel's restoration to the Ethiopian monarchy also marked the assimilationist assumptions of Western cultural superiority. Hopkins also effected a similar restoration of patriarchal authority routinely assumed within uplift ideology and among black leadership. Briggs's subsequent rule in Africa beside the black queen Candace, though troubled by "the advance of mighty nations penetrating the dark, mysterious forests of his native land," constitutes transcendence of the heritage of American slavery, with its horrific legacy of murder, rape, and incest rendered within the domestic American setting of the novel. The pan-African vision of *Of One Blood* linked domestic uplift ideology to the idea of the civilizing mission, but in a nostalgic manner that imagined black Americans' reclamation of an ancient African civilization as a refuge from contemporary domestic and imperial oppression of colored peoples. The novel's content reflected a long tradition of amateur scholarly productions by blacks which sought to Africanize prevailing notions of Western civilization, a tradition which endures today in the work of Afrocentric scholars.[30]

As Hopkins's writings shifted primarily to the terrain of race, attributes of imperial power and conquest became matters for praise as much as criticism. Hopkins reserved a central place in her series for Japan, in the wake of that non-Western imperial nation's recent victory in its war with Russia in 1905. Hopkins, like other black commentators of the day,[31] admired Japan's military conquest of a Western power as evidence that a nonwhite (and non-Christian) nation could break the West's apparent monopoly on military, scientific, technological, and imperial power. While noting that the "warlike" Japanese "surprised the entire world by their endurance and prowess," Hopkins viewed Japan's military success in terms of her belief in Christian teleology and her view of the messianic role that the darker races would play in world history: "Silently God demonstrates His power and the truth of His words: 'Of one blood have I made all races of men to dwell upon the whole face of the earth.' No amount of scientific reasoning, no strenuous attempts of puerile rulers or leaders can hope to prevail against Omnipotence."[32] Curiously, Hopkins did not perceive the need to reconcile the moral conflict between the aims of patriarchal imperial power and divine teleology. But imperial Japan, or the ideal of African nationhood—symbols of the reversal of Western dominance—epitomized the racial aspirations of black nationalists of her time.[33] Unable to conceptualize an alternative to social relations defined by imperial conquest, yet perhaps sensing the unlikelihood that blacks in America and Africa would prevail where only force would settle all disputes, Hopkins appealed not only to a plural combination of "darker races," but also, ultimately, to the cleansing authority of divine "Omnipotence," before which all else was powerless.

Hopkins sought to refute ideologies of racial difference by citing proofs of racial equality drawn from the Bible, also citing those scientific commentators she deemed most authoritative on the subject of the origin of races. Citing the black nationalist physician Martin R. Delany's study of racial origins, she claimed that differences in skin color were essentially a matter of different concentrations of pigmentation, whose presence in all races was portrayed as a trait more indicative of racial equality than difference. Moreover, she asserted, following Delany, that miscegenation did not decisively alter what she termed "original" races: as she put it, "the sterling races, when crossed, reproduce themselves in their original purity." Here Hopkins ventured a calm rebuke to prevailing taboos against miscegenation, as she did in the story "Talma Gordon," although she still seemed influenced by dubious notions of racial purity.[34]

Hopkins invoked the scriptures to make her case for racial equality and a universal human family, but at the same time, her evangelical piety prevented her from questioning the missionary component of imperialist ideology—the idea that the light of Christianity, civilization, and commerce would rescue so-called heathen peoples from barbarism. Ultimately, despite a religious vision of human brotherhood, Hopkins's writings showed a preoccupation with constructing an authoritative bourgeois persona, a concern which seemed to preclude a more consistent critique of imperialism and its racist assumptions. When she turned to a discussion of Africa, a denunciation of the atrocities of Belgian authorities in the Congo contended, in the same breath, with a generally benign, missionary view of colonialization: "The regeneration of Africa is upon us, but blood and tears flow in its train."[35]

Unlike many of the missionaries, travelers, and colonial adventurers whose writings accumulated to form the literature of Victorian anthropology, Hopkins did not conduct what professional anthropologists would have considered fieldwork. This in itself is no indictment of Hopkins; for many practitioners fieldwork has not been the antidote to ideology, and moreover, confinement to the metropoles hardly prevented many Western writers from overreaching themselves. While it was crucial that peoples of color intervene in public discussions of race and imperialism, the political inconsistency of Hopkins's writings resulted from the fact that her own ethnological accounts of the various peoples she discussed were not truly hers. Hopkins's ambivalent knowledge of imperialism was generally drawn secondhand from the imperialist texts that were likely her only sources of information. For example, in her discussion of Borneo, Hopkins quotes with approval a hagiographic view of its British imperial ruler, Sir James Brooke: "The personal courage exhibited by Mr. Brooke, and the firmness with which he put down the earlier conspiracies against his rule, won the better class of chiefs to his side." Hopkins endorsed the official imperialist myth of the British crown bringing peace and order to a region "in a chronic state of insurrection" so as to "open" the region for what was deemed "free trade" by the colonizers. To Hopkins, Brooke served as an "instructive" example of benevolent colonial paternalism and "humane" rule. "If our powerful American leaders," she observed, "might be brought to emulate the example of Sir James Brooke in dealing with the race question in the United States, how matters would be simplified, and peace take the place of suspicion and hatred." To Hopkins the terms of the "civilizing mission" served as a vehicle for her assertion of the middle-class agenda of racial uplift, as indicated by her reference to the alliance between Brooke and the "better class" of chiefs. Here, Hopkins was evoking the paternalism behind the self-described "better class" of black Americans' frequent appeals that white elites recognize their rights, bringing a truce to U.S. racial conflicts, or at least, sparing them, as elites, from the harmful effects of discrimination.[36]

In this sense, Hopkins's treatment of Borneo brought the imperialist rhetoric of the civilizing mission back home. Her very understanding of Borneo derived in part from an imposed domestic ethos of racial uplift, to a much different effect than that achieved by those for whom imperialism and debates on expansion informed their critiques of white supremacy in the American South. Hopkins's seemingly disinterested ethnological persona, claiming expertise in relation to the colonized peoples and cultures who were more often than not the object of her classifications, was akin to uplift ideology's self-serving representation of the black American majority as a more marginal, unassimilated "other," the antithesis of the progress embodied by the statistically small, but indispensable "Talented Tenth," to use the term for black leadership popularized by W. E. B. Du Bois. Hopkins's religious claims for the equality of races were not incompatible with the invidious worldly dimension of civilizationist ideology: that those races less advanced, or developed, on the scale of civilization were incapable of governing themselves. Presumably, Hopkins would have disagreed with this view that "undeveloped" races could only benefit from colonial tutelage. In any case, here is Hopkins, after noting physical similarities between African, Asian, and Celtic races:

> We contend that the characteristics supposed to be peculiar to the Negro are common to all members of the human species under conditions which tend to leave undeveloped the faculties of the mind. From this state of degradation all classes of men may be raised by the cultivation of the intellectual or spiritual part of this body. There alone is the difference; it is the portion of the spirit in every being which raises up to the heights of civilization and eliminates the purely animal, for man is a spirit shining within the body of an animal.[37]

Even as she opposed European dominance of the darker races, Hopkins's acceptance of the hierarchies of body and spirit, animal and man, all measured by the standard of Christian civilization, clashed with her claims of racial equality. Such contradictory declarations might be attributed not only to her education and background, but also to her defensive social position—she, like many other black commentators, was forced to refute the dominant stereotypes that consigned her and other blacks to the bottom of such hierarchies by demonstrating her affinity to the dominant ideals of civilization.

In Hopkins's nonfiction discussions of Japan and Africa, she ventured a more oppositional stance. Here, instead of the imperial vision of unbroken Western progress and of the material and cultural improvements of colonization, she offered a cyclical view of history marked by struggle between the forces of civilization and barbarism, and between imperial powers and their darker subject peoples. She sought to reverse the conventional wisdom of the correlation between race, namely "whiteness," and civilization and its moral authority. In light of Japan's triumph, Hopkins saw prophetic, teleological significance in her observation that "[t]hose barbarians were known to the dark races who ruled the world [in antiquity], as the 'white peril,'" implying that the darker races in their turn might eventually return to a dominant position in world affairs.[38] Here, and in closing her series with a discussion of Africa, Hopkins's treatment of race, and her use of the notion of uplift, took on a more confrontational tone, its messianism backed by a demographic recognition of strength in numbers, and an attempt to frame opposition to domestic racism with African nationalist movements such as the religious Ethiopianism of South African native churches:[39]

> The presumption of superiority by the Anglo-Saxon race is insolently arrogant. We mark the insinuating patronage of other races by them, the slogan of social equality, the gospel of racial purity, the dangers of the Ethiopian movement, as the outcome of a dread fear that is ever present with them and is tugging at their heartstrings. This is caused by the steady uplift of thousands of Blacks, Yellows and Browns. . . . That the ultimate desire of the Anglo-Saxon is the complete subjugation of all dark races to themselves, there is no doubt; but the persistent rise of the dark men in the social scale and their wonderful increase in numbers is a source of constant menace to the accomplishment of certain designs.[40]

Nowhere in the series did Hopkins more emphatically manifest a different destiny, one of social conflict and historical contingency, against naturalizing myths of Western progress and civilization. Hopkins's ambivalent discussion of racial ideologies of the period illustrates the dilemma of black writers torn between the desperate aspiration for the status of respectability, a strategy which tacitly endorsed prevailing assumptions of racial and social hierarchy, and the struggle to articulate an autonomous and oppositional racial group consciousness. Hopkins's genteel discourse on race was limited in its attempt to refute crudely irrational racist ideologies, which nevertheless possessed a formidable veneer of normalcy and authority.

While the act of claiming for themselves the status and functions inherent in "civilization" was central to their struggle against the dominant "whiteness" implicit in bourgeois citizenship, the preoccupation of many black leaders with racial uplift ideology as a sign of respectability restricted possibilities for effective resistance and constituted a measure of ideological collusion with discriminatory ideologies and practices. As such, it had devastating consequences for the lives of black Americans. The racialized terms of civilization upon which racial uplift ideology rested marked a compromised, *metaracist* antiracism that, needless to say, was not incompatible with the aims of empire or white domination in the South. Just as the violence instrumental to colonization was domesticated by the widely advertised wondrous progress of "civilization," the class bias inherent in black Americans' attempts to appropriate "progress" through the imperial terms of uplift and civilization helped legitimize black disfranchisement and the violence that enforced it. Uplift and its corollary, developmental ideology, eroded earlier abolitionist claims to a morally grounded natural rights. This Christian egalitarianism, which also animated the Reconstruction era's radical Republican ideology and its pursuit of voting rights and land reform for blacks, was eclipsed not only by the hegemony of scientific racism during the age of imperialism. What made the forces of racism and reaction all the more legitimate and formidable was the Christian imperialism of civilizationist ideology that affirmed the myth of political "unfitness" of both colonial subjects—and black Americans—for equal rights and self-determination.

Civilizationist ideology played a significant part in legitimizing what was a patriarchal, metaracist discourse employed, paradoxically, by non-racists: blacks, like Hopkins, who considered themselves opposed to racism! Many disfranchised and powerless bourgeois blacks sometimes showed a greater preoccupation with demonstrating their own entitlement to citizenship rights than with mounting opposition to the domestic repression of the black American majority. The complex character of Hopkins's writings on race suggests that, to paraphrase Lenin, imperialism at the turn of the century marked the latest stage of racism (as well as capitalism), not just in the colonies, or in European metropoles, but in the United States, as well.[41]

Contemporary commentators who plunge into the discourse on race without questioning its very terms, assumptions, and its historical contingency would do well to note that one cannot easily posit a fine distinction between racialized expression and racist practice, between the demeaning word and the hateful, violent deed. For verification of this, and as a postscript to Hopkins's series, we need look no further than the Atlanta race riot of 1906, in which white mobs, inflamed by a spate of newspaper accounts of alleged rapes of white women by black men, attacked Atlanta's black neighborhoods for four days after a gubernatorial election. A prominent black educator, William Crogman, vividly noted the tragic limitations of uplift ideology in an age of overt racism, as he recovered from injuries sustained in the violence: "Here we have worked and prayed and tried to make good men and women of our colored population, and at our very doorstep the whites kill these good men. But the lawless element in our population, the element we have condemned, fights back, and it is [to] these people that we owe our lives." Crogman was referring to the residents of "Darktown," Atlanta's black slum, who had fought off an invading white mob. Twelve lost their lives, and seventy were wounded, the majority of the victims African Americans. The riot displaced much of what had been a thriving black middle class in Atlanta, including institutions like the *Voice of the Negro*, which, not long after it fled to Chicago, ceased publication. From the time her series appeared in the *Voice of the Negro* to her death in 1930, during which she supported herself as a stenographer in Boston, there is little evidence that Hopkins was able to maintain her previous level of literary activity. Nor was there any indication that her views on race and imperialism changed in the heightened climate of race consciousness during World War I, when leaders in the black community once again faced the dilemma of sending black troops overseas, only to have the returning heroes greeted by forces of reaction on a domestic front that was anything but peaceful.[42]

Notes

This essay is an expanded version of "Black Americans and the Rising 'Darker Races': Pauline Hopkins' Re-Vision of Racial Ideologies," a paper presented at the annual meeting of the American Studies Association, November 2, 1991. I am indebted to Oscar Campomanes, Ann duCille, Linda Grasso, Matthew Jacobson, Amy Kaplan, Donald Pease, and most of all, Louise Newman, for their assistance and criticisms.
 1 Pauline Hopkins, *Contending Forces* (New York: Oxford, 1988).

2 Pauline Hopkins, "Talma Gordon," *The Colored American Magazine* 1, no. 5 (October 1900): 271–90; Hopkins, *Of One Blood*, in *The Magazine Novels of Pauline Hopkins*, ed. Hazel Carby (New York, Oxford University Press, 1988).

3 Henry Louis Gates, ed., *"Race," Writing, and Difference* (Chicago: University of Chicago Press, 1986); Michael Omi and Howard Winant, *Racial Formation in the United States from the 1960s to the 1980s* (New York: Routledge & Kegan Paul, 1986); Stuart Hall, "The Whites of Their Eyes: Racist Ideologies and the Media," in *Silver Linings: Some Strategies for the Eighties*, ed. George Bridges and Rosalind Brunt (London: Lawrence and Wishart, 1981), pp. 28–52.

4 Evelyn Brooks Higginbotham, "African-American Women's History and the Metalanguage of Race," *Signs* 17, no. 2 (Winter 1992): 251–74.

5 On the problems facing African American and Jewish writers seeking to challenge the idioms of scientific racism, whose presumption of the inferiority of racial minorities withheld the authority of science from their writings, see Nancy Leys Stepan and Sander L. Gilman, "Appropriating the Idioms of Science: The Rejection of Scientific Racism," in Dominick LaCapra, ed., *The Bounds of Race: Perspectives on Hegemony and Resistance* (Ithaca: Cornell University Press, 1991), pp. 72–103. Pauline E. Hopkins to John E. Bruce, April 6, 1906, in the John Edward Bruce Collection, Schomburg Center, New York Public Library.

6 See, for example, *America's Race Problems: Addresses at the Annual Meeting of the American Academy of Political and Social Science, Philadelphia, April Twelfth and Thirteenth, 1901* (1901; New York: Negro Universities Press, 1969).

7 On Anglo-American reunion, see William T. Stead, *The Americanization of the World, or The Trend of the Twentieth Century* (New York: Horace Markley, 1901), pp. 13, 23; Du Bois is quoted in George Shepperson, "Notes on Negro American Influences on the Emergence of African Nationalism," *Journal of African History* 1, no. 2 (1960): 307. Pauline Hopkins, "The Dark Races of the Twentieth Century, Part I—Oceanica," *Voice of the Negro* 2, no. 2 (February 1905): 108. In the same year, according to Richard Yarborough, Hopkins brought out *A Primer of Facts Pertaining to the Early Greatness of the African Race and the Possibility of its Restoration by Its Descendants—with Epilogue*. See notes to Yarborough's introduction to *Contending Forces*.

8 Several scholars have noted the assumptions of Western cultural superiority of early pan-Africanist intellectuals and leaders. See Wilson Moses, *Alexander Crummell: A Study of Civilization and Discontent* (New York: Oxford University Press, 1989); Kwame Anthony Appiah, *In My Father's House: Essays on African Philosophy and Culture* (New York: Oxford, 1992); and V. Y. Mudimbe, *The Invention of Africa* (Bloomington: Indiana University Press, 1988).

9 Nancy L. Stepan and Sander L. Gilman, "Appropriating the Idioms of Science" in LaCapra, ed.

10 George H. Blakeslee, "Introduction," *The Journal of Race Development* 1, no. 1 (July 1910): 1. The journal, edited by Blakeslee and psychologist G. Stanley

Hall, also represented antiracist positions, as it included on its board of contributing editors Franz Boas and W. E. B. Du Bois. For another instance of the professionalization of missionary discourse and race "problems," see *The Christian Mission in the Light of Race Conflict*, Report of the Jerusalem Meeting of the International Council, 1928 (London: Oxford University Press, 1928).

II Nell Painter, *Standing at Armageddon: The United States, 1877–1919* (New York: Norton, 1987), p. 161.

I2 Du Bois's statement at the London pan-African conference, which the black educator and intellectual Anna Julia Cooper also attended, is quoted in Williams, p. xiii.

I3 Willard Gatewood, *Black Americans and the White Man's Burden, 1898–1903* (Urbana: University of Illinois Press, 1975).

I4 Rayford Logan, *The Betrayal of the Negro* (New York: Collier, 1965).

I5 Kevin Gaines, *Uplifting the Race: Black Middle-Class Ideology and Leadership in the United States since 1890* (Chapel Hill: University of North Carolina Press, forthcoming). The origins of feminism and its ties to missionary and imperialist perspectives are explored in Louise Newman, "Laying Claim to Difference: Ideologies of Race and Gender in the U.S. Woman's Movement, 1870–1920" (Ph.D. diss., Brown University, 1992).

I6 Wilson J. Moses, *The Golden Age of Black Nationalism, 1850–1925* (New York: Oxford University Press, 1988), p. 28.

I7 Frances E. W. Harper, *Iola Leroy, or Shadows Uplifted* (Boston: Beacon Press, 1987), p. 116. Like Harper and others, Anna Julia Cooper invoked the missionary role in support of her argument for the inclusion of black women in racial uplift efforts. See Cooper, *A Voice from the South* (1892; New York: Oxford University Press, 1988).

I8 For a discussion of the ideological content and objectives of the Hampton-Tuskegee approach to industrial education, see James Anderson, *Black Education in the South, 1860–1935* (Chapel Hill: University of North Carolina Press, 1988).

I9 Booker T. Washington, *Up From Slavery* (New York, Penguin Books, 1986), pp. 16, 80, 111.

20 Walter L. Williams, *Black Americans and the Evangelization of Africa, 1877–1900* (Madison: University of Wisconsin Press, 1982); J. W. E. Bowen, ed., *Africa and the American Negro* (1886; Miami, Mnemosyne Publishing, 1969). On Crummell, see Moses, *Alexander Crummell*. For quotation of William T. Alexander, *History of the Colored Race in America* (Kansas City, Mo.: Palmetto Publishing, 1888), pp. 530–31, see Williams, p. 96.

21 William Loren Katz, introduction to George P. Marks, ed., *The Black Press Views American Imperialism, 1898–1900* (New York: Arno Press, 1971), pp. vii–xii. Louis Harlan, *Booker T. Washington: The Wizard of Tuskegee, 1901–1915* (New York: Oxford University Press, 1983).

22 Marks, ed., p. 109.

23 Dunbar is quoted in James P. Shenton and Jack D. Foner, *Blacks and the Military in American History: A New Perspective* (New York: Praeger Publishers, 1974), p. viii; Grimké quoted in Marks, ed., p. 203.

24 W. E. B. Du Bois, *The Souls of Black Folk* (1903; New York, Signet, 1969), p. 126.

25 Hazel Carby, *Reconstructing Womanhood* (New York: Oxford, 1987); Ann duCille, *The Coupling Convention: Black Woman Novelists and the Marriage Plot, 1853–1948* (Oxford University Press, forthcoming). For a useful reading of Hopkins's imaginative analysis of domestic race and gender oppression in *Of One Blood*, see Elizabeth Ammons, *Conflicting Stories: American Women Writers at the Turn into the Twentieth Century* (New York: Oxford University Press, 1991), pp. 81–85. On internal colonization of black women's bodies under U.S. slavery and segregation, see Carby, "'On the Threshold of Woman's Era': Lynching, Empire and Sexuality in Black Feminist Theory," *Critical Inquiry* 12 (Autumn 1985): 262–77.

26 Carby, *Reconstructing Womanhood*, pp. 121–62. Hopkins, "Famous Women of the Negro Race," *Colored American Magazine* [*CAM*] 4–5 (November 1901–October 1902); "Echoes from the Annual Convention of Northeastern Federation of Colored Women's Clubs," *CAM* 6 (October 1903): 709–13; "Toussaint L'Ouverture," *CAM* 2 (November 1900): 9–24. On the purchase of the Colored American Magazine, see also Richard Yarborough's introduction to *Contending Forces*, pp. xlii–xliii.

27 George W. Stocking, Jr., *Victorian Anthropology* (New York: Free Press, 1987).

28 Stepan and Gilman, pp. 81–82.

29 *Voice of the Negro*, vol. 2, no. 3 (March 1905): 189–91.

30 Carby, ed., *Of One Blood*, pp. 562–63, 621. On the Aryanization of ancient history, see Cheikh Anta Diop, *The African Origin of Civilization: Myth or Reality* (Chicago: Lawrence Hill Books, 1974); Martin Bernal, *Black Athena: The Afroasiatic Roots of Classical Civilization*, vol. 1, *The Fabrication of Ancient Greece* (New Brunswick: Rutgers University Press, 1987). See also Martin R. Delany, *Principia of Ethnology: The Origin of Races and Color, with an Archeological Compendium of Ethiopian and Egyptian Civilization* (Philadelphia: Harper & Brother, 1879); Pauline Hopkins, *A Primer of Facts Pertaining to the Early Greatness of the African Race and the Possibility of Restoration by its Descendants* (Cambridge, Mass.: P. E. Hopkins, 1905), and J. Max Barber, *The Negro of the Earlier World: An Excursion Into Ancient Negro History* (Philadelphia: A.M.E. Book Concern, n.d.).

31 For an interesting blend of Western ethnocentrism tempered by a keen respect for Japan's military success, see W. S. Scarborough, "Our Pagan Teachers," *Voice of the Negro*, vol. 2, no. 5 (June 1905): 404–6.

32 Hopkins, *The Voice of the Negro*, vol. 2, no. 4 (May 1905): 334.

33 In this regard, Hopkins anticipated the movement led by the Jamaican Marcus Garvey, which epitomized black nationalists' appropriation of the language of empire within their anticolonial struggles. See Judith Stein, *The World of Marcus Garvey: Race and Class in Modern Society* (Baton Rouge: Louisiana State University Press, 1986).

34 Delany, *Principia of Ethnology.*

35 Hopkins, "The Dark Races of the Twentieth Century, Part IV–Africa," *Voice of the Negro,* vol. 2, no. 5 (June 1905): 415. Hopkins's reference to the situation in the Congo is interesting in light of the criticism black leaders and editors were bringing to bear on Belgian atrocities. An American chapter of the anti-imperialist Congo Reform Association, based in Massachusetts, published its first report in 1904. Booker T. Washington and Robert E. Park lent their efforts to the association, publicizing King Leopold's reign of terror. See Booker T. Washington (ghostwritten by Park), "Cruelty in the Congo Country," *Outlook* 78 (October 8, 1904); and Robert E. Park, "Recent Atrocities in the Congo State," *The World To-day* 8 (October 1904): 1328–31. U.S. and African American opposition to Belgian imperialism is discussed in Stanford M. Lyman, *Militarism, Imperialism and Racial Accommodation: An Analysis of the Early Writings of Robert E. Park* (Fayetteville: University of Arkansas Press, 1992), pp. 57–76; and Wilson J. Moses, *The Golden Age of Black Nationalism, 1850–1925* (New York: Oxford University Press, 1988), pp. 205–6, 221–25.

36 *Voice of the Negro,* vol. 2, no. 3 (March 1905): 188–89.

37 *Voice of the Negro,* vol. 2, no. 4 (May 1905): 330.

38 Ibid., p. 334.

39 J. Mutero Chirenje, *Ethiopianism and Afro-Americans in South Africa, 1883–1916* (Baton Rouge: Louisiana State University Press, 1987).

40 *Voice of the Negro,* vol. 2, no. 7 (July 1905): p. 461. Cite study on Ethiopianism.

41 For an insightful discussion of the concept of metaracism, which holds great potential for illuminating and demystifying past and present racial ideologies, see Joel Kovel, *White Racism: A Psychohistory* (New York: Vintage Books, 1970). See E. J. Hobsbawm, *The Age of Empire* (New York: Vintage Books, 1989), pp. 59–60, which contains a judicious discussion of Lenin's analysis on imperialism. George Shepperson notes that elements of the Leninist analysis were foreshadowed by a pre-Marxist W. E. B. Du Bois. Du Bois's analysis can be found in "The African Roots of the War," *Atlantic Monthly* (May 1915), cited in Shepperson, "Notes on Negro American Influences," p. 307.

42 John Dittmer, *Black Georgia in the Progressive Era, 1900–1920* (Urbana: University of Illinois Press, 1977), pp. 127–28. Ray Stannard Baker, *Following the Color Line* (New York: Harper Torchbooks, 1964), pp. 3–15. On the domestic racial violence that resulted in the mobilization of black troops during World War I and black protest, see Mary Frances Berry, *Black Resistance/White Law: A History of Constitutional Racism in America* (New York: Appleton-Century Crofts Educational Division, 1971), pp. 142–43.

William E. Cain

From Liberalism to Communism

The Political Thought of W. E. B. Du Bois

We shall now proceed to construct the Socialist order.—V. I. Lenin, addressing the Second Congress of Soviets, 8 November 1917

There is no doubt that the world of the twenty-first century will be overwhelmingly communistic.—W. E. B. Du Bois, May 1960

he Soviet Union lies in ruins, and the communist ideology that buttressed it has been discredited, mocked, and derided, spoken of with grim humor or outright contempt. Yet for most of this century, the Soviet Union was a powerful symbol for the political Left and the anti-imperialist cause. It majestically represented the possibility of a better life than the majority of people led under industrial capitalism; it seemed a nation built by and for its workers, designed to liberate their energies and creative powers and at last end the misery, poverty, and exploitation that had always afflicted them; and, even after the harsh truth about Stalin's rule became widely known after World War II, it continued to give hope (along with material aid and diplomatic support) to the countries and colonies of the so-called third or underdeveloped world that were fighting for freedom and independence.

The collapse of the Soviet Union is a fact with which progressive critics and intellectuals must reckon. To be sure, one crucial task for them today, as in the past, is to detail the history of Western and American imperialism, a history that many Americans only thinly acknowledge and understand: America *is* an empire and yet its often brutal policies and practices are regularly discussed as though it were not. But a second task is imperative as well, and that is to pon-der the impact of the Soviet Union's dissolution and the meanings of socialism and communism, the complex bodies of thought that have been invoked throughout the twentieth century to signify what imperialism ruthlessly forestalls.

With a little careful research, it is not difficult to expose the realities of American and Western imperialism: the record of devastation is plain. But the importance of this project should not prevent intellectuals from seriously examining where they have placed, and where they will place, their belief in the prospects for change, for the transformation of capitalism and imperialism into something better.

Why haven't socialism and, especially, communism in the Soviet Union and China worked to bring real freedom and democracy and prosperity? Are these ideas, ultimately, beautiful abstractions that men and women can cherish only when the ideas are kept separate from the histories of the countries that have attempted to implement them? What precisely was the appeal of communism for twentieth-century intellectuals? What impelled them to fix their faith in the Soviet Union, trusting, even when they were told what Stalin had wrought, that somehow the ideals of socialism would eventually flower and flourish there? How, too, does the demise of the Soviet Union and its empire reflect on the long, painful struggle of oppressed peoples against Western imperialism? Where can they find examples of a better life than they have known?

In this essay I will begin to delve into these formidable questions by focusing on the single case of W. E. B. Du Bois, and by dwelling in particular on the trajectory of his political thought. He was a courageous man, a remarkable scholar, a renowned intellectual, a tireless foe of both capitalism and imperialism who during the course of his career moved from liberalism to socialism to communism, becoming by the 1940s an avid defender of Stalin and friend of the Soviet Union. This is where Du Bois's work took him, and I think it may reveal more than just his own mistaken judgments and personal tragedy.

As a scholar, educator, polemicist, world traveler, and diplomat, W. E. B. Du Bois was keenly interested in the history of slavery, colonialism, and imperialism. This deep, abiding concern is evident throughout his writings, from his Harvard dissertation and first book, *The Suppression of the African Slave Trade* (1896), to his posthumously published *Autobiography* (1968). Du Bois's struggle against imperial rule in Africa and his effort to empower the world's colored races began in 1900, when he participated in the first pan-African Congress in London and published an important essay, "The Present Outlook for the Dark Races of Mankind." Here he noted that "the color line belts the world" and stressed that "the social problem of the twentieth century is to be the relation of the civilized world to the dark races of mankind." He argued against injustice in the colonies and, celebrating the legacy of the French Revolution, identified the "Political Rights of the masses" and "the rule of the people" as incontestable truths.[1] Du Bois reaffirmed and extended this anti-imperialist, democratic viewpoint at the later congresses, meetings, and councils he attended and in such important books as *The Negro* (1915), *Darkwater* (1920), *The Gift of Black Folk* (1924), *Color and Democracy: Colonies and Peace* (1945), and *The World and Africa* (1947).

Du Bois's internationalism intensified during the crisis-ridden 1930s and, even more, in the aftermath of World War II with the founding of the United Nations, an organization Du Bois hoped would aid and uplift colonized people of color. By this point Du Bois was a socialist and, it seems, a communist in his ideas and values—though he was hostile, at least through the late 1930s, to both the Socialist party and the Communist party for their dim understanding of, and exploitative attitude toward, black Americans. Du Bois's absorption in Marxist texts (which he taught at Atlanta University upon his return there in 1934 after resigning from the NAACP), his commitment to pan-Africanism and hatred of colonialism, and his pained awareness of the grim economic conditions black workers faced in the Depression steadily pushed him to the left.

Du Bois advocated socialism nationally and internationally and pondered what a communist alternative to capitalism and imperialism would look like. As part of this project, Du Bois in *Black Reconstruction* (1935) reinterpreted nineteenth-century American history in order to foreground the agency of black men and women during the Civil War and Reconstruction, showing in the process that the oppressed had been, and could be again, the main force in their own liberation. And, in *Black Folk Then and Now* (1939) and countless other writings, he reexamined African history, exposing the myths and distortions of imperialism and, furthermore, identifying in the African past the communal, cooperative models for economic development that could spur reform and revolution in the United States and across the globe.

But it is not sufficient to call Du Bois a socialist and anti-imperialist: this makes him too easy to locate and comprehend. When the cold war broke out in full force in the late 1940s, Du Bois was in his seventies, yet he remained vigorous and prolific, and he said and did many important things in the midst of these difficult years that amplified themes he had accented earlier. Du Bois took his stand for peace, defended civil liberties, assailed inequality and segregation, and refused to buckle to right-wing attacks on freedom of speech. He denounced militarism and corporate tyranny, inveighed against American and European assaults on the third world, and championed national liberation movements. But he spoke and acted during the cold war as a Stalinist. This is the most troubling fact about his extraordinary career. It is hard to incorporate it in an assessment of Du Bois, and it marks a perilous difficulty in the anti-imperialist discourse American intellectuals have favored.

It is tempting to say that Du Bois's Stalinist violation of his democratic principles in the 1940s and 1950s should simply be overlooked today. Du Bois was wounded by America's antagonism toward equality and opportunity for all. America had sinned, and was continuing to sin, against its own ideals; and even many of the black elite and middle class were, Du Bois judged, unwilling to combat injustice and were consumed instead by the pursuit of wealth. Du Bois himself would not yield to triumphalist rhetoric about America, nor would he mute his protest against capitalism and imperialism because others had declared the Soviet and Chinese systems to be far worse. Perhaps he should not so much be criticized for his mistakes as admired for his tough, determined conduct, for the fervent sincerity with which he voiced his beliefs.

But this is not sufficient, either. One wishes Du Bois could have articulated an independent socialist position like that devised by Irving Howe, Lewis Coser, and their fellow editors of *Dissent* magazine, founded in 1954. Or that he could have aligned himself with the anti-Stalinist, cosmopolitan man-of-letters, C. L. R. James, who scorned both the "state capitalist" terrorism of the Soviet Union and the antidemocratic, imperialist practices of the United States and its Western allies. But Du Bois took neither path and defended Stalinist policy with alarming consistency. What should one say about this? How much should it shadow Du Bois's work and qualify his achievements? What is its connection to the books he wrote and his social activism in the decades before the cold war began?

Scholars have of course commented on Du Bois's pro-Stalinist position, yet they have not scrutinized it in adequate detail and depth. Until recently, Du Bois's embrace of communist theory and policy has been treated as an object of embarrassment, ripe for dismissal, or has served as the occasion for shallow descriptions of Du Bois's temperament. In a biography published in 1959, Francis L. Broderick suggests that Du Bois suffered from a persecution complex that mushroomed after his trial and acquittal in 1951 on the charge of being an unregistered foreign agent. Du Bois created an "epic," Broderick concludes, that depicted "all the elements of the ruling class" coordinating their efforts to hound, harass, and imprison him; he became "impervious to the rules of evidence" and, in his haunted state of mind, "fear appeared everywhere."[2] Broderick does concede that Du Bois's trial occurred in the context of cold war repression, but curiously this looms less prominently for him than Du Bois's expressions of pain and outrage—which Broderick records as proof of Du Bois's unchecked egotism.

In a biography published in 1960, Elliott Rudwick is not so eager to castigate Du Bois, but his study of Du Bois's political evolution is equally flawed. Rudwick's book consists of twelve chapters. Eleven survey Du Bois's activities before 1934, the year he resigned as editor of the NAACP journal, *The Crisis*, withdrew from the board of the NAACP, and made his way back to Atlanta University as the chairman of the sociology department. Only one chapter touches on Du Bois's work after 1934. Rudwick mentions but fails to explore Du Bois's Stalinist sympathies and eventual membership in the Communist party in 1961, remarking only that by this time Du Bois was in perpetual agony caused by a "virtually complete estrangement from America."[3]

Later scholars have given Du Bois's career as socialist, anti-imperialist, and communist more sophisticated forms of attention, but they, too, have been unable to account for Du Bois's steadfast praise of Stalin and apologies for Soviet crimes. In his excellent biography, Manning Marable crisply assesses Du Bois's shortcomings as a social and political theorist, in particular his failure to examine class rule within the one-party state.[4] But Marable oversimplifies his argument by defining Du Bois as a "radical democrat." If Du Bois indeed remained a radical democrat during the last twenty to thirty years of his life, he did so under Stalinist auspices and applied his radical, democratic critique only to the West. Du Bois exempted communist countries from his analyses; he did not find in them a trace of oppression, prejudice, police state supervision, or the curtailment of freedom.

Arnold Rampersad and Gerald Horne deal cogently with Du Bois's conversion to Stalinism, but they understate the challenge it poses to an evaluation of Du Bois and, beyond that, to the politics of anti-imperialist dissent. Rampersad outlines Du Bois's commitment to Marxism, which dawned with the outbreak of the Bolshevik revolution and climaxed with his "acceptance of the communist milieu in the United States" and decision to join the Communist party. "The wonder is not that Du Bois joined the party in 1961," Rampersad states, "but that he had not done so before."[5] Horne says what Rampersad implies: "Du Bois's joining the Communist party in 1961 was—contrary to the opinion of many—not a radical departure from his past praxis and, in actuality, a logical continuation."[6] But such a claim for a "logical" relationship between the radical democrat and the Communist party member cannot be made and then bypassed. How should one respond to a logic that portrays Stalinism as the natural result of Du Bois's labor for social change and anti-imperialist campaign against the West's lordship over the third world?

In his autobiographical writings, Du Bois frequently described his own perception of the unfolding logic of, and shifts of emphasis in, his political thought. He initiated his political work in the 1900s within the agenda that liberalism and progressivism had secured. As part of his effort to counter the accommodationist ideas of Booker T. Washington, Du Bois played a central role in establishing the Niagara Movement (1905–9) and, later, the NAACP (1909). In 1910 he withdrew from his academic post at Atlanta University, where he had taught since 1897, and became the editor of the NAACP journal *The Crisis,* a job he performed with distinction.

In the same year in which Du Bois helped to launch the NAACP and *The Crisis,* he decided to join the Socialist party, which had been organized in 1901 and was led by Eugene Debs. (Du Bois's earliest exposure to socialism probably occurred in 1892–94, when he was a student at the University of Berlin and attended meetings of the German Social Democratic party.) But he criticized the Socialist party's racism, soon gave up his membership, and endorsed Woodrow Wilson in the presidential election of 1912. Socialist ideas continued to attract him, however, and he traveled widely, including his first trip to Africa in 1923, learning much about radicalism and anti-imperialism and contributing to pan-Africanism. Yet in this phase of his career, Du Bois was less a full-fledged socialist than a brilliant left-leaning writer and agitator who characterized himself as "fighting the battle of liberalism" within the Western democratic order.[7]

In the late 1920s and 1930s, Du Bois discerned a serious weakness in the liberal enterprise: "the essential difficulty with liberalism of the twentieth century was not to realize the fundamental change brought about by the world-wide organization of work and trade and commerce."[8] During this period, Du Bois utilized Marxist terms and categories to depict the challenges of social reconstruction that the entire world and the West in particular faced. He tinged his arguments with Marxism while rejecting the official "Communist program" as "dogmatic" and "invalid."[9] To Du Bois the most sensible strategy for blacks was neither communism nor socialism but "economic organization within the Negro group"—a dynamic effort to consolidate business and commerce within a strengthened black community that would prepare it for entry into the industrial democracy of the future.[10]

This was not an adept response to the problems which blacks confronted in the midst of the Great Depression. It was an odd backward step that partially reiterated proposals for Negro advancement that Washington and Marcus Garvey had sketched, and it finalized Du Bois's break with the integrationist NAACP. The polemical and strategic weakness of Du Bois's proposal is apparent in the phrase he used to expound it—"segregation in economic lines."[11] To affirm the advantages of segregation ran counter to the mission Du Bois had undertaken for decades at the NAACP, and his appeal baffled his admirers. He hedged his argument, insisting that he still looked long-term toward integration, but he appeared to be counseling his followers to retreat from goals he and they had toiled to achieve.

For Du Bois's plan to prosper, it additionally required that the Negro church abandon its liturgical and theological cast and, instead, function as the center for business ventures and associations—surely not an adjustment that black churchgoers would ever favor adopting on a significant scale! As Du Bois admitted later in life, he also did not recognize that for economic cooperation to be successful, it had to be buttressed by the state: "without a socialist state, consumers' cooperation fails."[12]

Du Bois's emphasis in the 1930s on racial solidarity and economic cooperation proved momentous for his political development, however. It enabled him to grasp the unity that existed among exploited workers in America and throughout the world and made his anti-imperialism richer and more complex. Whatever their differences in race, ethnic background, and religion, all workers suffered under capitalism and imperialism, said Du Bois, and this common experience was a source of untapped power. In a commanding essay written in the mid-1930s, "The Negro and Social Reconstruction," Du Bois declared his belief in Marxism and related the ideals of socialism to his plea for an economic concord among blacks in America that would reverberate for workers worldwide.

"I am convinced of the essential truth of the Marxian philosophy," Du Bois states, "and believe that eventually land, machine and materials must belong to the state, that private profit must be abolished, that the system of exploiting labor must disappear, that people who work must have essentially equal income and that in their hands the political rulership of the state must eventually rest."[13]

If America's black people recoiled at the prospect of deliberate, planned segregation, Du Bois concluded, then they would be left with three choices, all of them unacceptable. They could fondly hope to gain entry into the capitalist system that the Depression had devastated, a system that had always denied access to blacks and that had enslaved their ancestors. Or else blacks could attempt to align themselves with the craft unions, which, Du Bois bitterly pointed out, had refused to enroll blacks as members. Or—the third option—blacks could enlist as "shock troops" for communist revolution and thereby pledge themselves to disaster and death. "Most American communists," Du Bois explains, "have become dogmatic exponents of the inspired word of Karl Marx as they read it. They believe, apparently, in immediate, violent, and bloody revolution and make it one of their main objectives. This is a silly program even for white men. For American colored men, it is suicidal."[14]

For Du Bois, the only prudent, pragmatic solution lay in acknowledging that blacks already formed "a separate nation within a nation" and should therefore develop an "inner organization for self-defense."[15] This view not only carried forward a long tradition of argument and activity on behalf of black self-reliance and independence, but it likely derived, too, from the Communist party's official policy, established in 1930 and widely discussed, that blacks in the South were a separate nation within a nation and therefore should be accorded the right of self-determination. While the idea of "separation" had a certain allure for the beleaguered masses and functioned as a useful organizing tool in the South, it contradicted Du Bois's integrationist stand and depended for its implementation on measures few black leaders endorsed.

Still, in Du Bois's judgment his proposal was geared toward unmistakable historical trends—the deterioration of capitalism, the undermining of imperialism and colonialism, and the emergence of socialism— and located blacks at the forefront of economic and political renewal: "Today there is a chance for the Negro to organize in fact the cooperative and socialistic state within his own group by letting his farmers feed his artisans and his technicians guide his home industries and his thinkers plan this integration of cooperation, while his artists dramatize and beautify the struggle to achieve economic independence."[16]

Du Bois emphasized that his plan resembled but essentially differed from the cooperative business and industrial schemes that the procapitalist Booker T. Washington had touted in the 1890s and early 1900s:

> Such cooperation as we have carried out within the race has been carried out in accordance with the private profit idea; that is, we have tried to make the incentive success and the enriching of our own owners of capital. What I propose is a complete revolution in that attitude; that we begin the process of training for socialism which must be done in every labor group in the world and in every country in the world, by organizing a nationwide collective system on a non-profit basis with the ideal that the consumer is the center and the beginning of the organization; and that to him all profits over the cost of production shall be returned.[17]

Blacks would thus commence a vanguard action against capitalism and incarnate the socialism that was the world's destiny; mobilized globally against imperialism, they would establish networks with white workers in America and Europe and with colored workers in the colonies:

> If American Negroes, taking the path of organizing their consumers' power, should be able to raise their working classes to dominate within their own group and to such a command of income and resources that they would not be objects of charity and dole, they can not only ally themselves with the white laboring classes in the United States and in Europe, but equally well with the black laborers of the West Indies and South America and of Africa; and with the colored laborers of India, China and Japan; and if this union could be cemented by mutual interests, by cooperative exchange of commodities made possible by lowering of the American tariff and the revision of the commercial rules which hamper British colonies, all this might lead to so strong an economic nexus between colored and white labor that the day of industrial imperialism would be over. It is a far-fetched dream, but it is worth the contemplation.[18]

Du Bois's closing sentence perhaps indicates how best to interpret him. He is not delivering proposals he expects readers will immediately embrace, but, rather, is offering wondrous, if "far-fetched," visions he trusts they will meditate upon. Yet for all its speculative dimension and practical weakness, Du Bois's position in the 1930s has behind it the body of historical research he had undertaken. One could even hazard that by the mid- to late 1930s, Du Bois's political thought was fitfully catching up with and augmenting the anticapitalist, anti-imperialist analyses he had articulated as early as the 1890s in his Harvard dissertation on the slave trade.

At the time of its founding and settlement, America "was a rich new land," wrote Du Bois in 1896,

> the wealth of which was to be had in return for ordinary manual labor. Had the country been conceived of as existing primarily for the benefit of its

actual inhabitants, it might have waited for natural increase or immigration to supply the needed hands; but both Europe and the earlier colonists themselves regarded this land as existing chiefly for the benefit of Europe, and as designed to be exploited, as rapidly and as ruthlessly as possible, of the boundless wealth of its resources. This was the primary excuse for the rise of the African slave-trade to America.[19]

Du Bois presented this argument more explicitly in *The Negro* (1915) and in later articles and books. He showed in detail that industrial capitalism had originated in slavery and colonialism and had relied for its exorbitant profits upon victimized labor. This was a radical insight whose consequences reached well beyond the liberal reforms within capitalism that Du Bois had stressed in his work for the NAACP.

By the time of *Dusk of Dawn,* which appeared in 1940 and recapitulated his "nation within a nation" platform, Du Bois extolled socialism as the inescapable alternative to capitalism and imperialism. "We believe," he averred in his "Basic American Negro Creed," in "the ultimate triumph of some form of Socialism the world over."[20] He insisted he "was not and am not a communist," but the insights he had gained from his journeys to the Soviet Union illuminated the nature of his past struggles, energized his current work, and colored his view of the future.[21]

"Russia was trying" to solve "the problem of poverty of the mass of men," Du Bois maintains: "[Russia put] into the hands of those people who do the world's work the power to guide and rule the state for the best welfare of the masses. It made the assumption, long disputed, that out of the downtrodden mass of people, ability and character, sufficient to do this task effectively, could and would be found. I believed this dictum passionately. It was, in fact, the foundation stone of my fight for black folk; it explained me."[22]

These words undercut the importance Du Bois had attached in prior decades to the "talented tenth," the elite group of intellectuals and leaders among whom Du Bois numbered himself and whose centrality in racial protest he emphasized. Yet even in his descriptions of the talented tenth and leadership class, Du Bois had honored the mighty motions of the masses. In 1909, for example, in his biography of John Brown, he referred not only to the "moral leadership from above" that distinguished the antislavery crusade, but also proclaimed the "push of physical and mental pain from beneath;—not simply the cry of the Abolitionist but the upstretching of the slave."[23] He dramatically concluded his account of "the legacy of John Brown" by affirming that the "great mass" of blacks in the 1900s was "becoming daily more thoroughly organized, more deeply self-critical, more conscious of its power," and stood on the frontlines of the battle for freedom.[24]

The really notable feature of the passage from *Dusk of Dawn*, however, is the linkage Du Bois contrives between Russia and his own identity: the Soviet experiment, and the faith that propelled it, "explained me." In part Du Bois is simply alluding to the spirit that animates the reforms the Russian people have inaugurated in marshaling their forces to eliminate poverty. The panoramic installation of democracy in Russia brings compellingly alive for Du Bois the character of his own work: it displays in action what he has been endeavoring to obtain and guarantee in America.

But Du Bois is also responding to the arduous effort by the Russian people to revamp their society along rationally planned lines. From the outset of his career, Du Bois had underscored the need for comprehensive organization, centralized authority, rational planning on a massive basis, exhaustive gathering and sifting of facts, and highly disciplined, tightly controlled attitudes toward work. Russia made Du Bois's love for democracy vivid and emblematized the regimented pattern of his intellectual commitments: it mirrored his consciousness, ratifying everything Du Bois's advanced scholarly training at Harvard and Berlin had instructed him to value and embody and that he had ambitiously promoted in his boldly designed, elaborately schematized sociological studies and conferences at Atlanta University.

Du Bois suffered, then, from a psychological vulnerability that led him to see in the Soviet Union yet another grandly planned form—a state built on orders dictated from above, a state in which life followed blueprints that visionary leaders and intellectuals had prepared. Du Bois often remarked that he had been blind to imperialism when he was a young man and wryly recalled his choice of "Bismarck" as the subject of his commencement address at Fisk University in 1888. But this choice says something important about Du Bois and the kind of strong leadership, centralized control, and disciplined national identity that he admired beyond the 1880s and 1890s. It is the foundation of his excessive regard for the Soviet experiment.

Another dimension of Du Bois's response to communism lies in the triangular relationship he perceived between America, Africa, and the Soviet Union. In "The Position of the Negro in the American Social Order," a major essay published in July 1939, Du Bois accented again the advantages of economic segregation and urged his people through their separate consumer groups to achieve "control of production" and thereby make "the interests of producers and consumers identical." "To do this," Du Bois adds, such groups

> must begin by creating a primary group of industrial democracy, correspond-
> ing to the New England town-meeting in political democracy. Indeed in medi-
> aeval Africa, just this development was carried out in the village council,
> where every family was represented, and where economic action was con-
> trolled and guided as well as social and political. This was the basic commu-
> nalism of the African tribe which the slave trade and colonial imperialism
> killed.[25]

Du Bois hoped to transfer the interdependent economic practices of African communalism to black America in the 1930s and 1940s, and he sought to couple them with the political traditions of small-town democ-racy he had witnessed when growing up in Great Barrington, Massachu-setts. When pressed in the final decades of his life to admit the absence of freedom in the Soviet Union, Du Bois said that the freedom that existed there in councils and discussion groups had once existed in America, too, back in the days when men and women candidly spoke their minds in regular town meetings: Americans plainly had forgotten what real free-dom looked like and how it operated.

Du Bois loved the huge master plan, the mightily organized and orchestrated scheme. Yet he also wanted to make the big picture inti-mate, and he appealed for small groups that would conduct political and economic business face-to-face. The Soviet Union, for Du Bois, recreated both African communalism—which imperialism had slain—and Ameri-can democracy—which capitalism had annulled. One can sense here the degree of Du Bois's emotional and intellectual investment in the Soviet Union, which ultimately mattered to him less because it put Marxist/Leninist theory into practice than because it restored beautiful customs and fair-minded, principled procedures that Africa had been denied and America had lost.

But by associating himself with the Soviet Union and connecting its fate to his own, and by seeing in it the distinctive virtues of Africa and America, Du Bois set himself on a tragic course. Serious criticism of Rus-sia could only come at his own expense: if he found flaws in it, he would be confessing he had read history wrongly and would sap the strength from his own hard-won identity. By 1939–40 there was no going back on the symbol that the Soviet Union had become for Du Bois, and, as the 1940s unfolded, he habitually invoked heightened language to praise it.

He called it "the rock on which rests apparently the salvation of the best culture of our day"—even as he reiterated that he was not a communist and did not believe in revolution.[26]

Du Bois may not yet have been a communist, but he was close to becoming a Stalinist. His sympathy and support for the Russian people hardened into rationalizations for Stalinism that skewed his critiques of imperialism and capitalism and prevented him from inspecting his own political ideas. The trouble is already brewing in *Dusk of Dawn*. In it Du Bois notes that the Soviet path "has been strewn with blood and failure." But the fundamental matter he emphasizes is Russia's herculean courage in combating the rule of the wealthy, ennobling the ranks of laborers, and equipping people to resist capitalist, imperialist regimes:

> Every honest observer must admit that human civilization today has by these very efforts moved toward socialism and accepted many of the tenets of Russian communism. We may, with dogged persistence, declare that deliberate murder, organized destruction and brute force cannot in the end bring and preserve human culture; but we must admit that nothing that Russia has done in war and mass murder exceeds what has been done and is being done by the rest of the civilized world.[27]

Du Bois wrote these words after the Moscow trials of 1936–38, the signing of the nonaggression pact between the Soviet Union and Nazi Germany in August 1939, the Soviet invasion of Finland in November 1939, and well after the enormous social and cultural disruption and appalling loss of life that Soviet collectivization had caused in the early 1930s. Du Bois gestures toward these shattering truths, which had stunned and alienated numbers of American communists and fellow-travelers, yet he is unable or unwilling actually to name them. His phrase "dogged persistence" sounds impatient, as though the rehearsal of Stalin's evils were tedious. Must "every honest observer" agree with Du Bois that the brutalities of Stalinism should be countenanced because the behavior of the capitalist, imperialist powers is worse?

By the 1950s Du Bois was captive to the cold war mentality he condemned. He repeated the cosmic melodrama that cold war liberals and McCarthyites adopted: all he did differently was place the Soviet Union, rather than the United States, in the realm of the uncriticizable. In 1953 Du Bois wrote a short essay in which he celebrates Stalin as "a great man"—"simple, calm and courageous." He attributes the poor performance of American liberals in the 1940s and 1950s to "naive acceptance of Trotsky's magnificent lying propaganda," presents a cheery picture of collectivization, labels the independent Russian farmers "rural blood-suckers," and trumpets Stalin's feats as universally acclaimed by "the common man."[28]

Du Bois developed these themes in a November 1956 article that conceded the human costs of Soviet reform but that exculpated Stalin:

> We could wish that all the men who in blood and tears have helped raise mankind out of the gutter had been scholars and gentlemen. But usually they have not been. Nevertheless even if their effort to raise the many has been stained by the oppression and murder of the few, we thank God that they lived and accomplished as much as they did. Not all the blame of the crimes of the Russian revolution can today be cast on the dead shoulders of Joseph Stalin, the struggling labor leader of Baku; they would rest more fitly on the head of Winston Churchill and Herbert Hoover who tried by every means to hold the nose of the Russian worker in the dust. For the glory of a great state founded on universal education and making the exploitation of a labor a crime is due to Joseph Stalin more than to any other human being.[29]

Du Bois's esteem for Stalin hence remained unshaken by Khrushchev's revelation of his predecessor's crimes and repudiation of the Stalin cult at the Twentieth Party Congress in February 1956. In fact, in an article published in January 1957, Du Bois bemoaned the assault on Stalin and described the attempt to "broaden the basis of democracy in the Soviet Union" as an "ill considered blunder" that damaged the socialist cause and recklessly reinforced anti-Soviet policies in the West.[30] He also seized this opportunity to flay the workers' uprising in Hungary as a shameful effort to overthrow socialism, and he defended the Soviet decision to send in troops and tanks to crush subversive "landlords and fascists" there.[31] So much for the revolutionary workers' councils.

Du Bois had objected in the 1930s to the dogmatism of American communists, yet by the 1950s he was dogmatic himself. He balked at de-Stalinization, brooded about the dangers of democracy in the Soviet Union, and hewed to the party line on the invasion of Hungary. The events of 1956 triggered a major crisis among communists in Eastern Europe and in the West and prompted many persons to reexamine the Soviet state and ask whether it could truly be said to advance socialist values. But Du Bois's political thought grew more uncritical of Stalinism and the Soviet Union than ever before. In his *Autobiography*, he devotes the opening chapters to laudatory accounts of the Soviet Union and China that jettison critical judgment. Where criticism does exist, Du Bois casts it in the form of ironic barbs at America and Western Europe. "China is no utopia,"

Du Bois admits: "Fifth Avenue has better shops where the rich can buy and the whores parade."[32] Du Bois's avowal of communism—"I believe in communism" and "shall therefore hereafter help the triumph of communism in every honest way that I can"—coincides with the breakdown of the critical discrimination and skeptical intelligence he had displayed earlier in his career.[33]

The *Autobiography* also exhibits Du Bois's double-think justifications for the Soviet denial of freedom, as when he comments on the art that the Soviet Union favors:

> The writer has a wide leeway and a rich applause, but he is limited by the aims of socialism to serve all and not a few, and by the fear of foreign attack which in the past has nearly ruined the Soviet Union. The recalcitrant writer, the idealists and dreamers disagree, but variety of opinion is becoming reassuringly common and open. As the Soviet Union becomes stronger and more self-confident, and less sensitive to that Western opinion which has so long ruled the world with a rod of gold, it will become freer. Never, I hope, so free as to betray the ideals of the land as French writers have betrayed France, and as American writers distort truth today.[34]

Du Bois's own freedom of speech in America was sorely limited. One wants to believe he wished to affirm "variety of opinion" and encouraged the Soviet Union to promote it. But Du Bois censors the inclinations of his better self, brandishing standard Soviet maxims in order to uphold the state repression that burdened writers under Stalin. He predicts the boundaries of freedom will grow wider, yet immediately adds that the "ideals of the land" will function as a control: the state will determine when these boundaries have been transgressed and—the part of the process Du Bois does not name—will clamp down on offenders.

At his best Du Bois was a "phenomenologist of imperialism" whose commentaries were polemical in nature and tied to the goals of political agitation and social change.[35] He exhorted readers and audiences to recognize the historical pattern of white European greed and exploitation and demanded they fight against America's mad desire to dominate Africa and Asia. But while Du Bois was a sharp critic of European and American imperialism, he saw neither the huge fact of Soviet empire nor the blood-stained history of Stalin's ascendancy and rule.

Perhaps what is crying out in Du Bois is a terrible feeling of personal betrayal: the promises that America has made to him and to his people it has not kept, and it has no intention of keeping them ever. Du Bois's angry disappointment at the dead end reached by the reforms he proposed drove him to reject America and accept the Soviet Union, in all its visionary grandeur, as though it were the Africanized America, the truly democratic community, that America itself should have become.

By the end of his life, Du Bois perceived himself as a stalwart materialist, yet it is one of the painful ironies of this intellectual's career that he was a heartfelt and headstrong idealist: he idealized Stalinism and the Soviet system because he imagined them as projections of African and American practices or, better, as reincarnations of social structures that had been lost or destroyed on their native grounds. Du Bois was one of the great pioneers of anti-imperialist scholarship, yet even as he exposed and corrected one form of bad history—the whitewashing of what imperialism had wrought—he transcribed another himself. He saw what he wished and needed to see, and thus he replicated the hard, domineering consciousness he condemned.

Notes

Epigraphs: V. I. Lenin, cited by John Reed in *Ten Days That Shook the World*, 1919, excerpted in *The Education of John Reed: Selected Writings*, ed. John Stuart (1955; New York: International, 1982), p. 204, and W. E. B. Du Bois, "Socialism and the American Negro," in *Against Racism: Unpublished Essays, Papers, Addresses, 1887–1961*, ed. Herbert Aptheker (Amherst: University of Massachusetts Press, 1985), p. 307.

1 "The Present Outlook for the Dark Races of Mankind," October 1900, in *Writings by W. E. B. Du Bois in Periodicals Edited by Others*, ed. Herbert Aptheker, vol. 1, 1891–1909 (Millwood: Kraus-Thomson, 1982), pp. 73, 79.

2 Francis L. Broderick, *W. E. B. Du Bois: Negro Leader in a Time of Crisis* (1959; Stanford: Stanford University Press, 1982), p. 223.

3 Elliott Rudwick, *W. E. B. Du Bois: Voice of the Black Protest Movement* (1960; Urbana: University of Illinois Press, 1982), p. 298. Rudwick makes the same point in a recent biographical sketch, "W. E. B. Du Bois: Protagonist of the Afro-American Protest," in *Black Leaders of the Twentieth Century*, ed. John Hope Franklin and August Meier (Urbana: University of Illinois Press, 1982), p. 82.

4 Manning Marable, *W. E. B. Du Bois: Black Radical Democrat* (Boston: G. K. Hall, 1986), p. 215.

5 Arnold Rampersad, *The Art and Imagination of W. E. B. Du Bois* (1976; New York: Schocken, 1990), pp. 263, 262.

6 Gerald Horne, *Black and Red: W. E. B. Du Bois and the Afro-American Response to the Cold War, 1944–1963* (Albany: State University of New York Press, 1986), p. 289. Horne does a masterful job of describing Du Bois's life during the cold war period, but for the most part he is surprisingly uncritical. In an essay that treats Du Bois as a historian, Herbert Aptheker also refers to the "remarkable

continuity" evident in Du Bois's career, though he argues that the term "Marxist" does not accurately reflect the shape of Du Bois's political and historical views. See "Du Bois as Historian," in *Afro-American History: The Modern Era* (New York: Citadel Press, 1971), pp. 47–67. For additional recent studies of Du Bois, see Sterling Stuckey, *Slave Culture: Nationalist Theory and the Foundations of Black America* (New York: Oxford University Press, 1987), pp. 245–302; Cedric J. Robinson, *Black Marxism: The Making of the Black Radical Tradition* (London: Zed Press, 1983), pp. 266–348; Joel Williamson, *The Crucible of Race: Black-White Relations in the American South Since Emancipation* (New York: Oxford University Press, 1984), pp. 399–413; Wilson Jeremiah Moses, *The Golden Age of Black Nationalism, 1850–1925* (New York: Oxford University Press, 1978); and Thomas C. Holt, "The Political Uses of Alienation: W. E. B. Du Bois on Politics, Race, and Culture, 1903–1940," *American Quarterly* 42 (June 1990): 301–23.

7 "A Pageant in Seven Decades, 1868–1938," in *Pamphlets and Leaflets by W. E. B. Du Bois*, ed. Herbert Aptheker (White Plains: Kraus-Thomson, 1986), p. 265.

8 Ibid., p. 269.

9 Ibid., p. 270.

10 Ibid., p. 271.

11 Ibid., p. 271.

12 "The American Negro and Communism," October 1958, in *Against Racism*, p. 296. In this essay, and in others he wrote during the 1950s, Du Bois emphasized that class division among American blacks endangered the promise of economic cooperation. Blacks were buying into capitalism: "the American Negro is today developing a distinct bourgeoisie bound to and aping American acquisitive society and developing an employing and a laboring class" (p. 297). See also "On the Future of the American Negro," a speech he delivered in 1953, in *W. E. B. Du Bois Speaks: Speeches and Addresses, 1920–1963*, ed. Philip S. Foner (New York: Pathfinder Press, 1986), pp. 268–77.

13 Ibid., p. 141.

14 Ibid., p. 142.

15 Ibid., pp. 144, 146.

16 Ibid., p. 149.

17 Ibid., p. 151. In "The American Negro and Communism" (1958), Du Bois recalls his own attempt in 1918–19 to launch a number of consumers' cooperatives, all of which failed because of the lure of private profit and "big business" opposition. See *Against Racism*, p. 296.

18 "The Negro and Social Reconstruction," p. 156. It is worth noting here that Du Bois wrote his essay for a series Alain Locke had organized. Locke asked for revisions of the first draft; Du Bois supplied them, and the essay seemed headed for prompt publication. But Locke reneged on his promise to publish Du Bois's work, and almost certainly did so, as Aptheker suggests, because he was wary of the radical ideas it contained. For a slightly earlier (and published) description

of Du Bois's segregationist views, one that skirts explicit mention of socialist and anti-imperialist goals, see "A Negro Nation within the Nation" (1935), in *Writings by W. E. B. Du Bois in Periodicals Edited by Others*, ed. Herbert Aptheker, vol. 3, 1935–44 (Millwood: Kraus-Thomson, 1982), pp. 1–6. Some sections of "The Negro and Social Reconstruction" were published in "Social Planning for the Negro, Past and Present" (1936), which is reprinted in this same volume, pp. 26–40, though here again a good deal of the forceful socialist and anti-imperialist message is absent.

19 *The Suppression of the African Slave-Trade to the United States of America, 1638–1870* (1896; Millwood: Kraus-Thomson, 1973), p. 194.

20 *Dusk of Dawn* (Millwood: Kraus-Thomson, 1985), p. 321.

21 Ibid., p. 302.

22 Ibid., pp. 284–85.

23 *John Brown* (Millwood: Kraus-Thomson, 1973), p. 121.

24 Ibid., p. 389. I treat this important book more extensively in "Violence, Revolution, and the Cost of Freedom: John Brown and W. E. B. Du Bois," *Boundary 2* 17 (Spring 1990): 305–30.

25 "The Position of the Negro in the American Social Order: Where Do We Go From Here?" July 1939, in *Writings by W. E. B. Du Bois in Periodicals Edited by Others*, vol. 3, p. 82.

26 "The Release of Earl Browder," May 1942, in *Against Racism*, pp. 202, 199.

27 *Dusk of Dawn*, pp. 287, 288.

28 "On Stalin," March 1953, in *Newspaper Columns by W. E. B. Du Bois*, ed. Herbert Aptheker, vol. 2, 1945–61 (White Plains: Kraus-Thomson, 1986), pp. 910–11.

29 "Colonialism and the Russian Revolution," November 1956, in *Writings by W. E. B. Du Bois in Periodicals Edited by Others*, ed. Herbert Aptheker, vol. 4, 1945–61 (Millwood: Kraus-Thomson, 1982), p. 275.

30 "Socialism and Democracy," January 1957, in *Writings by W. E. B. Du Bois in Periodicals Edited by Others*, vol. 4, p. 281. See also Du Bois's laudatory review of Anna Louise Strong's joyous account of "the Stalin era," in *Book Reviews by W. E. B. Du Bois*, ed. Herbert Aptheker (Millwood: Kraus-Thomson, 1977), pp. 249–52.

31 "Socialism and Democracy," pp. 281–82.

32 *The Autobiography of W. E. B. Du Bois*, ed. Herbert Aptheker (1968; New York: International Publishers, 1980), p. 51.

33 Ibid., p. 57.

34 Ibid., p. 36. I examine this text in greater detail in "W. E. B. Du Bois's *Autobiography* and the Politics of Literature," *Black American Literature Forum* 24 (Summer 1990): 299–313.

35 I borrow this phrase from Wolfgang J. Mommsen, who uses it about Rosa Luxemburg in *Theories of Imperialism*, trans. P. S. Falla (1977; Chicago: University of Chicago Press, 1980), p. 35.

Eric Lott

White Like Me

Racial Cross-Dressing and the Construction

of American Whiteness

t the start of a journey into the "night side of American life," which would furnish the material for his *Black Like Me* (1961), John Howard Griffin strikes up a relationship with a black shoe-shine "boy."[1] Griffin, a white investigative journalist turned black by medical treatments, sunlamp sessions, and black stain, asks for lessons in the ways of Negro life. The shine man, Sterling Williams, "promised perfect discretion and enthusiastically began coaching me." "'You just watch me and listen how I talk,'" says Williams. "'You'll catch on'" (27). Apparently he does catch on, for Williams soon certifies Griffin's racial transmutation. "Within a short time [Williams] lapsed into familiarity," Griffin writes, "forgetting I was once white. He began to use the 'we' form and to discuss 'our situation.' The illusion of my 'Negro-ness' took over so completely that I fell into the same pattern of talking and thinking. It was my first intimate glimpse. We were Negroes and our concern was the white man and how to get along with him" (28).

Griffin's narrative is only one relatively recent example of a blackface tradition that is fundamentally concerned with a forbidden "lapse into familiarity" between black and white men. No disembodied affair, the ventriloquizing or indeed purloining of black and other cultures has in many instances taken the form of a homosocial dance of white men and black. Whether blackface performers' fascination with slave singers and dancers, Carl Van Vechten's mimicking and brokering of Harlem Renaissance writers, or white-Negro

Norman Mailer's pursuit of Muhammad Ali and others, white men's intercourse with black men has been fraught with masculinist rivalry as well
as "compromising" desire. These instances have injected potent fantasies
of the black male body into the white Imaginary–and thence into the
culture industry. In thus giving shape to the white racial unconscious,
such homosocial scenarios actually found the color line even as they witness the latter's continual transgression. Griffin's "We were Negroes" is
the perfect summation of this dynamic: renegades together on the "night
side," Griffin and Williams enact a racial encounter that is both age-old
and implicitly affirming of the Berlin Wall they have momentarily agreed
to scale.

For me, this instance raises the question of why and under what circumstances a blackface tradition emerged and continues intermittently
to reemerge, if only briefly and in more or less ironized form. My assumption is that blackface is a charged signifier with no coincidental
relationship to the racial politics of culture in which it is embedded.[2] Why,
we might ask, this literal inhabiting of black bodies as a way of interracial male-bonding? There are, after all, alternatives to such a practice;
as Griffin's civil-rights-era contemporary Leslie Fiedler argued in *Love
and Death in the American Novel* (1960), our white male writers have been
stubbornly preoccupied with white male/dark male dyads (Ishmael and
Queequeg, Huck and Jim) which apparently fulfill a white need to be
"Negroes" together. The historical fact of white men literally assuming a
"black" self, the eternal and predictable return of the racial signifier of
blackface, is another matter entirely; and I would argue that it began and
continues to occur when the lines of "race" appear both intractable and
obstructive, when there emerges a collective desire (conscious or not) to
bridge a gulf that is, however, perceived to separate the races absolutely.
Griffin's *Black Like Me* and blackface minstrelsy both exemplify this structure of feeling, the former in its earnest antisegregationist politics, the
latter in its derisive but transparently obsessive attempts to try on the accents of "blackness." Blackface acknowledges a racial relationship which
to whites seems neither satisfactory nor surmountable; this acknowledgment owes in turn to perceptions of "race" and its signifiers that we would
now term "essentialist." To "black up" is to express a belief in the complete
suturing together of the markers of "blackness" and the black culture,
apparently sundered from the dominant one, to which they refer. John
Szwed observes of the withering-away of blackface: "The fact that, say, a
Mick Jagger can today perform in the [blackface] tradition without blackface simply marks the detachment of culture from race and the almost

full absorption of a black tradition into white culture."[3] Blackface, then, reifies and at the same time trespasses on the boundaries of "race." I see this doubleness as highly indicative of the shape of American whiteness.

Indeed, in the largest terms this racial trope obliges us to confront the process of "racial" construction itself, the historical formation of whites no less than of blacks.[4] Our typical focus on the way "blackness" in the popular imagination has been produced out of white cultural expropriation and travesty misses how necessary this process is to the making of white American manhood. The latter simply could not exist without a racial other against which it defines itself and which to a very great extent it takes up into itself as one of its own constituent elements. By way of several rather underhistoricized instances in the history of blackface miming and of imaginary racial transformation, I want to look at some American constructions of whiteness—in particular this curious dependence upon and necessary internalization of the cultural practices of the dispossessed. My title implies that Griffin's *Black Like Me* is precisely misnamed, that what Griffin uncovers in his trip through the black South are the contours of straight Caucasian maleness. But to engage this and other post-World War II texts of racial cross-dressing we must acknowledge the American racial histories and cultural products that implicitly structure them. By this of course I mean nineteenth-century blackface performance and other similar texts; but I mean also U.S. imperialism and its material and cultural transactions and results. Encounters with the other both at home and abroad easily become intertwined; as Griffin puts it early on, "the South's racial situation was a blot on the whole country, and especially reflected against us overseas" (8). In examining the racial unconscious of American imperial whiteness, I assume (absent the space adequately to demonstrate it) that the connection between internal and international is intimate. If national esteem in racial matters is related to international prestige—the ability to wield power among foreign races—it is also (or therefore) the case that representations of national racial difference often provide displaced maps for international ones. Not to put too fine a point on it, the domination of international others has depended on mastering the other at home—and in oneself: an internal colonization whose achievement is fragile at best and which is often exceeded or threatened by the gender and racial arrangements on which it depends.

"Brothers For the Time Being"

The minstrel show's great popularity with northern white urban audiences in the middle decades of the nineteenth century has been read as a fairly pat instance of financial and cultural manipulation. With its comic darkies, "plantation melodies," challenge dances, malapropistic wizardry, and general racial revanchism, minstrelsy long cried out for the revisionist critique to which it was only truly subjected in the 1960s and after.[5] In one of the most thoroughgoing and persuasive such critiques, Alexander Saxton surveys the social origins of certain major minstrel figures, among them T. D. Rice, Dan Emmett, E. P. Christy, and Stephen Foster. Many of the major innovators were northerners of urban origin (none from New England) who were raised in families with intimations of upward mobility. All of them rejected the Protestant ethic and escaped into the latitudes of the entertainment world. In the course of such escape they came into contact with/and stole—the music and dance of slaves and free blacks and first tasted theatrical success in blackface performances. While these "professionals" were sometimes class mutineers, passing up opportunities at a clerkship or better to immerse themselves in the underground world of blackface theater, they nevertheless shared with their families certain political ties to the elite of the Democratic party, the party of Andrew Jackson, antimonopoly, expansionism—and white supremacy. Henry Wood of Christy and Wood's Minstrels was the brother of Fernando Wood, Southern-sympathizing mayor of New York; another brother served three terms as a Democratic Congressman from Buffalo and one term as a state senator. Stephen Foster belonged to a family of ardent Democrats related by marriage to President Buchanan's brother, and Foster himself helped organize a local Buchanan-for-President Club.[6]

Yet it seems to me that one unfortunate effect of this necessary critique has been to reify and even reinforce the cultural domination taking place in the minstrel show. And evidence from performers themselves points to a more complex dynamic, in which such dominative tendencies coexisted with or indeed depended upon a self-conscious attraction to the black men it was the job of these performers to mimic. Billy Whitlock, banjo player of Dan Emmett's Virginia Minstrels, said that when on tour in the South he would, as the *New York Clipper* put it, "quietly steal off to some negro hut to hear the darkeys sing and see them dance, taking with him a jug of whiskey to make them all the merrier" (April 13, 1878). More revealingly, performer Ben Cotton claimed that he would sit with and study blacks on Mississippi riverboats: "I used to sit with them in front of their cabins, and we would start the banjo twanging, and their voices would ring out in the quiet night air in their weird melodies. They did not quite understand me. I was the first white man they had seen who sang as they did; but we were brothers for the time being and were perfectly happy."[7] Self-serving as this is, it nonetheless indicates that a major strain of American bohemia has its origins in blackface performers and enthusiasts. So much the worse for bohemia, perhaps; but in addition to the minor disasters bohemia has perpetrated from Walt Whitman to Carl Van Vechten to Jack Kerouac, there is in its activities an implicit tribute to, or at the very least a self-marginalizing mimicry of, black culture's male representatives. This hardly addresses the social *results* of such activities, which may be more or less harmful than the exoticism that generated them. But with antebellum blackface performers a set of racial attitudes and cultural styles that in America go by the name of bohemianism first emerged, and in this clumsy courtship of black men the contours of masculine whiteness as we know it began to take a definitive and recognizable form.[8]

Most minstrel performers were minor, apolitical theatrical men of the northern artisanate who pursued a newly available bourgeois dream of freedom and play by paradoxically coding themselves as "black." Indeed if, for men, sexuality is where freedom and play meet, "blackness" was for antebellum bohemians its virtual condition—a fascinating imaginary space of fun and license seemingly outside but in fact structured by Victorian bourgeois norms. This space seems to have arisen largely from encounters with black men—slave or dancer or vendor—to whom blackface minstrels had much access. For instance, according to legend—the closest we are going to get in the matter—T. D. Rice used an old black stableman's song and dance in his first "Jim Crow" act. Dan Emmett had left his Mt. Vernon, Ohio, home by the age of eighteen (in 1834) and joined the military, where he learned to play the infantry drum from a man nicknamed "Juba"—a black name, if not a black man, perhaps earned for the style of drum he played. Appearing as a banjo player in various circuses, Emmett was very soon teamed up with dancer Frank Brower, who had learned his dances directly from black men.[9] Stephen Foster no doubt had contact with black wharf workers and boatmen in his hometown of Pittsburgh, but according to his brother he experienced black church singing firsthand through a family servant, Olivia Pise, "member of a church of shouting colored people."[10] Ralph Keeler ran away from his Buffalo home at the age of eleven and wrote that as a dancer with Johnny Booker's minstrels in the 1850s he "wandered all over the Western country," keeping continual company with that troupe's Negro baggage handler, Ephraim.[11] E. P. Christy reportedly drew material in the late 1830s from One-legged Harrison, a black church singer in Buffalo; Christy said the two had often traded "down home talk."[12] Within the institution of minstrelsy itself, the renowned black dancer Juba (William Henry Lane) provided a link between the cultures, figuring centrally in many challenge-dance contests between black and white dancers.[13] The tableau reiterated in many of these scenes—a white man and a black man becoming, as Ben Cotton put it, "brothers for the time being"—shows up often enough to be a defining interest of these white Negroes, and we might pause over its role in the construction of American whiteness.

For what appears in fact to have been negotiated in blackface performance were certain kinds of masculinity. To put on the cultural forms of "blackness" was to engage in a complex affair of manly mimicry. Examples of this dynamic since the heyday of minstrelsy are ready enough at hand, but in the early nineteenth century it had yet to be given an available public form. To wear or even enjoy blackface was literally, for a time, to become black, to inherit the cool, virility, humility, abandon, or *gaite de coeur* that were the prime components of white ideologies of black manhood. T. D. Rice, said his friend F. C. Wemyss, in the event of a bad draw fell into a kind of black homespun when dealing with theater managers, as though indeed into a black-white dyad that reproduced his own felicitous exchanges with black men: "'Lookye here, my master, this has been a bad job—I don't think you ought to suffer to this tune; live and let live is a good motto—hand over ——, and I will give you a receipt in full, and wish you better luck another time.'"[14] How interesting that Rice should assume this humbled sense of masculinity precisely at the guilty moment of payment for expropriated goods, in the process authenticating his claim on the material; how fitting, too, that this disturbing moment of conventional masculinity in the public sphere—the hard bargain, the deal—could with a ventriloquial shift be evaded or at least better managed.

It is worth remarking the way minstrelsy traded on racialized images of masculinity if only because they have become so familiar, indeed ritualized. In *North Toward Home* (1967), white Mississippian Willie Morris remembers "a stage, when we were about thirteen, in which we 'went Negro.' We tried to broaden our accents to sound like Negroes, as if there were not enough similarity already. We consciously walked like young Negroes, mocking their swinging gait, moving our arms the way they did, cracking our knuckles and whistling between our teeth."[15] I would maintain that this dynamic, persisting into adulthood, is so much a part of most American white men's equipment for living that they remain entirely unaware of their participation in it. The special achievement of minstrel performers was to have intuited and formalized the white male fascination with the turn to black (manhood), which Leslie Fiedler puts this way: "Born theoretically white, we are permitted to pass our childhood as imaginary Indians, our adolescence as imaginary Negroes, and only then are expected to settle down to being what we really are: white once more."[16] These common white associations of black maleness with the onset of pubescent sexuality indicate that the assumption of dominant codes of masculinity in the United States is partly negotiated through an imaginary black interlocutor. If this suggests that minstrelsy's popularity depended in part on the momentary return of its partisans to a state of arrested adolescence—largely the condition to which dominant codes of masculinity aspire—one must also conclude that white male fantasies of black men undergird the subject positions white men grow up to occupy.

And this is no foregone conclusion—it is full of the fiercest anxieties and potential disturbances. There is evidence, for example, that performers and audiences also found in blackface something closer to a homoerotic charge. Eve Sedgwick has argued that nineteenth-century bohemia was a space, not of infinite heterosexual appetite, but of ambiguous sexual definition, through which young bourgeois men passed on their way to the "repressive, self-ignorant, and apparently consolidated status of the mature bourgeois *paterfamilias*."[17] Something of this situation applied in the case of minstrel men, certain of whose female impersonations appear, in the context of rough-and-tumble Jacksonian manliness, to have grown out of a sense of sexual ambiguity. Actress Olive Logan wrote that "some of the men who undertake this ['wench'] business are marvellously well fitted by nature for it, having well-defined soprano voices, plump shoulders, beardless faces, and tiny hands and feet. Many dress most elegantly as women."[18] While she is referring here to post-Civil War female impersonation—which as an American showbusiness tradition probably got its start in minstrelsy—there is no reason to believe that the wide renown of antebellum "wenches" (George Christy, Barney Williams) owed any less to their aptitude for or predisposition to such roles. And while it is inaccurate simply to read off homosexuality from effeminacy or indeed transvestism, same-sex desire does seem to have been registered by these performers. "Heaps of boys in my locality don't believe yet it's a man in spite of my saying it was," said a Rochester critic of Francis Leon, the most famous postwar female impersonator.

Leon was authentic enough as a female, this writer remarked, "to make a fool of a man if he wasn't sure."[19]

Other performers evinced homosexual attractions more obliquely. "A minstrel show came to town and I thought of nothing else for weeks," said Ben Cotton—this from the man who recalled the brotherhood of black and white singers.[20] George Thatcher, well-known later in the century, said of his first encounter with blackface performance in Baltimore: "I found myself dreaming of minstrels; I would awake with an imaginary tambourine in my hand, and rub my face with my hands to see if I was blacked up. . . . The dream of my life was to see or speak to a performer."[21] We might speculate a little as to the referent of the imaginary tambourine; the fantasy of racial conversion enacted in blackface seems to gesture at least toward sexual envy of black men (tambourine as penis), if not desire for them (tambourine as hymen). The fantasy may indeed direct us to a process in which homosexual desire is deflected by *identifying with* potent male heterosexuality. Perhaps the fantasy indicates only the usefulness of blackface in mediating white men's desire for other white men. In any case it did nothing to redirect myths of black masculinity, to say nothing of white men's attitudes toward women; and it only confirmed black men's status as bearers of black culture, objects of exchange. But it does bring to the surface a more submerged motive for racial intercourse, and it was (and is) probably one moment of most white men's enjoyment of black caricature.

These examples suggest that blackface performance reproduced or instantiated a structured *relationship* between the races, racial difference itself, as much as black cultural forms. They suggest moreover that this difference was as internal as it was external. To assume the mantle of whiteness, these examples seem to say, is not only to "befriend" a racial other but to introject or internalize its imagined special capacities and attributes. The other is of course "already in us," a part of one's (white) self, filled out according to the ideological shapes one has met in one's entry into the culture. The black male and fantasies about him supply the content of the white male Imaginary, they make up its repertoire. This (racial) splitting of the subject actually makes possible one whole area of white desire—but it also insures that the color line thus erected is constantly open to transgression or disruption.[22]

Several theorists have termed this predicament "abjection." Julia Kristeva writes of the abject that "'unconscious' contents remain . . . *excluded* but in strange fashion," clearly enough "for a defensive *position* to be established" yet "not radically enough to allow for a secure differentiation between subject and object."[23] This glosses very nicely the combined vigilance and absorptive cross-racial fascination of North American whiteness. Deviser of boundaries, "raced" signs and practices by way of an engagement with the other, the blackface performer or white-Negro heir, in Kristeva's words, "never stops demarcating his universe whose fluid confines . . . constantly question his solidity and impel him to start afresh" (8). The abjection so redolent of pre-oedipal archaism is reactivated amid the guilty pleasure we have witnessed in blackface performance, but it is masked with a racial logic. In rationalized Western societies, becoming "white" and male seems to depend upon the remanding of enjoyment, the body, an aptitude for pleasure. It is the other who is always putatively "excessive" in this respect, whether through exotic food, strange and noisy music, outlandish bodily exhibitions, or unremitting sexual appetite. Whites in fact organize their own enjoyment through the other, Slavoj Žižek has written, and access pleasure precisely by fantasizing about the other's "special" pleasure. Hatred of the other arises from the necessary hatred of one's own excess; ascribing this excess to the "degraded" other *and indulging* it—by imagining, incorporating, or impersonating the other—one conveniently and surreptitiously takes and disavows pleasure at one and the same time. This is the mixed erotic economy, what Homi Bhabha terms the "ambivalence," of American whiteness.[24]

In practice, this structure has meant, for one thing, that the dispossessed become bearers of the dominant classes' "folk" culture, its repository of joy and revivification.[25] And it is here that the agenda of pleasure meets that of domination, white male meets imperial subject. Whether it precedes or follows the dominative logic of imperialism, pleasure in the other is in fact its necessary twin. In the case of blackface these two agendas consorted in extremely complex ways, performance legitimating and sometimes subverting the politics of white supremacy, politics giving rise to an obsessive entertainment of racial difference. Berndt Ostendorf has written that the "lower class folk in Western society, and blacks among them, have served the dominant classes in two ways: first in setting up the material basis of high civilization, second in healing the injuries of that civilization by maintaining alternative life styles and cultures."[26] This double bind is the bedrock reality of racial cross-dressing, whatever its local habitation and name.

Elvis As Metaphor

Norman Mailer's "The White Negro" (1957), a text whose mythologies are as telling as its analysis, is of course the post-World War II reinvention of this structure of feeling. As none other than Norman Podhoretz observed in 1958 of the white-Negro discourse of which Mailer's essay was the centerpiece: "I doubt if a more idyllic picture of Negro life has been painted since certain Southern ideologues tried to convince the world that things were just fine as fine could be for the slaves on the old plantation."[27] Not a postdating or mere continuation of antebellum racial cross-dressing but its genealogical legacy, this postwar discourse—the Beat writers, Elvis Presley's early career, John Howard Griffin's *Black Like Me*, and others—did (despite its racial "modernity") reproduce the obsessions of certain nineteenth-century *Northern* ideologues. To the extent that these obsessions weren't wholly continuous with the dominant culture in the ensuing years of protest, they returned as farce in the late 1960s: Elvis's 1968 comeback TV special, Grace Halsell's *Soul Sister* (1969) (a second-generation simulacrum, for it imitates Griffin's *Black Like Me*), and, in a crowning blow (to which I will return), Melvin Van Peebles's *Watermelon Man* (1970)—in which Godfrey Cambridge in white-face plays a suburban racist who wakes up one morning to find himself black (too much time under the sunlamp). The almost "classical" resurgence of this trope and of white Negroism generally in the late 1980s and early 1990s—the movie *Soul Man* (1986); black-folk-filled music videos by Sting, Madonna, Steve Winwood, and many others; Lee Atwater's blues Republicanism (R.I.P.); Vanilla Ice;[28] *True Identity* (1991); Michelle Shocked's *Arkansas Traveler* (1992)—is as troubling in its ubiquity as it is bewildering in its ideological variousness, but I think these texts too confirm some of the remarks with which I began.[29]

Mailer's piece codifies the renegade ethic of male sexuality conceived out of and projected onto black men—and always "compromised" by white men's evident attraction to them—that informs the more than metaphorical racial romance underlying the construction of American whiteness:

> Knowing in the cells of his existence that life was war, nothing but war, the Negro (all exceptions admitted) could rarely afford the sophisticated inhibitions of civilization, and so he kept for his survival the art of the primitive, he lived in the enormous present, he subsisted for his Saturday night kicks, relinquishing the pleasures of the mind for the more obligatory pleasures of the body, and in his music he gave voice to the character and quality of his

existence, to his rage and the infinite variations of joy, lust, languor, growl, cramp, pinch, scream and despair of his orgasm.[30]

Mailer and other white Negroes inherited a structure of feeling whose self-valorizing marginality and distinction require a virtual imperson-ation of black manhood. It is revealing that while the specific preoccupa-tions of Mailer's existential errand are far from either Griffin's *Black Like Me* or Elvis Presley, the shape of this white mythology looks pretty much the same in all cases.

Its resonance is, for instance, succinctly articulated in white guitar-ist Scotty Moore's remark to Presley at one of the mid-1950s recording sessions in which Elvis first found his voice: "*Damn,* nigger!"[31] As Nelson George has observed, Elvis was the historical referent Mailer missed in limning the "white Negro." Bringing to the stage the sort of "symbolic fornication" that for whites denotes "blackness," his hair pomaded in imi-tation of blacks' putative imitation of whites, Elvis illustrates the curious dependence of white working-class manhood on imitations of fantasized black male sexuality.[32] It is true that in Elvis's case we must be clear about the precise nature of the indebtedness; nobody who thinks with their ears can dismiss Presley as merely a case of racial rip-off. I agree with Greil Marcus that Elvis's working-class origins already placed him as close to Bobby Bland as to Perry Como—that in creating what was after all a dis-tinctive rather than derivative sound he didn't so much steal the blues as live up to them.[33] Yet fantasies of "blackness" were unquestionably crucial in shaping a persona capable of such a task.

One image in particular stands out for its greater sublimation of this racial narrative. Much has been made of Presley's 1968 Christmas spe-cial, when after several years of silly movies and lifeless singing he roared back in black leather on network television. Marcus rightly identifies the central drama of the show as Elvis's attempt to win back his audience, and he demonstrates the way in which Elvis pulled all the stops out to do so. We might, however, also pause over the curious form of the show, in which Broadway productions of Elvis numbers (Elvis had not yet entered his Vegas period) alternate with an "unplugged" circle of Elvis and fellow musicians getting raw. In these latter scenes the black leather of his outfit defines the ambience; it refuses to slip from the viewer's mind; Presley himself remarks upon how hot it is. Both Elvis's look and the doubled structure of the show seem to me to call up the racial themes I have been developing. Particularly in a show dedicated to proving how foreordained and irrelevant is all the music since Elvis's early triumphs (stage patter at one point has Elvis damning with faint praise "the Beatles, the Beards, and the whoever"), its "blues" portions appear to mediate (against all odds and despite the artist's intentions) what had been going on in the streets by the time it aired in late 1968. That is to say, the split show structure suggests the meaning of the suit and the "blacker" performances: they are the "unconscious" of the production numbers—white as the whale— that surround them. In the leather-suited takes, and in songs such as the following year's "In the Ghetto," Elvis reveals his reliance even for resurrection upon "blackness." And his ever-increasing stature as *the* icon of white American culture, a fulfillment of the dubious potential augured by the comeback special's production numbers, only clinches my sense of the necessary *centrality and suppression* of "blackness" in the making of American whiteness.[34]

Black Like Me turns this structure into social criticism. While Griffin has "blacked up" to beat his forebears, his text is not a story of passing. In fact he has only spotty interest in what blacks think of him; his concern is with whites and how they will treat him in his adopted state. Whiteness is his standard: "'Do you suppose they'll treat me as John Howard Griffin, regardless of my color—or will they treat me as some nameless Negro, even though I am still the same man?'" Griffin asks some friends, among whom, incidentally, are three FBI agents (10). It is the position of "nameless Negro," not member of any community one might care to name, that interests Griffin. He passes less into a black world than into a "black" part of himself, the remissible pleasures of abjection, triggered or enabled by white distaste and aversion. (Some of which is his own—he speaks of the idea of turning black as having "haunted" him "for years" before undertaking his effort [7].) What he goes on to uncover are the contours of blackness *for whites:* contours he has externalized and thus indulges in his very disguise.

This racial logic underlies Griffin's whole enterprise. In revealing ways, *Black Like Me* is complicitous with the racial designs it sets out to expose. Griffin seems only dimly aware, for instance, that his disguise *is* an externalization, and yet there is evidence that his imagination of "blackness" colors him before his blackface does. Early on, pondering the dangers of his experiment, Griffin is gratified to find his wife ready, while he is gone, "to lead, with our three children, the unsatisfactory family life of a household deprived of husband and father" (9). That this is an unconscious reference to the much-bruited female-headed black family that would soon be mythologized in Daniel Patrick Moynihan's "The Negro Family: The Case for National Action" (1965) is indicated by Griffin's other mentions of the sadly depaternalized black family—as in: "[The black man's] wife usually earns more than he. He is thwarted in his need to be father-of-the-household" (90; see also 42). Even when Griffin is white, that is, he is "black" inside; it is this part of his "make-up" that he explores in *Black Like Me*.

One need not look far for the sources of this concern in Griffin's text. Early in his days of blackness, Griffin, for reasons that appear as unclear to him as they do to us, walks down his hotel hallway in the early hours of the morning (he can't sleep) to the men's room. There he encounters two black men, one in the shower and the other naked on the floor awaiting his turn. Griffin writes that the waiting man "leaned back against the wall with his legs stretched out in front of him. Despite his state of undress, he had an air of dignity" (19). This rather anxious (and certainly clichéd) assurance to the reader has its counterpart in Griffin's remark to the man: "'You must be freezing on that bare floor, with no clothes on'" (20). As if things weren't bare enough all around, the waiting man "flick[s] back the wet canvas shower curtain" and implores the bather to let Griffin wash his hands in the shower. (A nearby sink has been discovered to have no drain pipe.) Griffin hastily interjects:

> "That's all right, I can wait," I said.
> "Go ahead," he nodded.
> "Sure—come on," the man in the shower said. He turned the water down to a dribble. In the shower's obscurity, all I could see was a black shadow and gleaming white teeth. I stepped over the other's outstretched legs and washed quickly, using the soap the man in the shower thrust into my hands. When I had finished, I thanked him. (20)

Clearly the driving force here is the simultaneously fascinating and threatening proximity of black male bodies, beckoning, stretching, thrusting. If the accident of the scene's having occurred is not revealing, Griffin's retrospective mapping of it surely is. Moments like this put Griffin in the position of racial voyeur, allow him to confront the "shadows" of the white Imaginary. Paradoxically, as with his tutorials with the shine man, Sterling Williams, their result is to help Griffin identify with black men; "I fell into the same pattern of talking and thinking," he says of Williams (28). Whether or not as a defense against interracial homoerotic desire, Griffin in any case mentally assumes and impersonates—one might almost say he "masters"—the position and shape of black maleness. Poised in his disguise between white subject and black object, Griffin enters "blackness" according to the dictates of white desire.

This indeed emerges from the many pages that are taken up with conversations a hitchhiking Griffin has with white men who pummel him with questions about his sex life. "There's plenty white women would like to have a good buck Negro," says one (86); another man, with an "educated flair" (86), opines that blacks "don't get so damned many *conflicts*": "I understand you make more of an art—or maybe *hobby* out of your sex than we do" (87). Griffin's disgust at this predictable turn of events disguises the homosocial nature of the dialogues. For in these conversations, white men's interest in black male sexuality is mediated by but also identifies them with the white women black men are supposed to crave. In other words, the voyeuristic urge to expose the black man's body in congress with a white woman is quite cognate with fantasies of the forbidden coupling of black and white *men*—a coupling, after all, that Griffin has in effect been engaged in. These car scenes, of course, merely reiterate the shower scene, and implicitly place Griffin in the white male driver's seat as well as in that of the black passenger. Griffin's conscious distaste permits him both to distance himself from the debased discourse of which he is structurally the victim (the walking black penis that forms the object of white male desire) *and* to engage in that obsessive discourse through the pleasures of impersonation.

Leaving to one side *Black Like Me*'s stated intent of showing for the first time what it was like to be black in the segregated South—as though plenty of black-authored books had not investigated that predicament already—Griffin's text can be read as a story of what happens when this sexualized racial unconscious of American whiteness is not, as in the foregoing instances, kept suppressed or partitioned. It is all very well to fetishize black male bodies, as Griffin does above and also when he remembers seeing black dockworkers in Mobile "stripped to the waist, their bodies glistening with sweat under their loads" (99). But it is quite another thing, Griffin finds, to inhabit a black body. In a scene before the mirror that reveals his blackness to him for the first time, Griffin experiences total self-negation:

> Turning off all the lights, I went into the bathroom and closed the door. I stood in the darkness before the mirror, my hand on the light switch. I forced myself to flick it on.
>
> In the flood of light against white tile, the face and shoulders of a stranger —a fierce, bald, very dark Negro—glared at me from the glass. He in no way resembled me. (15)

The transformation, Griffin says, "was total and shocking"; he feels "imprisoned in the flesh of an utter stranger"; "all traces of the John Griffin I had been were wiped from existence" (15). "White skin," to play on Frantz Fanon, is here obliterated by "black mask"—a possibility only available to someone who imagines skin color in the way Griffin apparently does, as completely constitutive of identity and entirely divisive of the races. He fears he has gone too far: "the black man is wholly a Negro, regardless of what he once may have been" (16). Any sense of double perspective that chances to emerge—for instance, Griffin remarks that he "became two men, the observing one and the one who panicked"—melts away under the feeling of being "Negroid even into the depths of his entrails" (16). Fantasy here returns as frightening fact. What Richard Dyer calls the "hysterical boundedness of the white body" has been transgressed; while Griffin appears not to believe in the moral superiority of whiteness, he yet cannot let go of its powerful, life-preserving fixity.[35] Griffin's disorientation is true to Lacan's account of the mirror stage, though it produces a failed one, for his response reveals the (b)lack upon which whiteness depends but disallows an idealization of the mirror image that might heal the lack. Confronted with a "black" self-image, Griffin simply empties out the self. In what is perhaps an allusion to Ralph Ellison, Griffin writes that "The Griffin that was had become invisible" (16).

We ought, at this moment of crisis, to look at *Watermelon Man*, which, nine years after *Black Like Me*, alludes in turn to Griffin's travails. *Watermelon Man*'s white protagonist, Jeff Gerber, awakes in the middle of the night, stumbles to the bathroom, looks in the mirror, and experiences precisely Griffin's sense of self-negation upon learning that he has become black. In the first part of the film, Gerber (Godfrey Cambridge) is a jocular though devoted racist whose compulsive engagement with "blackness" undergirds or buttresses his whiteness. He exercises while singing blackface tunes ("Jimmy Crack Corn") and stages imaginary boxing bouts with Muhammad Ali ("you're a credit to your race," he says to an imaginary Ali). The film gives body to this fascination by way of Gerber's ongoing sarcastic banter with three black men: a bus driver, an elevator operator, and a lunch-counter waiter (played, in a stroke of casting genius, by an aged Mantan Moreland—the perennially frightened sidekick from the Charlie Chan movies). Disdainful of the black urban insurrections on television that comprise the film's soundtrack, yet everywhere dropping into "black" dialect and other "black" affectations, Gerber reveals that white supremacy has as one of its constituent (if unconscious) elements an imaginary closeness to black culture.

His sudden turn to black is thus both a logical and a scarifying one. Transfixed before the mirror, Gerber is at first frightened; he then hysterically acts out his subject/object split. He shadowboxes in the mirror the imaginary Ali he has now become; chants "how now brown cow"; robs his mirror image at gunpoint; drinks some milk; gets an idea and looks down his pants (but: "that's an old wives' tale," he says); soaps himself; and "proves" by his bridgework that the man in the mirror is really himself. The frenzied shifts in subject-position, from white to black to white again, point up what Van Peebles is ultimately after in the film—a state-of-the-race address on black self-hatred. Posed against *Black Like Me*, it offers, in other words, a perspective on the status of black masculinity apart from white male fantasy.

No simple affirmations are forthcoming, though. Much of the impact of *Watermelon Man* stems from its implication that the identities of both white and black men owe a heavy debt to a sort of displaced minstrelsy. Lamenting his new color, Gerber cries that his kids won't love him anymore, won't understand: "wait till I get down on my knee and I sing 'Mammy'!" The inevitable Jolson joke is actually a rather complex figure in this context. Surely it suggests a Gerber in blackface, referring once again to the obsession with blackness. But it also puts a *black* Gerber in blackface, lays a burden of white-filtered black images on his shoulders. As in Fanon, Gerber undergoes the self-othering attendant upon blacks in the West and devalues and ridicules his race accordingly. Soon Gerber is tracking down all the skin lighteners, hair straighteners, facial molds, and milk baths he can find. If as a white man he had wanted to be black, and dedicated many hours under the sunlamp to attain it, as a black man he wants just the opposite. No wonder Negroes riot, he says—the facial creams don't work.

Ultimately a simple attention to the facts of everyday life forces him to sympathize with the black militants and then become one. In fantastical form, then, Gerber experiences the transmogrification into "blackness" that the film perceives blacks generally to have experienced in the 1960s. Meanwhile Gerber's blackness comes between him and his wife, Althea (Estelle Parsons); she leaves and takes the kids to her mother's home in Indiana. The primal scene of the interracial marriage bed is crucial as well to the climax of Griffin's *Black Like Me*—but in light of *Watermelon Man* it carries a very different meaning. For Melvin Van Peebles's *Watermelon Man*, the way out of black racial mimicry or minstrelsy is into a militant blackness; its consequence is a refusal of desire for the white woman's body. (Jeff Gerber's chief moment of black self-understanding, a foretaste of the problematic gender politics of Van Peebles's *Sweet Sweetback's Baadasssss Song* [1971], occurs as he stares into the mirror of a black bar;

a topless black female dancer is visible above his head in the mirror; two white detectives conduct a vice raid in the corner.) Conversely, for John Howard Griffin, the way out of the threatening sexual return of black manhood (his own included) is into a despairing liberal whiteness; its consequence is a retreat to the politics of minstrelsy.

At a pivotal moment, under a great deal of stress, beset by racist harassers and black self-haters, Griffin finds himself alone in a Hattiesburg roominghouse contemplating his family. He spots some old film negatives on the floor; they are "blank." Griffin imagines a prior occupant having had them developed only to find them wasted. This negating of the negative is of course meant to be a kind of self-portrait of Griffin in extremis. The image does echo a remark Griffin earlier makes about "the world of the Negro" appearing to him as "a blank" (12); the lexical similarity of "blank" and "black" and their unfortunate metaphorical association in Griffin's mind (from negatives to Negroes) help Griffin to articulate his experience of self-cancellation. This glossing of the situation is, however, at odds with what happens next. Immediately after he spots the blank negatives, he tries to write to his wife: "No words would come. She had nothing to do with this life, nothing to do with the room in Hattiesburg or with its Negro inhabitant. . . . My conditioning as a Negro, and the immense sexual implications with which the racists in our culture bombard us, cut me off, even in my most intimate self, from any connection with my wife" (68). The page before him remains "blank" (68). Griffin means this as self-conscious, antiracist lament; the image he uses to describe himself under the reign of "blackness"—blankness—accords with the uncitizenly debasement he has wanted to experience. Yet I would suggest that he is himself actively suppressing the definite shape of (his) black manhood. For here and elsewhere, Griffin perceives the "immensity" of black men to be anything but blank. Indeed the "blank" page seems to loom for Griffin as a terrifying plenitude that must be sabotaged; its intimation of interracial sex, we note, "cut [him] off." Intoxicating if imagined, the fantasized black interlocutor is far too threatening as he rises up between white husband and wife. Griffin, haunted by a return of the racial repressed, in effect plumps for reifying or policing the color line. One suspects that the reason his family constantly feels so distant, why there is an absolute separation of self and other in the mirror, is because the transgressive racial pleasure Griffin everywhere imagines, and which he attempts to inhabit in his crossing of the line, must finally remain unbidden or refused. The rather flat film version of *Black Like Me* (1964) employs as one of its central cutting devices a highway's broken center line in motion, no doubt emblematic of Griffin's travels and transgressions. It appears that to cross the line is to encounter one's imagined other head-on, throwing whiteness into jeopardy.

Or into self-mimicry. One result of all this is that whiteness itself ultimately becomes an impersonation. The subterranean components of whiteness that so often threaten it require an edgy, constant patrolling. If *Watermelon Man* too easily leaves Jeff Gerber in a black, deminstrelized zone, his selfhood no longer routed through white fantasies of blacks, *Black Like Me* throws John Griffin back into a whiteness that has been decisively disrupted and must be shored up. At the end of Griffin's book, the citizens of his hometown try to run him out: "But I felt I must remain a while longer. . . . I could not allow them to say they had 'chased' me out" (155). This final imitation of white manhood, Griffin's righteous "last stand"—conceptually indistinguishable, as Richard Slotkin has shown, from notions of hegemonic whiteness and symmetrically opposed to the ending of *Watermelon Man*—is the goal toward which his text has tended.[36] "White like me" precisely names the internal division, the white self impersonating itself, that is the consequence of white men's fantasized proximity to black men. If Fanon's work and *Watermelon Man* give anti-imperialist force to the racist adage that "good" blacks are "white inside,"[37] the texts I've examined suggest that whiteness harbors some secrets of its own.

Notes

I would like to thank Amy Kaplan, Chris Looby, Jeff Melnick, Walter Michaels, Tania Modleski, Donald Pease, David Roediger, Kirk Savage, Werner Sollors, Gayatri Spivak and audiences at the Dartmouth Conference, William and Mary, and the American Studies Association convention in Costa Mesa.

1 John Howard Griffin, *Black Like Me* (New York: NAL, 1961), front cover, p. 14. For more on Griffin's adventure, see Jeff H. Campbell, *John Howard Griffin* (Austin: Steck-Vaughn, 1970); Bradford Daniel, "Why They Can't Wait: An Interview with a White Negro," *Progressive* 28 (1964): 15–19; and Ernest Sharpe, Jr., "The Man Who Changed His Skin," *American Heritage* 40, no. 1 (1989): 44–55. An early report on Griffin's trip appeared in *Sepia* (April 1960).

2 See my *Love and Theft: Blackface Minstrelsy and the American Working Class* (New York: Oxford University Press, 1993).

3 John F. Szwed, "Race and the Embodiment of Culture," *Ethnicity* 2, no. 1 (1975): 27.

4 Several scholars have begun to undertake such a task, and I am much in

their debt: Richard Dyer, "White," *Screen* 29, no. 4 (1988): 44–64; Walter Benn Michaels, "The Souls of White Folk," *Literature and the Body: Essays on Populations and Persons,* ed. Elaine Scarry (Baltimore: Johns Hopkins University Press, 1988), pp. 185–209; Alexander Saxton, *The Rise and Fall of the White Republic: Class Politics and Mass Culture in Nineteenth–Century America* (London: Verso, 1990); Tania Modleski, *Feminism Without Women: Culture and Criticism in a "Postfeminist" Age* (New York: Routledge, 1991), pp. 115–34; David Roediger, *The Wages of Whiteness: Race and the Making of the American Working Class* (London: Verso, 1991); Toni Morrison, *Playing in the Dark: Whiteness and the Literary Imagination* (Cambridge: Harvard University Press, 1992); bell hooks, "Representing Whiteness in the Black Imagination," *Cultural Studies,* ed. Lawrence Grossberg, Cary Nelson, and Paula A. Treichler (New York: Routledge, 1992), pp. 338–46; Vron Ware, *Beyond the Pale: White Women, Racism, and History* (London: Verso, 1992); and Michael Rogin, "Blackface, White Noise: The Jewish Jazz Singer Finds His Voice," *Critical Inquiry* 18 (1992): 417–53. See also the articles in "The White Issue," *Village Voice* 38.20 (1993): 24–41. On "race" generally I have been influenced by Homi K. Bhabha, "The Other Question: The Stereotype and Colonial Discourse," *Screen* 24, no. 6 (1983): 18–36; Stuart Hall, "New Ethnicities," *Black Film/British Cinema,* ed. Kobena Mercer (London: ICA, 1988), pp. 27–31; Andrew Ross, "Ballots, Bullets, or Batmen: Can Cultural Studies Do the Right Thing?" *Screen* 31, no. 1 (1990): 26–44; and Kobena Mercer's essays, for example, "'1968': Periodizing Postmodern Politics and Identity," *Cultural Studies,* pp. 424–38.

  5 Ralph Ellison, "Change the Joke and Slip the Yoke" (1958) in his *Shadow and Act* (1964; New York: Vintage, 1972), pp. 45–59; LeRoi Jones, *Blues People: Negro Music in White America* (New York: Morrow, 1963), pp. 82–86; Nathan Huggins, *Harlem Renaissance* (New York: Oxford University Press, 1971), pp. 244–301; Robert C. Toll, *Blacking Up: The Minstrel Show in Nineteenth-Century America* (New York: Oxford University Press, 1974). The next several paragraphs are reprinted from my *Love and Theft,* courtesy of Oxford University Press.

  6 Alexander Saxton, "Blackface Minstrelsy and Jacksonian Ideology," *American Quarterly* 27, no. 1 (1975): 5–7, 15–16. See also Saxton's "George Wilkes: The Transformation of a Radical Ideology," *American Quarterly* 33, no. 4 (1981): 437–58, for some of the other activities of the milieu that nourished blackface performers. Edward LeRoy Rice's *Monarchs of Minstrelsy from "Daddy" Rice to Date* (New York: Kenny, 1911) is the most comprehensive, if often sketchy, source for profiles of blackface performers.

  7 "Interview with Ben Cotton," *New York Mirror,* July 3, 1897.

  8 See the important account of French bohemia by Arnold Hauser, *The Social History of Art,* trans. Stanley Godman (New York: Vintage, 1951), 4:189–93; see also Richard Miller, *Bohemia: The Protoculture Then and Now* (Chicago: Nelson-Hall, 1977), pp. 29–78.

  9 Hans Nathan, *Dan Emmett and the Rise of Early Negro Minstrelsy* (1962; Norman, Okla.: University of Oklahoma Press, 1977), pp. 107, 110.

10 Morrison Foster, *My Brother Stephen* (1896; Indianapolis: Foster Hall, 1932), p. 83. William Austin disputes and complexifies this claim in *"Susanna," "Jeanie," and "The Old Folks at Home": The Music of Stephen Foster from His Time to Ours* (1975; Urbana: University of Illinois Press, 1989), pp. 238–39.

11 Ralph Keeler, "Three Years As a Negro Minstrel," *Atlantic Monthly* 24, no. 141 (1869): 77.

12 Quoted in Toll, *Blacking Up*, p. 46.

13 Eileen Southern, *The Music of Black Americans: A History* (1971; New York: Norton, 1983), p. 95.

14 F. C. Wemyss, *Theatrical Biography; or, The Life of An Actor and Manager* (Glasgow: R. Griffin, 1848), p. 179.

15 Willie Morris, *North Toward Home* (Boston: Houghton Mifflin, 1967), p. 81.

16 Leslie Fiedler, *Waiting for the End* (1966; New York: Stein and Day, 1972), p. 134. For some suggestive remarks on the interracial male bonding central to Fiedler's famous "Come Back to the Raft Agin', Huck Honey!" see Donald Pease, "Leslie Fiedler, the Rosenberg Trial, and the Formulation of an American Canon," *boundary 2* 17, no. 2 (1990): 155–98, esp. 172–77, 180–87. See also Christopher Looby, "'As Thoroughly Black As the Most Faithful Philanthropist Could Desire': Erotics of Race in Higginson's *Army Life in a Black Regiment*," *Race and the Subject of Masculinities*, ed. Harry Stecopoulos and Michael Uebel (Durham: Duke University Press, forthcoming).

17 Eve Sedgwick, "The Beast in the Closet: James and the Writing of Homosexual Panic" in *Speaking of Gender*, ed. Elaine Showalter (New York: Routledge, 1989), p. 251.

Revising René Girard's triangulated model of heterosexual desire in *Deceit, Desire, and the Novel*—in which rival men fighting over a woman engage in a more intense bond than either of the men share with the woman—and drawing on Gayle Rubin's reaccentuation (in "The Traffic in Women: Notes on the 'Political Economy' of Sex," *Toward an Anthropology of Women*, ed. Rayna R. Reiter [New York: Monthly Review Press, 1975], pp. 157–210) of an anthropological tradition that views women as objects of exchange in a male economy, Sedgwick explores some of the ways men maintain patriarchal domination by bonding through mediating women. "Homosocial" bonds are those heterosexual, homophobic relations that consolidate men's interests. But homosocial and homosexual desire are, in Sedgwick's words, "remarkably cognate." See *Between Men: English Literature and Male Homosocial Desire* (New York: Columbia University Press, 1985), pp. 1–27, and "Beast in the Closet," p. 246.

In the minstrel show, this dynamic extended in several directions. In addition to the traffic in women effected by minstrelsy's derisive "wench" characters (played by men), white male bonding occurred over the bodies of black men as well. This homosocial bonding was, oddly, mediated by white men's *appropriations of* "black" maleness—a peculiar kind of traffic in black men.

18 Olive Logan, "The Ancestry of Brudder Bones," *Harper's New Monthly Magazine* 58, no. 347 (1879): 698.

19 Quoted in Toll, *Blacking Up,* p. 142.

20 "Interview with Ben Cotton."

21 George Thatcher, "The Only Thatcher's Autobiography," Thatcher Minstrel Program, New York Public Library Theatre Collection, n.d.

22 Peter Stallybrass and Allon White, *The Politics and Poetics of Transgression* (London: Methuen, 1986), pp. 5, 193–94; see also Bhabha, "The Other Question."

23 Julia Kristeva, *Powers of Horror: An Essay on Abjection,* trans. Leon S. Roudiez (1980; New York: Columbia University Press, 1982), p. 7.

24 Slavoj Žižek, "Eastern Europe's Republics of Gilead," *New Left Review* 183 (1990): 57; Bhabha, "The Other Question."

25 Szwed, "Race and the Embodiment of Culture," p. 30.

26 Berndt Ostendorf, *Black Literature in White America* (Totowa, N.J.: Barnes and Noble, 1982), pp. 77–78.

27 Norman Podhoretz, "The Know-Nothing Bohemians," *Partisan Review* 25 (Spring 1958): 311.

28 Interestingly, Vanilla Ice's biographer argues for his subject's racial indeterminacy: "Ice's family life was hardly the 'white bread' existence of *The Brady Bunch.* With regard to the rest of his family tree he claims to be 'part Apache. I am also part Cuban, but other than that I'm really not sure.'" Mark Bego, *Ice, Ice, Ice: The Extraordinary Vanilla Ice Story* (New York: Dell, 1991), p. 22. But see Armond White on the same performer: "What Vanilla Ice has to say (nothing) leaves his representation of whiteness as his only point." "The White Albums: Is Black Music Under Siege?" *City Sun* 8, no. 49 (1990): 19.

29 Two striking images, one academic and one popular, underscore those remarks. The first, from the journal *Transition,* accompanies an article by Jerome McCristal Culp, Jr., which asks whether legal theorist Richard Posner would "come to the same conclusions about racial difference and the law"—that is, that race doesn't matter—if he were black; twin photos feature Posner as he is and Posner artificially blackened. This kind of essentialism (criticized by Culp himself in regard to gender), with intellectual positions the foreordained result of a writer's race, is somewhat surprising from a journal edited by Henry Louis Gates, Jr. and Kwame Anthony Appiah, who have devoted much of their work to contesting it. ("The Education of Richard Posner," *Transition* 52 [1991]: 114–22; quotation at p. 120.) The second, from *Insight* magazine, accompanies a news story critical of "discrimination testers," fake job applicants of various races who check the fairness of employment agencies' hiring practices. The photo, a man whose left half is white and right half black, refers to the "sameness" of the putative applicants in everything but pigmentation and imagines that such efforts toward racial justice themselves raise the specter of "race," willfully splitting the body politic—worse, one guesses, than the already existing racism the magazine apparently supports. (Elena Neuman, "Staking Out the Hiring Line," *Insight,* December 9, 1991, pp. 12–13, 36, 38.) This image is absolutely opposed to the thrust of, say, Michael Jackson's extraordinary video "Black or White" (1991) (though a foolish few have missed the point), whose racial "morphing" sequence melds races and faces even as it countenances the lived reality of racial particularity. Race, here, is imagined mutable; the burden of its construction is briefly thrown off, the line between self and other blurred. Unlike the thinking behind the blackface tradition, to which the *Transition* and *Insight* graphics are implicitly indebted, the video generally acknowledges the flawed and permeable, if not indeed inessential and constructed, character of the outlines of "race."

30 Norman Mailer, "The White Negro," *Advertisements for Myself* (New York: Putnam's, 1959), p. 314.

31 For the best account of Elvis's racial contradictions, see Greil Marcus, *Mystery Train: Images of America in Rock 'n' Roll Music* (1975; New York: Dutton, 1982), pp. 141–209; see also George Lipsitz, *Class and Culture in Cold-War America* (New York: Praeger, 1981), pp. 195–225. An acute reading of 1950s intellectual white-Negroism can be found in Andrew Ross, *No Respect: Intellectuals and Popular Culture* (New York: Routledge, 1989), pp. 65–101.

32 Nelson George, *The Death of Rhythm & Blues* (New York: Dutton, 1988), pp. 62–64.

33 Marcus, *Mystery Train*, pp. 186, 181.

34 The comeback special is available on video and record under the title *Elvis TV Special* (RCA 4088). On Elvis's afterlife, see Greil Marcus, *Dead Elvis: A Chronicle of a Cultural Obsession* (New York: Doubleday, 1991) and *I Am Elvis: A Guide to Elvis Impersonators* (New York: Pocket Books, 1991).

35 Dyer, "White": 63. Griffin did not, as is still widely rumored, die as a belated result of his skin treatments (Sharpe, "Man Who Changed His Skin," p. 55)—a rumor whose persistence (roughly half of those I spoke to about this essay repeated it) attests either to a continuing desire to punish Griffin for his transgressions and guard the color line or to a continuing fascination with white-liberal martyrdom. Either way, the tradition of all the dead generations weighs like a nightmare on the brain of the living.

36 Richard Slotkin, *The Fatal Environment: The Myth of the Frontier in the Age of Industrialism* (Middletown, Conn.: Wesleyan University Press, 1985). Cf. Amy Kaplan, "Romancing the Empire: The Embodiment of American Masculinity in the Popular Historical Novel of the 1890s," *American Literary History* 2.4 (1990): 659–90. For a pre-*Watermelon Man* take on Griffin that clarifies and ironizes this fact, see Dick Gregory, *What's Happening?* (New York: Dutton, 1965), pp. 94–97. Thanks to Doris Witt for bringing this to my attention.

37 Cf. Louis Armstrong's irony in "(What Did I Do To Be So) Black and Blue": "I'm white / Inside / But that don't help my case / 'Cause I / Can't hide / What is in my face." Filmmaker Leah Gilliam plays with some of these binaries in *Now Pretend* (1992), an explicit meditation on *Black Like Me*.

Imperial Spectacles

 IV

Michael Rogin

"Make My Day!"

Spectacle as Amnesia

in Imperial Politics

I

he thief hides the purloined letter, in Edgar Allan Poe's story, by placing it in plain sight. His theft is overlooked because no attempt is made to conceal it. The crimes of the postmodern American empire, I want to suggest, are concealed in the same way. Covert operations actually function as spectacle. So let us begin like Poe's Inspector Dupin and attend to the evidence before our eyes.[1]

The last Republican president of the United States was a Hollywood actor. His vice president, the man who succeeded him, was the director of the Central Intelligence Agency. To understand how the career paths of these two men, rather than discrediting either them or the political system in which they had risen to the top, uniquely prepared them for the presidency is to name the two political peculiarities of the postmodern American empire: on the one hand the domination of public politics by the spectacle and on the other the spread of covert operations and a secret foreign policy. "Going public," Samuel Kernell's phrase for the shift from institutionalized, pluralist bargaining among stable, elite coalitions to appeals to the mass public, coexists with going private, the spread of hidden, unaccountable decision making within the executive branch. How are we to think about the relationship between the two?[2]

It may seem that spectacle and secrecy support each other by a division of labor, one being public and the other private, one selling or disguising the foreign policy made by the other. The Iran/Contra exposure broke down that division, on this view, by revealing a secret foreign policy that not only violated public law against aiding the Contras but also contradicted public denunciations of the Ayatollah Khomeini and of bargaining with terrorists. The privatization of American foreign policy that characterized Iran/Contra signified, in this interpretation, the takeover of policy by private, unaccountable arms merchants and state terrorists by means of private, secret operations. Although the executive junta owed its power to officials in high public positions, the argument continues, it was not a public body.

Such an interpretation, which divides public image from secret operations, ignores secrecy's role beyond covert operational borders, producing signals for elite and mass audiences. To begin with, the "neat idea[s]" that produced Iran/Contra (to recall Oliver North's apt phrase) were acted out as a film scenario in the heads of the junta, who, along with the right-wing ideologues let in on parts of the story, formed the audience for their own movie. ("Ollie was a patriot," remarked former Reagan press spokesman Larry Speakes. "But I sometimes felt he thought he was playing some kind of role, that he was watching a movie on the screen with himself the star in it.")[3] And just as Iran/Contra was acted out as a spectacle within the junta, other covert operations have been intended to function as spectacle for relevant audiences—enemies and allies abroad, mass public and opinion makers at home. Political spectacle in the postmodern empire, in other words, is itself a form of power and not simply window dressing that diverts attention from the secret substance of American foreign policy.

To introduce the entanglement between the two apparent opposites, spectacle and secrecy, let us consider their conjunction in the modus vivendi of the two presidential figures, the Ronald Reagan of spectacle and the George Bush of covert operations. "Plausible deniability," as the phrase used to exculpate Reagan inadvertently admitted, points to a president whose operations in front of the camera were meant to render plausible the denial that he also operated behind it. That has been true since Hollywood, when President Reagan of the Screen Actors Guild engaged in two covert actions: first, he informed on his coworkers to the FBI and helped organize the anti-Communist blacklist whose existence he denied; second, he negotiated the exemption for Music Corporation of America that allowed it alone among talent agencies to produce movies and television shows and simultaneously to represent actors. The former covert action launched Reagan's political career. The latter, putting him in front of the camera on the GE Television Theater, moved him from movies to TV; helped him perfect the intimate, living-room image that would be crucial to his political success; and gave him the capital and capital-producing friendships that would underwrite his political career.[4]

These examples, which reverse the usual image of Reagan as mere entertainer, make covert action into the source of his power. Reagan's domination of American politics has come, however, not from his compartmentalized mastery of either covert action or spectacle but from his confusion of the two. Just as it facilitated his rise from Hollywood acting to Washington power, that confusion also protected the president from the worst consequences of the Iran/Contra exposure. When Reagan took responsibility for Iran/Contra with the words "It happened on my watch," he placed himself on the permeable border between public display and covert operation. "My watch" identified him as commander-in-chief, standing on the bridge as he did in the role of submarine commander in his last Hollywood movie, *Hellcats of the Navy*. Just as the script of that movie freed the fictional commander from responsibility for the loss of his ship, so "It happened on my watch" allows the real president to evade responsibility by assuming it. The line first separates the visible commander-in-chief from the guilty parties in charge of operations down in what one former presidential chief-of-staff has called the "engine room." Second, the line identifies the president not simply as the object at whom we look but as one of the watchers as well. "My watch" makes the president just another ordinary American spectator, as much or as little responsible as the rest of us—there and not there at the same time—as in the head and upper body shot of Reagan at the 1984 Republican convention. At once on camera and part of the television audience, the president lounged in shirt sleeves and watched his wife (a tiny image much smaller than he) raise her arms and, saying "Win one for the Gipper," turn toward the giant image of presidential head and torso lounging and watching his wife—an infinite regression that drew the convention and television audience into the picture, identifying that audience as one of and as subject to the one of itself it was watching. Reagan's managers planned every detail of that scene, including the special podium built without a single edge or straight line—"curves everywhere," as its creator described it, "brown, beige, nothing jarring. . . . The eye comes to rest there. Earth tones and rounded shapes are peaceful." "The podium was a giant womb," comments Garry Wills, "into which the country would retreat along with Reagan."[5]

The Reagan spectacle points, then, neither to the insignificance nor to the autonomy of the sign but rather to its role in producing power. By the same token, the former CIA director was no more a powerful invisible presence before he became chief of state than the former actor was a powerless visible one. That is not because, as Robert Dole charged, Bush is the perennial good-boy marionette who doesn't pull his own strings. Bush has had, after all, a substantial relationship to the CIA. He was, first, the former director who brought in Team B to politicize intelligence judgments, to exaggerate the extent of the Soviet military and political threat to the United States, and thereby to lay the groundwork for the massive military buildup and expanded covert operations that together define the Reagan Doctrine in foreign policy. And, second, his national security adviser, Donald Gregg, was (according to Congressional testimony) linked through CIA agent Felix Rodriguez to the illegal Contra supply operation, including the ill-fated Eugene Hassenfuss and probably to Contra drug running as well. Moreover, Bush has falsely denied his substantial involvement in trading arms for hostages. Bush's claims of ignorance and privileged communication, like Reagan's assumption of responsibility, evidence plausible deniability rather than the absence of either president or vice president from the scene of the crime.[6]

Bush, like Reagan, calls into question the distinction between mass spectacle and covert power. He does so in two ways. First, Bush's evasions exemplify the public use of the claim of secrecy, in the name of national security, that allows men like Bush, John Poindexter, and Oliver North to avoid political responsibility. And, second, Bush reminds us of the set of beliefs of the men (and women like Jeane Kirkpatrick) who carry out and defend covert operations. Whether or not Bush is a figurehead, he stands for fantasies about our enemies that—I have cited Reagan and the Reagan Doctrine, Bush and Team B to suggest—operate not in the first place in popular culture but at the most secret levels of decision making. These fantasies, reinforced by being shared among the covert operators, constitute the spectacle they produce for one another.

In a recent review, Ian Buruma agrees that Ronald Reagan's jokes, *Rambo,* and Jerry Falwell "tell us something about popular culture in America, but it would be simplistic to say that they directly account for United States foreign policy—even though the link might exist somewhere in the president's own mind."[7] In dismissing the organizing principle of the president's mind, however, Buruma is making a big mistake. For if the link exists not only in Reagan's mass mind—the public spectacle—but in the minds of those who think up and implement our foreign policy, then to separate fantasy from policy works simply to preserve a realm of public discourse for reasonable men like Buruma to speak to power.

The public Reagan/Bush relation to secret operations also introduces a third form of power, the power of amnesia. The secret, retroactive finding that President Reagan forgot he signed, like the incessant "I don't recall"s of John Poindexter and Edwin Meese, may seem merely to disconnect high public officials from secret, illegal activities. Amnesia of this sort slides into claims of privileged communication on the one hand— Bush cannot tell us what, as vice president, he advised the president about arms and hostages—and ignorance on the other—Bush denies he knew Noriega was trafficking in drugs although that was commonplace information in the CIA when he was in charge of it—"not a smoking gun," one former NSC staffer has remarked, "but rather a twenty-one-gun barrage of evidence." Amnesia here severs the link between what goes on behind the scenes and what in front of the camera, as when Reagan forgets the movie origins of the lines he delivers as his own or is just as surprised as the rest of us to learn that he never spoke to Mikhail Gorbachev the words that Larry Speakes attributed to him.[8] If we disbelieve those claims of forgetting, we see them as protecting secret complicity. If we believe them, the reality principle disappears. Let us not dismiss the latter hypothesis too quickly, for I am going to suggest that memory loss is not confined to the president and his men, and that it sustains not only the covert actions hidden from public view but also the imperial spectacles that we have all seen. Covert actions derive from the imperatives of spectacle, not secrecy. They owe their invisibility not to secrecy but to political amnesia. What is displayed and forgotten in imperial spectacle is the historical content of American political demonology.

II

If spectacle and secrecy define the political peculiarities of the postmodern American empire, racial and political demonology define the peculiarities of the historic American empire. Countersubversion and racism, I will argue, provide the content for the covert, specular form. But this content is hidden by the form that seems to reveal it. Racism and countersubversion, like the actor and the CIA director, are concealed from contemporary eyes by being in plain sight. I am calling this forgetting of what one continues to see political amnesia, in order to yoke together the arguments of Russell Jacoby's *Social Amnesia* with those of Fredric Jameson's

The Political Unconscious. [9] In this motivated forgetting, that which is insistently represented becomes, by being normalized to invisibility, absent and disappeared. Instead of distinguishing circuses for the mass mind from secret, elite maneuvers, as if the former merely covered over the forces that drive the latter, we need to see how the links between going public and going private are strengthened by amnesia. Consider two illustrations from a source I have been trying to legitimate, the movies that matter to Ronald Reagan. Instead of reporting only my own interpretations of these motion pictures, as if the films were self-enclosed texts, let me practice some informal reception analysis.

"Go ahead. Make my day!" President Reagan invited Congress, promising to veto a threatened tax increase. Reagan was quoting Clint Eastwood as Dirty Harry, of course. But it turned out to be hard to remember in which of the four Dirty Harry movies the lines appeared and in what context Eastwood delivered them. Like many others, I first thought the lines came from the original movie, *Dirty Harry* (1971), in the scene where Eastwood holds a gun on a killer and dares him to draw, neither the killer nor the audience knowing whether there is a bullet left in Eastwood's gun. But although that scene opens and closes the movie (the first time the killer fails to call Eastwood's bluff, the second time he is blown away), Eastwood says "Make my day!" neither time. He speaks that line in *Sudden Impact* (1983) to a hoodlum holding his gun to a female hostage's head. In the scene that closes the movie the hoodlum is a rapist; in the scene that opens the movie he is black. Eastwood is daring a black man to murder a woman, in other words, so that Dirty Harry can kill the black. No question this time about whether his gun is empty and Eastwood at risk. The lives he proves his toughness by endangering are female and black, not his own.

When the president says "Make my day!" he is aspiring to Eastwood's power, but the audience is in a more complicated position. Theories of the male gaze notwithstanding, viewers are passive spectators closer to the helpless, female hostage position than to Eastwood's. This is not only because of their passivity in theater or living room but because of their larger, political helplessness as well. "Make my day!" blames that impotence on the criminal threat to women. By reinscribing race and gender difference and identifying with the rescuer, Clint Eastwood, the film offers viewers imaginary access to power.

The audience's relationship to this particular scene, however, is more complicated yet. Eastwood made *Sudden Impact* during the Reagan presidency, as the racial and sexual antagonisms of the 1980s put women and blacks into the picture at their own expense. The president who quoted Eastwood's line had made women and blacks his targets, notably through the tax cuts that eviscerated their welfare-state benefits and that he was defending when he said "Make my day!" But my claim here is not only that women and blacks were present in the presidential unconscious but also that they were absent from the memories of those who had seen the picture. Whenever I spoke on Reagan and the movies after seeing *Sudden Impact*, to student and nonstudent audiences, in my own classes and in public lectures, I asked whether anyone remembered the context of the famous words. Everyone recognized the line, for it has become a cultural cliché. But those who thought they had seen the movie foundered on the scene. Some wrongly placed the words in the episode, between men alone, of the first movie. Others got the movie and general setting right, but forgot key characters. As my sample reached the thousands, only one person remembered either the black man or the woman. That exception was himself a black man; he forgot the woman. Amnesia allows Eastwood and Reagan to have their race and gender conflict and digest it too. The white hero is remembered; the context that produced him is buried so that it can continue to support *Standing Tall* (the title of yet another Reagan-quoted movie) in the world. In the American myth we remember, men alone risk their lives in equal combat. In the one we forget, white men show how tough they are by resubordinating and sacrificing their race and gender others. The white man dares Moamar Qadaffi to blow up a café (maybe he did and maybe he didn't) so that he can drop bombs on men, women, and children of color. "Go ahead. Make my day!"

My first example of political amnesia concerns race and gender; my second is about countersubversion. In his 1940 movie *Murder in the Air*, Ronald Reagan plays an undercover member of the Secret Service (forerunner of the wartime oss and the postwar CIA). The secret agent, Brass Bancroft, penetrates a Nazi/Communist plot to steal the plans for a secret, defensive superweapon that bears an uncanny (and, I have argued, not accidental) resemblance to Star Wars. I introduced my book *"Ronald Reagan," the Movie* with that film. But I told the story of sabotage, subversives, House Un-American Activities Committee investigation, and secret weapon as if I were describing history and not a movie. In the fall of 1987, after *"Ronald Reagan," the Movie* appeared, I visited a college freshman English class that was studying political writing and had read the Reagan essay. One student asked whether I had wanted readers to believe I was telling a true story, and since that was indeed my intention I asked other members of the class whether it had worked. An Asian-American responded that he had been taken in at first but realized the tale was fiction and not fact when I brought in the House Un-American Activities Committee. Relying on intelligence and common sense to compensate for historical ignorance, this student assumed that HUAC could only be made up; how could he know that it was also American history? It was a history, moreover, that operated with particular force, if not against the parents or grandparents of this student then against other Asian Americans who were, from the point of view of the makers of that history, indistinguishable from them.

These responses to *Sudden Impact* and *Murder in the Air* point to two amnesias whose forgettings are hardly identical. One is personal, the other social, since ignorance of American history is not the same as forgetting what one has actually seen. Millions of Americans familiar with "Make my day!" never have seen the movie, moreover. They may know the line from television trailers that do not show the actual scene, or from computer "toy" programs in which a digitalized voice speaks the words. As "Make my day!" enters the common culture its roots disappear, and HUAC and *Sudden Impact* come to resemble each other as instances not of individual forgetting but of historical memory loss. At the same time film, by functioning in Reaganite politics to confuse the historical with the imaginary, also preserves an objective memory of scenes that have now entered history. *Sudden Impact* allows us to hold to account the culture that voices the movie's most famous words.

That is not to damn all speakers of the line, however. "Make my day!" declares an aggression that leads back in American culture to racial and sexual inequality, even if many have used the phrase without knowing its filmic source or historical meaning. (The same would apply, for an earlier generation, to Theodore Roosevelt's injunction to speak softly and carry a big stick.) No one wants to be accused of knowing and forgetting the origin of "Make my day!" But instead of exculpating the innocently ignorant and sending those who have forgotten their guilty knowledge to hell, the concept of political amnesia points to a cultural structure of motivated disavowal. That structure will vary in implicating individuals (from those who want others to forget; to those who forgot; to those who, with varying degrees of wilfullness, never allowed themselves to know) and events (readers of earlier drafts of this essay have been more willing to acknowledge race and amnesia in Bush's use of Willie Horton, with which I will conclude, than in Reagan's invocation of Clint Eastwood).

It is not necessary to agree about who and what fit within the structure of political amnesia to understand how it works. Since amnesia means motivated forgetting, it implies a cultural impulse both to have the experience and not to retain it in memory. Political amnesia signifies not simply memory loss but a dissociation between sensation and ego that operates to preserve both. Amnesia signals forbidden pleasure or memory joined to pain. It permits repetition of pleasures that, if consciously sustained in memory over time, would have to be called into question. From this perspective, the political spectacle opens a door the viewer wants to close so that it can be opened again. There is, first, the forbidden pleasure in the sensations themselves, a sensory overstimulation that in political spectacle is more typically violent than sexual (or sexual by being violent). Amnesia disconnects from their objects and severs from memory those intensified, detailed shots of destruction, wholesaled on populations and retailed on body parts. There is, second, the historical truth exposed by the mythic effort to cannibalize it—that the white male sacrificed women and people of color, for example, in the name of his own courage. Historical amnesia allows race and countersubversion to continue to configure American politics by disconnecting current practices from their historical roots. Political amnesia works, however, not simply through burying history but also through representing the return of the repressed. An easily forgettable series of surface entertainments— movies, television series, political shows—revolves before the eye. The scopic pleasure in their primal, illegitimate scenes produces infantile amnesia once the images themselves threaten to enter the lasting, symbolic realm.[10] The recovery of historical memory exposes these processes.

Spectacle is the cultural form for amnesiac representation, for specular displays are superficial and sensately intensified, short lived and repeatable. Spectacle and amnesia may seem at odds, to be sure: *amnesia*, a term from depth-historical analysis, points backward, to the nineteenth century's concern with the past. *Spectacle*, by contrast, names the spatial pleasures of contemporary visual entertainment. But this opposition, underlined in modernist and postmodernist analysis, is what enables spectacle to do its work.

Spectacles, in the Marxist modernist view, shift attention from workers as producers to spectators as consumers of mass culture. Spectacles colonize everyday life, in this view, and thereby turn domestic citizens into imperial subjects. Spectacle goes private by organizing mass consumption and leisure; it attaches ordinary, intimate existence to public displays of the private lives of political and other entertainers. Spectacles, in the postmodern view, define the historical rupture between industrial and postindustrial society—the one based on durable goods production, the other on information and service exchange. With the dissolution of individual subjects and differentiated, autonomous spheres, not only does the connection between an object and its use become arbitrary, in this view, but skilled attention to display also deflects notice from the object to its hyperreal, reproducible representation. The society of the spectacle provides illusory unification and meaning, Guy Debord argues, distracting attention from producers and from classes in conflict. Simulacric games have entirely replaced the real, in Jean Baudrillard's formulation, and offer not even a counterfeit representation of anything outside themselves.[11]

Spectacle is about forgetting, for the Marxist modernist, since it makes the tie to production invisible. The historicizing concept of amnesia suggests that the forgotten link in political spectacle is the visible tie to the past. Spectacle contrasts to narrative, for the postmodernist, as fragmented and interchangeable individuals, products, and body parts replace the subject-centered story. Political spectacles display centrifugal threats—threats to the subject and threats to the state—to contain as well as to enjoy them. Instead of dissolving the subject into structures or discourses, the concept of amnesia points to an identity that persists over time and that preserves a false center by burying the actual past.

American imperial spectacles display and forget four enabling myths that the culture can no longer unproblematically embrace. The first is the historical organization of American politics around racial domination. Once openly announced, American political racialism must now give unacknowledged satisfactions. The second is redemption through violence, intensified in the mass technologies of entertainment and war. The third is the belief in individual agency, the need to forget both the web of social ties that enmesh us all and the wish for an individual power so disjunctive with everyday existence. And the fourth is identification with the state, to which is transferred the freedom to act without being held to account that in part compensates for individual helplessness but in part reflects state weakness as well.

Covert spectacles, the Reagan Era's main contribution to American imperial representation, display state-supported American heroes in violent, racial combat. Covert spectacles—movies like *Rambo* (which begins, "A covert action is being geared up in the Far East") and political schemes like aid to the Nicaraguan "freedom fighters"[12]—preserve the fiction of a center. It is not just that America occupies that center, but that international politics comprises a coherent narrative where secret agents—the word *agent* has a double meaning—are at once connected to a directing

power and also able to act heroically on their own. In a world of imper-
sonal forces, massive suffering, and individual helplessness, the covert
spectacle provides the illusion, through violence, of personal control. The
visual character of the story, moreover, encourages immediate audience
identification, elevating a visionary ideal above chaotic, ordinary, daily
existence.[13]

Political spectacles incorporate fragmentary surface pleasures—the
crotch shot in *Rambo*, for example, where the camera pulls back to reveal that it was showing not female private parts but the crease inside the
hero's elbow, now safely tucked between biceps and forearm; or the explosions of violence in *First Blood, Part I* and *Part II*—into a larger whole.
Resuscitating the center rather than disintegrating it, political spectacle
provides the pleasure of meaning-giving order. In so doing, political spectacle heals the rift between present and past. Mass advertising has marketed reassurance about historical connectedness since its origins in the
1920s.[14] The covert operator, bringing the past into the present, offers
that reassurance as well. Entering racially alien ground, he regresses to
primitivism in order to destroy the subversive and appropriate his power.

Two American histories support the covert spectacle, the history of
racial demonology and the emergence of a specular foreign policy. I want
briefly to outline those histories, suggesting at greater length how World
War II provides the missing link between them. World War II, by joining
demonology to the covert spectacle, configured both the first cold war
and its revival under Reagan. Finally, since amnesia itself must be historicized, I will conclude with the connection established in the 1960s
between racial demonology and imperial spectacle. For the display and
forgetting of that link produced both the Reagan Doctrine in foreign
policy and the Bush presidential campaign.

III

As with the career paths of President Bush and his predecessor, so with
our historical origins, the obvious is rendered invisible by being taken for
granted. The United States is a settler society. America began in European imperialism against people of color. The American empire started
at home; what was foreign was made domestic by expansion across the
continent and by the subjugation, dispossession, and extermination of
Indian tribes. Other settler societies—South Africa, now Israel—came
to depend on the labor of indigenous populations. The American colo-

nies, after experimenting with Indian workers, enslaved Africans instead. The United States was built on the land and with the labor of peoples of color.

Academic divisions between domestic and international politics separate the American empire from its domestic, imperial base. With the end of the continental frontier, the racial basis of American expansion carried forward into the Philippines, the Caribbean, Latin America, and eventually the Asian mainland, with full consciousness (since forgotten) of the continuity between the triumph of civilization over savagery at home and the white man's burden abroad. (Rudyard Kipling urged America to take up the white man's burden in the Philippines, connecting that war to European imperialism as well.) The distinction between European powers that held colonies and the United States, which generally did not, wrongly locates the imperial age in the late nineteenth century instead of three centuries earlier, at the dawn of the modern age. Imperial expansion to extend the area of freedom (in Andrew Jackson's words) was integral to American politics from the beginning. The linkage of expansion to freedom instead of to the acquisition of colonies prepared the United States to see itself as the legitimate defender of freedom in the postcolonial Third World.

To trace a line from Columbus to, say, Elliott Abrams hardly proves the racial motivations of America's Third World interventions—Iran in the 1950s, Zaire in the 1960s, Vietnam in the 1960s and 1970s, Nicaragua and El Salvador today, to name some prominent examples. Race enters in three ways, however. First, most subjects of American intervention are peoples of color, and the racial history of the United States makes it easier to dehumanize and do away with them. Second, American political culture came into being by defining itself in racialist terms. And third, categories that originated in racial opposition were also imposed on political opponents, creating an American political demonology.

To illustrate these three points, I borrow an example from Jonathan Kwitny's *Endless Enemies*. [15] Walter Cronkite opened the CBS evening news on May 19, 1978 with these words: "Good evening. The worst fears in the rebel invasion of Zaire's Shaba province reportedly have been realized. Rebels being routed from the mining town of Kolwezi are reported to have killed a number of Europeans." Easy to pass right over that remarkable "worst fears," which, as Kwitny says, makes it better to kill blacks than whites. Colored deaths, my first point, do not count the way white ones do. That is because the history of imperialism and slavery has encoded a nightmare of racial massacre so that it speaks even through Walter Cronkite. That nightmare of red and black murdering white inverts actual history, in which massacres (certainly in the big, world-historic picture and in most individual cases as well) were usually the other way around. There was, as Kwitny shows, neither a rebel invasion of Zaire nor a massacre of whites. Far more blacks were killed than whites in the fighting that did occur, and "the worst massacre of Europeans in modern African history" was a historically produced figment of the imagination of the *Washington Post*. It never happened.

Imaginary racial massacres make peoples of color not simply disposable but indispensable as well, for—and this is my second point— the fantasy of savage violence defines the imperial imagination. Racial inversions, in which victims metamorphose into killers, may seem at most to justify Euro-American interventions in the Third World, not to cause them. Surely the color of the minerals in Zaire, not the people, provoked the covert American intervention of the early 1960s that was responsible for killing Patrice Lumumba and making Joseph Mobutu the dictator of the postcolonial state. If Vietnamese oil won't do the work of Zairian copper, then geopolitical conflict will. Or the domino effect? Or anti-Communism? Or unconsummated male bonding? Why *were* we in Vietnam? As the procession of explanations moves farther and farther from solid, mineral ground, it moves closer to race. Not race as a natural category of difference (and even minerals acquire value from culture and not nature) but as a cultural field, inseparable from the economic and political forces it has helped to constitute.

Racial conflict, as Richard Slotkin, Richard Drinnon, and I among many others have argued, created a distinctive American political culture. It linked freedom to expansion in nature rather than to social solidarity, to violent conquest of the racial other rather than to peaceful coexistence. The covert operator, "consummating an act of racial revenge or rescue," is the mythic hero of American expansion.[16] The rescue of the helpless female hostage from peoples of color established sexual as well as racial difference—against the threats of racial uprising, female independence, and the feminization of helpless white men, *Sudden Impact* transports the frontier myth into the city as well. "Make my day!"

The impact of the racial history of the United States transcends race —my third point—contaminating our political culture as a whole. The conflict in the New World between Protestant bourgeois white men and peoples of color not only produced a racial demonology but underlies the broader countersubversive tradition in American politics. Racial and political demonology are often explicitly linked, as in the hostility to aliens in *Murder in the Air,* and as among the government officials and media spokespeople who fantasized a racial massacre in Zaire. Zaire illustrates the interconnection between race and countersubversion because Cuban troops in Angola were held responsible for a conflict with which they had nothing to do. Balunda who had fled to Angola after the defeat of their effort to create an independent state (which put them on the "Right" in the cold war procrustean bed during the 1960s) were in 1978 trying to return home (which put them on the "Left").[17]

"The crisis of ethnocentricity in the beginning of the sixteenth century (and for a long time afterward)," to borrow Carlo Ginzburg's phrase, came about when Europeans discovered other places and peoples that did not revolve around them. But Europeans in the New World used this Copernican revolution in politics to make themselves the center again.[18] The claims of the Reagan Doctrine to roots in American history should thus not be lightly dismissed. The distinctiveness of Reagan's foreign policy lies elsewhere, not in its demonological vision per se but in the character of its cold war revival. For the cold war, by centering countersubversion in the national security state, marked a break with the past. That shift, in turn, had its origins in World War II, both structurally at the beginning of the cold war and in the career patterns and mentality of those who revived the cold war under Reagan. World War II, moreover, is the distinctive historical moment when the United States seems innocent of the charges of racial and political demonology. The birth of the national security state from out of "the good war" (as Studs Terkel has labeled it) produced the cold war's specular foreign policy.[19]

IV

Beginning with the cold war's origins in World War II, demonology has been used to dramatize and justify the covert spectacle. But if racial demonology organized American politics before the war, and if the war has organized our politics since, then the grip of the good war has importantly to do with how it seemed at once to justify demonology and to free American politics from the stigma of race.

World War II justified demonology because in that war we confronted a truly demonic foe. It is easy enough to show how the presence of Nazism distorted postwar politics; how the concept of totalitarianism promoted a binary division between the extremes of Right and Left on the one hand and the Free World on the other; how the resulting distinction between

authoritarianism and totalitarianism, well before Jeane Kirkpatrick re-
suscitated it,[20] was an empty placeholder faithful neither to the actual
domestic qualities of the regimes it contrasted nor to their ambitions
abroad but rather to their relationship to the United States; and how anti-
Communism justified both coups against democratic regimes—Guatemala, Iran, Chile—to protect them from totalitarianism and the embrace
of merely authoritarian regimes that (with our help) use death squads
and massive bombing against their own populations. A thought experiment might be able to reproduce all these effects in the absence of World
War II. In real historical time, however, World War II offered an objective
correlative for the countersubversion that preceded and succeeded it by
providing a genuinely demonic enemy bent on world conquest.

In so doing, in addition, the good war shifted the stigma of racialism from the United States to its enemies, Germany and Japan. Jim
Crow continued at home, of course, notably in the armed forces. American participation in the war had nothing to do with saving European
Jewry, moreover, and was, as David Wyman has shown, actively hostile
to efforts to do so.[21] That was hardly the dominant postwar perception,
however, and since racial murder was the centerpiece of Nazism and at
worst a sideshow for America, the good war seemed to bring to an end
the racial underpinnings of American demonology. Racialism had spread
from peoples of color to Southern and Eastern Europeans during the
alien and Red scares of the industrializing United States; before 1930
American history was more dominated than was German by racism. But
the New Deal and World War II could be seen as reversing the racialist direction of American politics and as beginning to bring American racism
to an end.

That is its effect on Ian Buruma, whom I quoted earlier and to whom
I now want to return. John Dower's recent book, *War Without Mercy: Race
and Power in the Pacific War,* shows the brutalizing, murderous impact of
racial hysteria on American and Japanese policy. Buruma disagrees; he
believes that "Dower overstates . . . the moral equivalence of both sides";
that what racism emerged against the Japanese "was more the result of
war . . . than the cause of it"; that the propaganda required by a mass
war should not be confused with the causes of the war; and that the easy,
postwar resumption of friendship with Japan shows the superficiality
of negative racial stereotypes during the war. One has to distinguish,
Buruma writes, the Nazi war against the Jews and the American conflict with Japan. "Jews were killed because they were Jews. Japanese got
killed because they were part of a nation bent on military conquest." My

quarrel is not with the distinction between Nazi genocide and American racism, but with using that distinction to obliterate the racial character of America's war with Japan and—Buruma's explicit project—the character of subsequent American foreign policy.[22]

To take first the war against Japan: surely Buruma would at least acknowledge the racist basis for the internment of Japanese-Americans during the war. However, he suggests instead that the differing attitudes toward Germans and Japanese were based on "logical reasons that Dower does not take into account. Japanese-Americans, being relatively recent immigrants, still lived in highly visible, culturally distinct communities," explains Buruma. "'Good' Germans were acknowledged simply because there were more of them," that is, refugees from Nazi terror.[23]

Why does Buruma normalize Japanese internment? The good war has wiped out of his historical memory the exclusion of Japanese from America and the racially based residential segregation of those who were here. It has made him forget that the Italians, more recent immigrants than the Japanese, were not rounded up, deprived of their liberty and property without due process of law, and placed in concentration camps. Buruma suppresses not only the racially based exclusion of thousands of good Germans, Jews, from the United States but also the presence of many bad Germans, the thousands of organized and active supporters of Nazism in the German-American Bund who were not rounded up and jailed. He has forgotten that, underneath the fantasies about Japanese aliens, about the disloyalty not only of Japanese born in Japan but of those born in the United States as well, there simply were no bad Japanese. He fails to cite the racist justifications for Japanese internment by high United States and West Coast state officials who could cite no evidence at all of Japanese disloyalty or of any danger to American security. Buruma neglects one of Dower's most telling findings, that although cartoons and propaganda against Germany during the war depicted Hitler and Nazism rather than the Germans as the enemy, the demon in the Pacific war was the depersonalized "Jap." Thus a July 1942 *Washington Post* cartoon captioned "Mimic" shows Hitler destroying the towns of Lidice and Lezaky in the foreground, while in the background a gorilla labeled "Jap" tramples Cebu. Cartoon Japanese are apes and rodents; American leaders (sounding like cartoon figures but wielding real power) call for their extermination. "The Japs will be worried about all the time until they are wiped off the face of the map," warned Lt. Gen. John Dewitt, who headed the Western Defense Command and interned the Japanese-Americans. Marines wore "Rodent Exterminator" on their helmets, and a *Leatherneck* cartoon in March 1945 showed a Japanese "lice epidemic." "To the Marine Corps," reads the caption, "was assigned the gigantic task of extermination." That cartoon appeared the same month that the firebombing of Tokyo killed on a single night 80,000 to 100,000 Japanese—fewer than would soon die on a single night in Hiroshima, more than Nagasaki.[24]

Dresden and Hamburg were firebombed before Tokyo, to be sure; World War I's depersonalized, mass killing preceded them all. But instead of citing indiscriminate mass slaughter to minimize the significance of racism, one might better remember the racially imperialist prehistory of World War I, a war produced not only from imperialist rivalries in Lenin's sense but also from the brutalizations of colored peoples, Slavs, Jews, and others viewed as racially inferior.[25]

The Tokyo firebombing, defended as an effort to break the Japanese fighting will, was aimed at no material, military targets. It was psychological warfare, a spectacle to terrorize, demoralize, and destroy the civilian, Japanese mass public. And that firebombing produced another spectacular during the cold war. In the Hollywood, anti-Communist parable *Them!*, the Japanese rodents reappeared as giant ants, mutations from a desert atomic explosion. In history the atom bomb destroyed those labeled rodents; in fantasy it created them in order to destroy them again. At the climax of *Them!*, the ants are traced to their breeding ground, with its strong "brood odor," in the storm drains under Los Angeles. They are obliterated in a holocaust of fire. What looks like futuristic science fiction is actually, in the service of anti-Communism, a record of the firebombing of the past. Gordon Douglas, who had also directed *I Was a Communist for the FBI*, was putting on screen the injunction in *Leatherneck* that, "before a complete cure may be effected, the origins of the Plague, the breeding grounds in the Tokyo area, must be completely annihilated." Failing to accept responsibility for the hundreds of thousands of Japanese deaths by firebombs and atomic destruction, Hollywood made nuclear explosions reproduce the rodents who, now become Communists, had to be wiped out all over again.[26]

The firebombing of Tokyo also produced movies of another sort. Unlike *Them!*, which was made for a mass audience, these were part of a covert operation, "one of the better-kept secrets of the war, ranking up with the atomic bomb project." "Everyone who has ever seen a picture based on World War II" will, according to their narrator, recognize the briefing in which he supplied the voice-over. To prepare real pilots to bomb Tokyo, Hollywood special effects men built a complete miniature of the city for simulated bombing runs. They "intercut their movies of the model with real scenes taken from flights over Tokyo," thereby creating a series of movies that taught pilots about the real thing. Each movie concluded when the narrator said, "Bombs away." The narrator who has been describing his role in World War II is Capt. Ronald Reagan. After I read this account in his autobiography and then wrote about it, I stressed how, to make himself a participant in the war while he was actually stationed in Hollywood, Reagan had broken down the distinction between filmed war and real war, simulated bombing runs and real bombs: "As a result, none of the explosives in his account, from the bombs he narrates to the atomic bomb, fall on real targets."[27] But I was still being taken in, for Reagan is not simply pretending to have participated in a war but is also distancing himself from the real bombs his movie instructions helped drop. The actual people at risk were the inhabitants of Tokyo; as Reagan tells the story, he becomes the secret agent close to danger. Turning his covert operation into spectacle, Reagan has made invisible the real, obliterated Japanese. The white man, in no danger himself, cinematically participates in killing men, women, and children of color. "Make my day!"

When the Japanese government mercilessly bombed the civilian population of China in 1938, the United States Senate denounced "this crime against humanity . . . reminiscent of the cruelties perpetrated by primitive and barbarous nations upon inoffensive peoples."[28] The rhetoric of this condemnation blamed modern total war on American Indians. It helped prepare the United States, in the name of fighting savages, to imitate them, or rather, *Them!*—not historical Indians, but the monsters recreated in the imperial mind.

V

World War II laid the structural foundations in politics for the modern American empire. First, the good war established the military industrial state as the basis for both domestic welfare and foreign policy. Second, it made surveillance and covert operations, at home and abroad, an integral part of the state. Third, it drew the political parties together behind an interventionist, bipartisan foreign policy directed by Democrats during the major wars (World War II, Korea, and Vietnam) and by the former Democrat, Ronald Reagan, in the 1980s. Fourth, the good war's popularity linked the mass public to the structures of power. Mass enthusiasm for the national security state could not be mobilized for subsequent hot wars and was actually threatened by them. Nevertheless, only for a few years during and after the American defeat in Vietnam were the fundamental assumptions about America's role in the world established during World War II ever challenged by significant sectors within American politics. Finally, World War II celebrated the undercover struggle of good against evil, and thereby prepared the way for the covert spectacle.

World War II slid easily into the cold war, as Communism replaced Nazism and one Asian enemy, China, took the place of another, Japan (so that the Japanese demons of World War II movies could be recycled within the decade as Hollywood North Koreans and Chinese).[29] But the cold war was fought mainly with symbols and surrogates. It organized politics around ideology and conspiracy (Communists in government at home, secret interventions abroad) just as ideology was supposed to be coming to an end. It may be, as Fred Block argues, that the state recognized its need to play a foreign, economic role as the alternative to domestic social reconstruction and recast economic challenges as cold war and military ones to mobilize popular support. In any case, Richard Barnet suggests, the permanent mobilization of the American population—to sustain high taxes, foreign aid, interventionist state policies, and ongoing international alliances—marks a fundamental break with the peacetime past. The worry in the now famous National Security Council memorandum no. 68 as the cold war began—that America would be crippled by internal weakness at the moment of its greatest strength—reflected the state's new economic and security role and the fear that the population would not support it. Genuinely covert actions were one response to fears of popular flaccidity; the politics of spectacle as political mobilization was the other.[30]

The spread both of covert operations and of foreign policy as spectacle responded to the tensions among economy, state, organs of public opinion, and instruments of nuclear war that emerged in the shift from World War II to the cold war and that were accentuated at the end of the first cold war period with the American defeat in Vietnam. Postwar worries about the weakness of the American state nonetheless presumed an American hegemony that more recent economic and political developments have called into question. A multinational-dominated internationalized economy that resists state control sets the stage for defensive, American nationalism. The sources for that nationalism lie in state structures that lack the power either to control the economy or to mobilize the populace and so turn to covert action and the spectacle; in the political economy of the military-industrial complex; in a nuclear-dominated military strategy, where weapons function as symbols of intentions in war games rather than as evidence of war-fighting capabilities; and in the permeation of public and private space by the fiction-making visual media.[31]

Public anti-Communist mobilization operated alongside genuinely covert operations in the early cold war years, the one to engage masses, the other to serve the interests of elites. That separation broke down with John Kennedy, however, for whom the theory and practice of foreign interventions served less to preserve imperial interests than to demonstrate the firmness of American will. Vietnam functioned as the most important theater of destruction, from Kennedy's Green Beret adventurism through Nixon's expansion of the war to test our resolve to meet a future "real crisis."[32] But Vietnam failed as symbolic foreign policy, not just because the United States lost the war but also because American suffering and turmoil could not immediately be dissolved into spectacle.

The full-fledged absorption of American foreign policy by symbolic gesture, therefore, awaited the Reagan presidency. The men whose consciousness was formed by World War II revived the American empire after Vietnam—Paul Nitze and the other members of the Committee on the Present Danger, who prepared the ideological ground for the Reagan administration; William Casey, who moved from the wartime OSS to direct first Reagan's presidential campaign and then the CIA (and, as he shifted from electoral spectacle to secrecy, to subordinate intelligence collection to covert activities); and Reagan himself, who made training and morale movies during the war and who met the crisis in his personal and professional life after it by leading the fight against Hollywood Communism.[33] The Reagan Doctrine—inspired by the ideological adventurer Jack Wheeler, known as the "Indiana Jones of the right"[34]—recuperated in political theater what had been lost in imperial substance. A foreign policy run from the expanded, hidden, militarized National Security Council aimed, by reversing Vietnam ("Do we get to win this time?" Rambo wants to know), to reenact the good war as a movie.

The covert spectacle thus reflects the persistence of dreams about American dominance in the face of the erosion of the material and ideological sources for American preeminence in the world. The budgetary and political demands that the American government inflicts on its people in the name of military and national security contribute, to be sure, to trade and budget deficits and economic decay. But at the same time the decline in a solidly based American preeminence has generated efforts at symbolic recovery that center around military and national security. This combat with the Soviet Union takes two forms: a visible military buildup in weapons that cannot be used and low-intensity (as they are called) military interventions in the Third World. Together these demonstrate American resolution without substantial risks at home. Foreign policy is conducted by theatrical events—Grenada invasion, Libyan bombing, Persian Gulf flagging, Honduran "show of force"—staged for public consumption. These interventions may well succeed, but their significance lies less in stopping the local spread of "Communism" than in convincing elite and mass publics that America has the power to have its way. Substituting symbols for substance, these staged events constitute the politics of postmodernism, so long as one remembers that symbols produced for consumption at home and abroad have all too much substance for the victims of those symbols, the participant-observers on the ground in the Third World.[35]

Individual covert operations may serve specific corporate or national-security-clique interests, and the operations themselves are often (like Iran/Contra) hidden from domestic subjects who might hold them to political account. But even where the particular operation is supposed to remain secret, the government wants it known it has the power, secretly, to intervene. The payoff for many covert operations is their intended demonstration effect. The covert spectacle is a form of therapeutic politics. By focusing attention on itself, it aims to control not simply political power but knowledge.

Most obviously, the specular relation to political life has implications for democratic governance. Spectators gain vicarious participation in a narrative that, in the name of national security, justifies their exclusion from information and decision making. Covert operations as spectacle pacify domestic as well as foreign audiences, for they transform the political relation between rulers and citizens from accountability to entertainment. Vicarious participation, moreover, is also granted to the rulers themselves, for those who sponsor and promote covert action almost never place themselves at risk. Vicarious participation in the spectacle of the covert heals in fantasy and preserves in fact the separation of those who plan from those who kill and are killed, the separation that Richard Barnet has called bureaucratic homicide.[36]

Secrecy is a technique not just for vicarious inclusion and political exclusion, however, but also for defining the real. Covert actions, obscured by disinformation, require the state to lie. When John Poindexter denied that the Libyan bombing aimed to kill Qadaffi and defended the spread of disinformation about alleged Libyan terrorism as a strategy to keep the Libyan leader off balance, he also had a domestic purpose. He was orchestrating an entertainment that, in winning popular applause, would underline for the mass audience the need for secret planning, accountable to no one and to no standard of truth outside itself. Poindexter wanted a mass public that stopped asking what was true and what false because it knew which side it was on. The term for the psychology at which Poindexter aimed is *identification with the aggressor.* Destabilizing orienting cues from any source, the state was to become the single anchor in the midst of the shifting realities it displayed. And that would increase trust in government, for the less one experiences alternatives to power, the more one needs to see it as benign.

Aggression is thus not opposed to intimacy but rather a technique for producing it—much as, conversely, intimacy in the American president normalizes the violence he authorizes. The benign version of spectacle plays on our ontological insecurity by offering trust in the sources of information. That answers the question James Lardner recently asked in his review of *Broadcast News:* "Why are the networks' anchormen so much more vivid to us than the stories they present?"[37] Presidential intimacy, as in the "giant womb" Garry Wills described at the 1984 Republican convention, or Bush's call for a "kinder, gentler nation" four years later, offers us the security of trusting the head of state as much as we trusted Walter Cronkite.

The form promoted by political infantilization is reliance on central power; its content is reassurance that we can continue to live in the (fantasized) past. Aspirations to appropriate basic trust may well fall short, into mass cynicism and withdrawal. But they do succeed in investing the imaginary with as much truth effect as the real—or rather, I have been arguing, the other way around. Where political spectacles compel attention and are not turned off, they acquire the power of fiction. For why should the mass audience be able to tell the difference between TV series and movies and the political spectacles that also appear on the screen, so long as the reality principle never reaches, directly and forcefully, into their lives (as it did, for example, in the 1930s depression or the 1960s draft)? The spectacle aims either to keep the reality principle entirely at bay (Star Wars as invisible shield) or to seize control of the interpretations placed on its intrusions (Star Wars shifts the terms of political debate from aggressive American preparations to win a nuclear war to the pros and cons of nuclear defense).

The covert spectacle thus breaks down the distinction between politics and theater (or rather, movies)—from the one side in police, spy, adventure, and science-fiction thrillers (including old movies starring Ronald Reagan) where the audience is privy to the hidden world of counterinsurgency warfare, and from the other side in Reagan's invocation of lines from such movies and reenactments of their plots—in his praise to Oliver North on the day he fired him that the events that had made North a "national hero" would "make a great movie."[38]

This movie reenactment of history, whether directed from Hollywood or from Washington, puts few Americans at risk. Instead of actually refighting the Second World War, it enlists Third World peoples as surrogates. The covert spectacle is thereby grounded in the history of American expansion, not eastward against established European powers but westward and southward against vulnerable racial others. But the 1960s, by recovering imperial history in civil rights struggle and Vietnam, challenged the racial constitution of American national identity. The Reagan doctrine had to forget, therefore, the moment in which American history was remembered.

VI

"The crisis in ideological confidence of the 70s, visible on all levels of American culture and variously enacted in Hollywood's 'incoherent texts,' has not been resolved," writes Robin Wood in *Hollywood from Vietnam to Reagan*. "Instead it has been forgotten." Wood is referring to the shocks administered to the dominant (white male) politics and culture by black protest, Vietnam, and the emergence of a mass-based feminism. Two 1967 Sidney Potier movies, as Ed Guerrero has argued, represented Hollywood's last effort to incorporate race into liberalism. These twin celebrations of the black, middle-class professional, *Guess Who's Coming to Dinner* and *In the Heat of the Night*, together won seven Academy Awards. But Hollywood containment exploded the next year—in the Tet offensive, on the streets of America's inner cities, at the Chicago Democratic National Convention, and with the assassinations of Robert Kennedy and Martin Luther King, Jr. Wood analyzed the Hollywood movies that registered cultural breakdown without being able to resolve it. Ella Taylor has offered a comparable interpretation of the (more domesticated) space opened up on 1970s television, undercutting the traditional family and finding refuge in imagined workplace communities. The Carter presidency would lend itself to similar treatment.[39]

The Reagan regime put America back together again by exploiting and disavowing the 1960s. On the one hand, Reagan capitalized on the sharpest electoral polarization in American history along race and gender lines. Beginning in 1968, a large majority of whites (overwhelming in every election but 1976) has opposed the presidential choice of a large majority of peoples of color. Beginning in 1980 men have voted more strongly Republican for president than have women. No president since James Monroe has received as enormous a share of the white male vote as Reagan received in 1984—75 percent by my rough calculation, if Jewish voters are excluded—and the gap between men and women was as large or larger in the presidential vote four years later. On the other hand, since the 1960s subversive, colored, and female voices have called into question the racial and political demonology that often silenced such voices in the past.

The response to this double pressure, which undercuts the Reagan regime's claims to universality as they are being made, is regression. Hollywood in the 1980s has been dominated, writes Wood, by "children's films conceived and marketed largely for adults," an analysis that applies to Washington as well. Even if not technically science fiction (like *Star Wars*, the movie, and Star Wars, the weapon), 1980s films restore traditional race and gender divisions by abandoning pretensions to verisimilitude. "The audiences who wish to be constructed as children also wish to regard themselves as extremely sophisticated and 'modern,'" Wood explains, and they do so by admiring the skills with which they have been infantilized. Production is not hidden as the real source of power; it rather appears on the surface as one more display. Taking pleasure from production numbers, in film terminology, from the special effects of spin doctors, in the language of political campaigns, audiences enjoy at once the effects produced on them and the way those effects are produced. "We both know and don't know that we are watching special effects, technological fakery," Wood writes, suggesting that being in on the infantilizing tricks allows one to regress and enjoy them.[40]

The self-aware quality of the mass spectacle, to which postmodernism points, should thus be read not as a sign of maturity but as an escape from troubling depths so that their residues can safely appear on the surface. As the mass public withdraws from political engagement to spectacles, lo and behold it watches self-ironizing—*Indiana Jones*—or self-pitying—*Rambo*—displays of racial demonology. Fredric Jameson once distinguished entrapping displays of nostalgia, which emphasize the beauty and accuracy of surface reproductions, from self-knowing forms of pastiche that create distance from the past.[41] He wrote before the politics and the movies of the Reagan years used self-knowingness to allow us to return to the past (or go *Back to the Future* in another movie invoked by the president) without having time travel remind us of what we now know we must not do. When an imperial white male wins a white woman in violent combat with evil, dark tribes, as in the Indiana Jones movies, everyone knows that these surface cartoons are not meant to be taken seriously. So we don't have to feel implicated in their displays, can think they are send-ups of 1930s serials rather than precipitates of current covert operations, and forget what we have seen. "Go ahead. Make my day!"

VII

George Bush might have borrowed his film criticism during the 1988 campaign from Robin Wood. "We have turned around the permissive philosophy of the 70s," Bush boasted, so that a society that once enjoyed movies like *Easy Rider* now prefers "Dirty Harry" films. "Clint Eastwood's answer to violent crime is 'Go ahead, make my day,'" Bush continued. "My opponent's answer is slightly different. His motto is, 'Go ahead, have a nice weekend.'" Bush was invoking, of course, the Massachusetts weekend furlough program under which Willie Horton, the black convicted murderer, had been allowed to leave prison. Horton, as the Bush campaign was making sure every American knew, had terrorized a white couple and raped the woman. The black criminal and white rapist whom Eastwood had dared to make his day had merged in the figure of Horton; Bush was casting Dukakis as the impotent liberal who could not protect his wife. The buddies who went seeking America, according to the advertising campaign for *Easy Rider*, and "couldn't find it anywhere" had in Bush's movie reviews turned into Dukakis and Horton.[42]

Bush's campaign was not the first attempt to organize American politics around the specter of interracial rape. Repeated ads showing a revolving prison door, combined with the Horton victim's well-advertised campaign tour for Bush, reproduced *The Birth of a Nation*.[43] Attacking Dukakis as weak on defense as well as on violent crime, moreover, the Bush campaign linked imperial to domestic racial politics, for the Dukakis of Bush's television ads would make Americans vulnerable to aliens abroad and at home. Open racist appeals were now forbidden, however, and Bush (and his supporters in my presidency class) denied that Bush's version of "Make my day!" had anything to do with race. But the Republican candidate had succeeded in replacing Jesse Jackson with Willie

Horton as the dominant black face in the campaign. For the first time, several of my students then remembered the racial and sexual context for "Make my day!"

That memory of the racial antagonism he promoted posed a problem for Bush, however, to which he offered a solution after his victory. The solution was amnesia. Along with two other movie phrases popularized by President Reagan—"Win one for the Gipper," from *Knute Rockne, All American*, and "the Evil Empire," from *Star Wars*—"Make my day!" will be included in the new edition of *Bartlett's Book of Famous Quotations*. If Bush has his way, however, the words will be severed from their meaning. "The American people," the new president reassured us after his election, "are wonderful when it comes to understanding when a campaign ends and the work of business begins." Bush wanted Americans to believe that his campaign spectacle would have nothing to do with his conduct of government. He was making his business that "great act of American amnesia," as political scientist James Barber called it on election night, by which our politics forgets the forces that drive it. The new president brushed off Barbara Walters's questions about the campaign on the eve of his inauguration. "That's history," said George Bush. "That doesn't mean anything any more."[44]

VIII "Make My Day!": The Sequel

First presented in 1988, in the wake of Iran/Contra, the essay you have just read was revised and first published as the cold war was coming to an end. Far from exhausting the foreign policy of spectacle and secrecy, demonology and male heroism, the end of the cold war underlined its shooting location in the Third World. The campaign history that George Bush disavowed from the White House returned to organize the war against Iraq. The president who invoked the sexual harassment of a U.S. soldier's wife as the last straw justifying the Panama invasion went into what Elizabeth Drew called his "Clint Eastwood routine," boasting that Saddam (putting their relationship on a first name basis) "is going to get his ass kicked" because, in Bush's words, "Saddam Hussein systematically raped, pillaged, and plundered a tiny nation." The president's personalized involvement with the man whose name he mispronounced to suggest the biblical Sodom implied that the feminized object of rescue hid what really mattered, the fatal embrace between men. There was even a woman (ambassador April Glaspie) who, as in *Sudden Impact*, had led the rapist on and from whom the leader of the rescue operation would differentiate himself.[45]

But the very obviousness with which the Iraq war made Bush's day seems to subordinate the Hollywood spectacle of rape and rescue to the military-industrial complex, multinational corporations, and the national security state. Surely imperial interest explains the war, and imperial culture is simply its fig leaf and instrument.

Here one must distinguish the causes of the war from its character. The split in the national security bureaucracy about whether to support war (as opposed to sanctions) points to the difficulty, acknowledged since NSC-68 at the cold war's onset, of enlisting the American people behind American interventions abroad. That problem was intensified, of course, by the Vietnam syndrome, in which a country that "raped, pillaged, and plundered a tiny nation" blamed the lost war on home-front betrayal.

If mobilization of domestic support is inseparable from the push to war, then we can bring the causes of the war home. The effect of Iraq holding Kuwait hostage for a prolonged period was a domestic political threat, the sort that had destroyed the Carter presidency, and this at a moment when budget and tax humiliations had produced a precipitous drop in Bush's popularity. Acquiring a heroic identity based in violence, Bush replaced the self identified with class self-interest and domestic vacillation. In the terms that emerge from Susan Jeffords's and Lynda Boose's essays in this volume, he reintegrated the incoherent, hysterical, male self into a managerial structure of violence. From the beginning the decisive force for military intervention was the chief of state.

Given the central place of the home front in the push to war, foreign and domestic politics, national security and political security (to recall Nixon's Watergate defense) cannot be disentangled. Legitimate disagreements about the causes of the war, moreover, or about whether Bush and his circle were outside of the culture of war or produced and caught up in it, should not affect consideration of the war's character.

What, then, does the war culture mean? It means, first, the effort to replace the war actually being fought by a fictional, imaginary one. *The New York Times*, October 6, 1991, reports,

> President Bush provides a special introduction tonight in an ABC television movie called "Heroes of Desert Storm," which mixes news coverage of the Persian Gulf war with dramatic recreations of events. . . . The President also appear[s] several more times in the movie, in news reports. . . . Extensive videotape from the war . . . has been mixed with the scripted dramatic scenes in a format conceived to make indistinguishable the distinction be-

tween reality and movie. . . . Before it begins, ABC will televise a disclaimer that says the movie used this technique "to achieve realism." . . . "We're telling a real story," Mr. Ohlymeyer said, "When we show a tank being blown up, what's the difference whether it was news footage or whether we blew it up ourselves?"[46]

What's the difference, after all, between "Heroes of Desert Storm" and the staging of a mock battle during the Spanish-American War to exclude Filipino insurgents from the capture of Manila, in the war that, with its pseudo-documentary, filmed scenes, stands at the origins both of American overseas expansion and motion pictures? Or Captain Ronald Reagan's World War II Japanese bombing movie? Or military censors changing the quotes of air force pilots, deleting as well the information that pilots watched pornographic movies to psyche themselves up for their bombing runs? Or the military selecting from the hundreds of thousands of bombing videos produced each day one or two for televison viewing that showed bombs, especially smart bombs, hitting their targets (rather than releasing the 70 percent that showed them missing)? Or an international politics in which heads of state signal one another ("Make my day!") by their willingness to sacrifice other people's lives, what Christopher Hitchens calls the "epic movie," "Metternich of Arabia"? What's the difference between ABC's "The Heroes of Desert Storm" and the one Bush produced for domestic consumption?[47]

The president's Heroes of Desert Storm had to launder, at once use and deny, American expansion against and domination of peoples of color, the preparation, in Edward Said's terms, for the United States to succeed to the European, imperial role. Thus, the invocation of the racial rapist coexists with the incorporation of African Americans into the army, used, as they have been since Teddy Roosevelt's black regiments in Cuba (and, retrospectively, by *Glory,* for the Civil War), but with special urgency since the Civil Rights movement, the Vietnam War, and the increased devastation of the ghettoes, to show how America cares for and makes use of its former slaves. Colored troops are incorporated into the military, their loyalty and bravery (in what can now be called the *Driving Miss Daisy*/Clarence Thomas effect) contrasted, along the lines proposed by the Moynihan Report long ago, to the absent-father, matriarchally dominated, ghetto pathology (Clarence Thomas's sister on welfare, for example) of drugs and crime.[48]

Indians, like blacks, find a double place in Gulf War culture. Indeed, it took the Oakland Black Panther newspaper to point out that the ubiquitous yellow ribbon—worn, for example, by Los Angeles TV newscasters during the war's early days—invoked support for the Indian-fighting cavalry. The yellow ribbon entered cold war culture with John Ford's *She Wore a Yellow Ribbon* (1949), which used Indian massacre (beginning with Custer's last stand) to teach the country a hit song and the heroine to relinquish the female willfulness that cost soldier lives and to play her proper role of domestic support. Bush could not openly invoke Indian war, however. He introduced "Heroes of Desert Storm" in front of a picture of Andrew Jackson, evoking as well other generals "who led us in time of war." Four of these generals became presidents; Bush, Walter Goodman pointed out, was casting himself as the president who became a general. To name Indians, however, would have explicitly reminded viewers, as the yellow ribbon did only in the political unconscious, that the history of American heroism in war has mainly pitted white men against militarily weaker and racially stigmatized foes; Bush invoked Jackson as the Hero of New Orleans, not of the Creek War. Incorporated culturally, as forebears by the Apache helicopter used against Iraq, worthy opponents by the yellow ribbon, noble savages help render invisible contemporary Indians living unromantically and in poverty on reservations and in urban downtowns.[49]

World War II's racial reversal, the lynchpin connecting an expansionist, Jim Crow history at home to cold war foreign policy, was recycled for the Gulf war, since the quintessential racial victims of World War II were now found in the Middle East. Bush, moreover, may well have taken to heart Henry Stimson's address to his Andover graduating class that his generation would find its historical mission in fighting international aggression, thereby helping inspire the president to transfer World War II to the Persian Gulf and displace Reagan as the successor to FDR. In an inversion of Reagan at Bitburg, with the same insensitivity and political purpose, the presidential "Saddam is worse than Hitler" made obscene political use of Judeocide. The *New Republic* featured Saddam Hussein with his moustache subtly cropped to resemble Hitler's (the doctoring acknowledged only in fine print in the photo credits on an inside page).[50]

The debate over whether Saddam was being demonized, or was as bad as the war supporters painted him, missed the point three times over. No reader of Samir al Khalil's *The Republic of Fear* will want to defend Saddam Hussein against the Hitler accusation—just as accurate when, ignoring the Munich analogy it would later invoke, the administration was secretly selling arms and giving intelligence to Iraq, and looking the other way over the Iraqi threat to Kuwait. Demonization worked not to make Saddam Hussein worse than he was but to (1) take his regime out of the history of the Persian Gulf, from imperial interventions after World War I to U.S. support the day before yesterday, and to efface regional conflicts as well; (2) make him a monster on so large a world scale as to require war for our self-preservation, and dissolve overwhelming American military superiority ("Make my day!") into a contest of equals; and (3) reduce all Iraqis to pieces of Saddam Hussein's monstrous body. Sometimes that made Iraqi soldiers into "cockroaches," in the words of a U.S. Marine lieutenant colonel, scurrying for cover from his plane. More often, Iraqis simply disappeared. When the *Washington Post* compared "U.S. combat casualties" with "Iraqi losses," the newspaper listed American human beings on one side of the ledger, Iraqi planes, tanks and other military hardware on the other. Ted Koppel's "Quiet night in the Middle East," "aside from the Scud missile that landed in Tel Aviv," erased the 2,000 obliterating sorties on Baghdad. Bush's claim that our quarrel was with "Saddam" and not ordinary Iraqis was confirmed in the following way: Saddam Hussein is still in power, useful to the new world order as ongoing target and regional stabilizer, and hundreds of thousands of Iraqis and other Middle Easterners are stateless, devastated, dead or about to die.[51]

Satan's body on one side, Bush as God's instrument on the other. As Iraqis are the disappeared, atomized into their leader, the political spectacle mobilizes Americans in the simulacric body of the head of state. "At home war healed several wounds," was the *New York Times* front page headline the day after the Iraqi surrender. The war that, after Viet Nam, made America whole again inflicted losses, to be sure, but "A Region Suffers Grief," the headline of the smaller story inset into the larger one, referred not to the Middle East but to the Middle West, to, shades of *The Deer Hunter*, western Pennsylvania, home of thirteen army reservists killed in the final Scud attack of the war.[52]

In *The Origins of Totalitarianism*, Hannah Arendt described how racial thinking and an imperial bureaucracy imposed themselves on subjugated peoples, alternative to forms of popular accountability at home, and what happened when those structures and mentalities returned to domestic politics. The president of the United States claimed the right to make war without Congressional authorization; denied the plans for a troop buildup until it was a fait accompli that would foreclose alternatives to war (until, as with Vietnam in 1964, the election was over and the troops were on their way); and turned newspapers and television into instruments of the war state rather than investigators of it. The media itself, even without government censorship, devoted 1 percent of its news coverage of the Gulf crisis for the first four months to domestic opponents of Bush's policies, though a majority of the public opposed war. "'Make my day!,'" responding to the revival of covert operations—quintessentially, Iran/Contra—under the Reagan doctrine, gave central place to the spectacle of the covert. But although the Iraq war was a public spectacle, it was made possible by the hidden arrangements that led up to it, from the secret Reagan administration deals with Saddam Hussein through Bush's decision making after the Kuwait invasion. As in Arendt's analysis, the imperial hero, the secret agent, operates not only on alien ground but at the center of unaccountable power. The media functioned as the fourth branch of government to contribute to spectacle rather than to question the keeping of secrets.[53]

The Gulf war, to be sure, did not save President Bush from the economic reality principle at home. Nonetheless, it allowed him to leave office orchestrating military raids abroad rather than sunk in domestic disgrace. It bequeathed to his successor, moreover, not only the dance of death in Iraq but also an imperial culture at home that may well resurface should the new president fail to ameliorate America's enormous internal troubles.

Imperial culture brings home a discourse, of drugs, crime, quotas, family values, and male victimization, alternative to addressing the actual sources of domestic decay. Privatization referred, in "'Make my day!,'" to government unaccountability on the one hand and the invasion and political use of private life (replacing political judgment by personal identification) on the other. The word also points to efforts to seek private relief from public problems, in which identification with a nationalist state abroad facilitates the erosion of communal bonds at home.[54] Realpolitik, the term for the privatized, nationalist mentality in world politics, may stimulate fundamentalist rage around the world and separatism at home. Far from signifying the failure of Bush's war, however, the stimulation and repression of tribal passions (as they are called when other peoples express them) defines the new world order. That order returns us now to the days of yesteryear, to the homage *She Wore a Yellow Ribbon* pays to the professional soldiers "riding the outposts of the nation. Wherever they rode, and whatever they fought for [in the movie's final words], that place became the United States."

Notes

An earlier version of this paper was presented in the series "The Peculiarities of the American Empire," sponsored by the History Department, Rutgers University, April 29, 1988. The title of the session for which this paper was written was "The Postmodern Empire." I am grateful for the responses of Richard Barnet, Fred Block, Victoria de Grazia, and Michael Schaffer, who share responsibility for the differences between the paper they heard and this one. I have also benefited from the comments of Ann Banfield, Kathleen Moran, H. Bradford Westerfield, and members of the *Representations* editorial board. Reprinted (except for "The Sequel") from *Representations* 29: 99–123. Copyright 1990 by the Regents of the University of California.

1 There are risks in adopting the Inspector Dupin position, as D. A. Miller has pointed out to me most forcefully. It will position me as the subject supposed to know, detecting crimes that others overlook. Given the direction of the argument, this will cast me as the double of my white, male target, not only antagonizing white men who do not see themselves defined by imperial American political culture but also speaking for women and people of color in the name of coming to their defense. Acknowledging this risk hardly disarms it. But being unable to envision criticism without a place to stand, the best response I can make to such suspicions is the argument of the essay itself.

2 Samuel Kernell, *Going Public: New Strategies of Presidential Leadership* (Washington, D.C., 1986). The depiction of imperial political culture on which I am about to embark identifies operating mentalities, powerful forces, and individuals in whom they reside. I am concentrating on extreme tendencies that came to a head during the Reagan years and, as the current legal indictments facing some of these individuals attest, however powerful in our history and politics and however sanitized in respectable accounts thereof, they have not always gotten their way. Nonetheless, the Bush regime represents the normalization of the politics of the Reagan era, not their reversal. Anti-Communism undergirded the Reaganite shift from domestic welfare to military spending, the expansion of secret government, and the conduct of foreign policy as spectacle. The advertised end of the cold war has reversed none of these developments, and, insofar as the drug war and the defense of traditional family values inherit the role of anti-Communism, that will intensify what I link here to going public and going private in foreign policy, the racialist basis of American politics.

3 *San Francisco Chronicle*, March 19, 1987, p. 15.

4 The sources for this paragraph are Don Moldea, *Dark Victory* (New York, 1986); Garry Wills, *Innocents at Home* (New York, 1987); and Michael Rogin, *"Ronald Reagan," the Movie, and Other Episodes in Political Demonology* (Berkeley, 1987), pp. 1–43.

5 On *Hellcats* and the 1984 Republican convention, see Rogin, *"Reagan," the Movie*, pp. 40–42; Garry Wills, "More Than a Game," *New York Review of Books*, April 28, 1988, p. 3.

6 Robert Scheer, *With Enough Shovels: Reagan, Bush, and Nuclear War* (New York, 1982), pp. 36–65; *Contra Watch* 4–5 (May–June 1987): 3: Christopher Hitchens, "Minority Report," *Nation*, October 17, 1988, pp. 333–34.

7 Ian Buruma, "Us and Others," *New York Review of Books*, August 14, 1986, p. 24.

8 *San Francisco Examiner*, April 24, 1988, p. A-6; *New York Times*, April 30, 1988, p. 11; Rogin, *"Reagan," the Movie*, pp. 7–8; *San Francisco Chronicle*, April 13, 1988, p. 9; April 14, 1988, p. 20.

9 Russell Jacoby, *Social Amnesia* (Boston, 1975); and Fredric Jameson, *The Political Unconscious* (Ithaca, N.Y., 1981).

10 Thanks to Kathleen Moran for this argument, which is expanded in the following section.

11 Cf. T. J. Clark, *The Painting of Modern Life: Paris in the Art of Manet and His Followers* (Princeton, N.J., 1984), pp. 9, 68–69; Guy Debord, *Society of the Spectacle* (1967: Detroit, 1983); Jean Baudrillard, *Simulations* (New York, 1983), and "The Ecstasy of Communication," in *The Anti-Aesthetic: Essays in Postmodern Culture*, ed. Hal Foster (Port Townsend, Wash., 1983), pp. 126–34; Dana Polan, *Power and Paranoia: History, Narrative, and the American Cinema, 1940–1950* (New York, 1986), pp. 293–98; Fredric Jameson, "Postmodernism; or, the Cultural Logic of Late Capitalism," *New Left Review* 146 (July 1984): pp. 58–69.

12 For linking *Rambo* to Iran/Contra, I am indebted to Ronald Reagan, and I have analyzed the connection between Iran/Contra and *First Blood, Part I* and *Part II*, in "Ronbo," *London Review of Books*, October 13, 1988, pp. 7–9.

13 This formulation is indebted to Debord, *Society of the Spectacle*, and to Jacques Lacan, "The Mirror Stage as Formative of the Functions of the I as Revealed in Psychoanalytic Experience," *Ecrits*, trans. Alan Sheridan (New York, 1977), pp. 1–7.

14 Roland Marchand, *Advertising the American Dream: Making Way for Modernity, 1920–1940* (Berkeley, 1985).

15 Jonathan Kwitny, *Endless Enemies* (New York, 1986), pp. 11–14.

16 Richard Slotkin, *Regeneration Through Violence* (Middletown, Conn., 1973), and *The Fatal Environment* (New York, 1985); Richard Drinnon, *Facing West* (Minneapolis, 1980); Michael Rogin, *Fathers and Children: Andrew Jackson and the Subjugation of the American Indian* (New York, 1975), and *"Reagan," the Movie*. The quotation in the text is from Richard Slotkin, "The Continuity of Forms: Myth and Genre in Warner Brothers' *The Charge of the Light Brigade*," *Representations* 29 (Winter 1990), pp. 1–23.

17 Kwitny, *Endless Enemies*, pp. 13–15.

18 Carlo Ginsburg, *The Cheese and the Worms* (London, 1980), pp. 78, 92.

On the history of American demonology, see Rogin, "Political Repression in the United States," in *"Reagan," the Movie,* pp. 44–80 and passim.

19 Studs Terkel, *"The Good War"* (New York, 1984).

20 Jeane Kirkpatrick, "Dictatorships and Double Standards," *Commentary* 68 (November 1979): pp. 34–45.

21 David Wyman, *The Abandonment of the Jews* (New York, 1984).

22 See John Dower, *War Without Mercy: Race and Power in the Pacific War* (New York, 1986); and Buruma, "Us and Others," pp. 23–25.

23 Buruma, "Us and Others," p. 24.

24 Dower, *War Without Mercy,* pp. 34, 38–39, 78–92. See also Richard Drinnon, *Keeper of Concentration Camps: Dillon S. Myer and American Racism* (Berkeley, 1986); and Peter Irons, *Justice at War* (New York, 1983).

25 See Dower, *War Without Mercy,* p. 325; Buruma, "Us and Others," p. 25; Hannah Arendt, *The Origins of Totalitarianism* (New York, 1951).

26 I analyzed *Them!* in "Kiss Me Deadly: Communism, Motherhood, and Cold War Movies," *"Reagan," the Movie,* pp. 264–66, but did not make the connection to the Tokyo firebombing until reading *War Without Mercy;* see Dower, pp. 174–75; and, on depictions of Asians in Hollywood from World War II to Vietnam, Tom Engelhardt, "Ambush at Kamikazi Pass," *Bulletin of Concerned Asian Scholars* 3 (Winter–Spring 1971): 64–84.

27 Rogin, *"Reagan," the Movie,* p. 24.

28 Dower, *War Without Mercy,* pp. 38–39.

29 Engelhardt, "Ambush at Kamikazi Pass."

30 Fred Block, "Empire and Domestic Reform" (Paper delivered at the conference on "The Peculiarities of the American Empire," Rutgers University, April 29, 1988); Richard Barnet, comments at the same conference; James Fallows, *National Defense* (New York, 1981), pp. 162–63.

31 Of the enormous literature on these subjects, I have found particularly helpful Jonathan Schell, *The Time of Illusion* (New York, 1975); and Fallows, *National Defense.*

32 Cf. Garry Wills, *The Kennedy Imprisonment* (Boston, 1982); Bruce Miroff, *Pragmatic Illusions: The Presidential Politics of John F. Kennedy* (New York, 1976), pp. 35–166; Schell, *Time of Illusion,* pp. 90–95.

33 See Scheer, *With Enough Shovels;* and Rogin, *"Reagan," the Movie,* pp. 27–37.

34 Ben Bradlee, *Guts and Glory: The Rise and Fall of Oliver North* (New York, 1988), pp. 153–55.

35 Richard J. Barnet, "Reflections (National Security)," *New Yorker,* March 21, 1988, pp. 104–14; "Talk of the Town," *New Yorker,* April 4, 1988, p. 23.

36 Richard J. Barnet, *The Roots of War* (New York, 1972).

37 James Lardner, "Films," *Nation,* January 28, 1988, pp. 94–98.

38 *New York Times,* November 30, 1986, p. Y-12.

39 Robin Wood, *Hollywood from Vietnam to Reagan* (New York, 1986), p. 162; Edward Villaluz Guerrero, "The Ideology and Politics of Black Representation in U.S. Narrative Cinema" (Ph.D. diss., University of California, Berkeley, 1989), pp. 68–79; Ella Taylor, *Prime-Time Families* (Berkeley, 1989).

40 Wood, *Hollywood*, pp. 163–66.

41 Fredric Jameson, "The Shining," *Social Text* 4 (Fall 1981): 114.

42 Maureen Dowd, "Bush Boasts of Turnaround from 'Easy Rider' Society," *New York Times*, October 7, 1988, p. A-11; Elizabeth Drew, "Letter from Washington," *New Yorker*, October 31, 1988, p. 94; Wood, *Hollywood*, p. 228.

43 Cf. Michael Rogin, "'The Sword Became a Flashing Vision': D. W. Griffith's *Birth of a Nation*," in *"Reagan," the Movie*, pp. 190–235. Having written on the political significance of *Birth*, I was suffering from amnesia, and the connection between *Birth* and Willie Horton was pointed out to me by Martin Sanchez-Jankowski.

44 *New York Times*, November 28, 1988, p. B-4; *New Yorker*, November 21, 1988, p. 41; *International Herald Tribune*, January 21, 1989, p. 4.

45 Elizabeth Drew, "Washington Prepares for War," and George Bush, "The Liberation of Kuwait Has Begun," both in Micah L. Sifry and Christopher Cerf, eds., *The Gulf War Reader* (New York, 1991), pp. 182, 312. Subsequent citations will identify this volume as GW.

46 *New York Times*, October 6, 1991, p. 16.

47 Amy Kaplan, "Romancing the Empire: The Embodiment of American Masculinity in the Popular Historical Novel of the 1890s," *American Literary History* 2 (Fall 1990): 37; Robert Fisk, "Free to Report What We're Told," and Sidney H. Schanberg, "A Muzzle for the Press," GW, pp. 379, 370; Michael Linfield, "Hear No Evil, See No Evil, Speak No Evil: The Press and the Persian Gulf War," *Beverly Hills Bar Journal*, Summer 1991, p. 151; George Bush, "The Liberation of Kuwait Has Begun," and Christopher Hitchens, "Realpolitik in the Gulf: A Game Gone Tilt," GW, pp. 314, 108–9. I am especially indebted to the excellent article by Linfield, cited hereinafter as BHBJ.

48 On Roosevelt, see Alexander Saxton, *The Rise and Fall of the White Republic* (London and New York, 1990), pp. 372–74, and Amy Kaplan's paper in this volume. The Moynihan report explicitly proposed patriarchal discipline in the army as the alternative to black matriarchy in the ghetto.

49 Linfield, BHBJ, p. 150; Walter Goodman, "Using History to Serve Politics on TV," New York *Times*, October 7, 1991, p. B-2.

50 Drew, GW, p. 182; Linfield, BHBJ, p. 150.

51 Samir al Khalil, *The Republic of Fear* (Berkeley and Los Angeles, 1990); Murray Waas, "What Washington Gave Saddam for Christmas," GW, pp. 85–95; Fisk, GW, p. 379; Linfield, BHBJ, pp. 153, 150, 146.

52 *New York Times*, March 4, 1991, p. 1.

53 Hannah Arendt, *The Origins of Totalitarianism* (New York, 1973), pp. xvii–

xxii, 185–221; Theodore Draper, "Presidential Wars," *New York Review of Books* 38 (Sept. 26, 1991): 64–74; James Bennett, "How the Media Missed the Story," GW, pp. 355–61; Linfield, BHBJ, pp. 145–46, 149–50.

54 Cf. Lewis H. Lapham, "Onward Christian Soldiers," GW, pp. 458–59; Barbara Ehrenreich, *Fear of Falling* (New York, 1989).

Susan Jeffords

The Patriot System, or

Managerial Heroism

> He looked, Jake decided, like everybody else. It was as if the owner of that face had no personality of his own. The eyes stared out, slightly bored, promising nothing. Not great intelligence, not wit, not . . . Nothing was hidden behind the smooth brow, the calm, unemotional features.
>
>   Wrong. *Everything was hidden.*
> —Stephen Coonts, *Under Siege*

There have been numerous contextualizations of the 1990–91 war in the Persian Gulf. The most popular of these has been that voiced by President George Bush and General Norman Schwarzkopf, that the war would not be "another Vietnam." In such terms, the successes, rapidity, and advertised coherence of the war in the Persian Gulf could be seen as a kind of response to what is largely characterized as the failure, fatigue, and confusion of the Vietnam War. But while the Vietnam War has been the most frequently cited "history" of the Persian Gulf War, there have been other nominations as well for a historical referent to the war. Frederic Jameson has suggested that the war was in some ways a reaction to the Iran hostage crisis: "The collective defeat this war was supposed to make up for was not Vietnam but the endless media humiliation of the Iranian hostages."[1] Adam Meyerson has suggested that the war served at least in part as a response to the use of atomic bombs in World War II: "The Gulf war also lifts some of the burden of Hiroshima that has weighed so heavily on the Western psyche. The destructiveness of the atom bomb induced a tremendous sense of guilt among Western scientists who lost their moral self-confidence, and even began to question the search for knowledge itself."[2] What I would like to suggest here is a somewhat different contextualization of the war in the Persian Gulf, one that, I believe, holds more troubling and far-reaching implications than any of these cited above, that the war was sold and seems to have functioned as at least in part a response to the Iran/Contra scandal. To follow Oliver North's insight, "every new administration in Washington brings with it the memory of the worst catastrophes that affected its predecessors" (288).

Each of the contextualizations offers not only a historical referent for the war but figures a postwar future that is defined against what had come before. So, for those who perceive the war as a vindication of the U.S. military after the defeat of the Vietnam War, the Persian Gulf War marks a watershed, after which, presumably, no one will be able to lay charges of inefficiency, confusion, poor morale, or harassment at the door of the Pentagon or the U.S. government. Similarly, if the war serves as a response to the Iran hostage crisis, then the internal and external image of an international power held at its knees by a small, former "ally" will disappear. And, as Jameson argues, "the war is also supposed to serve as a warning to future Irans fully as much as to future Iraqs" (144). As for the Hiroshima connection, Meyerson goes on, "After the Scud attacks, it will be unconscionable for anyone to oppose missile defenses . . . [and] it will also be unconscionable to oppose the modernization of high-precision non-nuclear weapons that can defeat new Saddam Husseins" (2).

Military defeats, terrorism, missile defenses—each of these historical referents and overtures toward a redefined future speaks to overt U.S. activities. What I want to speak about here, and hope to address by suggesting the Iran/Contra connection, is the degree to which the war in the Persian Gulf functioned to reaffirm two activities in the public mind. First, and most straightforwardly, to reaffirm not simply the viability but the necessity for covert U.S. activities. I speak here not only of covert activities by the CIA or other U.S. government organizations, but also of what we might call the "covert" activities of U.S. culture in relation to the Persian Gulf War, looking finally at the "hidden" messages that the war's narrative was conveying both internally about the United States and externally about its relations to foreign governments (though as the circumstances surrounding Iran/Contra and the Persian Gulf War suggest, the lines between internal and external activities are increasingly blurred). Second, the war functioned to produce a "character" that will stand as the U.S. contribution to the New World Order, a character that serves as a quasi-technological imperial offering that reinforces U.S. interests in dominating that "new order." That character is one of management, operations, efficiency, and accomplishment. It came under challenge during Iran/Contra and resurged to make itself viable through the Persian Gulf War.

Let me begin by looking at one of the least covert elements of the military undertaking of the war, the Patriot missile.

Meyerson lists the "heroes" of the Persian Gulf War: Ronald Reagan, "whose military buildup made it possible"; General Schwarzkopf; the American and British troops (we might note in passing that Meyerson's estimations of troop performance fail to include any of the soldiers of other allied armies); President Bush; and "the designers of advanced weapons systems, whose pinpoint accuracy and near-perfect functioning destroyed the enemy's capacity to fight" (2). Writers John Huey and Nancy J. Perry of *Fortune* magazine summarize the public's changed attitude toward those weapons:

> Just a few months ago they were the furthest things from our minds, these deadly sleek appliances resting in what General Colin Powell calls his "toolbox" of war implements. . . . If we spoke of them at all, it was with pejoratives like "Pentagon toys" or "cost overruns." But suddenly . . . we know their nicknames, which are on our tongues in the fanciest restaurants and boardrooms, at loading docks, on factory floors, and in taverns.[3]

Huey and Perry go on to list those weapons: "We speak proudly of AWACS, Tomahawks, Hellfires, and Slams—above all, of the Patriot, the knight who parried the evil Scud right there in our family room" (34). As their imagery implies, the coverage of the Patriot missile—technically the U.S. Army/Raytheon Patriot weapon system—goes beyond the mere indication of a successful weapon and moves into the realm of the mythic, a rhetorical act not peculiar to these *Fortune* writers. Bruce A. Smith, in an article published in *Aviation Week and Space Technology*, describes the Patriot's performance like this: "The two systems [Patriots and Scuds] were part of a tense missile duel during the first week of the Persian Gulf War, pitting the relatively primitive Scud theater ballistic missile . . . against the sophisticated Patriot."[4] *Time* magazine even writes a role for the Patriot missile in the administration and media campaign to depict Saddam Hussein as another Adolf Hitler. In describing the history of the Scud missiles that were launched against Israel and Saudi Arabia, *Time* informs its readers that the "37-ft.-long Scud traces its lineage back to a 1940s design for the V-2 rocket, which the Nazis propelled into London in the waning days of World War II,"[5] thereby positioning the Patriot missile as the Allied effort to stop the extermination of the Jews.

The Patriot missile became a familiar image in U.S. television and print media during the Persian Gulf War. Television news programs carried action images much like the February 4, 1991, two-page photo spread in *Newsweek,* which depicts the firing of a Patriot missile over a Tel Aviv night sky. And photographs of Patriot missile cannisters, invariably with a missile emerging from its container, were used not only to illustrate stories about the missile or other weapons of the war, but came eventually to stand for the war itself, so that *Time* magazine identified its "letters" section on its war coverage with a Patriot missile firing, even though none of the letters referred to anything related to this weapon. And the Patriot missile was the second featured cover photo of the military technology magazine, *Aviation Week and Space Technology,* after the Navy Intruder plane, which was used in the first strikes against Iraq.

There are, indeed, some credible photographic reasons for the popular use of this weapon to illustrate and/or symbolize the war, especially in the print media. It is a somewhat less effective image to capture a plane dropping its bombs, and images from the video cameras aboard the "smart bombs" reproduced with a grainy quality, while images from the highly touted night-vision devices were equally difficult to discern. But the Patriot cannisters were stable, and the shot of the missile emerging from the cannister was dramatic, with the missile headed up to its target, exhaust exploding from behind, openly exhibiting the missile's power— something that a picture of a flying airplane cannot convey as well.

But there was, I suspect, more to the popularity of this weapon than simply that it was photogenic. What was equally if not more important was that the missiles were defined as *defensive* weapons. When the January 28, 1991, issue of *Time* magazine featured a story on the "High-Tech Payoff" of the military weapons of the war, its two-page spread showed photos of the Cruise missile, the Stealth fighter, electronic jamming, smart bombs, night-vision devices, and the Patriot missile. Breaking down its descriptions of each weapon into "purpose," "uses," "distinction," and "cost," *only* the Patriot missile's use was characterized as defensive, the "protection of ground facilities."[6] The full title of the weapon is often given as the "U.S. Army Patriot air defense system."[7] And, of course, the role of the weapon in the Persian Gulf War was depicted as explicitly defensive, defending first Israelis and then Saudi Arabians and U.S. soldiers from Iraqi missile attacks. As the title of one article put it, "Joint U.S.-Israeli Forces Use Patriots to Defend Against Iraqi Scud Missiles."[8] (We might also note here the use of "missile" to qualify the "Scud" title but not the "Patriot.") And in one of the great rhetorical reversals of the war, revealing the representational effectiveness of the defensive posture of this weapon, *Aviation Week and Space Technology* reported that "At least one of the Scuds shot down by Patriots in the first week of the war was headed for an area where 500 soldiers were located,"[9] placing the Allied soldiers, through metonymic connection with a "defensive" weapon, in a defensive position themselves, so that they can be characterized as the victims of Iraqi atrocities. To carry the "protective" function of the Patriot missile further, Angelo Codevilla extrapolates from the job the Patriot missiles did in the war to potential U.S. needs for antimissile systems at home.

> Patriot interceptors hit almost all of the 60 to 65 Scud missiles at which they were fired. . . . Every Israeli neighborhood, every allied unit, wanted a Patriot battery nearby. Americans at home asked whether, if Saddam had possessed long-range missiles, and had fired them at our homes, we would have been as well-protected as the Israelis? No, we would not have been protected at all![10]

Codevilla uses the Patriot missile's ostensibly clear "defensive" posture to appeal to Americans' felt needs for protection in order to justify enhancing U.S. antimissile systems.

The "defensive" characterization of the Patriot missile reinforces the image the United States wanted to convey of its own participation in the Persian Gulf War, as a defensive action prompted by the offensive attacks of Saddam Hussein. Whether depicting the United States as the ally of the victimized Kuwait—which had been "raped" by Saddam Hussein—or as a victim in its own right—losing oil resources—U.S. actions against Iraq could be seen as nonaggressive defensive necessities rather than aggressive, initiatory strikes. The popularity of the Patriot missile's defensive attitude worked as well to counteract some of the possible misgivings U.S. citizens might have had about the extensive bombings of Iraq going on at the same time. The images of "defensive" Patriot missiles could distract viewers from recognizing the U.S. bombings as outright attacks.

In the *Time* magazine essay on high-tech weapons, these missiles were referred to as the "Patriot system," acknowledging that the Patriot missiles did not operate individually or singly, but in concert with a series of other technological systems. The very operation of the missiles denies any single-combat idea, as the missiles are generally fired two at a time, from different directions, so that there is a higher chance of one hitting the target. But more than this, the missiles depend upon numerous other features. First, a crew that trains for thirty-six weeks on an Operator Tactics Trainer (in comparison, the training course for a battalion commander is eight to twelve weeks). Second, a radar system that depends upon an elaborate and sophisticated computer programming. And third, satellites that alert the missile batteries that Scud missile launches have occurred.

Each of these features of the "Patriot system" has its own manufacturers. The Patriot missile, made by Raytheon, is fired from a container built by Martin Marietta, who also assembles the missile and provides its controls, while the missile is propelled by a single-stage Thiokol solid rocket motor; the fuze is made by the Bendix corporation, and the warhead by Chamberlain. The Operations Tactics Trainer is made by Lockheed Sanders, while the operators are manufactured, if you will, by the U.S. Army.

More complex is the satellite system that alerts the Patriot missile batteries of a Scud missile launch. "In a typical scenario," *Aviation Week and Space Technology* explains, "USAF's Space Command informs the battalion's ICC [Information Coordination Central] of a Scud alert or Scud warning."[11] One satellite that was positioned over the Indian Ocean at all times during the war took infrared images of Iraqi territory every twelve seconds. If it detected the heat of a missile launch, it would send its data to an Air Force ground station in Woomera, Australia, and to the U.S. Space Command's Missile Warning Center near Colorado Springs. Information analyzed by computers at the Space Command Center would be sent, via satellite, to the Persian Gulf, both to alert air raid sirens and Patriot missile batteries. Some Patriot missile batteries were even equipped to receive the Scud missile launch information directly from the Space Command satellite. And, of course, these satellites must be put into orbit by a rocket, whether the Space Shuttle or a booster rocket, connecting them to NASA and the space system, as well as the companies that are involved in the manufacture of the rockets.

The $500,000 price tag on each Patriot missile is therefore, like most military expenditures, somewhat deceptive. What we need to look at is the "Patriot system," not just the individual missile. And while the cost of this entire system—Operation Tactics Trainers, soldiers, launchers, electrical connections, satellites, Command Center budgets, transportation, and manufacturing fees—is astounding, and certainly a lesson in how the military industry works, I am more interested here, not so much in what the Patriot missile itself costs, but in what it sells, what its "defensive" posture, its imagery, its professed statistics, and its price tag have been able to promote throughout and since the Persian Gulf War. The list is long and disturbing.

Most straightforwardly, the "success" of the Patriot missiles has sold, let's face it, more Patriot missiles. And not only to the U.S. Army. Israel and Saudi Arabia received Patriot missile batteries during the war, while the U.S. government decided later to sell them to Syria as well. Only two other countries were sold these weapons before the Persian Gulf War—Germany and the Netherlands—but there may be other potential buyers now. Each of the companies involved in the manufacture of these weapons will, in turn, be more profitable and be able to "sell" its stocks and productivity. In October 1991 the Raytheon Corporation opened a new company in Dubai—the Raytheon, Middle East Company—in order to increase its sales in the region.[12] The U.S. Army comes out well for training the crews that operated the batteries. And the initial apparent high percentage efficiency of the weapons could help to sell the satellites that enabled them to detect the Scud missiles so early.

But the list of what the Patriot missile sells is longer than this and relates to other weapons systems. As I mentioned earlier, Codevilla believes that the success of the Patriot missiles should sell the United States on an antimissile system for itself: "The lesson of the Scuds is that Americans ought to have as much protection against missiles as our technology can provide, and as soon as possible" (16). Others argue that the Patriot missile can support the flailing SDI program: "The success of the Patriot missile in knocking down the primitive Scuds . . . is certain to boost the budget hopes of those who back a far more sophisticated Star Wars system to shield the nation from ballistic missiles,"[13] an argument that President Bush made in his 1991 State of the Union address. As Ken Adelman, arms control director under Ronald Reagan, explains, "The Patriot is a sort of SDI Jr., based on the principles of the larger model."[14]

Certainly, like the entire war, the missile assisted in selling both George Bush and his foreign policy, while allowing that policy to be cloaked in nonaggressive rhetoric. (Acknowledging the connection between the Persian Gulf War and Bush's popularity, comedian Dana Carvey's *Saturday Night Live* impersonation of Bush's 1992 presidential campaign visit to a New Hampshire diner depicted Bush repeating the words, "Persian Gulf," every time he shook a voter's hand.) But the Patriot missile also accomplished something few thought possible, the redemption of Dan Quayle, since it was he who has been celebrated as "saving" the Patriot missile from Democratic budget cuts. As the conservative Codevilla explains it:

[I]n the early 1980s, grasping at the artificial distinction between "tactical" or short-range and "strategic" or long-range ballistic missiles, the Army set out to restore some of the Patriot's lost capability, with the help of then Senators Dan Quayle and Pete Wilson, and over the opposition of . . . the Democrat-controlled House of Representatives, which voted to kill the Patriot upgrade in 1986. It was restored by the then-Republican Senate. (17)

The role the Patriot missile plays in this scenario serves thus not only Dan Quayle but the entire Republican party and helps to malign the Democrats, without whom, Codevilla implies, thousands of Israelis would have died.

The installation of the Patriot missile batteries in Israel helped as well to enforce U.S. efforts to influence Israel's responses to Iraqi actions and to give the United States more control over its ally, while Germany's shipments of its Patriot missile batteries helped to alleviate any possible guilt its government may have felt over the sale of German manufacturing equipment to Iraq that was essential to the production of its poison gas (and could secondarily be linked to lingering historical guilts about German efforts to exterminate the Jews).

But there's still more. The Patriot missile is intertwined as well with network news programs, which brought entertainment images of Patriot missile launches and flashes of exploding Scuds in the sky; magazines, whose covers featured the forceful photographs of Patriot missile launches; videos, which feature U.S. weapons and military technology; baseball cards (the Patriot missile is #48 on the Operation Desert Storm trading cards checklist manufactured by Topps); Patriot missile rocket toys (manufactured by Estes Industries, whose earlier Scud model sold poorly compared to the "exceptional" demand for the Patriot missile toy);[15] the Desert Shield board game; the Desert Storm computer game, published by Interaction Software; even, in an oddly related way, journalist Arthur Kent, who became known as the "Scud Stud" during his broadcasts from Riyadh.

The "Patriot system" is then a pervasive and complex one that permeates not only military and military-industrial networks, but popular cultural representations as well. The Patriot system is more than an individual weapon, encompasses more than any single economic or foreign policy interest, and intersects with U.S. activities and interests both in the United States and abroad. It is through examining such a system as this, I would like to suggest, that we can begin to get a glimpse of how the New World Order that was the single greatest advertising campaign of the Persian Gulf War was being sold. In order to get a better look at how this sales pitch was worked, I want to turn now to another "Patriot system," this time one involving people instead of weapons.

During November 1985, when the office of the president was trying to engage in an arms-for-hostages exchange with Iran, the operation was bungled. Planes that were to originate in Israel, carrying the eighty TOW [tube-launched, optically guided, wire-tracked] missiles requested by Iran as barter for the U.S. hostages held in Lebanon, were unable to make their deliveries because they could not get clearance to land, change planes, and refuel in Lisbon. After a series of more direct U.S. interventions from the national security adviser, the CIA, the U.S. chargé d'affaires in Portugal, and members of the National Security Council staff, eighteen of the missiles were finally delivered by a plane chartered from a CIA proprietary in Germany and flown by West German pilots. When it was discovered that the wrong missiles had been sent by Israel—not those capable of hitting high-flying planes and containing Israeli markings—the Iranians involved declared that they had been betrayed and no hostages were released.

On November 26, Lieutenant Colonel Oliver North of the National Security Council staff and Vice Admiral John Poindexter, then deputy national security adviser and soon to be national security adviser, met to discuss these events. After a lengthy meeting, North made these notes:

—RR [Ronald Reagan] directed op[eration] to proceed
—If Israelis want to provide diff[erent] model, then we replenish
—*We will exercise mgt [management] over movmt [movement] if yr [your] side cannot do*
—*must have one of our people in on all activities* [16] (italics added)

As Theodore Draper assessed the position of those involved in the arms-for-hostages exchange at this point, "They [Reagan and Poindexter] were persuaded that the fault lay with the Israelis who had been in charge, not with the inherent folly of trading arms for hostages" (200). Or, as Draper put it more clearly later on, "Reagan and Poindexter were persuaded that the Israelis had bungled it and *that the Americans could do the same thing, only better*" (201; italics added).

In his autobiography, *Under Fire*, Oliver North exemplifies the attitude that "Americans could do the same thing, only better." He explains that McFarlane had asked him to "fix" the problems with the arms shipments: "'Fix it,' McFarlane had said, and that's all I needed to hear. It was the kind of challenge I thrived on, and I jumped right in. I can do it, I thought. I'm a Marine. This whole deal is screwed up, but I can take care of it."[17] Though others had "screwed up" the deal, North, with his special qualities, could "fix it."

What became apparent as the events that came to be known as Iran/Contra weaved on, was that the Americans couldn't do it "better," that, in fact, the Americans too had "bungled" the operation. What I want to get at in this section is how the Persian Gulf War and the popular culture that surrounded it struggled to repair the damages done to "American management" by the Iran/Contra affair, as well as the damages done to U.S. covert activities.

One of the figures whose role in the Iran/Contra activities still seems most muddled was, of course, George Bush, who seems still to have effectively escaped the brush that has painted lower-ranking members of the Reagan administration with blame for what happened in the arms-for-hostages deals.[18] But, as Hugh Sidey wrote for *Time* magazine, Bush's image was still not a strong one:

> Let's not forget those who derided [George Bush] as a wimp, a lapdog, every divorced woman's first husband, a terminal preppy. His painful politeness and unwavering loyalty to Ronald Reagan through mountainous deficits and Iran-*contra* bumbling raised the question of his backbone. He waffled on issues like abortion and taxes, and even his supporters wondered in dark moments about his inner stuff.[19]

But, in the wake of the changes brought about in Bush's image by the media presentations of the Persian Gulf War, Sidey goes on to conclude, not that Bush was ever really a "wimp," but that there's something wrong with current methods of forming political judgments: "What this may suggest is one more flaw in our system of political assessments" (55).

Media representations of popular opinion concur that Bush's performance during the Persian Gulf War was masterful, a performance that effectively altered his public image. In Adam Meyerson's words, "Whatever his many failures in domestic policy, George Bush will now go down in history as one of America's great commanders-in-chief."[20] But the way that Meyerson praises Bush is what relates the readjustment of Bush's image to Iran/Contra. As he goes on to say, "Primary credit [for the war victory] goes to President Bush, who prepared America and the free world for a war they did not initially want to fight, and gave the military the tools and the clear instructions it needed to get the job done" (2). Bush was to be praised, not as Lyndon Johnson would have been if the Vietnam War had gone differently, for personally making the correct strategic decisions about military targets and troop movements, but for giving "instructions," and for "preparing" U.S. citizens for a war "they did not initially want to fight." Bush's skills are then ones, not of military skill, but of management. Ann Reilly Dowd, writing for *Fortune* magazine, perceived this most clearly: "The President has focused his enormous energy on the *managerial tasks* proper to his role: setting goals, providing resources, monitoring progress, making strategic decisions, selling the war, and putting out periodic fires"[21] (italics added). As Dowd goes on to argue, it was precisely because Bush refused to act as Johnson and Carter had done—personally making military decisions—that he prosecuted the war so well: he has "effectively delegated the minute-to-minute conduct of the war to his generals" (12).

In prosecuting this "managerial style," Bush reaffirmed his power and that of the presidency, not through individual intervention and action, but through delegation, decision-making, goal-setting, and selling. What strikes me as important here is that Bush chose to respond to criticisms of him and of Reagan—both criticized for their roles in Iran/Contra—not through a negation of the Reagan hands-off management style, but through an effort to perfect it. To paraphrase what Draper says of Reagan and Poindexter, Bush was persuaded that he "could do the same thing, only better." Just as Reagan, Poindexter, and North had concluded that the problem with the Iranian deal was not its conception but its managers, Bush seems to have concluded that the problem with the Reagan foreign policy was not its philosophy, but its management. He would improve upon Ronald Reagan's presidency, not by altering its political judgments, but by improving its management effectiveness.

One of the reasons that Bush received such praise for this strategy and such support for his methods of pursuing the war was that he was not alone in propagating the importance of management style. "The Strong, Silent Type" that Northwest Mutual Life celebrated in its advertising during the war (*Newsweek*, February 4, 1991, p. 49) was being sold in supermarkets and bookstores all across the country in some of the best-selling novels of 1990 and 1991. While space prohibits discussing Stephen Coonts's *Under Siege* (1990) or Gerald Seymour's *Condition Black* (1990), it is Tom Clancy's 1991 novel, *The Sum of All Fears*, that best epitomizes the cultural frameworks that surrounded the Persian Gulf War and the management style that "won" it. Clancy's novel is especially appropriate because it addresses both the question of management style in an ineffective president and redeems the CIA as an intelligence service in the hero of the novel, Jack Ryan.

Briefly (though readers of Clancy's books know that this word is antithetical to his plots), the narrative hinges on a terrorist nuclear bombing of a Superbowl football game by Palestinians unhappy with a new peace arrangement in the Middle East. At the advice of a former member of the German Red Army Brigade who is unhappy with the unification of Germany, the bomb is detonated, not to gather attention for Palestinian demands, but to destabilize the new U.S.-Soviet rapprochements. As the terrorists designed, the bomb is taken to be a Soviet plot, and the United States is on the verge of launching an all-out "deterrant" first strike, when Jack Ryan, deputy director of the CIA, intervenes and prevents World War III.

The primary tension of the novel is between Jack Ryan and President Robert Fowler who, advised by Elizabeth Elliot, his national security adviser and lover, makes all the wrong decisions about the bombing. He disbelieves Soviet denials, misreads intelligence reports, and all-around bungles the job, so much so that he is impeached at the end of the novel. His biggest failure is not just listening to the hysterical Elliot, who overreacts to the bombing (because she and the president were supposed to go to the football game, she feels personally targeted and her fear takes over: when the president despairs, "All those people dead," Elliot thinks to herself, "And I could have been one of them"),[22] but *not* listening to the perceptive, informed, and highly reasonable Ryan, who is the only one present who understands what's going on (and who, to his credit in the narrative, has never liked Elliot). What is opposed in the novel, then, are two management styles: one, by the president, which listens only to the advisers personally (and intimately) connected to him; and the other, by Jack Ryan, whose strategy has always been to encourage dissenting opinions, especially on the part of those who openly disagree with him, and to coordinate the information provided by other reliable professionals. The president's worst move in this plot is to hang up the phone when Ryan tries to explain to him that the Soviets weren't responsible for the bomb and then to refuse to speak to him again. Ryan saves the day only by going against national security channels and speaking directly to the Soviet president on the hot line and asking him to back down his forces.

There are several things going on here. First, and most obviously, by having his hero be a rank-and-file member of the CIA, Clancy redeems the value, not only of the U.S. intelligence network (they do, after all, finally figure out who really set off the bomb), but also of the people who staff the chief intelligence-gathering agency in the U.S. government. While Clancy is obviously offering a justification for maintaining the CIA in a post-cold war era,[23] he is also redeeming the agency from its two biggest failures of the 1980s: having its director, William Casey, personally flaunt U.S. laws by prosecuting arms-for-hostages deals with Iran and failing to predict the downfall of the Soviet Union. And the way Clancy accomplishes this is important: not just through a validation of U.S. intelligence-gathering services, but through a celebration and heroization of the men who analyze that intelligence.

Significantly for Clancy, Ryan's is not a political appointment; he is instead a man who has learned the intelligence business from the ground up.[24] And, in the single most important word in Clancy's post-Iran/Contra vocabulary, Ryan is *professional*, or, as several characters phrase it, he does his job. This means, for Clancy, knowing how to gather information needed to make decisions and making those decisions without interference from personal emotions, especially fear. Professionals may feel fear, but they will not allow it to interfere with their ability to use logic, information, and experience to make the right decisions. In facing the Senate investigators of Iran/Contra, Oliver North says, "I was certainly angry, disgusted, embarrassed, and occasionally contentious, but fear didn't enter into it. The one time in my life when I had experienced real fear was in Vietnam, which may explain why I didn't feel it in the Senate Caucus Room. Once you've been shot at and hit in combat, everything else tends to pale by comparison" (355). Similarly, Jack Ryan's fearlessness is seen to stem from the fact that he's killed other people. In his tirade against the president's desire to drop a nuclear bomb on the Iranian city he believes sponsored the terrorist attack, Ryan reminds the president: "You need a better reason than that to kill people. I know. I've had to do that. I *have* killed people" (784). On this test of fear, Elizabeth Elliot fails. As one of the security guards assigned to guard the president concludes:

> Her face was—what? the Secret Service agent asked herself. It was beyond fear. Agent D'Agustino was every bit as frightened herself, but she didn't— that was unfair, wasn't it? Nobody was asking her for advice, nobody was asking her to make sense of this mess. Clearly, none of it made sense at all. It simply didn't. At least no one was asking her about it, *but that wasn't her job. It was Liz Elliot's job.* (739; italics added)

Now, in the novel, Liz Elliot *has* in fact "killed." The job as national security adviser is held at the beginning of the novel by Charles Alden. When

Elliot learns of a paternity suit pending against Alden by a former student at Yale, she rushes immediately to the president, who asks for Alden's resignation. But as a direct result of the stress of this scandal, Alden suffers a heart attack and dies. Of this, Ryan says, "Well, [Elliot] had the job she'd angled for, even if it had taken a death . . . to get it for her" (122). Unlike Ryan and North, Elliot's killing methods are indirect, actions which she doesn't have to take responsibility for. While North and Ryan were willing to face their enemies, Elliot cannot, marking her not only a coward but *unprofessional* as well.

Similarly, of the president, who "has lost control" (765), Ryan says, "He lost it. . . . Maybe anybody would have, maybe you just can't expect a guy to deal with this, but—but *that's his job,* man" (777; italics added). But even after Ryan has solved this international crisis and knows that the president is at fault, he agrees to talk to him on the phone, because not to do so would have been "unprofessional" (773). This is something that even the lowest-level government official knows better than the president. When a Secret Service agent is dispatched by the president to arrest Ryan for using the hot line, Ryan asks what charges are against him. When the agent replies, " 'He didn't say, sir,' " Ryan provides the lineage that made it possible for him to solve so many international crises: " 'I'm not a cop, but my dad was. I don't think you can arrest me without a charge. The law, you know? The Constitution.' " The agent then shows that he too knows his job: "He had orders from someone he had to obey [the president], but he was too professional to violate the law" (772). (Oliver North repeats this philosophy when he concludes about hostage negotiations with the Iranians, "I had given it my best shot, and now it was time to carry out my orders" [60].)

What makes Ryan a professional manager and not a Ramboesque lone wolf is that he depends upon many such "professional" people in his field. From FBI agents to local police officers to Israeli Mossad agents to Soviet intelligence officers to U.S. military commanders, Ryan's success depends, not upon his individual knowledge or skill (as was the case in spy thrillers of decades past), but upon his ability to gather information, analyze reports, and act professionally. This is, as *Fortune* magazine described it, the role that George Bush played in the Persian Gulf War. It is the "heroism of choice" of today's techno-thriller best-sellers. It is the redemption of those who took part in Iran/Contra. And it is what the United States offers the world as its contribution to the New World Order.

In *Intelligence Requirements for the 1990s: Collection, Analysis,*

Counterintelligence, and Covert Action, B. Hugh Tovar, a former senior official for the CIA, addresses what Bob Woodward has called the "identity crisis" confronting the CIA after Iran/Contra: "If such is the case, it must surely have been aggravated by what many observers saw as an unprofessional performance, of dubious legality, implemented by amateurs, with a disastrous impact on the intelligence community."[25] In responding to Tovar's statements, Eberhard Blum, former director of the German Federal News Agency, describes the kind of operators necessary for effective covert action: "This business, above all, must be handled by 'honorable men,' who, of course, are highly qualified. This standard is the sine qua non. . . . I use the words 'honorable and highly qualified' because the art of intelligence in its many facets is much too difficult and important a duty to be left to the average government employee."[26] What distinguishes good intelligence operatives is then not what they know or what kinds of skills they possess, but what kinds of men they are, what kind of character they have. Like the heroes of *The Sum of All Fears, Condition Black, Under Siege,* and many other 1980s best-sellers of their type, it is finally a professional quality—a "character"—that not only makes them successful but, in each case, resolves violent and desperate international crises. This is Jack Ryan (*The Sum of All Fears*). This is Bill Ehrlich (*Condition Black*). This is Jake Grafton (*Under Siege*). And this is George Bush (the New World Order).

In the face of decreasing U.S. prestige in areas of technologies, economies, education, social enforcement, territorial control, and international power, it is just these kinds of men—the managerial heroes—who, I would suggest, are being held out as the U.S. offering to the New World Order. Instead of money, goods, or brains, the United States is now selling services. But unlike the service workers upon whom the United States and so many other economies depend—noncitizens, the disenfranchised, migrant laborers, and so on—these services are of a different level, provided by top-level managers who may not know the materials or have access to the goods, but who can direct those under them and make effective decisions. But there is one feature that distinguishes U.S. managerial heroes from those of other countries and insures that, at least for the near future, there will be no competition for these jobs. It is, as Bush has most effectively shown, that the U.S. continues to have the military system to enforce the decisions its managers make.

These managerial heroes are, to return to the first section of this paper, part of the new U.S. "Patriot system," in which these high-level, world-crisis-resolving decision makers are at the pinnacle of an integrated network of information managers upon whom they depend. This network, like that which enables the Patriot missile to fire, is a complex one connecting intelligence agencies, information-gathering computerized systems, large corporations, government administrators, skilled field operators, and a wide-ranging police/military structure. And like the Patriot missile, the public "success" of these "Patriots" is used to validate all of these interconnected operations that accompany the Patriot/managerial hero. Additionally, those managerial heroes, like their Patriot missile counterparts, are effectively sold both to the U.S. public and to foreign nations as serving a *defensive* purpose. In each of the best-selling novels, the heroes are responding to some threat—whether it be of foreign or domestic origin—and are never portrayed as initiating their frequently destructive activities. Like George Bush's posture in the Persian Gulf War, these heroes proclaim themselves as defenders of innocent victims and never as complicit attackers. Both of these Patriot systems are oriented finally toward proving what many have said about the Patriot missile, that "America . . . is still capable of manufacturing something better than anyone else"[27] and are in this way a response to increasing anxieties about declining U.S. production capabilities in the face of Japan's increasing control of world market shares.

The importance of the reliance upon a "system" cannot be overlooked. As with the Patriot missile system, the managerial system suggests that it is not a uniquely heroic product or character that is "defending" (and selling) U.S. interests (as might have been the case in early twentieth-century celebrations of U.S. inventors and their products), but instead an integrated and interdependent network of "professional" workers and products, upon each of whom the fate of the world may depend, a burden each is, according to these narratives, more than capable of bearing. In this way, the managerial/war narrative can be used to encourage U.S. citizen/workers to feel that they are elemental, though perhaps unseen, parts of an efficient, valuable, life-saving, and professional system of U.S. Patriots.

In a time when U.S. corporations are cutting jobs here while building new factories in other countries where labor is cheaper, and when the workplace is becoming increasingly "taken over" by large transnational corporations and conglomerates, such feelings of an individual's value in a functioning system may serve as productive panaceas for many workers' increasing senses of alienation, anonymity, and displacement.

In such a context, being "professional" is a goal that helps to guard the operations of a managerial/war system from such worker alienation. In Clancy's novel, for example, the terrorist plot is finally uncovered, not through the single-handed and single-minded investigations of an individual intelligence operative, but through the routine reports of "professional" law enforcement officers across the country, from security guards to FBI agents to police officers, none of whom knows at the time what role their information will play in the eventual deterrence of World War III. Think of how reassuring such a message could be to an alienated and unhappy worker whose wages are being cut and whose union is losing more battles every year: "Though you may not know it, the job you do will form a link in a powerful chain of events, information, and products that could eventually contribute to the continuing security of the United States." And here's the catch: "You will probably never know the real role your work will play in world events, but be assured that it will." In such a context, being a "professional" amounts to being a "patriot," and doing a job that will contribute to the defense of the nation, whether militarily (terrorism, wars), economically (defeating Japan's economic takeover), or socially (antidrug campaigns). As with the Patriot missile batteries, this Patriot system is characterized as defending the nation against foreign onslaughts of multiple kinds.

Let me go back to that catch in the logic of professional patriotism: "You'll never know the real role your work will play in world events." Here's where the Patriot system can be linked back to covert action. Because I don't mean here so much covert operations themselves, though they form a large part of what the Persian Gulf War helped to revive, but the concept of covert activities in current U.S. cultural operations. In such terms, covert activities are not a subset of other CIA or government security actions, but a rationale for government operations as a whole. "There are things U.S. citizens simply cannot and should not know about the operations of their government." And the rationale for this? To prevent damaging sensitive negotiations, to keep enemies from knowing U.S. plans of attack, to deter terrorists (as in the occasional disclosures that there have been several thwarted terrorist attacks inside the United States), to guard sensitive scientific and product information from rival corporations/countries, and so on. One of the best examples of this technique of covert activities in the Persian Gulf War was in George Bush's failure to disclose planned U.S. troop movements while declaring to the U.S. public that he was committed to UN sanctions against Iraq. As Bob

Woodward reveals in *The Commanders,* Bush's only interest in promoting sanctions was to gain time to mobilize troops for a war. As the Bush administration later acknowledged, this was a necessary ruse, not so much to deceive the U.S. public, it was said, as to prevent the "enemy" from knowing U.S. war plans.

This is the most powerful redemption of Iran/Contra: not so much to revalidate specific covert operations against foreign governments or individuals (though the raids on Libya did a great deal to accomplish this), as to rationalize the coversion of U.S. public information systems and to present that rationalization *as a form of managerial necessity.*

The winter 1991 issue of *International Security* presents an article by Theodore Postol in which he argues that the Patriot missile system experienced "an almost total failure to intercept quite primitive attacking missiles." According to Postol, the declared 80 percent effectiveness rate for the Patriot missile in Saudi Arabia and its 50 percent success rate in Israel are illusions. In his analysis, the spectacular explosions that were witnessed by television audiences around the world were not actual destructions of Scud missiles by Patriot missiles but the fireballs of Patriot missile warheads detonating nearby already-fragmenting Scud missiles. Because of what Postol declares to be the poor designs of the Scud missiles, he claims that they began disintegrating on their own as the missiles descended through the atmosphere and were not, by and large, touched by Patriot missiles at all.

As Sut Jhally, Justin Lewis, and Michael Morgan's study of public opinion during the Persian Gulf War reported, the *only* piece of information about the war that television viewers knew more about than print readers was the Patriot missile,[28] suggesting that the missile's *visual* impact on viewers formed a large part of its perceived effectiveness. As those reporting on the missile put it, "The overwhelming visual impression, broadcast over television, was one of general success."[29] It is just this visual impression that Postol is attacking, declaring that the visual image was only an illusion. But precise information about the interceptions of Scud missiles has been declared "classified" by the government, so that Postol's assessments have had to come from close examinations of the available video footage of Patriot and Scud missiles. Since both the accredited success and failure of the missiles depends upon visual analyses of spectacular explosions, and since the manipulation of the imagery of the war was more successful than the Patriot missile was ever alleged to be, it is difficult to determine if Postol's declarations will have any real impact on the way that television viewers, at least, will "remember" the Patriot missile.

As Michael Rogin has so adeptly shown in his discussions of Ronald Reagan's use of the phrase popularized by Clint Eastwood's Dirty Harry movies, "Make my day," public memory of the details surrounding popular images is frequently inexact, especially to the extent that the recollection of a more specific context for the image would damage its ability to reinforce other popularly held beliefs or narratives. Rogin calls it "motivated forgetting . . . a cultural impulse both to have the experience and not to retain it in memory."[30] And, as Rogin goes on to say, this "motivated forgetting" takes place most easily in relation to spectacles of public imagery: "Spectacle is the cultural form for amnesiac representation, for specular displays are superficial and sensately intensified, short lived and repeatable" (106).

Like Rogin's "specular displays," the images of the exploding Scud missiles and the Patriot missile launchings are superficial, "sensately intensified," and short lived, all qualities that tend to reinforce them *as* images rather than as data. My guess is that more viewers recall the visually "successful" Patriot missile collisions than any of the military, government, or antiwar statistics that were repeated about the missile's target rates. In such a context, Postol's challenges of those rates, without the concomitant ability to challenge the imagery itself, may do little to disturb the overall impressions made by the Patriot missiles and, coincidentally, the war for which they have served as a spectacular emblem. In the face of continuing internal pressures to believe that "America . . . is still capable of manufacturing something better than anyone else," even if the "product" of that manufacture is war, the spectacular images of the Patriot missile explosions may well serve not only as a powerful local imagery that could counteract contradictory information about the missiles, but as a more powerful comprehensive imagery that would enable the "motivated forgetting" of other, less spectacular and less "successful" aspects of the war, specifically the statistics about the large numbers of Iraqi deaths resulting from the war, the CIA betrayal of the Kurds, or the continuing power of Saddam Hussein. The images of apparently clean, efficient, and effective Patriot missiles could provide for many a preferred imagery that would organize and focus the deliberate "forgetting" of the numerous "messy" parts of this war. In similar fashion, the cool, rational, and "understanding" images of U.S. managers could equally provide an imagery that would organize and focus a deliberate "forgetting" of many U.S. actions during the war, including but not limited to fighter pilots' detached elation over their "kills," April Glaspie's equivocal role in bringing about the Iraqi troop movement into Kuwait, a nationalistically fed anti-Arab racism, and so on.

In relation to the "overt" spectacles of technology and management that surrounded and made possible the Persian Gulf War, covert government and cultural operations have been reinforced and forwarded through the permissions granted by spectacle. As with the explosions of the Scud missiles, it is often very difficult for U.S. viewers to witness the actual interactions between U.S. technologies, operators, techniques, and managers. In a war in which very little was seen because "everything" was seen, coversion became the companion of spectacle as well as the beneficiary and, to some extent, the guarantor, of its "successes." The Persian Gulf War put to rest the memory of Iran/Contra,[31] not by rejecting covert operations, but by improving its strategies of spectacle for all Patriot systems.

Nothing was hidden behind the smooth brow, the calm, unemotional features.

Wrong. *Everything was hidden.*

Notes

1 Frederic Jameson, "Thoughts on the Late War," *Social Text* 28: 144 (subsequent page numbers are cited parenthetically).

2 Adam Meyerson, "The Limits of Tyranny, and Other Lessons from the Gulf," *Policy Review* 56 (Spring 1991): 2.

3 John Huey and Nancy J. Perry, "The Future of Arms," *Fortune,* February 25, 1991, p. 34.

4 Bruce A. Smith, "Scud Propulsion Designs Help Patriot System Succeed," *Aviation Week and Space Technology,* January 28, 1991, p. 28.

5 "The Dangerous Dinosaur," *Time* 137, no. 4 (January 28, 1991): 23.

6 Ed Magnuson, "High-Tech Payoff," *Time* 137, no. 4 (January 28, 1991): 30–31.

7 "Patriot System Exceeds Army's Expectations," *Aviation Week and Space Technology,* January 28, 1991, p. 34.

8 *Aviation Week and Space Technology,* January 28, 1991, p. 34.

9 "Patriot Antimissile Successes Show How Software Upgrades Help Meet New Threats," *Aviation Week and Space Technology,* January 28, 1991, p. 26.

10 Angelo Codevilla, "A Question of Patriot-ism," *Policy Review* 56 (Spring 1991): 16.

11 "U.S. Army Patriot Proven in New Role as Anti-Tactical Ballistic Missile Weapon," *Aviation Week and Space Technology*, February 18, 1991, p. 50.

12 "While Some Talk Peace, Middle East Buys Arms," *Seattle Post-Intelligencer*, November 4, 1991, p. A6.

13 Huey and Perry, p. 35.

14 Ken Adelman, "Star Wars in the Desert," *Newsweek*, February 4, 1991, p. 14.

15 Robert Weissman, "War Games," *Multinational Monitor*, March 1991, p. 8. The quotation is from Mary Roberts, head of Estes Industries.

16 Theodore Draper, *A Very Thin Line: The Iran-Contra Affairs* (New York: Hill and Wang, 1991), p. 200.

17 Oliver North, *Under Fire* (New York: Harper Collins, 1991), p. 34.

18 Bush's knowledge about the arms-for-hostages exchange became the subject of some debate during the 1992 presidential campaign. Though special prosecutor Lawrence Walsh has extended his investigation to include higher-ranking officials such as Casper Weinberger, to this date, George Bush has still eluded Walsh's efforts to pinpoint his role in the Iran-Contra activities.

19 Hugh Sidey, "The Presidency," *Time* 137, no. 6 (February 11, 1991): 55.

20 Meyerson, p. 2.

21 Ann Reilly Dowd, "How George Bush is Managing as Commander-in-Chief," *Fortune*, March 11, 1991, p. 12.

22 Tom Clancy, *The Sum of All Fears* (New York: G.P. Putnam's Sons, 1991), p. 721.

23 Senator Daniel Moynihan has suggested eliminating the CIA altogether, since its original purpose of fighting Communist domination has disappeared.

24 Clancy's assessment of operators versus politicians is echoed by another Iran/Contra figure, Major General John Singlaub (one of Casey's World War II trainees), who says this of the politicians who toured his World War II training camp: "We knew full well we would be involved in throat slashing in a matter of months, while this gentleman waxed eloquent over dry martinis at the Army-Navy club." *A Soldier Reports* (New York: 1992), p. 33.

25 B. Hugh Tovar, "Covert Action," in *Intelligence Requirements for the 1990s: Collection, Analysis, Counterintelligence, and Covert Action*, ed. Roy Goodson (Lexington, Mass.: Lexington Books, 1989), p. 211. This book is a collection of the proceedings of a colloquium at the National Strategy Information Center held in 1987.

26 Eberhard Blum, "Discussion," *Intelligence Requirements*, ed. Goodson. pp. 225–26.

27 Huey and Perry, p. 34.

28 Sut Jhally, Justin Lewis, and Michael Morgan, *The Gulf War: A Study of the Media, Public Opinion, and Public Knowledge*, Department of Communication (Amherst: University of Massachussetts, 1991).

29 "Faults Found in Gulf War Weapons," *Seattle Post-Intelligencer,* January 9, 1992, p. A1.

30 Michael Rogin, "'Make My Day!': Spectacle as Amnesia in Imperial Politics," *Representations* 29 (Winter 1990): 105.

31 In spite of the fact that the Iran/Contra indictments were revived in July 1991, with guilty pleas by Alan Fiers and Elliot Abrams, the nomination of Robert Gates, William Casey's principal deputy, to head the CIA went through the Congress with little trouble from Gates's possible Iran/Contra connections.

Donald E. Pease

Hiroshima, the Vietnam Veterans War Memorial, and the Gulf War

Post-National Spectacles

n the two years since the war's conclusion, media coverage of the Persian Gulf War has elicited at least as much critical commentary as the U.S. foreign policy authorizing the war.[1] Ambivalence over the appropriate focus results in part from official representations that tended to conflate incidents of war with their means of representation. From the outset, the Gulf War was constructed as a military enterprise designed, on the one hand, to forestall Iraq's aggression against Kuwait and, on the other, to solicit, following the breakdown of the cold war consensus, the public's spontaneous consent to an alternative enframement of historical events.

The cold war's authority as a consensus formation depended upon a dual capacity: to identify internal dissension as a threat to the national security and to recharacterize such dissension as the work of the national other, the imperial Soviet whose global ambitions enabled an extension of the cold war's powers of enframement to the entire globe. When it operated outside U.S. borders, the cold war configured the globe within a superordinate binarism that supervised a range of vertical rankings (North/South, First World/Third World, male/female, white/black, Euro-American/other) within and without the territorial U.S. borders. Because it always misrepresented internal divisiveness as if it were an external dualism, however, the cold war framework was inherently unstable. It constituted a coherent national identity out of diverse constituencies whose differences could only be partially and unevenly repressed through their projection onto a wholly exterior oppositional power. Throughout its forty-five year rule, the cold war's binary organization of the ideological differences between the U.S. and the USSR depended upon the successful repression of a multiplicity of internal differences between heterogeneous social groups but also *within* individual citizens. Overall, the coherence of the national identity was the result of a highly complex process. It entailed the condensation of these heterogeneous social materials into a single foregrounded entity, a nationality whose stability had to be constantly renegotiated in relation to such different matters as race, class, gender, and ethnicity.

The three proper names in the title designate crucial phases in the epoch of cold war rule and represent different symbolic resolutions of this constitutive instability. Individually and collectively they designate monumental national memories expressive of an ahistorical supranational essence as well as traumatic historical materiality unassimilable to the grand narrative of U.S. history.

As the medium through which the State Department had projected terrifying images of the "communist menace" onto the national imaginary, Hiroshima oversaw, in the years 1945–1968, the subordination of political dissent to the policy of containment abroad, and at home the emergence of liberal anti-communism as the new civil religion.

The Vietnam Veterans Memorial bears witness to two extremely different orientations to the breakdown, during the Vietnam era, of the cold war's powers of enframement. After the antiwar movement successfully recast the U.S. rather than the USSR as the aggressor in Vietnam, it was no longer possible to misrecognize domestic social protest as the work of the "other" superpower. From 1968 to 1980, patriotic nationalism was displaced with critical scrutiny of U.S. imperialism.

Following the 1980 election, the Reagan administration proposed a different understanding of the Vietnam era. He renamed the unwillingness to intervene in the Third World a national pathology, the "Vietnam syndrome," and associated this failure with other forms of social unrest. Characterizing the social contradictions that after the Vietnam War had become open to analysis and resistance, as likewise symptomatic of the nation's loss of resolve, Reagan activated widespread nostalgia for cold war certitudes. In campaigning against the Vietnam syndrome, Reagan summoned U.S. citizens to their collective refashioning in the transhistorical image of the self-reliant individualist he had previously represented in his screen roles, then deployed images from the cold war in an ongoing war of position he waged on heterogeneous social sites.

Reaganism set middle-class blacks against the black underclass, pro-life feminists against abortion advocates, straights against gays, U.S. workers against laborers from the Third World. When he baptized the Vietnam Veterans Memorial an official commemoration of the victims of world communism, Reagan accomplished a resolution of these self-divided and heterogeneous social spaces into a chain of interlinked connotations that reconstituted the national imaginary out of this collective memory of the Vietnam era.

To secure the linkage between the pervasive social logic whereby he reconstituted a unified national identity out of diverse constituencies, Reagan had to overcome internal adversity by reprojecting the object of social unrest onto a revivified national antagonist, the "Evil Empire." But with the end of the cold war in 1990, the Bush administration had lost the national other against which and through which Reaganism had articulated its "deterrence" hegemony. As a consequence, Bush was faced with the task of reconfiguring the iconography of cold war rule within the objectives of a New World Order. To accomplish this task, the Bush administration staged a military victory in Iraq to celebrate the end of the cold war and resuscitate its power to rule.

In its effort to solidify the Reagan administration's social formation, the Bush administration found in Saddam Hussein a new enemy in whose image U.S. publics were encouraged to misrecognize their internal differences. To complete the nation's recovery from the Vietnam syndrome, the State Department specified its origins in the antiwar consensus. The Bush administration, to overcome the Vietnam syndrome for which it had found the media largely responsible, thereafter not only limited media access to coverage of the Gulf War, but struggled to convert the events actually taking place during the war into the virtual reality of purely symbolic forms—instruments for the construction of a new consensus—rather than historical facts.

Following reports of Hussein's nuclear arsenal, Bush reinscribed the nation's governmentality in the totalizing image of its strategic defense against nuclear terror. In this alternative visual field, incidents of war could not be disassociated from the surveillance technology. Upon identifying the public's gaze with the war machine's surveillance apparatus, Operation Desert Storm short-circuited the relay between events and their factual observation. In thereby depriving individual viewers of critical distance, the official representations elided their historical witness. The surveillance system thereafter systematically displaced the negative images associated with the Vietnam War—body bags, critical commentary, civilian casualties, jungle warfare, faulty technology, guerilla insurgents—and condensed the remainder to the now of the New World Order.

A significant consequence of this loss of a critical standpoint was a disregard for the documentable facts about that war.[2] Keeping track of what he calls the "incontrovertible" historical facts, Christopher Norris has provided the following succinct account of that documentary record:

> 1) that Saddam Hussein was brought to power and maintained over a long period by US intelligence and "long-arm" strategic agencies; 2) that his regime was backed up *until the very last moment* by constant supplies of weapons and resources (not to mention diplomatic support) provided by the US and other Western powers; 3) that this invasion of Kuwait was prompted— or at least given what appeared to be the green light—by indications that the US would not intervene since it also wished to push up the oil-prices by exerting pressure on Kuwait; 4) that the Gulf War was fought *first and foremost* as a war of retribution against an erstwhile ally who had proved too difficult to handle; 5) that its conduct involved not only enormous military and civilian casualties but also—contrary to professed "Allied" war-aims— a full-scale campaign of aerial bombardment launched against electricity generating stations, water-supply systems, sewage disposal plants, and other components of the urban infrastructure whose collapse could be predicted to cause yet further death and suffering through the breakdown of emergency services and the spread of infectious diseases; 6) that the attacks on retreating Iraqi forces (along with civilian hangers-on and hostages) continued to the point where any justifying talk became merely a cover for mechanized mass-murder; and 7)—still within the realm of documentary evidence—that the war might well have been averted had the "Allies" held out against US pressure and listened to those well-informed sources who argued that sanctions were already (in early January) taking their toll in Iraqi war-fighting capabilities.[3]

In the remainder of this essay I shall not supply further critical commentary but briefly trace multiple logics at work in conflicting representations of that war as well as the other ("Hiroshima" and the "Vietnam Veterans Memorial") substitutive objects of cold war governmentality, as their power on the one hand to enforce its rule and on the other to effect strategic reversals. The massive scale of eventuation inferable from their trajectory calls attention to the difficulties these icons proposed individually and collectively to cold war historicity, which had developed sufficiently to include contradictory attitudes. I shall not be concerned primarily with a critical account of the imperialist ideology informing the cold war, but would remark at the outset that the cold war's powers of global enframement constituted in the United States' foreign policy of the last forty-five years the basis for such imperialist practices as the "formal" accumulation of territories, populations and markets, the control of economies, as well as the projection of political ontologies. In decomposing heterogeneous temporalities under the horizon of its binaristic totalization, cold war historicity expropriated plurality from history, reducing spatiotemporal differences to the homogeneous continuity of its contemporaneity, and historical signification to the double bind through which it became eventful.

As indicators of the unstable linkages between the plurality of histories each term connotes and the external antagonism onto which the cold war had only partially projected them, "Hiroshima," "Vietnam Veterans Memorial," and "Persian Gulf War" disclose the susceptibility of the cold war's totalizing historicity to a radical dismantling. When redescribed as unstable historical linkages, the second and third terms rehearse difficulties in commemoration and projection, respectively. The Vietnam Veterans Memorial was designed to restore to official national memory events which in fact undermined the assumptions informing the cold war frame and the Gulf War "took place" as if to make apparent the otherwise phantasmatic "end of the cold war." These brief observations attest to the fact that each one of these terms harbors ongoing contestations over its significance.

In denying such alternative historical significations, the cold war proposed a categorical reductionism that sublated all other possible meanings into one or another of its supervisory binarisms. In order to bear critical witness to a specific occasion wherein one of these terms, in coming delinked from its cold war framework, released a plurality of alternative memories of its historical significance, I shall analyze the so called "Rodney King Affair," as an *overdetermined* counter memory of the Gulf War.

When it was released on March 3, 1991, this eyewitness video of Los Angeles police officers brutally clubbing an unarmed black citizen, the tape filled in blanks—images of wounded civilians, excessive military force, ground combat—that during the Gulf War had been projected as visible absences. As it thus returned these repressed images of war to national visibility, this postwar spectacle restored as well the elided distance between facts and representations necessary for a critical standpoint.[4] With its interruption of U.S. spectators' previous identification with the surveillance apparatus of the New World Order, this postnational spectacle reversed the effects of U.S. disavowal of neo-colonialist brutality in the Gulf, and thereby enabled heretofore denied alternative knowledges as active forms of political resistance.[5] In the place of the images transmitted from Baghdad, a Third World spatiotemporal field, in an operation Homi Bhabha has analyzed intensively, had been relocated in Los Angeles:

> It is a process whereby the look of surveillance returns as the displacing gaze of the disciplined, where the observer becomes the observed and the "partial" representation rearticulates the whole notion of [national] identity.[6]

When rearticulated in relation to such unofficial scenes, the three proper names in the title render quite visible an otherwise occluded asymmetry between the national security state and an heterogeneously constituted nation state. Involved in a mimetic rivalry with the nation-state over appropriate representation of the United States, the national security state has depended for its legitimacy on the generalized fear of the nuclear holocaust which followed in the wake of Hiroshima. From 1945 until President Bush's January 28, 1992, State of the Union Address, the cold war supervised the nation's postwar recovery by securing the citizenry's willingness in peacetime to submit to wartime discipline. The beneficiary of this collective surrender of will was "the national security state," whose governmentality derived from Hiroshima. Not Hiroshima the actual, the historical event that took place on August 6, 1945, at the conclusion of the Pacific campaign and resulted in the deaths of over 100,000 Japanese soldiers and civilians, but Hiroshima as the *possible* fate of U.S. citizens if Soviet imperialism remained unchecked.

Because Hiroshima involved the near total annihilation of a civilian population, it was unassimilable to the assumptions underwriting a national narrative—wherein the United States had always liberated a nation from the totalitarian designs of Soviet imperialism. "Ultimate" responsibility was thereafter projected onto the potential nuclear aggression of the imperial Soviet, whereupon Hiroshima became a purely symbolic referent for a merely possible event and reassigned the duty to predict an anachronistic event, the what "will have happened" had not the United States already mobilized the powers of nuclear deterrence against the Soviets'.

Unlike other historical anachronisms, this nuclear holocaust from the future anterior entailed the destruction of any recollective agency capable of recording its historical actuality. In the following passage, Jacques Derrida explains the dizzying temporal status of such a nuclear holocaust whose *future* existence depends upon its anticipatory recollection from a present time, which is itself in danger of never being recorded as a memorable past:

> Unlike other wars which have all been preceded by wars of more or less the same type in human memory, . . . nuclear war has no precedent. It has never occurred itself; it is a non-event. The explosion of American bombs in 1945 ended a "classical" conventional war; it did not set off a nuclear holocaust. The terrifying reality of the nuclear conflict can only be the signified referent, never the real referent (present or past) of a discourse or text. At least today, apparently. And that sets us thinking about today our day, the presence of our present in and through that fabulous textuality. . . . For the moment, today, one may say that a non-localizable nuclear war has not occurred; it has existed only through what is said of it only where it is talked about. Some might call it a fable, then a pure invention, in the sense in which a myth, an image, a fiction, a utopia, a rhetorical figure, a fantasy, a phantasm, an invention.[7]

As the no-place the United States might have become had it not proleptically opposed, as the precondition for the postwar settlement, the Soviet Union's nuclear capacity, Hiroshima also presignified the geopolitical fate of those nation-states which had not identified the paradigmatic event of the U.S. national narrative ("liberation from imperial aggression") as the "political truth" of their nationhood. The name of the always already displaced event which every other cold war event at once deferred yet anticipated, Hiroshima held the place of what might be called the cold war's transcendental signifier. Because Hiroshima will have taken place only if the terrible reality of an all-out nuclear war did indeed take place *as such* in some possible cold war future, its historical "referentiality," at the conclusion of World War II would, according to the phantasmatic logic of the nuclear imaginary, also undergo derealization if the cold war lost *its* future.

Just such a symbolic return from the future informed the specular logic of the Gulf War. Capitalizing on the uncanny temporality informing the cold war and effected by a framing narrative which first disavowed any possible referent for Hiroshima within the U.S. national narrative and then identified Soviet totalitarianism as the potential historical agency for this non-event.[8] In the image of the Saudi Desert, which recalled the testing ground before and the nuclear winter after the holocaust, Operation Desert Storm enacted a simulacral return to the site of the first atomic explosion at Alamogordo, New Mexico, at 5:29:50 a.m. on July 16, 1945. Following this ex post facto deactivation of the nuclear device Saddam

Hussein was prevented from testing, the U.S. public was to have been relieved of a forty-six-year old nightmare, as President Bush reassured the
nation, in his January 28, 1992, State of the Union Address:

> And so now for the first time in 35 [sic] years, our strategic bombers stand
> down. No longer are they on round the clock alert. Tomorrow our children
> will go to school and study history and how plants grow. And they won't have
> as children did air raid drills in which they crawl under their desks and cover
> their heads in case of nuclear war. My grand-children don't have to do that
> and won't have the bad dreams children had once, in decades past. There are
> still threats. But the long, drawn-out dread is over.[9]

Bush drew upon this residual nuclear dread when he observed "that
the veterans of the Gulf War were safer in the Middle East than in the
streets of their own cities."[10] In correlating urban violence with Saddam Hussein's putative nuclear terrorism, President Bush was not simply
referring to the dangers of street crime but to the continued threat of
nuclear attack from Third World despots like Saddam Hussein. Bush
thereby reanimated an understanding of civil defense that presupposed
the sacrifice of urban population to the "first strike" capabilities of the
enemy. Dean MacCannell has described succinctly this "internal" foreign
policy as an aspect of the "nuclear unconscious":

> Nuclear technology, even without another Hiroshima, has already had a pro-
> found impact on social structure and consciousness, perverting them both in
> discernible ways. Beneath the surface of fear of the supposedly unthinkable
> prospect of millions of deaths in the United States of America, one can find
> growing evidence of the desire to experience the bomb. The United States
> official policy of . . . sacrificing our cities . . . suggests that the configura-
> tion of every detail of domestic life in the United States is the product of a
> transformation of our foreign affairs into a quasi-military nuclear foreign
> policy.[11]

Following the supersession of the cold war by the New World Order,
the nuclear anxiety originating from Hiroshima was to be understood as
if retrospectively crucial to the dismantling of the cold war mentality it
had engendered. As the actual *historical* enactment of the "spectacular
annihilation," which the cold war at once affirmed yet denied, Hiroshima
had acquired the U.S. public's spontaneous consent for the containment
ideology of the cold war epoch and a vivid justification for the policy of
nuclear deterrence. As a national spectacle, Hiroshima had turned the
entire U.S. social symbolic system into the afterimage of a collectively

anticipated spectacle of disaster, a self-divided (rather than self-present) instant, that had always not yet taken place (hence always anticipated) but had nevertheless always already happened (in the lived experience of anticipated disaster).

The difference between the cold war's phantasmatic ordering of events and social relations more usually attributed to the structure Guy Debord has called the society of the spectacle [12] entails a further transformation of the spectator. As the representation of an anticipated total disaster, Hiroshima transfigured cold war spectators into symbolic survivors of their everyday lives, able to encounter everyday events as the afterimages of ever-possible nuclear disaster. The spectacle of anticipated nuclear disaster activates a psychic logic able to convert events in everyday life into the screen memories of that unrepresentable scene. In the aftermath of disasters on the scale of Hiroshima, its actual survivors could never have exchanged their experiences for already existing national images. Such exchanges would have rendered the absolute singularity of nuclear disaster more or less continuous with other cultural representations. In place of a generalized exchange, the cold war derived its authority from the displacement of scenes of nuclear disaster, otherwise incommensurate with the official scenarios out of which the national narrative constructed its representations, with a global conflict. As a spectacle able permanently to deter the nuclear holocaust, for which it served as a screen memory, the East-West conflict reactivated the spectator as the national survivor, but also thereby authorized a division between what was representable and what was of necessity unrepresentable in the national narrative. As the official representation of an unrepresentable dimension of the national narrative, Hiroshima became the sociopolitical unconscious of the national security state.

In compensation for the continuous noneventuation of the nuclear holocaust, the national security state was tacitly granted the power to perform illegal covert activities. Exercising the power necessary to impede nuclear war, the national security state turned the U.S. publics' specular relations with nuclear holocaust into what Michael Paul Rogin has called their "vicarious participation" in the cold war spectacular:

> Most obviously, the specular relation to political life has implications for democratic governance. Spectators gain vicarious participation in a narrative that, in the name of national security, justifies their exclusion from information and decision making. Covert operations as spectacle purify domestic as well as foreign audiences, for they transform the political relation between

rulers and citizens from accountability to entertainment. . . . Vicarious participation in the spectacle of the covert secures in fantasy and preserves in fact the separation of those who plan from those who kill and are killed.[13]

When the cold war scenario positioned Hiroshima within this social logic, it transmuted nuclear panic into the opportunity to stage a technological spectacle corroborative of the nation's invulnerability. An invisible but pervasive supplemental scene accompanying their daily experience, "this end of the world" cold war scenario enabled U.S. citizens to reexperience everyday doubts, confusions, conflicts, and contradictions as the cold war's power to convert indeterminacy into an overdetermined opposition. Paul Virilio has spelled out some of the political consequences of this interidentification of personal with national security:

> There is no more need for an armed body to attack civilians so long as the latter have been properly trained to turn on their radios or plug in their television sets. No need for solid, laboriously moving bodies when their spectral images can be projected anywhere in an instant. From now on military assault is vaporous in time and the population's organic participation is no more than the irrational support of a technologistical supra-nationality, the final stage of delocalization, and thus of servitude.[14]

In its forty-five years, the cold war can thus be said to have assumed two distinct aspects. It was both a spectacle capable of organizing national life and a paradigm capable of determining international policy. Although these two cultural functions were certainly not equivalent, they were interlinked. As a spectacle responsive to the public's need for vicarious participation in the decision-making powers of the national security state, the cold war exhibited its powers of spectacular persuasion precisely in those historical moments when the cold war as a paradigm failed to account for political complexities. When the cold war as paradigm became productive of doubts, the cold war as spectacle represented that doubt as itself a threat to the national security and thereby effectively depoliticized the relations between U.S. citizens and their government. It displaced situations that citizens could change into an arena of decision-making wherein the unthinkable scenario of nuclear holocaust was a possible outcome. In refunctioning itself as a spectacle, then, the cold war did not articulate the significance of political events but reduced them to the status of ever-possible nuclear *afterimages* (arguably the fate of every event in the cold war epoch) hence in need of covert operations for their preservation.

The cold war as paradigm confined totalizing oppositions to the work of the other superpower, but as a spectacle the cold war identified its own totalization as that other at work. The paradigm thereby reduced freedom either to the activity of positioning oneself within the structured opposition or to the "freedom from" the need to decide, and it relocated U.S. citizens within a spectacle in which all discussion had been decisively premeditated if not quite settled and the only unfinished business that of becoming the "national character" through whom the paradigm could speak.[15]

I began this discussion of Hiroshima by describing its double register as at once the signifier of the cold war's powers of displacement as well as the counter-memory belonging to an order of events other than the official history regulated by the national security state. But thus far I have devoted all of my attention to the cold war's capacity to *deny* the difference between its powers of enframement and this different order of historical eventuation. As long as it functioned as the signifier of the cold war's power to appropriate and redescribe the agency responsible for nuclear holocaust, Hiroshima legitimized the suspension of the system of checks and balances underwriting the U.S. constitution, and authorized, in the name of national security, a shadow government comprised of unelected officials engaged in covert activities and *undeclared* wars. When successfully waged, these wars redeployed the containment power inherent to the cold war as the frame necessary for the unfolding of a formulaic drama (of an heroic democratic people overcoming a despotic, totalitarian power) whose entertainment value derived from a collective desire to find nuclear panic reduced to the dimensions of conventional warfare. Traditionally the beneficiary of such cold war spectacles was the national security state, but during the Vietnam War, the cold war's failure to correlate acts of war with this formulaic scenario resulted in collective national trauma. Combat veterans of the Vietnam War delegitimated the national security state's authority as in violation of rules of International Law and rendered suspect the cold war as the putative agency of ideological identification. Intense criticism of U.S. foreign policy during the Vietnam War explicitly associated military atrocities against civilian populations with Hiroshima. In an article which predicts obliquely the Gulf War, Marita Startkin has described the Vietnam Veterans Memorial as an unsuccessful attempt to overcome the national trauma resulting from actions incompatible with the prevailing representations in the national narrative:

The incommunicability of Vietnam War experience has been modified by the communicability of its memorial. Yet we cannot understand the role played by this memorial, by its *difference* as a memorial, unless we understand what made the war it memorializes different. In the Vietnam War the standard definition of warfare had no meaning. This was a war in which the enemy was not always known, and in which the master narratives of "free" world versus communism and First-World technology and Third World "peasantry" were no longer credible. The rupture in history made by the Vietnam War is . . . [of] the ability of this country to impose its will on others.[16]

The monument commemorated what was commonly referred to as the Vietnam syndrome, the loss of the nation's resolve to intervene overseas. When understood as an effort to disremember the Vietnam War, Operation Desert Storm could be redescribed as a deferred reenactment and subsequent working through of the traumatic events in this "unfinished war," and an attempt to relegitimize the foreign policies subject to intermittent reevaluation in the aftermath of Vietnam (and Hiroshima). If, Marita Startkin has concluded, "the memorial acts as a screen for projections of a multitude of memories,"[17] the Gulf War provided the figures capable of being projected onto that screen. When the United States failed to win the Vietnam War, the national spectacle lost the power to screen the memory of nuclear holocaust and as a direct psychological consequence of this failure, startling numbers of Vietnam veterans identified themselves with the survivors of Hiroshima. By way of a growing number of testimonials, autobiographies, and improvised narrative accounts, these combat veterans did not sacralize the nation's military violence by effacing its signs, but bore witness to images of war (charred bodies, dismembered limbs, eyeless skulls) that were utterly heterogeneous to the national narrative. But the technology of warfare displayed in the Gulf exceeded the needs of the individual soldiers. Unlike their predecessors in Vietnam, the combat soldiers in Desert Storm seemed surplus appurtenances whose bodily integrity was assured rather than betrayed by a war machine productive of a new chain of national memories, replacing the bodies in pain recollective of Vietnam with bodies shielded from danger. As the national public watched the war on television, the traumatic materials inherited from Vietnam seemed to have been "worked through" in the hyperreality of the Saudi Desert and thoroughly acted out of the national psyche.

As a "supplemental" recollection of the Vietnam War, the Gulf War can be described as having completed the screen memories projected onto the Vietnam Veterans Memorial. But it also stirred up traumatic materials (including the recollection of mass death at Hiroshima) those memories had only partially repressed. By commemorating the war, the Vietnam Veterans Memorial rendered it continuous with other national scars. In the Gulf War the Bush administration tried to project onto that screen of memorability such exemplary figures as the Vietnam veterans Norman Schwarzkopf and Colin Powell. Whereas the Veterans' Memorial had screened out negative images of Vietnam veterans, the Saudi Desert projected over 500,000 official substitute images of U.S. men and women whom the U.S. military had shielded from enemy attack.[18]

In linking the Gulf War to Hiroshima by way of the Desert Shield the Pentagon had hoped thereby to represent the nation as if it too were immune to nuclear attack. The U.S. public, the pictures transmitted from the desert suggested, should understand itself as liberated from the forty-six years in which it was the hostage of nuclear panic. But in its contradictory linkage of the Gulf War with Hiroshima, the Vietnam Veterans Memorial reactivated a way of remembering these forty-six years quite different from the selective amnesia authorized by the New World Order. W. J. T. Mitchell indirectly alluded to this alternative memory when he shrewdly observed that the power of the memorial derives from its violation of the cold war's conventional means of repressing (and expressing) violence:

> The Vietnam Veterans Memorial is antiheroic, antimonumental, a V-shaped gash or scar, a trace of violence suffered not of violence wielded in the service of a glorious cause (as in the conventional war memorial). It achieves the universality of the public monument not by rising above its surroundings to transcend the political, but by going beneath the political to the shared sense of a wound that will never heal, or (more optimistically) a scar that will never fade. Its legibility is not that of narrative: no heroic episode such as the planting of the flag on Iwo Jima is memorialized, only the mind-numbing and undifferentiated chronology of violence and death catalogued by the fifty-eight thousand names inscribed on the black marble walls. The only other legibility is that of the giant flat V carved in the earth itself, a multivalent monogram or initial that seems uncannily overdetermined. Does the V stand for Vietnam? For a Pyrrhic "Victory"? For the Veterans themselves? For the Violences themselves?[19]

Throughout this account, Mitchell draws attention to the difference between the figures it memorializes and their unassimilability to the national narrative. As does Hiroshima, the Vietnam War occupies the site wherein historical facts differ from their conflicting representations. As an undisputed fact, the Vietnam War refers to the historical events which took place during the U.S. occupation of South Vietnam between 1954 and 1973. As a cultural phenomenon, the Vietnam War refers to the massive transformation in the nation's self-understanding which took place during those same years. In *American Myth and the Legacy of Vietnam*, John Hellman explained this change as the nation's loss of its mythological rationale. That mythology which originated with James Fenimore Cooper's *Leather-stocking Tales* retold the story of America's origination in the savage wilderness and its violent regeneration through its many campaigns against the empire. But Vietnam brought this mythology to a conclusion when, instead of finding themselves able to take possession of their Vietnam experience by projecting this "inner romance" upon it, U.S. combat soldiers entered into a psychic landscape "that overwhelmed the American idea of frontier" as *liberated* territory.[20] When televised on the evening news, incidents in the Vietnam War refused to become referents in the composite national event which cross-identified Columbus's discovery of the New World with the American colonists' successful revolution against the British Empire. Unlike previous geographical sites on which the American Revolution was successfully restaged, Vietnam resisted this frame. Because the U.S. government could not provide a coherent justification for the American presence in Vietnam, combat soldiers, who lacked a moral rationale for their actions, lost the power ethically to discriminate between war crimes and incidents of war.

Their individual collective difficulties resulted in a profound change in the dominant cultural image of the American soldier, turning the heroic adventurer into an emotional cripple. This transformation in the agent of war was accompanied by related changes in cultural representations of the scene of battle and the narratives which appropriated it to the national mythology.[21] The belief structures informing the Vietnam combat veterans' understanding of the national mythology of war were incommensurate with their wartime experiences. Because their experiences could not gratify the national appetite for myth, they instead exposed the assumptions informing the national mythology, as well as the interests served by these assumptions. Their inability to identify the military's atrocity-producing activities with the official mythology led the vast majority to construe Vietnam as an unjust war. That construal resulted, in turn, in a reconceptualization of Hiroshima, as the first traumatic symptom of the Vietnam syndrome.

In an essay he published in the aftermath of the Russell International War Crimes Tribunal, Noam Chomsky designated "genocide" as the basis for their historical association:

Hoopes [a former under-secretary of the Air Force who resigned after the Tet Offensive] does not tell us how he knows that the Asian poor do not love life or fear pain, or that happiness is probably beyond their emotional comprehension. But he goes on to explain how "ideologues in Asia" make use of these characteristics of the Asian hordes. Their strategy is to convert Asia's capacity for endurance in suffering into an instrument for exploiting "a basic vulnerability in the Christian West." They do this by inviting the West "to carry its strategic logic to the final conclusion, which is genocide. . . ." At that point we hesitate, for remembering Hitler and Hiroshima and Nagasaki, we realize anew that genocide is a terrible burden to bear.[22]

Here and elsewhere in his analysis of the war, Chomsky refused official history's explanations of events. Identifying the characteristics assigned indiscriminately to all "Asian masses" as a symptom of "official racism," Chomsky interlinked this policy with U.S. efforts to construct the Japanese people as the nation's "official enemy" during World War II, and he associated the policy of genocide in Vietnam with the mass destruction of civilian populations in Hiroshima and Nagasaki. Following these recharacterizations, Chomsky argues that as the agency responsible for these war crimes, the national security state should be tried for violations of international law.

When combat soldiers involved in action in Vietnam struggled after the war to disavow their complicity in war crimes, their efforts only implicated them further in a chain of compulsive violence. In his commentary on the war, Jean-Paul Sartre provided the following account of their reaction-formation:

> They [the American soldiers] came to save Vietnam from "communist aggressors." But they soon had to realize that the Vietnamese did not want them. Their attractive role as liberators changed to that of occupation troops. For the soldiers it was the first glimmering consciousness. "We are unwanted, we have no business here. . . ." They vaguely understand that in a people's war, civilians are the only visible enemies. Their frustration turns to hatred of the Vietnamese; racism takes it from there. The soldiers discover with a savage joy that they are there to kill Vietnamese they had been pretending to save. All of them are potential communists, as proved by the fact that they hate Americans. Now we can recognize in those dark and misled souls the tenth of the Vietnam War: it meets all of Hitler's specifications. . . . Whatever lies or euphemisms the government may think up, the spirit of genocide is in the minds of the soldiers. This is their way of living out the genocidal situation into which their government had thrown them.[23]

According to Sartre's account, these combat soldiers constructed a false self-system which they divided off from their experience of the genocidal structure of the war. This false self (the figure in these soldiers only "pretending" to save the Vietnamese people from communist aggressors), however, was the only subject the United States government officially recognized. In his groundbreaking work with Vietnam veterans, Robert Jay Lifton discovered profound similarities between the combat veterans' collective experiences of social abjection—ontological insecurity, desymbolization, general distrust of the counterfeit nurturance of the environment, psychic numbing, flashbacks to the experience of death immersion, psychic disconnections between affect and experience, shock syndrome—and those of *hibakusha,* the survivors of Hiroshima, who were the subject of *Death in Life.* Neither the experiences of *hibakusha* nor the veterans Lifton examined could be represented in the image repertoires of their respective national narratives. As psychic materials in excess of any narrative's power to derive significance, these profoundly disturbing experiences remained unforgettable and unrepresentable somatic symptoms and returned *hibakusha* and Lifton's Vietnam veterans alike to the respective scenes of their traumas. Unable to surrender their past experiences to a narrative enchainment able to redescribe terror as valor, pain as courage, mutilation as integrity, and thereby transmute physical distress into the abstractions cultures reward, the survivors of Hiroshima as well as the Vietnam War, Lifton explained, instead felt absolutely disassociated from their culture's social symbolic orders. Without belief in the official narratives with which the government justified its Vietnam policy, the Vietnam veteran became, in the national mythology, the representative of a spectacle of atrocity—napalming, holocaust, assassination, torture—the official scenario could not recuperate.

The Vietnam veterans, in remaining unassimilable to the paradigmatic event structuring the national narrative, activated an order of discourse asymmetrical with the culture's habitual self-explanation. Their inability to justify their atrocity-producing activities in Vietnam with the imperatives of the national security state can be understood as partly responsible for the national adjudication of the difference between that shadow government and the U.S. constitution called the Watergate Trial. As it apprised the nation of the difference between its two constitutions (the U.S. constitution proper and the emergency measures of the national security state) that trial also suspended the cold war's power to enframe historical events.

The construal of the Vietnam War as unjust retrospectively enabled revisionist understanding of Hiroshima as the first symptom of what was to be called the Vietnam syndrome. With the following observations Robert Lifton proposed the My Lai massacre as the historical syntax able to bring Hiroshima into grammatical combination with the Watergate scandal as well as the Vietnam War:

> At My Lai the atrocity involved the killing of five hundred non-combatants, Watergate involved subverting the electoral process—an atrocity of its own— in a way that makes more likely the kind of military atrocity that occurred at My Lai. . . . Like Hiroshima and Auschwitz, My Lai is a revolutionary event: its total inversion of moral standards raises fundamental questions about the institutions and national practices of the nation responsible for it. . . . One finds in Watergate and My Lai a simplistic polarization of American virtue and communist depravity. . . . There was a self-perpetuating quality to the whole Watergate style [which also applies to My Lai and Hiroshima]. One had to keep on doing more things to prevent a recognition of what one had done from reaching oneself or others.[24]

Because such veterans as these experienced themselves, on their return home, as the objects of a generalized ostracism (for their failure to fulfill the imperatives of the national narrative and "liberate" Vietnam from totalitarian aggressors) comparable in its effects to social stigmatization, they reinvented themselves as if U.S. relatives of Japanese *hibakusha*.[25] Others represented the cause of the Vietnam people against the imperatives of the U.S. government, and they struggled for the rights of Asian minorities. Having discovered the Vietnamese survivor in their own psychic experience of the war, many veterans became antiwar dissidents, in open conflict with a government (and a public) which had betrayed them by refusing to understand their predicament. In assigning the moral responsibility both for the war's atrocities and their inability to recover to the national security state, these Vietnam veterans became representatives of the political alternative to the cold war mentality known as the Vietnam syndrome.

Astonishingly, that syndrome informed official foreign policy until Ronald Reagan took office in 1980 with an understanding of the cultural significance of the Vietnam veteran quite different from Lifton's. Throughout his presidency, Reagan recharacterized the combat soldiers in Vietnam as the prisoners of an antiwar sensibility which had deprived the U.S. public of its patriotic pride. His motives for commissioning the erection of the Vietnam Veterans Memorial entailed the psychological rehabilitation of these combat veterans and the nation's recovery from the

syndrome they represented. Reagan never wavered in his intention to return the United States to the psychological euphoria of the pre-Vietnam
cold war:

> Restoring America's strength has been one of our Administration's highest
> goals. When we took office, we found that we had ships that couldn't leave port
> [and] planes that couldn't fly. . . . In the last five and half years we've begun
> to turn that desperate situation around. We've restored the morale, the train-
> ing, and the equipment of our armed forces. And let me just say that around
> the world and here at home, I've met many of our young men and women
> in uniform over the last several years. It does something to you when you're
> standing up there on the demilitarized zone in Korea and a young fellow
> standing there in uniform says, "Sir, we're on the frontier of freedom." [26]

The Wall, as the Vietnam Memorial was commonly called, was to
have represented Reagan's new frontier of freedom. What W. J. T. Mitchell
described as a scar, memorializing the fact that the Vietnam experience
had been separated from any other official form of recollection, Reagan
understood contrastively as a badge of courage, a national war wound
representative of many acts of valor deserving of national commemoration. Erected during the second year of Reagan's presidency, the monument was intended to erase the negative chain of recollections and activated as the official national memory of the Vietnam era, the Vietnam
POW's as representatives of an imprisoned American citizenry, struggling
to return to the political certitudes of World War II.[27] The War Memorial
became the gigantic screen onto which U.S. citizens were encouraged to
project their collective wish to recover national pride.

The agency responsible for the success of this screen memory was
not Ronald Reagan the President but Ronald Reagan, the actor, who
provided the spectatorial public with representative heroic actions—
"freedom fighting" in Nicaragua, the bombing of Libya, the invasion of
Grenada—and encouraged U.S. citizens to realign themselves with the
doctrine of American exceptionalism and the moral imperative to fight a
Just War. One result of this realignment was the disavowal of any similarity between U.S. combat veterans and Japanese *hibakusha*.

Being recalled to the imperatives of the cold war entailed the nation's
collective amnesia of Vietnam and Watergate as condensed connotations
of Hiroshima, the "event" incommensurable with the cold war frame narrative. As long as the cold war scenario successfully recoded these historical events into its frame of reference, this collective amnesia remained
in force. But in the last two years of the Reagan presidency, *glasnost* and

perestroika threatened to bring the cold war itself to an end, thereby depriving Reagan of his habitual way of explaining away such illegalities as
the arms for hostages deal which surfaced in the Iran-Contra hearings. If
we understand the Gulf War as a spectacle in which the Pentagon aspired
to represent the end of the cold war as a U.S. victory, we can also understand it as the Bush administration's effort to justify the National Security
Council's role in Irangate. The Gulf War was after all a way of diverting
the national attention away from covert operations and redirecting it to a
purely symbolic war.

In trading arms to Iran in exchange for money to conduct unauthorized wars in Latin America, the national security state had turned an
ideological enemy into an ally in an illegal war. Because of this and related political contradictions it brought into the open, Irangate recalled
Watergate and encouraged an understanding of the Reagan presidency as
comparable with Nixon's. Without the cold war to justify its covert operations, the national security state had become the subject of more critical
scrutiny than in any other period since Vietnam. To recover the integrity of the national security state, the Bush presidency staged a scenario
which depended upon "arms for hostages" as its grounding rationale. As
combat soldiers returned home from the Gulf, they became representative as well of the hostages released from Lebanon and less directly of the
national citizenry released from the cold war.[28]

Following the U.S. military's systematic disarming of Saddam Hussein's nuclear capability, the U.S. public was invited to return to the Alamogordo Desert in 1945 but by way of the Saudi Desert in 1991 and thereby
witness the removal of the cold war from the U.S. national narrative, and
its miniaturization as the discourse exchanged by the principals in the
Middle East. Instead of remaining mnemically bound to the traumatic
historical materials—the Dresden and Tokyo fire-bombings, the Cuban
Missile Crisis, My Lai, Three Mile Island, Chernobyl, the Iranian Hostage
Crisis—secreted in the cold war mentality, official coverage of the Gulf
War "worked through" cold war hysteria by repeating all of these events
in the infinitely fast-forward of an "end of History" scenario, understood
this time as an overtaking of the cold war past by way of a U.S. future,
which rediscovered the cold war in an underdeveloped temporality (the
Middle East) understood as historically incommensurate with the New
World Order. In refinding the cold war in Kuwait's relationship with Iraq
(rather than the United States' with the Soviet Union), the televisual public might have undergone what could be called collective para-amnesia.
It was, as these representations suggested, to remember to forget its own

cold war history by learning to remember Middle Eastern history in the terminology of a miniaturized cold war.[29]

With the compulsive repetition of the troops' triumphant homecoming (from World War II, Korea, Vietnam, Grenada, and Panama as well as the cold war), the United States should have entered the New World Order with the same ideological assurance that had been accrued after World War II, and the cold war was to have been recycled as the history of the Middle East in the epoch of *Pax Americana*. [30] Able to see everything about the enemy without being seen, SDI was to have turned each viewer into an agent of a transnational security state, with surveillance responsibility for the globe. Invulnerable because invisible, this transnational consciousness was to have enabled viewers to transform Iraq into a peripheral U.S. border and the Middle East (as well as every other "developing" nation) into the United States' political unconscious.

But, as I have already argued, the concrete fantasy which underwrote the Gulf War entailed the projection of moral responsibility for Hiroshima onto Saddam Hussein and the symbolic disavowal (in SDI's systematic dismantling of Hussein's nuclear capability) of Hiroshima's ever having actually taken place. Through this symbolic undoing of the United States' role in the forty-five-year cold war, Operation Desert Storm repositioned the nation in the aftermath of World War II, a "war to end wars," and assigned it the responsibility for preventing nuclear wars in the future.[31] But since the United States was in historical fact the only nation ever to have used a thermonuclear device in wartime (and would have, and for the same ostensible reason [to save U.S. lives] used one again in the struggle with Hussein), this denial of responsibility exposed the United States' undeterred preeminence as a version of the Imperial Power that its national narrative was sworn to oppose. Which is to say that in the absence of the enemy superpower onto whom the United States was used to assigning responsibility for its crimes, the United States had become its undeterred other in the New World Order.

This historical fantasy depended upon the selective forgetting of the criticism directed against the Vietnam War as well as a new national mythology concerning the quest for MIA's held captive (in Vietnam, Korea, the Soviet Union) since World War II. As "hostages" released at the conclusion of the cold war, MIA's fostered an understanding of the nation itself as a hostage released after a forty-six-year captivity. The hostages released after the Gulf War fostered this identification.

At about the same time as the war's conclusion, however, the Rodney King incident activated an alternative memory. When the nation's public gaze was directed inwards at the spectacle of a black civilian beaten senseless as the result of a police action, the Gulf War lost its mandate to project internal dissension onto an external antagonism. The incident effectively detotalized the New World Order and triggered in the wake of this displacement an historical conjuncture discernible in the chain of contrary historical associations it enabled.[31] Reports of the rape of women in the U.S. military replaced Hussein's "rape of Kuwait," disclosures of the Bush administration's technological assistance both before and *during* the war severely compromised official accounts of Saddam Hussein's "secret" nuclear device, news of friendly fire in the Gulf recalled Vietnam, the yellow ribbons of endless homecomings were replaced following the first jury verdict with riots in South Central Los Angeles and purple ribbons signifying "No Justice, No Peace." Operation Desert Storm became Iraqgate. Bush lost the 1992 election.

Mike Davis underscored the historical dimensions of this alternative memory with the following observations about the Rodney King affair:

> The balance of grievances in the community is complex. Rodney King is the symbol that links unleashed police racism in Los Angeles to the crisis of black life everywhere, from Las Vegas to Toronto. Indeed, it is becoming clear that the King case may be almost as much of a watershed in American history as Dred Scott, a test of the very meaning of the citizenship for which African Americans have struggled for 400 years—as a veteran of the 1965 riot said while watching SWAT teams arrest some of the hundreds of rival gang members trying to meet peacefully at Watts's Jordan Downs Housing Project: "That ole fool Bush think we as dumb as Saddam. Land Marines in Compton and get hisself re-elected. But this ain't Iraq. This is Vietnam, Jack."[32]

Having taken place in an environment closer in its economy and demographics to Baghdad than say La Jolla, the King incident could not be enframed within the picture of a New World Order. As L.A. burned in May of 1992, as a protest against these unjust police actions, the Rodney King incident reanimated questions about the legality of events justified in the name of the national security dating as far back as Hiroshima.[33] The images of a city burning in protest against police brutality seemed in retrospect a response to the official representation of Baghdad, as the appropriate staging ground for U.S. prominence in the New World Order.[34] Like Hiroshima, L.A. represented one of those cities designated by nuclear strategists as expendable. Images of police brutally clubbing Rodney King recalled a residual series of related images left over from police actions in Vietnam, Korea, Panama, Grenada, and the Persian Gulf.

If Baghdad had been bombed to demonstrate U.S. technological superiority at the outset of a New World Order, the burning of buildings in South Central Los Angeles inaugurated a counter-demonstration. It raised important questions that recalled the related moral dilemmas attending the decision in the name of international security (and an earlier New World Order) to drop the atomic bombs on Hiroshima and Nagasaki at the end of World War II. Whereas the Bush administration had aspired to divert attention away from just such urgent moral dilemmas as these, the breakup of the cold war consensus has returned the nation to them as an unfinished collective task.

Notes

1 The best available critique of official coverage of the war can be found in Douglas Kellner's *The Persian Gulf TV War* (Boulder, Colo.: Westview Press, 1992).

2 In "Bombing Logic," *Marxism Today,* March 1991, p. 46, Dick Hebidge has cogently analyzed the official coverage in terms of the displacement of critical observation with a spectacle of consensus. For an example of a thoroughly postmodernist reading of the Persian Gulf War see Jean Baudrillard's "La Guerre du Golfe n'a pas eu lieu," *Liberation,* March 29, 1991.

3 This documentary account appears in Christopher Norris's *Uncritical Theory: Postmodernism, Intellectuals and the Gulf War* (Amherst: University of Massachusetts Press, 1992), pp. 110–11.

4 George Mariscal has described this counter memory succinctly: "The violence perpetrated against Rodney King cannot be disassociated from the massive destruction wrought by the United States Government against the Iraqui people." George Mariscal, "In the Wake of the Gulf War: Untying the Yellow Ribbon," *Cultural Critique* 19 (1991): 114.

5 This account of Reaganism was strongly influenced by Stuart Hall's "The Toad in the Garden: Thatcherism among the Theorists," in *Marxism and the Interpretation of Culture,* ed. Nelson and Grossberg (Urbana: University of Illinois Press, 1988), pp. 35–58.

6 In Homi Bhabha, "Of Mimicry and Man: The Ambivalence of Colonial Discourse," *October* 28 (1988): 129.

7 Jacques Derrida, "No Apocalypse, Not Now (full speed ahead, seven missiles, seven missives)," *Diacritics* 14 (1984): 23.

8 In "Sexuality in the Gulf War: Did You Measure Up," *Genders* 13 (1992): 3. Abouali Farmanfarmaian refers to the Gulf War as "Hiroshima on the Tigres" to call attention to the usage of the "just war" trope used to justify both events. Further evidence of this linkage can be found in Cal Thomas's "A Time to Think

Nuclear," *Boston Globe,* February 7, 1991: "The United States should use tactical nuclear weapons to . . . save the lives of American and allied fighters."

9 George Bush, January 28, 1992, *State of the Union Address.*

10 In the same State of the Union Address, Bush connected U.S. victory in the Gulf with an appeal for the funding of SDI "to protect our country from limited nuclear missile attacks . . . too many people in too many countries have access to nuclear arms."

11 Dean MacCannell, "Baltimore in the Morning . . . After: On the Forces of Post-Nuclear Leadership," *Diacritics* 14 (1984): 41.

12 Guy Debord, *The Society of the Spectacle* (Detroit: Black and Red Unauthorized Translation, 1970).

13 Michael Paul Rogin, "'Make My Day,' Spectacle as Amnesia in Imperial Politics," *Representations* 29 (1990): 116–17.

14 Paul Virilio, *Nuclear Democracies* (New York: Semiotexte, 1991), p. 77.

15 For a somewhat different account of the way in which this understanding of the cold war narrative functioned in the Construction of the Americanist Canon, see Donald E. Pease, "*Moby Dick* and the Cold War," *The American Renaissance Reconsidered,* ed. Walter Michaels and Donald E. Pease (Baltimore: Johns Hopkins University Press, 1985), pp. 115–17.

16 Marita Startkin, "The Wall, The Screen and the Image: The Vietnam Veteran's Memorial," *Representations* 35 (1991): 137–38.

17 Startkin, p. 137.

18 The hostages who had been held captive during the last days of Carter's presidency supplied the mythological relay connecting the Vietnam veterans to the Desert Stormers. See Farmanfarmaian, "Sexuality in the Gulf War," 14–17.

19 W.J.T. Mitchell, "The Violence of Public Art: *Do the Right Thing*," *Critical Inquiry* 16 (1990): 888.

20 John Hellman, *American Myth and the Legacy of Vietnam* (New York: Columbia University Press, 1986), p. 153.

21 For a more expansive overview of the literature of the Vietnam War see my entry "The Vietnam War" in *The Reader's Encyclopedia of American Literature,* ed. George Perkins (New York: Harper, 1992).

22 Noam Chomsky, "On War Crimes," *At War with Asia* (New York: Pantheon, 1970), pp. 298–99.

23 Jean-Paul Sartre, *On Genocide* (Boston: Beacon Press, 1968), pp. 81–82.

24 Robert Jay Lifton, *The Future of Immortality and Other Essays for a Nuclear Age* (New York: Basic Books, 1987), pp. 58, 71, 72.

25 See Lifton, pp. 31–73.

26 Department of State, Current Policy, No. 869.

27 In an interview with Mojtba Sadria, "The United States, Japan, and the Gulf War," published in *Monthly Review* 43 (1992), Doug Lummis spelled out this Pentagon strategy with remarkable precision: "The war had to be staged in such a way as to seem unambiguously just, with all the law and justice on the U.S. side, and it had to be winnable, which as they learned from the war in Vietnam, means that it had to be short. . . . The propaganda was Second-World-War language. . . . Their hope was clearly that by reenacting the Second World War, the society could become as strong and healthy and dominant in the world again as it was just before the Cold War began."

28 The identification President Bush ritualistically adduced between Saddam Hussein's "rape of Kuwait" and Adolph Hitler's invasion of Czechoslovakia fostered this association, and the administration's stakes in this representation: an imaginative re-investment of the symbolic moral and political inheritance of the Second World War onto a Middle Eastern topography previously the source of hostage and oil crises, religious wars, territorial disputes, and Irangate.

29 When such byproducts of the forty-five years of weapons buildup as smart bombs and Patriot missiles hit their targets, a civilian population (in Israel) was in fact defended against possible nuclear attack, and, as a consequence, the U.S. spectatorial public was encouraged to recognize the usage to which cold war history could be put in the explanation of Middle Eastern History.

30 For different accounts of the psychology informing the government officials who fostered this understanding, see *The Political Psychology of the Gulf War: Leaders, Publics and the Process of Conflict*, ed. Stanley A. Renshon (Pittsburgh: University of Pittsburgh Press, 1993).

31 In this account of an effective historical counter-memory, I have drawn upon Louis Althusser's notion of an "expressive totality" to explain how what I have called "critical witnessing" can detotalize the cold war's overdetermination of historical eventuation through the triggering of the alternative historical associations the cold war binarism repressed only partly. See *Reading Capital*, trans. Ben Brewster (London: New Left Books, 1970).

32 Mike Davis, *L.A. Was Just the Beginning: Urban Revolt in the United States: A Thousand Points of Light* (Westfield: Open Magazine, Pamphlet #20, 1992), pp. 5, 7.

33 In this focusing on race as the category through which to activate a chain of substitute memories, I do not intend a suppression, but the complication of the "gendered" and "class" reading of the war's mode of production.

34 For an analysis of the economic status of Los Angeles as a Third World city, see David Rieff, *Los Angeles: Capital of the Third World* (New York: Simon and Schuster, 1991).

Lynda Boose

Techno-Muscularity and the "Boy Eternal"

From the Quagmire to the Gulf

In a 1989 comparison of his own presidency to that of the legendary Abraham Lincoln, President George Bush emphasized that while Lincoln had been "tested by fire" in a war of "brother . . . killing brother," he himself had not yet had the opportunity for such a test. Considering the president's rhetoric of war and the family in which some apocalyptic trial by battle is necessary in order for him to compete with American history's preeminent forefather, something on the scale of the 1991 Persian Gulf War was almost predictable. For while invading Panama to bust Manuel Noriega may have bettered the scale of any of the "tests by fire" that had been staged by Bush's most immediate predecessor, for Lincolnesque historical stakes nothing so paltry would, obviously, suffice.

But George Bush was not alone in his preoccupation with an epic return to male conquest mythology; even before January 16, 1991, there were signs that American culture was literally saturated with such desire. The writer of an October 1990 *Newsweek* article on "The Civil War and Modern Memory," for instance, becomes so enthralled by the model of heroically confirmed sonship made possible by such "tests by fire" that, after briefly mentioning "nationhood . . . [and] the wounds of race and class," he goes on to find, as the core significance of the Civil War for modern Americans, that "it's to that moment of testing that Americans, especially American men, so often respond when they think of the Civil War: Would I fight? Would I die? Would I measure up?"[1]

So—forget about the fact that not all "Americans, especially American men" are white, as everything underlying the above reading of the Civil War assumes. Forget about slavery, the nation divided, and even the issue of union. For by October 1990, with the first American troops already in Saudi Arabia, American history was getting shoved aside by a refurbished mythology of manhood being tested. And what that test of manhood signified was, quite explicitly, the space in which sons confirm their authority with the fathers. For, as *Newsweek* goes on to say: "While Saudi Arabia is not Shiloh—at least not yet—the threads that connect them may be one reason so many people were drawn to the PBS series. Those ties that bind us to the Civil War are astonishingly short. . . . Former Secretary of State Dean Rusk recalls in his recently published memoirs that both of his grandfathers fought for the Confederacy. Rusk, a World War II veteran, went on to help plan the Korean War and the Vietnam War, the line unbroken."

And so the American parade is back in line: the war America fought to define the nation's moral geography collapsed together with—as if it could impart heroic meaning to—its imperialist intervention in Vietnam's civil war. Beneath the glibness of such ideological condensations,[2] history is pounded to oblivion under the hoofbeats of an imagined cavalry charge from the past, a father to son relay transmitted through war— the "line unbroken" through "threads that connect." Presumably, blest be such "ties that bind."

In *Newsweek*'s blithe transformation of the reproduction of sons into the reproduction of war, what has been conveniently elided is the glaring contradiction that the story itself invokes by its use of the Rusk family as a synoptic illustration of war's unbroken patrilineage. For while former Secretary of State Dean Rusk may have fought in World War II and had grandfathers who did so in the Civil War, Dean Rusk's son did *not* fight in Vietnam. The line was broken. Richard Rusk (as likewise, both the son and daughter of former Defense Secretary Robert McNamara)[3] was— and still is—deeply opposed to both the war in Vietnam and his father's role as "the architect of that murderous human tragedy." The Rusk memoirs that *Newsweek* glosses over are ones that Richard Rusk recorded in a series of painful, unresolving interviews which attempted to come to terms with the father whose authority he had twenty years ago rejected. Richard Rusk was intent, says his father, on trying "to find any ties that might still bind us together."[4] What had severed those ties was the war in Vietnam.

What *Newsweek* has elided in its narrative of war and sonship is the gap, the break, the halt to the parade that the Vietnam war threatened to insert in the nation's repetitive pattern of war every twenty to twenty-five years, one to allow each generation of sons its opportunity to be tested. In each of the mini-wars staged in the decade before the Persian Gulf crisis, America's primary goal was not, as had earlier been suspected, merely to undo defeat in Vietnam: it was to put to rest the legacy of resistant sons bequeathed by that conflict. January 1991 offered a unique opportunity. With Soviet power in collapse, a war in Iraq allowed America to demonstrate that it was the only big man around. There was now no one to impede American military muscle, block American control of the United Nations, or provide an alternative power base around which to rally any opposition. But simultaneously, through round the clock saturation bombing, subnuclear weaponry, tactics that flouted the Geneva conventions, overt censorship of media information, intransigence in all negotiations, and the rejection of all third-party ceasefire proposals—in short, through the repeated choice of high-violence options gratuitously disproportionate to the level of threat, an unfettered U.S. militarism was internally staging its own rebirth. Freed by history from external check, it was simultaneously demonstrating its freedom from and throwing off the inhibitions that had been imposed by antiwar sentiment residual from Vietnam. When in January 1991 the United States turned the full power of its conventional arsenal on several hundred thousand Iraqi soldiers trapped underground, George Bush did have a domestic priority: to bury in the desert the antiwar discourse signified by "Vietnam."

A key observation that the feminist perspective has contributed to the critique of culture is the recognition that every public power arrangement depends on the control of femininity and masculinity as concepts, from which notions the control of individual, sexed subjects becomes possible.[5] The road from the Quagmire to the Gulf was built upon the manipulation of just such concepts. It was, furthermore, built out of an antiwar discourse that was itself always comprised of two incompatible, strongly gender-marked narratives. Within the undifferentiated, widespread antiwar sentiment that compelled the 1973 withdrawal of American troops lay a range of potential contradictions that had managed to coexist not only within the loose antiwar coalition but even within the attitudes of single individuals. By the end of the 1980s, most Americans from the social class whose desires and memories define the nation's dominant discourse probably still remembered Vietnam as a "bad war" that "we didn't win and probably shouldn't have gotten into." But the key ideological issues that had constructed that opposition—just *why* Vietnam was a "bad war" that the majority wanted out of—had receded into oblivion, along with much of the rest of the era's history.[6] It was a public consciousness ripe for a surgically swift memory implant. And behind the official rhetoric connecting America's massive intervention in the Gulf with "overcoming the Vietnam syndrome" was a discernible effort to segregate remembered opposition to the Vietnam War into competing narratives so that one could be reclaimed from its antiwar affiliations and the other one anathematized. Behind the propaganda campaigns that had accompanied the various U.S. post-Vietnam mini-invasions of the 1980s lay a strategic objective to generate what the Gulf War finally produced on a large scale: the parades, the cheers, the public excitement over military hardware, and the popular sloganeering about a "new pride in America" that such cheap, easy victories progressively enabled. In short, a revivified militarism that could once again become self-reproducing.

As historian Marilyn Young eloquently illustrates and as U.S. government documents make explicit, the security establishment that the cold war entrenched in American government maintains a profound distrust of and determination to root out the pacifism that remained, even after World War II, a sizable factor in American attitudes.[7] Displacing that ethic in post-Vietnam culture depended on segregating the residual antiwar discourse along often unconscious, but deeply culturated associations of gender. In the recuperable one of these two narratives, issues about Vietnam were dealt with by strict containment: the war was restricted to a focus on the individual American soldier, discussion of U.S. involvement was isolated to issues concerned only with winning and losing, and geography was even relocated from Vietnam to the home front where revisionist history has staked its loudest claims. In this scenario, if Vietnam was a bad war, it was bad because we lost; and what we shouldn't have gotten into was a war that was doomed to failure by the refusal of the American people to support their troops.

In the other, more global narrative that the Gulf War was targeted to excise, the focus was on the morality of America's foreign policy and military conduct and its impact on both the Vietnamese people and American soldiers. The two narratives had been politically held together by consideration of the American soldier(s). But in the second narration, the importance of the individual American soldier was implicitly leveled and whether America "won" became almost inconsequential, since U.S. intervention in Vietnam was itself viewed as an unjustified act of political imperialism. At the core of this second narrative lay an ethic outside of the claims of patriotic nationalism—the claims for which the American soldier is signifier. Labeled during the Vietnam era as issuing from "bleeding hearts" and "sob sisters," it was a set of ethics that, by the very nature of its self-reflexivity, its internalization of guilt, and its antimilitarist, anti-violence ethos, had asserted—and for a time successfully promoted—an identifiably "feminized" structure of values against the distinctively "masculine" priorities of the other.

Teresa de Lauretis has argued that narrative is by definition masculine and Oedipal in structure.[8] And indeed, while the Vietnam counter-narrative may have been "femin*ized*," it stayed resolutely centered on the creation of male subjects, never deviating into anything that might be imagined as a "femin*ine*" story. Nonetheless, it effectively challenged the hegemony of American culture's traditional self-presentation. And while the long hair, flowers, and flowing robes disappeared from post-Vietnam male popular culture, what did not so readily disappear was the potential for an ethically reconstituted masculinity that those semiotics of resistance signified. What the debacle of America's masculinized, militarized policies on both fronts of the Vietnam War had opened up was the sudden space in American culture for an alternative to the mythology of a national self born in and valorized by a history of conquest and dominance.

Even given the problems of retroactively measuring cultural weight, it seems accurate to say that the 1970s were not spent in a national agony over having "lost the Vietnam War." As was then widely recognized, the putative "loser" had lost mostly pride while the uncompensated "winner" was left with millions of dead, missing, and homeless, cratered by bombs, saturated in chemicals, and punished for its victory by being cut off from all Western assistance for decades to come.[9] So long as repugnance was attached to the violence that had rendered the distinctions of "winner" and "loser" meaningless, America's so-called "loss" in Vietnam could not become a political rallying point—but culpability for the vast, continuing tragedy in Southeast Asia and the anguish of the men who had been sent there still decidedly could. In the late 1960s–70s the American people perhaps came as close as they ever have to considering America's global guilt in the promotion of war. But by the relentlessly underlying binary of gender, that space is already psychically constellated as a "feminized" site and one that the nation could occupy apparently only so long as repugnance remained at bay, associated with the opposite. And in a progression that fits the classic Freudian model of delayed traumatic experience, the newly aggressive, antispeculative American self that emerged as the driving force of 1980s American politics did so in convulsive reaction to the 1979 takeover of the American Embassy in Teheran—the event that was to define Jimmy Carter as a "wimp" and guarantee Ronald Reagan's presidency.[10] In that triggering recall of the humiliation and capture of an American Embassy, in those pictures of U.S. hostages again held captive by jeering Third World males, in the too-familiar nightly voice of Walter Cronkite spelling out the latest national debacle, and even in the image of the crippled American helicopters abandoned in the desert rather than the South China Sea—all the old, repressed humiliations came flooding back. And repugnance switched sides.

Throughout most of the 1970s, an antimilitarist discourse and the latent conditions for extending its impact did exist. Its influence in the culture at large is evident in such barometers as the 1970s market demise of military toys and G.I. Joe dolls—items that returned again in the mid-1980s and soared to market records in the wake of the Gulf War.[11] But while the Vietnam War had precipitated a crisis of gender that had opened up the myth of the so-called national character, since that persona both produces and is produced by the nation's understanding of masculinity, the attempt to change it was, finally, experienced very differently by women and men. American women emerged from the 1960s and 1970s with an optimistic sense of social/self liberation born in the streets along with the women's movement during the era of civil rights and anti-war protest.[12] For men, however, the pressure to reinvent manhood unavoidably threatened the destruction of a masculine selfhood tenuously acquired in negative differentiation from the feminine and socially constructed by a valorization of dominance. Given the profound personal and socio-historical investments involved, such change was thus always susceptible to recuperation. Faced with fundamentally rethinking an ideology of power, the masculine values instead retrenched. And from such trenches, the "problem" of Vietnam was reformulated. Thus reconceived, the problem was no longer the excessive deployment of militarized values but the failure to deploy them strongly enough. The problem became "fighting the war with one hand tied behind our backs," "kowtowing to the lily-livered liberals, peaceniks, and doves in the Congress who curtailed American bombing," and being too tolerant and not tough enough on protesters. And the language of the 1980s became an echo-box for reconfirming the ethics of "getting tough," "playing hardball," "being a winner," and not "flinching" or "wimping out."

This return to patriarchal values would be politically comprehensible were it limited only to a response from the right. To find it likewise a chosen ideological solution for liberal/progressive men like Robert Bly, premier anti-war poet of the Vietnam era and now founder of the "Men's Movement" in America, may suggest the profound extent to which a perceived threat to masculinity lies behind the revalorized aggressiveness of the national character. The "Men's Movement" is an odd political polyglot. Having apparently recognized the need for masculinity to reconceive itself, Bly's philosophy begins with values culturally identified with the feminine—the need for men to connect to their fathers and to acquire a greater openness, intimacy, etc) But the path into Bly's Jungian woods veers suddenly to the right, away from recognizing the inherent imperialism of patriarchal systems and toward an affirmed return to male privilege. As "Iron John" and Bly's newly masculinized "wild man" are celebrated in a reaffirmed hierarchy, the meaning of patriarchy for women goes wholly ignored. At least nominally, the abandoning father is held to blame for incoherent male identity. But any system that reflects as much fear of gender blurring as does Bly's inevitably ends up finding the real culprit in the mother, whose maternal affection he defines as a "baptism into shame" that undermines the father-son bond.¹³ Bly directly associates the problems of masculinity with the Vietnam War. He also associates them with that universal explanation for contemporary male angst, the feminist movement. And while I would argue that the pressure to reinvent manhood was not so much an effect of the women's movement as it was a synchronous event, when debate over U.S. aims and methods in Vietnam surfaced again in the 1980s, that very synchronicity, recycled as evidence of feminist castration designs, helped fuel the recuperation of a cultural ethic uncontaminated by values that might "feminize" it.¹⁴

The Hollywood movie has long been the popular culture site where America constructs and fine-tunes its self-mythologies to fit the libidinal exigencies of its foreign and defense policies. As America's military interventionism resurged in the 1980s, filmgoers concurrently began witnessing the reascendancy—with a vengeance—of a masculine ethos so narcissistic in its need for self-display that it progressively eroded most of the space hitherto even available for female representation. So considerable was the shrinkage in women's roles between 1980s films and those from 1930s and 70s, in fact, that in 1989, 1990, and 1991 the Academy Award industry actually had difficulty even coming up with five women in substantial enough roles to nominate for best actress. According to actress/writer Carrie Fisher's survey of Hollywood films produced between 1988 and 1990, only 28 percent of the speaking parts were written for women, less than 5 percent for women over forty.¹⁵

The films of the late 1980s and early 1990s—an oeuvre dominated by male buddy/cop films, boy's rite of passage films, son's quest for father films, and so-called adventure films populated by lone "terminators"—

spell out a metanarrative of violent masculine reassertion and feminine erasure that many of the films quite literally enact. Such a cultural meta-script is, furthermore, being written by dominant trends in the repre-sentation of the sexualized body. As women's roles have shrunk, their bodies have progressively become subjected to a chillingly literal evisceration: "slasher" films with their inevitably female victims have proliferated, and films featuring women raped or women assaulted included, by 1990, one out of every eight movies that Hollywood made.[16] Meanwhile, while female embodiment and female bodies were being whittled down, the screen has filled up with inflated male torsos of the sort that had, before the 1980s, been relegated to Tarzan movies. What dominated the 1980s screen iconography of gender was a determination to move male repre-sentation away from the new explorations of male sensitivity that had rather tentatively emerged in the first post-Vietnam decade. From Dustin Hoffman, Al Pacino, and the small, dark, vulnerable, often ethnically iden-tified bodies that Hollywood foregrounded in the 1970s, the cultural ethic visually embodied in the lead male figure had by 1990 done a 180-degree reversal.

What defines a newly dominant American film genre is the "techno-muscularity" packaged into films featuring incredible hulk stars such as Sylvester Stallone, Chuck Norris, their numerous grade-B video clones, and Arnold Schwarzenegger—the virtual apotheosis of the male mega-body and the highest paid actor in 1991 America. Yet as the masculine icon has undergone such literal inflation, the representation of maleness and the narrative in which it is imagined—which together constitute a set of culture-specific dreams, desires, and fears—has become progressively less adult as a projection and more and more the cartoon image of a little boy's fantasy of manhood. Inhabiting narratives that frequently belong to an identifiably post-Vietnam genre that imagines reshaping the future by changing the past, the fortresslike body image of the masculine hero who arose in post-Vietnam America reassures its audience of a masculine dominance made invulnerable by the arsenal of high-tech killing devices that this genre obsessively imagines as necessary extensions of male body power. Movies starring the Hollywood hulks are narcissistic and homo-erotic. They are focused on a male body image that signifies not hetero-sexual virility but potency over other male contenders played out within a graphics that writes female desire as a cipher and offers male bodies up to the gaze of other men. Such films are cultural isomorphs of the football game—an aggressive enactment of male bonding and competition played by males, for males, with women authorized only as cheering admirers of male prowess.)

It is Arnold Schwarzenegger who plumbs the deepest subtending fantasies of techno-muscularity. Both on screen and off, he inculcates the most unacknowledged (and unacknowledgeable) fantasy of domination embedded in the myth of not just of German but American history. Like the unspoken signified that lies behind the myriad U.S. interventions in Third World countries, the meaning of the fantasy is unavoidably present in everything an audience hears and sees in Arnold Schwarzenegger's phenomenally popular militarism. For American viewers weaned on Hollywood Nazis, the Schwarzenegger accent, physique, and even the mechanization of the characters he plays are undissociable from the Nazi dream of Aryan domination that America's wars in the Third World covertly play out. It seems equally impossible to miss the Third Reich allusion in the phrase "Desert Storm Troopers." And while associations between Schwarzenegger and Nazism are factually unfounded, they derive reinforcement from Schwarzenegger's widely publicized advocacy of right-wing politics.

The crossover in film from "sensitive male" to impervious behemoth is as much as recorded in the chronology of Sylvester Stallone's 1976–88 *Rocky/Rambo* sequence. The attempt in *Rocky* (1976) to construct a masculine hero in opposition to the macho ethic makes the film a definable product of the 1970s. In it the male fighter does not triumph in the ring but—with help from the woman in his life—achieves a moral victory by supplanting the "win" ethic with one that involves simply having the will to "go the distance.' But in subsequent *Rocky* films the woman's role is crowded out of significance, and the moral ethic disappears as the narrative of masculinity and the need to prove physical dominance nullify the ethic of 1976. By the time of *Rocky IV* (1985), the male hero's struggle had been enlarged to the international arena. There, morally impelled to avenge his fallen buddy, the American fighter is transformed into America's Fighter, embodied signifier of American valor who must single-fistedly stage America's comeback and show the world that an underrated America can defeat even the superhuman Russian(s).

In the counterpart Rambo film of that same year (*Rambo: First Blood Part II*), the militarized physique appears inside the fantasy that gave rise to it in the first place: the Vietnam War and the by-now obsessive concern over losing it that the Rocky/Rambo figure reinforces, even as his all-powerful body promises to undo its loss. And in *Rambo*—the most

popular of all Vietnam War films made up until 1991 when their production was abruptly suppressed by the arrival of a "good" war—the nearly
naked Stallone, visual signifier for the erect phallus and embodiment of
American techno-muscularity, strides in dominion through the jungles
of Southeast Asia, made invulnerable by the infallibility of his high-tech
American weaponry. But the feature of this movie that inspired a whole
subgenre of Vietnam War films is its fantasy of repetition, return, and
redoing. In this film the unjustly rejected Vietnam vet goes back to the
scene of America's loss to rescue the figural representation of a "missing" American masculinity embodied on screen as the emaciated and
emasculated versions of maleness who are imagined as having been left
behind, the "Missing in Action" that yet continue, even in the 1990s, to
haunt the filmic and the literal fantasies of the American public.[17] And
Stallone's most famous line in the film—"Do we get to win it this time?"—
helped to produce the angst it reflected over the issue that by 1985 had
come to traumatize the national psyche. Given the retroactive emergence
of that trauma and the concomitant obsession with a manhood imagined
as having been abandoned by American "withdrawal" (a term that itself
connotes masculine shame), the way Stallone's question plays out in the
movie does something more. By giving narrative reality to the fantasy
that forces located somewhere in American culture had not only deprived
men like John Rambo of their entitlement to heroism back in the Vietnam era but had afterward worked to perpetuate the imprisonment of
American manhood, Stallone's resentful line effectively rationalized the
amorphous male resentment that was increasingly adrift in American
culture by 1985.

Throughout the 1970s and early 1980s, the Vietnam War had been
shrouded in a silence born out of national shame. When it reemerged as
a topic in American society, it did so via film—surfacing at a site outside of argumentation or rebuttal and carried by the symbol-laden depiction of the male body. Through *Rambo*, Stallone's gleaming physique
became the virtual equivalent of an ideological stake onto which American masculinity became firmly lashed to a political stance on the Vietnam
War. After *Rambo*, the body of the hero in successive Vietnam films became a signpost for political perspective. Those films that construed their
position as "anti"-war represented the Vietnam experience through male
bodies filmed to seem small, vulnerable, and implicitly destructible—
bodies like those of Chris Sheehan, Michael J. Fox, Willem Dafoe, and
Tom Cruise. Meanwhile, the right-wing films of Norris, Stallone, Hackman, and Schwarzenegger, to which *Rambo* gave new life, used the mega-

bodied male to articulate the vision of an invincible America that did not "lose" the war so much as be prevented from winning it.

These highly popular MIA narratives served the recuperation of militarism extensively, supplying a format for fictitious projection into Central America during the years when U.S. invasion of El Salvador and Nicaragua seemed likely and even suggesting equivalencies between the plight of military Americans putatively held in Vietnam and civilians taken hostage in Lebanon from 1985 onward. The ante of American pride thus upped considerably, a pugnacious subtext bridging Vietnam and the Middle East was slowly becoming part of the popular baggage that American culture was inexorably acquiring. At its center was the image of the newly beefed-up American male, his right to dominate the world inseparable from his dramatization of the heroic will to redo.

If the widespread narrative of threatened masculinity helps explain why American men were lured back to the fold of militarism so shortly after the Vietnam debacle, women's response to the Gulf War (listed by Harris polls at 73 percent in favor on January 21) is less readily explainable. The most intriguing sign to consider is the widespread phenomenon of "yellow-ribbonism" and the belligerent demand to "love our boys" that the ribbons and the American flag displays encoded. Around those symbols, the nation's women as well as men were eventually mobilized, moving with alarming rapidity in less than six weeks from a widespread disinclination to fight a war for which not even the White House could articulate a compelling cause to a cheering reaffirmation of U.S. militarism, its essential causelessness swallowed up in a media-orchestrated roar of national self-confirmation.

The yellow ribbons served as a coalescent sign that both subsumed and offered to placate the peculiar anxieties that America had carried into the 1990s.[18] Used in the 1980s as a sign of remembering the hostages held in Lebanon, they were already correlated with unexpressed hostility toward the Middle East. But they served the nation's desires in an even more important way. Through the capacity of the ribbons to signify the feminine, they enabled the construction of a rigid binary of gender; and through that binary, all potential responses to the war could be contained. Noting the way that the gender gap measuring support for the war had shrunk from a substantial twenty-four point differential five days before the U.S. bombing of Iraq began to a mere ten points four days after it started, Cynthia Enloe commented that "In tying a yellow ribbon 'round an old oak tree—or car antenna, porch pillar, or shop sign—

most women probably do not see themselves as endorsing something so grandiose as a new world order. They probably see themselves as providing moral support to particular sons, daughters, neighbors, and friends. But, for the U.S. national security elite, they are voluntarily constructing a feminized 'homefront' to complement—28,000 American women soldiers notwithstanding—a masculinized battlefront." [19] By being positioned as the virtuously beribboned feminine, the civilian home front not only invoked the binary that reemphasized the exclusively masculine position of the military but effectively delegitimated resistance to the war from either men or women. The yellow ribbons helped to undo two alternative versions of gender that had first been imagined on a broad scale in the 1960s and 1970s: the masculinity that had been oppositionally constituted around resistance and militant pacifism, and the alternative femininity that had imagined divorcing itself from playing dutiful spouse/ maternal producer for the needs of the masculine, military state. During the Gulf War, with women soldiers for the first time at the combat front, conditions at least theoretically existed for a blurring of the strictly gendered binary through which war has traditionally been spatialized. But through a tightly policed feminization of the home front, masculinity was contained solely on the battle front and femininity at home as a gold-star mommy. As George Bush's target date for the display of American dominance came progressively closer, increasing pressures inside the culture began strictly dichotomizing all available civilian responses within the feminine options of the good mommy/bad mommy, loyal nurturer or unfaithful betrayer. Civilians could, in short, choose between playing Penelope or Clytemnestra, the archetypal good girl/bad girl models of Western culture's ur-war narrative.

America's entrance into the Gulf War abounded in ironies of gender which the media carefully avoided placing into juxtaposition before the American reader/viewer. For instance: while America—chivalric knight arrogant—was preparing to send its military to avenge the reported rape of Kuwaiti women by Iraqi military,[20] the reported rape and sexual assault of women recruits at U.S. military training installations escalated so dramatically in the months leading up to the war that both the Pentagon and the chairman of the Senate Armed Services Committee were finally embarrassed into ordering investigations.[21] And while intervention was being urged by the American president as an appropriate response to the murder of Kuwaiti infants who had been—according to stories later proven wholly false[22]—ripped out of incubators by Iraqi soldiers, the American war machine was at that very moment mapping out air strikes that would wipe out the majority of urban sanitation capabilities and would consequently eventuate—according to post-war United Nations estimates—in the 1992 death of some 170,000 Iraqi infants.[23] At stake in the media's avoidance of such enlightening ironies was the positive male persona that George Bush and company had so diligently crafted—the good father image that seemed consciously designed to suppress the identity of rapist and baby killer that had emerged as the defining signifiers of American troop actions in Vietnam. The media's willingness to reproduce the official Gulf War narrative unchallenged was in itself eloquent testimony to the impact that the revisionist narrative of the Vietnam War had made. Determined not to be again held accountable for the United States having lost a war,[24] the press and the public tacitly collaborated in a hear-no-evil/see-no-evil policy about Gulf War information. The mainstream press never really fought the imposition of government censorship and, as surveys showed, under the aegis of "protecting our boys," the majority of Americans would have approved of censorship that was even more stringent than that which was put in place. The American media and the public they play to may love violence, but the violence they love is only that which supports certain myths. As the press discovered two decades earlier from the outrage it provoked from approximately 80 percent of Americans by airing stories of the My Lai massacre,[25] American viewers make a critical distinction between "good violence" and "bad violence": bad violence is that which works to undermine or expose contradictions in the cultural myth for which good violence is the paradigmatic structure. And the sacrosanct story around which this nation's understanding of itself has been built and then adumbrated into millions of mediated narratives is the story of American masculine heroism. At the center of the story, within a semiotics defined by the male symbolic, lies the constructed image of the innocent American soldier. And American militarist ideology has been built on top of a public investment in protecting that image. As protesters of the Gulf War discovered, the threat to destroy the signified—the rectitude of American military action—is tantamount to attacking the boy himself. For while "supporting the troops" is recognized as a public sign of support for the war they signify, to withhold such affirmation situates the protester at the juncture where the society's two most negative figures are condensed: the national enemy and the withholding mommy.

With the media and the government acting as complicit mythographers of the scenario the public wanted to hear, the "bad violence" stories that were incompatible with the vision of America's innocent soldier boys were judiciously delayed in their release and/or soft-pedaled in mainstream media coverage. Quite unlike the obsession with quantifying the enemy "body count" that drove the Vietnam War, statistics on Iraqi troop deaths were left unreported and ultimately unknowable, registered only as perhaps several hundred thousand uncounted bodies, unmarked and unceremoniously bulldozed beneath the sand. By such action, America was flagrantly guilty of doing precisely what it had for twenty years accused the Vietnamese of having done: violating the Geneva convention mandating the identification, interment, marking, and transmission of information about enemy soldiers' graves. With the September publication of previously concealed information about U.S. tactics in the Gulf, the irony of U.S. accusations over Vietnamese treatment of America's putative "MIAS" reached cosmic proportions. The U.S. Army, as it crossed into Iraq, had conquered the enemy with specially designed plows that had buried alive some thousands of Iraqi soldiers dug into seventy miles of trenches. In the vocabulary of one of the American officers, the operation was "cost-effective."[26] In terms of another discourse, however, the incident literalized the most grotesque parody of the coming of universal peace as a "New World Order" biblically imagined as the turning of swords into plowshares.[27]

In spite of how thoroughly the technologized annihilation of a country with a GNP the size of Kentucky flew in the face of all mythology that defines the heroic, up until the more sobering facts of the economic recession began to be felt, post-Gulf War America seemed determined to celebrate its returning troops as exemplary American heroes. Nevertheless, such celebrations themselves were dominated by a distinctly hostile festivity. Instead of parades made up of the usual high school bands and bicycle brigades, the Gulf War victory was celebrated by a display of technologized, phallic aggression distinctly reminiscent of the old Soviet May Day shows or the fist-flexing of some Argentine junta, with massive tank formations, guns, armored personnel carriers, and missile launchers rolling across Memorial Bridge into the nation's capital.[28] But perhaps Washington, D.C., site of so many Vietnam War protests, was the appropriate space for playing out the veiled threat that is encoded in parading such military violence. The enemy that those tanks and guns were implicitly leveled at was the antiwar consciousness of twenty years ago—a consciousness that had been progressively demonized through the 1980s by association with all that is outside the masculine.

As the yellow ribbons began sprouting on front doors, in supermarkets, and used car lots across America, beneath all the excessive and anxious patriotism there was a particular underlying impetus that invested this sign of "homecoming" with its talismanic power. The ribbons, the parades, and "welcome home" celebrations still going on throughout the summer of 1991 weren't really even about the Gulf troops. Displaced responses to the 1980s' revisionist narration of Vietnam, they were half-conscious, guilt-ridden attempts to placate the by-now mythologized figure of the rejected and betrayed Vietnam veteran.

For the 1991 Gulf War, the Vietnam veterans once again got drafted. This time, however, their commander in chief ideologically evoked them to serve on the home front as accusatory signifiers of the son betrayed. Over the course of the 1980s, the Vietnam veteran had slowly been transformed from dangerous embodiment of ideological subversion into the sympathetic symbol of a war that had emasculated a generation of American men by stigmatizing them as losers. Inside this narrative, the figure responsible for all of the veteran's pain is the war protester. And simultaneously, the position of all those who had not "loved our boys in Vietnam" came to be anathematized as feminine. In story after story that began in the mid-1980s to pour forth from Vietnam veterans,[29] any and all rejection that some of them may have experienced upon return—together with guilt that such stories disguise beneath the figure of the external accuser—was remembered in the person of a woman: a wife, a sister, a girlfriend, an airline stewardess, or even, in the 1988 film *Hamburger Hill*, an invented account of being greeted upon return by Berkeley coeds throwing dog shit. The connection is most vividly dramatized through Jane Fonda, the condensed figure of antiwar activism who selectively bore the weight of a vilification that escalated even as the war itself receded. In 1990, Fonda was still the object of considerable negative media attention; at the Vietnam War Memorial, "Frag Jane Fonda" patches continued to be popular items of sale. But once Fonda had been romantically linked with conservative capitalist and sportsman Ted Turner, the image of her on Turner's arm apparently signaled her return to respectable femininity. Having been harassed for years over Vietnam, Jane Fonda was suddenly exempt from query: her views on the Gulf War were never even questioned.

By contrast, men who had opposed the Vietnam War seemed by the mid-1980s to be suddenly at a premium. What had faded out of the public narrative were men who acknowledged having been part of the large group of college-attending males whose resistance to the war combined with their political importance as a status group had been the single most important factor in giving the antiwar movement its national impact. Unlike their fathers, who had signed up the day after Pearl Harbor, this was a generation that resisted, whether tacitly or overtly. Yet because males of this status were for the most part able to use the system to resist the war from behind a draft exemption, they were left twenty years later still exempt from the necessity even to take responsibility for that resistance—exempt, in other words, from the major issue of their generation and all its ideological consequences. Men in positions of authority who had once been part of the massive white flight into protected statuses— men like J. Danforth Quayle—had by the late 1980s adopted a handy "pro-war" retropatriotism behind which their decisions to avoid Vietnam were conveniently hid. As the antiwar position lost respectability, it began retroactively to lose the now-middle-aged men who had once made it respectable. And as the public's sympathy for the rejected veteran grew, no one seemed to remember—or even notice the absence of any narrative about—the unsung heroism of those who had gone to prison or left their country in opposition to the war. Retroactively, the only hero-victims of the era were those who had gone to Vietnam, and this group was itself being remembered through 1980s distortions that eradicated the narrative of resistance that distinguishes these veterans in American history. Vietnam Veterans Against the War remained active as a postwar organization, trying to keep a history of that opposition alive. But the public at large no longer seemed aware of how powerful the antiwar movement within the active duty military had been or just how many veterans had returned to become a part of the civilian antiwar movement. Under such suppression had the history of male war resistance been that, in the mid-1980s when uniformed veterans gathered in protest outside of a Boston opening of *Rambo*, they were attacked by a horde of outraged teenagers. According to the teenagers screaming at the vets to go home, it was Sylvester Stallone—a real man—who was also "a real veteran."[30]

By 1991 not many of the veterans who had become part of the resistance nor men who had maneuvered to keep themselves out of Vietnam wanted to be identified with the newly negative and feminized position of war protest. While history was being rewritten and the Vietnam War brought back into the fold of masculine sacrifice, what was also getting conveniently forgotten was that the *real* mechanism that had enabled this return to a heroically militarized masculinity was a revised military recruitment system that no longer placed middle-class sons in harm's way. No longer threatened by a draft, the dominant class lost all memory of its role in the 1960s opposition and embraced the 1991 war enthusiastically, subsuming terms like "U.S. imperialism" under hypocritical euphemisms about all good men being willing to come to the aid of their country. The "all" no longer involved them.

As part of such rehabilitation, erased from public memory was any way of thinking that connected the widely publicized adjustment problems of the Vietnam vets to the real sources and agencies responsible for them. No one seemed to remember any more that it had been the government, not the peace movement, that had for years blocked treatment of posttraumatic stress disorder, impeded research into and denied responsibility for Agent Orange-related problems, welcomed the wounded home into shockingly understaffed and ill-equipped VA hospitals, failed to set up employment and loan provisions comparable to those given veterans of other wars, problematized Vietnam disability claims, and sharply cut services from the VA budget that were still needed by many of the returnees. These stories and the story of the greater catastrophe of the Vietnam War that inevitably surfaced in veterans' statistics on alcoholism, drug addiction, homelessness, cancer-related deaths, suicides, and birth-defective children became such anathema to the Reagan administration that they were finally just elided by a directive to cease recording Vietnam veterans' statistics separately and amalgamate them into the happier records of the returnees from World War II and Korea. By 1991 the American public remembered that the Vietnam veterans had had special problems, but they no longer connected such trauma to its basis in the memory of things seen and done in Vietnam.[31] All that anyone seemed to remember by January 1991 was that the Vietnam veterans, increasingly imagined as victims, had, upon return, been "spat on by war protesters" and "never got a parade."

The Gulf War marks a particularly disturbing conjunction of interests. It marks the moment when the media, having suddenly recognized the boundless commercial potential of war, began, in columnist Sydney Schanberg's words, to look "more and more like an arm of the government's executive branch."[32] Thus it would be easy enough to locate the source of America's militant new "pride in itself" strictly in the government and the media. But consumers as well as producers participate in national mythmaking. As Richard Slotkin points out, the consumers of an ideology are "respondents capable of either dismissing a given mythic formulation, or affiliating with it."[33] Popular desires were complicit with governmental policies, each one acting to reproduce the other, in what Claude Lévi-Strauss calls the "will to myth."

The narrative of the unsung Norman Schwarzkopf, victimized by the ingratitude of the American public that did not give him a parade, is merely one of many more like it. However, Schwarzkopf's Vietnam story—much publicized during the Gulf War—contained just the patriarchal resolution to appeal to the anxieties of 1991 America: faced with a sister expressing reservations about the war in Vietnam, Schwarzkopf threw her out of the house. Yet when this story was first told me, the figures were reversed and it became Schwarzkopf who, upon return from the war, was thrown out of the house by his hippie, war protester sister. So familiar with the female-assigned rejection of Vietnam veterans had the public become that the story had been unconsciously rearranged into the pattern that told it "right."

In such revisionary narratives as this the most remarkable transposition lies in the way that the American soldier who fought in Vietnam— not the hapless two million Vietnamese who by choice or accident got in his way—has become the victim. The physically real violence routinely directed against war protesters—evidence of which the nation had been forced to witness via televised broadcasts of the 1968 Chicago Democratic Convention—had been displaced by stories of veterans victimized by words and gestures. And photographic images as vividly definitive of the Vietnam era as the killings at Kent State, the Vietnam Veterans Against the War hurling down their medals on the steps of the capitol, the napalmed Vietnamese girl running screaming toward the viewer, or the young Viet Cong soldier being shot in the head by the Saigon police chief—images that had once visually formed a seemingly indelible counternarrative to the thoroughly discredited official one—had been all but evacuated from the remembered story. Perhaps they faded because they were not finally "about" nor did they enhance the all-important national story of American male heroism that unconsciously conditions how Americans rank the importance of data they take in. The only "event" in the revised narration that the nation seemed to remember in 1991 was a narrative of American male subjectivity constructed by an act of collaborative imagination: as the nation reacted against a national guilt that it had tentatively begun to confront in the 1970s, the only image that America "saw" by the late 1980s was the convincing picture of itself as the proverbially innocent American soldier, returning from the war and being victimized by the insults of "spitting and jeering throngs."[34]

A *Los Angeles Times* editorial entitled "Vietnam Vets Weren't Feted by Parades" by Robert McKelvey is in many ways a paradigmatic 1991 account. In its opening comparison, former Marine Captain McKelvey bitterly measures the Marine Corps Commandant's idealized tribute to "our wives and loved ones supporting us at home" against the irony of his own wife's having "joined tens of thousands of others marching on the nation's capital to protest U.S. involvement in Vietnam." Two distinct narratives are at work here. In one, the veteran registers an uneasy awareness of the moral issues that prompted opposition to the war: "It was a divisive, unhappy time. Few people believed the war could be won or that we had any right to interfere in Vietnam's internal affairs." Nor does McKelvey himself ever argue that the war was morally—or even strategically— valid. We learn, in fact, that after returning and living with the Quakers, he "felt almost ashamed of the uniform I was still wearing. . . . [and] began to feel as if I had done something terribly wrong in serving my country in Vietnam." But that narrative is continually at odds with another, decidedly more pugnacious, eventually determining story. In this other narrative, his wife's failure to play out Penelope in a prescribed story that was always about not her but her husband comes to stand for everyone who was not "supporting us at home." Eventually, this becomes the site where all of the latent, internalized blame in his first narrative gets displaced.

> Even though our family and friends meant us no harm by protesting our efforts, and probably believed they were speeding our return, their actions had a very demoralizing effect. Couldn't they at least wait until we were safely home before expressing their distaste for what we were doing? But by then, the military had become scapegoats for the nation's loathing of its war, a war in which draft dodgers were cast as heroes and soldiers as villains. . . . I recalled stories of comrades who had been spat upon in airports and called "baby killers." . . . Watching the Desert Storm victory parades on television, I was struck by the contrast between this grand and glorious homecoming and the sad, silent and shameful return of so many of us 20-odd years ago. . . . [For us] there were no family, friends, well-wishers, representatives of the Veterans of Foreign Wars or children waving American flags. . . . The feelings aroused in me by the sight of our victorious troops marching across the television screen are mixed and unsettling. Certainly they deserve their victory parade. But there is also envy. Were we so much different from them? . . . Seeing my fellow Vietnam veterans marching with the Desert Storm troops, watching them try, at last, to be recognized and applauded for their now-distant sacrifices, is poignant and sad; . . . a sense of hurt still lingers on and, with it, a touch of anger. Anger that the country we loved, and continue to love, could use us, abuse us, discard and then try to forget us. . . . It was our curious, sad fate to be blamed for the war we had not chosen to fight when in reality we were among its victims.[35]

The issues that defined the first narrative—whether "we had any right to interfere in Vietnam's internal affairs" (or, for that matter, in the Middle East)—pale to inconsequentiality beside the all-consuming desire that not only motivates this memoir and determines the writer's affirmation of U.S. militarism in the Gulf but ultimately convinces him that he and his brother veterans were really the war's "used, abused, and discarded victims." To McKelvey, he and his brothers are victims because they did not get the applause that he imagines as every soldier's basic entitlement, irrespective of the morality of the war in which he served.

Ex-Captain McKelvey's letter is written from the world of boyhood—the boyhood of a white American male growing up in the glorious aftermath of World War II, imbued with the unconditional promises life seems to have made to all such little boys. Gone from adult consciousness is any historical recall of just how grotesquely inappropriate it really would have been to applaud a show of U.S. military strength in 1973 or in any way assist the Nixon government's attempt to displace the sober national mood with symbolic practices affirming U.S. actions in Vietnam. In McKelvey's reconstruction, the political is overwhelmed by the personal and adulthood by regressive desire: all that matters is that he and his comrades went to war and came back—for which they are entitled to be heroes who get a parade. Even his insistence that he/they should not be "blamed for the war we had not chosen to fight" seems especially telling, for as an officer in the U.S. Marine Corps, McKelvey cannot wholly be exculpated from "choosing to fight." What he did not choose—and what seems grossly unfair to him—was to be born to a generation that didn't get offered any good wars, but that got instead the war that may have bequeathed American males the opportunity for agonized moral wisdom but refused them the hero's glory they had grown up to expect.

Because heroism must be conferred by a woman—without whose cheers it cannot be constituted—this perceived injustice ends up being peculiarly the fault of his wife/women. Angrily, McKelvey envisions the war as a rewards system "in which draft dodgers were cast as heroes and soldiers as villains." To situate the draft dodgers as "heroes" loses sight of the father's approval essential to the cultural definition of "hero" and suppresses the price paid by those who left the country or went to prison. Nonetheless, the affiliation between draft resistance and the feminine—in this case, his wife's literal alignment with war protest—compels the victimized veteran script into such a polarity. The draft dodgers, like the unworthy suitors Penelope denied as she dutifully awaited the return of Ulysses, are traditional figures in this myth. They appear in the U.S. Army marching song "Sound Off" condensed into the figure of "Jodie," the imagined feminized male who stayed behind and has now "got" the soldier's wife, his sister, and his Cadillac,[36] all of which are signifiers of the real object of social desire, which is male heroism.

This male-constructed myth of heroic destiny—along with several other cherished American self-conceptions—failed catastrophically in Vietnam. But McKelvey's story unwittingly demonstrates how such unconsciously held mythic models, reinvoked for the Gulf War, served to polarize the Vietnam veteran against the anti-war movement with which he actually shared a crucial history.[37] By degrading the deeds of the collective and hence the individual soldier, the antiwar position that refused to praise the slaughter in Vietnam and defined it instead as a large-scale atrocity became the agent that deprived the Vietnam soldier of what, within the myth, is construed as his entitlement. And that negative position, imagined back to the scene of its origin, is the space of the withholding mommy.

In the new narration that has been under labored construction for the past decade, the patriarchal military state has been returned to its pre-Vietnam status of wise father. Its executive branch and military brotherhood have disappeared from the list of the culpable, and blame for Vietnam is associated almost exclusively with everything outside of those two masculine locations: the unsupportive home front, the Congressional curtailment of U.S. military potency, the peacenik press, and an effeminate Pentagon leadership that General Norman Schwarzkopf describes as "a cottage industry [that] developed in Washington, D.C., consisting of a bunch of military fairies that had never been shot at in anger."[38] The general's uninhibited invocation of the homophobic lexicon in itself says a great deal about how, in the wake of the Gulf War and its affirmation of masculine ideology, the categories of gender and sexuality had, in effect, been retooled into social bludgeons.

By all outward appearances, the American public in 1991 had come full circle back to a militarism built upon the reinvestment of a national/personal selfhood in the image of the American soldier. But playing out the prodigal son's return to the fold has proved complex for the generation of American sons caught up in that compulsion. For what the Vietnam War set in motion was the radical truncation of the oedipal journey: a narrative, ultimately, of hollowed-out paternity and perpetuated sonship. Besides meaning a war that was lost and an era of committed and bitter political division in the country, what "Vietnam" signifies is the site of a traumatic break between the men of one generation and those of another—between the fathers and the sons. Something dimly understood to be occurring even at the time and termed "the generation gap" proved to be a systemic rupture on the scale of mass culture. America emerged from the Vietnam War still a patriarchal system—but a patriarchy with an unoccupied and no longer occupiable center. Chronologically bracketed by the assassination of the national father at one end, marked in the middle by his successor's forced retirement and culminating in the disgraced resignation, a few steps ahead of impeachment, of the final father figure of the era, the battles that America's sons waged in and over the Vietnam War were played out against a history repeatedly defined by a both literal and symbolic evacuation of authority.

The expulsion of the father has not, however, served to liberate the sons. For America's post-Vietnam narrative is stamped with the intensity of a generation stuck in its own boyhood and now playing out, with increasing violence, an unconscious cultural myth that attempts to recover the father. Within the drama of manhood being staged across the psyche of American popular culture, the Vietnam veteran functions as proleptic historical signifier of the moment when the father was lost, the moment of refusing the father's dictates, and the moment of failing them. And the veteran's story of striving and rejection has come to be weighted with such significance not because it reflects the actual experience of most veterans, but because it captures the shared, symbolic truth of what happened to American males of the whole Vietnam generation, veteran and nonveteran. Inside the oedipal framework of the only narrative through which the culture has been able to imagine itself, this whole generation of men shared the same fate, regardless of which side of the war they were on: none of them got a parade, none got heroized, none earned the father's approval, and all were stranded in a never-completed transition to manhood, left poised in one gap enroute to inheritance of the gap now signified by the father's vacated space.

The Vietnam War brought into being an historical collision of values that collectively compelled the nation's young men into severance from the fathers. Many severed themselves by rejecting their fathers' World War II reading of the Vietnam conflict, and many such sons were quite literally banished from their paternal houses. For defying the draft, some were forced into exile and others into federal prisons. But while back then the culture imagined the war protester versus the Vietnam soldier in terms of the classic Huck Finn/Tom Sawyer bad son/good son binary, the conditions of the Vietnam War made even the space of good son impossible. The young men of the Vietnam draft were forced by the dictates of the father-text to have to "choose," as a condition of masculinity, among a sadistically constructed series of virtually self-annihilating options: to fight a war for which no plausible ethical justification existed; to refuse induction and, as criminals, serve hard time in prison; or to banish themselves from the father's house and flee hunted in exile from their country. And if the second and third choices more obviously signify the father-son rupture, the choice to fight in Vietnam proved incapable of preventing it. Ultimately, not even those men who sequestered themselves in draft exemptions could escape the culture-wide severance from paternal authority.

The father is synonymous with the law that dictates patriarchal society and sets out its inflexible requirements for masculinity. He is unforgiving. Thus despite even the readiness of the dutiful sons to prove themselves heirs to the patrilineal "line unbroken," even the sons who went to Vietnam failed. They did not return winners, as had their fathers from World War II, but left an unforgivable blot on the unblemished war record they inherited. And the fact that some 120,000 of those who returned have by now committed suicide—twice over the number that even the war managed to kill[39]—strongly suggests that some far more powerful source of rejection was at work in American society than any bra-less hippie shouting "baby killers" could account for. It suggests that the sons of patriarchy unconsciously hear and obey a silent but omnipresent commandment written out in ancient Sparta as the edict to return from a war with one's shield or on it.

The Vietnam generation was, furthermore, compelled into the revelation that patriarchy disallows: that they had been lied to and used by the fathers. They, the youth, had been used by the old men who either did not go to Vietnam or who, if they went, betrayed their task of leadership;[40] the young men had been asked in the name of a tradition that bound them to personal, national, and historical fathers to kill, to die, and to taint their souls for mystified ideals they later discovered were shrouded in political lies. Some, while yet in Vietnam, took aim with grenades or rifles and tried killing the father. But even those who tried not to see the lies returned to America to stony rejection for failing to keep the fathers' myths intact. The popular, politically useful story would have it that it was the antipatriot who met and reviled the returning soldiers, but the unspeakable truth is that returning veterans were treated as pariahs by the Veterans Administration and were probably more scorned by groups like the American Legion and the Veterans of Foreign Wars than they were by war protesters.[41] Moreover, the whole generation of men was scarred by the war, including even those lucky enough to be outside the reach of the draft. Having been given the opportunity to undergo patriarchy's "test by fire," they had failed, for Vietnam was the war of their generation, the heroic moment they had grown up to anticipate, and the only war they had. And it is not in the least uncommon today for men who happily avoided the war to look back on Vietnam and find themselves with "the distinct feeling that they had missed a critical 'rite of passage' in coming to terms with their manhood."[42]

As the example of Richard Rusk's fruitless reunion with his father should suggest, it is not just the men who fought in Vietnam who find themselves inexplicably caught up twenty years later in the rhythms of repetition and return that mark out the psychic landscape of the son's always impossible quest for the father. It is all the men caught in the ten-year-long war—the generation that has now moved into power in this country and the one whose psychic needs are now dictating everywhere the shape of a deeply regressive national master plot. The quest for the father—which might seem to be a reparative ideal—is dangerously regressive and invariably futile because what was required at the time of transition to adulthood cannot, by very definition, be incorporated twenty years later. For a short space in the 1960s and 70s, American culture set out on the difficult and uncharted quest for new masculine narratives that might move beyond the father and the patriarchal world he defines, but such a progression was always in contention with the seductive impulse toward repetition and return. The Gulf War gave the clearest possible evidence that America had turned back, with compulsive desperation, regressing into boyhood deeds that demonstrate masculine loyalties and contempt for the feminine—the conditions for earning the oedipal validation that time has already rendered moot. In the four "tests by fire" that the United States has staged since its defeat in Vietnam, the pattern has been one of a progressively escalating use of force and an increasing reliance on weapons of mass destruction demonstrably disproportionate to any imputed threat. For the rest of the world, America's bildungsroman is dangerous, for the pattern strongly suggests a psychic quest that becomes compulsively more urgent with each successive proof of its impossibility.

Judging from such signs as America's heroized mythology of baby-faced gunfighters like Billy the Kid or from its traditional representation of its national historical self as the "young," "new," and "innocent" nation, one could say that this country has always valorized male adolescence. The choice of Audie Murphy as the national embodiment of the World

War II American soldier reflects the attraction; and certainly for Henry James, adolescent selfhood was a definitively American trait, producing a brashly honest, stubbornly innocent American character that James finally found culpable for his refusal to grow up. But the positioning of the father strongly differentiates the film models of American boyishness clustered around World War II from those made in the post-Vietnam era.

In the fictions of the filmmakers of the Vietnam generation, the father-son rupture gets repeatedly narrated, always from the consciousness of the son. Figures of authoritative, compassionate leadership like John Wayne's Sergeant Stryker of *The Sands of Iwo Jima* are simply gone, their absence narrated into post-Vietnam movies as either the father's betrayal of the son or the son's quest to revalidate the father or both. Films about World War II were generally organized as love stories and included girls/wives back home, but films about the Vietnam War—caught up in the regressions of the oedipal compulsion—are never love stories and their narratives are often violently inhospitable even to the presence of women. In these films the unresolvability of the father is frequently represented through an implicit accusation of him that is simultaneous with attempted exoneration, sometimes further complicated—as in *Apocalypse Now* and *Platoon*—by competition between several sites of vacated paternal authority within a narrative that impels the son to kill the father. In both these films the immediate position of the father is malevolently occupied and the good father displaced. But even when a benevolent father is put into the fantasy, as is the hero's mentor figure in the two Rambo films and Ron Kovic's father in *Born on the Fourth of July*, domestication has feminized him and his weakness and ineffectuality lead to a direct betrayal of the son anyway, leaving the father's position once again vacant. In the second Rambo film, blame is deflected away from the father by locating it with the pudgy, effeminate Pentagon civilian; in Stone's film, it is shunted onto the castrating mother, who is blamed both for sending her son off to war and rejecting him when he returns.

Most of the footage of combat units in Vietnam films suggests a total vacuum of authority. In a film like *Casualties of War* or *Apocalypse Now* or *Full Metal Jacket*, the war is a chaotic moral landscape with no fathers on hand, a war fought by boys led by boys, a space abandoned to the rule of frightened and lethally armed adolescents. *The Deer Hunter*—one of the few to include a focus on the hometown—lacks fathers in even that space. There are only brothers. But while the law of the (absent) father—represented by the "one shot" model of male ethics—is offered on the one hand as the highest ethical code available and that which saves the oldest/strongest son (Robert de Niro), it proves lethal to the sensitive son (Christopher Walken). Furthermore, the older son's attempt to move into and redeem the space of the father by going back to rescue the other sons proves bitterly insufficient to save or return them whole. The film's one literal father/son pair offers a bleak comment on the transition of the Vietnam sons into any paternity of their own: in this pair, the paraplegic veteran cut off at his manhood and returned from the war to a state of near infantile dependency is symbolically situated as the putative father of a son who is not his. And though much in this film seeks resolution in regression back to the myths of frontier individualism in which American imperialism was born, the film is nonetheless radical in its understanding of "Vietnam" as signifying the end of the idealized nuclear family. *The Deer Hunter* and *Apocalypse Now* were among the first Vietnam war films that emerged belatedly at the end of the 1970s; and the bleak integrity of their father-son representations reflects something of the attempt to confront and get beyond the father—the response that could still be imagined in that first decade. By the time of *Uncommon Valor* (1983), the need to recuperate the father and resecure patriarchal authority had become so pressing that this film, which features a military father (Gene Hackman) going back to Vietnam to rescue the son, even tries to situate the Vietnam War and the sense of abandonment and exile it bequeathed to American sons inside of a good father narrative. But even this fantasy of paternal affirmation stops short of staging the father and child reunion, tacitly conceding its impossibility through a narration in which the son dies in captivity before the father arrives.

The film that carried the most overt fusion of father and military state was *Top Gun* (1989), which locates its narrative impetus squarely in the losses of the Vietnam War. This film proved literally the best recruitment device the U.S. Navy has ever helped to produce. In it the Vietnam War exists as a memory through which to enact, both on and off screen, the seduction of sons necessary for any militarist state. On screen, in shots of high-tech military aircraft and jet pilot maneuvers that packed in young males across the country, the son (Tom Cruise) becomes a warrior in order to recuperate the honor of a father whose death in Vietnam was enmeshed in obscure charges that have left his name (and thus, his son's) falsely dishonored. What was simultaneously under recuperation was the reputation of the U.S. military, likewise sullied in Vietnam. Through the logic that only by going to war and redeeming their fathers can the sons of the Vietnam generation lay claim to their own honor among men, an unconscious script was being valorized for a nation to do likewise.

Neither *Top Gun* nor *The Great Santini* (1979) is usually categorized as a "Vietnam War film," but both should be. In their representation of the peacetime military playing out a model of war as game and flight squadron as fraternity, these two offer especially acute visions of the ethos that traveled from the high-tech warrior cadres of Vietnam to define the wholly technologized U.S. military operation in the Gulf. In Vietnam as well as World War II films, the paradigmatic soldier is characteristically remembered as an enlisted army or marine corps grunt embodying a certain moral seriousness associated with his proximity to killing and dying. *Top Gun* and *The Great Santini* explore a radically different ethos, that of the elite technicians of war, the studied *sprezzatura* and gamesmanship of the high-flying macho men of the air who are almost always officers and who experience war from the detachment of button-pushing technology. It is the ethos behind the sports-heavy metaphors through which interviewed American pilots reexperienced their aerial devastation of Iraqi ground troops as the scoring of points in some competitive contest; ultimately, it became the moral and linguistic visor through which the American public—who experienced the war as a military talk show—likewise conceptualized it.

Robert Duvall's "Lt. Colonel Bull Mechum," alias the Great Santini, is a type of the well-loved hero particularly valued within the conformity of the military—a hero whose leadership fuses with the kind of little boy risk-taking, nonconformist contempt for the rules that made legends out of Patton and MacArthur. For air groups, the code also involves a Rabelaisian mockery of moral seriousness and a studied disregard for regulations and bureaucracies. A rigid family disciplinarian who reveres the marine corps, Bull Mechum is also a forty-plus-year-old adolescent whose boyish pranks perform the highly important American fiction of nonconformist individualism through rebellions that never seriously question or attempt to overthrow the status quo. No one belongs more completely to the established national norms than does Bull Mechum, whose pranks and rebellions merely play out the time-honored drama of son against father/authority; and Mechum is himself driven by obsessions about masculinity that not only compel his son to play sports and be a winner but also dictate the father's compulsive need to compete against and defeat his own son in order to hold on to the position of boy eternal.

Masculine game mentality is hardly unique to this country, but the manic level of it that Bull Mechum represents may be. No matter how old the male nor how inappropriate it may be for him to constellate his sense of selfhood around athletic prowess, being able to defeat other males in various sports contests has become so overly invested a national feat that it quite openly affects even international interactions on the presidential level. Not only did George Bush thrive on setting up sports competitions as tests with which to challenge visiting foreign leaders but the mentality extended to even the parlance his administration coined for the device that launches nuclear war—a device inside of a black box that, with eloquent simplicity, became known as just "the football." For the president whose public fidgeting at world news conferences has been compared to that of an "elementary school student when [he gets] bored . . . a child inhabiting the body of an adult,"[43] the term presumably creates a nuclear sports joke about the nation's "quarterback" deciding to "throw the bomb."

It was through such a sports/game discourse with its underlying dictum of "win" that the American public was connected to the Gulf War. While the rest of the world may have been puzzled or even offended at hearing American pilots on CNN return from bombing runs and jubilantly relate the slaughter of Iraqi soldiers in terms of football and baseball metaphors, Americans understood the connections because they, too, had grown up in the uniquely American school system where sports take priority over academics, high schools produce sports heroes and colleges professional athletes, and the *real* curriculum that the system is tacitly organized to teach and test is one that could be called "Comparative (Competitive) Masculinity." No one but Americans probably recognized the dedication of Superbowl 1991 to America's boys in the Gulf as a genuine tribute of high seriousness in the culture. Quite obviously, the Italian player on Seton Hall College's basketball squad who returned to Italy under physical threat from the fans did not understand what sacred premise he had violated in declining to participate in the team gesture of sewing an American flag on his uniform to signify support for America's Gulf troops. But Americans understood: the drive to make sports a part of the public educational curriculum had even originated in America at the end of the Civil War as a substitute to provide "the moral equivalent of war."[44] And if Americans who did not grow up male did not wholly grasp the sacred connections that link a team of players and their playing field to the nation's warriors out on a battlefield, they had the opportunity to learn a critical lesson from the public outrage and presidential denunciation that Roseanne Barr provoked after a San Diego Padres baseball game where her rendition of the National Anthem seemed, wittingly or not, to mock the nation's sacred masculine investments in baseball. At least in President Bush's eyes, her gesture had mocked all of America.[45]

In films like *Big, Back to the Future, The Sure Thing, Dead Poets Society, Bull Durham, Field of Dreams, Home Alone,* and myriad others, filmmakers of the 1980s and 1990s have been writing out a culture's regressive desires into big screen fictions of the boy eternal. The opening programs of the 1990 fall television season were so marked by a childish "elevation of behavior that can only be described as irresponsible" that the *Baltimore Evening Sun's* television critic insightfully assessed the season as "a clumsy attempt by baby-boomer-aged producers to translate the generation gap that formed one of the main conflicts in their lives into a contemporary setting."[46] The world imagined by this TV sitcom fare is one in which male adolescents, evermore in subject position, move through misogynist narratives marked by domineering mommies and either ineffectual or absent fathers: *Get a Life,* where a thirty-year-old paper boy who still lives with his parents persuades his best friend to play hooky from work and spend the day in the park eluding the friend's killjoy wife—illustrates a representative plot. Nor did the victory in the Gulf allay the need for such regressive fictions. Post-Gulf male fantasies could still be read through their projection onto big screen narratives of men's boyhood heroes, a repertoire that included 1991's *Dick Tracy* and *Batman* and in 1992 expanded to produce *Captain Hook,* the ultimate fantasy of suspended boyhood, produced for a target audience of middle-aged Peter Pans. Writing in *The Washington Post,* Andrew Ward recognizes the film's mirroring of cultural production, seeing it as "of a piece with what my entire generation has done to childhood itself. We have ruined it by refusing to let it go."[47]

For the past decade, Americans have been devouring movie after movie about reclaimed sonships and perpetuated boys' rites of passage. But however enamored of the adolescent his own countrymen may be, all this boyishness in American behavior has costly consequences for the rest of the world. In Graham Greene's Vietnam novel, *The Quiet American,* the culpability of the boy-man version of American diplomacy is depicted through the fifty-five-year-old title American who is out planting bombs on bicycles in order to save the Vietnamese from communism, yet whose "young and unused face . . . gangly legs and his crew-cut and his wide campus gaze . . . seemed incapable of harm, . . . impregnably armoured by his good intentions and his ignorance. . . . as incapable of imagining pain or danger to himself as he was incapable of conceiving the pain he might cause others."[48] As Greene's novel about Vietnam of the 1950s prophetically recognized, America's "crew-cut" version of itself as the righteously innocent adolescent is a mythic self-image that allows the nation to behave in just such massively irresponsible ways as its foreign policies reflect. To the American boys on the sports field/battlefield and to Boy George, the overaged preppie in the White House whose film tastes run to the cartoon heroics of Stallone, Schwarzenegger, and Norris,[49] being a bully is apparently fun—as much fun, for instance, as the international American prank that was staged in Panama under direction from Washington with American soldiers bombarding the Papal Nuncio and his staff inside the Vatican Consulate with ear-splitting, round-the-clock rock music until Manuel Noriega was handed over from sanctuary. As for the some 1,000+ civilians who got in the way of America's little 1989 military Christmas show in Panama and were apparently then dumped in unmarked mass graves, the U.S. Army clearly felt annoyed by any imputation of moral responsibility. Leaving it up to the Panamanians to sort out the aftermath, America picked up its planes and trucks and went home to have a parade.

Yet even though such 1980s American "victories" were transparently the ego-driven posturings of an overgrown bully beating up the smaller kids, Americans in the late 1980s seemed incapable of registering anything but glee over actions that, in the mid-1970s, would more likely have provoked a challenge to the government that ordered them. Outside of remnant peace organizations that the press came increasingly to ignore, by 1990 the American public registered neither a sense of moral responsibility nor even curiosity about the price that civilian populations routinely pay for America's enjoyment of watching its own deadly technology go bang in the night. To be concerned for the plight of the many hundred civilians killed by a laser-guided hit on an Iraqi bomb shelter or to question the orders that selected that target would introduce exactly the kind of potentially emasculating ambiguity that war films educate their male viewers to discard. Ambiguities and doubts belong to the feminine; and American heroes from the western movie onward have always been heroes precisely because their masculinity depends on having the fortitude to stand firm against all such compromising complexities as those with which the "Vietnam syndrome" had threatened permanently to mar America's discourse of war.

The annihilation of the Iraqi army and the "Willie Horton" tactics of the 1988 U.S. presidential election together attested that winning—whenever and by whatever means possible—had clearly replaced all other possible ethics in America's reassertion of manhood. But the compulsions that drove the "win" mentality signified anything but adulthood. The short-lived adulthood that had once visited the Vietnam generation, and through their experience had offered the nation a chance to grow up, had come in the form of sobering loss and painful self-knowledge, not as the movie ending of a cheering parade. The Gulf War provided the counteroffer of the parade. But in turning back to that option and enacting its regressive desires into full-scale war, what America produced and televised for the world to admire was, ironically, an all-too-appropriate depiction of the culture of American masculinity that the latter half of the twentieth century had shaped: an image of wanton boys, killing for their sport.

Notes

1 Jonathan Alter with Lucille Beachy, "The Civil War and Modern Memory," *Newsweek,* October 8, 1990, p. 64.

2 The Chrysler Corporation's advertisement that appears on the H BO video-cassette preceding *Platoon* employs the same strategy. As Lee Iacocca comes upon a World War II army jeep, he tells us: "This jeep is a museum piece, a relic of war. Normandy, Anzio, Guadalcanal, Korea, Vietnam. . . . It was the same from the first musket fired at Concord to the rice paddies of the Mekong Delta: they were called and they went. That in the truest sense is the spirit of America. The more we understand it, the more we honor those who kept it alive. I'm Lee Iacocca." See Harry W. Haines, " 'They Were Called and They Went': The Political Rehabilitation of the Vietnam Veteran," in *From Hanoi to Hollywood: The Vietnam War in American Film,* ed. Linda Dittmar and Gene Michaud (New Brunswick and London: Rutgers University Press, 1990), pp. 81–97, esp. p. 81.

3 See James Reston, Jr., *Sherman's March and the Vietnam War* (New York: Macmillan, 1984).

4 Dean Rusk, *As I Saw It,* as told to Richard Rusk, ed. Daniel S. Papp (New York: Norton, 1990).

5 Susan Jeffords has written widely and richly on connections between post-Vietnam America and anxieties about masculinity. See esp. her book, *The Re-masculinization of America: Gender and the Vietnam War* (Bloomington: Indiana University Press, 1990).

6 My paraphrasing condenses the typical responses my Dartmouth College students received when they quizzed their parents about their attitudes toward the Vietnam War. A similar point about the antiwar coalition is made by David W. Levy, *The Debate over Vietnam* (Baltimore: Johns Hopkins University Press, 1991), p. 172.

7 See Marilyn Young, *The Vietnam Wars, 1945–1990* (New York: Harper Collins, 1991).

8 Teresa de Lauretis, *Alice Doesn't: Feminism, Semiotics, Cinema* (Bloom-

ington: Indiana University Press, 1984), p. 108; see also Michael Selig's use of this model in "Boys Will Be Men," Dittmar and Michaud, pp. 189–202, as a tool for analyzing Jane Fonda's role in one of the earliest of the (1978) Vietnam War films, *Coming Home*. Selig notes the displacement, midfilm, of Fonda's narrative by Voight's. It needs also be noted, however, that *Coming Home* is one of the few Vietnam films to allow women so substantial a place in the story at all.

9 Philip H. Melling in *Vietnam in American Literature* (Boston: Twayne, 1990) documents the vindictiveness with which the U.S. government throughout the 1970s and 1980s not only refused help to Vietnam but refused to allow any other nation to give it. A representative incident is: "When India [in 1977] tried to send a hundred buffalo to Vietnam to replenish the herds destroyed by the war, the United States threatened to cancel 'food for peace' aid to India." The sympathies of the American people in the late 1970s, however, ran in direct opposition to those of their government. According to a *New York Times* poll of July 1977, two-thirds of Americans supported sending food and medicine to Vietnam and a majority favored economic assistance to help the country rebuild (87).

10 In light of the evidence presented in 1991 by historian Gary Sick implicating the Reagan-Bush campaign in a secret deal to ensure that the hostages not be released until after their continued captivity had guaranteed Jimmy Carter's election loss to Ronald Reagan, the event has a complexly ironic history in America as a signifying event in the circulation of masculine power.

11 James William Gibson's "Paramilitary Culture," *Critical Studies in Mass Communication* (March 1989): 90–94, offers insightful comments on the connections between consumerism and paramilitary culture in the circulation of "a powerful myth [of] warrior heroes operating at the various margins of large-scale bureaucracy" (93). See also Susan Spillman, "Rambomania: Action Dolls, Other Tie-ins Spark Toy War," *Advertising Age* 5 (1985): 3–63. In June 1991 the Associated Press reported on the boom in Gulf War toys and games that had continued unabated, even three months after the shooting stopped, the most popular item being the Patriot missile model. See David Disheau, "War's Over, Let the Games Begin," for A P; rpt. *Valley News* (Lebanon, N.H.) June 1, 1991, p. 7.

12 See Sandra M. Gilbert and Susan Gubar, *No Man's Land: The Place of the Woman Writer in the Twentieth Century* (New Haven: Yale University Press, 1988) on women's liberation in the wake of male wars.

13 Bly's book, *Iron John: A Book About Men* (Reading, Mass.: Addison-Wesley, 1990), became a national best seller in the fall of 1990 and his "wild-man movement" received the media attention of a cover story in *Newsweek*. One of the first places Bly aired his "Iron John" story and the place I initially encountered it was at the first national retrospective on the Vietnam War held at Salado, Texas, in October 1982. For Bly's presentation and my summary of the conference, see *Vietnam in Remission*, ed. James F. Veninga and Harry A. Wilmer, Texas Committee for the Humanities and the Institute for the Humanities at Salado (College Station: Texas A&M University Press, 1985). See also Suzanne Gordon's *Los Angeles Times* editorial, "Patriarchy, in Any Form, is Anti-Woman," rpt. *Valley News* (Lebanon, N.H.) September 7, 1991, p. 14, from which I have in part drawn my summation of Bly's book.

14 Again, see esp. Susan Jeffords's groundbreaking book.

15 Carrie Fisher, interview, *Fresh Air*, National Public Radio. According to an October 1991 report by Women in Communications, only 13 percent of the people referred to in *Time, Newsweek*, and *U.S. News and World Report* during 1991 were women (qtd. in *The Progressive*, January 1992, p. 17).

16 "U.S.A. Number One" was certainly accurate as far as international pre-eminence in rape statistics: 4 times higher than Germany, 13 times higher than England, and 20 times greater than Japan. See *Newsweek*, July 23, 1990, p. 52.

17 Although *Rambo* chronologically followed the MIA fantasies of *Uncommon Valor* and *Missing in Action*, it was the popularity of Stallone's film that retro-actively invested its predecessors with increased public credit. On the whole issue of the Vietnam MIA/POWs see especially H. Bruce Franklin's essay, "The POW/MIA Myth," in *Atlantic Monthly*, December 1991, pp. 45–81. According to a *Wall Street Journal*/NBC News poll cited by Franklin, 69 percent of Americans believed even as late as 1991 that U.S. prisoners of war were still being held in Southeast Asia.

18 At the conference on "Cultures of U.S. Imperialism" (Dartmouth College, November 1991) Michael Rogin connected the yellow ribbons to the U.S. Army's campaign against the American Indian, thus defining their origins within a racist military policy.

19 Cynthia Enloe, "Tie a Yellow Ribbon 'Round the New World Order," *Village Voice*, February 19, 1991, p. 370.

20 Any concern over the literally raped Kuwaiti women often became displaced by its translation into the metaphoric "the rape of Kuwait." On the use of the rape discourse in the Gulf War, see Susan Jeffords, "Protection Racket," *Women's Review of Books*, July 1991, p. 10. As Jeffords points out, "the rape-and-rescue scenario metaphor is hardly new in American thought" and can be traced back as far as the captivity narratives about the abduction of American women by Indians.

21 The ensuing U.S. Navy study showed reported sexual assaults and rapes had risen by 55 percent between 1989 and late 1990. Furthermore, ¾ of the women and ½ of the men surveyed acknowledged sexual harassment within their commands, with junior enlisted women being the most frequently targeted recipients. The report implies that overt sexism seemed to have been more widespread in the Navy because women's assignments were more restricted in that military service than in any other (Molly Moore for *The Washington Post*; rpt. *Valley News* [Lebanon, N.H.] April 4, 1991, p. 10).

22 The stolen incubators story, which George Bush cited repeatedly and which apparently had a major impact on rallying both popular and congressional support for a war, had originated in testimony at a Congressional hearing and, before being proven false by Kuwaiti hospital officials, was circulated by Amnesty

International as fact. The mysterious witness who had provided the testimony then turned out to be the Kuwaiti ambassador's own daughter, who had been coached in advance by Hill and Knowlton, the public relations firm hired for ten million dollars of Kuwaiti royal family money to sell the war to the American people (CBS-TV "60 Minutes," January 20, 1992).

23 See Alexander Cockburn's "Beat the Devil" in *The Nation*, November 25, 1991, pp. 658–59 and May 5, 1991, pp. 1–22. See also "Report Criticizes Bush for Post-War Actions," by Robin Wright for the *Los Angeles Times*; rpt. *Valley News* (Lebanon, N.H.) May 5, 1991, p. 1.

24 This line of the revisionist scenario focuses especially on media coverage of the Tet offensive of February 1968, the moment from which a decline of public support for the war can be dated. See especially Peter Braestrup, *Big Story: How the American Press and Television Reported and Interpreted the Crisis of Tet 1968 in Vietnam and Washington* (Garden City, N.J.: Anchor Press, Doubleday, 1978). Most mainline Vietnam war historians reject the revisionist model of an "anti-war press" and point to the way that the mainstream press advocated U.S. participation and blocked stories that might undermine support. Neil Sheehan's experience as Saigon UPI chief supplies evidence for this in *A Bright Shining Lie: John Paul Vann and America in Vietnam* (New York: Random House, 1988). See also Charles Mohr, "Once Again—Did the Press Lose Vietnam?" *Columbia Journalism Review* Nov./Dec. 1983.

25 The 1968 massacre at My Lai of some 350–500 civilians and the attempted military coverup first entered the news via the print media, breaking into the *New York Times* in the final months of 1969. After a serious editorial debate about whether or not to do so, *Life* magazine did publish the photographic evidence. Charges were originally brought against fourteen army officers, including two generals and two colonels, but only Lt. William Calley was convicted. He was given a life sentence that was subsequently commuted by Richard Nixon. The most diligent investigative reporter of the massacre was Seymour M. Hersch, in *My Lai 4: A Report on the Massacre and Its Aftermath* (New York, Random House, 1970) and, two years later, *Cover-Up: The Army's Secret Investigation of the Massacre at My Lai 4* (New York: Random House, 1972).

26 Patrick J. Sloyan, "Iraqis Were Buried Alive," for *Newsday*; rpt. *Valley News* (Lebanon, N.H.), September 12, 1991, p. 1; and Patrick J. Sloyan, "U.S. Annihilated Iraqi Division After Cease-Fire," for *Newsday*, rpt. *Valley News* (Lebanon, N.H.), May 8, 1991, p. 1.

27 "They shall beat their swords into plowshares"—probably the best-known model of peace in Western heritage—appears in both Isaiah 2.4 and Micah 4.3.

28 In a coincidence that seems less than coincidental, the Washington, D.C., homecoming parade was suddenly scheduled on the same day as—and thereby thoroughly displaced—the scheduled lesbian and gay rights day celebrations.

29 See esp. the returning vet narratives collected in Bob Greene's *Homecoming: When the Soldiers Returned from Vietnam* (New York: Putnam, 1989). The accounts were themselves solicited by Greene's asking, in a weekly *Chicago Tribune* column, for any veteran who had been spat upon by a war protester to send him his story.

30 The incident is cited in Kevin Bowen, "'Strange Hells': Hollywood in Search of America's Lost War," in Dittmar and Michaud, pp. 226–35, esp. p. 230.

31 Peter Marin's "Living in Moral Pain," *Psychology Today*, November 1981, pp. 68–80, the best psychological analysis I have read of the Vietnam veterans, discusses why traditional psychology has dealt so poorly with this group.

32 Sydney H. Schanberg's editorial for *Newsday*, "Another View of the Gulf War 'Victory,'" rpt., *Valley News* (Lebanon, N.H.) July 10, 1991, p. 16. The documentaries that Bill Moyers has produced since the mid-80s—including "After the War," his June 1991 report on Gulf War television coverage and the film footage that none of the major channels would air—likewise indicate Moyers's growing concern over the increasing chumminess between the White House and the media.

33 Richard Slotkin, "Gunfighters and Green Berets: The Magnificent Seven and the Myth of Counter-Insurgency," *Radical History Review* 44 (1989): 65–90, 65. Of the various cultural assessments of Vietnam and its aftermath, *The Vietnam War and American Culture*, ed. John Carlos Rowe and Richard Berg (New York: Columbia University Press, 1991), offers a particularly rich collection.

34 The phrase comes from an otherwise unquoted letter to a local newspaper.

35 Robert McKelvey, editorial for the *Los Angeles Times*, "Vietnam Vets Weren't Fêted by Parades," rpt. *Valley News* (Lebanon, N.H.), June 20, 1991, p. 22.

36 David Rabe invokes these lyrics in the first play of his Vietnam War trilogy, *The Education of Pavlo Hummel*. "Jodie" is likewise the name given to the Jon Voight figure—the war protester who, in the 1978 Vietnam film, *Coming Home*, does in fact "get" the wife of the soldier (Bruce Dern).

37 Here and elsewhere, my use of the term "the Vietnam veteran" refers to the public perception of such a figure that has emerged from dominant representation and whose image works to subsume the multiplicity of political perspectives that are, of course, actually held by the many different men and the women (never included in the public image of the veteran) who served at different times, places, and in widely different circumstances in Vietnam. As Cynthia Enloe points out, the model of "the Vietnam vet" has taken "15 years and a lot of celluloid and paper to create, but today he is a potent figure inspiring complex emotions, . . . [and] it is the unappreciated, alienated male Vietnam vet whose image looms over the present war" (as cited in note 19).

38 Qtd from *Newsweek*, May 27, 1991, p. 17.

39 Barry Romo, National Coordinator of Vietnam Veterans Against the War lecture, Drake University, Des Moines, Iowa, 24 October 1990.

40 The failure of any military leadership in Vietnam and the widespread careerism amongst senior officers is well documented. See esp. Loren Baritz's description in *Backfire: A History of How American Culture Led Us into Vietnam and Made Us Fight the Way We Did* (New York: Ballantine, 1985), pp. 276–318.

41 See esp. D. Michael Shafer, "The Vietnam Combat Experience: *The Human Legacy*," in *The Legacy: The Vietnam War in the American Imagination*, ed. D. Michael Shafer (Boston: Beacon Press, 1990), pp. 80–103. In discussing Vietnam veterans' "cruel . . . often callous treatment by the VA hospital system" Shafer points out how the acute care needs of the several hundred thousand young, seriously wounded Vietnam combatants were essentially ignored in favor of the chronic care needs of aging World War II veterans, the constituency that had numerical and political clout (96). The Legion and the VFW—veterans in the father position to the Vietnam returnees and also men who "strongly supported the American cause in Vietnam and often blame Vietnam veterans for defeat"—further protected such interests by aggressively lobbying to block funding of outreach, drug rehabilitation, and psychological counseling programs for Vietnam veterans (97).

42 Sam Brown, "The Legacy of Choices," in *The Wounded Generation*, ed. A. D. Horne (Englewood Cliffs, N.J.: Prentice-Hall, 1981); rpt. in *The American Experience in Vietnam: A Reader*, ed. Grace Sevy (Norman, Okla.: University of Oklahoma Press, 1989), pp. 195–203, esp. p. 201.

43 Maureen Dowd, "Tame Latins and No Eggs Greeted Bush," *New York Times*, December 9, 1990, international ed., p. A3.

44 *Newsweek*, October 8, 1990, p. 64. Much has been written on the Gulf War and its sports metaphors. See, for instance, Molly Ivins, "Super Bowl in the Sand," *The Progressive*, March 1991, p. 46.

45 See "Chronicle," *New York Times*, July 27, 1990, p. B4; "Roseanne Strikes Out! The Whole Crazy Story of How She Turned into a National Disgrace," *National Enquirer*, August 14, 1990, pp. 28–29, 36; and Carolyn Marvin, "Theorizing the Flagbody: Symbolic Dimensions of the Flag Desecration Debate, or, Why the Bill of Rights Does Not Fly in the Ballpark," *Critical Studies in Mass Communication* 8 (1991): 119–38.

46 Michael Hill, "New Fall Season Glamorizing a Lot of Irresponsibility," for *The Baltimore Evening Sun*, rpt. *Valley News* (Lebanon, N.H.), September 11, 1990.

47 Andrew Ward, "Paunchy Peter Pans," editorial for *Washington Post;* rpt. *Valley News* (Lebanon, N.H.) December 31, 1991, p. 16.

48 Graham Greene, *The Quiet American* (London: Penguin Books, 1973), pp. 17, 179, 62.

49 *Newsweek*, April 16, 1990, p. 25.

Mary Yoko Brannen

"Bwana Mickey"

Constructing Cultural Consumption

at Tokyo Disneyland

> We really tried to avoid creating a Japanese version of Disneyland. We
> wanted the Japanese visitors to feel they were taking a foreign vacation by
> coming here, and to us Disneyland represents the best that America has to
> offer.—Toshiharu Akiba, spokesperson, Tokyo Disneyland

 hough the Walt Disney Company wished to diversify its first foreign
theme park by including some home-country attractions such as a
"Samurai Land" or a show based on a Japanese children's tale like
"Little Peach Boy," the Japanese owners of Tokyo Disneyland, the
Oriental Land Company, insisted that the original park be dupli-
cated as closely as possible. The phenomenal success of the theme
park, which opened on April 15, 1984, suggests that the Japanese
owners' reading of consumer preference was correct. In 1988 attendance reached 13,382,000, making Tokyo Disneyland one of the
most popular diversionary outings in Japan. The Japanese spend
more money at Tokyo Disneyland than do their American counterparts at either Disneyland, in Anaheim, California, or Disney World,
in Orlando, Florida—most of it on such souvenirs as Mickey Mouse
dolls, pins, T-shirts, and designer accessories.[1] The theme park is
not only a sensational hit among Japanese consumers of leisure-
time activities but also a favorite destination of students on school
pilgrimages (*shūgaku ryokō*). Previously such groups had preferred
to visit traditional historical areas such as Kyoto or Nikko, the sites
of ancient temples and shrines referred to in their history books and

classical literary texts. In 1988 some 1,171,000 of the park visitors were students on such organized school outings.

The Tokyo Disneyland annual report of 1989 attributes these substantial attendance and sales figures in part to Japan's rapid rise in economic status over the last decade, resulting in a significant increase in per capita disposable income and a new attitude toward relaxation and recreation. Another major factor in Tokyo Disneyland's success is that the Disney philosophy of creating a "dream world" coincides with the current consumer trend of *yuttarism* (from *yuttari*, meaning easy, comfortable, and calm), an attitude of attaching importance to relaxation and comfort. According to the Dentsu Advertising Agency, which handles the Tokyo Disneyland account, consumers are "seeking quality in this world rich with things, [and] are starting to pursue affluence of the mind, time and environment."

But these explanations of the success of Tokyo Disneyland fail to take account of the Oriental Land Company's insistence on maintaining the cultural purity of the original American theme park and its efforts to turn the experience of visiting the theme park into a "foreign vacation" for Japanese visitors. What is remarkable about Tokyo Disneyland is that the Japanese owners wanted an exact copy and think of it as an exact copy, even though they have in fact adapted the Anaheim Disneyland to suit the tastes of Japanese consumers.[2] Ultimately, it is the Japanese, not the Americans, who have defined Tokyo Disneyland. That is to say, it is the *importation* of the artifact rather than its *exportation* that begs to be analyzed.[3]

Why do the Japanese prefer a copy of the original Disneyland to a version incorporating their own history and culture? Broadly speaking, there are two ways of answering this question. One I call context-free and the other context-bound, though neither of these explanations alone is adequate. The context-free account derives from a certain discourse of symbolic domination in the West that is put forth by such Marxist theorists as Frederic Jameson and Jean Baudrillard[4] who, despite their different perspectives, both see the spread of postmodern consumerism as leveling the particularities of local or national cultures. In this view, the Japanese fascination with representations of American popular culture implicitly exemplifies the Westernization of Japan by effacing the particular context of its national traditions and self inventions. While this account does not explicitly address cross-cultural domination, it implies that the West is the major global power from which late capitalist consumerism emanates; therefore as it gains power over other cultures, it dominates them in the same way it dominates people in the West—namely, by homogenizing culture through the same material and symbolic practices of consumerism. Thus Disneyland, as a product of a free-floating transnational capitalism, means the same thing in Japan as in the United States. In anthropological terms, this view suggests that the transferred popular cultural artifacts have the same meaning for the Other as for the home-country consumers.

The alternative, context-bound account, recently articulated by Yoshimoto Mitsuhiro (1989), argues that Japanese society is based on a postmodern order of mimesis in which incongruous cultural artifacts are a facet of everyday life.[5] In contrast to theorists like Jameson and Baudrillard, who argue that late capitalism or the simulacrum unleashes free meaning from the specific national or local context, Yoshimoto argues that the meaning of cultural artifacts is context-dependent and therefore nonexportable. The symbolism of Disneyland works only within the greater context of its relationship with American society. The theme parks in Anaheim and Orlando reproduce the hegemonic ideology of Middle America by calling attention to the distinction between the imaginary (Disneyland) and the real (America)—a distinction American customers intuitively understand.[6] Disney cultural simulacra consequently are meaningless in Japan because Tokyo Disneyland is decontextualized, surrounded by a people whose cultural logic is different from that of the originally intended audience.

The problem with these two accounts is their assumption that exported cultural artifacts retain their original cultural symbolism. Either Tokyo Disneyland means the same thing in Japan as in the United States (the context-free account), or it can only mean what it means in the United States and therefore is meaningless when transferred to Japanese culture (the context-bound account). Yet if Western domination of the global economy has produced a singular consumer appetite, thereby creating a homogeneous market for Western symbolic capital in the context-free account, why is it that the Japanese owners themselves asked to import an exact replica? And if the exported cultural artifacts, severed from their contextual meaning in the homeland, become meaningless to the Other, as in the context-bound account, why would millions of Japanese go to an incongruous theme park to participate in activities that mean nothing to them?

In contrast to these views, I argue that the commodified cultural artifacts of Disneyland are recontextualized in Japanese terms at Tokyo Disneyland. This recontextualization of Disneyland is a specifically Japanese construction of cultural consumption and takes two forms: making the exotic familiar and keeping the exotic exotic. The first appears in the many accommodations in service and consumer orientation that have made the park more comfortable and accessible to its primary client base, the Japanese—despite the owners' initial insistence on fashioning an exact replica of the original park.[7] The second, keeping the exotic exotic, is a way of distancing the self from the Other, or, in Japanese terms, a way of maintaining the *uchi-soto* dichotomy—the distinction between inside and out.[8] What is significant about this recontextualization of Disneyland is that it complicates the usual way we understand cross-cultural hegemony. In the Western imperialist model of hegemony, exported cultural artifacts are either imposed intact onto the Other's culture or are domesticated by the Other; in either case the exotic is made familiar. But, in the case of Tokyo Disneyland, the owners have insisted upon constructing an exact copy of the original, thereby keeping the exotic exotic to the point of effectively denying that they have familiarized it. My explanation for this apparent paradox is that it represents a specifically Japanese form of cultural imperialism. The process of assimilation of the West, the recontextualization of Western simulacra, demonstrates not that the Japanese are being dominated by Western ideologies but that they differentiate their identity from the West in a way that reinforces their sense of their own cultural uniqueness and superiority, or what we might call Japanese hegemony.

We can begin to see how this process of assimilation works by looking first at how the Japanese recontextualize Western cultural artifacts to make sense of them in their own terms. A reading of the Anaheim and Tokyo Disneylands as cultural texts reveals the contextual differences in the modes of commodification.[9]

The original Disneyland layout (figure 1) follows a distinctly modern progression in which guests may relive the American romantic journey by heading "out West" from Main Street."[10] They first fight their way through the turbulent waters of Adventureland, encountering savages and beasts along the way. They relax for a while in the civilized settlement of New Orleans Square before they push forward on their quest for the American dream through the rough terrain of Frontierland. Finally, they reach Fantasyland, where their dreams come true. Tomorrowland is a fantasized extension of this limitless dream—the new frontier.

Whereas the original Disneyland can thus be read as a romantic narrative, Tokyo Disneyland yields no such neat reading. Themes nostalgic for Americans but meaningless for the Japanese have been renamed and recontextualized to capture the attention of the new clientele; in the pro-

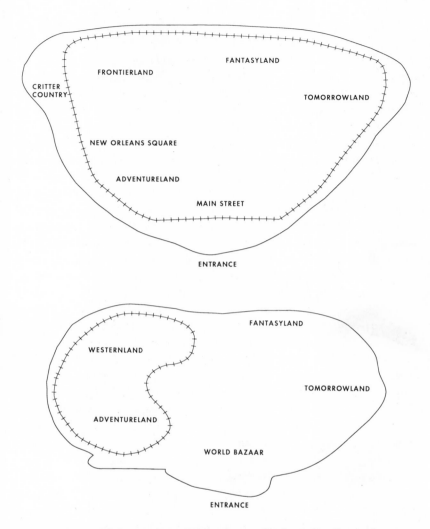

Figure 1. Disneyland in Anaheim (top) and Disneyland in Tokyo (bottom).

cess, the logic of Disneyland's romantic metanarrative is broken.[11] Main Street U.S.A. becomes the World Bazaar; Frontierland becomes Westernland; the Golden Horseshoe Revue becomes the Diamond Horseshoe Revue. Perhaps the most obvious visual break in the Disney metanarrative is the course of the railroad; whereas the original Disneyland's railroad encircles the entire theme park, Tokyo's version cuts off Adventureland and Westernland from the rest of the park.[12]

A Western postmodernist reading, such as the context-bound account put forth by Yoshimoto, would explain this by saying that the decontextualized cultural artifacts have lost their meaning in Japan; therefore, for the Japanese, the Disney metanarrative simply breaks down into meaningless simulacra. I want to show, however, that although the Western metanarrative does break down, the cultural artifacts are recontextualized and function as new mininarratives at Tokyo Disneyland.

Much of the exotica of Disneyland is already familiar to the Japanese. Disney movies and paraphernalia have been a part of the Japanese experience since the late 1940s. Japanese parents I have interviewed say they can relate to the wholesome virtues embodied in the Disney philosophy and therefore feel secure about the positive educative effects the theme park will have on their children. In addition, the park is safe and kept meticulously clean, and the employees are always courteous—all characteristics that fit in the Japanese visitors' own high standards and expectations of service. Disney University, the forty-hour apprenticeship program for those newly hired at Disneyland in the United States, turns out employees (or "cast members," as they are called by insiders) socialized in the Disney corporate culture. Their demeanor is governed by the following three rules: "First, we practice the friendly smile. Second, we use only friendly and courteous phrases. Third, we are not stuffy." [13] The same three rules (among numerous others) can be found in any Japanese training manual for new employees in service-oriented jobs. These are the formulas that have produced the ever-present Japanese "service voice" (a slight adjustment on Disney's version, which involves speaking in a pitch at least one octave higher than one's regular speaking voice) that greets customers as they enter a department store, take a ride on an elevator, or ask for assistance at an information counter. Everyone at Tokyo Disneyland uses the service voice—the guide who leads tours of the park, the crowd-control staff, the food-service people, and of course those in charge of public announcements. Other slight adjustments intended to accommodate Japanese clientele include name tags at Tokyo Disneyland featuring the last name of the employee rather than the first, street signs and signboards with Japanese subtitles, and Japanese sound tracks to all the attractions.

There are also many small but obvious ways in which the owners have made concessions to the Japanese consumer. In spite of Tokyo Disneyland's claim to be a pure copy of the American original, the product has in fact been carefully adjusted to its target market. Looking at these adjustments, we begin to get a sense of the difference between consumer capitalism in Japan and the United States.

Main Street U.S.A. has become the World Bazaar. Although Tokyo's version has retained the quasi-Victorian architecture of the buildings, the storefronts are full-size, as opposed to the three-quarter scale of the original ones, and the facades face Main Street directly, rather than being set at an angle, resulting in a less intimate welcome. The enlarged scale of the buildings, the changes in their angle of placement to the street, plus the covered walkways and glass roof over the entire World Bazaar (a necessary protection against central Japan's often rainy weather) give Tokyo's Main Street the feel of a large suburban shopping mall rather than a quaint town center. In fact, Tokyo Disneyland has more commercial space than the Disney complexes in Anaheim or Orlando, and the owners complain that it still is not enough. There is much more emphasis on shopping; each visitor to Tokyo Disneyland spends an average of six thousand yen (about forty-two dollars) on souvenirs per visit.

Another architectural change reflecting the strong consumer emphasis of Tokyo Disneyland is Cinderella's Castle, situated at the end of the World Bazaar. The original Disneyland features Sleeping Beauty's castle, but in the midst of Japan's newfound economic prosperity, it is no wonder that Tokyo Disneyland chose to feature Cinderella instead, whose rags to riches story relates more directly to the Japanese historical experience.

Whereas stores on the original Disneyland's Main Street sell mostly Americana items, the World Bazaar features gifts from around the world. In addition, the gifts at Tokyo Disneyland are of higher quality and consequently cost more. This is in keeping with what the Dentsu Advertising Company has identified as the key words characterizing Japan's current consumer-product trends: *personal, high function, high quality, global,* and *genuine.*

Rather than appeal to nostalgic sentiment, as Main Street does for Americans, World Bazaar serves the gift-giving needs of the Japanese. The Japanese system of *senbetsu* obliges the traveler to repay the traditional farewell gift of money with a return gift which must conform to three rules: it must be worth half the yen value of the original gift; be a specialty of the locale visited on the trip—a *meibutsu;* and have a legitimating mark—a *kinen,* the tag or wrapper proving that it was purchased on site. At the World Bazaar one can buy mementos that serve the functions of both meibutsu and kinen—all Tokyo Disneyland souvenirs have TOKYO DISNEYLAND marked on them, whereas U.S. Disneyland mementos have no such identification. Visitors to Tokyo Disneyland make it a point to mail postcards to family and friends from the Tokyo Disneyland postbox because all mail is stamped with a special Mickey Mouse *kinen* stamp, reminiscent of the rubber stamps available at virtually all travel sites throughout Japan. Visitors often stamp their travel diaries with these legitimating mementos which feature the name and a picture of a locale.

By far the most popular of legitimating mementos is some commodified form of Mickey Mouse. The cartoon character's popularity in Japan is neither recent nor accidental. Like their American counterparts, many Japanese under the age of forty-five watched the "Mickey Mouse Club" on television as children and when prompted will readily join in a Japanese version of the Mickey Mouse song. In addition to these shared meanings of Mickey, however, the Japanese have other recontextualized meanings for him. For example, whereas in the United States Mickey Mouse is a symbol used predominantly on children's items, in Japan he is a common symbol on items for both adults and children. When an American adult sports Mickey Mouse attire, usually in some form of casual wear, such as a T-shirt or sweatshirt or watch, it can be understood as a nostalgic reference to a childhood experience of sitting in front of the television set with Mickey Mouse ears on, being a part of the Mickey Mouse Club, and wearing one's first watch—a Mickey Mouse watch, of course. Or an American adult may wear a Mickey Mouse item in order to be camp or antiestablishment—witness the business person who wears an expensive Mickey Mouse quartz watch.

On the other hand, when a Japanese adult sports Mickey Mouse attire (and this would more likely be a female adult), this can be understood as nostalgia for childhood in general rather than as a reference to a specific experience. Further, Japanese wear Mickey Mouse paraphernalia because they think it is cute (*kawaii*), not as an antiestablishment statement. In addition to adult clothing items, Mickey Mouse can be found on guest towels and adult-size bed and futon sheets; at present he is being used as the mascot for money market accounts because of the similar alliteration of Mickey Mouse and money market. (What sound-minded American would entrust her money to a Mickey Mouse account?)

The restaurants at Tokyo Disneyland originally served only Western food, but there were too many complaints from visitors who were accustomed to enjoying *bentō* (Japanese boxed lunches) on outings. In response, the Hokusai Restaurant on Main Street now serves tempura and sushi, and the Hungry Bear Restaurant in Westernland has added curried rice (a favorite luncheon item for the Japanese) to its menu.

There are not as many food vendors on the streets of Tokyo Disneyland as at the Anaheim Disneyland. Whereas visitors to the original theme park can buy hot dogs, ice cream, snow cones, cotton candy, hot pretzels, and churros, the only option at Tokyo Disneyland is popcorn. The scarcity of food stands in the Tokyo version can probably be explained by the fact that Japanese consider it impolite to eat while walking.

Traveling west from the World Bazaar, one encounters Frontierland, which has been renamed Westernland. A spokesperson for Tokyo Disneyland commented, "We could identify with the Old West, but not with the idea of a frontier."[14] Interviews with Japanese men between the ages of twenty-eight and forty-five help to explain this identification with the West. Each reported growing up with such television Westerns as "The Rifleman," "Laramie," "Wyatt Earp," and "The Lone Ranger." What drew them to these shows, they said, was the simple, nonreligious, yet moral content—the good guy triumphs over evil (*seigi wa katsu*).[15] Many of those interviewed likened the morality in the Western television shows to that of a long-running samurai program called "Mitokōmo."

Disneyland's Golden Horseshoe Review is called the Diamond Horseshoe Review at Tokyo Disneyland. The original made sense in terms of the Disney metanarrative—the adventuresome American travels west on horseback to find her or his dream—in this case, gold. The renaming upsets this Western narrative, but gold does not have much cultural significance in modern Japan. Traditionally Japanese do not wear wedding rings, but if they do, they favor silver or white gold because they feel it is less ostentatious than yellow gold. In addition, silver is indigenous to Japan (it was formerly mined in northern Japan). Of course, diamonds are generally considered ostentatious, but when pressed with this contradiction, Japanese I have queried have simply responded by saying that "diamonds are a sign of wealth."

Although most of the narrations delivered by ride operators and tour guides at Tokyo Disneyland are direct translations of the original Disneyland versions, there is a substantial amount of ad-libbing by the Japanese facilitators. These adaptations usually take the shape of Japan-specific puns, jokes, and creative explanations. For example, when the trunk of a huge (strategically positioned) African elephant fails to spray the cruise boat's passengers with water, the Tokyo Disneyland ride operator explains that luckily for them the elephant's trunk is stopped up with *hanakuso* (snot). Humorous references to *kuso* (a vulgar generic suffix attached to the names of various bodily orifices from which mucus or excrement is expelled) are commonplace among children and adults in

Japan, where people are much less inhibited about bodily functions than in the United States. The American version is that the elephant did not have time enough to get a refill.

A second example of narrative adaptation is the ride operator's explanation that the bwana dressed in safari attire beating an alligator on the river's shore is playing *jan ken pon* (a game of "paper, scissor, rock"—the Japanese equivalent of "eenie, meenie, minie, mo") for his life. "Since we Japanese have legs too short [a common self-deprecating complaint among the Japanese] to facilitate a swift escape, we must use our wits and negotiate for our lives. Everyone knows that an alligator's choice is limited to paper as he can't make a fist [for the rock] or scissors."

Western theories of hegemony generally assume that cultural imperialism operates in one way: the dominant West colonizes and subordinates the Other. The following examples, however, show a different type of cultural imperialism at play at Tokyo Disneyland. Here, Japan appropriates a cultural artifact from America (Disneyland) and uses it in relation to its Western and Asian Others in such a way as to retain its own unique identity.[16] This Japanese form of cultural imperialism operates by continually reinforcing the distinction between Japan and the Other, by keeping the exotic exotic. By preserving the experience of Tokyo Disneyland as a foreign vacation the Japanese owners attempt strategically to ward off any threat to their identity from the West. Nevertheless, this strategy is not completely successful, as closer examination of the contradictions in the Japanese response to the exotic will show.[17] The Japanese view the Other dualistically: positive responses include everything from respect to condescending appreciation; negative responses range from ridicule to outright omission.

"Meet the World" is an attraction specific to Tokyo Disneyland. The name of this attraction would seem to suggest that it is about various countries of the world (in the fashion of Disney's "It's a Small World"). On the contrary, "Meet the World" is about the Japanese; more specifically, it is a sixteen-minute crash course on Japanese history.[18]

The show, which combines film and audio-animatronic technologies, begins as a young brother and sister sit on a beach and view the sea. The sister asks her brother a question on the history of Japan. When he cannot answer it, a white crane (a Japanese symbol of longevity) appears and recounts the history of Japan and its relationship to the world. This attraction is really about Japan's relation with the Other. The hidden agenda is to show that the Japanese, despite their numerous encounters with other cultures through trade, remain a unique people.

The first encounter with the Other (according to this history) is with China: Japan's first emissary to China, Shotoku Taishi, returns to Japan with many gifts, which are flashed across the screen. They include pottery, artwork, religious scrolls, artifacts from Persia and India, and the Chinese characters, from which the Japanese develop their unique phonetic symbols—*hiragana*. Then the statue of the Great Buddha (a Japanese architectural treasure in Kamakura) flashes across the screen, and the brother cries out in protest, "You mean that's not really Japanese?" The crane explains that Japan never borrowed cultural artifacts directly but brought back the seeds from other countries to plant in its own soil. "This is how we developed our own unique culture over the years." The crane then narrates, as Yaji-san and Kita-san,[19] the Japanese equivalents of Mutt and Jeff, trace the intensive development of Japanese arts and crafts during Japan's period of isolation from other cultures (1636–1853) by rapidly opening and closing *fusuma* (sliding partitions) on which the artistic treasures are displayed.

The boy's fear that there might be nothing uniquely Japanese is shared by many Japanese. Among the gifts the Japanese received from China, as reported in the narrative, are its writing system, the beginnings of its culture, its political administration, Confucianism, and Buddhism.[20] Having learned culture at the feet of the Chinese, the Japanese have long felt somewhat inferior to them and have therefore strived to distinguish themselves as unique.

This attraction illustrates that Japanese cultural identity is never separate. The entire narrative is framed within the subjectivity of the Asian Other—always in unsettled relations. This is evident from the emphasis on Japan's uniqueness in relationship to China and from the complete absence of any mention of Korea in Japan's history. The attraction treats China positively, paying respect to its role as a source of Japanese culture (in much the same way that the West pays homage to Greece and Rome), but at the same time it distances Japan from China by emphasizing Japan's development of the transplanted cultural seedlings.

This attraction treats Korea negatively by omission.[21] Korea is excluded because it is the Asian country most similar to Japan and therefore the one most difficult for the Japanese to differentiate themselves from. Or, to extend Emiko Ohnuki-Tierney's classification system of outsiders, though the Chinese and Koreans are both "marginal outsiders" and therefore more threatening than the Western Other, Koreans are the closest to the margin and therefore the most problematic. Korea is the Asian country nearest to Japan and is similar in size; Koreans are the largest population of foreigners in Japan and represent the greatest number of aliens who have obtained Japanese citizenship; and archaeological as well as linguistic evidence suggests some common origin for the Japanese and Koreans.[22] Moreover, the Japanese imperial line can be traced to Korea.[23]

Some of the telling omissions in the narrative of "Meet the World" are: (1) Buddhism first came to Japan in 552 from Korea, not China; (2) Korea's role in keeping trade alive with the outside world after Japan closed its doors to trade and travel in 1636 is never mentioned (the crane's version explains that this function was provided by the Chinese and the Dutch alone); and (3) Korea has been exporting goods and culture to Japan intensely since the middle of the ninth century, including such everyday items as rice, beans, cotton, hemp, and handcrafted articles; temple paraphernalia such as Buddhist images and temple bells; smelting, weaving, and pottery techniques; and religious, scientific, and scholarly knowledge.[24]

"Meet the World" deals with Japan's relationship with the West on two occasions. Japan first encountered the West through the Portuguese, who are reported to have introduced guns and Christianity. The second encounter was with the United States; Commodore Matthew Perry arrived in Japan in 1853 and announced to the Japanese that "we didn't come here to fight but to trade." Then, in a cursory treatment of World War II, the screen and theater are completely darkened for thirty seconds; the little boy cries out *"Kurai"* (it's dark); and quickly the crane changes the subject away from the war by saying, "We've been looking at the past— what about the future?" The attraction ends with a slide show of forecasts for the future, accompanied by the theme song "We meet the world with love/*Ai no fune de* [in our love boat]/We meet the world with love."

Westernland features an outdoor show in which a confidence man, Dr. Barker, and his two sidekicks, a dolled-up woman and a male flunky, trick the audience into buying magical healing potions. When I viewed the show, one of the customers asked to come on stage was a Japanese actor dressed up as an American Indian. The confidence man began a hard-sell routine to coerce the Indian to buy a potion. Whereas the doctor and his assistants spoke in the standard Japanese dialect (*hyōjungo*), the Indian spoke in a southern Japanese dialect that immediately categorized him as a hick. The doctor, remarking on the Indian's accent, insulted him by asking, "What are you, an Indian or a Chinese?" The comment was met with a round of laughter from the crowd. Here, it is the Chinese Other who is on the wrong end of Asian Orientalism.

Cinderella's castle at Tokyo Disneyland is a repository of all the sinister themes and characters from Walt Disney's stories. The Tokyo Disneyland brochure invites you to this attraction with the question "Can you capture the evil forces of the Disney villains in the castle?" Upon entering the castle, one is surrounded by evil images from such Disney movies as the *Black Cauldron, Fantasia, Sleeping Beauty,* and *Snow White.* As I walked through the castle I had a nagging sense that something was strange but couldn't quite grasp what it was until I ventured upon the "Mirror on the Wall" from Snow White. The image in the mirror was reciting "Mirror mirror on the wall, who's the fairest of them all?" in Japanese, of course, but in a foreign (*gaijin*) accent.[25] Evil is represented as foreign. This is not unlike our custom of giving evil characters in spy movies foreign (usually German or Russian) accents and personae.

The treatment of gaijin at Tokyo Disneyland is complex. The Japanese have wholeheartedly welcomed Disneyland to Japan, praising it as "the best America has to offer" and gaijin employees at Tokyo Disneyland are treated with respect, both of which suggest a positive attitude toward the West. Yet the above example of evil gaijin voices at Cinderella's castle suggests a negative attitude. Although gaijin employees occupy high-status positions at Tokyo Disneyland, they are not integrated into the Disney experience of the customers like their Japanese counterparts. Instead they are treated as exotic specimens.[26]

There are two categories of gaijin employees at Tokyo Disneyland: cast members who dress up as Peter Pan, Snow White, or Cinderella and authentic craftspersons such as Swiss clock makers, glassblowers, and silversmiths. These gaijin employees function as "authentic artifacts" with whom the Japanese guests can have their pictures taken to legitimate the experience of the foreign vacation. To maintain their distinction as exotic, gaijin employees are asked to speak only in English and not to wear name tags, presumably so that guests do not relate to them as individuals. Rather than function (like their Japanese counterparts) as facilitators of the Disneyland experience, gaijin employees are put on display. Gaijin cast members appear as a group in the place of honor at the front of the daily Disneyland parade, and gaijin craftspersons are displayed throughout the day at their boxed-in workstations, not unlike animals in a zoo.

My account of Tokyo Disneyland allows for difference in the present postmodern moment to show that Western cultural imperialism is neither the only nor the most prevalent form of imperialism at Tokyo Disneyland. Moreover, I have tried to show that cultural imperialism works in a more complicated way than previous theories have allowed. They assume that there is either a systematic encoding of "Us" by the "Other" or a totally incoherent reencoding that fractures the American narrative and makes nonsense of it. Both accounts limit our understanding of the way in which the politics of culture works, especially in terms of cultural imperialism.

By contrast, I have undertaken an anthropological cultural critique.[27] In my account, the process of encoding is neither completely systematic and noncontradictory nor completely unsystematic and contradictory; rather, it is an inconsistent process by which meanings get negotiated. By allowing for inconsistencies in the process of encoding cultural artifacts, I have shown how the Japanese encode (as in the case of the United States and China) or do not encode (as in the case of Korea) other cultures and then reincorporate them for their own purposes, in some case to stimulate and satisfy consumer desire, in others to advance their own hegemonic national narrative.

Further inquiry in this area demands a rethinking of the very conception of domination that has commanded recent accounts of international hegemony. This would, of course, demand that capitalism itself be understood as a nonunified practice, as Japanese versions make clear. Current accounts of hegemony assume that one group is dominant and the other subordinate. In terms of cultural imperialism, they play out a relationship of colonizer and colonized that assumes a one-way imposition of power. But the case of Tokyo Disneyland suggests that the opposition between dominant and subordinate groups does not apply to the Japanese and American (or Western) groups. The exported cultural artifacts are not necessarily imposed onto a passive Other. Disney, as colonial emissary for the West, has not succeeded in colonizing and subordinating the Japanese at Tokyo Disneyland. In fact, the selective importation of Disney cultural artifacts works in the service of an ongoing Japanese process of cultural imperialism. Let me formulate this problem as a question: How is the concept of hegemony to be modified to account for the struggle between two dominant powers?[28]

Notes

A version of this chapter appeared in *Re-Made in Japan*, ed. Joseph Tobin (New Haven: Yale University Press [©], 1992).

I   The Walt Disney Company receives 7 percent of Tokyo Disneyland's profits from admissions, food, and merchandise. Within the first five years of Disneyland's operation, the Japanese had already spent over ten billion yen on Disneyland paraphernalia.

2 The plan for the Paris Disneyland, which opened in 1992, has from the outset incorporated many European adaptations to the Anaheim Disneyland.

3 My point is borne out by the fact that though Tokyo Disneyland started as a joint venture of the Walt Disney Company and the Oriental Land Company, the Japanese company bought out the American interest well before the park opened in 1984.

4 Although Jameson is a classical Marxist and Baudrillard a post-Marxist—which explains their different views of the economy—their theories of cultural domination and the views that they imply of cross-cultural domination are similar in their emphasis on the spectacle and the commodity as a transnational leveling phenomenon. See Fredric Jameson, *Postmodernism, or, The Cultural Logic of Late Capitalism* (Durham: Duke University Press, 1990); Jean Baudrillard, *Simulations*, trans. Paul Foss, Paul Patton and Phillip Beitchman (New York: Semiotext(e), 1983).

5 For a comprehensive discussion of postmodernism in relation to Japan, see Miyoshi Masao and H. D. Harootunian, "Postmodernism in Japan," *South Atlantic Quarterly* 87, no. 3 (1988): 388–444. For discussions of the postmodern in Japan by other Japanese commentators, see Karatani Kōjin, *Hihyō to posuto-modan [Criticism and the postmodern]* (Tokyo: Fusanbo, 1985) and Asada Akira, *Kōzo to chikara: Kigōron o koete [Structure and power: Beyond semiotics]* (Tokyo: Fusanbo, 1985).

6 Jean Baudrillard deconstructs the opposition between "real" and "imaginary" Disneyland by asserting that Disneyland's ideological function as imaginary is to "save the reality principle," and to hide the fact that the rest of America is as imaginary as Disneyland (*Simulations*, p. 25).

7 Although I read this move to make the exotic familiar as an example of good marketing know-how (see my discussion below), it is perhaps also possible to interpret it by means of the group model. If one seeks to understand this type of recontextualization using Doi Takeo's psychobehavioral model, one might see it as fulfilling what he calls the dependency need, or *amae*, of the Japanese people—the expectation of care given to the nurturance of group needs. See Doi Takeo, *Amae no kōzo [The structure of amae]* (Tokyo: Kobundo, 1971).

8 On the uchi-soto dichotomy, see Takie Sugiyama Lebra, *Japanese Patterns of Behavior* (Honolulu: University of Hawaii Press, 1976), p. 112–13. For a discussion of distinctions between types of outsiders, see Emiko Ohnuki-Tierney, *Illness and Culture in Contemporary Japan* (Cambridge: Cambridge University Press, 1984), p. 40–46.

9 Clifford Geertz, *The Interpretation of Cultures* (New York: Basic, 1973).

10 I am using Habermas's notion of the modern to mean that there is a connection between the self or subject (in this case the guest) and a historical progression and moral improvement; see Jurgen Habermas, *The Philosophical Discourse of Modernity*, trans. Frederick Lawrence (Cambridge: MIT Press, 1987).

11 Jean-François Lyotard defines the postmodern as "incredulity toward metanarratives"; breaking up modern metanarratives, which are then replaced by disjoint mininarratives, is a characteristic of the postmodern era. See Jean-François Lyotard, *The Postmodern Condition*, trans. Geoff Bennington and Brian Massumi (Minneapolis: University of Minnesota Press, 1984), pp. xxiv, 31–37.

12 A Tokyo Disneyland spokesperson told me that the structural reason for limiting the path of the Tokyo Disneyland railroad involved maintaining a sense of fantasy: if it had been constructed around the entire circumference of the park, the elevation of the tracks at various points along the route would have allowed guests to catch glimpses of the surrounding Chiba area, thereby disrupting their foreign vacation experience.

13 Quoted in John Van Maanen, "Whistle While You Work: On Seeing Disneyland as the Workers Do." Paper presented at the panel on the Magic Kingdom, American Anthropological Association Annual Meetings, Washington, D.C., November 16, 1989.

14 It is understandable that the Japanese, whose borders have always been well defined by water on every side, might not be able to identify with the concept of the American pioneer spirit of expanding a seemingly endless frontier. Nevertheless, the concept of expanding their national border by colonizing other countries is hardly novel to the Japanese experience. See Raymond Myers and Mark Peattie, eds., *The Japanese Colonial Empire, 1895–1945* (Princeton: Princeton University Press, 1984).

15 To understand the extent of the Japanese identification with the American Old West, one need only observe the Japanese "cowhands" on the Japanese-owned cattle ranches in the United States and Australia (a recent area of Japanese foreign investment); they are enthusiastically dressed in chaps, boots, spurs, kerchiefs, and cowboy hats.

16 This penchant for asserting Japan's uniqueness is directly related to a genre of literature called *Nihonjinron* (theories about Japanese people). For a historical account of *Nihonjinron*, see Kawamura Nozomu, "The Historical Background of Arguments Emphasizing the Uniqueness of the Japanese Society," *Social Analysis* 5/6 (1980): 44–63. For a comprehensive treatment of the subject, see Ross Mouer and Yoshio Sugimoto, *Images of Japanese Society* (London: Methuen, 1986).

17 I am indebted to Emiko Ohnuki-Tierney's discussion of the inside-outside distinction in *Illness and Culture*, pp. 40–46. She argues that in the case of Westerners the inside-outside distinction has a dual nature: Westerners are sometimes seen negatively as the enemy or carriers of germs and sometimes seen positively and received by the Japanese with unsurpassed hospitality. Non-Japanese Asians, on the other hand, are seen as "marginal outsiders toward whom the Japanese feel ambivalent or downright negative." My examples of Japanese hegemony at Tokyo

Disneyland add to Ohnuki-Tierney's classifications of treatment of the Other by further breaking down the non-Japanese Asian category to account for specific differences in the treatment of Chinese and Koreans.

18 This sort of confusion between title and content is not a rare occurrence in Japan. A recent Japanese book entitled *People the Japanese Know*, put out by the Japan *Times* publications department, turns out to be a Who's Who of the Japanese people.

19 These are the popular names of the Yajirobe and Kitahachi, characters developed by Juppensha Ikku, a famous comedy writer in the Tokugawa period.

20 Many of these "gifts" were actually received indirectly through Korea. The writing system, for example, was brought to Japan by Korean priests, and the great Daibutsu (statue of Buddha) was constructed by Korean artists.

21 This negative treatment of the Koreans by omissions is not limited to Tokyo Disneyland. An even more poignant example is that the monument for Koreans who died in the August 6, 1945, bombing of Hiroshima (one-fourth of the 100,000 people killed) was not permitted to be constructed inside the Peace park and therefore lies at a separate location across the river (statistics cited in the *New York Times*, April 29, 1988.)

22 Japanese explain that the Koreans remind the Japanese of their recent past, the bleak period of economic hardship in the wake of the war, and that therefore reference to Koreans is often omitted in popular accounts of Japanese history. Although this explanation awaits empirical confirmation, my hypothesis is reinforced by DeVos and Lee, who report that the "Chinese were always [since the seventh century] given greater deference than their Korean counterparts, since they were thought to be the originators while the Koreans were carrying a borrowed culture." See George DeVos and Changsoo Lee, *Koreans in Japan* (Berkeley: University of California Press, 1980), p. 15. Again, it is the *shared status* as borrowers of another culture that prejudices the Japanese against the Koreans.

23 Archaeological findings in ancient Japanese tombs, in particular artifacts from Takamatsuzuka's tomb, support the theory that Japan's dynastic line includes Korean rulers. In addition, there is strong evidence that Prince Shōtoku's mother was Korean; see DeVos and Lee, pp. 1–14.

24 In fact, trade between Japan and Korea was so intense in the ninth century that the Japanese posted Silla interpreters on Tsushima Island. See Ki-baik Lee, *A New History of Korea*, trans. Edward W. Wagner (Cambridge: Harvard University Press, 1984), p. 95. See also pp. 191–96 for references to items exported from Korea to Japan.

25 Though *gaijin* literally means outsider, in popular usage the meaning has been narrowed to refer more specifically to Caucasian foreigners.

26 This is in keeping with Ohnuki-Tierney's observation that "the Japanese demonstrate [a] favorable attitude [toward Westerners] as long as Westerners can be kept at a distance," see *Illness and Culture*, p. 42.

27 Here I refer to the notion of cultural critique as put forth by George E. Marcus and Michael M. J. Fisher, *Anthropology as Cultural Critique* (Chicago: University of Chicago Press, 1986), p. ix–x.

28 My notion of hegemony of course assumes the absence of outright conflict, as in the case of the cold war.

Deborah Gewertz and Frederick Errington

We Think, Therefore They Are?

On Occidentalizing the World

I n her recent book, *Gone Primitive*, Marianna Torgovnick provides a fascinating examination of the way ideas of the primitive are structured in a variety of Western texts, ranging from art to anthropology.[1] Two of the photographs she includes are of particular interest to us. The first (figure 1.6 on p. 39), appears initially to be a relatively conventional rendering of the primitive: a bare-breasted young black woman is posed against a background of thatch and mud huts. However, on closer inspection, the woman can be seen as wearing both a cross and cassette headphones. Furthermore, it can be seen that a number of large, mass-produced metal pots are scattered about in her "traditional" village. The second photograph (figure 3.2 on p. 80), significantly included as well in James Clifford's *Predicament of Culture*, is also of a young dark-skinned woman.[2] Festooned as though for a ceremony, her necklace is composed of large flashbulbs.

Torgovnick, we must note, neither identifies the cultural groups nor even the parts of the world from which the young women come (Clifford tells us, at least, that the woman wearing flashbulbs is from New Guinea). She is illustrating two importantly related ideas with these photographs: The first picture demonstrates that we in the West tend—indeed, are strongly motivated—to ignore signs of the modern when we look at "primitive" people. Thus, her caption, "What's 'primitive,' what's 'modern'? Increasingly it becomes difficult to tell," suggests the distinction between what is modern and what is primitive is of continuing importance to us. The second picture reveals a more general Western cultural preoccupation: it is to appropriate the "primitive" for our own cultural ends. In this case, the photograph is making, according to her caption, "A visual pun—on the young girl, the forms of breasts."

Both of these photographs cast light on the process of "Orientalizing"—a process that has been the subject of considerable discussion in recent years. Orientalizing is the presentation of the "other" in *essentialized form* as "absolutely different . . . from the West" in order for the West to "intensify its own sense of itself by dramatizing the distance and difference between what is closer to it and what is far away."[3] (Indeed, Clifford displays this second photograph to make somewhat the opposite point— in order to illustrate the "Affinities *not* [our emphasis] included in the MOMA [Museum of Modern Art] 'Primitivism' show."[4])

Torgovnick contributes to this discussion by arguing that we structure ourselves in opposition to a primitive, non-Western, frequently ubiquitous "other" primarily in order to deny the realities of our contingency in a postmodern world—a world we no longer experience as ordered by the imposition of clearly defined, largely patriarchal, moral and scientific principles. In Torgovnick's view, ideas of the primitive have been constructed and manipulated to uphold Western male conceptions of themselves as in control, as dominant over those they define as the less-developed "other," primarily women and non-Westerners. Thus, the second photograph Torgovnick includes conveys, not only a pun at another's expense, but also, it seems to us, a plural denial of full humanness. In accord with the conventions for representing the primitive, the young woman should appear bare-breasted; however, as a child (she is little more than a girl) and as primitive, she is sufficiently naive not to realize that the breasts she displays are as multiple as those of an animal and as artificial as those of a machine.

We very much share Torgovnick's concern with the political implications of representations and largely agree that representations of the primitive reflect broad sociocultural interests of the sort she discusses. We must stress, however, that as ethnographers, our concerns go well beyond the textual. At the most specific level, we are troubled that, for instance, we do not know where that woman in the first photograph lived and what her participation in a world system was such that she and other villagers had acquired manufactured pots. So too, we know far less than we would like about those in the West who are consuming these images of the generic primitive and to what effect.

At a more general level, we are worried that the *textual focus* Torgovnick adopts has the *political implication* of rendering virtually irrelevant to us the lives that *actual*—nongeneric—others *in fact* lead. Her view, that our renderings of them determine their existence for us, establishes them as products of our imaginations. This places them, in effect, as inhabiting realms essentially disconnected from our own. (We live in the world; they live in our imagination.) In other words, we fear that a textual focus on Orientalizing, like Orientalizing itself, may curtail our understanding of more fundamental processes. It may curtail our understanding of those sociohistorical forces of systemic connection, those forces which *articulate* between, and *shape*, our lives and theirs in a world system. (Said himself, of course, acknowledges the forces that link them to us.) In fact, such a textual focus on the process of Orientalism may well foster another kind of distortion, that of Occidentalism.

The term "Occidentalism" was coined by James Carrier to refer to the fact that anthropologists' views of the West are often both central to their exposition of the other and tend to be "naive and commonsensical."[5] He warns that reliance upon what is, at best, a partial understanding of the West is dangerous "because knowledge of the Alien is produced through a dialectical opposition with knowledge of the West. . . . [Thus Occidentalisms] cannot be treated as curios. . . . Indeed, if we are to understand anthropological Orientalisms we have to take account of anthropologists' Occidentalisms" (199). Both the West and the other become "understood in reified, essentialist terms, and each is defined by its difference from the other element of the opposed pair" (196).

It seems to us that by defining the lives that others *actually* live as irrelevant to our own, Torgovnick engages in a subtle form of Occidentalizing. She makes the other so unknowable—and thus, in effect, so different—as to deny (at least, to ignore) connection. Thus, perhaps ironically, Torgovnick's approach to the very real political problem of Orientalizing fails to explore sufficiently the relationship—the *connection*—between them and us that this process of constructing the other not only establishes, but masks. That we are all, although of course in significantly different ways, caught up in a world system, means that getting the other wrong (as in Orientalizing) has different and more pervasive implications than Torgovnick recognizes. A view of ourselves as disconnected— as absolved from the obligation to struggle to know the other—is, given the nature of a system, to Occidentalize by misinterpreting who we are, including the effects we have in the world.

To put it simply, "they" are related to "us" in ways other than through the texts we have written about them. Their lives and our lives have significance for, and influence on, them *and* us in ways that are not exhausted by regarding them as constructs reflecting our fears and hopes. In other words, it is useful but it is not sufficient to demonstrate that we create the "other" for our own purposes. It is also necessary to show that these purposes *may also be well served* by regarding "others" as only constructs, rather than as real lives, in complex interaction with our own.

In order to consider in more detail the manner in which Torgovnick's textual focus on Orientalism becomes an Occidentalism, which generates its own form of Orientalism—which gets both us and them wrong—let us turn our focus to several texts in which both Orientalisms and Occidentalisms are more overt, more straightforward. We wish in particular to comment on works by Margaret Mead—some of which are discussed by Torgovnick herself—and Mary Catherine Bateson. These reveal, if not establish, the basis of the position that Torgovnick adopts. It is the particular Occidentalisms that Mead and Bateson so evidently utilize, those that define us as having the freedom to shape our lives, which allow Torgovnick (and others) to ignore the nature of systemic interconnection and constraint.

On Margaret Mead's Occidentalisms

Perhaps more than any other anthropologist, Mead not only Orientalized the "other" but Occidentalized "us."[6] In her voluminous anthropological writings, her regular column for *Redbook,* and her published discussions with figures such as James Baldwin, Mead actively formulated (and criticized) a Western culture and society that was in contrast to the non-Western cultures and societies she knew from her fieldwork.

For example, in *Male and Female* she describes the different gender arrangements and modes of child socialization she found in Papua New Guinea, Bali, and Samoa and contrasts them to those she believed existed in the United States. Her explicit aim was to help us rethink and rearrange those gender role assignments she felt unduly constrained the temperaments of Western individuals, whether male or female. She writes thus:

> A recognition of these possibilities [for flexibility within gender role assignment] would change a great many of our present-day practices of rearing children. We would cease to describe the behaviour of the boy who showed an interest in occupations regarded as female, or a greater sensitivity than his fellows, as "on the female" side, and could ask instead what kind of male he was going to be. We would take instead the primary fact of sex membership as a cross-constitutional classification, just as on a wider scale the fact of sex can

be used to classify together male rabbits, male lions and male deer, but would never be permitted to obscure for us their essential rabbit, lion, and deer characteristics. Then the little girl who shows a greater need to take things apart than most of the other little girls need not be classified as a female of a certain kind.[7]

It is significant that Mead directed this view of the future to us, not to those Papua New Guineans, Balinese, Samoans among whom she had done fieldwork. For us, unlike for them, it might be possible to create such a breadth of expectation and encouragement that individuals could be free to construct (dare we say compose?) lives of personal significance. Hence, in *Sex and Temperament*, Mead writes: "If we are to achieve a richer culture, rich in contrasting values, we must recognize the whole gamut of human potentialities, and so weave a less arbitrary social fabric, one in which each diverse human gift will find a fitting place."[8]

That we have the capacity to create a future which maximizes personal gifts and individual potentialities, Mead suggests, lies in the fact that in many of its aspects—although not yet in areas of socialization with respect to gender temperament—our lives are already quite varied. Thus she writes in *Coming of Age in Samoa*:

> For it must be realized by any student of civilisation that we pay heavily for our *heterogeneous, rapidly changing* civilisation; we pay in high proportion in crime and delinquency, we pay in the *conflicts of youth*, we pay in an ever increasing number of neuroses, we pay in the lack of a coherent tradition without which the development of art is sadly handicapped. In a list of prices, we must count our gains carefully, not to be discouraged. And chief among our gains must be reckoned this *possibility of choice*, the recognition of many possible ways of life, where other civilisations have recognized only one. Where other civilisations give a satisfactory outlet to only one temperamental type, be he mystic or soldier, business man or artist, a civilisation in which there are many standards offers a possibility of satisfactory adjustment to individuals of many different temperamental types, of diverse gifts and varying interests.[9]

Although in contexts such as her book appendices and unpublished field notes, Mead often revealed exceptionally subtle and detailed social and cultural insight,[10] in her published, popular work, she presents both the "other" and "us" as diametrically opposed categories. For all their obvious differences from one another, Bali, Samoa, and the various societies of Papua New Guinea are each, as a manifestation of the "other," homogeneous, stable, and standardized. In fundamental contrast, the

West is heterogeneous, rapidly changing, and diverse. For Mead, the primary significance of this essentialist contrast—the politics of her representation—was that it enabled her to argue that the members of "primitive groups" (8) have determined futures, while members of our complex society may choose the lives they will lead.[11]

As has been implied, and we will now see more clearly, Mead was sometimes willing to flatten and simplify her ethnography in order to present arguments which would enable members of her (our) society to seize what she saw as their potential to change their world. In a political milieu in which views of biological determinism and social Darwinism were forcefully advocated, one can sympathize with the use to which she put her ethnographic authority. Yet, we will argue, the particular essentialisms she chose sustained rather than subverted existing sociopolitical arrangements. The misrepresentation of the "other" contributed to the misrepresentation of ourselves.

The Orientalizing of Chambri Temperament

In the following discussion of Mead's rendering of the Chambri, among whom both she and we have worked,[12] our primary intention is not to evaluate her analysis of Chambri society, including its gender constructs. This we have done elsewhere.[13] Rather, we wish to discuss the political implications of her essentialisms because they are continuous with—indeed perhaps can be seen as establishing and framing—a politics of representation which ignores the nature of systemic interaction between them and us.

Mead's analysis of sex and temperament among the Chambri (Tchambuli) of Papua New Guinea is well known. In her preface to the 1950 edition of *Sex and Temperament* she summarizes Chambri men as conforming in their temperament to "our stereotype for women—[they] are catty, wear curls, and go shopping, while the women are energetic, managerial, unadorned partners." She contends that Chambri women dominate Chambri men by reason of their economic activity (women controlled the fishing and constructed an important item of trade) and that Chambri men misapprehend the nature of their subservience to their women. Chambri society tells a man that: "he rules women, [yet] his experience shows him at every turn that women expect to rule him. . . . [T]he actual dominance of women is far more real than the structural position of men and the majority of Tchambuli young men adjust themselves to it, be-coming accustomed to wait upon the words and desires of women" (253).

Significantly, though, the particular Chambri men she specifically does discuss do not fit her characterization—indeed they would be hard to characterize in terms of common temperament. Consider, for example, those she names and describes in *Sex and Temperament*.

> Walinakwon: "[a] beautiful, a graceful dancer, a fluent speaker, proud, im-perious, but withal soft-spoken and resourceful" (253).
>
> Tchuikumban: "an orphan; his father and mother having both been killed in head-hunting raids, he belonged to a vanishing clan. But he was tall and straight and charming, although more arrogant and masterful than Tchambuli men usually are" (p. 260). After his foster father tells him he cannot marry the woman of his choice, he is "reduced . . . [to] sulking misery" (261).
>
> Kalingmale: "sits with his eye on an ax the women are keeping from him. His wife has accused him of being responsible for . . . [their] child's straying in the water; he wants that ax to kill the mother of the child who was with his dead child but who was not drowned. Twice he has already assaulted her" (269–70).
>
> Taukumbank: "was covered with tinea; during a short period away from his own village he forgot his own language and had to speak to his father in the trade-jargon of the middle Sepik. (His confusion was further intensi-fied by an irregular marriage between his father and his mother, which made him a member of conflicting social groups and completely blurred his understanding of the working of his society)" (272).
>
> Yangitimi: "had a series of boils, and grew lamer and lamer, and more reces-sive" (p. 272). During the pregnancy of his wife he took little interest: "he sulked and his boils grew worse. She retaliated by continual fainting-fits, in the most public and conspicuous circumstances" (273).
>
> Kaviwon: "a fine muscular youth, the son of the government-appointed Luluai, tried to realize through his father's position his desire to rule. . . . Kavi-won, seated on the house floor, was seized by an ungovernable desire to thrust a spear into a group of chattering women. . . . He said simply that he could bear their laughter no longer. The spear, pushed compulsively through a crack in the floor, pierced his wife's cheek" (272).
>
> Tanum: "a violent, overbearing, thoroughly maladjusted man" (275).

Far from conforming to a single temperamental type, the Chambri men Mead so describes appear quite diverse. To the extent Mead acknowl-edges their differences in temperament, she regards them as aberrances, as manifestations of deviance springing from neurosis: "Neurotic symptoms, unaccountable acts of rage and violence, characterize these young men whose society tells them they are masters in their home, even after any such behaviour has become thoroughly obsolete" (272–73).

We recognize, of course, that there were many Chambri she does not describe. But those she does, cannot simply be regarded as the exceptions that prove the rule. Without going into their cases in detail, it seems to us that the men she portrays are indeed various, but hardly aberrant.

Some, for instance, were under stress: Kalingmale had just lost a child. It is also clear that he was not making a very serious effort to kill the mother of the child who had been with his own at the time of death. Kaviwon, whom we came to know well from our own Chambri research, was being thwarted by his powerful father in his wish to sign on as a migrant worker.[14] Tanum was engaged in a bitter political struggle with a former clansman. This clansman had broken away from Tanum's control and was subverting the loyalties of Tanum's remaining allies. He did this by patronizing them with the European valuables he had acquired from relatives working as migrant laborers.[15]

Moreover, some of those Mead mentions were or came to be regarded by other Chambri as men of remarkable power, as the embodiment of the desirable: Walinakwon controlled two extremely beautiful and ritually significant water drums which were crucial to the success of Chambri initiations. (These are now to be found in the National Museum of Papua New Guinea.) Kaviwon has become the most powerful and respected man now living in the three Chambri villages—and was obviously working toward this end when Mead knew him. Yangitimi was described to us as the most powerful man ever to live at Chambri. He "had so much power that he could make anything happen," and it was his magical intervention during World War II that protected Chambri from bombs.

Others exhibited behaviors which, from our knowledge of Chambri culture, would have been acceptable, indeed expected: Taukumbank's refusal to speak Chambri was a means by which he and other migrant laborers distinguished themselves from those who had not braved life far from Chambri. Moreover, Taukumbank was not unusual by virtue of the "irregular" marriage of his parents: in a society that is highly (over 90 percent) endogamous, such marriages were not only common, but potentially advantageous in that multiple group membership could be used to maximize political options.

Once again, we wish to point out that in her book appendices and unpublished notes Mead has provided much fine-grained data. Nonetheless, in many of her publications, we think she made a double error: Because she believed their culture to be homogeneous, their temperamental variability was a manifestation of neurosis. In contrast, she believed our civilization to be heterogeneous, and, therefore, it was possible for us to learn to cultivate our temperamental variability. They had few choices; we had many. They were constrained; we were free to be you and me.

Through a Mother's Eye

In a recent, eloquent portrayal of five women's lives, inspired by feminist concerns about "relationships and commitments, and about gender," Mary Catherine Bateson seems much influenced by her mother, Margaret Mead.[16] Bateson's *Composing a Life* is explicitly designed to teach us in the West how to live more fulfilling, more creative lives. To assure us that such is both feasible and desirable, she begins her book with the following Orientalizing and Occidentalizing essentialisms:

> In a stable society, composing a life is somewhat like throwing a pot or building a house in a traditional form: the materials are known, the hands move skillfully in tasks familiar from thousands of performances, the fit of the completed whole is understood. . . . In a society like our own, we make a sharp contrast between creativity and standardization, yet even those who work on factory production lines must craft their own lives, whether graceful and assured or stunted and askew.[17]

In this passage, as in the work of Mead, there is the assumption that they—members of this generalized "stable" society—are determined, whereas we—members of a society where (Bateson continues) "fluidity and discontinuity are central to the reality in which we live"—are free to, and indeed must, "craft" our lives. But it is not simply that Bateson characterizes them and us in much the same way as did her mother which is worthy of note: it is the politics of promulgating this dichotomy in the late twentieth century to our increasingly stratified and, yes, diverse society that we find of special significance.[18] After all, one might well question whether the just mentioned production-line worker has the same option to craft a graceful or a stunted life as do the women Bateson describes, all of whom have advanced degrees and, we estimate, annual household incomes in excess of $100,000. Indeed, one might wonder whether the constraint of the one at least to some degree subsidizes the freedom of the other. In order to explore these politics a bit more thoroughly, let us turn to the question of work itself and see how our freedom to engage "in a day-to-day process of self-invention" is actually experienced by some of us.[19]

Ellen Bassuk, one of the women Bateson describes, is a psychiatrist who has held a variety of jobs, including director of psychiatric emergency services at a major metropolitan hospital. Because of her two young children, she resigned her position as director and gave up most of her clinical work. At the Bunting Institute of Radcliffe College when Bateson met her, she was devoting herself largely to research, in particular, to understanding better the psychosocial circumstances of homeless persons and to consulting. Bateson applauds her decision to "orchestrate her own life" (175):

> Just as the capacity for sex or nursing or exercise is not governed by an arithmetic of addition and subtraction, so the possibility of combining these activities should be looked at in terms of synergy rather than competition. Having an active sex life at night does not necessarily make a man or a woman less productive on the job, yet even sex can become difficult and laborious or be overdone. The self-reinforcing effect of exercise works within a certain range, which can be adjusted but is always liable to be disrupted by extremes. When schedules become rigid, adjustment is impossible and the level of effort that can be sustained over time drops.
>
> One of the things that has fascinated me during my interviews is discovering how many things the women in this project fit into their days. Ellen is the only one with pre-school children now, and she repeatedly described simplifying her life and reducing her commitments so that she can concentrate on caring for her son and daughter. But with a little probing, out comes a long list of activities including joint projects with a number of women friends. In fact, Ellen did not so much reduce her professional life to have children as change the way that life was organized, learning to compose the disparate elements in novel and less rigid ways (174).

We agree with Bateson that this woman and the others she depicts are to be commended for achieving a creative and synergistic balance between personal satisfaction, social commitment, and family responsibility. Our criticism is not of them as individuals. We also agree with Bateson that these women are in a "very different situation from that of thousands of women whose employers offer no flexibility, who are *caught in a model* that assumes that work shaped in response to multiple commitments must be inferior work" (177, emphasis ours). Yet we must ask if the entrapment of the latter is simply the consequence of constraint by an inappropriate cultural model. Is the primary difference between those women who are successful in composing their lives and those who are not a matter of attitude and metaphor, as Bateson suggests when she describes creative lives as being like jazz improvisation, cooking Middle Eastern food, and quilting?

Bateson's is a possible interpretation of the way lives acquire form, and indeed she employs it well to illuminate the joys and sorrows in the lives of those particular women she describes. But it seems to us incumbent on those who adopt this approach also to explore the question of how and for whom attitude and metaphor come into being, and how attitude and metaphor might be changed for those persons who cannot craft their lives as easily as the woman who switched from hospital administration to consulting. In the absence of such an examination into the nature of power, interest, and systemic constraint, Bateson's politics are strikingly reminiscent of her mother's. Mead, as mentioned, believed that "chief among . . . [the] gains of our civilization must be reckoned this possibility of choice, the recognition of many possible ways of life, where other civilisations have recognized only one."[20]

A very different conclusion concerning the possibilities of choice for many Americans is reached by Arlie Hochschild in *The Second Shift*. Hochschild examines the pressures and constraints experienced in dual-job families—145 people altogether, including husbands, wives, daycare workers, babysitters and schoolteachers, from all socioeconomic classes and educational backgrounds. For most, the likelihood is remote that they would become sufficiently free to compose lives in ways comparable to those Bateson discusses. Many are constrained not only by class and race, but by such factors as the denial (based on their employers' analyses of costs and benefits) of on-the-job daycare. They are, as well, constrained by gender ideologies and strategies. Significantly (but not surprisingly) only 20 percent of the men Hochschild interviewed helped at all with domestic labor, including child care. For those women who returned home after a full day's work, responsibility for what was in effect a second shift was experienced more in terms of exhaustion than synergy.

These multiple constraints do not seem simply expressions of free-floating cultural values, but rather are anchored in complex factors including early experiences, economic dependency, and, sometimes, economic prospects.[21] Ironically, as "good Americans," many in Hochschild's sample share Bateson's ideology of choice: they frequently view their incapacity to compose lives that are "graceful and assured" as denoting personal failure.[22]

What's Primitive, What's Modern?

Thus far, our argument concerning Mead and Bateson has been that by Orientalizing the "other" as culturally determined, it has been possible for them to Occidentalize "us" as free to choose our destinies. It is possible, as we have suggested, that this conclusion was politically justifiable for Mead in an earlier era. Then it served as a counter to biological determinism, invoked by many during the 1920s and 1930s to justify both Nazism and racial eugenics. However, we wonder whether this perspective has any justification today. In a postmodern world in which "primitives" wear crosses, cassette headsets, and necklaces of flashbulbs, should not such talk of their stability and determination versus our flux and the freedom to choose be viewed as anachronistic? Should not, instead, this world system be characterized in terms of determination *and* flux, with freedom available only for the few? Consider, in this regard, the following, all too depressingly familiar, account:

Norma, who refused to give her last name when she was interviewed by Sandy Tolan for a recent article in the *N.Y. Times Magazine*, says she has a dream she tries to remember whenever she "get[s] tired and can't go on." Her dream is to be her "own provider and not be a burden on others."[23] In order to accomplish this dream she has moved north from her home in southern Mexico to Nogales, two miles south of the Arizona border. Like others who were "drawn by the radio advertisements in the center of our country, saying that in Nogales, there is work," Norma fled poverty: "They come with big dreams. Where they come from, there is no work and they're dying of hunger." Norma has taken a job at an American-owned factory where she makes hospital gowns on an assembly line.

She is one of thousands of Mexican workers known as "maquiladoras," a term referring to an old arrangement whereby a miller keeps a share of the grain ground for a farmer. (We base our account of the lives of maquiladoras exclusively on Sandy Tolan's *New York Times* article. In so doing, we wish to make the point that knowledge about the social and economic inequities with which workers like these live is not restricted to specialized scholars.) The maquiladora industry is flourishing as a result of a drastic decline in the Mexican standard of living, itself caused by what is referred to as "la crisis," that is the plummeting of oil prices, the devaluation of the peso, and the immense foreign debt. These factors make Mexicans desperate for jobs and Mexico desperate for foreign currency. Official rhetoric describes the maquiladora industry as production sharing. It is, however, a sharing that especially benefits American industries: in Mexico such industries have relaxed environmental controls and cheap labor. A worker at an American-owned factory earns an average of 55 cents an hour (in Guatemala, such a worker earns 27 cents; in Bolivia, 24 cents). Living in desperately crowded squatters' settlements, lacking running water and adequate sanitary facilities, and facing prices as high as across the border in the United States, Norma and her compatriots find basic survival difficult. One man, for instance, budgets the $36 a week he earns folding hospital gowns in the following manner: $4 for fresh water, which must be shipped in by truck; $12 for rent of his lot in the squatters' settlement; $9 for his wife who, eight months pregnant, returned home because she could not endure the cold of an unheated shack; and $11 for food.

Given these circumstances, many workers simply leave. (Annual job turnover in these factories ranges between 100 and 400 percent.) Many others take extra jobs. Here is the work day of one young man: "[H]e gets up at 4:30, arrives at the Magnetic Metals Factory No. 6, leaves work at 3:30 P.M. for his second shift job at the garage-door opener factory, and returns home by 1:30 in the morning" (21). This work day is fairly representative for workers who make garage door openers for Sears, sunglasses for Foster Grant, uniforms for Kimberly Clark, or medical products for C. R. Bard.

Robert Reich, then of the Kennedy School of Government at Harvard University, described the labor of these maquiladoras thus: "The emerging global company is divorced from where it produces its goods. It has no heart, and it has no soul. It is a financial enterprise designed to maximize profits. [Such a global company—RCA, Xerox, Chrysler, United Technologies, ITT, General Instruments, Eastman Kodak, IBM and General Electric—saves, relative to its American plants, an average of $16,000 a year per worker in its Mexican factories.] Many of the people who inhabit it may be fine, upstanding people, but the organization has its own merciless logic." One of these people—the manager of the Foster Grant sunglasses plant—evaluates his work in response to this criticism: "Even though wages are low, that's the structure. We don't develop the structure. That's how it was. Some people feel we're taking advantage of the people. I have a hard time dealing with that" (31).

From our perspective, the lives of Norma and her compatriot maquiladoras are all *too* determined, but clearly not because they live in a culturally "stable," "primitive," society with a structure already given.[24] This is not to say, however, that their lives are *altogether* determined. Their tough grace of resilience, indeed, their negotiation and, sometimes, resistance must be recognized and applauded. But, unmistakably, their agency is sharply circumscribed by a world system in which power is unequally distributed and the economic interests of some sharply constrain, at least in broad outline, the destinies of others.

We Think, Therefore They Are?

We have a photograph rather like the one Torgovnick includes in her book with the query: "What's 'primitive,' what's 'modern'? Increasingly it becomes difficult to tell." It is the picture of a Papua New Guinea man, a Chambri named Godfried Kolly. We took this picture in 1987 when we were sharing a wood and cardboard shack with him in a squatters' settlement in Wewak. He is wearing a large cross around his neck, stereo headphones, and a pair of sunglasses. (For the sake of our narrative, we would like them to be Foster Grant's made in Mexico, but we do not know if this is so.) Godfried, standing in the doorway between his room and ours, had come to speak to us about his project of writing Chambri myths down so as to create what he termed a "Chambri Bible." By so preserving indigenous truths he hoped both to counter pernicious aspects of Occidental influences on Chambri youths and to establish a direct analogy—indeed identity—between Chambri truths and Christian truths.

More than fifty years earlier, Mead must have known Chambri much like Godfried. When she worked at Chambri in 1933, 52 percent of the men (between the ages of fifteen and forty-five) from the village in which she lived were away working as migrant laborers.[25] Virtually all Chambri by this time had been exposed to missionization, and many had become at least nominal Catholics.[26] That she did not take these articulations with a larger system into consideration in her analysis in *Sex and Temperament* reflected her essentializing perspective.

Our criticism of Mead here is significantly different from Torgovnick's criticism of her. (Torgovnick does mention, though, in a footnote that "Mead's Samoa . . . [was] already exposed to Westerners and Western values at the time . . . [she] studied" it[27] [293].) In Torgovnick's book, Mead is paired with Malinowski in a section entitled "Physicality." Torgovnick argues that both studied primitives to explore, perhaps to resolve, the "transcendental homelessness," the profound, psychosocial alienation they experienced from their bodies. They were, to themselves, strangers in a strange land. Malinowski used the primitive to learn "to live with the fact of alienation, perhaps coming to repress the body as a matter of course and, ultimately as a matter of pride" (228). The primitive became for Malinowski a projection of his physicality, and the theories—the grand, scientistic ones—he devised about primitives became his sublimated resolution.

Mead's case was different. Torgovnick suggests that she protested "against alienation from the body . . . and [sought] other ways of relating to the bodily self" (228). However, Torgovnick criticizes Mead for not going far enough:

> Mead is a classic example of a woman who succeeded largely by virtue of having internalized her culture's dominant and therefore masculine values and attitudes. Mead was a feminist and yet (in her acceptance of a Freudian view of women) not a feminist, a radical, and yet not so radical after all [she did not, Torgovnick notes, openly write her bisexuality into her work], someone who wrote and thought like what her culture called a woman—but also like a man. (242–43)

(One leaves Torgovnick's discussion of Mead and Malinowski with the implication that they would have been better ethnographers if he had slept with the Trobriand women for whom he lusted and she had openly acknowledged her sexual attraction to Samoan women.)

Yet Torgovnick thinks that Mead was more complex and more honest than scientistic male ethnographers like Malinowski. In "her popularizing use of primitive societies to comment on the United States, Mead grasped the essential point: whether 'Manus' or 'Samoa' or 'Bali' ever existed or existed any longer as she portrayed them mattered less, in a way, than the messages they conveyed to American society now" (241). And, Torgovnick thinks, what Mead conveyed was, with respect to her audience, sometimes remarkably prescient.

Indeed, Torgovnick applauds Mead for at times pinpointing "rather precisely, what the postmodern West seems to want most from the primitive: a model of alternative social organization in which psychological integrity is a birthright, rooted in one's body and sexuality, and in which a full range of ambivalences and doubts can be confronted and defused through the culture's rituals, customs, and play" (240).

At this point we can perhaps see more clearly the ways in which Bateson and Torgovnick still embody Mead's perspective: that we can construe our lives in essentialist terms, apart from the "others" from whom we may, however, learn. Yet, in certain regards Bateson leaves off where Torgovnick begins. Whereas Bateson has worked her way through to the position that the lives "others" *actually live* are irrelevant, Torgovnick begins with this assumption.

Bateson encourages the reader to frame a life, at first through reference to Occidentalist and Orientalist essentialisms. But, then, "they" drop away entirely. Is it perhaps because she suspects that her vision of them is too simple actually to apply to anyone, or perhaps because she knows how many of them in fact live alongside us in the United States—how many of them are without the incomes that allow her and her friends to compose their lives as they do? And with their disappearance she is freed from serious consideration of the political and economic complexities, inequalities, and interconnections of the modern world system. Her Occidentalism, in other words, depends on an Orientalism in which the actual "other" is fundamentally irrelevant.

Torgovnick's argument is similar, if more subtle. She is correct that to construct ourselves through the construction of the primitive cannot remain an innocent drama. Yet, it seems to us that she does not go far enough: although the nature and determinants of the lives of such as the maquiladoras are no surprise to her, her focus on ethnography as text effectively constrains her political concerns about non-Western people to the politics of representation.[28]

It is, of course, true as Torgovnick states that Mead and Malinowski have written ethnographic accounts which construct the primitive in ways that reflect their own psychological dilemmas and sociocultural concerns. And we agree with her that the deconstruction of their ideas (as well as those of others) of the primitive is valuable. However, it should also be recognized that Mead and Malinowski *have* provided us with information about various peoples which later ethnographers, presumably with somewhat disparate psychological dilemmas and sociocultural concerns, have found largely accurate.

In this regard Torgovnick, given her focus on Malinowski's depiction of the Trobrianders, might have considered Weiner's important discussion of the fact that despite significant theoretical differences between herself and Malinowski (and taking into account the changes in Trobriand life during the some sixty years which separated her work from his), her data substantially *do* agree with his.[29] That Torgovnick did not consult, or at least comment on, this particular reference, is excusable in itself. However, such an omission does point to an important limitation in her position: as far as we can tell, as a matter of policy she did not consult what other ethnographers, working in the same places as Mead and Malinowski, have written.[30]

For Torgovnick to say that she "would not at all deny the reality and multiplicity of the societies we have tended to call primitive, but would deny that such societies have been, or could be, represented and conceived with disinterested objectivity and accuracy" (20) is, we think, inadequate. That there are Trobrianders, Samoan, and Chambri who exist as more than our literary products, who exist beyond our ethnographic texts, suggests to us that we must not be completely preoccupied with issues of textual representation: we must not forget that they are also people whose lives are affected in important ways by our Western power, interests, and ideas, including those ideas of the primitive that Torgovnick so ably discusses. To put it simply, in her focus on how we have gotten them wrong, Torgovnick's concern remains exclusively on the implications our errors have for *our* lives; moreover, she argues as if our lives could be understood in isolation from theirs.

It seems to us, in contrast, that to be other than passive agents of a Western hegemony that links and, at least partially, determines us and them, we must do more than reveal through the deconstruction of our texts the innocence or corruption of our concepts. We suggest that to further a politics of representation which would be appropriate in a world system—a politics that would work both to increase our self-knowledge and to sustain the concerns of peripheral peoples, like the maquiladoras, like the Chambri—we must separate (to refer to the language of the preceding quote) a concern with disinterest and objectivity from one with accuracy and, we must add, efficacy. Resisting, if we can, either epistemological hypochondria or simplistic essentializing contrasts, we must with passion—at times, with outrage—convey, as best we can, complexities of life that both differ from and articulate with our own.

Torgovnick does write of passionate complexities as well. She locates herself among those in the postmodern West who wish from the primitive "a model of alternative social organization in which psychological integrity is a birthright, rooted in one's body and sexuality," (240), and we think this would be nice too. But here, she invokes just another essentialism—the opposite of the one we have discussed earlier in this paper, with them teaching us to be freer to be you and me than Mead ever dreamed was possible to admit in public. The irony, of course, is that our world is one in which our political and economic interests have increasingly constrained those from whom we now wish to learn to be free.

In the name of development, a luxury tourist hotel is being built by an Australian conglomerate on Chambri territory. The hotel is primarily expected to attract wealthy Americans, who are familiar with the peoples of the Sepik through the works of Margaret Mead, and wealthy Germans, who are aware of the region through knowledge of their colonial history and through trips to their museums which are filled with Sepik *kunst*. At this hotel, the Chambri will work as maids and caretakers; moreover, for the edification and entertainment of the guests, they will also be paid to present themselves as professional primitives. In so doing, Chambri will not only experience class inequalities for the first time within their home territory, but also will be engaging in a form of indigenous ethno-Orientalizing—portraying themselves in response or, perhaps, in resistance, to images they think we have of them. And these images, of course, may well, in one transformation or another, reflect what Margaret Mead (and even we) once wrote about them.

We do not know what will happen. But we are glad that as ethnographers we have the privilege and responsibility to be there to try to tell the complex story.

Notes

This paper originally was published in a slightly different version in *Anthropological Quarterly* 64 (April 1991): 80–91. We thank the editors for permission to republish it here. A shorter version was presented by Deborah Gewertz at Amherst College as a Five College Twenty-fifth Anniversary Lecture. We wish to thank our colleagues in the Five College Consortium, particularly Debbora Battaglia, Sylvia Forman, Alan Goodman, and Elizabeth Hopkins for both nominating her to this honor and providing comments on the paper. She also presented this shorter version at the Graduate School of the City University of New York as the Anthropology Program's Second Annual Alumni Lecture and thanks to Leith Mullings and her colleagues for the invitation. We also wish to thank Don Brenneis, James Carrier, Jane Nadel-Klein, Marilyn Strathern, and the anonymous reviewers for helpful and perceptive comments on the version that appears here.

1 Marianna Torgovnick, *Gone Primitive* (Chicago: University of Chicago Press, 1990).

2 James Clifford, "Histories of the Tribal and the Modern," in *The Predicament of Culture* (Cambridge: Harvard University Press, 1988), p. 211.

3 Edward Said, *Orientalism* (Hammonsworth: Penguin, 1978), pp. 96, 55.

4 Clifford, p. 210.

5 James Carrier, "Occidentalism," *American Ethnologist* 19 (1992): 205 (subsequent page references are cited parenthetically).

6 As Carrier makes clear, most anthropologists generate implicit Occidentalisms. Indeed, it would be difficult or even impossible for any Western anthropolo-

gist to characterize a culture different from his or her own without establishing at least an implicit Occidentalism. Carrier also points out that many eminent anthropologists have relied on unexamined essentialisms to make their arguments: Mauss contrasted "them," as archaic gift economies, to "us," as modern commodity economies; see Marcel Mauss, *The Gift* (London: Routledge, 1990). Durkheim opposed them, with mechanical solidarity, to us, with organic solidarity; see Emile Durkheim, *The Division of Labor in Society* (New York: Macmillan, 1933). Lévi-Strauss differentiated them, with a cold historicity, from us with a "hot" one; see Claude Lévi-Strauss, *Savage Mind* (Chicago: University of Chicago Press, 1969). Implicit in all of these oppositions is, of course, an evolutionary model in which they preceded us in developmental time. For a discussion of evolutionism implicit in much anthropology, see Johannes Fabian, *Time and the Other* (New York: Columbia University Press, 1983).

7 Margaret Mead, *Male and Female* (New York: Morrow, 1949), p. 142.

8 Margaret Mead, *Sex and Temperament* (New York: Morrow, 1963), p. 322.

9 Margaret Mead, *Coming of Age in Samoa* (New York: Morrow, 1961), p. 247; emphases ours.

10 Perhaps the best testimony to Mead's thoroughness as a field worker is the superb ethnography by Nancy McDowell, *The Mundugumor* (Washington, D.C.: Smithsonian Press, 1991). She relies primarily upon data drawn from Mead's unpublished notes.

11 Mead, *Coming of Age*, p. 8.

12 We worked among the Chambri of the East Sepik Province of Papua New Guinea, as Mead did, and we are grateful to the granting agencies that supported our research. During 1987, we were joint recipients of the Interpretive Research Grant #RO–21584–87 from the National Endowment for the Humanities; in addition, Errington was awarded a Grant-in-Aid from the American Council of Learned Societies, and Gewertz a Faculty Research Grant from Amherst College. We also wish to thank the Department of Anthropology of the Research School of Pacific Studies at the Australian National University for sponsoring our research among the Chambri during 1983. Gewertz had, prior to 1983, made two trips to the East Sepik Province of Papua New Guinea. On the first, from 1974 through 1975, she was supported by the Population Institute of the East-West Center, the National Geographic Society, and the Graduate School of the City University of New York. The second, during the summer of 1979, was paid for by the National Endowment for the Humanities and the Miner D. Crary Fellowship from Amherst College. She expresses gratitude to each of these institutions as well as to the Wenner-Green Foundation for Anthropological Research which enabled her to investigate archival material during 1981.

13 See, in particular, Deborah Gewertz, "The Chambri View of Persons," *American Anthropologist* 86 (1984): 615–29. See also Frederick Errington and Deborah Gewertz, *Cultural Alternatives and a Feminist Anthropology* (Cambridge: Cambridge University Press, 1987); and Frederick Errington and Deborah

Gewertz, "The Remarriage of Yebiwali," in *Dealing with Inequality*, ed. Marilyn Strathern (Cambridge: Cambridge University Press, 1987).

14 For an analysis of this case, see Deborah Gewertz, "Deviance Unplaced," *Sexual Antagonism, Gender, and Social Change in Papua New Guinea*, ed. Fitz Poole and Gilbert Herdt, *Social Analysis* 12 (Special Issue: 1982): 29–35.

15 Errington and Gewertz, "The Remarriage of Yebiwali," 71–5.

16 Bateson acknowledged that "key ideas" in her book "echo" the work of her parents, Margaret Mead and Gregory Bateson: see Mary Catherine Bateson, *Composing a Life* (New York: Atlantic Monthly Press, 1989), p. x. We discuss echoes of her mother in the body of our paper. For echoes of her father see, primarily, her discussion of "synergy" in *Composing a Life*, pp. 162–86.

17 Bateson, pp. 1–2.

18 Many studies have indicated that dating from the Reagan years to the present, the American population has become increasingly polarized in terms of income. See, for example, Kevin Phillips, *The Politics of Rich and Poor* (New York: Random House, 1990), p. 14.

19 Bateson, p. 28.

20 Mead, *Coming of Age*, p. 247.

21 Hochschild explains that it is not only economic need but also economic opportunity that draws women into the paid work force. Once there for whatever reason, they require help with housework and childcare and frequently request it from their husbands. In approximately 80 percent of all cases, men resist giving this help. Different women deal with this fact differently. Many—afraid of precipitating divorce and the downward mobility that accompanies it—eventually give up asking for help and simply do the "second shift" themselves. Working at least two shifts means, in effect, that they work at least a month per year longer than do their husbands. Many women soon feel exhausted; few can keep up the pace indefinitely without becoming dissatisfied with their performance both at home and at work. See Arlie Hochschild, *The Second Shift* (New York: Viking, 1989).

22 Bateson, p. 2.

23 Sandy Tolan, "Border Boom: Hope and Heartbreak," *New York Times Magazine* (July, 1990): 40.

24 The degree to which the interests of international capital *actually did* create the "structure" of inequality in Latin America is convincingly demonstrated by Andre Gunder Frank, *Capitalism and Underdevelopment in Latin America* (London: Monthly Reader Press, 1969).

25 These statistics were derived from a comparison of Mead's household surveys with Gewertz's genealogies.

26 For a discussion of the degree to which Sepik people were, by the time Gregory Bateson and Margaret Mead worked among them, heavily influenced by Christianity, see Mary Huber, *The Bishop's Progress* (Washington: Smithsonian Press, 1988); and John Barker, "Christianity in West Melanesian Ethnography," in *History and Tradition in Melanesian Anthropology,* ed. James Carrier (Berkeley: University of California Press, 1992).

27 Torgovnick, p. 293.

28 Torgovnick does write powerfully, if briefly, about the systematic inequalities and injustices that connected the colonized to the colonizers and that continue to connect the postcolonized to the postcolonizers; see Torgovnick, pp. 40–41. She does not, however, sustain a concern for these articulations throughout her book.

29 Annette Weiner, *Trobrianders of Papua New Guinea* (New York: Holt, Rinehart and Winston, 1988).

30 We concur here with comments from an anonymous reviewer of this paper: "Torgovnick's surmises on what motivated these personalities and the nature of their actions seems rather to be poorly grounded speculation masquerading as profound biography; an irony, given postmodernists' special attention to the way the Other is exploited in ethnographic writing."

Index

Contributors

Lynda Boose is Professor of English at Dartmouth College. She has published essays on the British Renaissance Theatre, feminist issues, and the Vietnam era, and is editor of *Fathers and Daughters*.

Mary Yoko Brannen is Assistant Professor of International Business, Organizational Behavior, and Human Resource Management at the University of Michigan. She is currently working on a cultural critique of Euro-Disneyland and on an ethnography of Japanese-owned U.S. work organizations.

Bill Brown, who teaches at the University of Chicago, has written on baseball and the American (and post-American) imaginary in *Cultural Critique* and *Public Culture*. He is completing a book titled *The Material Unconscious: American Amusement, Stephen Crane, and the Economies of Play*.

William E. Cain, Professor of English, Wellesley College, is the author of *The Crisis in Criticism* (1984), *F. O. Mathiessen and the Politics of Criticism* (1988), and *American Literary Criticism, 1900–1950* (forthcoming).

Eric Cheyfitz is Professor of English at the University of Pennsylvania. He is author of *The Transparent: Sexual Politics in the Language of Emerson* and *The Poetics of Imperialism: Translation and Colonization from The Tempest to Tarzan*. He is currently working on a book entitled *Cultural Collaborations: The Literature of Euroamerican and Native American Conflict*.

Vicente M. Diaz, a native of Guam, received his graduate training at the University of Hawaii at Manoa and at the University of California at Santa Cruz. Currently he teaches Pacific History at the University of Guam and conducts research at the University of Guam's Micronesian Area Research Center.

Frederick Errington is Charles Dana Professor of Anthropology at Trinity College. His most recent books include, jointly authored with Deborah

Gewertz, *Cultural Alternatives and a Feminist Anthropology: An Analysis of Culturally Constructed Gender Interests in Papua New Guinea* (1987) and *Twisted Histories, Altered Contexts: Representing the Chambri in a World System* (1991).

Kevin Gaines is Assistant Professor of History and African American Studies at Princeton University. He is author of the forthcoming book, *Uplifting the Race: Black Middle-Class Ideology and Leadership in the United States Since 1890.*

Deborah Gewertz is Professor of Anthropology at Amherst College. Her most recent books include, jointly authored with Frederick Errington, *Cultural Alternatives and a Feminist Anthropology: An Analysis of Culturally Constructed Gender Interests in Papua New Guinea* (1987) and *Twisted Histories, Altered Contexts: Representing the Chambri in a World System* (1991).

Donna Haraway is Professor in the History of Consciousness Board at the University of California at Santa Cruz, where she teaches feminist theory, technoscience studies, and women's studies. Her books include *Primate Visions: Gender, Race, and Nature in the World of Modern Science* (1989), and *Simians, Cyborgs, and Women: The Reinvention of Nature* (1991). She is currently working on a book called *Worldly Diffractions: Feminism and Technoscience.*

Susan Jeffords is Associate Professor of English and Director of Women's Studies at the University of Washington. She is author of *The Remasculinization of America: Gender and the Vietnam War* and *Hard Bodies: Hollywood Masculinity in the Reagan Era,* as well as co-editor of *Seeing Through the Media: The Persian Gulf War.* She is currently completing *National Victims: Rape, Heroism and U.S. Identity.*

Myra Jehlen is Board of Governors' Professor of Literature at Rutgers University. She is author of *American Incarnation: The Individual, The Nation and the Continent,* and has just completed *The Literature of Colonization, 1590–1800.*

Amy Kaplan teaches English and American Studies at Mount Holyoke College. She is author of *The Social Construction of American Realism* (1988), and is writing a book on the culture of American imperialism at the turn of the century.

Eric Lott teaches American Studies at the University of Virginia. He is the author of *Love and Theft: Blackface Minstrelsy and the American Working*

Class (1993), and his work has appeared in *American Quarterly, Representations, The Nation,* and *The Village Voice* among other publications.

Walter Benn Michaels is Professor of English at The Johns Hopkins University. He is author of *The Gold Standard and the Logic of Naturalism* and editor of *The American Renaissance Reconsidered,* and is currently working on a book called *Our America: Nativism, Pluralism and Modernism.*

Donald E. Pease holds the Ted and Helen Geisel Chair in the Humanities at Dartmouth College. He is the author of *Visionary Compacts: American Renaissance Writings in Cultural Contexts,* and is editor of *The American Renaissance Reconsidered; New Americanists: Revisionist Interventions into the Canon;* and *New Essays on The Rise of Silas Lapham.*

Vicente L. Rafael is Associate Professor in the Department of Communication at the University of California, San Diego. He is author of *Contracting Colonialism: Translation and Christian Conversion in Tagalog Society under Early Spanish Rule* (1993).

Michael Rogin teaches political science at the University of California, Berkeley. His most recent books are *"Ronald Reagan," the Movie and Other Episodes in Political Demonology* (1987) and *Subversive Genealogies* (1983).

José David Saldívar, an Associate Professor of Literature at the University of California, Santa Cruz, is the author of *The Dialectics of Our America* (1991) and *Border Matters: Sites of Cultural Contestation* (forthcoming).

Richard Slotkin is Olin Professor and Director of American Studies at Wesleyan University. He recently completed the last volume of a trilogy on the American Myth of the Frontier, *Gunfighter Nation: The Myth of the Frontier in Twentieth Century America* (1992). The first volume is *Regeneration Through Violence, the Mythology of the American Frontier, 1600–1860* (1973), and the second, *The Fatal Environment: The Myth of the Frontier in the Age of Industrialization, 1800–1890* (1985). He has also published two historical novels, *The Crater* (1980) and *The Return of Henry Starr* (1988).

Doris Sommer is Professor of Romance Languages at Harvard University. She is author of *Foundational Fictions: The National Romance of Latin America* (1991).

Gauri Viswanathan is Associate Professor of English and Comparative Literature at Columbia University. She is author of *Masks of Conquest: Literary Study and British Rule in India* (1989). She is currently writing a book on religious identity and colonial culture.

Priscilla Wald is Assistant Professor of English at Columbia University. "Terms of Assimilation" is part of a larger project, entitled *Constituting Americans*.

Kenneth W. Warren is Associate Professor of English at the University of Chicago. He is author of *Black and White Strangers: Race and American Literary Realism* (1993).

Christopher P. Wilson is Professor of English and American Studies at Boston College. He is author of *The Labor of Words: Literary Professionalism in the Progressive Era* (1985), and *White Collar Fictions: Class and Social Representation in American Literature, 1885–1925* (1992).